Web Design

ALL-IN-ONE

FOR

DUMMIES®

2ND EDITION

by Sue Jenkins

WILEY

John Wiley & Sons, Inc.

Web Design All-in-One For Dummies® 2nd Edition

Published by
John Wiley & Sons, Inc.
111 River Street
Hoboken, NJ 07030-5774

www.wiley.com

Copyright © 2013 by John Wiley & Sons, Inc., Hoboken, New Jersey

Published by John Wiley & Sons, Inc., Hoboken, New Jersey

Published simultaneously in Canada

WILEY

About the Author

Sue Jenkins is a professional web and graphic designer, illustrator, fine art photographer, and owner/creative director of Luckychair.com (www.luckychair.com), a full-service web and graphic design studio serving businesses across the U.S. since 1997. An award-winning Adobe Certified Expert/Instructor, Sue is the instructor in several Adobe Software Training programs from ClassOnDemand and Lynda.com. She is also the author of numerous *For Dummies* instructional books on web design, Dreamweaver, Illustrator, and Photoshop, including *Dreamweaver All-in-One For Dummies* (John Wiley & Sons, Inc.) and *Smashing Photoshop CS5: 100 Professional Techniques* (John Wiley & Sons, Inc./SmashingMagazine). Sue holds an MFA in photography and works as an Assistant Professor of Graphic Design at Marywood University in Pennsylvania. For questions, tips, and fun ideas, follow her on Twitter @LuckychairNews.

Dedication

To Phil.

Author's Acknowledgments

In the making of this book, my humble thanks go out to my kind and hardworking agent, Matt Wagner, who keeps surprising me with fun projects; to executive editor Steve Hayes, for his patience and flexibility with my schedule during the course of this book; and to my project editor, Rebecca Senninger, who has an amazing ability to look at the big picture and move all the pieces around until they fit together beautifully. Special thanks also go to Virginia Sanders, my copy editor, and my technical editor, John Chastain, for their excellent comments and suggestions. Thanks also to all the other folks at Wiley who were a part of this project for their fantastic effort at making this book look great. I'd also like to thank my husband, Phil, and son, Kyle, whose support and humor helped me write this book.

Publisher's Acknowledgments

We're proud of this book; please send us your comments at http://dummies.custhelp.com. For other comments, please contact our Customer Care Department within the U.S. at 877-762-2974, outside the U.S. at 317-572-3993, or fax 317-572-4002.

Some of the people who helped bring this book to market include the following:

Acquisitions and Editorial

Project Editor: Rebecca Senninger

(Previous Edition: Kim Darosett)

Development Editors: Jean Nelson, James Russell, Beth Taylor

Executive Editor: Steven Hayes

Copy Editor: Virginia Sanders

Technical Editor: John Chastain

Editorial Manager: Leah Michael

Editorial Assistant: Leslie Saxman

Sr. Editorial Assistant: Cherie Case

Cover Photo: © iStockphoto.com / Noam Kahalany

Cartoons: Rich Tennant (www.the5thwave.com)

Composition Services

Project Coordinator: Sheree Montgomery

Layout and Graphics: Jennifer Creasey, Christin Swinford

Proofreader: Christine Sabooni

Indexer: BIM Indexing & Proofreading Services

Publishing and Editorial for Technology Dummies

Richard Swadley, Vice President and Executive Group Publisher

Andy Cummings, Vice President and Publisher

Mary Bednarek, Executive Acquisitions Director

Mary C. Corder, Editorial Director

Publishing for Consumer Dummies

Kathleen Nebenhaus, Vice President and Executive Publisher

Composition Services

Debbie Stailey, Director of Composition Services

Contents at a Glance

Table of Contents

Book II: Designing for the Web 125

Book III: Building Websites 205

Chapter 1: Adding Text, Images, and Links 207

Chapter 2: Organizing Content with Tables and Lists 251

Introduction

Welcome to *Web Design All-in-One For Dummies*. This reference book is ideal for both the entrepreneur looking to design his own site and the new web designer who plans to make a career of this exciting profession. For simplicity, this book uses many Adobe products to demonstrate common web design techniques. Specifically, all the graphic examples are done exclusively in Photoshop, and all the web page–building examples are done in Dreamweaver. That said, many other software programs are mentioned and recommended throughout the book, and the examples are easily adaptable to your preferred software tools.

Web design is a unique occupation because it combines the best parts of visual creativity with modern technology. A web designer, in essence, is a graphic designer, a creative organizer, a visual communicator, a markup language technologist, and a cutting-edge trendsetter. What sets web design apart from other careers is that, as the designer, you play a key role in helping businesses connect with their customers in positive and meaningful ways. A good design can help attract the right target audience, sell more products and services, communicate new ideas, and change people's lives.

As a web designer, you have the opportunity to put your visual and organizational spin on the world, taking the complex puzzle of each web project and turning it into a visually pleasing, easy-to-navigate web solution for your client. What's more, you're inextricably part of the worldwide network of web professionals who help shape the visual realm of communication in the 21st century.

Whether you've designed a site before or you're brand-new to the world of web design, this book takes you through each step of the web design process. By the final chapter in the last minibook, you'll have all the skills you need to design, build, and publish your own websites.

About This Book

Because this is a reference book, you have the luxury of reading it any way you like. You don't have to remember anything you read because the answer you're seeking is always at your fingertips. Feel free to jump around from chapter to chapter, reading particular sections of the book as the needs arise, or go ahead and read from cover to cover like a sort of how-to manual to understand the craft of web design. The book is divided into five minibooks, which are each divided into several self-contained chapters on a variety of topics.

Everything you find in this book is written simply and straightforwardly so that you can get right to the task at hand instead of having to wade through complicated technical details. When there is something of note, such as the introduction of a new term, a special tip, or some geeky technical information that I think you should discover, I let you know by putting an icon in the margin so that you can choose whether to read or ignore that material. Other than that, you find detailed, step-by-step instructions and easy-to-understand descriptions of each topic.

Above all, this book is written to help make you comfortable with all the aspects that relate to the process of web design. It is my sincere hope that you'll use this book frequently and consider it the main go-to resource of your web design library.

Foolish Assumptions

This book presumes that even though you may have some technical experience using computers and accessing the Internet, you might be a newcomer to the field of web design and the relevant ideas presented here. It is further presumed that you're a hobbyist, a do-it-yourself entrepreneur, or a person looking to become a web professional, and that you're seeking a professional-level understanding of web design from an experienced web designer and software instructor. That's exactly what you'll get.

Creating websites, as you soon discover, is an extremely enjoyable, challenging, and rewarding process. You can control (or help to influence, if you're working for someone else) which content will be displayed on the site, how it will all be organized, what the site will look like, and how the site will function. You get to engage your creativity, your knack for organization, your ability to visualize, and your artistic sensibilities all at once. Plus, if you have a flair for discovering technology, you can soon impress your friends with your vast web vocabulary and your understanding of how websites work behind the scenes. Best of all, when you build a website, you have the unique opportunity to effectively communicate your (or your client's) ideas with the world in one of the coolest mediums available.

Conventions Used in This Book

To help you understand all the new terms and concepts that relate to web design (and you'll find lots of them!), the following typographical rules or *conventions* are used in this book:

✔ **New terms:** New terms are set apart with italics. For example:

Your *meta tags* are the special lines of HTML code that you add to your web page between the opening and closing <head> tags to communicate important information about the site to web browsers.

✔ **Reader entry:** For times when you are instructed to enter your own content to replace sample content, those parts are listed in bold, as in

```
<img src="images/yourimage.gif">
```

✔ **Code examples:** The HTML, CSS, and JavaScript code examples in this book either are listed in monospaced text within a paragraph, like this: <img src="images/taxi.jpg">, or set apart from the text, like this:

```
<!doctype html>
<html>
<head>
<meta charset="utf-8">
<title>Untitled Document</title>
</head>
<body>
</body>
</html>
```

How This Book Is Organized

By design, this book enables you to get as much (or as little) information as you need at any particular moment. Need to know something fast about how to mock up a web design before you build a site? Read the part of Book II, Chapter 2 that applies. Whenever some new question about web design comes up, you can reach for this book again and again.

This book is divided into five minibooks, each of which is further divided into relevant chapters about the process of web design, organized by topic. If you're looking for information on a specific topic, check the headings in the Contents at a Glance or skim the Table of Contents. In the following sections, you find an overview of what each minibook contains.

Book 1: Getting Started

This minibook covers all the behind-the-scenes work you need to do before you design and build a website. Topics include planning your site goals, creating a site image, defining the target audience, building wireframes, gathering and creating content, building a site map, and choosing the right tools for the job, including a web editor to build your pages, a graphics program or two to design and optimize your web graphics, shopping cart software (when applicable), and knowing when to hire others to assist you. By the end of this minibook, you'll understand how to create a site that best projects the site's identity and attracts the ideal site visitors.

Book II: Designing for the Web

Designing for the web is a special task that blends the visual with the technological because your designs must conform to the rules of HTML, CSS, JavaScript, jQuery, and other markup and programming guidelines. If you're looking for information about defining a site's look and feel, choosing the right layout and navigation scheme, mocking up a design, and optimizing graphics for the web, you definitely want to read this minibook.

Book III: Building Websites

This minibook is all about website construction. Using your preferred HTML editor, here you find out how to set up a basic web page; add text, images, hyperlinks, and multimedia files; work with semantic HTML; organize your data with tables and lists; style your pages with CSS; create layers-based layouts; build customized navigation systems; build, validate, and test web forms; and work with templates and Server-Side Includes to build smarter, more efficient websites.

Book IV: Web Standards and Testing

After you've built a site, it isn't necessarily ready for publishing. Before you put your finished work online, spend some time reading the chapters in this minibook to find out about working with web standards and making your pages accessible to the widest possible audience. You also find information here about using the proper DOCTYPE, writing semantic code, testing on multiple platforms in multiple browsers and devices, validating your code to ensure that your markup meets those web standards, and resolving any issues that may come up during testing before you share your work with the world.

Book V: Publishing and Site Maintenance

After your site is fully built and tested, you will be ready to publish it on the Internet. This minibook details the process of choosing and registering a domain name for your site, setting up a hosting plan, creating a custom placeholder page for your site, and publishing your site to your host server using FTP (File Transfer Protocol). Post-launch, you may also need to make further changes and enhancements to your site. Here you find an entire chapter devoted to enhancing your site with Search Engine Optimization techniques, performing routine site maintenance, and finding out ways to keep your site up-to-date so that visitors will be more likely to return to it again and again.

Icons Used in This Book

To make your experience with the book easier, the following icons appear in the margins to indicate particular points of interest.

Tip icons alert you to interesting techniques and hints that can save you time and effort when planning, designing, building, and publishing your websites.

This icon is a friendly reminder or a marker for things to keep in mind when performing certain tasks. It's also used to alert you to important facts, principles, and ideas that can help you become a better web designer.

Watch out! This icon is the equivalent of an exclamation point. Warnings are placed next to information that can help you avoid making common mistakes. They also give you important directions to help keep you from experiencing any web design nightmares.

Throughout the chapters, this icon shows up next to particularly technical information. Although this kind of geek-talk may be interesting to some, it's not essential reading for everyone. That said, please do consider at least glancing at the text marked with the Technical Stuff icon just in case it applies to your situation.

Where to Go from Here

This book is written so that more experienced web designers can skip around to the parts they need. Novice users probably need to start with Book I, which gives a good foundation of building web sites, before proceeding to the other minibooks. If you're one of those experienced designers, scour the index for the material you need and then read those sections.

Read through the Table of Contents to find what interests you. Otherwise, consider the following jumping-off topics:

- ✔ To find out about site planning, check out Book I, Chapter 1.
- ✔ For tips on choosing the right web editor and graphics software programs, see Book I, Chapter 4.
- ✔ For help in creating a mock-up of your web page, see Book II, Chapter 2.

- ✔ To find out about optimizing graphics for the web, see Book II, Chapter 3.

- ✔ For information about adding text, graphics, and links to your pages, read Book III, Chapter 1.

- ✔ To discover everything you want to know about working with Cascading Style Sheets, look at Book III, Chapter 3.

- ✔ If you want to know more about creating a layers-based layout and building a navigation system, see Book III, Chapters 4 and 5.

- ✔ To find out about web forms, see Book III, Chapter 7.

- ✔ To get help with testing and validation, see Book IV.

- ✔ For information on publishing your site, see Book V.

Book I
Getting Started

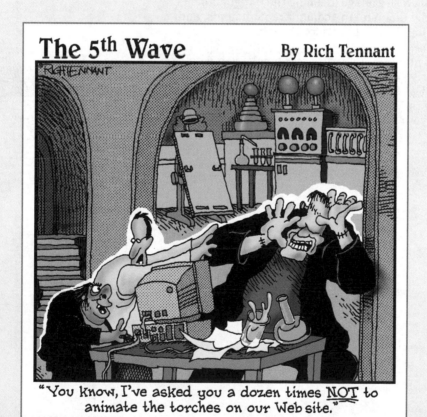

The 5th Wave   By Rich Tennant

"You know, I've asked you a dozen times NOT to animate the torches on our Web site."

Even though the best-laid plans might often go awry, for websites they don't necessarily have to if you do your homework. A good web plan includes figuring out the site's purpose, building a site image, defining the target audience, carefully planning the content requirements, and choosing the right tools for the job.

In this minibook, you discover how easy it is to properly get started with any new web project. Armed with the information you find in these chapters, you'll be totally ready to design and build your site.

Chapter 1: Starting with a Plan

In This Chapter

- Determining the site's purpose
- Building a site image
- Determining site content
- Diagnosing the site's dynamic requirements

A t the start of any website project, you — and your client, if you're designing for someone else — should sit down to think about (or discuss) your ideas about the final product. If those ideas are vague, you need to flesh them out, and if they're specific, you need to keep them organized and understand the purpose behind them. In other words, you need a plan.

To get the project off to a good start and ensure that all of your ideas and issues get the consideration they deserve, begin by pinpointing the purpose for building the website. The purpose is like an arrow that points you in the right direction. Some people build websites to sell a product or service. Others create sites to share ideas and information. One might also create a site to promote a good cause, educate the public, or simply have a place for family and friends across the country — or across the planet — to visit, share information, and catch up with one another.

Because the answer to "Why build a site?" is largely determined by the specific needs of the website owner, this chapter includes a handful of brainstorming exercises that you can use as a guide to discovering why you are building any particular site. By defining the site's purpose, you develop a foundation for the rest of the site-planning process. By the end of this chapter, you'll have all the tools you need to establish a plan for building almost any website.

Understanding the Different Phases of a Web Project

Before you begin any website, you must first have a good understanding of the project as a whole, as well as all the different steps or phases that you will move through during the web-development process.

Most website projects have a logical flow of development, a type of evolution with distinct phases that, when followed, can streamline the entire design process. Here's the general order in which most website projects evolve:

1. **Planning phase:** Define the goals and purpose of the site; construct a site identity; determine what content should go on the site; diagnose dynamic site requirements, if any; and figure out ways to attract visitors to the site after it gets published on the web.

2. **Contract phase:** If you're designing a website for a client, this is the phase where you'd draft and submit a proposal to the client for the project. The proposal outlines the scope of the work in written form so that both you and the client have a clear understanding of the expectations and outcome of the project, as well as financial agreements, time frame, and deliverables. Upon approval, the proposal gets converted into an official contract that both parties sign, and a deposit is paid to the designer to begin work.

3. **Design phase:** Characterize a target audience; construct an identity for the ideal site visitor; gather information about the target audience's computer usage and demographic preferences; determine the benefits to site visitors; make design decisions about layout, color, organization, and content; and finally mock up a design in your preferred software program, such as Adobe Photoshop, Fireworks, or Illustrator. If you're designing for a client, be sure to present your completed mock-up to the client for approval.

4. **Building phase:** Convert the website mock-up into a functional web page using HTML, CSS, and JavaScript in a WYSIWYG web editor such as Adobe Dreamweaver; create and optimize web graphics; organize content in visually pleasing ways; add dynamic capabilities to the pages with JavaScript, jQuery, and other programming languages when warranted; and ensure that all the pages on the site look good and function well in a variety of browsers (and browser versions) on both the Mac and PC, as well as other web-enabled devices, as the pages are being built.

5. **Testing phase:** Test the design on a remote host or testing server in the most popular browsers and browser versions on Mac, PC, and Linux platforms in the most popular operating systems (Windows XP, Vista, 7, 8, Mac OS X, and so on) at a variety of monitor resolutions; also test on web-enabled devices, such as smartphones and tablets; validate the code; check for spelling errors; fix coding errors; and otherwise ensure that each visitor can navigate through the site with no technical problems.

6. **Site launch:** Register a domain and secure a hosting plan, upload the site's files to a host server, retest the site, and be ready to maintain the site post-launch. Launch the site by submitting the URL to search engines. If desired, post to social media accounts and send out press releases, newsletters, and e-mails announcing the launch.

7. **Post-launch site maintenance:** Ensure that the site's content stays relevant and up-to-date by adding new and editing existing content, as well as making improvements and other enhancements to the site.

Determining the Site's Purpose

Before you begin any new web project, you need to first develop a plan. With a plan, you will know in advance what you're going to do and the order in which everything needs to be done. Furthermore, when designing sites for others, a plan can help keep both you and your client on the right track.

If you've never created a website plan before and aren't sure where to begin, the very first thing you should do — before you even start to think of designing the site — is to determine the ultimate purpose of the site. To do that, start by asking a few simple questions and jotting down the answers:

- Why are you building this site?
- Will the site be professional, fun, trendy, educational, informative, or something else?
- Will the site sell products or services, provide information or ideas, or combine some of these things?

If you think of any other questions that can help you determine the site's purpose, add those to the list. When you're finished, continue reading.

Checking out the competition

In the *age of the Internet,* anyone who owns a business, wants to stay competitive, and wants to be taken seriously by web-savvy consumers needs to have an attractive website. If you agree with this premise, you have to know what the competition is doing right now, both online and off.

Take a look at your competitors and make notes about what they're doing on their websites. What are they doing that works and what are they doing that doesn't? Pay attention to color, graphics, format, layout, content, and the tone of the writing. This information can help you determine the type of content to include on your site and understand how to deliver it.

Gathering information

In your career as a web designer, oftentimes your client will rely on you to assist with determining the site's purpose. If you or your client hasn't discussed this issue yet, read through the following questions and take careful note of your client's answers:

✔ **Will the site showcase biographies, histories, and other informational data?** Some websites show a listing of employees and board members, biographies, historical timelines, and general information about the company and its key players.

✔ **Will the site market services?** A company, group, or sole proprietor (such as a nonprofit arts organization, a law firm, an artist, or a marketing consultant) might want an informational or *brochureware* website to help spread the word about its services. How many services will be offered? Will pricing information be made available online, too?

✔ **Will this site provide in-depth information about a particular topic?** The function of a political news blog or nonprofit organization is to share ideas and information with the public, while a business that sells products may be more focused on sharing information relevant to a particular industry. For example, a lawn mower company might want to offer lawn-care advice in addition to selling mowers.

✔ **Will the site be someone's personal website?** Personal websites are often created just for family, friends, and schoolmates. It could be a digital family photo album, a blog, or an outlet for personal expression.

✔ **Will the site be someone's professional portfolio?** Professionals use portfolios to generate new business and showcase their talents. People who use portfolios include artists, illustrators, designers, crafts people, writers, singers, photographers, videographers, film and television producers, musicians, poets, and academics.

✔ **Will the site sell any products, and if so, what kinds?** If the site will sell lots of products, find out how many product categories are needed and whether the products will be sold wholesale, retail, or both. Will the products be sold online or through an outside distributor?

After discussing these and other questions with the site owner, you can figure out what you need to design the site to accomplish. The site may need to attract business, share information, provide feedback and advice, be a blog with text and photographs, provide a dating service, sell moving and relocation services, provide virtual secretarial services, supply wholesale products to retailers, or some combination of these and other things.

Developing a statement of purpose

A *statement of purpose,* such as the example shown in Figure 1-1, is a brief summary of the goals for the site, including who the site is for, what the site hopes to accomplish, how it will look, and most importantly, how it will function. Statements are often one or two sentences long, but never longer than a paragraph. Think of the statement of purpose as a type of mission statement. Use the answers to the questions in the preceding section to begin forming a vision of how the site will look and function. For example, a Realtor's website that markets rental properties and realty services will look and function much differently than a nonprofit site for disabled veterans or one that showcases a watercolor artist's portfolio.

After you have all the information for your site (as discussed in the preceding section), you just need to take this information and boil it down into a statement of purpose. Table 1-1 gives examples of several types of businesses and statements of purpose that those business owners might come up with for their sites.

Statement of Purpose for a Graphic Design Studio

This site will be an online portfolio to showcase and promote the design services of *CUSTOMER* to art directors, editors, publishing companies, and others who regularly hire graphic designers for various projects including branding, corporate identity, brochures, letter head, book jackets, web design, and packaging design. In addition to generating new business, the site will also promote *CUSTOMER's* services by including client testimonials, a list of industry related awards, a biography, and a short history about the *CUSTOMER's* studio and work ethic. The design will be clean, open, and minimalistic, with interactive features like jQuery sliders, rollover effects, and accordion panels.

Figure 1-1: A good statement of purpose can help guide the web design process.

Table 1-1	Creating a Statement of Purpose
Type of Business	*Example Statement of Purpose*
Sole proprietor or entrepreneur (such as a business consultant, family therapist, life coach, or private detective)	This site will market services to a wider audience, provide advice about a particular topic, lend a sense of legitimacy to the business, generate more clients, and allow customers to register for a monthly newsletter.
Creative entity (such as an artist, a designer, a crafter, a photographer, a writer, an actor, or a band)	This site will be an online portfolio/showcase for displaying and promoting work (art, music, photos) to art directors, editors, and other people in the industry. Additionally, it will help generate new business, share news and information, and sell a limited number of creative works.
Nonprofit organization	This site will promote services, provide industry-related information, educate the public, collect donations, offer public and private programs and events, list classifieds for members, and supply registration information for fund-raising events.
Personal/non-business blog site (such as a blog that covers the local music or arts scene)	This blog site will report on the local scene, providing information about current and upcoming events, news, popular venues, and important people around town, as well as allow visitors to submit feedback and questions to the authors of the various posts. In addition, the blog will allow visitors to subscribe to an RSS feed, get updates by e-mail, and research topics of interest in the blog's archive.
Small- to medium-sized business (such as a greeting card company, a computer hardware manufacturer, a low-flow showerhead wholesaler, or an adventure tour company)	This site will be an online storefront to sell products and services, answer FAQs, have a library of information related to products and services, provide client testimonials, and allow visitors to contact the business, receive customer support via e-mail and live chat, and subscribe to a weekly newsletter.

Think about the purpose(s) of your website project and write your answers on a sheet of paper or in a new word processing document using the format shown in Figure 1-2. (If you don't have a project in mind, pretend that you're planning a site for a marketing consultant who promotes art books so that you can practice generating ideas for a statement of purpose.) Whatever your answers happen to be, turn them into a statement of purpose that you can keep handy as you read through Book I; the statement can help you organize your ideas and plan the best website for your needs.

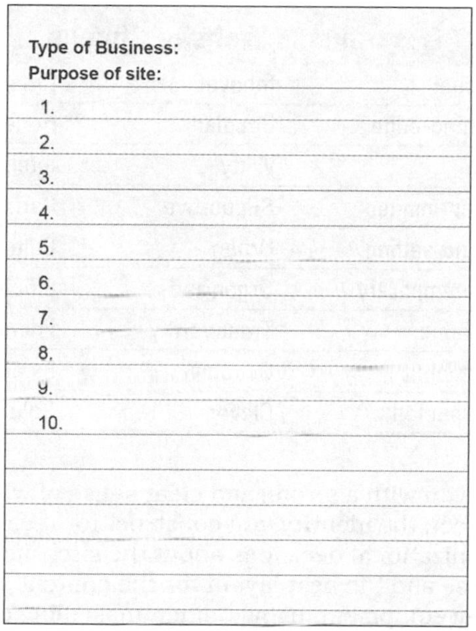

```
Type of Business:
Purpose of site:
1.
2.
3.
4.
5.
6.
7.
8.
9.
10.
```

Figure 1-2: Write a statement of purpose for each site you create.

Building a Site Image

The next important step to take with your project is to define and build the image that the website will project to the consumer. This image establishes the unspoken identity or personality of your website to visitors — an identity that they will (hopefully) respond to both intellectually and emotionally.

To help construct this identity, follow these steps:

1. **Think of the site as if it were your number one salesperson, someone who fully represents the best about the company.**

2. **Come up with as many words as you can to describe this "person's" traits.**

   Is the person professional or laid back, serious or fun, creative or traditional? If the salesperson angle is a bit awkward for you and/or your client, think about the ideal image you'd like the website to project and find adjectives that describe that image. Table 1-2 lists descriptive terms you can use to begin defining the website's image; it's by no means complete, but it should get you started.

Table 1-2	Describing a Website's Image		
Professional	Casual	Innovative	Creative
Traditional	Cutting-edge	Popular	Honest
Open	Fun	Witty	Intelligent
Smart	Open-minded	Supportive	Caring
Technological	Trend-setting	Urban	Cultured
Educated	Contemporary	Organized	Efficient
Cost-effective	Reliable	Trustworthy	Friendly
Talented	Confident	Capable	Established
Savvy	Respected	Clever	Solution-oriented

In addition to providing you with a strong and clear sense of what you're doing with this web project, the identity you construct for it can help you make aesthetic and organizational decisions about the site, such as what colors and graphics to use and the best layout for the content. For example, if your client sells hockey equipment, using bolder, masculine colors will work better than pastels in the design. Or if your client is a medical consultant looking to advertise her services to hospitals and medical centers, advise her to invest in some good royalty-free, industry-specific artwork for the site rather than display the often-overused and amateurish-looking illustrations from the Microsoft Word Clip Art archive. You find out more about creating and licensing artwork for your site in Book I, Chapter 3.

Right now, on a blank piece of paper or in a new word processing document, write a list of at least ten adjectives that describe the company identity or *site image* for your current website project. These are the words that should automatically come to mind when a person visits the website for the first time.

Determining Site Content

After you've identified the site's purpose and made the initial steps toward defining an identity for the site, you should have a pretty good idea about the site you need to develop. Now you're ready to start thinking about what content needs to be presented on the website.

Though there is technically no such thing as an industry standard on the web, logic tells you that certain content should be on every website, regardless of the site's purpose. Beyond that, anything else that goes on the site is up to you — the designer — and, if you're working for someone else, your client.

The more informed you are about the whole web design process, the better the finished product. Even if you already know how a web page should look or how it should function, being able to explain these things can help you clarify your goals as well as educate your client. The client, in turn, might also be able to give you input that is more constructive if she understands the *concepts* behind your design and the principles that drive content selection.

The following general guidelines assist you in figuring out what, at a minimum, should go on a website.

Minimum requirements

At a minimum, your web project needs to supply basic information to site visitors, so your job during this planning phase is to decide what content you need for the pages on your site.

The following information is commonly found in some variation on most websites.

Home page information

The home page is the first page on a website that visitors see when they type your web address, such as www.*yourwebsite*.com. In addition to setting the visual tone of your site through the use of graphics and Cascading Style Sheets (CSS), this page should include the company name and/or logo, navigation to the rest of the pages on the site, and text describing the site's products or services. It is also the most important page on the site because this is where you introduce the site to visitors and search engines. For this and other reasons, the home page should contain at least a paragraph or two of descriptive, keyword-rich, search-engine-friendly HTML text (not a graphic) that generally outlines what visitors can expect to find on the site. Whenever possible, any *keywords* (descriptive terms used to find information on a specific topic) in the text should be hyperlinked to other relevant pages on the site. For example, if you say, "Please contact us for more information," the words "contact us" can be a hyperlink to the site's contact page.

In the not-too-distant past, many sites used the home page as a place to play introductory flash animations, have one giant graphic with an Enter or similar hyperlink, or have a different set of graphics and layout than found on the rest of the website. Though these strategies may have contained a bit of the old "Wow!" factor, they never were a good idea, particularly because they lacked meaningful, searchable content (text) on the home page that can prevent the site from being fully indexed by the most popular search engines. More importantly, when visitors can't find what they're looking for by quickly scanning the home page, they leave. Therefore, make the most of the home page by including relevant text, hyperlinks, and graphics, using the same layout found on the rest of the site. Consistency is key!

Contact information

Visitors will want to know how to get in touch with the owners of the website via phone, mail, or e-mail. Be ready to provide the physical address of the company, the mailing address (if different), telephone and fax numbers, Skype usernames, social media site links such as Facebook and Twitter, and at least one contact e-mail address. You may also want to include special contact information for various employees, departments, and services, as well as local geographical area maps, transportation directions, and hours of operation. Some sites even provide a form on the contact page where visitors can submit personal information, answer survey questions, provide comments and feedback, and/or request information. If you plan to collect data from visitors on the contact page, make a list of the data you intend to collect so that you can have it handy when you build a web form for that page.

Privacy policy

Perhaps you intend to collect any personal information (e-mail address, name, telephone number, and so on) from site visitors on a form, during registration, or for purposes of responding to an inquiry. If that's the case, the site would benefit greatly from including some kind of *privacy policy* that explains to visitors why their data is being taken and what the site will or will not do with that private data.

In the most general terms, a privacy policy should state how the company will care for the collected data, including any *cookies* collected from the computer used to visit the site. (Cookies contain personal data, such as name, address, phone, username, password, IP address, shopping cart contents, and so on, collected by a visited site's server and saved to the visitor's computer so that future visits to that site will run more efficiently.) For example, if the company will share the data with or sell the data to other vendors, you need to state that expressly. Conversely, if the company plans to honor the privacy of visitors and closely guard collected information as if it were a priceless gift, state that clearly.

For a clear example of a simple privacy policy, see www.freeprivacy policy.com/privacy-policy.html. Alternately, www.findlegal forms.com has a generic policy (Privacy Policy Agreement #28152) that you can purchase online for only $8.99 (at the time of this writing). Or, if you want to generate a policy to match your specific business, you can use the Policy Wizard at http://privacyaffiliates.com for just $19.95.

Site map

A site map is the often-forgotten web page that contains a list of organized text links to all the pages on the website. If you want your site to be accessible to as many visitors as possible (including visitors with disabilities using assistive devices, as well as search engine robots and spiders), regardless of how simple or complex the site is, include a site map page. Alternatively, if your site has many pages with multiple categories, consider adding key site map information to the footer area of every page.

Footer

At the bottom of every page of a site, you should include the company name, copyright information, and a series of *footer links,* which are navigation links to the most important pages on the site. At a minimum, include links to such pages as Home, About, Services, Contact, and Site Map. This information not only reminds visitors whose site they're visiting but also provides additional ways for visitors to navigate to other pages on the site.

To really harness the full power of this valuable web real estate, treat this area like a mini site map and list links to not only high-level navigation destinations but also to more detailed subnavigation category pages. Figure 1-3 shows an example of a site that includes all these features. To find out more about making your sites accessible, see Book IV, Chapters 1 and 2.

Footer links

Figure 1-3: Smart websites include footer links.

Marketing and sales content

Whether the website you're designing is for yourself, a sole proprietor, an entrepreneur, a nonprofit organization, or a small- to medium-sized business, the rest of the site content should be geared toward promoting the business and attracting new customers from the pool of site visitors. Therefore, be sure to provide ample information about the company, organization, person, or entity and all the skills, talents, materials, services, and/or products offered, plus anything else you can think of that can benefit the visitor and positively impact business.

Developing an enthusiastic awareness of the website's online and offline competition can greatly assist you in making decisions about what information should (and should not) be included on a website. For example, if you're designing a site for a children's gymnastics program, the site should probably include the necessary information that can help visitors choose to enroll their children as students, such as a schedule, photographs of the facilities and smiling children, a teaching philosophy with instructor bios and certification, parent testimonials, and perhaps a price list. If the school's offline competitors happen to give students free tote bags, perhaps your client's gymnastics school should offer students free T-shirts and balloons that include the company logo and web address.

The following list of potential website pages is not meant to be comprehensive; rather, you may use it as a starting point for brainstorming about the particular content needed for each specific website you create.

Company information

This part of the site, usually called About Us or something to that effect, typically consists of either one page of company-related information or several pages of logically organized company details. The information here should describe the company to the visitor and include some form of the company's mission statement. In addition, this section might include a corporate history and philosophy statement, a directory of employees with bios of the management team, and/or information about available internships and career opportunities at the company.

Biography

Similar in scope to the Company Information section, the biography page (called About Me, Bio, or Biography) usually includes historical and other interesting information about the artist, sole proprietor, educator, or small-business owner. This page, or series of pages, provides information to stimulate interest in the services, skills, work, products, and so on being presented on the website. This might also be a good place to include a résumé or curriculum vitae (an academic's work history and accomplishments) or listings of awards, publications, clients/customers, and upcoming projects or events.

Product/service information

Every product and service offered on a website should have its own detailed description. If the business is service-oriented, describe what the business does, who needs this service, and how long the business has been operating.

If the business sells products, the products need to be organized into logical categories and subcategories, such as Electronics⇨Digital Cameras⇨Nikon Digital Cameras.

In addition to a description for each main category, every individual product deserves its own description, including any information that might be interesting or necessary to purchasers, such as size, dimensions, color, weight, materials, ingredients, nutritional information, care instructions, technical specifications, country of manufacture, and warranty information. Whenever possible, also try to include client/customer testimonials.

Keep in mind that for any copyrighted material you intend to use on the site — including intellectual property, photographs, and illustrations — you must have permission to use it. This means paying royalty fees for rights-managed work, requesting and receiving written permission for non-rights-managed work, and otherwise obtaining the right to use and display the work created by another person or entity. To find out more about copyrights and permissions, see Book I, Chapter 3.

News and press information

This section of the site typically contains current and recent press releases or newsletters, a press release/newsletter archive, articles about the business or industry, and/or any news items in the form of media coverage. This area might also include information about upcoming programs, trade shows and exhibitions, gifts and collections, relevant technology, works in progress, white papers, a historical corporate timeline, an image gallery or media library, and a listing of literary publications.

Video and podcasts

With the advent of YouTube, Vimeo, and other video sharing sites, it's never been easier to insert video into your website. Video clips can be used to sell products, promote services, highlight ideas, offer news and information, and even provide training and tutorials to interested visitors. In addition to adding video directly to the individual pages of your websites, many blogs now include plug-ins that allow you to insert video clips directly into your blog posts. You find out how to add multimedia files to your web pages in Book III, Chapter 8.

Portfolio

When the site belongs to an artist, designer, or other creative professional, the Portfolio area displays an online version of a portfolio, including photos and graphic examples of their work, a résumé or curriculum vitae, video clips, sound files (MP3s), and other types of media files. The online portfolio is fast becoming the best way to market services to a global audience, generate new business, and share news and industry information with the public.

Frequently asked questions (FAQs)

Most visitors have questions — lots of questions — and to convert those visitors into customers, it's a smart practice to answer those questions. When you make common questions and answers available online on FAQ pages, visitors can often find what they need without having to spend extra time making a phone call or sending an e-mail — a big plus in this fast-paced world. Most FAQ pages cover information about contacting the site, searching for information on the site, customizing site preferences or membership accounts, getting more information, using the site, and accessing customer service. Alternately, the FAQ page may contain answers to common questions about products, services, and business-specific information.

 If you don't have a list of information to create a FAQ page yet, start keeping track of questions the business gets asked. When a pattern begins to emerge, add those questions and answers to the FAQ page.

Site search

Though not required, providing a means for searching an entire website's content with keywords can improve the site's *stickiness* (the ability of a site to entice people to stay on the site longer and return often). The most popular free search tool is Google Site Search. Get the code from Google at www.google.com/sitesearch. Google also offers a custom search engine tool at www.google.com/coop/cse that allows site owners to customize the look of the search box as well as host the results on the same site. Two other free site-search tools worth looking at include Bravenet's Site Search (www.braveapps.com/search2) and FusionBot's Free Package (www.fusionbot.com).

Of course, as an alternative to these types of site-search tools, you could hire a PHP programmer to build a custom server-based search tool, complete with a search results page, though the cost might not be justifiable for smaller sites. Or, even better, CMS (Content Management System) tools such as WordPress have built-in site-search features created with PHP, and it's much simpler to install WordPress than hire someone for custom PHP work.

Terms of service

Similar in importance to the Privacy Policy page, the Terms of Service page should state how the site provides services to — and the conditions under which those services must be accepted by — visitors. This may include concepts of intellectual property rights, usage, registration, security, payment, advertising, applicable law, legal compliance, indemnification, and more. Because the Terms of Service page should contain legal content specific to the website's offerings, the best way to create the page is to consult with a lawyer. Do-it-yourselfers can download a generic website Terms of Use Agreement from www.findlegalforms.com for only $8.99.

Shopping cart

Depending on your needs, several kinds of web shopping carts are available for you to choose from. The most basic is a cart that uses PayPal or Google Checkout to process payments. These options require no merchant account, special software, or secure server licensing fees; however, they may require all purchasers to create their own PayPal or Google account before their transaction can be processed. Another option is to create an online store through Yahoo! Shops, which uses the Yahoo! proprietary shopping cart system (see http://smallbusiness.yahoo.com/ecommerce). This service, however, is pricey and doesn't have the easiest interface to use, but it has the benefit of automatically being listed in the Yahoo! shopping directory.

For more customized solutions that include some kind of inventory management system, you'll want something that's tailored specifically to your site's needs. With a simple search, you can find several decent online shopping carts that are free and customizable, carts that are controlled by host providers, and carts that are powered by third-party software manufacturers. There are even free shopping cart plug-ins for WordPress and other CMS systems.

In a 2012 Shopping Cart Software Report on TopTenReviews.com (http://shopping-cart-review.toptenreviews.com), the top-rated shopping cart software programs on the market included Volusion, Shopify, Ashop Commerce, BigCommerce, 3DCart, and Shopsite Pro.

Whatever shopping cart software solution you decide to use, you must take extra care to ensure that visitors' personal information is safe and secure during the purchasing transaction. If your website will process credit card payments (instead of processing them through an outside service such as PayPal or Google Checkout), you need to set up a special merchant account with a qualified bank, as well as purchase an SSL (Secure Sockets Layer) digital security certificate for your domain. Your host provider should be able to assist you in both finding a bank to set up your merchant account and licensing and installing the SSL certificate. You can find more information about merchant accounts, SSL certificates, and working with the different types of e-commerce shopping carts in Book I, Chapter 4.

Customer service (Help)

Any site that plans to sell products or services must have a place for visitors to go to get more information about customer service, including how to contact you, ask questions, and resolve problems. Try not to think of this section of the site as a liability but rather as an opportunity to get to know and serve your customers better. Look at other successful websites to gather ideas on how to set up this valuable area of your site. Consider having sections for ordering information, privacy issues, shipping and delivery, dealing with returns or damaged items, and accessing account information, just to name a few.

The easier you make it for visitors to get answers, the more positive their experience on your site will be. Furthermore, the better the customer satisfaction, the more likely that can quickly translate into free word-of-mouth advertising and repeat customers.

Site credits

Though site credits by no means need to be included on a website, why not toot the horn of the designer or design team (you!) that turned a site concept into a web reality? If you've included a clause in your client contract to do so, add a Site Credit or Web Design By [Yourname] link on the site, preferably embedded somewhere in the footer links. Otherwise, ask your client for permission to include the link. The Site Credit link itself can go directly to the website of the designer or open a page similar in layout to the rest of the site with designer contact information.

XHTML, HTML, HTML5, CSS, CSS3, and 508 compliance information

If the site has been built to be accessible to any and all web visitors, consider proudly displaying compliance information somewhere on the site, such as in the footer, on the Contact page, or in some other logical section of the site. You can find out more about how to adhere to the accessibility guidelines set by online web standards organizations in Book IV, Chapter 1, which is entirely devoted to working with web standards.

RSS feeds

Sites that include blogs may want to consider syndication of the blog content through an RSS feed, which can be used to automatically notify registered readers (by e-mail, web portal, and news readers) of new posts and information. There are some really good RSS feed services such as FeedBurner (owned by Google), as well as products you can use yourself, such as the RSS Feed Creator application from `http://sourceforge.net`. To find out more about RSS, check out the Google help pages at `www.google.com/support/feedburner`.

Diagnosing the Site's Dynamic Requirements

A dynamic website refers to any site that uses a programming language — such as PHP, ASP, ASP.NET, JSP, CGI, Perl, Oracle, Java, Ajax, or ColdFusion — to gather specific records of information from a database, such as Microsoft Access or MySQL, and displays that data on a web page. A *database* is any collection of information, such as a spreadsheet, that organizes the data into categories that can be easily retrieved by a computer program or programming language on a website.

Many sole proprietors, small businesses, and nonprofit organizations with limited-content sites might have little (if any) need to offer a website with dynamic capabilities. Having dynamic content on a website largely depends on the goals and budget of the site's owner.

For sites with lots of content, a dynamic site with a database and CMS system should be a serious consideration. By organizing and storing data in a database, the content can be selectively pulled according to different scenarios or rules set up in advance. For instance, one business might want to display the ten most recent news items about the company on a page. Presuming that new data is regularly being entered into the database, the programming language can be set to check article publication dates and always pull and display the ten most recent files on a particular page.

Databases should almost always be used if you're selling products on your site; however, you can also use databases to store and retrieve all kinds of information. For instance, you might decide to use a database on your (or your client's) website to display the following:

- Articles, papers, and documents sorted by date, author, and so on
- Lists of services and service detail information
- Calendar of events, schedules, contact information, and important dates
- Categories of products for sale and product detail information
- Customer data such as a purchase log, order records, and account information
- Customer membership information or saved shopping cart details
- Store locations, hours of operation, and contact information
- Tracking information for uploads and downloads to and from the site
- A glossary of industry-related terms or FAQs

In addition to dynamically accessing and using data, databases can be used to assist with adding, deleting, and editing content on a website. For an added fee, many programmers and host providers can now build a custom Content Management System (CMS) for a site, which allows site owners to easily manage specific parts of the site's content — without having to know any programming languages or HTML — through a customized web interface. Depending on the size of the project and the complexity of the dynamic needs, a CMS website component can cost from as little as $1,000 to as much as $15,000 or more. This type of cost-effective tool can be extremely useful for sites that require frequent updates.

A more convenient, affordable, and popular option is to build your site using a free CMS system, such as WordPress. Many host providers now offer one-click installation of the WordPress software, which is helping to make it one of the preferred methods for building small-scale websites, either with or without a blog component. Other popular CMS systems besides WordPress include Drupal, Joomla, and ExpressionEngine.

Though admittedly slick and cool, not every site needs to use a database (unless the site includes a blog, in which case a database is a must, or if you want to use a particular predesigned WordPress template). To determine whether the site you are building needs one, take a good look at the type of content you intend to display and ask yourself (or your client) these questions:

- ✔ **How often will the content need updating?** Sites with daily and weekly update requirements might benefit from a database, whereas sites requiring less frequent modifications might be better off without the added expense. Non-database site updates can be performed by the designer who built the site (you!) or by the client using simple web-editing software, such as Adobe Contribute.

- ✔ **Are more than 20 products or services being sold?** If the site is selling only a handful of products, each product can have its own web page, although that method is time-consuming. However, if more than 20 products will be sold or if the client anticipates increasing its product line to over 20 in the foreseeable future, using a database to dynamically create each product page is more efficient.

- ✔ **What kind of growth does the company expect to achieve in the next year, three years, or five years?** For some sites, little to no anticipated growth will be expected, and therefore you have no real cost justification for using dynamic features. On the other hand, sites that project to grow their products and services over the coming months and years might greatly benefit from building a site that can accommodate such growth.

- ✔ **Does the company need to collect and use visitor data?** E-commerce sites, such as the www.dummies.com website shown in Figure 1-4, have good reason to collect data from purchasers to both streamline the ordering process and provide future sale and promotional information. By contrast, a small business could just as easily manage that information by using a simple HTML form and an Excel file.

- ✔ **Is there or will there soon be enough dynamic content — such as a listing of store locations or the ten most exciting daily news articles — to justify the added cost of making the site dynamic?** If you have the budget and foresee a need for dynamic content, setting up a data-driven site from the start can be more cost effective than adding one to a static site down the road. Certainly the old adage "to make money, you need to spend money" pertains, but not everyone can afford to spend the money up front, even when he or she wants to.

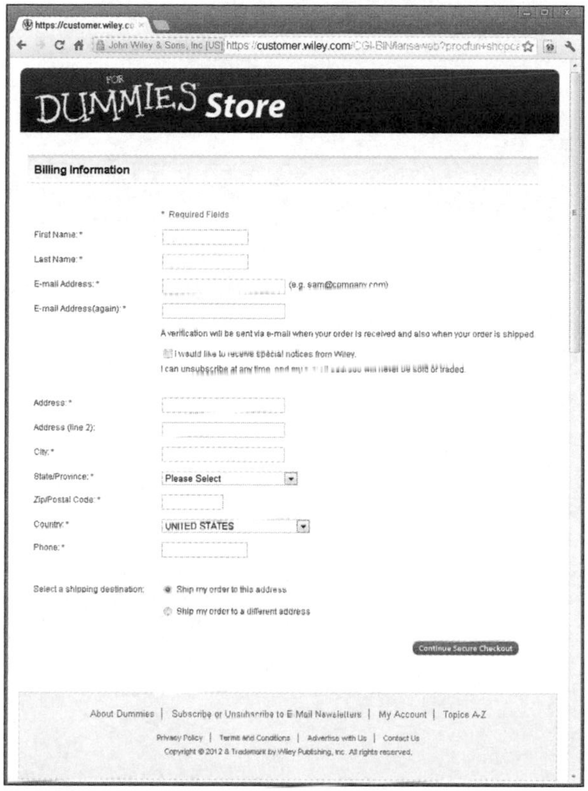

Figure 1-4: An e-commerce website collects data from its visitors.

In some cases, a blog site might be the best solution. For instance, you may be able to accomplish everything you need (daily entries, content management system, e-commerce, and so on) with a WordPress or Tumblr blog site. For details about working with these platforms, see *WordPress For Dummies* by Lisa Sabin-Wilson and *Tumblr For Dummies* by yours truly, Sue Jenkins.

Ultimately, the decision about whether to create a dynamic site should be fairly clear after answering these types of questions. If you're still unsure about whether to use a database for your site, get quotes from programmers or hosting companies to see how it will impact the budget for your project. Money can often be the great decider.

Chapter 2: Defining the Audience

In This Chapter

✔ **Performing market research**

✔ **Gathering information on the target audience's computer use**

✔ **Assessing a site's competition**

✔ **Understanding how to characterize a target audience**

✔ **Determining benefits to site visitors**

After the planning phase of your web project, as explained in Book I, Chapter 1, you should have enough information to successfully move into the contract phase, where you estimate fees for the project and draft and submit a proposal to the client.

When the client gives verbal or written approval of the proposal, you can write an official contract and present it to the client for signatures. If you don't already have a contract, check out the article about web design contracts at http://webdesign.tutsplus.com/articles/workflow/writing-the-perfect-web-design-contract/, which links to a few sample contracts you can use as a starting point. After you draft your own copy, you can modify it as needed to suit your individual projects. If desired, and if you can afford it, you may want to have the contract checked over by a lawyer first.

www.komiorganics.com

BALANCI

MENU   RESEARC

At the same time as you receive the signed contract from your client, you can also collect financial retainers or deposits, along with any content or materials needed to begin development of the site. Ask for at least a 25 percent deposit from the client before you do any work. This shows good faith on your part for doing the work and good faith on the client's part that he is serious about having you do the work and is willing to pay part of the fees to retain your services.

After you get the contract and deposit, you can safely enter the design phase, which you begin by identifying the target audience. This is an information-gathering process that helps you make an effective website design. The *target audience* for a website is the ideal group of visitors site owners hope to attract in an effort to increase web traffic and thereby improve sales. In other words, they're the intended visitors of a website, as defined by their common interests, habits, and demographics. This ideal group might be of a certain age or gender; come from a particular part of a neighborhood, city, county, state, region, or country; and have very specific interests, as well as particular likes and dislikes.

This chapter shows you how to define your target audience by finding out everything you can about them — what their computer usage and Internet surfing habits are, where they fall demographically, what their buying preferences are, and what special interests they may have. To determine these and other characteristics, you (and your client if building a site for someone else) should carry out certain pre-design tasks. This includes performing a bit of informal (or formal) market research, gathering Internet usage statistics, and taking a look at what the competition is doing so that you can create a more attractive design for the site and ensure that the site includes the relevant content and user experience that the target audience is likely to seek. You also spend a little time doing your own informal market research by taking a good look at the competition to give your web project an extra edge.

Doing Informal Market Research

Market research is a type of research performed when information about a particular group of people is gathered as an aid to making strategic marketing decisions. Whether performed in a formal or informal manner, market research is one of the best ways to begin the design phase of any website project.

With your particular web design project in mind, be sure to complete the following three tasks, from the checklist shown in Figure 2-1, to make the most of your market research time:

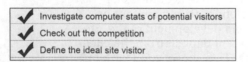

✔ Investigate computer stats of potential visitors
✔ Check out the competition
✔ Define the ideal site visitor

Figure 2-1: Create your own marketing research checklist to gather information about your project.

✔ **Gather general information about the computer usage and Internet browsing habits of Internet users.** This knowledge about the people using the Internet can greatly help you make important decisions about the site's design measurements, organization, layout, color palette, image usage, navigation scheme, and accessibility features.

✔ **Find out what other businesses in the same field have already done with their websites.** By looking at competitors' websites, you can quickly assess what was already done poorly and take steps to avoid those same mistakes. In addition, you can find out a lot from what the competition has already done successfully and make plans to implement similar (though not identical — that would be plagiarism or copyright infringement) ideas in your web project.

✔ **Define the ideal site visitor based on the demographic and other statistical information you gather from your own informal marketing research.** The clearer your understanding of your target audience — their ages, income levels, buying habits, and interests — the easier it is to customize your site design to their tastes. (See Book II, Chapters 1 and 2, for more on implementing your design.)

If you don't know much about market research, take a look at KnowThis.com (http://knowthis.com), which bills itself as the Marketing Virtual Library — a place where visitors can find out about market research, marketing, advertising, and more. Besides the general marketing information, you can also find many useful articles, tutorials, and even free research reports there. Another great resource on marketing and market research is the Marketing section on About.com (http://marketing.about.com).

Gathering Internet Usage Statistics

Before you gather any specific demographic information about your target audience (which you define later in this chapter), do research and gather some general information about what folks are on the Internet and what kinds of computers, mobile devices, operating systems, and browsers they use.

Finding statistics online

You can easily find out more about Internet users by reviewing the latest statistics regarding their computer usage and Internet-browsing habits. Here are some guidelines to get you started:

✔ **Visit one or more online resource websites that offer information on computer usage and browsing.** One of the best is www.w3schools.com, shown in Figure 2-2, where you can find a list of detailed, long-running (since January 2002), up-to-date browser, mobile device, operating system (OS), and computer usage statistics.

For additional, comparative statistical data on general Internet usage and browsing habits, visit these sites:

- http://www.w3counter.com/globalstats.php
- http://gs.statcounter.com
- http://www.netmarketshare.com

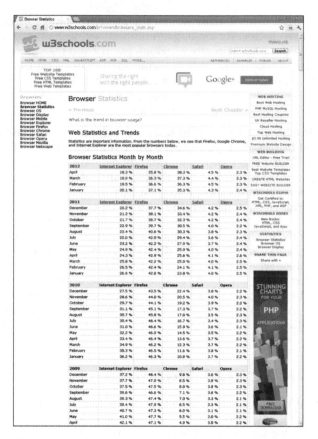

Figure 2-2: Gather Internet usage statistics from reputable sites like this one.

✔ **Jot down the information you find out about browser usage.** Look specifically at the percentage of users on the most popular browsers, including Firefox, Chrome, Safari, Opera, and Internet Explorer (IE). For mobile/tablets, pay attention to Safari, Android, Opera Mini, and Symbian Browsers.

✔ **Find out which operating systems are the most popular among people accessing the web.** For computers, the ranking is Windows, then Mac, then Linux. You might be surprised at how few Internet users are on a Mac versus a PC. By contrast, with mobile/tablet operating systems, you'll find that iOS has the lion's share, with Android, Windows, Blackberry, Java ME, and Symbian following behind.

✔ **Find out the monitor resolutions and bit depths of Internet users.** This data is often referred to as *Browser Display Statistics*.

The *bit depth* is the grayscale or color depth of an individual pixel of an image displayed on a monitor. An 8-bit-depth monitor can display only 256 colors, whereas 24-bit and 32-bit color monitors display 16.7 million colors!

Display resolution refers to the number of pixels, organized horizontally and vertically, that are used by a computer monitor to set the screen size of the monitor. The most common factory default size is 1,024 x 768 or higher. When the resolution size is set to a particular size, the monitor uses bits — actual tiny squares — of color to create the on-screen display. The more bits that are used, the clearer the image and the more colors that can be displayed. Higher resolutions result in more pixels being used onscreen. In other words, you can fit more on your screen at a higher resolution, though everything will be displayed proportionately smaller.

✔ **Note what percentage of Internet users (98 percent as of January 2010) leave JavaScript enabled in their browsers.** JavaScript is an easy-to-use, easy-to-learn, simple scripting language that, when added to a web page's HTML code, can perform dynamic and interactive functions in a browser window, such as opening new browser windows, changing an image when a visitor moves the cursor over a graphic (*rollover buttons*), and displaying the current date. Plus, when combined with HTML and CSS, JavaScript can add fun and interesting interactivity to a web page with elements such as galleries and image sliders.

Though the percentage is small, some site visitors either don't have browsers or other web-reading devices that support JavaScript or have chosen to disable it. To make a site accessible to all possible visitors, the site should be accessible in a web browser even when JavaScript is turned off.

Interpreting statistics

Going by the analytic data from www.w3schools.com, as of August 2012, the following percent of computer users surfed the Internet with the following browsers:

Browser	Percentage of Internet Users
Google Chrome	43.7 percent
Firefox	32.8 percent
Internet Explorer 8	7.8 percent
Internet Explorer 9	6.2 percent
Safari	4.0 percent
Internet Explorer 7	1.8 percent
Opera	2.2 percent

The computers and operating systems Internet users have is as follows:

Operating System	Percentage of Internet Users
Windows 7	54.5 percent
Windows XP	24.8 percent
Mac OS X	8.7 percent
Linux	5.0 percent
Windows Vista	3.2 percent
Mobile	1.8 percent

And, because new monitors come with factory-preset resolutions of at least 1,024 x 768 pixels (13 percent) or higher (85 percent), nearly all of these computer users who go online leave their monitors' resolution at the factory setting.

This kind of information clearly tells you that, at a minimum, you need to test your web page development in Chrome, Firefox, and Internet Explorer JavaScript-enabled browsers on a PC with a 24-bit-depth monitor with a resolution set to 1,024 x 768 or higher prior to site launch, because these are the facts about most of the online population that is likely to visit the website. In other words, though your ideal site visitor will have certain characteristics, the majority of visitors will have certain characteristics in common, as listed in Figure 2-3. In addition, to make the site accessible to the widest possible audience, you should also test in all the operating systems and in the different browsers on both the Mac and PC, as well as testing to see how your site appears in mobile and handheld devices such as smartphones and tablets.

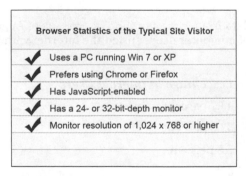

Figure 2-3: A majority of Internet users have several things in common.

Using real-time Internet traffic reports

After a web project is completed and published on the Internet, the site can harness the power of real-time Internet traffic reports to gather statistical data about actual site visitors, including geographic origin, search term usage, entry and exit pages, and more. Two well-respected, fee-based services that provide web statistics and analysis are Opentracker (www.opentracker.net) and Omniture (www.omniture.com; now owned by Adobe). Although costly, this kind of sophisticated data mining can help site owners quickly identify marketing strategies that aren't working so that they can make site improvements based on actual visitor preferences such as search term usage (which search term led the user to your site), entry page, exit page, and time spent on the site. For a wonderful free alternative, consider using Google Analytics. Visit www.google.com/analytics to set up your free or premium account and learn more about your visitors, how they interact with your site, and ways you can improve your site to attract more visitors and convert them into paying customers.

Sizing Up the Competition

No matter what business you or your client happens to be in, you're bound to find other websites that represent competitors in the same field that can be evaluated for their apparent successes and failures. The beauty of this market research strategy is that it's free, and as long as you have access to a computer, you can do this kind of business investigation online anytime you want.

Performing keyword searches for similar companies

Begin your research by opening your favorite search engine and doing several keyword searches for similar businesses in the local, regional, state, national, and global arenas, regardless of your web project's anticipated marketing scope. For example, if you're working on a web project for a local catering company that does business only within a 100-mile radius of its office, don't limit your searches to local competition only. Instead, make sure that you also search for catering company websites across the country. If you do this, you're more likely to find some great catering websites in other geographic regions that can be used for design inspiration as well as a springboard for defining and refining your project's site content and design requirements.

Keywords — if you didn't already know this — are any specific words or phrases that define the object, person, or place a site visitor is searching for in a search engine, database, or catalog. For example, if you want to find a new hairdresser, you might do a search-engine search for the keywords *hair salon* along with the name of your city and state, such as *hair salon, San Francisco, CA*. After submitting the keywords to the search engine, the browser then displays a search results page that lists all the results that contain those same keywords. The results are culled from all the websites on the Internet that include those keywords in their page content, page titles, headings, and metadata, all of which were purposefully placed there to drive additional traffic to a website.

How do you know which keywords to use to find these competitors' websites? The answer is simple: Just think of the words you would use to find your client's business online.

Another way to find relevant keywords for your site is to take a peek at the competition's keywords, which are typically placed in the `Keywords` and `Description` meta tags inside the HTML code of the website's home page. Not all sites use them, but the good ones do. To locate these keywords, open a competitor's website in a browser window and choose View⇨Page Source from the browser's main menu. If you can't find a view option, look for Tools⇨View Source, or try right-clicking to access the option from a contextual menu. The browser opens a separate window that contains the HTML code of the page displayed in the browser. Scroll down just a little from the top until you see the `title` and the `meta` tags, and review the `Keywords` and `Description`. The tags should look something like this example from www.komiorganics.com:

```
<title>Komi Organics :: Balanced homemade kid's meals, fresh to your doorstep! ::
    We deliver in Manhattan :: Order today!</title>
<meta name="Keywords" content="organic, kids, children, food, meals, healthy,
    delivery, new york, manhattan, nyc" />
<meta name="Description" content="Komi Organics LLC, manufactures organic
    children's meals in a certified kitchen, and then delivers meals to residents
    of Manhattan, NY. This service is sold as a five day meal plan, which
    consists of a balanced lunch and dinner for Monday through Friday. Delivery
    of meals occurs three times per five day delivery period (M/W/F)." />
```

You can find out more about working with meta tags in Book I, Chapter 3, but if you're eager to find out even more about them, read Google's Webmaster Tools blog post on meta tags at `http://support.google.com/webmasters/bin/answer.py?hl=en&answer=79812` and check out Search Engine Watch's article on meta tags at `http://searchenginewatch.com/article/2067564/How-To-Use-HTML-Meta-Tags`.

To illustrate how to perform keyword searches at the local, state, and global market levels to assess the competition, I use an example client who owns and operates an antique shop in Hartford, Connecticut, that specializes in Victorian furniture. Here's what you should do:

1. **In the search field of your favorite search engine (such as Google, Bing, Yahoo!, Ask, or AOL), type the local search keywords, including the commas and spaces.**

   Using the antique shop example, you would use the keywords *antique furniture, victorian, hartford, connecticut*, as shown in Figure 2-4.

   The local search includes the name of the client's city and state, which can help the search engine narrow the focus of the returned results. Results should include a listing of other antique stores in the same town that also specialize in antique Victorian furniture. Take a look at the top 10 or 20 links and review each site, making notes about the content and layout.

Figure 2-4: Use your favorite search engine to find competition at the local, state, and global market levels.

2. **For the next search, expand the results listing to a statewide search by entering appropriate keywords into the browser search field.**

   In this example, you enter the keywords *antique furniture, victorian, connecticut*.

   This search doesn't include the city of Hartford, so the results include antique furniture stores throughout the state of Connecticut. The results are now geared more toward antique businesses within the state; dealers, buyers, and collectors; antique search directories; and antiquing blogs. Again, click through to the top 10 to 20 links in the search results listings and note any interesting content and layout features that appeal to you and might be useful to mention to your Hartford antique shop client.

3. **For the last search, which is national or global in nature, omit any geography in the keywords.**

   For this example, you would use the keywords *antique furniture, victorian.*

   This last search provides links to other antique furniture businesses across the country, as well as to sites that sell other kinds of antiques besides Victorian furniture, antique buying guides, home furnishing stores, appraisers, reproduction services, and showrooms. In this search results listing, you might want to explore sites deeper than 20 entries to find other relevant competitors' sites, because this search result includes a wider variety of results that may or may not suit your needs.

As you can see, the results listings for each of these keyword searches are geared to the specific geographic areas contained in the keyword string, providing you with more insight to the world of antique Victorian furniture across the city, state, and country. By doing wider searches like this, you're likely to find that companies doing national and even global business tend to have the better-looking, better-functioning sites when compared to their state and local counterparts.

Evaluating competitors' sites

As you evaluate the sites in the search results listings, look closely at the content presented and work with your client to ensure that his or her site includes content that visitors will want to read. In the case of BBQ catering, that might mean including sections on the site like Company Information, Menus, Directions to the Restaurant (if the catering is part of the main business of running a restaurant), Press Releases and Awards, Visitor Comments, Specialty Sauces for Sale, and possibly Dine-In Coupons.

Here are some questions you might want to ask when reviewing competitors' sites:

- Can you determine where the target audience lives: in the suburbs, the countryside, in the city, in a particular region, or all over the world?

- What kinds of photographic and graphic images appeal to the target audience?

- Do competitors' sites use any particular colors repeatedly in an attempt to appeal to their target audience? Should you copy them or stray from the pack?

- What is the target audience's age group: Kids? Teens? Adults? Seniors?

✔ Does the target audience have any particular hobbies or group interests, such as being an avid reader, sports fan, cook, artist, or gamer?

✔ Can you guess what kinds of values (religious, ethical, political, and so on) the audience might share?

✔ Can you identify any specific needs of the target audience (such as seeking green solutions for living in a better world)?

Pay particular attention to website details, such as colors, shapes, fonts, photographs, and other design elements that are consistently used on competitors' sites. When you know what everyone else is doing, you have the opportunity to decide whether to follow suit or break the mold in a unique and interesting way. If you're developing a new site for a company in the finance industry, for instance, and you notice that almost all the competitors use navy blue as the primary color and burgundy as the secondary color, consider using two different but similar colors for your design, such as a light blue and a rusty tan.

Also pay attention to the marketing messages other sites use to sell their products and services. These messages often shed revealing light on the target audience's buying preferences, habits, likes, and dislikes.

Even when your client provides you with all the content before you begin the design phase of the project, you should still perform a keyword review of the competition to ensure that the client hasn't forgotten anything that might make his or her website more attractive to visitors. This research can also help you to make important decisions about layout and design so that the site will stand out from the competition.

Other good resource areas for gathering market research on a particular topic or business are the industry-related associations and organizations, as well as government agencies. You can often find websites for these groups by doing a search in your favorite search engine using terms like "*Industryname* Association of America," "American *Industryname* Association," or "Association of *Industryname* of America."

Summarizing your results

When you're done with your research, organize the information into logical categories and summarize the details into a few definition-packed sentences. For example, if you perform keyword searches about a new website you'll be designing for an interior design company based in San Francisco, you might discover that many other interior design websites do three things: They favor using black, white, gray, and earth tones in their website designs; they display lots of photographic examples of their work; and they target their services to an audience who is well-educated, cultured, and moneyed.

With this information, you can write a summary of facts such as

> "Black, white, gray, and earth tones; clean, linear layouts; and a sophisticated audience that needs to be wowed with photographic examples of the client's work."

You can then use this summary to assist you in both defining the ideal site visitor and then coming up with a design that will appeal visually to that target audience. In fact, if you want to take things a step further, you can quickly mock up a visual profile of the target audience, like the one shown in Figure 2-5.

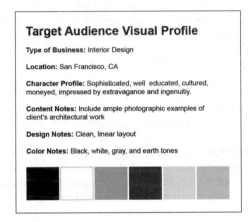

Figure 2-5: A quick visual profile of the target audience can help you make important decisions about a site's content, layout, and design.

Defining the Ideal Site Visitor

After you've done your demographic research to define your target audience, you can take things one step further and imagine a single ideal site visitor who would want to buy whatever products or services your site offers. Having a clear understanding of the ideal site visitor is an essential element of the design phase because that refined, detailed description guides you in making important decisions about the site's design. For instance, if you're developing a health care website for an audience composed mostly of seniors, you might deduce that a larger font size is an important issue and thus choose to make special modifications to the site's Cascading Style Sheets (by using percentages or other scalable measurement units for the font size rather than pixels, which are fixed in size) that can allow those visitors to adjust font sizes in their browsers. This also provides you with the opportunity to ensure that the site layout looks good both when the fonts are normal size and when they're increased in the browser.

At this stage, after gathering general computer usage information and doing some informal research about the competition (as described earlier in the "Sizing Up the Competition" section), it's time to figure out who the ideal visitor is for your website. If you're lucky, the company hiring you as a designer will have already done some of its own market research and can quickly tell you the detailed demographic information about the people using its products or services. Your role here is one of gathering and distilling the demographic data into an *identity description* of the ideal site visitor.

Start by asking your client for a demographic profile of his target audience. If that information isn't available, you can do what I call *research by proxy,* which is essentially harvesting information about the target audience by looking at competitors' websites and other industry-related sites. Perhaps you already got a sense of that audience as you performed your keyword searches (as described earlier in the "Sizing Up the Competition" section). Or, if you haven't done any keyword searches on your own yet, do them now.

To assist you, use the following questions to help define the ideal site visitor for your web project. Ideally, if you're working for someone else, your customer should perform this task, not you. In many cases, however, a customer is hiring you to help figure out all this stuff. After all, you're supposed to be the web design expert. To illustrate how you might answer each question (or guide your customer to answer them for you), I use the example of a client seeking a website to sell his designer, screen-printed, organic cotton, men's and women's T-shirts.

✔ **Is the ideal visitor a man or woman, or does that matter?**

A website for a mostly male audience might look very different from one that has a mostly female audience, whereas a site that should appeal to all visitors, both male and female, can (and probably should) use more gender-neutral colors in its design.

T-shirt site: Because the client is selling both men's and women's T-shirts, the audience must include both men and women. However, because women shop more often than men, the ideal visitor is probably female.

✔ **Is the ideal visitor young, old, or somewhere in between? What age range does he or she fall in?**

Having a target age or age range for the ideal site visitor can assist you with making artistic and accessibility decisions. For example, a site for mostly college-aged student visitors can be more alternative in design layout, color, and font usage than a site that needs to appeal to white-collar businesspeople in their 40s or 50s.

T-shirt site: Designer T-shirt wearers tend to be in the 12–42-year-old age range, depending on the grade of cotton, the sophistication of the design, and the intended retail outlets, if any. Presuming that the client wants celebrities like Justin Bieber and Kim Kardashian wearing them, narrow the age range to 16–35-year-olds.

✔ **Answering the next set of questions, which might rely solely on your imagination, can assist you in making other design and layout decisions. Does the ideal visitor**

- Smoke or drink alcohol?
- Attend a place of worship?
- Eat organically?
- Participate in sports?
- Clip coupons?
- Watch TV?
- Read newspapers?
- Vote and get involved with politics?
- Own any pets?

Really get down to particulars and describe your ideal site visitor as clearly and vividly as you would a person sitting next to you. The more you understand who will be visiting a site, the better that site can look and function as well as provide the information the visitor seeks.

T-shirt site: Because trendy people often break the rules, presume that the ideal visitor is a female who loves to shop, goes to parties, attends church on holidays, occasionally eats organically, doesn't play team sports but does yoga and Pilates, snowboards in the winter, barely watches TV or reads newspapers, spends most of her free time with friends, and has (or really wants to get) a tiny pet dog.

✔ **Using adjectives or descriptive statements, create a list of ten or more identity traits that define the ideal site visitor, similar to the exercise you perform in constructing an image for the website in Book I, Chapter 1.**

Is the ideal site visitor smart or of average intelligence? Is he or she urban or suburban? Is he or she organized or messy, confident or timid, silly or serious? Who is this person?

T-shirt site: Single, urban, confident, a little irresponsible, fashionable, outgoing, makes good grades, image-conscious, sassy, and fun to be around.

✔ **Using the ten or so adjectives you generated in the previous point, write an identity statement for your project's ideal site visitor.**

The identity statement becomes your guiding statement of who to design the website for.

T-shirt site: A single, 22-year-old female who is an urban, confident, sometimes irresponsible, fashionable, outgoing person who overspends on fashion; likes to dance, have fun, meet new people, and try new things; goes to parties; drives a fun car; and lives with roommates.

When you are finished, you may want to round out your visual profile of the ideal site visitor with a photo, like the one shown in Figure 2-6.

**Target Audience
Visual Profile**

Type of Business:
T-Shirt Designer/Manufacturer

Location:
Brooklyn, NY

Character Profile:
Ashley is a single, 22-year-old female who is an urban, confident, sometimes irresponsible, fashionable, outgoing person that overspends on fashion, likes to dance, have fun, meet new people, and try new things, goes to parties, drives a fun car, and lives with roommates.

Content Notes:
Include photos of cool young people wearing merchandise

Design Notes:
Simple design with large text, and bold areas of flat color punctuated with sample tshirt designs

Color Notes:
purples, aquas, black, white, and some neutral tan tones

Figure 2-6: Add a photo to your target audience visual profile to put a sample face on the ideal site visitor.

Table 2-1 offers some additional examples of identity descriptions for a variety of businesses. Each description is unique to the type of business it represents, and each speaks to the creation of a different look and feel for the site's design. Remember, the specific account of the ideal site visitor for your project can help you make intuitive, informed decisions about the site's colors, fonts, navigation, images, and more when you start working on the site's design.

Table 2-1	Sample Identity Descriptions
Type of Business	*Description of the Ideal Site Visitor*
Life coach	Committed, somewhat educated, lower- to middle-class male or female who is or will soon be making a major life change and needs assistance getting organized, making decisions, meeting deadlines, and setting and achieving goals.
Alternative rock band	Urban, hip, trendsetting, open-minded, cutting-edge, casual, friendly 20- or 30-something person who wants to hear new music in clubs, download music, and/or write/create positive reviews about us for blogs, tweets, YouTube videos, e-zines, magazines, and newspapers. Also professional, honest, intelligent, open-minded, efficient, friendly, capable, and respected A&R music executive who is looking to sign record contracts with new alternative rock bands.
Global warming awareness nonprofit organization	Smart, informed, educated, caring, concerned, active, supportive, reliable, and solution-oriented person (of all ages, races, sexes, and religions) who will take steps in his or her life to reduce global warming, as well as take an active role in educating others about this serious issue.
Start-up greeting card company	Fun, open, honest, witty, creative, professional, 20–80-year-old woman owner of retail gift store who is looking to buy new greeting card lines and establish long-term wholesale buying relationships with a start-up greeting card company.

Determining Benefits to Site Visitors

Now you can put all the pieces together. Taking the site's general purpose, which you created in Book I, Chapter 1, and combining it with the keyword market research you did on the competition and the identity description you just created for the ideal site visitor, you can begin to construct ideas about the tangible benefits to visitors.

Benefits can help persuade visitors to purchase products, use services, tell all their friends about it, and return to the site often. To really understand what those benefits are, put yourself in the shoes of consumers and look at the website from their perspective.

Before you design and build any website, you should always determine what that site's visitors can gain from visiting that particular site and hopefully purchasing its particular products or services. The benefits of doing this are what can set your site apart from your competitors' sites. For example, when you're designing a site for a organic children's meals delivery service in New York City, if you know that its distinguishing benefits are the quality of the organic ingredients they use, the fact that their meal plans ensure your child gets 100 percent of the RDA of nutrients, and that each meal plan is carefully researched and approved by a nutritionist, you can highlight those details in the design for the company's site, as illustrated in Figure 2-7. If you don't have this knowledge at the onset of the project, you might encounter design revision setbacks further down the line.

Figure 2-7: Understanding a company's benefits to visitors can help you with the site's design and layout.

Defining the true benefits

A *benefit* is something that is useful, helpful, or advantageous and enhances or promotes health, happiness, and prosperity.

Whereas opinions won't necessarily provide any tangible benefits to the customer, benefits can sway a buyer to favor one product over another. For example, every pizza parlor across the country will tell you it has the best pizza. And to stay competitive in business, each parlor probably has a legion of regulars who will swear up and down that the pizza there really is the best in their neighborhood, town, state, or country. To claim that the pizza is the best, however, is only an opinion.

Having the best pizza in town, while true, might benefit the consumers only if their lives are improved by eating it. Therefore, rather than boasting on a website to have the best pizza in town, it makes more sense to market verifiable facts about the parlor — and build those elements into the design. For example, you might say that it uses the best reduced-fat mozzarella, makes its own low-cholesterol pizza sauce from tomatoes grown fresh at local farms, is rated number 1 in the ZAGAT survey, and that two slices of its famous Italiano salad pizza contain only 390 calories.

What are some of the tangible benefits your web project's target audience might get from visiting that site? What will make them happy, prosperous, and healthy? What can they find there that is useful, helpful, or advantageous? What would be important to you if you were that visitor? Write it all down.

Taking the visitor's perspective

To give you the experience of taking the visitor's perspective to come up with a solid list of benefits to the visitor, try this next example in which you take a look at one type of business to see how you can convert someone's skills into benefits and clearly state why visitors should want to use the business's products or services.

Here's the scenario: Suppose that your client is a professional digital photographer looking to increase business by putting a portfolio website online. She has extensive studio and field experience, has won some important industry awards, has completed hundreds of fashion shoots around the world, and is willing to travel for the right project.

What's in it for me?

When you purchase a product or service online, the benefits you hope to receive from the item are part of what makes you decide to make the purchase in the first place. Good online marketers know that those benefits need to appear front and center so that you can decide quickly whether a product or service is right for you.

Take a few minutes to visit the following sites to see whether you can quickly identify at least two product or service benefits:

✔ Dreamweaver: www.adobe.com/products/dreamweaver

✔ Firefox: www.mozilla.com/firefox

✔ Epson: www.epson.com (In the Products area, note how features and benefits are highlighted for individual products.)

✔ The Nature Conservancy: www.nature.org

Hint: Benefit statements often begin with action verbs such as *create, manage,* and *develop.*

The benefits to those visitors making their way to this client's website might include the following:

✔ **This photographer is Equipped.** She owns her own studio and digital photographic equipment, so there will be no hidden equipment fees if a site visitor hires her.

✔ **This photographer is Accomplished.** Hiring this award-winning photographer means that visitors can feel confident that their projects will have quality results when using this photographer's services.

✔ **This photographer is Experienced.** With over ten years' experience in the fashion industry, visitors can rely on this photographer's skills, talent, and professionalism.

✔ **This photographer is Global.** She has traveled around the world in the past with *Elle, Vogue,* and *Sports Illustrated,* and she is willing to travel anywhere in the world. Visitors can rest assured that this photographer will probably go anywhere for the right assignment.

To discover some benefits that your particular website project can offer to its ideal site visitors, try asking yourself what you would want to know if you wanted to do the following tasks:

✔ Hire someone who does what your client does. (For instance, your client might be an artist who paints faux finishes for home interiors, a clown who specializes in children's birthday parties, or a private marketing consultant for the knitwear industry.)

✔ Find a company that sells what your client's company sells.

✔ Find a business that provides services like your client's company.

✔ Find an artist or designer with your client's particular skills and experience.

✔ Get information about a nonprofit agency like your client's organization.

You can then easily convert the answers to these types of questions into a list of site benefits or a more formal benefit statement. In addition, think about why visitors might want to use the products or services on your client's (or your own) website and add those reasons to your list. The better you can predict what will appeal to your target audience, the more you can cater to that audience's true wants and needs.

Chapter 3: Gathering Content

In This Chapter

✔ **Determining a site's content needs**

✔ **Gathering existing content and obtaining new content**

✔ **Organizing site content**

✔ **Creating a visual site map**

A t this point in the process, you've created an identity for the site, have a clear understanding of the target audience, know who the ideal site visitor is, and recognize the benefits that can be offered to site visitors. You're now at the stage where you can begin guiding the client in the task of gathering and organizing content for the site in a useful and meaningful way. Content includes any text, logos and branding, graphics, icons, photos, illustrations, animations, Flash movies, QuickTime videos, MP3s, and so forth that will appear on the site.

Why would you (and your client) want to determine the site's content needs before you begin working on the design? Because the content can help determine the design, organization, navigation, and layout of the site. You need this information now, before you start the design.

With luck, the client has already prepared a lot of this material for you, and your work is just a matter of helping the client organize that information in a way that's best suited for the web environment. What's more likely, however, is that the client has only a vague, fuzzy idea of what should go on the site, how that content should be organized, and what a visitor's experience on the site might be like.

Please try not to feel too overwhelmed by this task. Yes, a lot of content may be available, but this chapter is designed to give you the techniques you need to gather the right content for your site. In fact, to make it even easier, I start with the following guidelines:

✔ The client should be responsible for gathering and providing all the website content to you. If the client wants your help with gathering and/or generating content, he needs to pay you additional fees for these services.

✔ You should have no redundancy in the content on the site.

✔ Everything should be logically placed into hierarchical categories.

✔ The client must create original work or else obtain the rights for any text, images, graphics, and photos used on the site.

✔ If it doesn't make sense or isn't necessary, don't use it.

To assist you with this large — and what some think of as a tiresome task — I've created some helpful tools and techniques for you in this chapter. For starters, you find a series of questions you can ask your client (or yourself, if you're designing your own site) to help the client generate ideas for content, page order, metadata, and site navigation. Then you discover information and suggestions about where to obtain help with copywriting and editing and where to license or purchase photographs and illustrations needed for the site. The latter part of the chapter deals with a website architectural technique called *wireframing,* and it ends with a few sections on content organization and the creation of a graphical site map of the entire project.

Defining Site Content Requirements

Before you design or build any web pages, you must first gather everything you can from the client to really lock down what content will go on the site. The reason for this is twofold:

✔ You want to know what will go on the site so that you can create a design tailored specifically to the site's content.

✔ You need to set tangible boundaries for your client (for example, gather all the content now, and after that, no new pages can be added to the site without incurring additional costs) so that the project can move ahead successfully and stay on schedule through completion.

Specifying content

The content-gathering process includes getting all the text for the pages, logos and branding graphics, photographs (either in electronic format or as images that need to be scanned), illustrations, Flash movies, MP3s, QuickTime videos, PDFs, and anything else that will appear on, or can be downloaded from, the site. Some of these items will already be prepared by the client, but other items might need to be created, licensed, and otherwise obtained. Most of this content-gathering stuff is really the client's responsibility, not yours. However, because many clients don't yet know what they're supposed to do (having never created their own website before) and may be unsure of how to do it, your role as the designer might include educating and guiding them through the content-gathering process. Of course, if you're working on a web redesign project rather than on a brand-new website, most (if not all) of the content has already been gathered for you. Still, a redesign is a good time for a virtual spring cleaning, so be sure to check with your client about any content edits, additions, and deletions.

If you're billing your client by the hour, be sure that you include any time spent on these content-gathering tasks as part of your billable services. However, if you're working for a flat rate, make sure that you don't overdo it with the time you put into this part of the process. A few hours here and there to oversee the client should be part of your overall rate. But if the client somehow expects you to do more of or all the legwork, renegotiate your contract with an addendum so that you get paid for any extra time you put in.

Crafting the vision of the site

To begin the process of gathering content, set up an in-person hour-or-so long meeting with the client (or schedule a telephone or Skype conversation if you can't meet in person) so that you have a formal time in which you can question the client about his or her vision for the site. During this conversation, take careful notes of the client's answers.

The following sections include some of the questions that you might find helpful to ask your client during this meeting.

In addition to a home page, what other main pages do you want on the site?

Most sites have, at a minimum, both About and Contact pages. After that, the remaining pages depend on the site's purpose and goals.

Because part of the content-gathering task includes helping the client make decisions about what to put on the new site, try to get the conversation started by suggesting ideas, such as which words might be beneficial to use for the labels on all the main navigation buttons. You can then move on to ideas about how to identify each web page with elements like the page header, the page filename, and the page title. For example, if the client owns a hair salon and wants to have a section on her new website for "hair styling trends for long hair and summertime events," you might want to guide her to shortening the main navigation button to something like Styling Trends. You may then suggest including several subpages under Styling Trends for each trend she'd like to discuss on the site, such as Men's Summer Styles, Women's Summer Styles, and Summer Weddings.

Pay close attention to what the client says because he or she might not realize the long-term implications of choices made now. In the case of the hair salon example, be sure to ask the client whether she really meant that she wanted to offer only summer trends or if, in fact, she wants to display new trends each season, which would mean the navigation for those subpages would need to be updated quarterly. If she wants to display only summer trend information, she needs to be okay with the idea that for a substantial part of the year, that summer trend information may be irrelevant. With that in mind, the client can then decide whether she truly wants to update this section four times a year, for each of the seasons, or change the navigation and subnavigation sections to simply Trends for Men, Trends for Women, and Wedding Trends, leaving off any reference to the season. As you can see, the latter option is more generally labeled and would still allow the client to update the page content to match the season without having to edit the navigation. Alternatively, updates like these might help you decide to build the site dynamically, using a database or some type of Content Management System (CMS).

Do you want an About page or section to provide company information?

Find out what the client would like to call this page/section — About, About Us, or About Our Company? What subpages, if any, might go in this section? How about a page for listing a Board of Directors, Donors, or Sponsors; a Staff Directory; a Mission Statement; a Corporate History; Testimonials; or some other information?

What do you want to include on the Contact page?

This presumes, of course, that the client wants a Contact page. While it is highly recommended all sites include a page like this, you may occasionally get a client who wants to break the rules by including contact information in the footer of all the pages rather than dedicate an entire page to listing an address, e-mail, and phone number, as shown in Figure 3-1.

However, for everyone else, the Contact page might list a physical address, telephone and fax numbers, links to social media sites such as Facebook, Twitter, LinkedIn, and Pinterest, and a single contact e-mail address or several department-specific e-mail addresses. In addition, this page may have a contact form to collect contact information, comments, questions, and feedback from visitors. If you have a lot of contact information to impart to visitors, this page may warrant having subsections or even subpages for details such as transportation information, directions, maps, or other facts, as well as retail and wholesale buyer information and sales representative contact details.

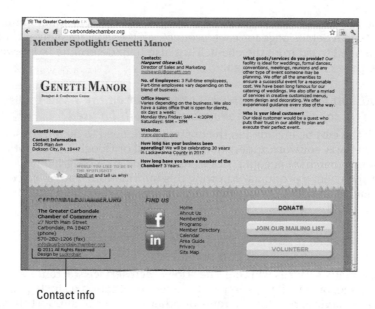

Contact info

Figure 3-1: Forgoing the traditional contact page and putting contact information in the page footer.

Do you want to have a Clients page that lists past and current clients?

A Clients page might contain a list of past and current clients, including links to recent projects and links to client websites, and all this data can be listed in alphabetical order, by vertical industry, or by project type. Some client pages also include client case studies, and if so, you want to find out how many case studies will appear in this area and whether they'll be bunched together on a single page or displayed on separate pages.

WARNING!

Before posting any client information, be sure to get approval from each client. You might get the occasional "No, thanks," but most clients say yes in exchange for the free publicity.

If you're selling products, do you want to have a Products page?

When considering this page, discuss whether the products will be merely described or both described and sold on this site. Be sure to find out how many products will be displayed and whether multiple product categories will be shown, because the decision to use a database may have an impact on how the pages need to be designed. For instance, having a small number of products gives you the freedom to design each page in a different way, whereas having a large number of products often begs for a data-driven template.

The Products page may include subpages, such as a product detail page and technical details page for each product. All these factors impact the content you need to get from the client. They also help determine (somewhat) how the pages need to be designed.

Will you have an e-commerce component on the site and, if so, what kind of shopping cart will be used?

Will the cart be included in the hosting plan, need to be purchased as a third-party software application, use PayPal or Google CheckOut to avoid using a merchant account, or be custom-built by a programmer specifically for the client's products? Knowing this information in advance can help you organize and design a site that's optimally suited to the products or services being sold.

Do you need a Services page to list all the services your company provides?

How many services will there be? Does each service warrant its own subpage, or can all the services be listed together on a single page? Do any of the services require diagrams or other graphics to support them? Will you list the pricing of these services on the site? Can services be purchased online?

Do you want a page that describes what the company produces?

For example, this page might be titled Our Work, What We Do, or Portfolio. You can break down this page into categories that match the client's particular offerings, such as Planning & Urban Design, Landscape Architecture, and Interior Design; or Illustrations, Paintings, and Sculpture. Find out how many sample images, if any, will be shown in each category and how the client wants these images to be displayed — in a slide show, as thumbnails in a gallery that link to larger close-up images, or in some other format.

How about a page for news or press releases?

How many news items and/or press releases will you have, and how often will they be added to the site? How will the list of news items or press releases be displayed? By date, by topic, or by title? Will they need to be sortable by the site visitor (which means that you'll need a database)? If many news items will be posted regularly, does the client need a news archive?

What about an Events page?

What kinds of events will there be? How often will the Events page be updated? Enough to justify having subpages in this section? Will events need to be presented by separating them into current/upcoming and past categories, or will only upcoming events be listed? Does the site warrant having some kind of interactive calendar? Will visitors be able to register and pay for events online?

What about other industry-specific pages?

Do other pages on the site call for having their own sections, with or without subsections? In other words, are any pages or sections so important that they should become part of the main navigation, or can they be logically tucked into some other section of the site?

What about including an RSS feed?

Do you want to allow visitors to subscribe to an RSS feed so that they can be notified automatically of new events, news items, products, and press releases? Setting up an RSS feed is quite easy to do. Most news-related sites, blogs, and e-zines often syndicate their site content through an RSS feed, but any site that has relevant news and content to offer visitors can create one.

Will the site need any other pages?

Some pages don't need main navigation links but should still be included on the site, which means that they'll need to be accessible through footer links on every page, through the site map page, or through regular text links on other pages throughout the site. Examples might include pages for Articles, Links, a Résumé, Partners, Affiliates, Terms of Service, Privacy Policy, FAQs, a Site Map, or a page that links to an external blog.

Does the text on the site need to appear in multiple languages?

If so, how many other languages do you need and what are they? What technology will be used to create these sister websites? Does the client need to purchase translation software or hire a translation service? If you expect a lot of pages, will each site be separate or does the client prefer that the content is organized with a database and displays dynamically based on a visitor's language preference? How can visitors switch between languages on the site? If the different language sites are dynamically generated, you could use a drop-down list to toggle between them, like they do at Dreamstime (www.dreamstime.com). Another less expensive idea, as illustrated in Figure 3-2, is to include the Google Translate tool (http://translate.google.com/translate_tools?hl=en), which converts an entire web page into the language selected from a drop-down list.

Finding a good translation service may be difficult because services vary in quality, ability, and price, and because the translation service providers' sites, although helpful, aren't always the best indication of quality. Services that seem to have a good reputation, competitive pricing, and nice websites (in my opinion, a big factor in determining whether to do business with that company) are Welocalize (http://welocalize.com), FreeTranslation.com (www.freetranslation.com), Translation Central (www.translationcentral.com), Translation Cloud (www.translation-services-usa.com), and Verbatim Solutions (www.verbatimsolutions.com).

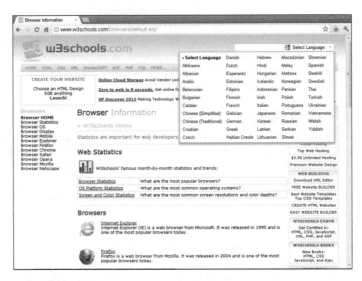

Figure 3-2: When you present a site or even a single page in multiple languages, give visitors an easy way to switch between languages.

What elements — textual and graphical — should appear on every page?

Definitely include any branding information, including logos, tag lines, and the main navigation links in the same location on every page. However, what other things should be accessible from anywhere on the site? How about Join Our Mailing List, Location/Store Finder, Site Search, Request a Brochure, Help, Customer Service, My Account, Login, Online Chat, an e-mail address, or a toll-free telephone number? These items can be graphics or text links anywhere on the page, such as at the upper-right corner of the page or down in the footer, depending on their importance.

If the site's design includes one or two sidebars on most of or all the pages, elements like these can be placed there. (A *sidebar* is a section of a web page, usually along the left or right margin, that contains content separate from the main body text of a page, often used for subnavigation, advertising, feature articles, and other site content that the site owners want you to pay particular attention to.) The sidebars typically have different background colors, borders, text treatments, and graphics to visually distinguish them from the main content area. The repeating elements on the CouponConnector (www.couponconnector.com) website, shown in Figure 3-3, include a logo and tagline, a site search form, a navigation bar, and footer.

Figure 3-3: Repeating elements, like the logo and a site search form, should be in the same location on every page.

Who will provide all the graphics, photos, and illustrations for the site, as well as branding information?

The branding information includes logos and other brand-identity graphics. If the answer to this question isn't *the client,* you should definitely find out about some of the resources discussed in the "Hiring freelance artists" and "Licensing stock images" sections, later in this chapter.

Does anything else need to go on the site?

Make sure that you've covered everything the client or group you're working with has in mind for the site. Be clear with your client that there should be no last-minute surprises; otherwise that could create both timeline delays and additional charges.

Other content might include a photo gallery, sliding banner, advertisements, special password-protected members-only section, bookstore, class listing, or registration form. Every detail must be thought out in advance and planned for.

At the end of the conversation, thank the client for his time and let him know that there is still much to do during this stage of the web design process with regard to gathering content, the responsibility of which mostly falls on the client's shoulders before you begin the actual design.

Concurrent with gathering the content for the site — which may include generating new content as well as culling content from existing company sources and/or hiring a copywriter — the client needs to produce, acquire, and/or license photographs and illustrations for the site.

In addition, after the content areas have been discovered and outlined, all that information must be organized to assist with creating a layout for the site. This can be done through the creation of *wireframes,* as you read about in the next section, to help identify what content is needed for each page on the site. Oftentimes, putting everything down on paper helps the client to better envision what content to display on every page and how the site will function.

Building Wireframes

Creating *wireframes* is an interesting technique that helps many clients when they're trying to determine what content to put on each of the individual pages of their website. In addition to understanding what each of the pages should contain, a wireframe helps site owners plan how their sites will function and gives a general overview of what the layout might look like. Designers often play a key role in the development of wireframes, because most clients aren't familiar with the types of graphics and wireframing software programs that are often used to create them.

As you can see in Figure 3-4, a wireframe is a text-only diagram, or blueprint, of a particular page in the website, and it typically includes the following elements:

- **General site navigation:** Using text only, the wireframe diagrams the navigation and subnavigation elements, buttons, links, form fields, and other functional elements that show or describe how the visitor can enter and exit the page.

- **Content that appears on every page:** In addition to the navigation menu, the site may include components such as corporate identity and branding, search boxes, mailing list or newsletter signup buttons, links, or form fields, page headers, page footers, and other page elements.

A *page header* is a word (such as Contact or About), phrase (such as Contact Us or About Our Services), or short line of text (such as Sign In to Use the Control Panel) that identifies the content that can be found on the page and is placed above or away from the main body of text on the page. Page header text can be formatted with CSS using the <h1> through <h6> tags, or it can be a graphic that includes text and is inserted onto a web page in roughly the same location to serve the same purpose.

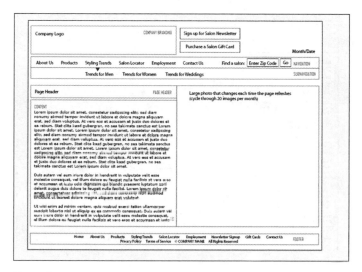

Figure 3-4: Wireframes are text-only depictions of a website's navigation, interactive features, and content areas.

✓ **Interactive components:** This can include hyperlinks, rollover buttons, navigation menus, hidden layers that pop up and disappear, games, rotating banner ads, rotating graphics, photo galleries, slide shows, tab panels, accordion panels, sortable elements, animations, video clips, movies, and other multimedia files.

✓ **Dynamic functionality:** Any data, images, or other site content that will be dynamically pulled from a database and displayed on the web page should be indicated on the wireframe to assist with the site layout and programming.

✓ **Content for a particular page on a website:** For each individual wireframe, include the page title, placeholder graphics, and text for that page (or if text is unavailable, dummy or greeking placeholder text can be used instead). *Greeking text* looks similar to Latin (refer to Figure 3-4) and is often used to show how text in a particular font will fill the desired space within the layout. It is also sometimes used as placeholder text in graphic layouts until the real content becomes available. Greeking text usually begins with the famous "Lorem ipsum dolor sit amet . . ." and looks similar to English in its word size and distribution within sentences.

All these temporary elements will be replaced with actual graphics and text on the web page. For example, your client might include notations such as "About Us page content" and "Boardroom Photo" within the wireframe, as shown in Figure 3-5, and replace that with real content on the website.

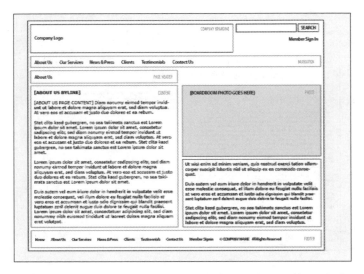

Figure 3-5: Greeking text and dummy graphics can be used in a wireframe.

When designing for others, you may find that most of your web clients will have never heard of wireframes before. Make it part of your job to educate your client about how she can use wireframes as a time-saving, cost-effective, content discovery tool, and consider creating a sample wireframe for the client's home page as your special web design value-added service. Who knows? The client might appreciate it so much that she'll consider paying you a little extra to help create additional wireframes for the rest of the pages on the site.

Because the wireframe typically contains only block outlines and text, one of the key benefits of making wireframes for all the pages on the site (or at least the most important ones) is that the client can focus on user experience and content without having to think about design and layout decisions or coding and development issues. That stuff comes later. It is only after the content has been gathered and the wireframes created that the client should tackle what actual text the visitors will see on each page.

To create the wireframes, your client (or you) can draw them by hand on plain or graph paper, mock them up in a graphics program like Adobe Illustrator (as was done in Figure 3-5), throw them together in PowerPoint or Keynote, or use any other application that allows the insertion and arrangement of text and shapes. For instance, you might consider using one of the free or affordably priced online collaborative wireframing tools, such as those available at http://mockflow.com, www.gliffy.com, http://iplotz.com, https://gomockingbird.com, www.balsamiq.com, or www.hotbgoo.com. For a list of completely free wireframing tools, visit `http://speckyboy.com/2011/02/23/10-completely-free-wireframing-and-mockup-tools/`. Alternatively, if your client has a bigger budget, he might consider purchasing one of the software applications on the market, such as Microsoft Visio or Axure RP Pro, that are specifically designed for creating HTML wireframes. These programs contain buttons, form fields, menus, and other web page elements that can easily be dragged onto the wireframe diagram, making it easier for the client to foresee the content and its functionality pre-design. Or, if your client would rather go low-tech due to budgetary or time constraints, he or she can certainly create wireframes in a simple word processing or spreadsheet program such as Microsoft Word or Excel, or simply draw the wireframe by hand on a whiteboard and take digital photos of it.

You don't need to create wireframes for every page on a website unless this is something the client expressly asks for and is amenable to compensating you for. A more likely scenario is that you or your client will create a wireframe for the home page and possibly one or two additional wireframes for any subpages with distinct content and layout requirements, such as a shopping cart page, a product detail page, or a search results listing.

The wireframing technique is meant to assist with gathering content for a website. Similar in concept to a book's table of contents, the wireframe merely outlines or hints at the content in a particular section, not how it's supposed to look. With the wireframe, you can focus on the general rather than the specific by noting what information should be displayed, even when the information (such as text and graphics) isn't available or hasn't been created yet. For example, if the website will offer products for sale, plan to have at least a main product listing page and a product details page, both of which can be wireframed to show how the individual products and product details will appear in the browser. In the absence of real content, the details page wireframe can include information placeholders such as greeking text for the full description, technical specifications, customer reviews, and photos of the item.

Gathering Text and Graphics

Whether you're designing for yourself or working for someone else, you might already have some of the materials you need for your website. If you're lucky, your client is likely to have some or perhaps all the textual content for her website already created in the form of existing newsletters, press releases, brochures, and other marketing collateral. Ask the client to start pulling all these materials together for the site, as well as to generate any new content that is needed and to rewrite any existing copy that needs updating to fit into the specific pages you discussed in the content-gathering meeting.

When the website will use a database and have some kind of dynamic functionality, or even a CMS, you or your client would also be wise to begin entering that data into an Excel spreadsheet for later importing into a database of some kind. Because each dynamic site uses a unique combination of coding, it is very important to know in advance how the data should be entered into the spreadsheet (how files are named and numbered), because that may depend on the programming language (such as ASP, JSP, PHP, or CFML) chosen to make the site dynamic, and this decision will most likely be made by the person who is programming the site, whether that's you or a contracted programmer. For instance, to ensure that the wines are listed appropriately on their site, as shown in Figure 3-6, the folks at Rockwood & Perry (`http://rockwoodandperry.com`) must have the name, manufacturer, size, bottle and case price, and description for each wine in their rotating inventory. Making this decision before you design and build a site can save everyone time later on when you import data from the database into the web pages.

Figure 3-6: Some database-driven websites use spreadsheets to update their inventories of products.

Likewise, if you know that you will need to pull together text and graphics from someone other than your client, now is the time to look into hiring a copywriter and freelance artists, licensing stock images, and generating appropriate page titles and metadata.

Hiring a copywriter

Although you may have some of your own or your client's website content ready to go, some other text for the site might simply not exist yet. In such cases, you or your client needs to decide whether to write the missing information or to hire someone to do it. If you're confident in your copywriting skills, you might want to offer your services for an additional fee. However, if writing isn't your thing (or if the client rejects your offer to do copywriting and the client isn't capable of it), he needs to hire an outside subcontractor or find someone through a service, agency, job-listing site, or writing organization.

The more promising-looking national copywriting services include Freelance Writing (www.freelancewriting.com), Guru.com (www.guru.com), Elance (www.elance.com), and Writerfind.com (www.writerfind.com); however, you (or your client) should unquestionably still search online to see whether you can find someone to do the work locally. For example, if you are looking for a copy editor in a particular geographical region within the United States, visit www.freelancedesigners.com/dir/writers (shown in Figure 3-7), where you can find regional listings of copywriters, many of whom have web copyediting experience.

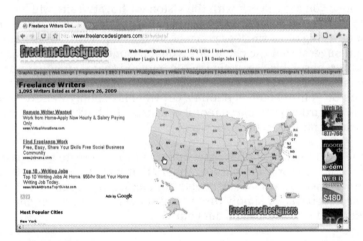

Figure 3-7: Locate a web copy editor in your area by checking an online directory.

Above all in your search, be skeptical: Not everyone who thinks he can write can really do a good job. Ask for writing samples, see whether you like the way they communicate in print, and compare fees to ensure that you get the best service for the price.

Hiring freelance artists

Despite how creative noncreative people may think they are, you should — without hesitation — insist that your client use professional artists, illustrators, and photographers to create any custom visual graphics and photographs that will appear on the site. The only exception is if the client is a graphic designer, illustrator, photographer, or artist, in which case you may welcome her own graphics and other artwork.

Ask the client whether he intends to use established contacts for the graphic art that will go on his site. Some clients already have an established relationship with other graphic designers, artists, illustrators, and photographers and will gladly get any needed site graphics, such as icons and illustrations, directly from those people. Other clients, however, will look to you for direction on these things. If you're an artist, illustrator, or photographer as well as a web designer, definitely offer your services to the client for an additional fee. Otherwise, be ready to suggest some local artists, illustrators, and photographers who would be happy to create the needed art and photos.

Of course, you could leave the hiring of such people solely to the client, but many times the client will want or need you to take on this responsibility because you are the one with the vision for how the site will look and function. Fortunately, your role in this part of the content-gathering process can be as big or as small as you feel comfortable with. For instance, you might suggest that the client buy a digital camera and create her own photographs. Likewise, you may recommend that your client purchase or license specific stock art (see the next section in this chapter) for the site based on your recommendations. Or, you may simply want to steer your client toward a particular handful of artists you have worked with before and are confident in their services.

Whatever the client's preference turns out to be, create a list of freelance artists, illustrators, and photographers that you like and keep this list handy. You can then choose to selectively contact people from the list on a project-by-project basis, or simply turn your list over to your client and let her vet, select, and hire someone from your list.

To generate this list, you need to do some homework by doing any of the following:

- ✔ Post ads looking for artists on Craigslist (`www.craigslist.com`) or some other local online community website that has a job board.

- ✔ Search for specific artists on sites such as Directory of Illustration (`www.directoryofillustration.com`).

- Join the local chapter of the Graphic Artists Guild (www.gag.org) or at least look through their online links to member websites.

- Join a MAC user group (www.mugcenter.com or www.apple.com/usergroups).

- Join some other local arts organization where you can network with other artists, illustrators, photographers, and designers.

You may even find some up-and-coming artist types through a local university; lots of student artists are eager to work for a reduced fee — sometimes even for free — while they build their portfolio.

Above all, remember that each project is unique, so be open to making suggestions and let the client decide what works best for her, given her project's time frame, needs, and budget.

Licensing stock images

For your fixed-budget and quick-turnaround-time projects, a good alternative to hiring a freelance artist is to either license or purchase stock imagery directly from an online service. You have two general options with stock images:

- **Royalty-Free (RF):** Royalty-free photographs, illustrations, and other artwork are images that you purchase, usually for a one-time fee, to use for a given project, as long as that project does not include the reselling or redistribution of the image in some other form. Some stock art services charge different rates for royalty-free art, depending on its size, quality, and intended usage. With all royalty-free artwork, the image being licensed still belongs to the creator of it under U.S. property and copyright laws, which means that if you were to use the image in some unlawful way, the creator of that image could sue you and you could be fined, jailed, or otherwise punished for any improper usage.

- **Rights-Managed (RM):** Rights-managed images are licensed photographs and other artwork that you can purchase from an online service or agency (or directly from the creator), with the exclusive usage rights for a given period of time. While it is a much more expensive option than royalty-free stock art, rights-managed work cannot be used by anyone else, competitors included, until the contract period ends.

Both royalty-free and rights-managed images can be purchased online. For projects that require several images along a particular subject, consider purchasing an entire CD of royalty-free images on a particular theme, such as diet and exercise, architectural marvels, or growth economy. Most CDs cost between $299 and $799 for anywhere from 50 and 100 images.

Respecting the copyright

Before you search for images to use on a website, you should know a little about copyright protection laws. All the images that you see online — whether they're on a royalty-free image site, in an online store, in somebody's Facebook page, blog, or Flickr account — belong to somebody. Someone took the time to take that photograph, draw that illustration, build that animation, and design that icon. Savvy art makers have registered their own custom artwork, illustrations, and photographs with the U.S. Copyright Office. Likewise, smart website owners make the necessary arrangements to legally license or purchase the work of others. For the rest of the world, what are the implications if you or someone else copies an image from another site, without permission or payment, and then uses that image for another project? What rights might have been violated? The answers depend on your usage and intent.

Suppose that you go to the Disney website and see a picture of Goofy that you love and want to turn it into your desktop wallpaper so that you can look at it every day. In this case,

your usage intent is for private use and isn't for profit; therefore, your use of that Goofy image isn't harming anyone or earning you any income. Disney knows that many visitors might use its graphics for personal use, so it includes a clause in its Privacy Policy and Terms to allow that, but it forbids visitors from taking images from its site to use in any way for profit. Of course, it has no way of tracking this information because no reliable way of accurately monitoring images that are copied from the website exists. Nonetheless, by stating its rights on the website, Disney is protecting those rights to the images in case it needs to file suit against someone who knowingly violates the copyright.

Therefore, if you need an image for your site — say, a photograph of a sunset on Waikiki beach that you use as part of the home page design for a luau event and catering company based in Los Angeles, California — the right thing to do is to create it yourself, hire someone to create it for you, or license the image from one of the many stock-art or clip-art websites.

For projects where you only need a handful of images on a particular theme, single images can be licensed from several royalty-free stock art websites for as little as $1 per image, depending on the image size and quality, license time frame, and usage parameters. Corbis (www.corbisimages.com) is the leading provider of rights-managed and royalty-free stock photography and illustration. Veer (www.veer.com) and iStockphoto (www.istockphoto.com) are also reputable services with similar price structuring. For those looking for a less expensive, purchase-what-you-need option, check out two of my personal favorites, Fotolia (http://us.fotolia.com) and Dreamstime (www.dreamstime.com), shown in Figure 3-8, as well as Clipart.com (www.clipart.com), Fotosearch (www.fotosearch.com), Getty Images (www.gettyimages.com), RoyaltyFreeArt.com (http://royaltyfreeart.com), Shutterstock (www.shutterstock.com), and Inmagine (www.inmagine.com).

Figure 3-8: Find interesting and affordable stock art at sites like these.

Another useful source of stock art comes from regular folks from around the world who have decided to license their work through Creative Commons, a nonprofit organization (http://creativecommons.org) that offers an "alternative to full copyright." For instance, if you visit www.flickr.com/creativecommons, you can find graphics for your projects that have Attribution, Noncommercial, No Derivative Works, and Share Alike copyright assignments.

Another great alternative is for you or your client to subscribe to one of the royalty-free online image services, such as Thinkstock (www.thinkstock photos.com), Jupiterimages (www.jupiterimages.com), and Photos.com (www.photos.com), where, for a flat rate, you can download an unlimited number of images on a monthly, biannual, or annual basis.

The only real drawback to using online royalty-free images is that they carry a high likelihood of other businesses — including potential competitors — having also licensed and used the same images for their projects.

If you want to go the super DIY route (which means, of course, that an even higher likelihood exists that someone else might use the same images), consider buying a box of royalty-free clip art on CD. You can find something like Nova's Art Explosion 300,000 Clip Art and Nova's Art Explosion 800,000 Clip Art on Amazon.com for anywhere from $29.99 to $109.99. If you decide to do this, just be sure that the set you're purchasing will work on your specific computer and operating system, because some clip-art CDs are out-of-date and may be PC-only for Windows NT/95/98/2000/Me/XP, but not for Windows Vista/7/8.

Wherever the client decides to get images for his site, be sure that you, as the designer, add only legally licensed artwork to your design for the site. Ethically, you should also be sure that the images provided by the client are also legally licensed. In other words, don't make yourself liable to any copyright infringements made by your client. In fact, you might want to add to your contract some kind of Permissions and Releases regarding Copyrights and Trademarks clause. This clause could state that the client agrees that he either own the rights to all images provided to you, or that he shall be responsible for obtaining all permissions and rights for the lawful usage of images created by others for use on his site. The clause should also clearly state that you, the designer, will be held harmless for using any and all client-provided images in your design, should they be found to be unlawful. For more information about copyrights, trademarks, and fair use, visit the websites of the U.S. Copyright Office (www.copyright.gov) and the U.S. Patent and Trademark Office (www.uspto.gov).

Creating page titles and meta-tag data

In addition to all the text, photos, illustrations, and other graphics that will appear directly on the pages of your website, you also need to create two other important bits of information, namely unique page titles and meta-tag data, both of which go into the HTML code of all the site's pages.

If you're creating a site for someone else, ask your client to provide the titles and metadata for you. Otherwise, if you're designing a site for yourself, you can easily create this content.

Page titles

Page titles are pretty self-explanatory. Each page on a website needs its own unique title, which, after being placed appropriately in the head area of the HTML code, will (in most browsers) appear in the browser window's title bar or page tab. Page titles are set between opening and closing <title> tags in the HTML code of a web page. Each page on a website should have its own unique title because this information assists search engines and web crawlers in indexing pages and entire sites. For example, if you go to Amazon.com, the title of the home page is "Amazon.com: Online Shopping for Electronics, Apparel, Computers, Books, DVDs & more." As you can see in Figure 3-9, the title appears at the top of the browser window.

Title appears in the title bar

Figure 3-9: The title appears in the browser's title bar at the top of the browser window or on the page's browser tab.

Titles need to identify the site, as well as the content displayed on each page by using a maximum of 70 to 80 characters, including any letters, numbers, symbols, spaces, punctuation, or other text entities, such as A, 23, ©, ⅜, and #. For example, "NY Bests: Best Breakfasts for Under $6 in New York City" would be a good title for a web page called NY Bests that had a page with reviews of restaurants serving cheap breakfasts. Titles longer than 70 characters might get truncated, or cut off, by the browser, so if titles are a bit longer, put the most important words in the first 70 characters. When writing your page titles, a good rule is to pack each one of them full of keywords that visitors are likely to use when searching for pages that contain desired information.

Meta tags

Meta tags are special HTML tags that also go inside the head area of the HTML code on a web page, but rather than appear somewhere on or in the browser window, this information is strictly used by search engines, indexing spiders, and robots and is hidden from the visitor's view. Specifically, these tags provide search engines and web browsers with informational content about the client's company and code settings, which helps those search engines rank the site in search results listings and helps those browsers accurately display the code inside the browser window.

Keep in mind that meta tags aren't magical search engine ranking-improvers; on the contrary, they're merely assistive code bits that can help people find your site. Truth be told, Google and some other search engines don't use this kind of information as much as some of the other search engines, spiders, and robots do. Nonetheless, even though they aren't as important as they once were, using them is still worthwhile.

 You may be wondering why it might be important to ask for this data from the client at this stage of the site development. The answer is because the client is focused right now on getting the content to you, and he will be more likely to comply with your request now rather than later. In my experience, if you wait until you start building the site to ask for titles and meta tags — even though realistically it should only take your client about ten or so minutes to generate them — the chances of you receiving them are slim.

While a lot of different kinds of meta tags can be added to the HTML of the pages, for search engine optimization (SEO) purposes, the following two tags should be placed on every page of a site — the meta description and the meta keywords:

- **Description:** The description of the site is a single sentence that concisely describes what can be found on the site. Normally, it should be written as a single sentence or short phrase and should contain no more than 150 characters, including spaces and punctuation. This information is critical, because this exact copy is often (though not in all search engines) what appears in a search engine results listing when the site is found after a keyword search. As a matter of fact, you may even want to create unique descriptions for each page of your site to further assist visitors in finding relevant information on the site's different pages.

- **Keywords:** While many web crawlers ignore this meta tag, some still do use this information, so you may as well plan to include keywords in the code of your pages. Keywords should include the words or short phrases that you feel would be helpful when searching for this site. Keywords (and/or key phrases) should be separated by a comma either with or without a space, such as "bread,cakes,pies." or "bread, cakes, pies." Place the seven most important words first, in order of importance. Any more than seven words will probably be ignored.

If you're coding the meta-tag information yourself, be sure that you understand the proper use of syntax, because if you code it incorrectly, it won't be read by the search engine crawlers and spiders. To illustrate proper coding, here's an example of the meta-tag HTML code used by Oceana Surf, shown in Figure 3-10, a private surf instruction and surfing retreat company based in Santa Monica, California:

Figure 3-10: A good meta description should help search engines properly index the page for potential site visitors.

```
<head>
<title> Oceana Surf :: Los Angeles :: 310.500.9605 :: Lessons, Surf Camps,
    Women's Travel, Retreats</title>
<meta http-equiv="Content-Type" content="text/html; charset=iso-8859-1">
<META NAME="keywords" CONTENT="surf lessons, learn to surf, santa monica, malibu,
    surf retreat, surf travel... ">
<META NAME="description" CONTENT="Beginning through intermediate year-round surf
    instruction, from Santa Monica to Hawaii, Costa Rica to Indonesia. Private
    one-on-one training. Includes equipment. Los Angeles: 310-500-9605 info at
    oceanasurf.com">
<META NAME="Publisher" CONTENT="Oceana Surf">
<META NAME="Copyright" CONTENT="Copyright, Kim Welsh for Oceana Surf. All Rights
    Reserved. ">
<META NAME="Author" CONTENT="oceanasurf.com">
<META NAME="Language" CONTENT="en-US">
<META NAME="Robots" CONTENT="All">
</head>
```

The limited power of keywords

If you do any online research about meta tags and their usage, you'll quickly discover that keywords are much less useful on a site than the description. This is because, for a time a few years ago, keywords were widely abused by unethical site owners looking to improve their website rankings and increase site traffic by padding their keyword meta tags with irrelevant search terms. Soon after this abuse was discovered by the major search engines, the importance of keywords quickly diminished. Today, only a couple of search engines still use a database that supports the usage of keywords as a ranking tool, but in my opinion, even one is enough to justify keeping the keywords listed in the code. As an alternative to listing the seven most important keywords in the meta keywords tag, some designers simply duplicate the meta description content there instead.

As you can see, many different kinds of meta tags can be added to the head of a web page, but these are less critical to the function of indexing the site on a search engine and instead are used more for informational purposes should anyone decide to look at the code. In addition to the meta tags shown here, many others can be used for a variety of purposes. For instance, one meta tag can forward a page to another URL, and another can prevent the browser from caching the content on the page. You find out more about meta tags in Book III, Chapter 1, including how and where to add them to your web pages.

Organizing Site Content

Depending on how organized you are, you can use several methods to arrange the content — the text, logo, branding graphics, photos, illustrations, icons, animations, Flash movies, MP3s, QuickTime videos, plug-ins, and so forth that will appear on the site — in a meaningful and useful way. The best practice, of course, is to have the client begin to organize the content for you before he hands it over to you. Notice I say *begin to*. That's because the client isn't always the best judge of how to effectively organize everything. The client might, for example, want to have a staff contact page on the site that lists the names, telephone numbers, and e-mail addresses of everyone in the company and might think this information should go on the site as part of a Company History page under the About Us section. That just doesn't make sense. You may have to step in and think about the site from a visitor's perspective. Where would you expect to find this information? A more logical location for a staff directory would be as a separate subpage under either the About Us or the Contact Us page.

To begin your part of the content-organization process, follow these general steps:

1. **Write all the names of the main pages across the top of a sheet of paper.**

   These represent the main navigation buttons or links that will enable visitors to navigate their way through the site. For example, the main pages might include Home, About, Services, Testimonials, and Contact.

   If the site you're working on is fairly large in scope and breadth, another useful technique for content organization is to write all the page names on individual index cards and then, on a table or other flat surface, order the index cards into the main navigation and subnavigation categories. The final order of the index cards can then be transcribed on a single sheet of paper.

2. **Look at all the other pages of content that the client has provided to you, and decide where each page would best be placed relative to the main pages.**

   This way, you can both establish logical categories and subcategories of information and create the navigation scheme that you will use when building the site.

During this process, take extra care not to make too many levels of subnavigation in your page organization. Three levels should be your maximum depth (that is, main, subnavigation, sub-subnavigation). In fact, an extremely important web usability principle states that it's better to have a wide navigation than a deep navigation. In other words, rather than embed subnavigation that has subnavigation on top of subnavigation with even more subnavigation (deep), it is more user-friendly to site visitors to keep most of the content close to the top level (wide) so that *all the content on a site is accessible in no more than three clicks from the home page.* This technique works great for most sites with less than ten main categories of information. Over ten, and the site might need to use a directory type of navigation system, where users can click a category (think the Yahoo! home page) with hypertext links to narrow what they're looking for and can then be taken directly to that section of a larger site.

For your smaller website projects, organizing the content is much simpler and quicker because most sites have at least three of the main pages in common: Home, About, and Contact. However, for your medium-sized sites — over 15 pages, say — exactly where in the site architecture each of the main page and subpages should go becomes a matter of logical organization. Try to arrange the content from the top down, starting at the home page; then move on to the main navigation categories and finally the subpages. If you happen to run across a page of content that doesn't seem to have a logical place to fit on the site, ask the client where he thinks it should go and be prepared to make a suggestion to the client about where it might fit in. If there truly is no logical place for the content, the site might benefit from combining that content with the information on another page that already does fit within the site architecture. Otherwise, that content may need to be removed from the site. Just because the client thinks something might be a good idea doesn't necessarily make it so. What matters is the visitor's experience on the site. The site should be well organized, easy to navigate, and only contain information that is interesting, useful, and meaningful to site visitors.

As a little practice test, take a few minutes to try assembling the following pages into a logical layout for a website using the paper or index card methods described in the preceding paragraphs:

Contact Information

About Us

Our History

What We Do

Our Goals and Values

Publications

Upcoming Events

Home

Links

Events

Donate

Our Mission Statement

Staff Directory

To begin the page-ordering process, follow these steps:

1. **Select which pages will be the main navigation pages.**

2. **Pick the pages that will become subpages.**

Did you find any pages that didn't quite fit anywhere? If so, what would you recommend that the client do with the page(s)?

When you're finished with the organization, compare your solutions with the following potential answers for each step:

✔ For the main pages, include Home, About Us, Events, Donate, Publications, and Contact Information.

✔ For the subpages, under the About Us page, include What We Do, Our Mission Statement, Our History, and Our Goals and Values. Place Staff Directory as a subpage under the Contact Information page, and place Upcoming Events as a subpage under the main Events page.

✔ The Links page doesn't quite fit in anywhere and may not be necessary to site visitors. Recommend that the client either remove it from the site, add it as a subpage of the About Us section, or add it as a new main page called Resources, which sounds better than Links.

Having something like this written on paper is a good first step in preparation for creating a design mockup for the site. However, if you really want to impress your client, consider building a graphical site map.

Building a Site Map

A *site map* is a visual illustration or representation of a website's architecture or structural design. By reducing the site to its most important components, such as pages and page names, you can pay special attention to the placement and ordering of the pages relative to each other. In addition, you can add other relevant information to the site map, such as notes regarding the dynamic functionality of the site and which fonts and colors will be used in the site's design.

The site map serves a totally different function than the wireframes that you or your client may have created for the site to outline and organize the content for the pages. Instead, the site map becomes your guide to designing the mock-up for the site's layout and look and feel, as well as your road map for building the web pages as you construct the entire website. Therefore, the site map should be created by you, the designer.

Site maps can be sketched by hand or produced in any software program that allows you to add text and draw rectangles and lines. Acceptable-looking site maps can be created by the non-designer in Microsoft Word, Excel, PowerPoint, Keynote, and Visio. Those with more design experience can create a site map in programs like Illustrator or Photoshop by using the various line, shape, and text tools. Your site map can be as simple or elaborate as you want, as long as its main function to diagram the site is accurate and complete.

When designing client site maps, my preference is to use the drawing tools in Adobe Illustrator. This is because Illustrator allows me to create more elegant site maps by using unique shapes, like rounded rectangles, ovals, and polygons, as well as to display the specific fonts and colors that will actually be used in the site's design, giving me the opportunity to customize each site map to the client's project. Figure 3-11 shows an example of a site map I created for Evergreen Printing & Graphics, an environmentally responsible graphic design, offset and digital printing, and mailing and fulfillment company in New Jersey, which hired me to create its website back in June 2007.

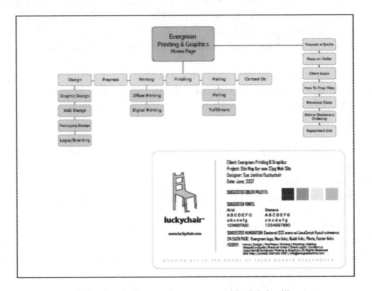

Figure 3-11: This visual site map was created in Adobe Illustrator.

When you're ready with a list of information about your particular site, use the following steps to guide you in creating your site map:

1. **Using a standard 8.5-x-11-inch letter-size page with a landscape layout, create and center a 2-inch-wide rectangle at the top of the page and label it "Home page."**

   A good site map shows how each of the pages on a site is connected from the home page as well as through the site's navigation and subnavigation menus.

2. **Directly below the Home page rectangle, draw a row of equally sized rectangles to represent all the main pages on the site, and label each of them according to your notes about the site.**

   For example, your main pages might include About Us, Events, Donate, Publications, and Contact, or in the case of the Evergreen Printing & Graphics website, the main pages are Design, Prepress, Printing, Finishing, Mailing, and Contact Us.

TIP

Make sure that these main pages are listed in the exact order you intend them to appear on the website — from left to right for the main navigation and from top to bottom for any pages accessed through subnavigation links. This order can assist you in the site's design and building phases.

3. **Connect all the page rectangles by drawing straight connector lines. One line should flow horizontally behind each of the main page rectangles, and another line should connect the Home page to the horizontal line.**

   Connecting the pages in this manner can aid you in identifying to the client how a visitor will interact with the navigation and experience visiting the site.

4. **Add the subpages and subpage connector lines.**

   Add additional rectangles and text labels to represent each of the subpages that falls under each of the main pages on your site. Then draw a vertical line behind each column of subpages to connect them to the main page that they fall under, as well as connect them to the main horizontal line that links the main pages. (Refer to Figure 3-11.)

   The line behind the subpages shows that the subpages will be accessible through the main navigation buttons. If any sub-subpages exist in your site, use this same technique to add them to your site map.

5. **Most sites have at least one or more special pages, such as Terms & Conditions, Privacy Policy, or Site Map, that is not accessible through the main navigation but needs to be accessible through footer links, sidebar links, and/or regular hypertext links. If this applies to your site, add more page rectangles to your layout, perhaps off to the side of the site map page, and label them accordingly.**

   Though you could if you wanted to, you don't need lines to connect these odd pages to the rest of the site map; they are indicated merely to show you and the client that these pages exist and are accessible through means other than the main navigation.

6. **In a blank area of the site map page, type in any special notations you may have about site details that should be appearing on every page, such as the logo, company slogan, toll-free telephone number, footer links, site search features, and so on.**

   If desired, you may also want to include design information about what colors, fonts, font sizes, layout attributes, and page dimensions to use.

7. **On another part of the site map page, preferably on the lower-left or lower-right side, add the date the site map was created, along with your company name, logo, and contact information.**

   This information clearly identifies you, the designer, as the author of the site map for this project.

8. **Save the file in its native format. Then, if you own a copy of Adobe Acrobat Professional or similar PDF-creating software, convert the page into an Adobe Acrobat PDF document, which you can use to present the site map to the client.**

    PDFs are wonderful tools to use because they don't require the client to own or purchase any design software to view them. If anything, the client may need to download and install the latest version of the free Adobe Acrobat Reader software, which is readily available online at www.adobe.com.

    If you don't own Acrobat Professional, consider using a free online PDF file-conversion tool, such as the one found at www.pdfonline.com.

Each time you make contact with your clients — whether by e-mail, in person, or by phone — you have the opportunity to make another positive impression on them about you and the quality of your web design services. Friendly banter and a professional work ethic definitely go a long way toward fostering a good rapport with your clients, but so does the unspoken look of all your web-related paperwork, e-mails, PDFs, and other correspondence. Therefore, make the most out of every nonverbal communication opportunity you have by consistently adding your name, company logo, and contact information, including telephone numbers and e-mail address, to every document you present to your clients.

When you have the chance, the completed site map should be reviewed by the client to make sure that it meets his or her expectations, and that it includes and diagrams all the pages of the site in a logical manner. If any changes need to be made to the architecture of the site, making those changes now can save you valuable time after you begin creating the site design. After the site map is reviewed and approved by the client, get approval in writing before you proceed to the next step in the design phase — creating the design.

Chapter 4: Choosing the Right Tools

In This Chapter

✓ Using a web editor (HTML versus WYSIWYG)

✓ Choosing graphics software

✓ Using color effectively on the web

✓ Choosing the right shopping cart for your e-commerce site

✓ Determining when to hire a programmer

*B*y now you should have pulled together and organized all (or most of) the content required for the site, and you're nearly ready to begin working on the site design. Before you can do that, however, you must first make a few important decisions about which development tools to use. After that, you need to be sure that you understand some fundamental techniques for using those tools.

You begin this chapter by discovering the basics of coding and working with HTML. You can hand-code your pages using a simple text editor, or even better, you can build your pages with some kind of HTML or web editor. Although not all web-editing programs insist that you know HTML before you use them, having a simple understanding of HTML's structure and syntax can definitely help you build the pages for the site more quickly and efficiently. It's important, too, that you understand how to save your HTML files using the proper naming conventions and correct file extensions. Plus, when you have a basic grasp of HTML, you can easily start using the more advanced features of XHTML and HTML5.

After you've selected your web-editing tool, you need to look into and purchase (or download a free copy of an open-source application) at least one or two graphics programs. Some programs are better than others at certain tasks, so having an understanding of what each program can do can help you in selecting the right tools for the job. I highly recommend having at least one vector and one raster graphics program. You will use them to create the website design and for the optimization of all the images that will appear on the website. While you're creating your web graphics, it's critical that you know how to work in the RGB color space at the low resolution of 72ppi (that's Pixels Per Inch), use web-safe color palettes if needed, and understand hexadecimal color values. This attention to color inside the program you choose to work with can help ensure that the colors in your design look just right.

In addition to finding a good web editor and the right graphics software programs, when you're creating a site that has an e-commerce component or needs a way to process credit card payments, you also need to look into finding the right shopping cart solution. Your options range from a simple PayPal setup to third-party software or host-provided carts to custom-built shopping carts. All of these options — with the exception of PayPal, Google Checkout, or some host-provided shopping cart sites like Etsy and BigCartel — require the site owner to get a merchant account from his bank and an SSL (Secure Sockets Layer) certificate from the host provider to securely process online payments.

Finally, although you may want to design and build the site entirely by yourself, some sites have such customized and complex data-processing needs that you'll want or need the assistance of a professional web programmer. For example, if your client wants a custom-built shopping cart that caters specifically to her products, hiring a professional programmer is a very good idea. The last part of this chapter examines some criteria that can help you determine when it is time to call on a programmer and offers some suggestions on good places to look online to find one.

Working with Web Editors

HyperText Markup Language, or HTML, is the foundation code of any web page. The code is comprised of a simple tag-based *markup language* for the World Wide Web that communicates information about how the text, graphics, links, and other content formatting, as well as the page structure of a document, should be viewed in a web browser. Almost anyone can learn HTML in a short period of time because its rules are reasonably straightforward, it isn't a full-scale programming language, and its structure is fairly uncomplicated.

The HTML code for any web page can either be typed using a plain-text editor, such as Notepad for the PC or TextEdit for the Mac, or written using the specialized tools in a dedicated HTML (code) or web (visual) editor. An editor is really the better choice for creating web pages because an editor can help you create the HTML quickly, as well as integrate other important technologies with the pages, such as adding CSS (Cascading Style Sheets), JavaScript, and jQuery, as well as other scripting and programming languages to the code.

Selecting a web editor

You can choose from two basic types of web-editing programs — code editors and visual editors — to build your web pages in HTML:

✔ **Code editors:** These kinds of HTML editors are perfect for people who already know some HTML and prefer to hand-code their HTML pages. Code editors can be as simple as the text-editing program that comes with your computer — whether that's Notepad or Notepad++ on a PC or TextEdit on a Mac — or as complex as a program dedicated to writing HTML, such as BBEdit, shown in Figure 4-1, or Coda from Panic (www.panic.com), which has special tools, buttons, and other code helpers to assist with the tasks of coding your pages. If you're looking for a free coding editor, you might enjoy using the TextWrangler, Aptana, or the CoffeeCup free HTML editor. Any of these and other editors you might find online are fine to use, as long as the editor you choose assists you in writing standards-compliant code, whether that be HTML 4.01, XHTML 1.0, or HTML5.

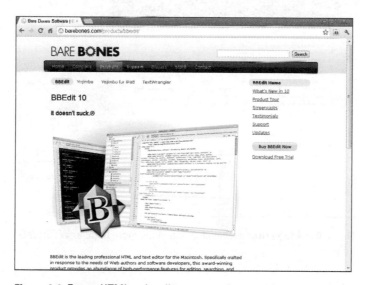

Figure 4-1: For an HTML-only editor, use a robust tool like the Bare Bones BBEdit software.

Do not use a word processing application like WordPad or Microsoft Word as a code editor. These programs tend to add extra characters and unnecessary markup to the HTML code that can drastically increase the file size of the saved .html document.

✓ **Visual editors:** Also sometimes called *design, drag and drop,* and *web* editors, these types of HTML editors, like Adobe Dreamweaver shown in Figure 4-2, allow designers to build pages by using a friendly WYSIWYG user interface. (*WYSIWYG,* pronounced "wizzy-wig," stands for *What You See Is What You Get.*) Visual editors provide you with easy-to-use buttons, tools, special shortcuts, and drag-and-drop features that allow you to easily add text, graphics, and other content to a web page. This means that you don't need to know much HTML to use an editor like this (though the more you know, the faster you can code and edit, and the better designer you'll ultimately be). Besides their user-friendly interfaces, visual editors have working offline design views, or *rendering engines*, that closely mirror what the page will look like when displayed in a browser window (either with or without a live Internet connection), making the web page–building process much more fun and easy to do.

Figure 4-2: Adobe Dreamweaver is one of the more popular WYSIWYG editors.

Another great benefit to using a visual editor over a code editor is that most visual editors have built-in coding editors, so users can easily switch back and forth between the code and visual editing modes, or in the case of Dreamweaver, work in both modes simultaneously using a Split Code display that shows both the code and the design views of a page.

The most popular visual editors being used by professional designers today are Adobe Dreamweaver, CoffeeCup, Microsoft Expression Web, and Nvu (pronounced "n-view"). Of course, other web editors are out there for you to choose from if none of the options presented here suit your fancy. Freeware seekers might like Kompozer or OpenOffice's BlueFish editor. Alternatively, some developers prefer to use browser-based editing tools and extensions such as Firebug for Firefox and Safari's built-in developing tools for the web.

This book uses Dreamweaver and hand-coding methods exclusively as the basis for providing instructional steps in later chapters on how to build your web pages. You also find instructions for using Photoshop and a few other software tools preferred by professional designers. No matter which software programs you ultimately choose to use, all the instructions are easily adaptable so that you can follow along with the examples provided.

Understanding HTML and CSS structure

Even if you are somewhat uncomfortable right now with the idea of working with HTML code, as a web designer, you can greatly benefit from having a basic knowledge and understanding of it. When you get the hang of the basics of HTML, comprehending the rest of the syntax rules should be a snap.

Before you get to learning syntax, however, you should understand the general difference between regular HTML, XHTML, and HTML5. HTML is the original language for marking up pages viewed in a browser on the World Wide Web. XHTML and HTML5 are more recent, advanced versions of HTML that follow slightly different syntax rules and offer additional features and functionality. Most people new to web design start by learning the rules of HTML 4.01.

What makes HTML easiest to learn is that it is fairly straightforward to comprehend and the coding rules are somewhat more forgiving than other coding methods, should you make any organizational mistakes or code omissions. XHTML, which stands for eXtensible HyperText Markup Language, is a stricter version of HTML that allows the data on a web page to be used as an application of XML. Because mistakes made in XHTML coding can throw off the entire display of content on a page in a browser, definitely begin your journey into the world of web coding with HTML, and only advance into XHTML if you intend to use XML. For a friendlier, more robust, and newer alternative to HTML, consider advancing to HTML5, which is almost identical to HTML 4.01 but includes many new tags, advanced audio, video, and graphics support, support for CSS3, and a bunch of other amazing features for improved visitor interactivity.

All HTML code, whether HTML, XHTML, or HTML5, uses small components called *tags* to mark up your text, graphics, and other content on a page that is viewed in a web browser.

Tags are essentially predefined words or acronyms written in all lowercase letters and surrounded by left (<) and right (>) angle brackets, as in the tag <html>. Understanding a few fundamentals about HTML tags can help you understand much of the HTML code that you'll see as you begin creating web pages.

Most HTML tags come in tag *sets,* or *pairs,* to mark the start and end of a text block or other object, such as an image, table, or layer, that appears on a web page. Think of each tag pair as a kind of container that can hold certain kinds of content as well as inform a browser how to format and display that content. Closing tags look identical to the opening tags with the exception of having an added forward slash directly before the tag name after the opening bracket. For example, a sentence might be marked up with opening and closing paragraph, or `<p>`, tags like this:

```
<p>HTML tags make your documents viewable on the Internet.</p>
```

In HTML, the opening/closing tag rule has a few exceptions. These exceptions include the use of meta tags, line breaks `<br>`, image tags `<img src="filename.extension">`, and a few assorted others, like the tags used to add form fields and embed media files on a web page. Because these exceptions can be somewhat confusing to people who are new to HTML, unclosed HTML tags can be closed out either by closing all unclosed tags with a closed tag, thereby creating a tag pair, like this:

```
<br></br>
```

or by borrowing from one of the syntax rules used in XHTML, namely, adding a space and a forward slash before the ending right angle bracket of the opening tag in question, as in this example:

```
<br />
```

Before designers started using Cascading Style Sheets to style and position their web page content, simple formatting rules used to be applied directly to the opening HTML tags. These formatting elements or attributes would tell the browser how the tag or the contents between the opening and closing tags should appear in the browser window. Formatting attributes like these included such things as color, alignment, width and height, and style. These attributes appear only in opening tags (never in the closing tags) using the syntax `x="y"`, where `x` is the attribute and `y` is the value of that attribute, as in the following example:

```
<hr width="500">
<p align="center">This sentence will be centered on the page.</p>
```

If desired, you can list multiple attributes in the opening tag should the need arise:

```
<div id="main" align="center">
```

Many HTML tags deal with semantically identifying the different parts of the web page content. You can use the basic tags like `<p>` for paragraphs and `<h1>` through `<h6>` for headings; character formatting tags, like `<strong>` for bold and `<em>` for italics to add emphasis; and then all the rest of the tags —

including tags for inserting links, images, lists, tables, frames, and forms — for adding graphics, objects, programming, styles, and metadata to the page.

For a complete listing and description of all the HTML tags you can add to your web pages, visit the following sites:

- ✔ www.w3schools.com/tags/ref_byfunc.asp
- ✔ www.webmonkey.com/2010/02/html_cheatsheet
- ✔ www.html.net
- ✔ http://reference.sitepoint.com/html

Looking at web page structure

Every web page uses a similar fundamental structure. All tags are hierarchically nested between opening and closing <html> tags, and all the code in the page falls between either the <head> or the <body> tags:

```
<html>
<head>
<title>The page title goes here and displays in the browser's
  title bar.</title>
</head>
<body>
This part of the web page contains all the content that will
appear in the browser window, including text and graphics
marked up by HTML tags and CSS.
</body>
</html>
```

Figure 4-3 shows how this HTML code appears in a browser. The head area of a page contains certain information about the web page that is interpreted by the browser, such as the page title (which appears in the browser's title bar), meta tags used for page indexing by a search engine, style definitions in the form of CSS (Cascading Style Sheets) to control how content appears on the page, and JavaScript to manage simple site interactivity, such as rollover buttons and form processing. All the head data, with the exception of the title definition between the <title> tags, is hidden from view in the browser window and does not appear anywhere on the finished web page. Rather, this information is used strictly by search engine spiders, robots, and crawlers.

By contrast, the body area of the code is where all the page's text, graphics, and other objects go. All content included between the opening and closing <body> tags — unless marked up with special comment tags — appears as content on the page in the browser window. Therefore everything in the body of the page should be marked up with additional CSS markup to specify its style and position.

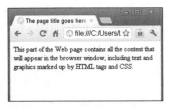

Figure 4-3: The content that appears on a web page is determined by the markup positioned between the opening and closing <body> tags.

Building a web page

Building a simple web page is easy. To prove it, the following steps show you how to create your first web page by hand-coding it in HTML.

Follow these steps to see how easy HTML is to understand and use:

1. **Open a new document in your computer's text-editing program.**

   On a PC, choose Start⇨All Programs⇨Accessories⇨Notepad.

   On a Mac, launch your Applications folder and double-click the TextEdit icon.

   A new, untitled document should open automatically. If that doesn't happen, choose File⇨New to open a new file.

2. **Type the following HTML tags into the document window:**

   ```
   <html>
   <head>
   <title></title>
   </head>
   <body>
   </body>
   </html>
   ```

3. **Between the opening and closing `<title>` tags, type** My First Web Page.

   Your code should now look like this:

   ```
   <html>
   <head>
   <title>My First Web Page</title>
   </head>
   <body>
   </body>
   </html>
   ```

4. **Between the opening and closing `<body>` tags, type** Hello world.

Now your code should look like this:

```
<html>
<head>
<title>My First Web Page</title>
</head>
<body>Hello world.
</body>
</html>
```

5. **Choose File⇨Save to open the Save As dialog box.**

   If you're using simpleText, choose Make Plain Text from the Format menu before saving the file as .html.

6. **Set the Save In location to your computer's desktop.**

7. **In the File Name field, type** index.html.

8. **In the Save as Type field, select All Files.**

9. **Click the Save button to save the file with the settings you just entered and close the file.**

10. **Launch your favorite browser and resize the browser window to roughly half the size of your desktop.**

11. **Drag and drop the icon of your new index.html page into the open browser window.**

    Your new web page appears with the words "Hello world." in the body of the page, and the title, My First Web Page, appears in the browser's title bar. Figure 4-4 shows a side-by-side comparison of your HTML code file and the browser window that displays your page.

Congratulations! You've just created your first web page. Of course, you already know that you can do a lot more to a page than include text, which you find out how to do in future chapters. For now, feel free to experiment by adding more text between the body tags or changing the title.

Saving web files

I need to add a quick word about saving web files that you may not know about. When saving your files, you can save them with any name you like, but you should follow some simple rules to ensure that your files can be displayed on all types of web servers. Filenames can be any length, but it's more common to use all lowercase letters, to keep page and filenames fairly short and succinct, and to avoid using spaces or odd characters with the exception of the underscore (_) and hyphen (-). Many host servers follow strict syntax rules and will display files only when the URL or HTML exactly matches the name of the file on the server. For example, a page filename may be something like about.html or email-signup.html but not About Me.Html or Contact & Directions page #1.html. If you fail to follow these rules, there's a good chance your pages won't display at all.

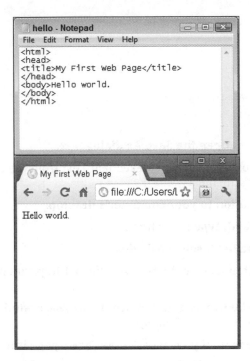

Figure 4-4: A side-by-side comparison of your code and web page can help you visualize how your code works.

Likewise, if you save an image as `MyProfilePic.JPEG` but then in your HTML list it as `Myprofilepic.jpeg`, that image simply won't show up on the page. Stick with all lowercase, no spaces, and short, descriptive filenames for best results.

In addition to choosing a descriptive filename that matches the contents of the page, you should save all your web page files with the appropriate file extension. It's important to remember to do this because the extension informs the browser about the type of code used in the file so that the browser knows how to process and display the file's contents. Acceptable extensions for HTML, XHTML, and HTML5 are `.html` and `.htm`. Either one works; however, I strongly recommend that you select a single extension (I use `.html`) and use it exclusively for all the pages on a single site.

Though most of your pages can be named anything you like, your home page must be deliberately named so that it appears as the default page when visitors go to the site. In most cases, you should save the home page as either `index.html` or `index.htm`. Because the filename *index* is the default page name in a web directory on most web servers, visitors do not need to type the filename and extension when they want to access the first (home)

page on a site. For example, if I want to see the home page of the Museum of Modern Art, rather than typing the URL and the filename plus the .html extension into my browser's address bar — www.moma.org/index.html — I only need to type www.moma.org (or simply **moma.org**, which most browsers can interpret) to get there.

Though it's almost always the case that your home page should be named index.html, some websites might be hosted on different types of web servers that require the home page to be named either default.html or default.htm instead. In my experience, this happens so infrequently that I can usually figure this out by testing the index.html naming convention with a test page on the live server. If index.html doesn't work, default. html should. To save time, however, if you're unsure which filename to use, check with your (or your client's) host provider or system administrator.

When your pages use programming languages or Server-Side Includes (a page containing HTML code that's embedded inside another HTML file, which you find out about in Book III, Chapter 9), other file extensions may need to be used instead of .html. For example, articles.shtml, contact_us.php, products.jsp, and services.cfml are all acceptable filename plus file extension combos. Table 4-1 outlines the file extensions you can use for different types of pages.

Table 4-1	Saving with the Correct File Extension
Type of Page	*Extensions*
HTML/XHTML/HTML5	.html, .htm
HTML/XHTML/HTML5 pages with Server-Side Includes	.shtml, .shtm
Microsoft Active Server page	.asp, .aspx
JavaServer pages	.jsp
PHP script pages	.php
ColdFusion Markup Language pages	.cfml, .cfm

Choosing the Right Graphics Software

One of the nice things about being a designer, in my opinion, is the fact that you get to make lots of important decisions throughout the web design process, including what software to use to create the design mock-up, optimize all the graphics, and build all the pages on the site. Whether amateurs or professionals, all web designers need a few of the right software tools to successfully design and build websites. In the following sections, you find out about how to choose the right graphics software.

Graphics programs

To work with and create images for the web, designers can freely use both raster and vector programs:

- **Raster:** A raster or bitmap program, such as Adobe Photoshop, shown in Figure 4-5, uses pixels to represent each bit of an image at the size used to create the image. Raster/bitmap programs are great for photographic retouching and for building website mock-ups. While it is okay to scale down (make smaller) a raster image, you should definitely try to avoid enlarging a raster file because the larger version needs to use a computerized guessing technique called *resampling* and tends to look, well, pixelated. Alternatively, web designers on a tight budget might enjoy working with Adobe Fireworks, a dedicated web graphic image editor, or with a free raster application such as GIMP.

- **Vector:** By contrast, a good vector program, such as Adobe Illustrator, shown in Figure 4-6, uses mathematical algorithms to draw shapes and paths. This means that vector images can be scaled up and down a zillion times and still retain the sharpness and clarity of their original lines and shape. Vector programs should always be used to create branding and corporate identity such as logos and other artwork because the work can be scaled with no loss of resolution. In addition, vector graphics often have smaller file sizes than their raster-based bitmap counterparts.

Figure 4-5: A good program like Adobe Photoshop is perfect for creating raster graphics and editing digital photographs.

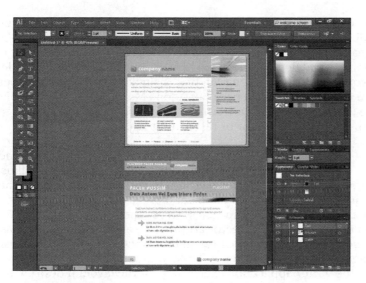

Figure 4-6: Use a program like Adobe Illustrator to create your vector illustrations and graphics.

By far, the most popular raster graphics software application in use today is Adobe Photoshop, which, while primarily being a raster (or bitmap) application, can also create vector shapes and incorporate placed vector graphics or *SmartObjects* from vector programs such as Adobe Illustrator. Originally developed as a digital photo retouching and image-editing program, Photoshop has since evolved its capabilities for use as a nice web graphics design and optimization tool. To get the most from Photoshop, use the full or extended version. Alternatively, if you're on a budget or you already own a copy of Photoshop Elements, it should suffice. For vector art, most designers use Adobe Illustrator because it's a feature-rich drawing program that allows you to draw just about anything for use in print, web, animation, mobile devices, and video.

Though some graphic designers use Photoshop and Illustrator as page layout programs for print projects like postcards, brochures, and business cards, most tend to use software programs designed specifically for multi-page layout, such as Adobe InDesign or QuarkXPress. Unless you're using InDesign CS6, which offers limited support for creating e-books and other digital publications for tablets and other devices using Adobe Edge technology, do *not* use a page layout program for your web layouts. Page layout programs were designed for print, not the web, and therefore don't necessarily have all the same features you'd currently find in Photoshop, Illustrator, and Fireworks. To be fair, Quark 7 and 8 allow you to export graphics into HTML, as well as perform a few other optimization-like features similar to the things you can do with graphics in Photoshop and Fireworks. As for InDesign, versions CS5 and below offer nothing in the way of exporting HTML or graphics optimization. What some of those earlier versions of the software can do is allow you (since the CS version) to export only an InDesign-tagged XML file. That file can then be imported into a predesigned Adobe Dreamweaver template, which inserts tagged data into preset areas on a web template and doesn't allow you to take advantage of your own design layout. If you're looking for a program that is similar to InDesign but doesn't require you to learn any code, check out Adobe Muse, a new program offered with the CS6 suite of tools. Otherwise, upgrade to InDesign CS6 or create your web graphics in a vector or raster program.

At a minimum, I suggest that you have access to at least one good raster and one good vector art program, preferably Photoshop and Illustrator, respectively. Use the raster program to lay out all the parts of the web page in the mock-up (which you find out more about in Book II, Chapter 2), and if the design requires any special logos, shapes, drawings, or illustrations, you can create them in the vector art program and then copy and paste them as *SmartObjects* (graphics that retain their vector scalability while sitting as an object inside a raster program) into your raster mock-up. You could also use the vector application exclusively for the layout if desired, but many designers find the filters and effects in a vector program somewhat limiting compared to the special effects that can be applied to your work in raster programs. Today, roughly two-thirds of all web designers use Photoshop for creating their web mock-ups. The other one-third use either Fireworks or Illustrator.

You can, of course, use other vector and raster image-editing programs to create your web graphics:

- ✔ Adobe Fireworks is an excellent all-in-one web image-editing and image-optimization tool that integrates beautifully with Adobe Dreamweaver.

- ✔ Paint.NET is a free, open-source, easy-to-use, powerful, bitmap-image and photo-editing software program for PCs running Windows, available for download from www.getpaint.net.

- ✔ DrawPlus from Serif (www.freeserifsoftware.com) is a nice tool for vector drawing, editing, and text manipulation.

- ✔ PhotoPlus, also from Serif (www.freeserifsoftware.com), is a decent digital photo editing program.

- ✔ For a super low-end, cookie-cutter graphics option, check out NetStudio's Easy Web Graphics program or Xara's Photo & Graphic Designer MX software.

- ✔ If you have no budget for purchasing software, you can use several free online applications, such as the image editor at www.myimager.com. You can also find some good freeware (like the Gnu Image Manipulation Program, or GIMP), shareware, and 30-day trials of image-editing software programs (like CorelDraw) through download web services like www.download.com and www.zdnet.com.

That said, I highly recommend that you make the investment and buy Photoshop and Illustrator if you don't already own them, or update them to the newest version if you own old copies. These programs really are the best tools available right now, and the quality of your website may be relative to the quality of the graphics you can create for it.

If you don't own either of these programs yet, or if you have old versions of them and are in need of an upgrade, a smart choice would be to buy the Adobe CS6 Creative Cloud directly from Adobe. Alternatively, students who can prove they are enrolled in a K–12 school, privately licensed training center, community college, or four-year college or university can qualify to purchase this software at a discounted rate. For example, a regular subscription to the Adobe CS6 Creative Cloud costs around $49.99 per month, whereas the educational version of the same software costs only $29.99. Table 4-2 shows a cost comparison of the bundled Adobe product, standalone versions, and some truly useful, free, open-source products.

Table 4-2	Side-by-Side Software Cost Comparison		
Product Name	*Product Type*	*Cost*	*Website*
Adobe CS6 Creative Cloud comes with versions of Dreamweaver, Photoshop, Illustrator, Fireworks, Flash, Acrobat, InDesign, Bridge, and many others.	Full suite of products to help design mock-ups, create optimized graphics, make vector-based animations, convert files to PDFs, build websites, and more.	$1,899 or upgrade from $749	www.adobe.com
Adobe CS6 Web Premium comes with versions of Dreamweaver, Flash, Photoshop, Illustrator, Fireworks, InDesign, Acrobat, Bridge, and Media Encoder.	Full suite of products to help design mock-ups create optimized graphics, create vector-based animations, convert files to PDFs, and build websites.	$1,899 or upgrade from $375	www.adobe.com

(continued)

Table 4-2 *(continued)*

Product Name	Product Type	Cost	Website
Dreamweaver CS6	WYSIWYG HTML web dditor	$399 or upgrade from $125	www.adobe. com
Photoshop CS6	Raster/bitmap graphics editor	$699 or upgrade from $199	www.adobe. com
Photoshop Elements 10	Raster/bitmap graphics editor	$99 or upgrade from $79	www.adobe. com
Illustrator CS6	Vector graphics editor	$599 or upgrade from $249	www.adobe. com
Fireworks CS6	Web graphics editor	$299 or upgrade from $149	www.adobe. com
CorelDraw	Graphic design and illustration vector/bitmap software	$499 or upgrade from $199	www.corel. com
Microsoft Expression Studio 4 Web Professional	WYSIWYG HTML web editor	$149 or upgrade from $79	www.micro soft.com/ expression/
BBEdit	HTML web editor	$49 or upgrade from $39	www.bare bones.com
TextWrangler	HTML web editor	Free	www.bare bones.com
CoffeeCup	WYSIWYG HTML web editor	Free	www.coffee cup.com/ free-editor/
PageBreeze	Open-source web authoring system	Free	http:// pagebreeze. com
KompoZer	Open-source web authoring system	Free	http:// kompozer. net
NVU	Open-source web authoring system	Free	http:// net2.com/ nvu/
BlueFish	Open-source web authoring system	Free	http:// bluefish. openoffice. nl

Product Name	Product Type	Cost	Website
Paint.NET	Open-source digital photo retouching and image editor	Free	`www.get paint.net`
InkScape	Open-source vector graphics editor	Free	`http://ink scape.org`
DrawPlus	Open-source graphics editor	Free	`www.free serifsoft ware.com`
PhotoPlus	Open-source digital photo retouching and image editor	Free	`www.free serifsoft ware.com`

Web graphic optimization programs

After you've finished creating your mock-up for the site design, you need to *optimize* your graphics (which is covered in detail in Book II, Chapter 3). Optimization means compressing the graphics into acceptable file formats, such as `.gif`, `.jpg`, and `.png`, that are small enough to be displayed on the web without losing too much image quality.

In the past, the application most frequently used for image optimization by Photoshop and Illustrator users was Adobe ImageReady, which used to come bundled with Photoshop. Then, several years ago, the ImageReady optimization engine was integrated into both Photoshop and Illustrator (using the File⇨Save for Web command), eliminating the need for a separate program for the optimization process. If you happen to have an old copy of ImageReady, you can certainly still use it, but if you've already migrated to CS3 or higher in Photoshop or Illustrator, you don't need to.

Another option is to design and optimize or just optimize your web graphics with Adobe Fireworks or any number of the free or affordable optimization programs for a PC or Mac, like DeBabelizer Pro, ImageOptimizer (`http://www.imageoptimizer.net/Home.aspx`), and RIOT (`http://luci.criosweb.ro/riot/`), or the AIR application called Shrink-O-Matic (`http://toki-woki.net/p/Shrink-O-Matic/`). What makes the Save for Web dialog box and Fireworks applications so good, though, is that they can both optimize graphics and export either tables- or layers-based HTML files with CSS. This can greatly reduce the time it takes to build a website using an HTML or web-editing program such as Adobe Dreamweaver. For non-Adobe alternatives, including some truly fantastic, free, open-source image-editing software programs, refer to Table 4-2.

Working with Color

In the following sections, you find out how to work with RGB color on the web using hexadecimal values.

Using web-safe colors

Of necessity, the web-safe color palette was born in the early days of the Internet (coined by Lynda Weinman of www.lynda.com) because computer monitors at the time were only capable of an 8-bit display, which meant they could only handle showing a maximum of 256 colors onscreen. Unfortunately, the 256 colors that were viewable in an Internet Explorer, Netscape, or Mosaic browser on a PC running Windows were somewhat different from the 256 colors viewable in an Internet Explorer, Netscape, or Mosaic browser on an 8-bit monitor connected to an Apple computer running the Mac OS. As it turned out, a total of 40 non-overlapping colors out of the total possible 256 colors were visible on both platforms. This left a total of 216 colors, shown in Figure 4-7, that would render uniformly on an 8-bit monitor in those early Internet browsers on both Mac and PC platforms.

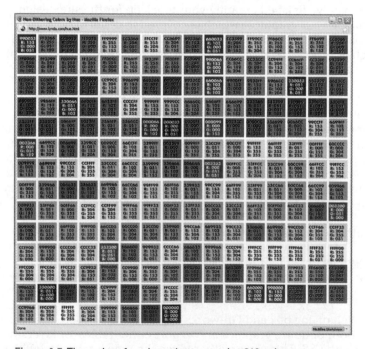

Figure 4-7: The web-safe color palette contains 216 colors.

To help ensure that visitors on PCs and Macs would have uniform visual experiences when they visited a particular website, web designers had to limit their web design colors to this web-safe or *browser-safe* color palette. As you can imagine, this web-safe color palette was somewhat restrictive in scope. And to make matters worse, the palette didn't necessarily have a wide range of visually appealing colors in it, having been developed mathematically by programmers, not aesthetically by artists.

But, one must work with the tools and technology available at any given time and make the best of it. And thankfully, these color limitations were somewhat short-lived because of improvements made to monitor resolutions and browser capabilities. Today, monitors capable of 16-, 24-, and 36-bit displays can render millions of colors onscreen, which means that the web-safe palette is now pretty much a thing of history.

Nonetheless, for the rare, occasional web project, you may be asked to create designs for (or at least consider) viewers of the lowest common denominator — the audience members still using old computers, old monitors, and old versions of old and perhaps now-extinct browsers — and thus choose colors from the web-safe palette for their web designs. At the time of this writing, Internet users with monitors having an 8-bit display or using handheld computers with 8-bit displays represent 0 percent of the installed base. In fact, only 2 percent of users have monitors with 16-bit displays showing a maximum of 65,536 different colors, while the remaining 98 percent of users have 24- and 32-bit displays showing 16,777,216 different colors. In most cases these days, the web-safe palette simply isn't an issue.

As a general design rule, if monitors can display the colors, you should use them, but you might for certain projects still consider using the web-safe colors smartly in ways that might not be so obvious to the occasional visitor using old equipment. If you do get a project that caters to users who might only have 8- or 16-bit monitors, the prevailing "recommendation" for the web-safe palette is to use these 216 colors for large, flat areas of color on a site, such as background colors (for pages, tables, and layers), logos, and illustrations saved as GIF files. For other parts of a site, such as photographs and graphics that can be saved as JPGs, using other colors might be fine, as long as you and the site owner understand the ramifications of potential color shift in different browsers on different computer platforms when viewed on older computer equipment. That said, plenty of contemporary web designers out there use the exact colors they want to use without regard to the web-safe palette, and their sites look just fine. In sum, it's an old rule, and breaking it causes little to no visual trouble.

Using hexadecimal colors

When you're creating graphics for the web in your preferred vector or raster software program, you need to do two things to ensure that your color looks good on the web:

  ✔ **Check that you're working in the RGB (red-green-blue) color mode (not CMYK).** CMYK color is used exclusively for print whereas RGB is used for any onscreen presentations, such as PowerPoint, PDFs, and the web, where light is transmitted through a device to display colors on a screen or other device.

  ✔ **Specify all the color in your mock-ups and other graphic files using hexadecimal values.** Of course, you could specify color in RGB values if you wanted to, but it uses a lot more code, and most code editors currently only recognize hexadecimal values.

As you'll soon discover, when you're working in an HTML code or web page editor, all colors — web-safe or otherwise — must either be hand coded in RGB values or be specified in hexadecimal values preceded by the number symbol (#) to display properly on a web page. The hexadecimal numbers, often called simply "hex colors," "hex numbers," or "hex values," refer to the six-letter/number combination RGB (red-green-blue, the additive colors used to display color on a computer monitor) values written in three pairs of numbers (from 0 to 9) or letters (from *a* to *f*), as shown in Table 4-3. As you can see, the RGB value of white is R=255, G=255, B=255 where the hexadecimal equivalent is simply written as #ffffff.

Table 4-3	Sample Hexadecimal Values			
Color	*Hexadecimal Value*	*Red*	*Green*	*Blue*
Black	#000000	0	0	0
White	#ffffff	255	255	255
Gray	#c0c0c0	192	192	192
Red	#ff0000	255	0	0
Green	#00ff00	0	255	0
Yellow	#ffff00	255	255	0
Blue	#0000ff	0	0	255

If you like gadgets, you might enjoy playing around with the online Color Mixer at www.mathisfun.com, shown in Figure 4-8. As you move each of the sliders, you can see the RGB and hex equivalents. There are a ton of free color mixers like this online, such as the ones on www.w3schools.com and www.design-lib.com, so be sure to bookmark the ones you like.

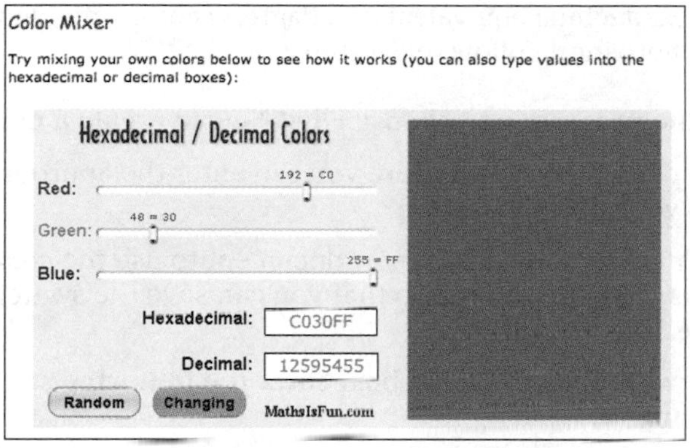

Figure 4-8: Use the hexadecimal color value when specifying a color on the web.

Believe it or not, of the millions of monitor colors that have hex values, a handful of them have named equivalents that are supported by most web browsers and can be used in HTML and CSS code instead of the hex values, such as LightCoral for #f08080 and DarkSeaGreen for #8fbc8f. For a listing of color names, see `www.w3schools.com/html/html_colornames.asp`.

To find the hexadecimal value of any RGB color or the hexadecimal equivalent of a CMYK (cyan-magenta-yellow-black, the subtractive ink colors used in four-color process printing) color, you must use a software program that has a value conversion tool installed. Photoshop, Illustrator, Fireworks, and Dreamweaver all include web-safe palettes and color tools that display and can convert RGB, CMYK, and Pantone (a color-matching system used by designers and printers; see `www.pantone.com`) colors into hexadecimal values.

If you want to use a standalone color-conversion tool, you can find several freeware applications by searching online for the term *free color picker*. ColorPic, Color Cop, Color Spy, Huey, and ColorPickerPro all provide excellent RGB, CMYK, and hex conversions. You can also use the free online color-conversion tool at `http://web.forret.com/tools/color.asp`.

When building websites for others, you may occasionally encounter customers who provide you with Pantone colors instead of CMYK or RGB values. In those cases, you need to find the RGB equivalents to use within your web designs. If you're using an Adobe product, the Pantone matching system is built in to Photoshop and Illustrator. Non-Adobe users, however, might enjoy using the special Pantone program, PANTONE COLOR MANAGER. The cost is $49 for a standalone program or free for anyone who purchases a qualifying Pantone product.

To find the hexadecimal equivalent of a Pantone color provided by your client using Photoshop, follow these steps:

1. **Launch the program and choose File⇨New to create a new document.**

   The New dialog box opens. Here you can enter the appropriate settings to set up your document.

   You don't necessarily need a new document to use the color-picker tool, but in this exercise you will so that you can save the swatches for future reference.

2. **In the New Document dialog box, enter the following settings for the new document:**

   Enter **960 x 640** pixels for the web page width and height dimensions and **72** pixels/inch for the Resolution. For the Color Mode setting, choose RGB, enter **8** bit, and for the Background contents, set that to White.

   These settings are typical for web design, and you can use them for most of your web page mock-ups.

3. **Click the OK button to close the dialog box and return to the new, blank document.**

4. **With the rectangular marquee tool selected in Photoshop, click and drag inside the top-left edge of the document window to create a small rectangular shape (about 1 x 2 inches) and release the mouse button.**

   The rectangular marquee tool creates a selected area that you can fill with any color.

5. **Click the Foreground Color icon at the bottom of the Tool palette.**

   The foreground/background color selector icons are the overlapping squares. The foreground is on the upper left, and the background is on the lower right.

   This step opens the Color Picker dialog box, shown in Figure 4-9, which has several options for selecting and viewing color.

6. **Deselect the Only Web Colors check box at the bottom of the dialog box.**

   Because you're looking at RGB, Pantone, and CMYK colors to find their hexadecimal equivalents, you don't need to be restricted to the web-safe palette. You want to see millions of colors.

7. **To look up an RGB color, enter the following values in the R, G, and B fields, respectively:** 246, 180, **and** 0.

   As you enter the numbers into the R, G, and B fields, notice how the color shifts inside the Color Picker.

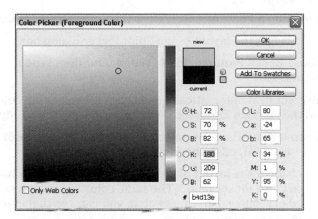

Figure 4-9: The Photoshop Color Picker displays colors in RGB, CMYK, Pantone, and hexadecimal values.

The hexadecimal value of your entered color appears as a combination of six letters and numbers in the hex field at the bottom of the Color Picker, beginning with a # symbol.

The hexadecimal value of this RGB color is #f6bf00.

8. **Click the OK button to close the Color Picker dialog box.**

   The rectangular shape is still selected. Next you fill it with the new hex color you just specified the RGB values for.

9. **Choose Edit⇨Fill to open the Fill dialog box and, from the Use menu, select Foreground Color. Then click the OK button.**

   The yellow color fills the selected rectangle.

10. **To the right of the yellow rectangle in your document, repeat Steps 4 and 5 to create another rectangular shape and open the Color Picker dialog box.**

    You use the same process to look up the hex value of a CMYK color.

11. **Look up the CMYK color by entering the following values in the C, M, Y, and K fields, respectively: 52, 15, 98, 1.**

    The hexadecimal value of this CMYK color is #89ac40.

12. **Repeat Steps 8 and 9 10 to fill the second rectangle with the new hex color.**

13. **To the right of the green rectangle, repeat Steps 4 and 5 to create a third rectangular shape and open the Color Picker dialog box.**

    You use the same process to look up the hex value of a Pantone color.

14. **To look up a Pantone color, click the Color Libraries button.**

    This changes the layout of the Color Picker dialog box.

15. **Choose Book⇨Pantone Solid Coated, and then type a Pantone color number:** 297.

    The color field automatically displays a range of blue color swatches with the Pantone 297C (the C stands for coated) color highlighted.

16. **To convert the Pantone color to a regular process color and find its hex equivalent, click the Picker button.**

    This changes the layout of the Color Picker dialog box back to the normal Color Picker mode. The same color blue is still selected, but now instead of seeing a Pantone swatch, you can see that color's RGB, CMYK, and hexadecimal equivalents!

    The hexadecimal value of this Pantone color is #78c7eb.

17. **Repeat Steps 8 and 9 to fill the third rectangle with the new hex color.**

18. **Choose File⇨Save to save the document.**

    Select a location on your computer to save your new file, name your file `hexswatches.psd`, select the Photoshop format, and click the Save button.

Choosing a Shopping Cart

When the site you are building will be selling any products or services online, the site needs some kind of shopping cart or payment-processing system for payments coming from the purchasers. Payments can be processed in many ways, depending on the needs and budget of the site owner.

The most basic kind of shopping cart uses a payment-processing service such as PayPal. The next tier of service is to create an online store using a specialized shopping cart service's proprietary software, such as Yahoo! Merchant Solutions. Some of these carts, however, must reside on the service's server away from the site owner's main URL, which can at times make purchasers feel uneasy, unless the carts are hosted by a reputable service like Yahoo!, which can elicit instant trust from purchasers. Other shopping cart services include building more customized carts from either web-host-provided services or out-of-the-box shopping carts from third-party software manufacturers. You can even find cart tools for WordPress and other CMS systems. Though fancier, some of these solutions also have limitations and can be very frustrating to customize, even for the most experienced designers.

For clients looking for something really slick, the best option is to have a shopping cart custom built so that it's tailored specifically to the site's needs. This, however, can cost significantly more money and take a lot more time to build than the other shopping carts.

In the following sections, you find some general information about each of these shopping cart options.

Using PayPal shopping carts

One of the great things about PayPal is that it offers several payment solutions for individuals and businesses. The PayPal shopping cart is great for everything from sites working within a budget or selling only a handful of products to sites with existing shopping carts and sites where a customized cart will be integrated with the PayPal payment system. What's more, PayPal accounts are affordable, easy to set up, and easy to use.

To use any of PayPal's services, follow these steps:

1. The client needs to set up a Merchant PayPal account linked to the bank she'd like to use to accept credit card and other online payments.

2. The client must also input data about all the products she'd like to sell on the site so that PayPal can generate "Add to Cart" or "Buy Now" PayPal buttons and the HTML button code for each product.

3. When that's done, as the designer, you need to copy and paste the code for each of those buttons from the PayPal site into the HTML pages that list the products on the client's site.

   That's all there is to it.

To use the PayPal shopping cart online, visitors click the PayPal button of the item they want to purchase, as illustrated in Figure 4-10, and after clicking, a special PayPal payment-processing page opens. Registered PayPal users can simply enter their payment information to complete the transaction. Unregistered visitors can either choose to set up a PayPal account or simply enter their credit card information to proceed with the transaction without creating a PayPal account. After the transaction is complete, PayPal sends an automated e-mail to the site owner about the purchase. The site owner then has the responsibility of processing the order for the customer. PayPal processes Visa, MasterCard, American Express, Discover, eChecks, and PayPal payments.

Checking out Google Checkout

If you already advertise with Google AdWords (or plan to), you might be interested in Google Checkout, a PayPal-like button-activated checkout payment-processing system that can process credit and debit cards free of charge. The system does require visitors to have their own Google account to complete the transaction. To find out more about Google Checkout, visit `https://checkout.google.com/sell`.

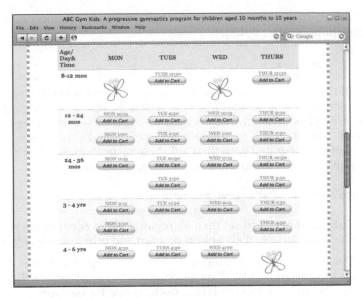

Figure 4-10: PayPal offers free Add to Cart and Buy Now buttons for e-commerce sites that want to process payments off-site.

Looking into third-party and web-hosted shopping carts

Two additional payment-processing alternatives for e-commerce websites include using a host-provided shopping cart system or purchasing a third-party software solution.

Most reputable web-hosting companies offer some kind of shopping cart service in one or more of their hosting plans. Host e-commerce plans often use their own specialized, custom-built applications that allow site owners to add all the required products to their site and manage those products through some kind of online Control Panel or other web interface.

These kinds of systems are typically fairly easy to set up, configure, and use; however, site owners should be aware of the greater fees associated with these types of e-commerce hosted plans. In addition to the monthly or annual hosting fee, site owners also need to get a merchant account to process credit cards through their shopping carts, as well as pay for an SSL certificate to ensure that online transactions through their websites are secure. These extra fees and capabilities can increase the total cost of a hosting plan considerably (say, from $25 per month to upwards of $200 per month). Because host-provided carts can vary drastically in functionality and visual appeal, be sure to test-drive any of the carts you're considering before committing to using the service.

Alternatively, if you're an artist, designer, musician, or craftsperson, you might be interested in using a marketplace shopping site Etsy or BigCartel. These sites allow you to set up shop and sell your products to their registered customer base. If you're really on a tight budget, you may even decide to forgo building a custom website yourself and instead create a website using WordPress, which can easily include a shopping cart module through the use of a plug-in such as the one offered at `http://getshopped.org`.

For those looking for a more customized but still reasonably inexpensive e-commerce solution, a third-party software application could be the answer. However, finding a good software package might prove challenging. In the "2012 Shopping Cart Software Report" on TopTenReviews (`http://shopping-cart-review.toptenreviews.com`), Volusion, Shopify, and Shopping Cart Elite were rated the best shopping cart software programs on the market, but be sure that you take these recommendations with a grain of salt.

Believe it or not, some free, open-source, and inexpensive shopping cart applications are fantastic and ready for downloading. And though they require a bit of coding to configure the cart, a few of them are quite reputable. Check out Zencart, Magento, osCommerce, CubeCart, and PrestaShop. Definitely do a web search to find out more about your shopping cart options if you decide to go the third-party route.

Building custom shopping carts

Though by far the most expensive solution, my favorite way to add a shopping cart to a site is to build a custom cart that meets the client's exact specifications. (If you don't have any technical know-how, you'll have to enlist the help of a programmer.) With a custom-designed shopping cart, every aspect of the ordering and checkout process can be customized, from the color scheme and user interface to the checkout confirmation page. This kind of detailed customization is possible because a tailored database is typically developed and integrated into the site as part of the e-commerce solution while the site is initially being built. All the e-commerce page layouts can be customized to the products being sold and have the same navigation, look, and feel as the rest of the site. Not only that, but using the customized database means being able to customize the payment-processing tasks, including sending e-mail receipts to the purchasers and creating administrative reports for the client.

If you don't have a background in database development and integration, you could either figure out how to do these things yourself or hire a programmer to do them for you. If you have good split-brain power and are motivated to learn, go for it. Personally, I'd much rather have someone who enjoys this kind of left-brain data manipulation do the work for me than to spend my own right-brain power trying to figure out how to do it myself. You discover more about hiring a programmer later in this chapter.

Planning for secure transactions

Whichever solution you decide to use to process payments online, take extra time and care to ensure that the site visitors' personal information is safe and secure during the purchasing transaction. If credit card payments are going to be processed on the website (instead of through an outside service such as PayPal or Google Checkout), the site owner needs to set up a business merchant account through his bank, as well as purchase and install an SSL certificate from his host provider for the domain.

A *merchant account* is a special bank account that handles the processing of credit card transactions. In fact, oftentimes, a bank will require business owners with both online and "brick and mortar" stores to have two separate merchant accounts: one for online sales and another for in-store, phone, and fax orders. If you or your client plan to sell online only, you only need the one merchant account. Either way, the merchant account collects payments electronically from the purchaser and then transfers the funds into the business owner's local business checking account. If you or your client decide to set up a merchant account, keep the following facts in mind:

- ✔ **Setup and application fees:** Merchant accounts can be set up through local banks, through host providers, and through billing software websites such as the Intuit site for QuickBooks. Most accounts cost $25–$250 in setup and application fees.

- ✔ **Monthly processing fees:** Fees for merchant services can add up quickly! Most merchant accounts charge a minimum each month, in the $15–$30 range (this is sometimes called a gateway or statement fee) when the number of transactions processed is below a preset minimum, plus a nominal charge, $0.20–$0.30, on all transactions processed. If the monthly minimum is met in transaction fees, the monthly minimum fee is often waived. Thirty dollars might be merely a token savings if you do a lot of business online. For instance, at $0.30 per transaction, if you sell $10,000 in products a month, you'd pay $300.00 in transaction fees.

SSL stands for *Secure Sockets Layer* and refers to the digital security web certificate that needs to be purchased from the host provider by the site owner and configured for the domain by the host provider. A valid SSL certificate guarantees that the site uses 128-bit or higher encryption methods to keep both visitors' personal information and credit card numbers secure and to protect the website from hackers and credit card thieves.

The leading brand of SSL certificates is VeriSign, but several others are available at varying costs. Annual rates vary from vendor to vendor, depending on the bit encryption rate. You might also check with your host provider to see if they offer any special discounts for SSL certificates purchased through them. Here are the current annual rates for three popular SSL providers:

✔ VeriSign, $798–$2998

✔ Thawte, $149–$699

✔ GeoTrust, $199–$499

All certificate issuers charge a one-time or annual fee, and the host provider might charge about $50 as a set-up fee to obtain the certificate for you, though sometimes with specials, host providers will waive the set-up fee. The first year always costs more than the renewal rates for subsequent years.

Knowing When to Hire a Programmer

In Book I, Chapter 1, you discover a little bit about diagnosing a site's dynamic needs. Adding dynamic features to a site adds cost and time to the project, and not all sites truly need it. Budget is often the primary factor for determining whether to add dynamic functionality to a site. Other considerations include expected growth of the site, the projected schedule for making updates, and the amount of data to be served on the site.

Taking a look at your dynamic content needs

You might need to hire a programmer if you . . .

✔ Have information stored in a database (or intend to) and want to have that data dynamically served on the pages of the website.

✔ Want a site-search feature on the website that accesses the site's database and returns search results based on selected search criteria, such as an alphabetized listing of store locations.

✔ Want a custom-built shopping cart for the site's products or services that allows you to customize the user's experience throughout the entire purchasing process from product selection to payment confirmation and order tracking.

✔ Would like a Content Management System (CMS) built for the site so that you (or your client) can manage content on the site through an easy-to-use web interface. This includes building a site with WordPress, Joomla, Drupal, or some other CMS system.

✔ Need to create an area of the site that requires a username and password for secure login to a database of accessible records or to other password-protected and members-only areas of the site.

✔ Want to allow visitors to choose how data will be displayed and sorted on a page by clicking the category heading of a table of data to re-sort the records, as with the Sort by Price shopping feature found on most e-commerce sites.

✔ Want to collect information from site visitors who have completed an online form, add that data to a database, and use that data to generate newsletters and e-mail blasts.

✔ Would like to dynamically display information, such as product descriptions, course listings, job opportunities, and real estate listings.

Dynamic sites are truly useful, and some things on the web just can't be done without a database and some programming. Keep in mind that a matter of degree exists here. For instance, if you're truly completely rolling your own site Search and Content Management System (CMS), you need one sort of programmer and will probably pay a big ticket. But you can hire a totally different type of programmer and pay a much smaller ticket to have someone get Google's custom search integrated with your site or get WordPress up and running for you. Similarly, in advertising campaigns, if you're going to roll your own advertising solution, that's one thing, but getting someone to integrate Google AdWords into your site, while possibly still requiring outsourcing, is a different type of resource.

Fortunately, you can learn and handle the simpler programming-like tasks. For example, you can figure out how to hard-code hyperlinks to individual pages and add the appropriate actions, hidden fields, and script-configuration settings to a web form so that a Perl or CGI script provided by a web host can process the data entered into the form by a site visitor.

Perl and CGI scripts are often used to process data collected in online forms, but they're also extremely vulnerable to spam. The scripts themselves must typically be placed inside the CGI (Common Gateway Interface) or cgi-bin folders at the root level of the web host server to function properly. You discover more about forms and form processing in Book III, Chapter 7.

The two most common types of databases are created with MySQL and Microsoft Access, both fairly easy programs to learn. After the database has been constructed to meet the needs of the website, you can easily figure out the appropriate code to add to the HTML of a web page so that the browser can pull the right data from a database on the fly.

On the other hand, if programming is something that doesn't interest you, you might want to hire a programmer to do the work for you. Finding a good programmer may take a little time, so be sure to start the search well before you actually need a programmer's services.

Finding a good programmer

Here are some suggested steps you can follow to help find a good programmer for your project:

1. **Write a "programmer wanted" ad. In your ad, be as clear as possible about your exact programming needs and how you'd like applicants to respond.**

   For instance, if you know you need to collect e-mail addresses so that the site owner can generate and mail monthly e-newsletters, state that. Also, if you know the language you want the programmer to work in, whether it's .NET, JSP, PHP, ColdFusion, or something else, say it.

   Similarly, if you really need someone who can come to your office and work with you side by side, specify in your job posting that the applicant must live in your town and clearly state that you're seeking on-site help only. If you want to hire only seasoned programmers, request to see evidence of the programmer's portfolio and references. Always ask for references from everybody, even the student who might be charging next to nothing to build his or her portfolio.

2. **Post your ad. Fortunately, some of the best places to look for a programmer are online.**

   You can find programmers through an agency like Monster (www. monster.com) or the less-formal job-listing sites like Elance (www. elance.com) and GetACoder.com (www.getacoder.com). Other, perhaps smarter, places to look are Craigslist, local programming school job boards, programmer blogs, and forums. Also consider word of mouth in programmer chat rooms.

3. **Ask each of the applicants who responds to your ad (who, by the way, will be responding from around the globe) as many questions as you want about their experience, fees, and the time frame it may take them to complete your project.**

   Use your e-mails with applicants as a way to weed out the less-capable candidates. A good way to screen candidates is to see how they respond to questions. Pay attention to grammar, spelling, and how polite they are in their responses. Applicants with good answers should stay in the running, while applicants with bad or incomplete answers get tossed. It's truly fascinating to see how some people completely ignore your specific requests and try to hound you into hiring them. Stay away from those types.

4. **When you've whittled your list to two or three promising programmers, try them out, if you can, on a small test project (different from the reason you're hiring them) to see whether they're reliable, friendly, hard working, accountable, responsible, and capable.**

   If you're lucky, you'll end up with at least one, but hopefully two, programmers who you can begin working with on all your dynamic projects.

Paying a programmer

Payment is another issue to consider before a project begins. When a web project requires the help of a programmer, you have two basic options:

- Make the programmer's part of the job separate from your own work and have your customer pay the programmer directly for those services.

- Include the programmer's fees with your own fees in your overall cost to your customer. Some designers even include a 15 percent markup of programmer's services when adding the programmer's fees with their own.

Programmers typically charge anywhere from $45–$100 per hour, and their projects can range from as little as 1–4 hours to as much as 40 hours or more. Do the math and ask yourself whether you can afford to pay the programmer before the client pays you. Otherwise, you may elect to have the client pay the programmer directly.

Chapter 5: Attracting Visitors to Your Site

In This Chapter

✓ **Using e-newsletters to attract visitors**

✓ **Writing free tips and articles**

✓ **Blogging to attract site visitors**

✓ **Holding contests and sweepstakes**

✓ **Linking and sharing with social media**

*O*ne of the best ways to figure out what will attract visitors to a particular site is to think about the site from the visitor's perspective. When most people visit a website, they're typically looking for *specific* information about a *particular* product or service, such as a 16.6-cubic-foot refrigerator or a Promaster 28–210mm f3.5–5.6 MF lens for a Nikon camera. Finding that information is important — presuming the products or services are the online company's bread and butter.

To make those customers happy and keep them coming back, a website should also provide other relevant information that supports the product or service, such as the answers to frequently asked questions, company information, customer support, and contact information. Beyond this kind of expected customer service content, any other information on the site is strictly optional — unless, of course, the site owners want to drive more traffic to the site, which they should.

Statistically speaking, the more traffic a site gets, the greater the likelihood that some of those visitors will either want to purchase the products and/or services being offered or feel confident telling someone they know about the site, which in turn can increase traffic!

Fortunately, you can use lots of nice techniques to increase visitor traffic that have nothing to do with the product or service being sold. For instance, you or your client might decide to start a newsletter that offers industry-related tips, free downloads, or coupons, or the site owner (or you, if she hires you to do post-launch site maintenance) might begin to post weekly articles on a variety of topics related to products or services. Other sites might post blogs; serve up news items through an RSS feed; display the ten most recent Twitter tweets, Facebook posts, or Pinterest pins; or even have frequent contests with fun prizes — all designed to attract and keep visitors coming back, day after day.

In the following sections, you get a chance to look at a few of these techniques in greater detail. As you compare them and decide which one(s) you might want to include in your plan, keep the site's purpose, benefit to visitors, and image at the forefront of your (and your client's) mind. These factors should help identify the best ways to make the site attractive.

Communicating Regularly with Visitors Using E-Newsletters

E-newsletters, whether sent weekly, monthly, quarterly, or sporadically, are a fantastic way to communicate regularly with customers through e-mail. In addition to keeping the company name, brand, products, and services in customers' minds when they read it, each issue creates a new opportunity to have a positive and meaningful exchange with site visitors, who either are, or soon could become, customers or clients.

If you or your client plan on having a newsletter, make sure that you set aside space on the website, preferably in the same location on every page of the site, for a form that visitors can fill out to sign up for the newsletter, as in the example shown in Figure 5-1.

Most e-newsletters are graphically formatted in HTML with CSS styling (but they might also be plain text, or you can offer both) and typically include the following:

- Some kind of topical news
- Sale offers
- Information about new products and services
- Upcoming events listings
- Links to articles or products online
- Company information, the date, instructions on how to subscribe to and unsubscribe from the newsletter, and a few website links

Figure 5-1: Savvy websites send newsletters that get readers to visit the site.

Giving readers the choice to subscribe and unsubscribe is an important part of *netiquette* and can help the site avoid looking like a spammer. With that in mind, I highly recommend that when sending e-newsletters, you take extra care to ensure that

✔ You ask permission of your site visitors to add their e-mail address to your customer list *before* sending them anything.

✔ You include a link to your site's privacy policy so that interested visitors can learn more about how you will use their e-mail address and other personal data.

✔ You include, in every mailing, a simple method for visitors to unsubscribe from your list.

See the nearby sidebar for more about the art and practice of netiquette.

For exceptional information about writing, designing, and sending out e-newsletters, visit the MailChimp Resource Center, shown in Figure 5-2, at `http://mailchimp.com/resources` and be sure to download a free copy of MailChimp's Email Marketing Field Guide. You may also want to get a copy of *E-Mail Marketing For Dummies* by John Arnold.

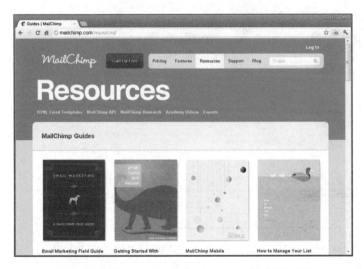

Figure 5-2: Discover free e-newsletter tips at the MailChimp Resource Center.

To send newsletters, you can choose from a variety of e-mail programs, though the best-supported applications often only allow the sending of one e-mail to a maximum of 50 addresses at a time. A better solution is to outsource the management of your e-mail list to one of several online services that can handle the job. Table 5-1 lists three popular newsletter services that have great reputations.

Table 5-1	Third-Party E-Newsletter Services
Service	*Website*
MailChimp	`http://mailchimp.com`
Constant Contact	`www.constantcontact.com`
Vertical Response	`www.verticalresponse.com`

The importance of netiquette

Nowadays, when you purchase anything online, your e-mail address will probably be automatically added to the selling company's e-newsletter mailing list. If you enjoy learning more about towel sales, electronics equipment, or office supplies (for instance), seeing these e-mails in your inbox might be a pleasant surprise for you each time they arrive. But when unwanted newsletters arrive — especially when you didn't expressly authorize the enrollment to the e-mail list — these kinds of missives can seem downright spammy.

When sending e-mails and otherwise communicating over the Internet, do you always use your best online manners?

Network etiquette, or *netiquette,* is the set of unspoken rules that everyone online should follow, whether sending personal or professional messages. Think of it as the art of being respectful on the Internet. Each online interaction should be polite, courteous, kind, and considerate — using a sort of "do unto others" set of e-ethics to guide all your online correspondence and transactions.

To find out how your Internet manners rate, take the Netiquette Quiz at www.carnegiecyberacademy.com/funStuff/netiquette/netiquette.html.

Attracting Visitors with Free Tips and Articles

If marketing products or services is the driving force of a website, e-mailing industry-related tips to subscribed members and publishing regular articles on the site are both smart ways to provide tangible benefits and build a positive relationship with visitors. And remember, the more positive contact a site has with its audience, the greater the likelihood that audience will want the site's products or services.

Finding ideas for these tips and articles is quite easy. Just think of all the details you know about the business that could help visitors and then jot them down. For example, if you're designing a site for a dog-grooming business, the tips might include the following:

- How to choose a dog-grooming brush
- A review of the best dog shampoos
- How to keep a dog's teeth clean
- Exercise tips that keep dogs fit

Quick tips within the e-mail can also help bring visitors to your site to read more detailed tips online, as well as find out more about and potentially purchase the site's products and services. Take the CliffsNotes website (www.cliffsnotes.com) for example, shown in Figure 5-3. Visitors can sign up for newsletters; browse for literature, test prep guides, and other titles; share the page with a friend via e-mail, Facebook, or Twitter accounts; and get advice on studying and student life — all for free.

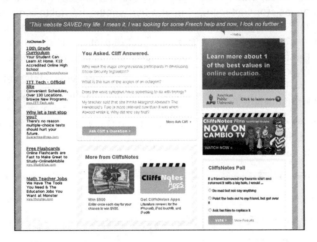

Figure 5-3: Savvy websites send e-mails to subscribers that encourage readers to visit the site.

To help generate more traffic to your website, be sure to regularly update the content on the site. Fresh content often translates into more visitors — and possibly more sales or more customers. At the very least, fresh content draws good search engine attention so that more people can find you on the web. For a fast approach, sit down now and come up with at least 12 ideas that you could conceivably use for tips or articles over the next 12 months. Then all you have to do is write them out and add them to your site at the appropriate time each month. Keep in mind that if you intend to archive the old news items as you update information on your site, you may want to seriously consider using a database or blog to both manage that content and help you to display the new data dynamically on your site.

Blogging to Bring 'Em In

Blogging is now the single best way for Internet readers to find out about and provide feedback on nearly every topic of interest. That's because blog news travels just about as fast as news items on social media sites such as

Facebook and Twitter. Blogs encourage instant feedback from readers and are the place for readers to share information and experience. Best of all, participation in the blogosphere provides instant cachet in the Internet world. When combined with business goals (such as increasing web traffic and online sales), blogs provide business owners with the opportunity to communicate directly with their target audience.

Understanding what a blog is

So what is a *blog?* The term is short for *web log,* and it typically refers to a database-driven website that publishes articles (which are some combination of text and/or media) related to particular or general topics (or a series of topics along a central theme). Almost all blogs solicit feedback from visitors. The articles, commonly called *posts,* tend to be published on a regular basis (daily is most popular, although weekly, biweekly, or monthly is okay too) and listed on the site in reverse chronological order, with the newest articles at the top of the page and older articles below. In addition to newer articles, most blogs contain archived articles, pictures, and links to other sites and blogs of interest in the same or related fields.

A person who has a blog or writes for one is called a *blogger.* Thus, *to blog* means to post entries on your own blog. When you respond to an entry on another person or company's blog, that's called *commenting.* The term *blogosphere* refers to the entire movement of blogging and all things pertaining to the world of blogs.

One popular feature of blogs is the ability to allow visitors to respond directly to any given post by entering their comments to it, thereby creating a forum for online exchanges between the blogger and the blog's audience. Having a blog that offers advice and feedback from other consumers can be a very effective site tool for attracting and keeping visitors.

Using a blog on your site

As you consider whether to include a blog on the site you're designing, here are some important points to keep in mind:

- A successful blog requires one or more people who can add new content on a regular basis. To maintain attractiveness, or *stickiness,* to visitors, your site must be able to post new and interesting content frequently. It's what keeps people coming back to your site. Some blogs post one or more short articles per day, while others post content a few times per week.

- To spread out the responsibility of authorship, blogs can be set up for groups or businesses, where there can be multiple blog authors in addition to full participation in commenting and feedback.

✔ Be sure that you understand some basic blogging rules and authoring styles prior to starting your blog. One great resource is *Blogging For Dummies,* 4th Edition, by Susannah Gardner and Shane Birley, which takes you through the steps of setting up a blog, explains how to generate revenue and build an audience, and even covers how to integrate you blog with social media and how to generate revenue with advertising.

✔ A visually appealing blog makes a good impression. Besides the content, the look of the blog is all-important because a visually captivating blog is more welcoming than one that obviously took no care in its design. Fortunately, blogging services such as WordPress, Tumblr, and Blogger offer several free layouts, scripts, graphics, and more to assist you with the blog look and feel.

✔ Adding pictures, illustrations, video, and music to individual posts increases appeal. Though having images or other media on a blog isn't a requirement, it is a nice feature, and most blogs allow you to quickly upload photos and other media to each post as a way to enhance or editorialize it. Some even let you upload media files straight from your mobile phone or social media account.

Figure 5-4 shows how the folks at Vandelay Design seamlessly incorporate a blog into the site. As you can see, the design of the blog is similar but not identical to the rest of the site. This provides the most flexibility when creating the blog and allows for a nice flow of traffic between the blog and the website.

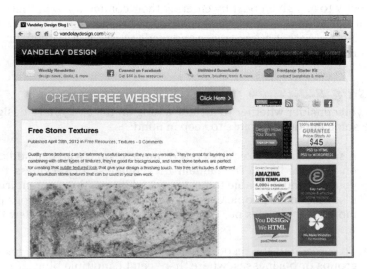

Figure 5-4: Some websites use a blog as a way to communicate more directly with visitors.

Choosing a blogging tool

Before you create your blog or add one to your site, take some time to decide which blogging tools you'll use. When you add a blog to your site, you can do so in the following ways:

- You can host the blog on your own domain by using blog software (such as the free WordPress.org software) on the server used to host your site (www.*yourcompany*.com)

- You can install the blog in a directory on your own domain, such as www.*yourcompany*.com/blog.

- You can have it hosted by a blog-hosting service, so that your web address would be a subdomain of the hosting service, such as www.*myblog*.wordpress.com. The five most popular services are WordPress (www.wordpress.com), Blogger (www.blogger.com), Tumblr (www.tumblr.com), LiveJournal (www.livejournal.com), and Movable Type (www.movabletype.org). For a brief overview about each of these platforms, see www.itechcolumn.com/2012/02/5-best-blogging-platforms-2012.html.

Of all the blog tools that I've used, my two favorites, by far, are Tumblr and WordPress.org, shown in Figures 5-5 and 5-6. Tumblr is free and has an easy learning curve, allowing you to post text, photos, quotes, chats, videos, and audio files with ease. You can post updates from a browser, by phone, and by e-mail. You can even link up your Twitter, Facebook, and other social media accounts to your blog, ensuring all your followers get instant updates each time you post to Tumblr. WordPress.org is also free, but takes a little more patience to set up, configure, and maintain. Both platforms provide you with hundreds of free templates, scads of user support, and other technical information, and they're relatively easily to customize should you decide you want your blog to closely match your website's design.

Adding a profile

To help draw visitors to a new or existing blog, add a profile. When the blog is live on the Internet, you can create a profile (like an About page on a website) for yourself or the blog's authoring group. The profile typically includes a picture or an avatar, and it provides room for a short description that identifies your interests. This profile helps people with common interests find the blog. It's also an opportunity to further your brand identity by helping visitors associate your blog with your profile's avatar.

Examining the pros and cons of a blog

Blogs have their good points and bad points.

Figure 5-5: Use Tumblr if you want an easy-to-use, simple blogging platform.

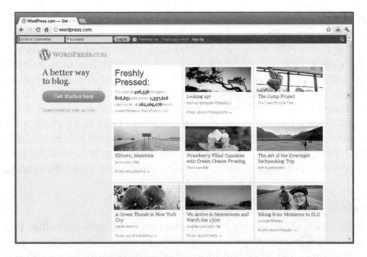

Figure 5-6: Use WordPress.org if you plan to host your own blog on your domain. Use WordPress.com to get a free blog hosted there.

On the plus side, with very little overhead, blog posts can and often do spread news and information faster than most traditional media sources, such as TV, newspapers, and radio. Similar to some forms of guerilla marketing, where information is passed through word of mouth, blogs far surpass traditional marketing avenues because they're global and typically reach audience members who are interested and take active participation in getting the news rather than passively having advertising and ideas presented to them.

Taking your blog to the next level

In addition to posting relevant articles, news, and information, other elements can be added to a blog to enhance the visitor experience and generate revenue for the blog owner. For example, you can use Google AdSense, a tool that automatically places content-relevant ads on registered users' blogs. Each click of an ad by a visitor earns money for the blog owner. You can also globalize content through blog syndication (news feeds with Atom or RSS), whereby the blog host generates machine-readable versions of the blog for display on special newsreaders, handheld devices, and websites. Bloggers might also benefit from enrollment in blog services (such as www.bloglines.com or http://technorati.com) that allow enhanced blog searches and shared news feeds, among other things.

On the minus side, regularly posting to blogs can be a very time-consuming task, so you'll need to consider in advance what kind of posting schedule to maintain — be it daily, a few times a week, weekly, or monthly — and then be ready to stick to it. Remember your site's statement of purpose? (See Book I, Chapter 1 for help writing the site's statement of purpose.) If you're planning on blogging as a way to keep your site relevant and interesting to visitors, make sure your commitment to keep the blog content current is part of your mission statement.

An abandoned or unkempt blog can be more injurious to a business identity than no blog at all. A blog with little to no content — as well as one with little to no feedback — can give visitors the impression that the blogger doesn't care about visitors, which in turn can make visitors not care about visiting. And, if no one cares, why bother reading posts, exploring the adjoining website, and possibly using the site's products and services?

The bottom line: Adding a blog to your site is a good idea only if someone is willing to devote time to regularly updating and improving the blog, to driving relevant traffic to it, and to saying something interesting and saying it well.

Giving Them Free Stuff: Contests and Sweepstakes

Having a contest, sweepstakes, or some kind of giveaway on a site is a great way to attract visitors and keep them coming back month after month. For example, www.cookinglight.com (shown in Figure 5-7) offers several different contests and sweepstakes to visitors each month.

Figure 5-7: Contests are a great way to bring in visitors to a site time and again.

Contests can be for nearly anything you can think up. Raffle off a car. Give away a free computer class. Send winners on an all-expenses-paid vacation. Affiliate your company with a worthy cause and offer cash to winners while increasing awareness about an important issue. Sponsors of events often provide valuable prizes for relevant and worthwhile contests at no cost in exchange for the free publicity, such as offering winners a $500 T-Mobile gift card, guest passes to the latest IMAX movie, or coupons for $1.00 off a latte. Enrollment in the contest can be at the visitor's discretion through an online contest entry form, or it can happen automatically after a visitor signs up for an e-newsletter or registers for membership.

Most online contests and sweepstakes require the following:

- ✔ A set of rules and regulations outlining who can and cannot participate in the contest
- ✔ A defined contest time frame, with entry dates and award dates
- ✔ A list of prizes and the odds of winning
- ✔ A way, both online and off, for visitors to enter the contest
- ✔ An objective third-party administrator
- ✔ Proper insurance

If you decide to have an online contest or sweepstakes on your site, be sure to follow the strict federal and state legal guidelines to ensure that your contest is fair. You might also want to seriously consider hiring an outside firm, such as National Sweepstakes Company (`http://nationalsweeps.com`) or Odds On Promotions (`www.oddsonpromotions.com`), to organize and administer the contest for you.

Spreading the Word with Social Media Links and Share Buttons

There's no denying the power of social media platforms and the potential they have to help increase traffic flow on websites. In fact, it may even secretly be your dream as a business owner (or your client's dream) to share something online that *goes viral,* getting seen by millions of people all over the world and garnering you/your client instant stardom, respect, and zillions of dollars in new business. Of course, in reality that rarely ever happens. But you can improve your chances of getting a little more traffic on your website by creating lots and lots of interesting content that is (hopefully!) share-worthy.

What makes content share-worthy? Often, it happens when the content has value or resonates in some way with the viewer. Of course, it would be unrealistic to expect that every little thing you place on your website will be interesting enough for a visitor to share. What is more likely is that only a few things will ever be shared, but that's certainly better than nothing. Think of your own browsing habits and the kinds of content you like to share online. Then think about what kinds of content your target audience might find interesting. Videos are often big hits, as are infographics, unusual photographs, funny cartoons, step-by-step tutorials, freebies, coupons, and articles or tips about your site's special area(s) of interest.

The current most popular social media platforms are Facebook, Twitter, LinkedIn, Pinterest, and Google+. One of the main reasons for their popularity is the fact that people, in general, love sharing their ideas, thoughts, dreams, creations, and interests with the group of people they're virtually connected to. Those connections include their friends, family, acquaintances, and co-workers, as well as current and potential business partners, employers, clients, and customers. Another interesting reason for the popularity of social media is that participating on these sites is fun and can be somewhat addictive. That's where you come in.

The following is a list of ways you can participate in the social media frenzy:

✔ **Create business accounts for your website on all the relevant social media sites** to develop an Internet traffic loop that feeds back to your website, making sure to include your web address on each of your social media profiles. For instance, on Twitter, you can insert your site's URL in your profile, as shown in Figure 5-8.

Include your web address.

Figure 5-8: Invite more traffic to your website by including your web address in all your social media profiles.

✔ **Add social media icons somewhere on your website** that link to your social media accounts. Many designers add these icons in the header or footer of every page so that visitors can easily become fans and follow you outside of your website.

✔ **Share your social media account posts on your website** to encourage visitors to follow you outside your website. Most social media sites offer free code and instructions on how to insert social media content into your site, such as the five most recent tweets from your Twitter account.

✔ **Give your site visitors an easy way to share your web content** with their friends on their own social media accounts. Facebook, for instance, offers free social plug-ins such as Like Buttons, activity feeds, and comments boxes. You can add these features to as many pages on your site as you like. The easier you make it for visitors to share your content, the more likely they are to do it.

✔ **Add a whole slew of share buttons to your site** through a sharing service such as www.addthis.com or http://sharethis.com. Sites like these not only provide you with the free code to add the desired icons to your site, but they also help you build an audience for your marketing message and often provide free reporting with statistics about the visitors using your share buttons. This information can be very helpful from a marketing standpoint.

After you've integrated your website with your social media accounts, remember to keep your fans happy by updating your social media accounts frequently.

Book II
Designing for the Web

The 5th Wave   By Rich Tennant

RURAL WEB DESIGN

"What you want to do, is balance the image of the pick-up truck sittin' behind your home page, with a busted washing machine in the foreground."

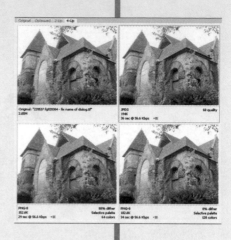

One of the funnest things about being a web designer is actually creating the website. But a lot more goes into this process than meets the eye. To best design a website, you must first choose the right layout and navigation scheme, mock up a design for your site that will best promote the company while attracting the ideal target audience, and optimize all the graphics so that you can add them to your web pages.

This minibook helps make sure that you know everything you need to know about defining the look and feel of your site, mocking up a web design, and creating and optimizing your web graphics.

Chapter 1: Defining the Look and Feel

In This Chapter

✓ Generating design ideas based on client and target audience profiles

✓ Making design size and layout orientation decisions

✓ Choosing appropriate site colors, fonts, and other design elements

✓ Selecting the best navigation system for the site's design

*I*n this chapter, you find out how to develop the site's look and feel based on the information you gathered about the client's target audience profile and site identity. You also use the information you gathered from your client about his or her preferences for fonts, colors, layout, size, orientation, and other design elements, as well as the site's navigation.

Working with the Client to Make Design Choices

By making important design and layout decisions with the client now, before you begin your design work for the site's mock-up, you can save yourself and the client valuable time. In fact, if you do this step with all your projects, you will quickly discover that generating a *design theme* based on your conversations with the client can significantly jump-start the design process when you get to the mock-up phase in Book II, Chapter 2. Furthermore, by involving the client in finding the answers to these fundamental design questions, the issue of the site's design becomes a co-creative effort that can both enhance your relationship with the client and strengthen your role as designer.

Give your gear Safe Passage.

Safe Passage® Rolling Vented Duffle

photo: Marco

Besides being very useful, this process should also yield some interesting and sometimes unusual information about the client's preferences, which until now you would not have known, such as a particular distaste for the color red or a penchant for center alignment. While some of these preferences can be catered to, others may need to be avoided from an aesthetic point of view and to ensure that the site appeals more to the target visitors than any one person in charge of a company. In other words, even though your client is the Owner, Vice President of

Marketing, or the de facto person of the department in charge of the new website, your "client" is a mere human with his own particular aesthetic preferences, and though he might need to have you follow some company-set design initiatives to keep the new site in line with the company's other marketing materials, this person's subjective tastes might also strongly influence what will and won't be done with the site's design and layout.

To illustrate, a few years ago I designed a site for a large traditional bakery that provides breakfast pastries to the hotels, retail food stores, and corporate dining rooms in the New York metropolitan area. At the look-and-feel defining stage, the owner said that although he didn't have any specific ideas of how his new site should look, he did want the site to have a slick, clean edge to it, similar to a fine luxury car website like the ones BMW and Mercedes-Benz had at the time. Armed with this specific knowledge, I had a clearly defined starting point for the design and layout: Create a linear, modern design with the use of fine lines within a fixed-width layout and include crisp photos throughout the site. I then combined those ideas with a sophisticated yet neutral color palette based on collected data from the target audience profile to create an elegant site that the client absolutely loved and is still using to this day, over ten years later.

Occasionally, you might be hired to create a site's design around a client's preexisting marketing materials, which means you don't need to develop a new look and feel. If that's the case, read through this chapter's sections on layout and design decisions, selecting appropriate fonts and choosing the right navigation scheme. Then continue on to mocking up the design as outlined in Book II, Chapter 2, at which time you can get the specific color values (Pantone, CMYK, or RGB, for example) from your client along with the logo and any other photos and graphics you may need to use.

The choices you make now will dictate much of what the client sees when you're finished creating your design mock-up. Therefore, before you begin your "look and feel" conversation with your client, read through the different sections in this chapter to discover the specific questions you'll need to ask and to understand how you can use the answers to assist the client in making the best decisions about the site's look and feel.

Defining a Site Theme Using Target Data

Now, finally, it is time to really use the target audience information and ideal site visitor profile you gathered and created, as described in Book I, Chapters 1 and 2. As the designer, you can take this information and convert it into a visual theme. You can use this information to anticipate the preferences and needs of the ideal visitor, and to make design and layout decisions specific to those needs. Everything about the ideal site visitor can influence the decisions you make about layout, navigation, color, image usage, and even reading level. It's like you have a secret design assistant right there in the site's profiles.

In a way, these thematic decisions are fairly straightforward to make if you take a little time to think logically about what might appeal to the target audience. Wouldn't you agree that the navigation, layout, and color scheme for a business coach's website should be very visually different from that of a hard-core heavy metal rock band's site? Of course you would. Both businesses conjure up totally different mental images, and it's the ideas that those images bring to mind, plus the ones that come to mind when you reread the target audience description, that you want to use for your design inspiration.

Take, for instance, the following information about this ideal site visitor from a target audience profile:

✔ Male, aged 20–60

✔ Annual income from $30,000 to $65,000

✔ Outdoorsy, active, and an avid fisherman

For this ideal site visitor, you might choose to make the following thematic design and layout decisions:

✔ Keep the navigation simple and easy to use.

✔ Ask the client to set the writing tone of the text at around a high school reading level (suggested by the average income level).

✔ Use bold, woodsy colors like hunter green, brown, and navy blue, contrasted with white and neutral colors, and have lots of photographs of trees, rivers, sunsets, camping, and fishing scenes throughout the site (the ideal visitor is active and outdoorsy and likes to fish, so nature photos and this rich color palette will be appealing).

A helpful example of a site that already uses a similar theme for its ideal visitor is www.orvis.com, depicted in Figure 1-1.

As the designer, try not to influence the look and feel of the site too much with your own aesthetic. The idea here is to let the target audience profile determine how the site should look before you apply your own sense of order and style to it. On the other hand, you might begin to develop your own aesthetic style and want to include certain features in all the sites you build, such as making them all center aligned and fixed width. Nonetheless, some sites must be built to specifications that fall beyond the bounds of your own preferences, and you need to stay flexible enough to be able to build a site that has elements in it that you might not choose. Remember, too, that the client might have very specific and unwavering needs that must be catered to.

In the following sections, you discover more about how to use the target audience information to make design and layout decisions with your clients for upcoming web projects. Specifically, you need to discuss colors, fonts, navigation, layout, size, orientation, and graphics. At the end of this chapter, you have an opportunity to put all your newly acquired skills to good use by filling out a simple Layout Checklist for your project based on the ideal site visitor and target audience profile.

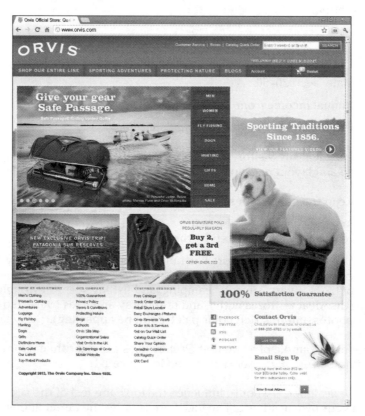

Figure 1-1: Use the ideal site visitor profile to generate a design and layout theme that appeals to the target audience, as this site does for its audience.

The client is not always right

You may have heard the familiar phrase, "The customer is always right." In web design, however, that is not always the truth. Yes, the client is paying you for your design services, and he may have specific requirements for the website, such as making sure that you include certain graphics and text, but how those items look and function should really be up to you, the one with the web design experience.

Now, in a perfect world, you'd have 100 percent authority to make all the aesthetic and design decisions, but because you're a hired hand, you don't. This doesn't mean, however, that you need to bend to every one of your client's whims. On the contrary, you should use your expertise as both a designer and Internet user to guide your client into making the best design decisions for the site.

For instance, your client may be the kind of person who is still for some reason wowed by cheesy Flash intros and primitive GIF animations. Clients like this will have definite ideas about what they think the site should look like and may even make some pretty awful suggestions to you, such as telling you they want "a big, spinning globe on the home page and text that flies in from the left and right that says something like Professional . . . Reliable . . . Fast . . . Affordable . . . and then everything fades into a big photograph of the company's president."

If your client makes a strange suggestion, let him know in a kind and gentle way why the suggestion is not a good idea from the visitor's perspective (especially because Flash animations are neither search engine–friendly nor accessible to visitors with disabilities), and then be ready to make suggestions about what will appeal to the target audience. As long as you frame your comments around promoting the company in the best way possible to visitors, your criticism should be well received.

In this example, I'd suggest to the client that the home page needs to be a place where visitors can find what they are looking for without having to wade through unnecessary information. I might even go so far as to say, "Please do not put a spinning globe on your home page. Customers will think it looks old-fashioned and unprofessional." Animations may be interesting to some people, but they often tend to be more sparkle than substance, which can detract from the overall goals of the site and take up valuable visual real estate that could have been better used to promote the site's products or services. Instead, the home page should have clearly defined areas for company branding and navigation, descriptive text about what can be found elsewhere on the site that can be read by both visitors and search engine crawlers, and lead articles or teaser introductions to other information the site visitors may want to find out more about.

If your client is still a little resistant, tell him that you've done extensive research and have consulted with seasoned professionals (like me) who have years of experience with creating sites that appeal to the target visitors their company wants to attract. You might also say that you want to build a standards-compliant site that appeals to the target audience *and* conforms to best practices outlined by the W3C. Hopefully, both you and your client can come to an agreement that will satisfy the goals for the site and the needs of the target audience.

Making Basic Layout and Design Decisions

You and your client definitely need to make a few decisions about the site's look and feel well before the design gets under way. In particular, you should determine how the website layout will be positioned inside the browser and how it will fill the browser space. That means deciding whether the layout will be fixed in width (like Yahoo!'s home page) or expandable (like Amazon. com), what its orientation will be relative to the top-left edge of the browser window, making the site either centered, left, or right aligned, and whether the pages will be printer friendly on their own or whether you'll need to build a second CSS file to handle how the pages will print. In the following sections, each of these layout issues is addressed, starting with the layout size, and each of them both forms a general framework for creating the mock-up and provides a glimpse at how the site might potentially be built in HTML and CSS.

Some designers help their clients make decisions about the layout based on foreknowledge of HTML/HTML5, CSS/CSS3, JavaScript, jQuery, and the site-building process. This is something I do quite often because my first-hand knowledge about building navigation systems can greatly help the client envision how some parts of the site will look before the design is even started. For instance, you can have the client look at select websites to preview how different navigation systems and layouts look and function and assist him in making the right decisions for his site.

Even if you have little to no experience with building websites, you can still help your clients make informed decisions about their sites at this stage in the process. Specifically, you should try to get them to make decisions about the layout width, expandability, orientation, and printability, as well as help them choose appropriate color and font palettes that will be appealing to the target audiences.

Choosing a size for your site

With the current trend toward developing websites that are responsive and flexible enough to be viewed on a variety of devices (including desktops, notebooks, tablets, and smartphones), fixed-width websites have suddenly become less popular than their *fluid-* or *flexible-width* counterparts. Nonetheless, it's still important to choose the maximum width for your site's layout before you design it. You find out more about responsive web design in Book III, Chapter 5.

As you probably found out from your market research, most computer monitors come with a factory preset resolution of 1366 x 768 pixels or higher. Though most people never adjust this setting, some do increase or decrease the monitor resolution from as low as 640 x 480 to as high as 2560 x 1600 with some of the new widescreen LCD monitors.

Here are some examples of typical resolutions for LCD monitors:

- ✔ **14–15-inch:** 1024 x 768 (XGA)
- ✔ **17–19-inch:** 1280 x 1024 (SXGA)
- ✔ **17-inch:** 1280 x 800 (WXGA, Widescreen)
- ✔ **18-inch:** 1366 x 768 (WXGA, Widescreen)
- ✔ **19-inch:** 1440 x 900 (WXGA, Widescreen)
- ✔ **20-inch+:** 1600 x 1200 (UXGA)
- ✔ **20-inch:** 1680 x 1050 (WSXGA+, Widescreen)
- ✔ **24-inch:** 1920 x 1080 (HD 1080)
- ✔ **24-inch:** 1920 x 1200 (WUXGA, Widescreen)
- ✔ **30-inch:** 2560 x 1600 (WQXGA, Widescreen)

Here are some examples of typical device sizes for smartphones and tablets:

- ✔ **Smartphone:** 240 x 320 (portrait)
- ✔ **Smartphone:** 320 x 480 (portrait)
- ✔ **Smartphone:** 480 x 640 (portrait)
- ✔ **Smartphone:** 480 x 800 (portrait)
- ✔ **Tablet:** 600 x 800 (portrait)
- ✔ **Tablet:** 640 x 960 (portrait)
- ✔ **Tablet:** 640 x 1136 (portrait)
- ✔ **Tablet:** 768 x 1024 (portrait)
- ✔ **Tablet:** 800 x 1280 (portrait)

With no control over this visitor variable, how do you select a layout width for a client's website without alienating or infuriating some of the visiting audience? Follow these tips:

- ✔ For a general audience on the Internet (which is a public network, accessible to anyone with a computer, browser, and Internet connection), the answer to the layout width-versus-resolution question in most cases is pretty simple: Design for a size that can display readable text to all viewers, regardless of monitor resolution. By creating a design for monitors set to an 1024 x 768 resolution and making columns of text (with font sizes set to 10 pixels or larger) no wider than 500–600 pixels if you can help it, everyone should be able to read content on the site. Furthermore, when you take into consideration that most of the *browser chrome* (those browser elements like scroll bars, the status bar, the navigation bar, and the Favorites bar) takes up some of that design space, the actual "safe" design size for a monitor set at 1024 x 768 becomes more like 960 x 640 (or taller).

Figure 1-2 shows a screen shot of the Logohause website (`www.logo hause.com`), which has an overall width of 960 pixels and two columns of content with widths set to roughly 560 and 280 pixels, leaving a little room for spacing between the design's edges and the two columns of content.

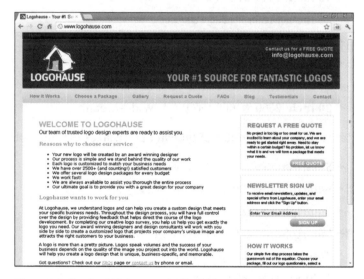

Figure 1-2: Fixed-width layouts designed for 1024 x 768 resolutions can range as wide as 950–980 pixels and can contain one to three columns of content.

✔ For clients who have a limited or very specific audience, you may need to gather more information. Picture, for example, that you've been contracted to design a web *intranet* (a private network of interconnected local- and wide-area networks using web protocols to share information among the members of an organization) for the human resources department of a large corporation. You might learn from the client that the target audience consists of only PC users with desktop monitors set to 1024 x 768, and all the users access the intranet site using only Firefox 14.0. Armed with these details, you may help the client choose to create a much wider design with multiple columns that maximize the use of the known usable browser space for the employees' PC monitors in Firefox — about 1000 x 580 pixels.

When in doubt, go for the 1024 x 768 design size. To see a breakdown of the most popular screen resolutions by size, check out the listing at `www.w3schools.com/browsers/browsers_resolution_higher.asp`. For a more expansive discussion on monitor resolution and actual design space, turn to Book II, Chapter 2.

Selecting a fixed-width or flexible layout

Next, consider whether to make the site's design using a fixed-width or an expandable design layout:

✔ **Fixed-width layout:** A fixed-width design means that the content on the web page will remain fixed within a predetermined content area and that any overflow content will expand the page vertically rather than horizontally, like on the The Weather Channel website (`www.weather.com`) shown in Figure 1-3. Everything outside the fixed-width layout is considered part of the background design of the page, which can include color and graphics.

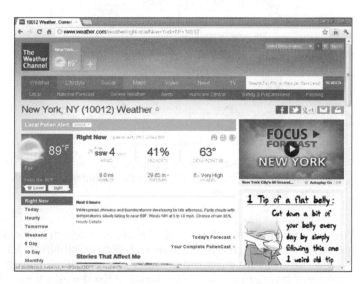

Figure 1-3: Fixed-width layouts can expand vertically when you have more content than can fit inside an expanded browser window.

✔ **Expandable layout:** By contrast, an expandable-width design is one in which the website layout spans the full breadth of the browser window and includes one or more columns of information that can expand and contract with the width of the browser window, displaying the page as you'd see on the Google Shopping search results listings, like the one shown in Figure 1-4. The expandable layout uses percentages relative to the browser window's width. Some designers refer to this technique as *liquid design* or *fluid design*. This is also the technique used with responsive web design.

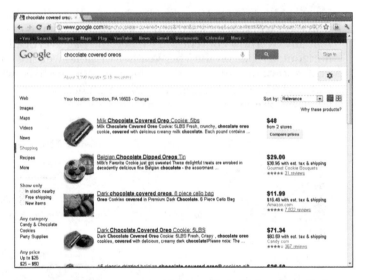

Figure 1-4: Fluid layouts expand horizontally to fill the entire window width as well as expand vertically to handle content that overflows past the window's height.

The expandability or lack thereof of a website design helps determine which techniques you can and should use to build the site in HTML. For example, a fixed-width site with a left/top browser orientation can easily use absolutely positioned layers in the layout, whereas a fixed-width design with a center alignment or a site with a liquid design often uses a combination of relatively and absolutely positioned layers. Table 1-1 outlines the pros and cons of each format.

Table 1-1	Fixed-Width versus Expandable-Width Designs	
Type of Design	*Pros*	*Cons*
Fixed-width	The designer can predict how content will look on a web page before the site gets built in HTML.	Visitors with larger monitor resolutions will see more blank space surrounding the fixed-width design than those with smaller monitor resolutions. Not a drawback, but a design consideration that can be creatively utilized.
Expandable-width	The site will always fill the entire browser window, regardless of the visitors' monitor resolution, and whether the browser is minimized or maximized.	The text in the main area of the page can become so wide and extended (set to 100% of the browser window) that it's difficult to read. While this type of layout is good for news and commerce, it doesn't always work well for simple "brochure-ware" sites.

With the popularity of iPads and other handheld devices, fluid designs have had a slight resurgence in the past few years. More often, however, what you're actually seeing are sites that automatically resize using CSS3 @media queries. To find out more about this type of responsive web design, turn to Book III, Chapter 5, and see http://coding.smashingmagazine. com/2011/01/12/guidelines-for-responsive-web-design/ and http://webdesignerwall.com/tutorials/css3-media-queries.

If you and your client do choose the fixed-width design size, the next aesthetic design issue that you need to decide upon is the orientation of the page relative to the browser window. Will the design begin fixed to the upper-left corner of the browser window, leaving empty space to the right of the design, like www.bedbathandbeyond.com, or will it be anchored to the top of the page but aligned to the center of the browser window with empty space to both the left and right of the fixed-width design, like www.home depot.com? Figure 1-5 illustrates the general differences between each layout.

Figure 1-5: The top site has a fixed-width layout with a left browser alignment, and the bottom site has a fixed-width layout with a center browser alignment.

Neither solution is better than the other, so choosing the right one is simply a matter of taste. In recent years in the United States, the prevailing trend has been to create fixed-width designs that are center aligned to the browser. However, trends change. Ultimately, you should choose a design layout that will suit the client's needs and the website's content, and above all, a design that will cater directly to the target audience's preferences.

Choosing a method for printing the layout

When designing a page with content that site visitors might want to print and keep, you need to think about how the design layout will print. Many web pages contain navigation, images, banners, advertisements, and other page elements that the visitor probably doesn't need on the printout, and you don't want visitors to use more paper (save a tree!) by printing redundant, unnecessary page elements.

To help solve this issue, do one or both of the following:

✔ **Make sure that all the key parts of the printable content fall within the leftmost 700 pixels of the design layout.** That should work for both fixed and flexible layouts to prevent the content from getting cut off of the right side of the printed page without the visitor needing to adjust her printer's scale percentage settings. Navigation buttons or other elements in the layout might get cut off on the printed page if they extend past the 700-pixel mark, but that might be insignificant to the visitor if the main content gets printed intact.

✔ **Design a second Cascading Style Sheet for the site that can be used automatically anytime a visitor wants to print a page.** By creating and using a secondary CSS for print (that includes a custom class style with the block display set to None for the elements contained in layers that should be hidden from view on the printed page) in addition to the default media type for all media, certain page elements can be blocked from displaying on the printed page. Book III, Chapter 4 explains Cascading Style Sheets in more detail. For now, you just need to know that this is an option you can include in your design.

A third option is available, but its inefficiency should sway you against using it as a regular solution unless it only applies to a handful of pages on the site or for sites that are database driven, in which case these alternative printable HTML pages could be automatically generated on the fly. The third option would be to create an alternative printer-friendly version of the page in HTML that is set to a fixed width so that the content won't be cut off along the margins by the average home or office printer.

Picking a color palette

The colors you choose for a website project do more than just decorate the content. They can also communicate ideas, evoke emotions, alter moods, and convey unspoken psychological messages about the owners of the site and who they're trying to appeal to and the professionalism and quality of any services and products being offered and/or sold.

When you pay attention to the details about the ideal site visitor, you should be able to translate that identity, that personality, along with the other demographic information you collected, into a tangible and at times obvious web color palette. In other words, to choose an effective color palette, you need to select colors that are consistent with the target audience's cultural, social, and industry-standard preferences.

When presenting your client with a color palette, you can create a simple graphic in Photoshop, Illustrator, Fireworks, or some other graphics application and then send the client a PDF, JPG, GIF, or PNG file to preview and approve. Figure 1-6 shows an example of how you might present your client with a sample color palette so that she can decide whether it matches her vision of the ideal site visitor.

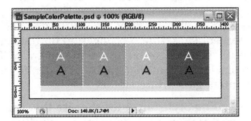

Figure 1-6: Presenting the color palette in GIF format.

The following steps outline a basic process you can follow to select an appropriate color palette for your web project:

1. **Refer to your notes about the site's identity and consider what colors are (or are not) compatible with that identity.**

   With many businesses, the nature of the work tends to evoke consistent mental images from which an appropriate color palette can be created. For instance, if you are creating a site for a health spa and yoga retreat, you might stay away from reds (which evoke feelings of love, heat, and excitement) and opt instead for calmer, earthier colors like brown (natural), beige (calming), light blue (truthful), and green (harmonious).

2. **Refer to your market research to see whether you'd like to copy (or avoid) any industry standards.**

   When used effectively, colors can help sell a product or services and engender brand loyalty among consumers. However, when used inefficiently, color can distract from a product or service message and work against the goals of the site.

   Some industries even seem to have publicly accepted color schemes that, if veered away from, might adversely affect business. Financial institutions, for example, seem to favor navy blue, red, and burgundy as their colors of choice, so unless the client is a true rebel, the idea to use pink or purple as the primary color for a bank's website might not be such a good idea.

3. **Using the target audience data, note any cultural preferences or special considerations that the site should reflect.**

   Colors represent specific meanings in different cultures across the globe. For instance, black is the color of mourning in the United States, but in other cultures, mourning is represented by blue (Iran), red (South Africa), white (Japan and China), and yellow (Burma). Therefore, if your client is based in the United States but sells products or services worldwide, she might do well to use neutral or industry-standard colors on the website rather than select a color palette that might accidentally offend or give the wrong impression to international visitors.

4. **If you know your target audience's demographics, use that data to assist you with color selection, too.**

   The target viewer's age, sex, income, and education can provide some great cues for selecting color.

   For example, younger audiences tend to like brighter colors, whereas mature audiences are more drawn to pastels and neutral palettes. Likewise, men tend to be drawn to cool colors like blues, purples, and greens, and women to warmer colors such as orange, pink, and red. If the target audience belongs to some kind of social subgroup, like motorcycle riders, organic gardeners, sports fans, or scrapbooking enthusiasts, you can more easily tailor the color palette to those groups' particular preferences.

5. **After considering your notes and the ideal site visitor, select a primary color to dominate the site design.**

   The primary color of the site is the design's main color, like the wall color in a room of a house. This color typically helps delineate the site's layout against the page background, like having a swatch of color across the top of the page, behind a navigation area along the left margin, and/or behind a sidebar area along the right.

6. **Based on the primary color, choose a secondary color.**

   The secondary color is often complementary to the primary color of a website's design. Secondary colors can help offset content areas from navigation areas, and these colors can be used for decorative accents for things like the page background color (behind a fixed-width design), other page subdivisions, and/or page and section headings.

7. **Choose a third color (the accent color) for elements such as buttons, bullets, hyperlinks, headlines, and other decorative elements.**

   Any more than three colors might be overkill and distract the visitors from finding the information they're looking for. However, sometimes a larger selection of colors might work well within the context of a particular site. I've seen plenty of great-looking sites that have a primary, secondary, and accent color, plus several other colors used within the navigation system to differentiate the different sections of the site or to otherwise help organize the content being displayed.

TIP

If for some reason you don't feel confident in your color-selecting abilities yet, consider using a special color selection software program that can take a more scientific approach to choosing a color palette. For example, Color Cache (www.colorcache.com) and Color Wheel Pro (www.color-wheel-pro.com) are two color programs that generate complementary accent colors based on your choice of a primary color. You might also check out Adobe's free Kuler theme site at http://kuler.adobe.com. The more you work with color, the more you will come to develop your own sense of what works and what doesn't. The right colors can make or break a site, so be sure to choose your colors well!

Choosing the right fonts

For the most part, all the text that appears on a website needs to follow certain guidelines:

✔ **Text must be marked up as HTML text.** This means that a primary HTML font should be selected for the bulk of the selectable text visible on a website. If desired, you can use a secondary HTML font for headings, and you can use additional fonts if desired to set content in certain specific regions apart from other areas on the site, as with advertisements in a sidebar.

✔ **The use of graphics that contain text should essentially be limited to those rare occasions when you must to use a specific font.** Images containing text can't be "read" by search engines, web crawlers, or other assistive web devices, so if you want your copy to be easily found in a search engine, avoid using graphics containing text. By contrast, when a site uses HTML text rather than graphics containing text, the text becomes automatically "indexable" by search engines and the pages load faster in a browser window. Plus, with CSS, you can easily differentiate your body text from your headings, headlines, pull quotes, and other text, without making the page load time slow down. While it is true that image HTML tags can include attributes such as alternative text and long descriptions, images containing text should be the exception on a site rather than a rule.

✔ **The fonts you choose for your site need to be either cross-platform (PC and Mac) "web safe" fonts, Google fonts, or Typekit fonts.** In other words, the fonts you select for your project must be either preinstalled on the visitor's computer (web safe) or they must be hosted by a font provider like Google or Adobe (Typekit) for the page to render the text in the desired font(s).

In the past, most designers had resigned themselves to using the limited set of "web safe" HTML fonts for their sites. That list of safe-to-use HTML fonts, as shown in Figure 1-7, includes Verdana, Arial, Helvetica, Courier, Courier New, Times, Times New Roman, Georgia, Geneva, Tahoma, Trebuchet, Comic Sans, Impact, Serif, and Sans-Serif. Other fonts that have cross-platform equivalents include Palatino Linotype, Book Antiqua, Lucida, Arial Black, Symbol, Webdings, and Wingdings.

TIP

The three most popular primary fonts in recent years have been Verdana and Arial for the sans-serif fonts (unornamented fonts) and Georgia for the serif fonts (fonts with decorative ascenders and descenders on the stems and ends of letter shapes), all displayed as black text on a white background. Thankfully today, with Google fonts and Typekit fonts (see the nearby sidebar on "Google and Typekit fonts" for more), you can now choose from thousands of fonts for your web designs!

Figure 1-7: Use one or two of these web-safe fonts for all your site's HTML text.

Despite these web-safe and hosted font guidelines, you can still add quite a bit of pizzazz to your text with the magic of CSS. The different elements of the content (headings, bylines, footers) can be made larger, smaller, bolder, or italicized, and you can display them in different colors, among other things.

When setting up your pages in HTML and CSS, you have the option of creating *font sets,* whereby text on any web page on your client's site is rendered in a browser window based on the font availability of the computer system viewing the page. One such typical font set is Verdana, Arial, Helvetica, and

Sans-Serif. When this font set is used, Verdana would be the preferred font to view the web page in. If that font were missing from the visitor's computer, the text would be rendered in Arial, the next font in that set, and so on.

Google and Typekit fonts

In September 2009, a company called Small Batch, Inc. started a web type subscription service named Typekit that let you embed special non-web-safe, high-quality fonts into your web designs. Subscriptions cost roughly $25–$100 per year, which included access to hundreds of fonts, a search engine to help you find suitable fonts for your projects, and the guarantee that those fonts would be hosted by Small Batch for guaranteed 100 percent uptime. Needless to say, this service caught on big with web designers and developers, and in October 2011, Adobe purchased Typekit with intentions of making it part of the Adobe Creative Cloud service sometime after releasing CS6.

While all that was going on, in 2010, the folks at Google also gave web designers a much-needed reason to cheer with the introduction of their free Google Web Fonts. Essentially, they decided that they'd host free fonts that designers could easily use in their designs to break away from the monotony of using web-safe fonts. These specialty Google fonts are easily viewable on any website from nearly any device including desktop computers, notebooks and laptops, smartphones, and tablets. Best of all, the entire process is seamless to the visitor, giving designers the ultimate control over how their sites look.

With the improvement of computers and browsers being able to render fonts better and better each year, the introduction of hosted fonts such as Google and Typekit has been a boon to designers. That said, browsers do still render fonts differently, and you're likely to see these types of fonts look better in one browser over another. Differences that will be most notable upon browser comparison are clarity, anti-aliasing, kerning and tracking (letter spacing), and how type flows (and wraps) within a container element.

As you can see in the following figure, Google currently offers over 500 free font families to choose from, and Typekit makes it easy to choose the right fonts for your projects. To discover more about using free Google fonts and subscription-based Typekit fonts, visit `www.google.com/webfonts` and `http://typekit.com`.

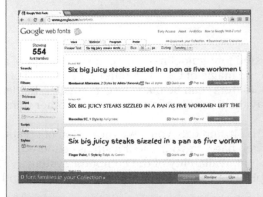

Up until very recently, browsers running on OS X rendered web fonts much differently than browsers on PCs. If you were to do a side-by-side comparison, you'd see that the Mac browsers displayed true PostScript fonts with anti-aliasing, which makes each of the letter shapes appear sharp and smooth, especially around the curved edges. By contrast, PC browsers used a different technology to render text in a browser, which displayed fonts in a more pixilated, not anti-aliased way. At the time, the recommendation was to test and show your clients the look of your site on both Mac and PC so that there wouldn't be any surprises about the way the text looked in each scenario. Today, while you should always still test and preview your site on both platforms (and in as many browsers as possible), what you'll see is a drastically improved method for rendering fonts on the web on both Mac and PC and in nearly all the newest, most popular browsers including Chrome, Firefox, Safari, Opera, and Internet Explorer.

Even with all these wonderful font options, you may still occasionally have a client request that a particular non-cross-platform-available font be used on the site. In these cases, explain the cross-platform font issues to your client and suggest a workaround that includes using HTML text for the bulk of the content and using Google or Typekit fonts for creating page heading graphics. If they still insist on a particular font, make the graphics you need containing that font and try to use them sparingly. For example, you may need a special font for a section heading (In the News) or some kind of sale or promotion (Take $25 off), such as the images shown in Figure 1-8. Whenever possible, though, insist that your client use HTML text marked up with CSS, especially because it will make the site load faster and be more search-engine friendly.

Figure 1-8: You can use special fonts as graphical elements on a website.

Selecting a Navigation System

The navigation system on a web page is typically the primary tool that visitors use to jump from one page of a website to another. The key ingredient to a good navigation scheme is *usability*. The navigation should be easy to understand and easy to use, and the information on a site should be easy to locate, even by the most inexperienced web visitor. This is different from *accessibility,* which has more to do with the HTML coding of the elements presented on the page rather than how the site is designed. In addition, the placement and functionality of the navigation system should be consistent throughout the entire site so that visitors aren't forced, even on one page, to guess how to access the different pages on the site.

Thankfully, most Internet visitors today are familiar with using the most common types of navigation systems. Navigation schemes usually consist of a set of text or graphical button links, with or without subnavigation menus, and visitors know they must click the links to navigate from one page to the next. Some navigation types have more intuitive interfaces than others, but they all tend to provide links to other pages on the site or external to the site. A drop-down form style "jump menu" (where the visitor selects a destination from a drop-down menu and is instantly taken there upon release of the mouse button), for instance, would arguably be easier for an Internet novice to figure out how to use than a navigation system that uses shapes, symbols, or other graphics as links to other pages on a site.

In your own Internet experience, you've probably already seen examples of the most popular types of navigation systems, and although they might look graphically different from one another — you find navigation menus, navigation trees, navigation lists, and navigation buttons — each of them functions essentially in the same way. Figure 1-9 illustrates simple examples of each of these navigation types.

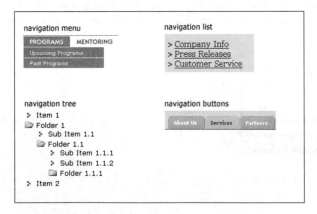

Figure 1-9: Web page navigation comes in a variety of styles.

Choosing a location and style

The placement of most website navigation systems tends to be either at (or near) the top of the web page or along the left or right margin of the page layout. When a site is larger than just a handful of pages, some of or all the navigation elements might serve as both links to their respective pages and triggers that open a submenu to additional navigation links, which themselves might also have additional submenu navigation links to their respective pages.

Submenus tend to drop down, pop up, or fly out to the left or right of the main navigation option being selected. How any one submenu system functions largely depends on the technology powering it, such as JavaScript, jQuery, Java applets, Flash, DHTML, CSS, or some combination of these.

Talk with your client about your ideas for the navigation, and plan to have some example URLs handy that you can refer to when defining which navigation systems you think might work best for the client's site. To be sure, many clients will already have a general idea of how they'd like the navigation to function, and they may even present you with sample URLs of the type of navigation they'd like to have. Whether you can create a comparable navigation system is another question, however.

When researching someone else's navigation system, take a look at the source code to see whether you can identify whether the navigation is using CSS, JavaScript, jQuery, Flash, or some kind of applet or plug-in to drive its functionality. If you can't quickly figure it out, you may need to suggest some kind of alternative to your client that you know you can easily create. Some of the fancier, super-dynamic navigation menus you might find are often built by third-party providers using Java, a programming language (not to be confused with JavaScript, a scripting language), but in all likelihood, you should be able to find an attractive menu system that is easy to create using simply HTML, CSS, and a bit of JavaScript or jQuery.

Not all fancy navigation menus require programming, however. Many third-party menus these days use HTML and CSS. OpenCube (`www.open cube.com`), for example, offers an affordable ($389 for web developers) CSS menu solution that allows you to use both graphics and text to create multilevel cross-browser-compatible menus to suit nearly any website. If you're looking for a free simple CSS menu or a free robust CSS3 menu generator, check out `www.cssmenubuilder.com` and `http://css3menu.com`.

Determining how to handle submenus

If you or your clients are having difficulty choosing the right navigation and subnavigation system for the site, take the following steps:

1. **Determine the best location for the navigation on the page.**

   Across the top and down the left side of the page are the most common locations for the navigation. However, some sites have begun to use a combination layout where the main navigation falls across the top and the subnavigation falls along the left or right margins. Some fluid design sites have even put the entire navigation system on the right, submenus and all. When in doubt, think of the site visitor's perspective and ask yourself where it would be easiest for him or her to find it.

2. Decide how the subnavigation, when needed, will function.

When the main navigation is on the left, the subnavigation typically displays to the right of the main navigation as a fly-out menu. By contrast, when navigation is located near the top of the page, the subnavigation tends to vary quite a bit more:

- The most common top-menu subnavigation type is the drop-down list, such as on the Cooking Light website (www.cookinglight.com). In some cases, if the top menus are positioned low enough on the page, the subnavigation menus might pop up above the navigation bar.

- The second most common submenu type, which is very popular on large ecommerce sites such as Target (www.target.com) and Barnes & Noble (www.barnesandnoble.com), is the rectangular multi-list, multi-column box navigation menu.

- The third most popular type of submenu tends to be a horizontal submenu directly below the main navigation links, usually placed atop a color bar that matches or compliments the background color of the main navigation link or button, such as the Apple iPad and iTunes landing pages (www.apple.com/ipad and www.apple.com/itunes).

A newer solution that designers have been using quite a bit more in the past couple of years is to make subnavigation accessible through links styled with CSS along the left, but more typically the right, margin of the page.

 Oftentimes, the site map can provide clues about which type of navigation is most suitable for a site, so if you're feeling stuck or undecided, look to the site map. Websites with multiple categories and subcategories might benefit from relying on more straightforward navigation systems using drop-down menus, whereas sites with fewer pages overall can take more creative risks with how they display their navigation to the visitor.

While I'm on the topic of navigation and drop-down menus, there is an important issue you should know about when using this sort of navigation with touch-based devices, such as the iPhone and iPad. Even though rollovers and hovers are commonly used to expand submenus on websites viewed in a browser on a desktop or laptop computer, most handheld devices have no rollover or hover state. This means that any rollover buttons and hover states, whether crafted with JavaScript or CSS, are nonfunctional on the handheld device. As a work-around, many web designers now use separate lists for main navigation and subnavigation, each of which is easily accessible on most touch-based devices.

Whichever navigation scheme you choose with your client, make sure that it makes sense within the context of the overall layout and the content being presented. Above all, navigation should be both professional looking and user friendly.

Organizing the Site's Look and Feel

One of the most fun and challenging aspects of creating a website's look and feel is to figure out how all the pieces of the puzzle fit together. The *look and feel* is a general term that refers to the *GUI* (graphical user interface, pronounced *gooey*) of a website, which defines the overall design appearance and functionality of a site before the site is designed. Within the GUI, you have the main navigation and subnavigation, the logo and other branding, possibly a tag line, some photographs, some copy, illustrations, and other miscellaneous bits of content that need to go on the page. You also have your chosen fonts and colors, and you have made a few decisions about layout size and orientation to assist you in creating a design that can project the image that the client wants while attracting the target audience that the client wants.

Fortunately, you can discover a few tricks about how to put all the pieces together in a visually pleasing way. Two factors, in particular, can greatly help get the design going in a positive direction, namely, positioning the brand and designing your site on the grid system.

Positioning the brand

The brand is the site's identity, which usually consists of a logo or logotype, a tagline or catch phrase, and occasionally some kind of photo, illustration, or other graphic treatment.

On a web page, the most important part of the layout is the top 400 pixels. As long as you position the branding within this area, the visitor can see it when first arriving on the website. Most sites position the brand in the top 150 pixels, aligned either to the top left (such as www.youtube.com), top center (such as http://pinterest.com), or top right (such as http://altpick.com) area of the layout, as illustrated in Figure 1-10.

No one perfect position for the branding exists. Instead, you need to find the right place for your particular logo and branding information within the context of your particular site. In essence, you have three popular choices, so try them all and pick the one that looks the best! On the other hand, the answer may come directly to you from your client's marketing standards, which may prescribe the exact location of the branding for you.

Figure 1-10: Position the brand to the left, center, or right along the top area of the site.

Designing layouts on the grid

If you've done any design work, you've probably heard about working on a grid. Each layout (and this goes for print projects as well as web designs) has a defined space on top of which a grid can be placed to divide the space into equal parts. For example, if your design will be fixed width at 960 pixels wide and roughly 640 pixels high, you can split the workspace in half down the middle both vertically and horizontally. You can then add additional divisions between the new dividers, as shown in Figure 1-11, to further carve up the space into even increments. To further control the layout, you could carve up the space into multiple subdivisions with equal subdivisions between columns to suit the specific needs of your design, such as 12 columns that are 60 pixels wide each with 20-pixel gutters, as illustrated in Figure 1-12. For free grid templates and CSS for your site, visit the 960 Grid System website at http://960.gs.

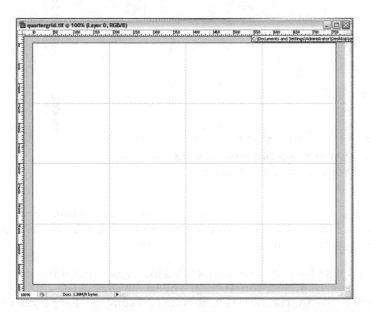

Figure 1-11: Evenly divide the space in your layout using the grid system.

When you place your content elements within a grid system, a natural ordering of those elements begins to emerge. Navigation buttons can be equally distributed, graphics can be placed strategically in visually harmonious spots, and the whole layout can begin to take on an otherwise missing sense of cohesiveness. Of course, you don't have to design on a grid, but it can be a good jumping-off point if you're more of a rebel designer.

Making a layout checklist

To help you begin to get a sense of what is needed for each individual web project, you may want to create a general layout checklist that you can use to guide you in the process of preparing to create your design mock-up.

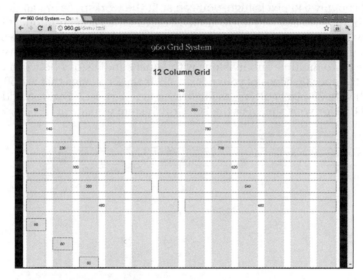

Figure 1-12: To have even greater control of your layout, divide the space into equal columns and gutters.

There are no right or wrong answers to the checklist questions. Each project has its own set of circumstances, requirements, and guidelines, given the descriptions for company and ideal visitor.

Your checklist should look something like Figure 1-13. If you use a form like this for each project you work on, you can take each site's design ideas right into the mock-up phase. Then, as you're creating the design, you can regularly check the form to see whether the design is consistent with the site's design goals.

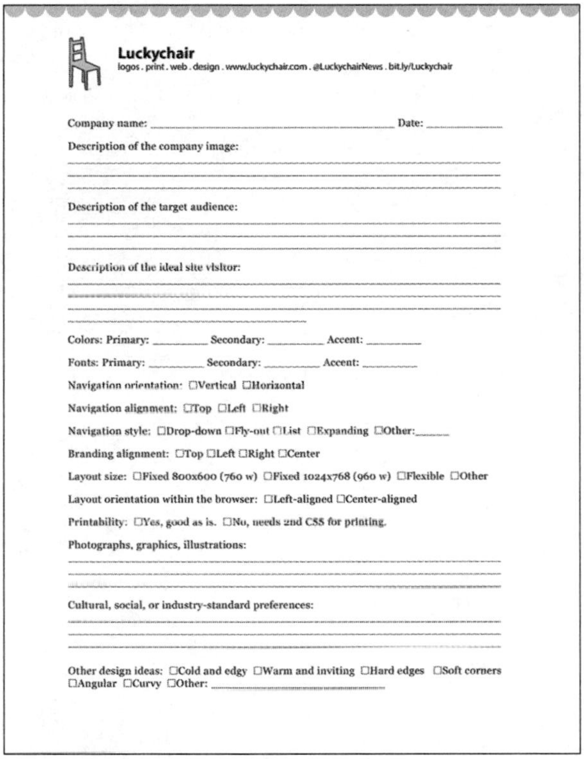

Luckychair
logos . print . web . design . www.luckychair.com . @LuckychairNews . bit.ly/Luckychair

Company name: _____ Date: _____

Description of the company image:
_____
_____
_____

Description of the target audience:
_____
_____
_____

Description of the ideal site visitor:
_____
_____
_____

Colors: Primary: _____ Secondary: _____ Accent: _____

Fonts: Primary: _____ Secondary: _____ Accent: _____

Navigation orientation: ☐Vertical ☐Horizontal

Navigation alignment: ☐Top ☐Left ☐Right

Navigation style: ☐Drop-down ☐Fly-out ☐List ☐Expanding ☐Other:_____

Branding alignment: ☐Top ☐Left ☐Right ☐Center

Layout size: ☐Fixed 800x600 (760 w) ☐Fixed 1024x768 (960 w) ☐Flexible ☐Other

Layout orientation within the browser: ☐Left-aligned ☐Center-aligned

Printability: ☐Yes, good as is. ☐No, needs 2nd CSS for printing.

Photographs, graphics, illustrations:
_____
_____
_____

Cultural, social, or industry-standard preferences:
_____
_____
_____

Other design ideas: ☐Cold and edgy ☐Warm and inviting ☐Hard edges ☐Soft corners
☐Angular ☐Curvy ☐Other: _____

Figure 1-13: Use a checklist to help guide you in creating the site mock-up.

Chapter 2: Mocking Up the Design

In This Chapter

⮡ **Using the visual site map as a guide for the layout**

⮡ **Mocking up the site design**

⮡ **Placing page elements strategically in the mock-up**

⮡ **Designing additional graphics for the site**

*1*f you already read the previous chapters in the book, you've covered quite a bit of ground laying the foundations for your project. With the site's purpose, a grasp of the target audience, and the definition of the ideal site visitor, you should now have a firm identity for the site that includes ideas about colors, fonts, graphics, photographs, layout, navigation, and other design-related site components. You may now take all that information, combine it with the content on the home page and your visual site map, and jump feet first into your chosen graphics software program to create the actual mock up for the design.

In this chapter, you mush all that information, your research, and your design decisions into a one-of-a-kind layout for your web project. With a little effort, some patience, and a sprinkling of creativity, you should quickly find that using the project's site map as your guide can help you easily generate a unique, creative, and compelling web page mock-up that best represents the project goals, the client's vision for the site, and the most appealing look for the target audience. Sounds like a tall order, but it's really not. All you must really do is put all the parts of the site together in a visually pleasing way — whatever that means to you — given your aesthetic preferences, the client's specific requests, and the visual pieces you have to work with. Think of the design as representing a balance among your own aesthetics, what the client wants to see, and what the site actually needs to look like to be successful.

Creating a good design, no matter what project you're working on and how many design restrictions you feel you have, requires that each of the elements for the site — text, fonts, colors, design elements, and so on — is strategically placed on the page. For some sites, this can be somewhat like solving a complicated puzzle, but if you take your time and follow the basic organizational rules outlined in this chapter, you should be able to come up with at least one, if not two or three, suitable layouts. One extremely useful rule is to include on the mock-up a graphic example of the type of navigation system the site will use, preferably with one of the navigation links shown in its "rollover state" when applicable. This can greatly help your client envision how the completed web page will look and function when converted into HTML.

 If you'd like to find out about some of the more popular navigation options before building the mock-up, turn to Book III, Chapter 6. After you have chosen the best navigation system for your project, return to this chapter to complete your mock-up.

Understanding the Value of a Mock-Up

There are several very valuable reasons why you should create a mock-up (or mock-ups, if you've contracted to create more than one for your client to choose from) of a website in a graphics program before you build it in HTML and CSS. Here are the top four reasons:

- **Visual representation:** First and foremost, the mock-up is meant to provide your client with a visual representation of how the completed site will look in a browser window before you actually spend any time generating the graphics or building the web pages in HTML, CSS, JavaScript, jQuery, and any programming language you may decide to use. In other words, the mock-up becomes a kind of blueprint that both you and the client can refer to when communicating about the specifics of how the site will look and function. It's also a great way to communicate dynamic needs to programmers and other web developers who may be assisting you with the construction of your site.

- **Easy modification:** Should the design require any adjustments (which it inevitably will), you can more easily modify a single graphic mock-up than rebuild or modify the code on all the pages on a website. Most clients do like to have some say in the design process. Allowing for client feedback during the design phase is a nice way to share the decision-making power and arrive at the best possible final design. Of course, you only want to show your client your very best work so that the choices he can assist you in making will be ones that are acceptable to you from a design and production perspective.

- **Design unification:** Ultimately, the mock-up allows you to put all your design ideas in one place, providing a single, unified vision of the site's look and feel that you can constantly refer to as you build the site. You will also use the layout as a guide from which you can generate all the additional necessary graphics for the remaining pages on the site.

✔ **Satisfaction:** For many clients, the site mock-up has an emotional component. Not only is an approved mock-up a clearly definable milestone within the web design process, but it also provides the client with a great sense of accomplishment toward the finished project.

You should expect, after presenting the initial design to the client, to go through one to three rounds of revisions before the client approves the design. Two rounds are often sufficient, but given the fact that many designers now communicate with their clients exclusively through e-mail and voice mail, three rounds should give you ample time to resolve any possible miscommunication that might naturally occur.

Whether you'll be designing one, two, or possibly more mock-ups for your client's web project, be sure to limit the number of revisions the client can make to her preferred design, and gently remind your client of this limit so that the project stays on track within the predefined site budget and time frame. Some designers allow unlimited changes until the client is satisfied. However, in my experience, limiting the number of revisions to three or less (or a maximum of five in special circumstances or if the client is paying by the hour rather than a flat fee) helps keep the project moving forward.

If you include some kind of clause in your design contract that states the maximum number of revisions to the design before any additional fees kick in, you can inform the client of her responsibilities and your expectations in advance. For example, you might want to state that the contract "allows a maximum of three rounds of revisions to the initial design and that any additional work beyond this maximum shall be automatically billed at $X/ hour." This simple clause can greatly help you prevent the more aggressive clients from asking more from you than they've agreed and contracted you to pay for.

In addition to using the mock-up as the foundational graphics you need to build the site, the mock-up also provides you with all the necessary design elements you would need for creating other graphics for the site, as well as for other projects the client may hire you to perform. For instance, your client may decide that he wants to place some banner ads on some other websites and decides to hire you to create those graphics. Because you already have a style guide embodied in your mock-up, generating these new banner ads should be a piece of cake.

Working from a Site Map

When you're staring at an empty canvas (or blank page or whatever you want to call a new file), the task of putting all the elements together can seem so overwhelming that you don't know where to begin. To help you get started, go to the visual site map you create (as described in Book I, Chapter 3) and use it to guide you in creating your site mock-up. Remember, the site map is an agreed-upon, client-approved document about the site, and as you can see in Figure 2-1, it also contains at-a-glance information about all the navigation links, subnavigation elements, the page order, and all the other bits and pieces of content that need to be added to the mock-up. This content includes elements such as the logo and other branding or company details, footer links, a copyright notice, and certain site-wide dynamic functionality (for example, a site-search feature, blog link, or e-mail sign-up form).

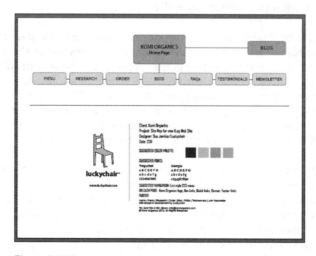

Figure 2-1: Use your site map as a starting point for designing your site mock-up.

As long as you start by putting all the necessary content onto the design canvas before you start thinking about the layout and design, you should have an easier time arranging all the elements when you start to move them into the position consistent with the design decisions you made about the page layout, size, orientation, color panel, and font selection. In the following sections, you find out how to translate the information in the site map into an organized graphic mock-up worthy of presentation to the client.

Creating the Mock-Up

A thousand times better than any sketch, your graphic mock-up is the single best way to show the client what the finished website will look like. The *mock-up* is the graphical representation of the website layout used to communicate the look, feel, and functionality of a site before the graphics are optimized and the site gets constructed using HTML, CSS, and other development coding, scripting, and programming techniques.

Of course, if the idea appeals to you, feel free to sketch a mock-up by hand before generating the graphical version of it in your preferred graphics program. However, do not use a sketch in lieu of the graphical mock-up, because sharing a sketch with a client often creates too many opportunities for miscommunication.

What makes the graphical mock-up so powerful is that it can clearly demonstrate a unified vision that pulls together all the site's elements, including precise color selection, accurate representations of fonts and font sizes, and specific placement of the navigation system and textual and graphic content on the site. Furthermore, this precision assists with discussions between you and the client about revisions to the design should any need to be made. With luck, your client will like what you have done and will only have a handful of minor suggestions to improve the layout.

In the sections that follow, you find some important suggestions about creating the mock-up, including how to block out different parts of the page, strategically place your most important design elements "above the fold," and unify your design with graphic elements.

Blocking out the parts of the page

Because the most important page of any website is the home page, you should plan to mock up that page for the client (or for yourself, if you're designing your own site). If you and your client agree in advance that you, the designer, will mock up a different internal page (that is, any pages on the site other than the home page) instead of or in addition to the home page, doing so can be helpful if the budget and time frame allow this. Generally, though, the home page sets the standard for the design of the rest of the site, because it includes most if not all the repeating graphical elements that will appear in the same location on the other pages throughout the site.

As you discover in Book I, Chapter 4, you can use any of several graphic applications (Photoshop, Illustrator, Fireworks, and so on) to create the web mock-up, depending on your specific needs, budget, and personal preferences. Begin the mock-up process by following these steps in your graphic application:

1. **Add, in any order you like, all the site elements to a blank, appropriately sized document in your chosen graphics editor.**

    For example, if you decide to work in Photoshop (like I do), create a new, blank RGB, 8-bit, 72-ppi document in the agreed-upon size, such as 960 x 640 pixels.

2. **After you have added all the elements to the page, begin to reposition each of them around the document window into a visually pleasing order consistent with the agreed-upon design directives.**

Use rulers, grids, guides, and any other software-specific tools to assist you in organizing and aligning your content, and be sure to apply consistent spacing between elements.

Figure 2-2 shows an example of how a budding mock-up might look.

Figure 2-2: After adding the home page logo, text, and graphics, move each element to its approximate location.

To better envision how the final website will look, set your monitor resolutions to 1024 x 768 or 1280 x 1024, take a screen shot of a maximized browser window, and then paste the screen shot into your mock-up file before returning your monitor to your preferred working resolution. Not only does this method show approximate available design space, but seeing the design as it might appear in a browser can assist in selling the layout to the client when it's time for review and approval.

Here are a few important points to keep in mind while blocking out parts of the page:

✏ **Navigation links:** As a general rule, navigation links are often placed either somewhere across the top of the layout directly below or to the right of the company logo, or along the left margin of the layout beneath the company identity. (Of course, you're welcome to break the rules and place your navigation elsewhere, but it's good to know the standards before you veer away from them!)

Each of the navigation text links, in both the header and footer, should be clearly delineated by designing button graphics behind, around, or to the sides of the link text or by adding some kind of dividing symbol like a bullet (•) or pipe (|) between them. Footer links at the bottom of the layout, which often include navigational links and other text such as a copyright notice (as shown in the footer example in Figure 2-3), are also often part of the mock-up.

Figure 2-3: Separate links in the footer with graphics or a dividing symbol.

- **Text:** For any text on your mock-up that will be rendered in HTML when you build the site, be sure to choose a cross-platform-compatible, Google, or Typekit font. Acceptable cross-platform fonts include Verdana, Arial, Arial Black, Helvetica, Courier, Courier New, Book Antiqua, Lucida, Palatino Linotype, Times, Times New Roman, Georgia, Geneva, Tahoma, Trebuchet, Comic Sans, Impact, Serif, and Sans-Serif. In addition, try to include examples in the main content text of any formatting styles that will be included on the site, such as headings, subheadings, bylines, paragraphs, and bulleted and/or numbered lists.

- **Color:** Apply color as needed to help define the different areas of the layout, such as background page color and/or design background color, regardless of whether your final site will be fixed in width or fluid. Color can be used as stripes, blocks, bars, lines, circles, squares, triangles, parallelograms, blobs, and other customized shapes. For instance, you might want to have a horizontal band of the primary color across the top of your layout with the company logo over it; another band of the secondary color just below that for a row of navigation buttons; and an accent-colored box or series of boxes off to the left or right below that for subnavigation page links, ads, and other sidebar information.

Expect to put in at least 8–12 hours for the initial design if you're an experienced designer — more if you're new or relatively new to the web design process.

Designing above the fold

A web page has certain areas that visitors are more likely to drink in and linger upon, similar to the upper-front page of a newspaper. The most valuable real estate on a web page, therefore, is the area from the top edge of the browser window down to the bottom edge (in a maximized browser window), before a visitor needs to scroll vertically to see any additional content. Though this area will be different for visitors viewing your site on other web-enabled devices such as tablets and smartphones, this area is still a top priority.

The actual area of this part of a web page, which is commonly referred to as the area *above the fold,* is determined by each visitor's monitor resolution setting, which varies from one monitor or device to the next.

To help you accurately determine the size of the area that is above the fold for your target audience, take a look at Table 2-1. In general, you need to take into account the resolution the target audience uses, and within that resolution, allow space for browser chrome — the stuff that takes up space inside the browser window, such as the scroll bars, navigation buttons, the status bar, and the address bar.

Table 2-1	Find the Design Area above the Fold
Target Audience's Monitor Resolution	*Approximate Design Space above the Fold*
800 x 600	760 x 420 pixels
1024 x 768	1000 x 600 pixels (typical design size is 960 x 640)
1280 x 1024	1260 x 800 pixels (typical design size is 1100 x 700, sometimes 1000 x 700)

Because you truly have no control over what resolution visitors' monitors, tablets, smartphones, or other devices are set to, the recommended standard is to put the most important information in your web design in the top 420–700 pixels, with less critical information beneath that.

Your above-the-fold design area should include the following:

- Company branding (logo, company name, tagline, and so on)
- Navigation links or buttons
- Text and graphic information to tell the visitors about the products, services, and benefits the site has to offer

What should not be included above the fold? Typically, you should avoid including Flash intros and banners, advertisements, unnecessary text, and too many navigation links. Besides taking up valuable space, these unnecessary components can increase the size of the page, causing it to load more slowly in the browser window. If each page on a site should take fewer than 15 seconds to load (ideally, it should be more like 8 seconds), you really can't afford to waste any space putting unnecessary information above the fold that could be just as easily placed elsewhere on the page.

What's more, visitors should be able to scan the above-the-fold area within five to ten seconds to determine whether your site has what they are looking for. The home page needs to visually lure visitors into the rest of the site. At a quick glance, visitors should be able to do the following:

- Identify the site by its name or logo

- Get an overall flavor for the company by the site's layout and use of fonts, colors, and graphics

- Scan the navigation links for keywords that might help visitors find a particular page (such as products, services, or a contact)

- See quickly whether any specials or items of interest are available or on sale

- Scan or rapidly read introductory headlines or short comments about the company, key products, services, or news items

- Find quick-access links to customer service, shopping carts, help, coupons, site search, login, and other dynamic features

Including all this important information above the fold encourages the visitor to stay on the site, keep looking around, and click through to the other pages on the site. That is the main goal of the home page!

If visitors cannot find what they are looking for when they first enter the site, or if the site looks unprofessional and unorganized, they are very likely to leave without further exploration.

If you don't believe this, think about your own browsing habits. How long does it take for you to decide whether a particular site has what you're looking for? Five seconds? Ten seconds? Thirty? The human brain processes so many calculations per second that, relatively speaking, ten seconds is a lot of time. Seasoned Internet users know exactly what they are looking for. They are an impatient bunch (when it comes to surfing the Internet) and will gladly keep searching elsewhere until they find what they're looking for.

To assist you in your design mock-up for the area above the fold, keep the following tips in mind:

- Add headlines, subheadings, bylines, and other visual design elements that clearly communicate the site's benefits to visitors. Think of a newspaper: The name of the newspaper is the first thing you see, then the main story headline and text with a picture or two. You also find information about news items in different sections of the paper, a few bylines, and introductory text to three or four stories.

- Other good elements for the area above the fold (besides your navigation and key content) are links that allow visitors to sign up for a newsletter, contact the site, search the site, access a shopping cart, log in to an account, and bookmark the page.

✔ As you're arranging all the elements on the page in your mock-up, refer often to the words selected to identify the ideal site visitor as well as the identity for the site. Also keep the overall purpose for the site in mind because that concept can sometimes provide cues to positioning things in the layout.

As long as you can accomplish these goals within the top 420–700 pixels or so, depending on your chosen layout size, you can pretty much do whatever you like for the remaining areas of the layout. For example, after you set the tone of the mock-up, you can repeat design ideas such as pinstriping, custom bullets, header treatments, and unique image cropping throughout the rest of the layout, as illustrated in Figure 2-4. As you can see, the sidebars each have a title and striped background, which echo other design elements within the layout.

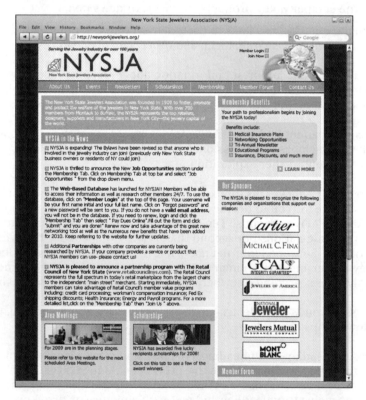

Figure 2-4: Use repeating design elements throughout the mock-up to create a sense of visual unity.

Unifying the layout with design elements

The design process doesn't stop when all the elements are in the layout. Your next task is to start to add design elements to the mock-up that can really make the design unique. This includes adding design elements such as horizontal rules, vertical divider lines, customized bullets, rounded or specially angled graphical corners, unusual textures, drop shadows, outer glows, special effects, buttons, borders, arrows, widgets, symbols, shapes, borders, and backgrounds to delineate the different areas of the layout, and other target-appropriate graphical embellishments.

The design process is a time of exploration and play. Take some design risks if they make sense in your layout. Repeating certain elements can provide instant unity to a design, but so can adding contrasting elements like using different-sized fonts and accent colors. You might even want to try making several versions of the mock-up to try out different text treatments and content-alignment options. If you get stuck for ideas during the design process, spend time looking at other sites for inspiration.

Above all, remember to be thorough. Each and every element in your web layout needs to seem like it was meant to be in the position it is, in the color it is, in the size it is, and in the font it is, all relative to the other objects in the design. Make the layout interesting, original, and creative. Here are some ideas that can help you pull together the rest of the site's design:

✔ Organize the content so that the site will be easy to navigate.

✔ Have a single focal point for the visitor's eye to rest upon.

✔ Leave white space in the layout to balance out the areas with content.

✔ Use no more than three different font faces in the design.

✔ Use consistent spacing between like objects such as bullet points, navigation links, and table rows.

✔ Make the text easy to read by using a single column no wider than 600 pixels or by breaking the layout into two or four columns.

✔ Add headers, subheads, pull quotes, photographs, illustrations, and other graphic elements to break up large text areas.

To help you create a sense of visual unity within the design, consider doing any of the following to your mock-up:

✔ Use photographs and illustrations to add visual appeal.

✔ Add horizontal and vertical rules to create divisions between different areas on the layout.

✔ Use rounded edges, angles, and other shapes to break up the linear quality of the design.

✔ Show hypertext links with underlines in the same color they will appear on the finished site.

TIP

If you're ever feeling stuck, remember that a simple design is usually more compelling than one that is overcrowded with bells and whistles. Try the squint test. If the page seems organized and balanced when you squint at it, you've done a good job. If parts seem too jumbled or too heavy on one side and too light on another, keep playing with the pieces of the layout until you can find a nice balance. Remember, too, to keep spacing and alignment among the elements consistent or deliberate throughout the layout. Good design allows the eye to flow from one area of the page to another, with areas of white space surrounding the content so that the eye has somewhere to rest as it moves among the important items in the layout. Figure 2-5 shows an example of the completed mock-up that incorporates all these design principles.

Figure 2-5: Good design is often balanced and organized, like this layout for a New York–based organic meal site.

Finalizing the Mock-Up

After you have completed the design to the best of your ability, put it away for a day or two and then return to it to be sure that it still looks fresh and finished. Not looking at it for a couple of days can provide you with a little objectivity. If you find any inconsistencies in the design's spacing, alignment, coloration, or sizing, now is the time to make your corrections and adjustments. Use the following questions to help you review your design:

- ✔ Does the layout look unified?
- ✔ Is the navigation system easy to identify, and does it look clickable?
- ✔ Have you used too many fonts?
- ✔ Can any redundant elements be removed from the layout?
- ✔ Did you place the most important information above the fold?
- ✔ Does the site have more than one focal point?
- ✔ Are the visitor benefit messages clear and easy to identify?
- ✔ Does the eye have any white space to rest upon?
- ✔ Are any design elements repeated throughout the design to give it a look of cohesiveness and professionalism?

Book II Chapter 2

Mocking Up the Design

In addition to this checklist, the following sections help you finalize your mock-up and provide tips on how to best present your design to your client.

Showing the subnavigation

The navigation system in your mock-up will be consistently placed on all the pages throughout a site, allowing visitors to easily navigate to the different pages of a website. Navigation systems range from the simple to the complex and can be created using HTML, JavaScript, jQuery, DHTML, Java, and/or other programming languages. The most popular systems are text based, list type, and JavaScript-enabled navigation. Some navigation systems, as you've likely seen in your own exploration of sites on the Internet, include subnavigation to help organize the destinations that visitors can select from. While you may know how you intend the navigation and subnavigation system to look and function, your client may not until the navigation has already been built, which would not be a smart thing to do.

One of the best secrets that can help you sell the finished mock-up to your clients is to add one special element to your mock-up. Namely, you should try to show at least one of the navigation buttons in the layout in its *rollover state* or *mouseover state* — that is, how the link will look when a visitor moves her mouse over one of the links on the main navigation, complete with a hand cursor pointing to the link and including the look and feel of any drop-down or tiered subnavigation menus, when applicable. The more realistic the mock-up, the more easily you can help your client visualize the final product. Rollover graphics or link effects generally appear on the fly due to the activation of CSS or JavaScript in the page code when the user moves the cursor over the link. Likewise, when the visitor moves the cursor away from the rollover link, the link (and any submenus that may have appeared) typically returns to its normal state immediately or after a predetermined delay measured in milliseconds.

Remember, however, that mobile and any touch-based devices don't have rollover state capabilities and therefore can't expand submenus. For more about creating websites that are mobile- and tablet-friendly, see Book III, Chapter 5.

By adding this one simple graphical element to the layout, you can help your client get a feel for how the site's navigation will function when the site gets built in HTML. Figure 2-6 shows an example of a mock-up that includes how the subnavigation menu will look when a visitor mouses over a navigation link.

Figure 2-6: Include an example of rollover or subnavigation functionality on the website mock-up.

Presenting the mock-up to the client

If you are truly satisfied and proud of your design after you've added a sample of the rollover state to the mock-up, you are finally ready to present the finished mock-up to the client.

Avoid a red herring

Though it's not a practice I use, some designers intentionally add some kind of noticeable error to the layout — a *red herring* — before presenting the mock-up to the client. The idea behind this technique is that by including something obviously wrong in the layout — like using the wrong font or color — the client will almost assuredly point out that error during the mock-up review ("Why is *that* blue?"), recommend a change of some kind ("Make it red"), and come away from the process feeling valued for making a contribution to the design process. This sounds good in theory, but I've witnessed some clients say they actually liked the "bad" element, and removing something can be tough after the client has seen it. It's kind of like a Murphy's Law of Design: When given three options, the client will almost always choose the worst-looking design!

Web mock-up presentations can take many forms, including the following:

- E-mailing a JPG, GIF, PNG, TIFF, or PDF file to the client for review
- Uploading a JPG, GIF, PNG, or PDF file of the mock-up to a test server or online collaborative space and sending the client the URL to view it
- Uploading a JPG, GIF, PNG, or PDF file of the mock-up to a free drop site (such as www.dropbox.com) and sending the client a link and password to retrieve the file
- Meeting with the client in person to present the mock-up on a laptop, projector, or computer screen in its native graphics program format, or as a JPG, GIF, PNG, or PDF file
- Meeting with the client in person to show the mock-up as a printout (or series of printouts) that's been mounted to an archival presentation board

Unless the client wants to confer with other members of her team, or with friends and family before giving you her opinion, she should be able to review the mock-up in a reasonable amount of time, say, one to five business days. After the review, she'll either provide you with feedback on what revisions she'd like you to make or grant you written approval of the mock-up so you can begin building her new site in HTML.

Getting written client approval on the design

If I could share only one tip with you about working with clients, it would be "Get everything in writing." When communication is clear and both you and the client agree in writing about each of the steps of the design process, the project magically stays on track and within budget.

Start each project with a contract (and get a deposit), and tell the client in advance that you will be obtaining her signature of approval at key points during the development process. Get written approval on the site map, definitely get written approval on the completed mock-up before you begin building the site in HTML, and be sure to also get a final signature at the end of the project when the site is finished before sending the client your final invoice. These signatures are your insurance should the client change her mind about the site requirements while the project is under way. They also show the client that you're committed to meeting your responsibilities as outlined and defined in the contract.

In my experience, most clients are great to work with and treat the designer with respect. Nonetheless, clients occasionally push for more and don't want to pay for any additional services. Do *not* be tempted to do any extra work for free, just to be nice, even when the client begs you to do something in a kind and gentle way. Your time is your livelihood, and you deserve to earn money for every minute you spend working on the project. Should additional changes be required beyond the scope of the project, the signatures allow you to feel confident about requesting more time, more money, and more materials to get the job done.

During your mock-up presentation, communicate to the client why the layout looks the way it does. Sell your ideas. Explain your reasons for selecting particular fonts, colors, and alignments. Point out all the key elements of the design, being sure to mention how it captures the identity of the site as well as caters directly to the target audience. Identify the focal point of the design and any other key elements you're particularly proud of. The more you show that you have thoroughly thought about each of the design elements, the more your client will understand your visual point of view. Good luck!

Be prepared to make some changes. Most clients will have at least one thing to say about the mock-up that requires revision. If you disagree with anything a client wants to have changed, respectfully give reasons for why you believe the mock-up works the way you've designed it. If the client still disagrees and insists you make a particular change, say you'll try her suggestion (even if you're sure it won't work well or look right). With bad ideas, many clients can actually see how your version looks better than their suggestions when the two versions are compared side by side.

Above all, however, remember that the client is paying you for the project, and she needs to be happy with the results. Be willing to compromise, be open to making changes, and keep working to the maximum number of allowable revisions in your contract until the design is approved. If additional changes are requested beyond the scope of the project, remind the client of your fee for these extra services before you provide them to ensure that both you and the client are in agreement. Many clients will rein in their desire for multiple revisions in an effort to stay within budget and keep the project moving forward toward completion.

Creating Additional Web Graphics

Websites often include additional page-specific graphic elements that must be designed to be consistent with your mock-up. After the client approves the web mock-up and provides you with written acceptance of the design, you may begin creating these other graphics before you start to optimize the rest of the site's graphics and move into the site-building phase of the project.

These additional graphics, for lack of a better term, include items such as the over states of rollover buttons; social media and other icons; bullet graphics for customized lists (with CSS, you can use your own graphics for bullets!); background images; navigation elements; curved or specially angled decorative graphic elements; graphical horizontal and vertical rules or dividers; animated GIFs; page headers using fancy non–web safe, Google, or Typekit fonts; illustrations; and photographs.

For some of the additional graphics, like rollover graphics and background patterns, you can create new layers in the existing mock-up file. For the rest of them, feel free to create as many new RGB, 8-bit, 72-ppi appropriately sized documents as you need. For example, you may create one file for rollover buttons, another file for header graphics, one for background images, and another for sale item graphics.

In the following sections, you find out about creating other graphics for your site, including header graphics, rollover graphics, background images, social media icons, and others, such as diagrams, photos, and illustrations.

Header graphics

Also called page *headers*, *headings*, or *A-heads*, header graphics refer to graphical renderings of page titles, often using specialized fonts, that are placed at the top of the page content in lieu of creating headings using cross-platform-compatible or web-hosted fonts styled with CSS.

If your layout calls for specialty font headers instead of headers styled with CSS, create and save these graphics in a file separate from the mock-up. This way, if any new pages are added to the site during the page-building process or at some time down the road after the site has been launched, you can easily go back into this header graphics file and quickly create the new headers that you need. When working in Photoshop, you can easily add new layers for each new bit of text, as illustrated in Figure 2-7, and then hide and show the layers as needed to generate the individual optimized graphics.

Figure 2-7: Use a single file repeatedly to create multiple versions of a graphic.

Rollover graphics

Rollover graphics change from one look to another when a visitor interacts with the graphic in some predetermined way, such as mousing over the normal graphic. The most common form of rollover graphic is the rollover button used in navigation or for some other function on a site, such as a submit button on a form. Rollovers can be any color or combination of colors; can be styled with special effects like bevels, drop-shadows, and stroked edges; and can include any content such as text, illustrations, and photos. In fact, as long as you make sure that both the normal state and rollover state graphics are exactly the same size, they can look like whatever you want them to.

To create rollover graphics, feel free to design them with color, text, and special effects using either a vector or raster graphics program, whichever suits your needs at the time. When your graphics are finished, you will optimize the two rollover state graphics as GIF, JPEG, or PNG files. Book II, Chapter 3 shows you the ins and outs of web graphic optimization. After you have optimized your graphics, the next step is to make the rollovers functional. To do that, you need to use a little bit of JavaScript with your HTML, which you find out how to do in Book III, Chapter 6.

Background images

Cascading Style Sheets (CSS) give you the amazing ability to use background images on your page, as well as inside any HTML container, such as the body of the page, a table, a table cell, or a layer using the <div> tag. Background images can be set with CSS to repeat along the X axis, the Y axis, or both the X and Y axes, or to appear once and not repeat. You can also position a background image precisely by using X/Y coordinates relative to the upper-left corner of the parent container, such as the browser window or a DIV tag. This means that background images no longer need be miles tall or wide to tile seamlessly horizontally or vertically within your layout. Wahoo!

Two other things you can do with background images, now that CSS3 works in most of the newest browsers, are creating a "full page" background image that fill the entire browser window without scrollbars, and making "resizable" background images that will automatically scale downwards based on media queries that detect the size of the viewing device, such as a computer monitor, a tablet, or a smartphone. For details about using these techniques, visit the CSS-Tricks website at http://css-tricks.com.

Social media graphics

With social media sites such as Facebook, Twitter, Tumblr, LinkedIn, and Pinterest, among others, being so popular these days, it would be almost foolish to not include both Share and Follow links on a new website. If the site owner you're designing for has social media accounts, you can add Follow links to those accounts either manually or through a sharing service such as AddThis (www.addthis.com) and ShareThis (www.sharethis.com). Likewise, you can also include Share links to visitors' social media accounts to encourage visitors to share site content among their own social networks.

If you choose to add links manually, you should be able to easily find free social media icons by searching for *free social media icons* in your preferred search engine. Alternatively, you can always create your own icons to give them a sense of personal flair or to better match the look of your site's design. Either way, having them on the site will give the impression of a well-connected site owner.

Other graphics

Before you head off into the land of graphics optimization, look again at your site map and continue creating all the graphics you think you will need for the various pages of your site. Most of the graphics you'll need to make will be obvious when referring to the content the client intends to use on the individual pages of the site, such as ribbons, banners, photos, illustrations, icons, bullets, gallery images, maps, diagrams, and board member portraits. Then, later on, while you're building the site, if you discover that you've forgotten to create a graphic or determine the need for a new one, you can come back to your graphics program and create one.

Chapter 3: Slicing and Optimizing Web Graphics

In This Chapter

✓ Selecting the appropriate web graphic format

✓ Choosing the right optimization program or tool

✓ Slicing and optimizing techniques

✓ Choosing the proper optimization settings

✓ Outputting optimized files and graphics

*B*efore you begin the optimization process of your web graphics, you should have a clear understanding of how the graphics and photos you use on your website need to be different from the ones you might use in a print project, such as a brochure or annual report. For one, print graphics are high resolution, whereas web graphics must be set to a low resolution. For another, print graphics depend on the CMYK color mode, whereas any graphics used for onscreen, handheld devices, and web presentation must use RGB color.

In this chapter, you find out about all the differences between web and print, as well as everything you need to know to create graphics that are ready for web optimization. Without this preparation — and especially without optimization — the graphics and photos on your websites would simply be too large to transmit over the web and display in a browser on a visitor's computer monitor in an acceptable time frame.

In the following sections, you find an overview of web graphics as compared to print graphics. You also discover tips about choosing an optimization program. Following that, you find out about the different web file formats, including how to select the right format for different graphic types. The later sections of this chapter include the finer points about selecting different optimization settings, slicing up images before optimization, and finally, choosing the right optimization output options to produce the desired output results.

Web Graphics 101

When people talk about web graphics versus print graphics, what they're really referring to are the different ways in which web graphics must be formatted compared to graphics intended for print.

Graphics, whether for print or the web, can be created with a variety of software programs, the most popular among them being Illustrator, Photoshop, Fireworks, Edge, Muse, and Flash for the web and Illustrator, Photoshop, QuarkXPress, and InDesign for print. The finished graphics may then be saved in a variety of file formats, depending on their intended usage.

Of all the applications you can choose from to create your graphic images, one primary consideration is whether the artwork needs to be developed and saved as either vector or raster:

- **Vector:** A vector program uses mathematical equations to generate paths, lines, and shapes, which enables the image to be scaled up and down with no loss of resolution. Logos, for example, are best created in a vector program. When created as vector graphics, the logo artwork can be colored and scaled for any medium — online, newsprint, embroidered on a hat, printed on the side of a pen, and so on — and still look great at any size.

- **Raster:** Raster (or bitmap) programs represent images as a collection of tiny pixels or little squares of color, the size and quantity of which are determined by the file's resolution. The number of pixels in an image determines the image's quality; typically, the higher the number, the sharper the image, and the lower the number, the fuzzier the image. An image set to 300 dpi (dots per inch), for instance, has a high resolution and therefore is fine and clear enough to use in a printed piece, whereas an image set to 72 ppi (pixels per inch) has too few bits of information to print crisply, even though the image might look fine and clear on a computer monitor.

Table 3-1 shows a comparison of web and print graphics based on a variety of key criteria. As you can see, some features of web and print graphics are so different from one another that you must take extra care that you don't mistakenly set up your files incorrectly at the start of each new project. For instance, your web and print graphics use different color spaces because print requires CMYK inks and the web relies on RGB technology to display color. In the next section, you discover details about each of the features listed for web graphics in Table 3-1, along with a few others that can assist you in creating your graphics appropriately for the web.

Table 3-1	Web and Print Graphic Comparison	
	Web Graphics	*Print Graphics*
Color mode	RGB	CMYK (including CMYK and Pantone colors)
Resolution	72 ppi	300 dpi or higher
Unit of measure	Pixels	Inches, points, picas
File size	Smaller file sizes make images display faster on the web.	Larger file sizes may produce sharper images in print.
Page size	Images can be placed on an adjustable-size web page.	Images are placed in layouts with a fixed page size.
File format	GIF, JPG, or PNG (PNG-8 and PNG-24)	TIFF, EPS, PSD, PDF, BMP, AI, INDD, QXP, PPT, DOC

Color mode

Graphic artists use two color modes, or *gamuts,* to create and save their work for the web and for print design: RGB (Red, Green, and Blue, which are additive colors) and CMYK (Cyan, Magenta, Yellow, and Black, which are subtractive). Typically, you should select the appropriate color mode for your graphic file at the start of each project when you create the new document.

If you forget to choose the correct color mode for your graphic files and you create some or most of the layout or image adjustments before realizing the mistake, be forewarned that converting a file from one color mode to another can cause noticeable shifts in color in the image that might render the image color inaccurate and possibly unusable. This is especially true for images created in RGB but intended for CMYK print.

Figure 3-1 shows how the different color modes achieve their color and what happens when all colors in that mode are combined.

RGB colors are the additive colors of the visible spectrum, which means that when combined, the resulting color is white light. RGB is used primarily for onscreen (computer monitor) presentations, such as web pages and PowerPoint slide shows, because computer monitors and most handheld devices use RGB technology to display color.

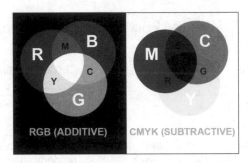

RGB (ADDITIVE)   CMYK (SUBTRACTIVE)

Figure 3-1: RGB should be used for the web and any other onscreen presentations, whereas CMYK is used primarily for print.

CMYK colors are the subtractive print colors used mainly for four-color reproductions. When cyan, magenta, and yellow inks are combined and printed on paper, the resulting color is technically black, which represents the absence of light. I say "technically" here because in reality, combining these three inks creates a sort of muddy gray-black that isn't quite as rich and saturated a color as you're used to seeing when you think of black. This is where the K (for black) in CMYK comes in. To get a true rich black in any print job, the printer must add a separate black ink to the printing process, thereby combining black with a little bit of cyan, magenta, and yellow to create that deep, rich black.

Color gamut warnings

Compared to the visible spectrum and the 16.7 million colors you can see on a 24-bit computer monitor, the CMYK color mode is somewhat limited. The current U.S. standard CMYK technology, or SWOP (standard web offset press), simply cannot reproduce with inks on a printed page the same full range of color you can see on a monitor. Any color that can't be reproduced in print, therefore, is referred to as being *out of gamut*. *Gamut* refers to the range of reproducible colors on any given device, such as a printing press or computer monitor.

In addition to the bucket of colors that are out of gamut for print, another thing you might want to watch out for when creating graphics for the web are the colors that don't fall within the web-safe palette. The web-safe palette, as I describe in Book I, Chapter 4, refers to the 216 non-dithering (solid) colors that can be accurately displayed in browsers on both Mac and PC computers with 8-bit monitors set to display a maximum of 256 colors. (The web-safe palette has only 216 colors instead of 256 because 40 of the 256 colors appear differently on a Mac than they do on a PC.) Following this same gamut logic then, any color that can't be represented onscreen on an 8-bit monitor is considered non-web-safe and would be called out of gamut for the web.

As I also describe in Book I, Chapter 4, using the web-safe palette is no longer as critical an issue in web design as it once was in the early days of the Internet because today's computers have monitors capable of rendering millions of colors. Though it might still occasionally be good to use a color from this palette when coloring large, flat areas of a web page, such as a page or container background or when specifying the color of styled text with CSS, it's no longer a general web recommendation.

So how do you know whether a color you have selected for a web or print project is out of gamut? Thankfully, both Photoshop and Illustrator (the two programs used by most professional web and print designers) have a feature within the Color Picker dialog box that alerts designers when a selected color is either out of gamut for print or non-web-safe. To demonstrate how this works, follow these steps in Photoshop:

1. **Launch Photoshop.**

   You can access the Color Picker tool without opening a new document, but feel free to open a new document if desired.

2. **Click the Foreground Color box at the bottom of the Photoshop Tools panel.**

   The Color Picker dialog box opens, which has several options for viewing color.

3. **In the R, G, and B text fields, enter the color values of** 0, 200, **and** 200, **respectively.**

   After entering these numbers, the hollow circle icon within the large foreground color field moves to near the upper-right corner of the square, thereby selecting a turquoise color.

   To the left of the OK and Cancel buttons, you can see a rectangle with the new color on top and the previously selected color on bottom.

   Directly to the right of those color swatches, you see two sets of small warning icons, as shown in Figure 3-2. The top two icons indicate that the selected color is out of gamut for print, and the bottom two icons indicate that the selected color is not web safe.

4. **Click the top triangular out-of-gamut warning icon to have Photoshop locate the nearest in-gamut print color that you could use instead.**

   The new suggested color should have the RGB values of 50/191/194, which is now in gamut, but it isn't web safe.

5. **Click the bottom cube-like, non–web-safe color warning icon.**

   You now have a color that is web safe (RGB values of 51/204/204) but is out of gamut for print!

   Though it may be tough at times to find a particular color that is both web-safe and printable, you have two ways to find such a color. First, you could click several times inside the large square color field until you find a color that is both in gamut and web-safe. The alternative is to select the Only Web Colors check box at the bottom of the dialog box. When this option is enabled, the nearest web-safe color is automatically selected. Then try clicking one of the other web-safe colors in the same color range and toggling on and off the Only Web Colors option until you find a value that is both web-safe and in gamut, such as RGB 102/204/204.

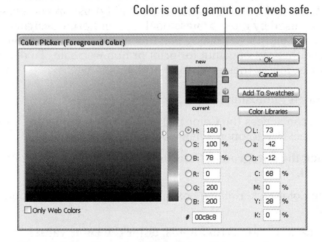

Color is out of gamut or not web safe.

Figure 3-2: The Photoshop Color Picker dialog box shows warnings for any selected color that is either out of gamut for print or not web safe.

If you train yourself to get in the habit of paying attention to the gamut warning icons as you're selecting your colors for your print and web projects, you can eliminate possible headaches that might occur if you show your client the mock-up with irreproducible colors. From now on, when you see an icon in the warning area, click it to ensure that the selected color meets your needs for print and the web.

Resolution

Resolution refers to the number of *pixels per inch (ppi)* onscreen that are used to display an image. Though computer monitors can display different ppi settings, such as 640 x 480, 800 x 600, 1024 x 768, 1280 x 1024, and 1600 x 1200, web browsers can display images only at a maximum of 72 ppi.

By contrast, your print graphics use *dots per inch (dpi)* to determine the quality of the printed output. To print a graphic at a high quality, you must set the resolution of your file to at least 300 dpi (though depending on the audience, in some cases, 150 dpi might be enough). Figure 3-3 illustrates the differences between dpi for print and ppi for the web.

In print, the more dots there are, the larger and clearer the image. On the web, however, increasing the number of pixels per inch is unnecessary because browsers, handheld devices, and most regular computer and video monitors can't yet display images at resolutions higher than 72 ppi. Furthermore, a resolution higher than 72 ppi not only increases the file size but may also increase the dimensions of the graphic, making the image take longer to download and be potentially larger than intended. That said, if you're going to be creating graphics for other output, such as projected PowerPoint presentations or images to be displayed on high-def monitors and TV screens, you could create graphics and 92 ppi and 96 ppi, respectively, for slightly improved quality output.

Figure 3-3: Print graphics are displayed in dots per inch, whereas web graphics are displayed in pixels per inch.

This brings up a conundrum if you plan to create graphics that can do double duty for web and print, as ideally you'll want your web graphics to look great in a browser while also printing crisply for the visitor. Here are two suggestions you can use alone or in tandem for creating print-worthy web graphics:

✔ **Set the resolution to 96 ppi.** When creating new graphics for the web, set the resolution of the files to 96 ppi instead of 72 ppi. This tiny bump in resolution might make the web graphic look a tad crisper when printed without drastically increasing the size of the graphic. Remember that the higher the resolution, the larger the file size, and the larger the file size, the slower the image transmits and displays on the web. The bump in resolution may also affect the file's dimensions, so be sure to keep an eye on that, too.

✔ **Add a print media CSS.** This technique presumes that you understand CSS and can configure it to correctly format and display the content on your website. After the master CSS file has been created, you could generate a second print media CSS that could replace the source code of the web graphic files (`images/sample.jpg`) with higher resolution print graphic files (`images/print/sample.jpg`) when the visitor prints a web page.

Though this book only covers general CSS techniques, I highly recommend you begin your journey to finding out more about advanced CSS techniques by reading Eric Meyer's influential article on CSS Design, "Going to Print," at `www.alistapart.com/stories/goingtoprint`. You might also enjoy reading *HTML, XHTML, and CSS All-in-One For Dummies* by Andy Harris.

Unit of measure

Print graphics can be measured in any unit your graphics program supports, such as inches, points, pixels, picas, millimeters, ems, exs, and percentages, though the most popular units for graphic designers tend to be inches, points, or picas. The unit you choose to work in determines the size of the image when printed. By contrast, almost everything on the web is measured in pixels, ems, or percentages. For instance, instead of saying, "Move that logo about a quarter-inch to the right," you'd probably say something like, "Move the logo 37 pixels to the right."

To change the unit of measure in your graphics program, check the preferences to adjust the program's default unit of measure, or if you're using an Adobe program, adjust the measure unit through the Ruler's context menu.

File and page size

The size of a graphic file largely depends on the dpi or ppi settings and the dimensions of the image in inches or pixels. For example, a file set to 500 x 400 pixels at 72 ppi might only be around 6 x 5 inches in print size with a 585.9K file size, but an image set to 7 x 5 inches at 300 dpi might have a pixel dimension of 2100 x 1500 and a 12MB file size. On the web, file sizes should be as small as possible while retaining the best-quality image, whereas in print, file size is somewhat irrelevant as long as the printed output is sharp and clear.

If you're used to working in print, the main thing you need to do differently for your web graphics is to pay close attention to the document settings each time you create a new file. If you're new to both web and print, as long as you select the appropriate color mode, resolution, file dimensions, and unit of measure for each new document you create before you begin designing your graphics, you'll do just fine.

Optimizing and Slicing Graphics

Up until the release of Adobe CS3 in 2007, design and optimization programs were separate. The software program you used to create your web graphics, such as Photoshop or Illustrator, was different from the program you used to optimize your web graphics, such as Fireworks, which was specifically designed for the creation and optimization of web graphics, or ImageReady, which came bundled with Photoshop and the Adobe CS Suite. Today that is no longer the case, because Adobe has incorporated ImageReady's optimization engine into Photoshop and Illustrator. Of course, if you still have an old copy of ImageReady, feel free to use it, or any optimization program you happen to have handy. If you're new to the optimization process, however, you might want to stick with the optimization tools that I recommend in this and the following sections.

The following sections explain what optimization is, help you choose the right optimization program for your needs, and offer tips for optimizing and slicing graphics.

Understanding optimization

Optimization is a process whereby the software program applies an adjustable compression method to the digital information in an image to assist you in producing an output graphic in the smallest possible file size with the best possible quality. In other words, to be suitable for the web, a graphic must be put through a compression process that takes the original image data and condenses it in such a way that the file size gets reduced to a point where the image quality is still acceptable. The smaller the file size, the faster the image can be transmitted over the Internet and displayed on a web page. Even when the source file is already set to 72 ppi, the graphic must still be optimized and saved in an acceptable web format.

In the simplest terms, optimization means reducing file size while trying to retain quality. During the optimization process, you can control how much compression to apply to an image. Remember, the ppi of the file is a requirement of web graphics but a separate issue from the optimization process. Thus, when you create a new file at 72 ppi, that doesn't mean the file is already optimized. Rather, the file is at the correct size and resolution for optimization. If you need, therefore, to create a web graphic from a high-resolution image, you must first reduce the resolution of the file to 72 ppi and then check the pixel dimensions to ensure that the size of the graphic is suitable before you optimize the graphic.

Choosing an optimization program

The following overview of the optimization tools and programs available can help you decide which one will work best for your needs:

✓ **Save for Web in Photoshop and Illustrator:** Accessible from the File menu, the Save for Web optimization command (formerly called Save for Web & Devices), which has been incorporated into Photoshop and Illustrator since Adobe CS3, launches a dialog box, shown in Figure 3-4. It has 2-Up and 4-Up panel tabs for comparing optimization settings before selecting one, a toolbox, a preview pop-up menu, and a Preview in Browser button, and it allows you to select individual slices to apply different optimization settings. The dialog also offers several graphic output options, including saving optimized graphics along with a tables-based or CSS and layers-based HTML page.

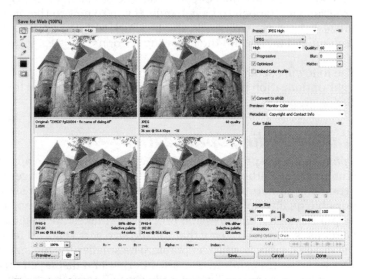

Figure 3-4: Optimize web graphics directly within Photoshop and Illustrator in the Save for Web dialog box.

✓ **Fireworks:** With Fireworks, you can design, edit, and optimize graphics all in one application by using a variety of tools similar to those found in Photoshop and ImageReady. Fireworks graphics, which are created and saved in the PNG format, can be sliced, optimized, and exported. Fireworks even has a preview tool that shows any cross-platform differences in color display. Fireworks users can create graphics for JavaScript rollover buttons, pop-up menus, and other interactive features that Fireworks can generate with the optimized files. Output includes HTML, images only, or both. Even better, Fireworks integrates seamlessly with Adobe Dreamweaver for easy round-trip editing.

✓ **ImageReady:** Formerly available as a standalone software package or as a freebie bundled with the sale of Photoshop or the Adobe CS Suite up until the release of Adobe CS3, ImageReady has an interface nearly identical to Photoshop. This software allows the creation of simple rollover graphics and GIF animations, has a special 4-Up panel for comparing optimization settings before selecting one, and offers several graphic output options, including saving optimized graphics along with a tables-based HTML page that includes prewritten JavaScript code for any rollover graphics you may have created.

✔ **Other optimization tools:** Several other less expensive and free web optimization tools are available, so feel free to use whichever ones you think will produce the best results, given your budget. For example, you might enjoy using the free GIMP (GNU Image Manipulation Program; www.gimp.org), which also doubles as a full graphics program, or the free Image Optimizer (www.imageoptimizer.net), Resizr (www.resizr.com), and RIOT (http://luci.criosweb.ro/riot). Other programs you may look into using include Corel software (www.corel.com), Xara's Photo & Graphic Designer (www.xara.com), and NetStudio's Easy Web Graphics (www.netstudio.com).

Optimizing using Save for Web

Illustrator and Photoshop users can quickly and easily optimize graphics for the web using the built-in Save for Web dialog box, accessible through the File menu.

In the following set of instructions, you see how easy it is to use Adobe's Save for Web tool to optimize and save your web graphics. Follow these steps to optimize an image:

1. **Create your web graphic in Illustrator or Photoshop, taking care to set the document resolution to 72 ppi, the color mode to RGB 8-bit, and (when applicable) the background to transparent or white.**

2. **To optimize and save a file for the web, choose File⇨Save for Web.**

   The Save for Web dialog box opens. (Refer to Figure 3-4.)

3. **Select either the 2-Up or 4-Up tab at the top of the dialog box to view your original image side by side with one or three versions of the image with different optimization settings.**

4. **Set your optimization preferences for each comparison version of your graphic on the right side of the panel.**

   You find detailed descriptions of all the optimization settings, including output options, in the sections "Choosing Web Optimization Settings" and "Optimization Output Options," later in this chapter.

5. **Click the Save button to save the graphic to the specified location on your computer.**

   The dialog box automatically closes as the graphic is saved.

You can also use the Save for Web dialog box to generate graphics for rollover buttons and GIF animation if you are familiar with configuring those features in Photoshop. Alternatively, you can do these same tasks quite easily in Fireworks and most of the optimization programs referenced earlier in this chapter.

If you want to improve your Photoshop skills, check out my training program, "Complete Training for Adobe Photoshop" from Class On Demand (www.classondemand.com), available in DVD and online streaming. To find out more about working with Fireworks, see *Adobe Fireworks Classroom in a Book* by Adobe Press.

As you discover in the next few sections, most optimization engines have settings that allow users to select the output file format and control the quality of the compression. But first, a word about slicing up graphics.

Slicing up graphics

When I teach Photoshop, Illustrator, and Dreamweaver classes, one of the most frequently asked questions I get from students is, "How do I take my website mock-up and turn it into optimized graphics?" And it's a great question.

For most small graphics, such as buttons, background images, or a single photograph, the optimization process is fairly straightforward. However, if you want to optimize several graphics within a single file at once, you will need to slice your graphics before you optimize.

Slicing and *optimizing* describe the process of dividing a large image into individual pieces, or *slices,* that are then compressed into GIF, JPEG, or PNG graphics and reassembled on the web page with HTML and CSS, much like the pieces of a puzzle. Of course, the fewer graphics you have on a page, the faster the page will load in a browser. The second best thing if you do have a lot of graphics is to carve them up into smaller pieces so that each piece can load more quickly than one or two larger ones. For example, if you had mocked up a sale graphic complete with photo, some text, and a rollover button, you could slice up the file in such a way that each of the individual pieces would become their own, separate graphics when the file is optimized.

When you digitally slice up your graphics, whether you're creating rollover buttons, banners, bullets, or other decorative elements, you are essentially dividing the larger rectangular whole into smaller rectangular pieces that can be easily reassembled on a web page, usually inside some kind of container tag like a table cell (<td>) or a layer (<div>). Images are often sliced to help create rollover buttons and decorative graphics.

Previewing your files in a browser

After you have optimized and saved a GIF, PNG, or JPG graphic for the web, you don't need to wait until it's on a web page to see what it will look like. To preview any of your optimized graphics in a browser window before you add them to a web page or upload them to a remote server, simply drag and drop the web graphic from its saved location (such as your desktop or inside a folder) to any open browser window, regardless of whether you have a live Internet connection. The image will appear at its full size in the browser.

Photoshop, Illustrator, Fireworks, and ImageReady all have a similar Slice tool that you can use to slice your larger mock-ups and graphic files into smaller pieces. The Slice tool's icon looks sort of like an Exacto blade, making it easy to identify from the other tools on the Tools panel. In Photoshop, the slice tool is located in the Crop tool's flyout menu.

To slice your graphics using the Adobe Slice tool in Photoshop, Illustrator, Fireworks, or ImageReady, use any of the following techniques:

✔ **Drag and release:** Select the Slice tool from the Tools panel and drag the cursor through the image to create a rectangular marquee-like selection. When you release your mouse button, the previously whole image is sliced into pieces where you made the incision marks with the Slice tool. For instance, if you were to drag the Slice tool to create a shape about 3 inches wide through the center of an image, when you released the tool, you'd end up with three slices, like the example shown in Figure 3-5.

Figure 3-5: Slice your image into pieces before you optimize your graphics.

✔ **Create slices from guides:** In Photoshop, Illustrator, or ImageReady, set your document to display rulers (choose View⇨Rulers) so that you can use guides as boundaries from which slices will be generated. Drag guides from the top and left rulers and release them into the file where you'd like the image to be sliced, as in the example shown in Figure 3-6. Place as many guides as needed into your file so that the application can use them to divide the larger image into smaller parts. Slice commands in various programs are as follows:

- *Illustrator:* Choose Select⇨Select All to select all the objects in your layout. Choose Object⇨Slice⇨Create from Guides.

- *Photoshop:* Select the Slice tool and click the Slices from Guides button on the Options bar.

- *ImageReady:* Choose Slices⇨Create Slices from Guides.

If, after creating slices from guides, you find that the application has created too many slices, or if the slices don't quite meet your needs, you can combine and further divide slices horizontally and vertically to your liking using the program's other Slice tool features.

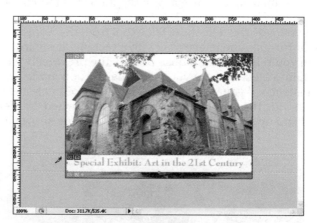

Figure 3-6: Drag guides into your layout to help you slice images with precision.

✔ **Create slices from guides:** In Fireworks, set down guides as you would in Photoshop, Illustrator, or ImageReady to divide the larger image into smaller pieces. Next, use the Slice tool to create the individual slices. As you drag with the Slice tool, each slice snaps to the Slice Guides.

To further illustrate how easy it is to slice up an image in either Photoshop or Illustrator, open your image and then follow these steps:

1. **With your file open in the document window, select the Slice tool from the Tools panel.**

2. **Drag a rectangular marquee shape around the first area in your file that you want to convert to a slice.**

   As you release the mouse button, the program adds a slice border and slice number to the slice area. You might also notice that the remaining parts of your layout suddenly have grayed-out *auto slices.* The auto slices aren't actual slices, but rather are a way for the application to anticipate how the rest of the file will be sliced up. You can use these auto slices as a guide to create actual slices. Slices are numbered automatically from top to bottom and from left to right.

   Photoshop users can use the Slices from Guides button to automatically create slices from the guides placed in the layout or create slices from the contents of individual layers by choosing Layer⇨New Layer-based Slice.

   To toggle on and off the visibility of slices on the artboard, do one of the following:

   - *In Illustrator:* Select View⇨Hide Slices or View⇨Show Slices.

   - *In Photoshop:* Select View⇨Show⇨Slices.

3. **Repeat Step 2 to finish slicing the rest of your graphic, like the example shown in Figure 3-7.**

   You can also slice your image in any of the following ways:

   - Select one or more objects in your layout and choose Object⇨ Slice⇨Create from Selection.

   - Select one or more objects in your layout and choose Object⇨ Slice⇨Make.

   - Let Illustrator create slices based on the document guides by choosing Object⇨Slice⇨Create from Guides.

4. **(Optional) Select an output option, such as Image, No Image, or HTML Text (Illustrator only).**

   You can program image slices before optimization to support a variety of output options:

   - *In Illustrator:* You can set slices to Image, No Image, or HTML Text by choosing Object⇨Slice⇨Slice Options.

   - *In Photoshop:* You can set slices to Image or No Image by accessing the Slice Options dialog box. To open this dialog box, click the Set Options for Current Slice button on the Options bar, or right-click on the slice and choose Edit Slice Options.

Book II
Chapter 3

Slicing and Optimizing Web Graphics

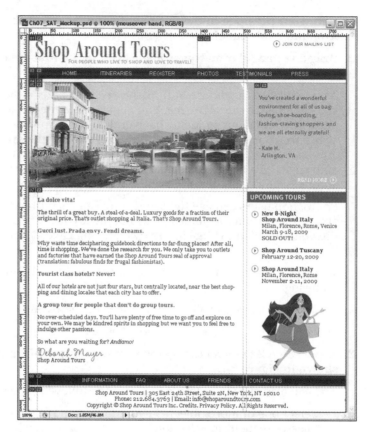

Figure 3-7: To optimize properly, slices should carve up the entire area of your layout.

Here's the lowdown on the output options:

- *Image:* Slices with this setting are optimized as regular web graphics. To assist with coding in CSS after the graphic has been optimized, enter a Name or ID for each slice, and if needed, set the URL of the HTML page that the graphic will link to when clicked. Linked slices should also include the Target for the URL, which can be set to _self so that the linked URL page opens in the same browser window. If desired, enter a short message that will appear in the browser's status bar when a cursor is positioned over the graphic. Finally, add Alt text to identify the slice with a word or two; the words entered here are useful as text that can be read by a screen reader for visitors who are visually impaired. To set the background color of the slice, select one of the options from the Background type drop-down menu at the bottom of the dialog box.

- *No Image:* A slice with this setting does not optimize any graphics within the slice but instead sets the background color of the slice dimensions to match the background color specified, or when no background color is set, the slice remains blank. To add placeholder text to the slice area in the output HTML file, select the Text Is HTML check box if applicable and type your text into the Text Displayed in Cell field. Take care to only enter a few words that do not exceed the dimensions of the slice. If desired, apply any of the other settings available.

- *HTML Text (Illustrator only):* This option only becomes active if text is turned into a slice using the Object⇨Slice⇨Make command. When activated, Illustrator converts the text and any of its basic formatting into HTML code during optimization.

5. **(Optional) To adjust the borders of any of the slices, you must select all the slices that are touching to make the adjustments without breaking the order of the slices.**

   To shift the slice borders, select the Slice Selection tool (Illustrator) or the Slice Select tool (Photoshop), click once on the inside of the first slice that needs to be adjusted, and then Shift+click to add any additional slices as needed to the selection. Next, by placing your cursor above the slice boundaries, your cursor temporarily turns into a double-sided adjustment arrow that you can click and drag to move the slice boundaries to a new position. Repeat this select-and-drag process until the slice boundaries are in the desired position.

6. **(Optional) If you want to combine, divide, duplicate, move, resize, align, distribute, release, delete, or lock selected slices, right-click (Windows) or ⌘+click (Mac) a slice to choose an option from the context menu and/or click any of the slice-specific buttons on the Control panel (Illustrator) or Options bar (Photoshop).**

7. **After you finish slicing your graphic, you can optimize and output your file in the appropriate file format by choosing File⇨Save for Web.**

Selecting the Right Web Format

You can choose from three different file formats — GIF, JPEG, and PNG — when optimizing graphics for the web. Each has different strengths and weaknesses, as described in Table 3-2, making it quite easy for you to identify which format will work best for your individual web graphics.

Table 3-2		Graphics File Formats		
Format	*Is Best For*	*Maximum Colors*	*Transparency and Animation*	*Compression*
GIF	Images with large, flat areas of color, and animated GIFs	256 colors (8-bit) and grayscale (8-bit)	Supports both animation and background transparency	Lossless LZW compression
JPEG	Photographs and graphics with lots of color and gradient blends	Millions of colors (24-bit) and grayscale (8-bit)	No support for animation or transparency	Lossy compression
PNG	Images with large, flat areas of color; recommended replacement for GIFs by the W3C	PNG-8: Maximum of 256 colors (8-bit) and grayscale (8-bit) PNG-24: millions of colors (48-bit)	Supports background transparency but not animation	Lossless LZW compression

During the early years of the Internet, web browsers supported only the GIF (Graphics Interchange Format) and JPEG (Joint Photographic Experts Group) formats. However, it has only been since about 2006 that the PNG (Portable Network Graphic) file format increased in popularity enough to be supported by most new browsers. Today, all the popular browsers provide excellent support for GIF, JPG, and PNG files. The only older browser still occasionally in use that doesn't is Internet Explorer 6 (IE6), which displays the transparent areas in PNG files as blue instead of clear.

All three of these web file formats use different compression algorithms to crunch data and produce smaller graphic files. The format you select for your images ultimately determines how the final optimized graphic looks. Referring again to Table 3-2, it's quite easy to grasp which format you should use for each graphic you optimize. Choose JPEG for all your photographic images, and use the GIF or PNG-8 format for images that contain large, flat areas of no more than 256 colors. The PNG-24 format, which all modern browsers support, is also wonderful because it supports background transparency, like the GIF format, and displays millions of colors, like the JPEG format; however, it still tends to produce large files, so keep that in mind when using this format.

Web files that include additional information data like video, sound, or other multimedia must be compressed by other software applications for transmission over the web. File formats for those types of web objects include PDF, MP3, MPEG, Flash SWF, and Shockwave.

Saving your graphics in the correct web file format is easy if you follow a few basic rules that will ultimately determine the final image's quality and file size. Take a look at Figure 3-8. The simplest way to decide which format to optimize it in should be based on the contents of the image:

✔ If the image is a photo or has a lot of gradient blends in it, choose JPEG.

✔ If the image has large, flat areas of color or text, or contains areas of transparency, choose GIF or PNG.

Figure 3-8: Optimize your web graphics with photographs and gradients as JPEG (top) and all others as GIF or PNG (bottom).

To better evaluate the benefits of each format and help you choose the right format for your graphics, here is a bit more information:

✔ **GIF (Graphic Interchange Format):** This format, created by the folks at CompuServe, is officially pronounced *jif*, like the peanut butter brand, but it's more commonly pronounced *giff*, with a hard *g*, as in *get*. The GIF format supports a maximum palette of 256 colors and is great for images with text and large, flat areas of color.

Using a special LZW (Lempel-Ziv-Welch) lossless compression algorithm to shrink the file without removing detail, the GIF format can reduce file size up to about 60 percent of the original size during optimization. Colors in a GIF image that aren't part of the 256-color palette can be *dithered* (two colors alternated in a grid pattern) to approximate the missing colors. For more on dithering, see the "GIF and PNG-8 optimization" section, later in this chapter.

GIFs support transparency, which means that parts of the image can be fully opaque (solid) while other parts are fully transparent, allowing you to see through to any objects or colors behind the image when placed on a web page.

GIFs also support animation through a rather crude optimization technique that saves multiple images to separate frames inside a single GIF file. To create a simple GIF animation, place each of the different images in the animation onto layers inside any graphics program that supports the creation of GIF animation, such as Photoshop or Fireworks. You can then use the Make Frames from Layers command on the Timeline panel (formerly the Animation panel) options menu to create a frame-based animation sequence, as illustrated in Figure 3-9. Optimize the file as you would a regular GIF file. When viewed in a browser window, each frame of the animated GIF file plays one after the next (either with or without looping at the end), giving the illusion of a little movie.

Figure 3-9: Create simple GIF animations from multiple layers in your file.

✔ **JPG (Joint Photographic Experts Group):** Choose the JPG/JPEG format, pronounced *jay-peg,* for any image that includes a photograph or a significant area of gradient color. The JPEG format, which always uses the `.jpg` file extension, supports a palette with millions of colors and can help create photographic images for the web with smaller file sizes than a GIF or PNG file would, because these other formats would resort to dithering to create any colors beyond the 256-color palette, thereby increasing the file size. JPEGs use a compression method called *lossy,* whereby some digital information in the image is removed and becomes irretrievable (lost) after the compression.

As good as they are for photos and gradients, JPEGs do not support transparency or animation. Should you need either or both of these features, you must save the file as a GIF image (for animation and/or transparency) or PNG image (for transparency only) and potentially suffer some loss of image quality in lieu of the gain of transparency and/or animation.

✔ **PNG (Portable Network Graphics):** This file format, pronounced *ping,* was created as a royalty-free raster alternative to GIFs, TIFFs, and occasionally JPEGs, combining the best features of compression algorithms, such as *lossless* compression and support for millions of colors and transparency. You find two flavors of PNG files:

- *PNG-8:* Because it also supports a maximum of 256 colors and grayscale images, the PNG-8 format has been recommended as a replacement for the GIF format by the World Wide Web Consortium (W3C). Most modern web browsers (Chrome, Firefox, Opera, IE7+, and Safari) support this format without issue; however, earlier browsers may not.

- *PNG-24:* The PNG-24 format, by contrast, is superior to the PNG-8 because it supports background or alpha transparency and millions of colors (but not animation), and this format should be supported by the newest browsers (Chrome, Firefox, Opera, IE8+, and Safari).

Nonetheless, before you go saving all your files as PNG-8 and PNG-24, be sure to test the images on a sample web page in all your favorite browsers on both the Mac and PC to ensure that your files will be properly supported.

Probably the best way to really understand how web graphics will look when compressed by one format or another is to see what each compression algorithm does to the image during the compression process. Figure 3-10 shows what happens to a graphic with flat color and text when saved as a GIF, JPG, and PNG. Figure 3-11 shows what happens to a photographic image when saved in the same three formats.

Figure 3-10: Save images with transparency and with large, flat areas of color and text as a GIF or PNG for best results.

Figure 3-11: Photographic images and files that contain gradients are best saved as JPGs.

As you can see, the GIF format is the better choice for the graphic with flat areas of color because JPGs and PNGs tend to pixelate the flat areas, especially around the edges of letter shapes. Likewise, JPG is the better choice for the photograph because it handles gradients and shadow areas better than GIF and PNG formats, which tend to display those areas as bands of color rather than a single smooth transition of color. PNGs are good replacements for many GIF files, but if you decide to use them, pay attention to file size and be sure to test how they display in all the browsers your target audience will be likely to use. In most cases, PNGs provide a higher-quality compression than GIFs with a lower file size. However, transparency can often be better on the GIF and PNG-24 than on the PNG-8. When in doubt, try them both and use the format that looks best.

Choosing Web Optimization Settings

Most web image optimization programs allow you to either choose from a preset list of default optimization settings or customize your own settings to create the optimized graphics to your specifications. The particular settings you choose determine several things about the output graphics, including the file format, size, number of colors, and quality.

Your main goal when optimizing graphics is to create the best-quality image with the smallest possible file size. If you reduce the file size too much, the quality might suffer, and if you make the quality high so that the image is sharp, the file size might be too large. With every image, a balancing point of good quality and decent file size exists, and you'll soon figure out which settings work best for all your different kinds of graphics.

As you're discovering which format and settings are best, take advantage of your Photoshop or Illustrator optimization tool's 4-Up panel, which allows you to compare three different optimization configurations side by side so that you can easily select the one with the optimization settings that create the best-quality image at the smallest possible file size.

For best results with your image optimization, try using the following guidelines:

- Try to make your images as small as possible. Each image should be in the 10K or less range, though for larger graphics and photos, up to 30K should be fine.

- Add up the file sizes of all the images on your page. For quick display in a browser, the display time for an entire web page should not exceed 8 seconds even on an old, slow Internet connection such as one using a 56K modem. Ideally, each page should have no more than approximately 40K in images.

The following sections help you decide which format to choose and how to configure that format's settings so that you get the best possible optimized file every time.

GIF and PNG-8 optimization

The Save for Web dialog box in Photoshop and Illustrator has a special optimization panel that allows you to customize the settings for your web graphics prior to optimization. If you plan to use the ImageReady program as a standalone application, configure the optimization settings through the program's Optimize panel. Fireworks users can apply optimization settings through the Optimize panel and export directly or with the help of the Export Wizard. When using any other web graphic optimization tools, feel free to refer to the following list when choosing your optimization settings.

GIF and PNG-8 graphics share the following optimization settings:

Book II
Chapter 3

Slicing and
Optimizing Web
Graphics

- ✔ **Color Reduction Algorithm:** The color algorithm establishes how the colors in the GIF or PNG file will be compressed. The algorithm is calculated by the color reduction type and the number of colors selected in the Colors field. You find four general algorithms:

  - *Adaptive:* Produces a color palette in the image by sampling colors from the image itself. By reducing the number of colors in the palette, the reduction algorithm produces a smaller file.

  - *Selective:* Produces a color palette like the Perceptual palette while preserving any web-safe colors in the image and using only colors found in the graphic. This is the default option for GIF compression and tends to produce the most realistic color in the final output graphic.

  - *Perceptual:* Produces a color palette that favors colors that the human eye is sensitive to.

  - *Restrictive (Web):* Produces a color palette in your image that favors the 216 colors in the web-safe palette and prevents colors in the image from being dithered. This means your graphic's colors will be automatically converted to web-safe colors when choosing this algorithm. You can, however, adjust the percentage of colors that Web Snap in an adjacent slider. Unused colors are discarded from the palette.

- ✔ **Lossy (GIF only):** This compression format used for GIF files removes image data, reducing the file size by as much as 60 percent. The larger the lossy number, the more data is removed. Typical lossy settings range between 0 and 10 with little noticeable image degradation. You cannot, however, adjust the lossy feature with interlaced GIFs or when the Pattern or Noise Dither options are selected.

- ✔ **Colors:** Use this setting to adjust the total number of colors that appear in the image, as indicated in the corresponding Color Table at the bottom of the panel. The maximum number of colors in a GIF or PNG-8 image is 256, and the minimum is 2 (black and white). Web-safe colors, when detected, appear in the Color Table with a tiny white diamond in the center of the color square; non-web-safe colors appear as solid color squares.

Internet connection speeds

Even though well over half of all users on the Internet have cable, DSL, T1, or some kind of fiber optic access, believe it or not, some (roughly 10 percent or less, according to a 2008 Pew Internet and American Life Project study) are still visiting web pages with 28.8K and 56K dialup modems, which means pages for these visitors download at only about 4K per second. That's r-e-a-l-l-y slow. For visitors to see the graphics on a web page, all the images must be transferred to the temporary cache area of the visitor's computer. For instance, a 30K file takes about 7 seconds to load on a computer with a 56K modem. For a lot of visitors — especially the ones using older equipment with slower connection speeds — if the page takes longer than 8–10 seconds to load, the visitor might lose patience and leave the site before even seeing it! Unless you know for a fact that your target audience has a high-speed Internet connection, try your hardest to ensure that your pages (including HTML, images, CSS, JavaScript, jQuery, and any other multimedia plug-ins or page enhancements) load within the 8–10 second time frame.

✔ **Dither:** Dithering is a color-simulation system whereby two colors are alternated in a checkered or random noisy pattern that tricks the eye into seeing a new solid color based on the combination of the two colors used. A dithered green color, for example, could be created by dithering blue and yellow pixels. This effect, while at times improving the image quality, does add to the overall file size.

Dithering can be good for images with flat areas of color and for images containing gradient colors that need to be saved in GIF format, because without it, the colors in the gradient tend to band out into stripes of color. This banding effect also occurs when viewing a web page on a monitor with a resolution set to 256 colors.

The Dither setting has four different options:

- *No Dither:* No dither is applied to the image.

- *Diffusion:* A diffusion dither applies a more random dither pattern than the Pattern dither option. You can adjust the percentage of the dither in the Amount field on the Optimize panel to control the amount of dithering in the image. The larger the percentage, the more dithered colors are in the resulting image.

- *Pattern:* A Pattern dither creates dithered colors in a square-ish pattern that might be more noticeable to the eye than a Diffusion or Noise dither. You can control the amount of dither by adjusting the dither percentage.

- *Noise:* A Noise dither uses a more random pattern for the dither than Diffusion or Pattern. Set the dither percentage.

✓ **Transparency:** Both the GIF and PNG formats allow you to save images that contain transparent pixels. The transparent parts of the image appear as see-through when placed on a web page, and any underlying colors on the page (such as the page background color, a table, or a DIV layer) show through those areas. The amount of transparency, on a scale of 0 to 100 percent, determines how many of the pixels will be transparent, semitransparent, or opaque. The transparency setting has the following four options:

- *No Transparency:* In images that contain transparency, any transparent and semitransparent pixels appear as opaque or semi-opaque against the color selected in the Matte color field (see the following Matte description). For example, if the Matte color field is set to black, the transparent and semitransparent pixels in the image appear as if they are sitting on a black background.

- *Diffusion:* This option controls the dithering pattern of semitransparent pixels along the edge of the transparent area(s) in the graphic. When selected, a random dither pattern is applied to semitransparent pixels.

- *Pattern:* With this option, semitransparent pixels along the edge of the transparent area(s) in the graphic are dithered with the selected matte color in a square-like pattern.

- *Noise:* This option creates a more random dithering pattern than Pattern and Diffusion by blending semitransparent pixels with the selected matte color in an irregular, almost haphazard pattern.

✓ **Matte:** If you know what color the image with transparency will be sitting on in a web page, select a matching matte color to ensure that semitransparent pixels in the image blend smoothly with the background color. For example, if you know the background color of a page is a particular red with the hexadecimal value of #cc3333, set the matte color for your image with transparency to the same hexadecimal value.

✓ **Interlaced:** Selecting this option causes the image to be downloaded in the visitor's browser in multiple passes, giving the viewer something to see as the image gets drawn in the browser window. This option is good for larger images but not so necessary for individual images smaller than 10K.

✓ **Web Snap:** The percentage number you select for Web Snap determines the number of colors in the color table that snap to the web-safe palette. The higher the number, the more the colors in the resulting optimized image will be forced to snap to colors in the web-safe palette. Although the web-safe palette is no longer a major concern for designers, visitors with older monitors who view web pages that include non–web-safe color will likely see a big color shift.

PNG-24 optimization

The PNG-24 setting only has three options to configure:

- ✓ **Transparency:** When the transparency option is selected, the image is optimized with transparent parts. When the transparency option is deselected, any transparent areas in the image are filled with the specified matte color.

- ✓ **Matte:** Choose the default white matte or specify another color to ensure that semitransparent pixels in the image are evenly filled in.

- ✓ **Interlaced:** Select this option for larger files to make the file automatically download in the visitor's browser in multiple passes, giving the viewer something to see as the image gets drawn in the browser window.

JPG optimization

The JPG file format has many more different settings than the GIF and PNG formats. The following is an overview of the different JPG optimization settings:

- ✓ **Optimized:** (Optional) Select this setting to enhance the compression of the resulting image. Though this option may slightly reduce the image file size, optimized graphics might not display well, or at all, in some older browsers.

- ✓ **Quality:** The Quality slider controls the amount of compression applied to the resulting optimized image. Choose from five preset quality options (Low, Medium, High, Very High, and Maximum) from a drop-down list, or use the Quality slider to manually select the quality on a scale from 0 to 100 percent. The higher the percentage, the better the image quality and the larger the file size. To find the best quality with the smallest file size, compare three different qualities using the optimization tool's 4-Up panel.

- ✓ **Blur:** Images that use the lower-quality compression settings begin to produce jagged areas in the image. These *jaggies* are especially noticeable around the edges of contrasting colors, on flat areas of color, and along the edges of text. Jaggies can be somewhat reduced by applying a slight blur to the image, thereby reducing the file size. However, the more blur you add, the less crisp the resulting image. If you do choose to apply a blur to your file, keep the setting below 0.5 for best results.

- ✓ **Matte:** When the original image has any areas that are blank (such as a transparent background layer), those pixels will be filled with the opaque color selected in the Matte field. If you can, try to match the matte color to the background color the image will be placed on top of on the web page. For example, if the image will sit in a table cell with a red background with a hex value of #bf3b3b, set the matte color to #bf3b3b before optimization.

✔ **Progressive:** Like the interlaced option for GIFs and PNGs, the progressive setting creates JPG images that display in multiple passes as the image downloads by displaying a low-resolution version of the file until the high-resolution version is finished downloading on the visitor's computer. Some older browsers might not support this feature, so be sure to test at least one progressive image in your target browsers on both Mac and PC before optimizing all your graphics with this setting.

✔ **ICC Profile:** The ICC profile describes information about the graphic's RGB or CMYK color settings so that the color displays as intended. Select this option to preserve the image's ICC profile and have it embedded in the image to assist some browsers with color correction of the image.

Optimization Output Options

Whether you're optimizing a single graphic file or a fully sliced mock-up, you'll probably encounter a few of the same choices when it comes time to save your optimized files. For example, when using the Save for Web dialog box in Photoshop or Illustrator, you begin the optimization process by configuring the options for your graphic, whether it's a JPG, GIF, or PNG file. Then, to create the actual optimized graphic, you need to click the Save button and make a few output decisions regarding the file's extension, selected slices, output location, and output file types. For example, to automatically generate an HTML file and have all your sliced and optimized graphics placed into an images folder on your Desktop, choose the following Output settings:

✔ **Save As:** `test.html`

✔ **Location:** Desktop

✔ **Format:** HTML and Images

✔ **Settings:** Default Settings

✔ **Slices:** All Slices under Slices

The HTML file and images folder that the Save for Web dialog box outputs can be the starting point for your web-building process when you're ready to build your first web page, though you can certainly use your own code if you prefer. If you do intend to use the HTML code from this dialog box, rather than send the optimized files to your desktop, send them to the location on your computer where you'd like to save all the files for that specific web project.

To keep your files organized, you might want to use some kind of naming convention, such as always calling your web project folders `COMPANY_HTML` so that they are easy to identify from other files and folders. In fact, if you organize your client projects into individual folders, you can keep better track of all your projects and their attending documents. Consider, for example, keeping your files organized by using the method shown in Figure 3-12. Feel free to use this same naming and organization convention if you think it will help you keep track of your projects.

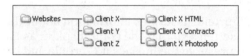

Figure 3-12: Using a uniform naming and filing convention.

Because each optimization program has similar, though possibly slightly different, options regarding how and where the files will be optimized and output, use the following steps (which are roughly the same for Photoshop, Illustrator, and ImageReady) as general guidelines:

1. **Launch your program's Save for Web optimization dialog box and click the Save button to access the optimization output options in the Save Optimized As dialog box, shown in Figure 3-13.**

2. **In the Save In drop-down list, choose a location on your local computer or network where the optimized file will be saved.**

   This can be on your desktop or in a folder somewhere else on your computer, such as a folder for this particular web project.

3. **In the File Name field, enter the name of the graphic file.**

   This filename will be used to save the graphic or graphic with HTML with the selected file type.

   Filenames can be anything you like as long as they use the proper file extension such as `.gif`, `.png`, `.jpg`, or `.html` (for example, `contact.png` or `about.html`).

4. **In the Save as Type field, choose one of the following options:**

   • *HTML and Images:* Saves the image or selected slices as optimized graphics in your selected file format, along with a tables-based or CSS/Layers-based HTML file that includes the optimized graphics you are about to optimize inside a folder called Images.

   • *Images Only:* Saves just the image or selected slices as optimized graphics in your selected file format into a folder called Images.

   • *HTML Only:* Saves just an HTML file formatted with a table to support the graphics in your document.

Figure 3-13: Choose a file type and format for your optimized graphic output.

5. **From the Settings drop-down list, choose Default Settings.**

   These settings determine the various output settings, such as placing all of the optimized graphics into a folder called images. If desired, you can customize these settings by selecting one of the other options from the drop-down list (Custom, Background Image, XHTML, or Other).

6. **For multisliced images, choose an option from the Slices drop-down list.**

   Your options are All Slices, All User Slices, or Selected Slices. If you're unsure which option to select, choose All Slices. That way, you get a folder full of optimized images based on all the slices in your layout.

7. **Click the Save button to complete the optimization output process.**

   Your optimized files are saved to your computer in the location specified in the Save In location.

After the Save Optimized As and Save for Web dialog boxes close, you can preview your graphics in a browser window. To view the HTML page that contains the optimized graphics, double-click the HTML file or drag and drop the file into any open browser window. To preview any individual optimized graphic, drag and drop the file into any open browser window.

Book III
Building Websites

The 5th Wave — By Rich Tennant

"Ooo — wait! That's perfect for the clinic's home page. Just stretch it out a little further...little more..."

*W*hen it's time to build your site, you'll delve into the world of HTML, CSS, and JavaScript, and possibly also XHTML, HTML5, CSS3, jQuery, and more. Using your preferred HTML editor, you'll be creating all the individual pages of your site from the optimized graphics you created from your mock-up.

Here you find chapters about adding content to your pages, including text, images, hyperlinks, layers, tables, lists, and media files. You also discover a host of information about working with Cascading Style Sheets to style and position your content in the most user-friendly, accessible, standards-compliant manner. This minibook is rounded out by additional chapters on creating layers-based layouts, working with navigation systems, designing web forms, making your site interactive with JavaScript and jQuery, and discovering how to work efficiently with templates and Server-Side Includes.

Chapter 1: Adding Text, Images, and Links

In This Chapter

✔ **Understanding HTML basics**

✔ **Working with semantic markup**

✔ **Inserting text and graphics**

✔ **Hyperlinking text and graphics to other pages**

✔ **Labeling objects in preparation for using CSS, jQuery, and JavaScript**

✔ **Making page content accessible with HTML**

At this point in the design process, you've already discovered a little bit about HTML coding, syntax, and structure. To complement that knowledge, you've also made several important decisions about the look and feel of your design and have hopefully already mocked up the home page in your preferred graphics software program and presented your design to your web client for review and approval. In this chapter, you find out how to put all those pieces together into a single HTML document.

To start, you find out about setting up a basic, bare-bones HTML page, which you can use for any web project. After that, the specifics of your particular website come into play. The first couple of times you put a website together can certainly feel daunting, to say the least. That feeling of building a website from scratch can be similar to the feeling a painter has when looking at a fresh blank canvas. Where should you begin? What should you do first? Although no perfect solution exists, try not to let the options overwhelm you. Instead, focus your energies on building that first page. After the first page is built, constructing the rest of the site should come relatively easily.

In addition to the basics, this chapter also covers using meta tags; adding content (such as text and graphics) to the body of the page; creating hyperlinks to other pages from text and graphics; marking up content and labeling objects properly in preparation for using CSS and applying jQuery and JavaScript; and improving page accessibility for all web visitors, both human and machine.

Setting Up Basic HTML

To ensure that your web pages display properly in a browser window, your HTML code must include several necessary components, each of which must be placed in the correct order. As you'll probably discover with a mistake, when the order is incorrect, whether a tag is misspelled, or whether any of the parts of the code are missing — such as a period (.) or slash (/) — the page will probably not display correctly (or at all) when viewed in different browsers. Even more annoyingly, some browsers might display the page fine, while in other browsers the page looks all crazy and crooked. In fact, the more you understand about building web pages, the quicker you'll discover that a single page can look very different in different browsers, even when all the HTML, CSS, and JavaScript code is perfectly written!

A good, well-structured web page has six core parts that should flow in the following order:

1. DOCTYPE
2. HTML tags
3. Head tags
4. Title tags
5. Meta tags
6. Body tags

As long as your web page includes all these parts in the proper order, the page will have a solid foundation upon which all of your other content can gently rest. Without them, your page may not display properly in a browser, nor communicate clearly to the person, browser, or device displaying the page, and perhaps worst of all, not provide the details necessary to help visitors find the site in a search engine. Because you clearly would want none of these problems, you need to follow a few simple rules to ensure that your pages are properly coded.

Adding the title, DOCTYPE, and metadata

As you find out in Book I, Chapter 4, a web page uses a simple structure whereby HTML tags are hierarchically nested between opening and closing <html> tags, and between those, all the code in the page falls between either the <head> or the <body> tags, as follows:

```
<html>
<head>
</head>
<body>
</body>
</html>
```

In addition to these, which I call the "bones" of a web page, you also need to include the page title, the DOCTYPE, and the meta tags for your page in the correct location to be considered properly structured.

Adding a page title

The page title is the code that allows you to name and display a title for the page in the browser's title bar. You can use up to about 70 characters, including spaces and punctuation, to describe the contents of the page. Designers often include the name of the site along with the name of the page and a few keywords that might help visitors find the page, such as *"Jet-Stream" Showerhead(r) - Frequently Asked Questions about Low-Flow, High-Quality, Water-Saving Showerheads.*

You may (and should!) use unique, descriptive page titles for every page on your website because the title helps visitors find your site when using a search engine. When creating the page titles, use a short, descriptive phrase that reads well, like the example shown in Figure 1-1, and keep the character count to about 70 characters or less; otherwise, the title may be truncated (cut off) in the title bar of the browser.

Adding a DOCTYPE

A DOCTYPE, also often referred to as a Document Type Definition (DTD) and sometimes called a Document Type Declaration (again, DTD), is a set of instructions to a web browser or device that identifies the type of code that the page was written in, such as HTML, HTML5, XHTML, or Frames. More importantly, a DOCTYPE informs the browser how the document should be interpreted as an application of the XML programming language.

Title for the web page

Figure 1-1: For best SEO results, each page on your site should have its own unique page title.

The DOCTYPE generally consists of two parts:

✔ The first part defines (to the browser) the type of code that is used on the page, such as HTML, HTML5, or XHTML.

✔ The second part displays the URL of a text file on the W3C website (`www.w3.org`) that further describes how the DTD is used. The only current exception to this is the HTML5 DTD, which uses the abbreviation html instead of a URL.

You can choose from seven different DOCTYPES, depending on whether you're creating an HTML, HTML5, or XHTML document: HTML 4.01 Transitional, HTML 4.01 Strict, HTML5, XHTML 1.0 Transitional, XHTML 1.0 Strict, XHTML 1.1, or XHTML Mobile 1.0.

If you're unsure of which DTD to use, select 4.01 Transitional when writing HTML code, pick HTML5 for making HTML5 pages, and choose XHTML 1.0 Transitional when writing XHTML code because these are the three most forgiving and flexible DTDs of the bunch. For detailed explanations about all the HTML, HTML5, and XHTML DOCTYPES, turn to Book IV, Chapter 1.

When using a visual editor, such as Dreamweaver or an HTML code editor like BBEdit, those programs should automatically allow you to select which DOCTYPE DTD to include in the page, such as HTML 4.01 Transitional, HTML5, or XHTML 1.0 Transitional, and then insert what I call the *bones* of a web page into the code each time you create a new HTML document.

Here's an example of the HTML bones you'd see if you created a new HTML document in Dreamweaver CS6 with the HTML 4.01 Transitional DTD:

```
<!DOCTYPE HTML PUBLIC "-//W3C//DTD HTML 4.01 Transitional//
    EN" "http://www.w3.org/TR/html4/loose.dtd">
<html>
<head>
<meta http-equiv="Content-Type" content="text/html;
    charset=utf-8" />
<title>Untitled Document</title>
</head>
<body>
</body>
</html>
```

By contrast, here are the bones for an HTML5 document:

```
<!doctype html>
<html>
<head>
<meta charset="utf-8" />
<title>Untitled Document</title>
</head>
<body>
</body>
</html>
```

As part of the bones, Dreamweaver also drops the `Content-Type` or `Charset` meta tag into the page, which identifies the type of characters being used in the code. That tag can reside in the code either above or below the `<title>` tags, as long as it sits somewhere between the opening and closing `<head>` tags.

Adding metadata

Your meta tags are the special lines of HTML code that you add to your web page between the opening and closing `<head>` tags to communicate important SEO information about the site to web browsers and search engines.

What's great about meta tags is that they're invisible to site visitors and do not appear in the browser window. The information you put in the various meta tags placed in your page can help with the indexing of a single page or an entire website in a search engine's database, as well as provide informative data, comments, and contact information to any visitors clever enough to view the page's source code.

To function properly, the meta tags themselves must be placed in the code somewhere between the opening and closing `<head>` tags of your page. More often than not, meta tags are inserted in the code directly after the closing `</title>` tag and before the closing `</head>` tag, like the example that follows. When using a visual or code editor, however, you may at times see the `Content-Type` meta tag automatically placed above the `<title>` tag, which is fine too:

```
<head>
<meta http-equiv="Content-Type" content="text/html; charset=utf-8">
<title>Snorkeling and Diving Adventures of Southern Florida</title>
<meta name="Keywords" content="Snorkeling, scuba diving, scuba divers,
    snorkelers, glass bottom boats">
<meta name="Description" content="Plan your aquatic vacation with SDASF. We
    offer snorkeling and diving adventures throughout southern Florida. Private
    charters and passenger vessels available.">
</head>
```

To generate a comprehensive set of meta tags for your website online, use the free meta tag generator at `www.metataggenerator.org`.

The two most important meta tags (besides unique page titles) to include on every page to improve search engine indexing and ranking are `Description` and `Keywords`, as shown in the preceding example code:

✔ `Keywords`: Although the `Keywords` meta tag is no longer read by Google or most other search engines, the tag is still worth including in your code because it provides at least one search engine — Yahoo!— with keywords to help visitors find your site. In addition, you can use this meta tag to list obscure keywords or misspellings of commonly misspelled industry-specific terms. That said, you should only use the seven most important keywords, listed in order of relevance; any more than seven keywords will likely be ignored.

✔ `Description`: By contrast, the `Description` meta tag can use a maximum of 250 characters, including spaces and punctuation, to clearly describe what visitors can expect to find on the website. What's more, `Description` actually appears in the search engine results when the URL is listed after a visitor performs a keyword or key phrase search in his or her favorite search engine. That search will likely include a list of words, possibly separated by commas, that visitors might use to find the website's products or services.

Besides the `Description` and `Keywords` meta tags, you can add several other optional meta tags to your pages for communicating vital information to visitors and search engine robots and spiders:

✔ `robots`: This is probably the third most important meta tag you can add to your pages. The robots meta tag tells search engine spiders/ robots whether the site should be indexed and whether links on pages should be followed when indexing is allowed. The default option is `"index,follow"`, which both indexes the submitted URL and follows any hyperlinks to internal pages and external site links. You can customize the tag in any one of the following ways, depending on your preferences:

```
<meta name="robots" content="All">
<meta name="robots" content="index,follow">
<meta name="robots" content="noindex,follow">
<meta name="robots" content="index,nofollow">
<meta name="robots" content="noindex,nofollow">
```

Some search engines use proprietary meta tags and tag attributes (such as `"content="all"`) to help filter content for search engine results. For a list of Google specific robots tags, see `http://support.google.com/webmasters/bin/answer.py?hl=en&answer=79812`.

✔ `Content-Language`: This tag defines which written language is used for the content presented on the page, such as English, French, or German:

```
<meta http-equiv="Content-Language" content="en">
```

Get further information about language declarations from the W3C website: `www.w3.org/TR/i18n-html-tech-lang/#ri20050208.091505539`.

✔ `Content-Type`: This meta tag instructs browsers about the type of character encoding, or set of letters, being used on the web page, such as the A–Z alphabet or Chinese characters. Dreamweaver automatically includes this meta tag as part of the bones of a new HTML 4.01 Transitional web document:

```
<meta http-equiv="Content-Type" content="text/html;
    charset=iso-8859-1">
```

For HTML5 files, the content type is shortened to a simple character set tag:

```
<meta charset="utf-8">
```

To find out more about character encoding, visit the W3C website at `www.w3.org/International/questions/qa-html-encoding-declarations`.

✔ `refresh`: This meta tag instructs the browser to reload the page in the browser window at the specified number of seconds, such as 120 seconds for 2 minutes. Refreshing the page can be a useful tool for sites that provide up-to-the-minute data or sites that need to redirect visitors to a different URL. In the following example, the page would refresh after 30 seconds:

```
<meta http-equiv="refresh" content="30">
```

In recent years, this meta tag has sadly been misused by unethical web bandits, and some search engines have begun penalizing sites that use it. Therefore, if you'd like to use the `refresh` meta tag to redirect visitors to a new permanent web address, a *301 redirect* is a smarter solution.

For detailed instructions on creating a 301 redirect for your website, visit `www.webconfs.com/how-to-redirect-a-webpage.php`.

✔ revised: Displays the date the site was last revised:

```
<meta name="revised" content="Jenny Pfister, Jenny
    Pfister Design, 8/23/12">
```

Unless you use some kind of programming or scripting language to automatically update the date for you, this meta tag must be updated manually.

✔ **Other tags:** Create and use other meta tags, such as `Publisher`, `Copyright`, `Author`, and `Reply-to`, to provide information about the publisher and author of a web page:

```
<meta name="Publisher" content="Joann Coates Creative
    Inc. ">
<meta name="Copyright" content="Copyright 2010-2012,
    Joann Coates Creative Inc. All rights reserved. ">
<meta name="Author" content="Joann Coates Creative Inc.
    for www.joanncoates.com">
<meta name="Reply-to" content="info-at-joanncoates.
    com">
```

Figure 1-2 shows an example of how you might combine several of these meta tags onto your web page.

Figure 1-2: Meta tags help to identify site content to browsers for page indexing.

Coding pages by hand

If you are hand-coding your web pages, the easiest place to begin building your first page is at the very top. Follow these steps:

1. **In a blank text file in your preferred text or code editor, insert the desired HTML, HTML5, or XHTML DOCTYPE for your page.**

The DOCTYPE (DTD) needs to go at the very top of the code, above the opening <html> tag.

2. **Add the opening and closing <html> tags to your page if your editor hasn't done so already.**

When creating XHTML files with Dreamweaver, the program should automatically add the xmlns attribute with the opening <html> tag when it drops in the DTD, as shown in the following example. If you're hand-coding an XHTML page, therefore, be sure to also type that attribute.

```
<!DOCTYPE html PUBLIC "-//W3C//DTD XHTML 1.0
Transitional//EN" "http://www.w3.org/TR/xhtml1/DTD/xhtml1-
   transitional.dtd">
<html xmlns="http://www.w3.org/1999/xhtml">
</html>
```

When hand-coding an HTML5 page, the DTD is simpler:

```
<!doctype html>
<html>
</html>
```

3. **Enter the opening and closing <head> tags between the <html> tags.**

The head area is where information that won't appear in the browser window goes. This includes the page titles, CSS styles, JavaScript code, and links to external CSS, jQuery, and JavaScript files, as well as any meta tags you might want to add to your page to provide information about the site to search engine robots.

```
<!doctype html>
<html>
<head>
</head>
</html>
```

4. **Directly above the closing <head> tag, enter the content type or character set meta tag:**

For XHTML:

```
<!DOCTYPE html PUBLIC "-//W3C//DTD XHTML 1.0
Transitional//EN" "http://www.w3.org/TR/xhtml1/DTD/xhtml1-
   transitional.dtd">
<html xmlns="http://www.w3.org/1999/xhtml">
<head>
<meta http-equiv="Content-Type" content="text/html; charset=iso-8859-1">
</head>
</html>
```

For HTML5:

```
<!doctype html>
<html>
<head>
<meta charset="utf-8">
</head>
</html>
```

5. **Between the opening and closing `<head>` tags, enter opening and closing `<title>` tags, and between those, insert the text that will appear in the browser title bar.**

```
<!doctype html><html>
<head>
<meta charset="utf-8"><title>Snorkeling and Diving Adventures of Southern
    Florida</title>
</head>
</html>
```

6. **Beneath the `<title>` tags but before the closing `<head>` tag, add the `Description` and `Keywords` meta tags, as well as any other `<meta>` tags you would like the page to include.**

```
<!doctype html><html>
<head>
<meta charset="utf-8"><title>Snorkeling and Diving Adventures of Southern
    Florida</title>
<meta name="Keywords" content="Snorkeling, scuba diving, scuba divers,
    snorkelers, glass bottom boats">
<meta name="Description" content="Plan your aquatic vacation with SDASF.
    We offer snorkeling and diving adventures throughout southern
    Florida. Private charters and passenger vessels available. ">
</head>
</html>
```

7. **Place the content for the site between the opening and closing `<body>` tags.**

```
<!doctype html><html>
<head>
<meta charset="utf-8"><title>Snorkeling and Diving Adventures of Southern
    Florida</title>
<meta name="Keywords" content="Snorkeling, scuba diving, scuba divers,
    snorkelers, glass bottom boats">
<meta name="Description" content="Plan your aquatic vacation with SDASF.
    We offer snorkeling and diving adventures throughout southern
    Florida. Private charters and passenger vessels available. ">
</head>
<body>Page content goes here.
</body>
</html>
```

The details of this last step are what the bulk of this chapter is about — making sure that the text, images, tables, links, and more are all added to your HTML page. By the end of this chapter, you should have a simple web page with code that is valid and ready to be formatted in CSS.

All this metadata is invisible in the browser window. If you were to view this page in a browser, all you would see would be the words Pagecontentgoeshere., as shown in Figure 1-3.

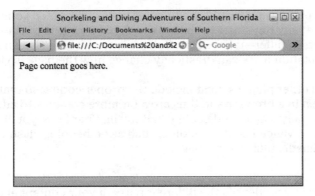

Figure 1-3: Metadata doesn't appear in the browser window.

Coding Your Pages

As you enter the code into your HTML files, here are a few important points to keep in mind:

✔ **If you plan on hand-coding your pages, be extra careful about entering all the code correctly.** You'd be wise to invest in an HTML book and/or spend as much time as you can learning HTML from an online tutorial to ensure that your HTML markup is compliant with the latest rules for HTML 4.01, XHTML 1.0, and HTML5. To code an image into a page by hand, for example, you need to insert the HTML tag for the image as well as include any attributes for it. *Attributes* are how you apply special characteristics to a tag using the syntax `attribute="x"`. Attributes can be applied to any tag and can include the width and height; the alternative text of an image; the title of a hyperlink; the alignment of a table cell; and the style of a bullet in an unordered list.

✔ **If you'll be using a code editor of some kind, be it a WYSIWYG code editor or an HTML-only editor, the application should do some of the coding work for you.** For example, when inserting an image with an editor, all you'll probably need to do is select the desired graphic file listed on your computer in a dialog box and, after it's inserted, add any desired attributes for the graphic through a special panel (such as the Property inspector in Dreamweaver) that can then apply those attributes automatically to the code.

Regardless of the way you choose to enter your code, you'll soon naturally discover that any tiny mistake you make can have a big impact on how the page renders in different browsers. Believe it or not, a single extra space or a missing quotation mark can drastically change how the page is viewed!

Movies and other plug-ins must include the proper coding so that visitors can see them in a browser and thus are a bit more complex to add to your pages, especially when hand-coding. In Book III, Chapter 8, you find out about more advanced content adding, such as embedding Flash movies and other multimedia plug-ins in a page.

When it comes to coding pages, the more you use *semantic HTML,* the easier it will be for you to identify the different parts of your content and use that content for a variety of purposes, such as applying CSS styles, pulling collected form data from visitors into a database, and adding JavaScript to objects to make the page more interactive.

Semantics refers to the proper usage of HTML 4.01, XHTML 1.0, and HTML5 tags based on those tags' contents. For example, when adding a paragraph of text to your page, you'd mark up that paragraph with opening and closing <p> tags. Likewise, when creating a page heading, you'd use the <h1> through <h6> tags, and when creating lists, use <ol>, <ul>, and <li> tags. You get the general idea. What semantics doesn't refer to is how and where the contents of an HTML page will appear in a browser; the presentation of the page should, as much as possible, be defined with Cascading Style Sheets.

In addition to proper usage of tags, semantics also refers to avoiding the use of any deprecated tags, such as the old <center> tag for center alignment of objects on the page and <font> tags for applying text styling. In fact, most books and online tutorials do not even cover these deprecated tags anymore. However, they're important to know about because you might, in the course of doing business, inherit an old site from a client for either site maintenance or a site redesign and need to know how to update those tags and attributes to the current semantic standards.

Deprecated refers to any HTML tag or tag attribute that has been phased out of usage in favor of better coding and styling methods. Most deprecated tags and attributes are not supported in HTML 4.01, XHTML 1.0, and HTML5 markup and thus might not work in newer browsers. Table 1-1 lists the more well known deprecated HTML tags along with suggestions for replacement methods.

Table 1-1   Deprecated HTML Tags and Suggested Alternatives

Deprecated Tag	Usage	Suggested Alternative
`<center>`	Centers objects	Use the `<div>` tag with the alignment (align) attribute, as in `<div align="center">`.
`<font>`	Applies styles to fonts	Style using CSS.
`<basefont>`	Sets default font style	Style using CSS.
`<blockquote>`	Applies indents to text and other objects	Style using CSS.
`<menu>`	Creates menu lists	Use `<ol>` or `<ul>`.
`<dir>`	Creates directory lists	Use `<ol>` or `<ul>`.
`<s>` and `<strike>`	Applies strikethrough	Style using CSS.
`<b>`	Bold	Style using CSS `<strong>`.
`<i>`	Italics	Style using CSS `<em>`.
`<u>`	Underlines	Style using CSS.
`<frame>`	Defines a frame	Use the `<div>` tag with CSS.
`<frameset>`	Defines a frame set	Use the `<div>` tag with CSS.
`<applet>`	Inserts applets	Use `<object>`.
`<isindex>`	Adds search fields to a page	Use `<form>`.

In addition to all these deprecated HTML tags, several HTML tag attributes, such as using `vlink` as an attribute of the `<body>` tag, have also been deprecated in favor of using CSS for styling text and other elements on a web page. To avoid accidentally using any of these deprecated tag attributes, use CSS as much as possible to style the content and to position objects in your pages. That said, even if you do accidentally use a deprecated tag or tag attribute here and there, you have a chance before you publish your site to identify and fix it. As part of your prelaunch testing process, you'll verify the accuracy of your HTML/XHTML/HTML5 code with some online tools to ensure that the code meets the minimum standard requirements to be compliant with the DTD you selected for your pages.

Adding Page Content

Your *page content* refers to all the text, images, links, navigation, Flash and QuickTime movies, Flash and GIF animations, MP3 files, and other media files and plug-ins that can be viewed on a web page. As long as your content is properly coded and everything is placed between the opening and closing <body> tags of the page, it should appear in the body of the page in a browser window, though keep in mind that different browsers may display the content, especially text, in slightly different ways.

In the following sections, you discover all the basics about how to add text and graphics to a web page.

Inserting text

Text is, by far, the easiest thing to add to a page because you can quickly transform it into paragraph text and headings, organize it into a list, or place it into rows and columns within the structure of a table or <div> layer.

As you add your copy to the page, try not to be too concerned about how the text looks (the font face, size, color, and so on), because the styling of the text happens later with CSS.

Follow this simple process to add text to your web page:

1. **Type or paste all your text onto the page before you do any formatting.**

   It is much easier and faster for you to do all the formatting at once using CSS after the content is in place. The same goes for adding any dynamic functionality (such as JavaScript rollover buttons) to the page; get the content on the page first and then add the dynamic functionality.

    Be careful pasting in text copied from Microsoft Word documents. It often contains miles and miles of extra proprietary useless "code" when pasted directly into an HTML editor. Dreamweaver has an option, under the Edit⇨Paste Special menu, that lets you choose your paste preferences to help avoid adding this unwanted extra code to your pages.

   Take the following sample text, for example:

   ```
   Creating Custom History Panel Commands
   The History Panel is one of those tools in Dreamweaver that many users
   don't take full advantage of. When the panel is open, it records all the
   actions you make in an open document, up to a certain number of steps
   (as specified in the General category of Dreamweaver's Preferences), and
   lets you take multiple steps backward with the use of the panel's
   slider.
   ```

2. **Mark up the text with the appropriate HTML tags to define the different parts of the content.**

Semantic tags have been added to the following sample text to identify both the main heading (<h1>) and the general paragraph (<p>) text, as well as adding bold (<strong>) and italic (<em>) tags to two key words:

```
<h1>Creating Custom History Panel Commands</h1>
<p>The <strong>History Panel</strong> is one of those tools in
    Dreamweaver that many users don't take full advantage of. When the
    panel is open, <em>it records all the actions you make</em> in an
    open document, up to a certain number of steps (as specified in the
    General category of Dreamweaver's Preferences), and lets you take
    multiple steps backward with the use of the panel's slider.</p>
```

When viewed in a browser, this code is automatically formatted like the example shown in Figure 1-4.

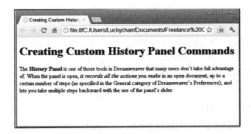

Figure 1-4: Semantic HTML means using the appropriate tags to mark up content on your pages.

In the following sections, you find out about the different tags you can use to mark up your text.

Headings

Heading tags are special preformatted tags that identify the important parts of your text that are different from the regular paragraph text, such as headings, subheadings, and bylines. Headings look different from regular paragraph text in that their default style is always bold and either slightly larger or slightly smaller than regular paragraph text, all without the use of CSS. Heading tags range from <h1> through <h6>, with <h1> being the largest preformatted text and <h6> being the smallest. Figure 1-5 shows how each of the following heading tags automatically transforms the content in a browser:

```
<p>This is normal paragraph text</p>
<h1>This is heading 1</h1>
<h2>This is heading 2</h2>
<h3>This is heading 3</h3>
<h4>This is heading 4</h4>
<h5>This is heading 5</h5>
<h6>This is heading 6</h6>
```

Keep in mind that this kind of preformatting determines only the default look of content styled with these tags within a browser; with the magic of CSS, you can easily *redefine* the attributes of these preformatted tags.

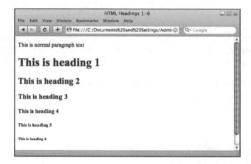

Figure 1-5: Use appropriate HTML tags to identify the different parts of the content, such as headings and paragraphs.

Bold and italic emphasis

When your text includes a word or phrase that isn't a heading yet still needs to stand out from the rest of the content, use the bold or italic structural tags.

If you're familiar with the old HTML `<b>` and `<i>` formatting tags, *do not use them!* Those tags are deprecated. Although they may still be backward-compatible in HTML in some browsers, they won't be viewable in XHTML and HTML5. Instead you should exclusively use `<strong>` for bold and `<em>` (which stands for emphasis) for italics. Use these newer structural tags in all your new web pages and convert any old bold and italic tags to the strong and emphasis tags when inheriting an old site for maintenance or redesign.

You can use strong and emphasis tags independently or in tandem. When you need to make something both bold and italic, be sure to use proper tag nesting in the code, where the closing tags mirror the order of the opening tags, as follows:

```
<h1>Creating Custom History Panel Commands</h1>
<p>The <strong>History Panel</strong> is one of those tools in Dreamweaver that
    many users don't take full advantage of. When the panel is open, <em>it
    records all the actions you make</em> in an open document, up to a certain
    number of steps (as specified in the General category of Dreamweaver's
    Preferences), and lets you take <strong><em>multiple steps backward</em></
    strong> with the use of the panel's slider.</p>
```

One interesting fact about bold and italic emphasis that you may not know, especially because you can create CSS styles with these attributes rather than add these tags to your code, is that screen readers actually inject different inflections into words that use the `<strong>` and `<em>` tags! Even more interestingly, search engine algorithms sometimes pay more attention to the contents between these tags than the other words on the page, which can both identify and improve the SEO rankings of the page within a particular search engine.

Text alignment

Text can be aligned left, center, right, or justified, relative to the browser window or any container tag (such as paragraphs, headings, table cells, and layers created with `<div>` tags) inside which the content sits. To illustrate, the contents in Figure 1-6 use the `left`, `center`, `right`, and `justify` alignment tag attributes. However, keep in mind that not all browsers support these attributes (as with the justify alignment shown here) when added to the HTML.

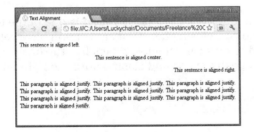

Figure 1-6: Text can be aligned to the left, center, right, or justified.

In the past, the `align` attribute would have been added to the opening tag, as in `<p align="left">`. Today, however, rather than using this attribute, you should leave the paragraph tag with no alignment markup and apply the alignment using CSS, which you explore in Book III, Chapter 3.

In addition to setting the alignment, you can decide on the font face, size, and color of text on a web page when styling your content with Cascading Style Sheets, which you find out about in Book III, Chapter 3.

Adding graphics

In Book II, Chapter 3, you see how to optimize graphics for the web into one of the three acceptable web file formats: GIF, JPG, and PNG. With those images at hand, you're now ready to find out how to add them to your web pages.

One of the best ways to keep all your web graphics organized is to put all of them into a folder called images or img and place that folder inside (at the root level) that project's HTML folder on your local computer. You can then repeat this same organizational structure for each project you work on, giving each project a root HTML folder (perhaps named something like EmilyK.HTML) and placing a generic images folder inside it. When you create a folder for your images, it will be much easier for you to locate and insert them into your pages as you build your site. If your project requires that several categories of images need to remain separated, organize them into subfolders within the main images folder, such as a folder for images of skylines (images/skylines/newyork.jpg) or a folder for images of button graphics (images/buttons/continueshopping.gif).

Each time you add an image to your page, you'll always use the same simple <img> tag, regardless of the particular file format of your web graphic. That is because the <img> tag specifies the source (location) of the file, the filename, and the file format, as in the following:

```
<img src="images/filename.gif">
```

What is most unusual about the <img> tag is that it is one of the few tags in HTML that doesn't require a closing tag. That said, if you have selected the XHTML DTD, you need to close any unclosed tags like the image tag using the XHTML syntax of an extra space and slash before the right angle bracket of the tag itself:

```
<img src="images/filename.gif" />
```

For each of your images inserted onto a web page, be sure that the filename and extension of each graphic in your code are spelled correctly using all lowercase lettering. This helps you establish a uniform naming convention as well as ensure that your pages are XHTML compatible. Likewise, you must also be sure that the filename in the code exactly matches the filename as it is written in the images folder. Therefore, if your images folder has a file called AmericanIdolJudge.jpg and the code in your page refers to an image called americanidoljudge.JPG, you must rename both the file and the code so that both instances use all lowercase lettering, as in american idoljudge.jpg. This tip is extremely important to remember because some servers simply won't display an image on a page if the filename is written one way in the code (sjNav_03.GIF) and another way in the images folder (sjnav_03.gif). Figure 1-7 shows an example of what happens to an image in one browser when the filename in the code is different from the filename of the actual file.

Figure 1-7: When the code and filename don't match, the image may not appear in the browser.

After your image has been inserted onto the page, you can add any of the following attributes to your code to further specify how the image should be displayed in a browser. Although many of these attributes have been superseded by CSS styles, you should still know what you can do with regular HTML formatting before you veer away from it to the more robust capabilities of CSS.

Alternative text

Identify the contents of the graphic by adding a textual description to the `<img>` tag with the alternative text (`alt`) attribute:

```
<img src="images/popcorn.gif" alt="popcorn">
```

Size

After listing the source location and filename of the image in the image tag, include the `width` and `height` attributes of the graphic in pixels to ensure that the image displays with the correct dimensions:

```
<img src="images/popcorn.gif" alt="popcorn" width="100" height="100">
```

Image sizes can also be noted in percentages. For instance, if you want to stretch a 1-x-1-pixel image to span the entire width of the browser window or the width of a smaller area like a table cell, specify the width in percentages using the following syntax:

```
<img src="images/line.gif" alt="" width="100%" height="1">
```

Border

With the `border` HTML attribute, you can apply a uniform black border to or remove any hint of a border from your images. Borders can be of any thickness by changing the number of pixels in the quotation marks:

```
<img src="images/car.jpg" alt="car" width="100" height="100" border="1">
```

By default, most images include a 1-pixel invisible border, like padding, around the outer edges of the graphic. This invisible border becomes active (and visible in some browsers) only when the graphic gets hyperlinked to another page, as demonstrated in Figure 1-8. If desired, you can remove this invisible border attribute by setting the `border` attribute to `"0"`. This ensures that the padding is removed from the outer edges of the graphic, allowing graphics that sit side by side on a page to touch each other cleanly with no hidden space between them. Setting the `border` attribute to `"0"` in the code looks like this:

```
<img src="images/brochure.png" alt="Request a Brochure " width="100" height="100"
    border="0">
```

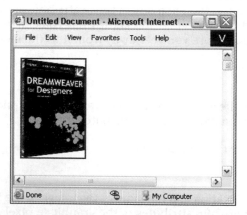

Figure 1-8: Hyperlinked graphics display a border unless you zero out the border attribute.

Using alternative text attributes for images

Although you can add many HTML formatting attributes to your images with CSS, there is one, the alternative text (`alt`) attribute, that you should add to each of your images every time, even when styling the image using only CSS. Alternative text does not appear on the web page.

Rather, it is a code tip that screen readers, other assistive devices, and search engine robots and spiders use to identify the contents of the graphic for visitors with disabilities viewing your pages with assistive devices and to help index the content on your website for future visitors. As a matter of fact, many Internet browsers display the alternative text attribute as a screen tip when a visitor's mouse hovers over a graphic that has an alternative text attribute.

Here's an example of a graphic with the `alt`, `width`, `height`, and `border` attributes:

```
<img src="images/filename.png" width="100"
     height="50" alt="Alternative
     text here" border="0">
```

Alternative text attributes should be short, descriptive phrases, no longer than about 50 characters or so, that define the contents of the graphic, such as `alt="On Sale Now"` or `alt="Photograph of Half Dome, Yosemite, CA"`. If you find that you simply need more space to describe the contents of the graphic, use another image tag attribute, called the long description, or `longdesc`, which links to a separate web page that contains a longer description of the image:

```
<img src="images/dfddvd.jpg" alt="Dreamweaver
     for Designers Training DVD"
     width="100" height="156"
     longdesc="dfddvd.html">
```

You can then put more detailed information in the linked file. For example, in `dfddvd.html`:

Dreamweaver for Designers Training DVD:

Dreamweaver for Designers is the Telly Award–Winning ClassOnDemand self-paced, 10-hour instructional DVD that provides users familiar with design concepts but new to the Dreamweaver application with a step-by-step approach to building a professional website. Instructor Sue Jenkins is a Dreamweaver expert, Adobe Certified Expert/Instructor, and industry-renowned author of several web-related instructional books. The DVD takes students through the fundamentals of website and application creation with Dreamweaver.

To be standards compliant, always add the `alt` text attribute to your images. That said, there are bound to be several images on your pages that are used solely for decorative purposes and don't really need to have the `alt` text attribute. For those types of images, still include the `alt` text attribute to keep the tag HTML 4.01 and XHTML 1.0–compliant, but leave the attribute's contents blank, as in this example:

```
<img src="filename" width="100"
     height="100" alt="" border="0">
```

To add the blank `alt` attribute to an image in Dreamweaver, select the inserted graphic on your page in Design view and type **<enter>**, including the brackets, in the Alt text field in the Property inspector. Or, when accessibility features are enabled for graphics, simply enter the alternative text (and a long description link, if desired) into the Image Tag Accessibility Attributes dialog box when it appears before the image gets inserted on the page.

Decorative images may include, but are not limited to, corner graphics for tables (to create a curved corner effect without using the CSS3 border-radius style, though CSS would certainly be smarter), horizontal and vertical dividing lines, spacer GIFs (transparent 1 x 1 pixels often stretched out to hold open empty table cells to specific sizes), custom bullets, and nontextual ornamental borders and graphics.

When you take care to include the `alt` text attribute, whether with descriptive text or blank, you're helping to make your pages accessible to the widest possible audience of visitors and compliant with the current recommended standards set forth by the W3C.

**Book III
Chapter 1**

**Adding Text,
Images, and Links**

Now that you know what the `border` attribute does, other than zeroing out the border, you should never use this attribute to apply a border to your graphics (unless you absolutely have to) for three important reasons:

✔ The border attribute color in HTML is limited to black.

✔ Using border attributes in HTML is old school and may not be supported by every browser, device, tablet, or smartphone; instead use CSS for all your styling and formatting.

✔ With CSS, not only can you create a border in another color besides black, but you can also apply different colors to each of the four sides of your graphic as well as specify the border's thickness and style (solid, double, grooved, dashed, and so on).

For more on CSS, refer to Book III, Chapter 3.

Image padding

Padding is the extra space around the outer edges of an image that can be used to help keep text and other objects from butting right up against it. For instance, padding can be useful when trying to separate an image from any text that wraps too closely around the image edges.

Before CSS enabled you to add padding to any or all four sides of an image, the only way to add padding to an image was by using the old hspace (as in horizontal space) and vspace (as in vertical space) HTML tag attributes. For example, to add even spacing around the entire image using this old method, you would need to use the same number of pixels for both tag attributes:

```
<img src="images/applepie.jpg" alt="Award Winning Apple Pie" width="175"
    height="175" hspace="10" vspace="10" border="0">
```

The main drawback to adding padding with HTML is that the attributes uniformly apply padding to both the left and right sides of the graphic and both the top and bottom sides of the graphic, which may not cause surrounding content to wrap around the image as desired. Thankfully, these attributes are now considered deprecated. Therefore, for best control over padding of your images, including being able to independently style each of the four sides of the graphic, use CSS.

Alignment

Always use CSS to position your images on the page relative to other content, such as text and other images. To find out how to make text wrap around an image using CSS, see the section about box properties in Book III, Chapter 4.

Creating Hyperlinks

If you've ever clicked an underlined word or button graphic and have been taken to another page on a website, you've experienced the magic of hyperlinks. Simply put, a *hyperlink* is any link in a file that leads you to some other file on the web, whether that file is located on the same website as the linking page or on another site on the Internet, such as clicking a link in a Google search results listing and visiting a website that has the information you were seeking.

Hyperlinks, or links, are typically created by pairing the href attribute with the <a> anchor tag. The href part is short for "hypertext reference" and defines the destination, whereas the anchor tag converts the contents between the opening and closing <a> tags into a link. Here is an example of a hyperlink that converts text into a link to another web page:

```
<a href="about.html">Read More</a>
```

Hyperlink code is very versatile and can be used for a variety of purposes. In the following sections, you find out about local and global links, link targets, linking graphics, e-mail links, image map links, and named anchor links.

Understanding local and global links

Book III Chapter 1

Adding Text, Images, and Links

Your hyperlinks can point to any location on the Internet; however, the destination often determines the syntax that must be used to code the link. You find two general types of links:

- ✔ **Local:** A local link is a hyperlink that points to a different page within the same website, such as going from the about.html page to the contact.html page.

  When the linked file is local, only the filename (and relative location when other than at the root level) needs to be listed, as in the following examples:

  ```
  <a href="services.html">Services</a>
  <a href="about/mission.html">Our Mission</a>
  ```

  Most websites contain primarily document-relative local links that refer to other pages within the site, either through the navigation menu or embedded naturally within the text, as shown in Figure 1-9.

Links to other pages on the site

Figure 1-9: Most navigation links are local links.

✔ **Global:** A global link, also called an *external* link, is a hyperlink that points to a page outside the current domain to some other website on the Internet and requires the specification of the full path of the file being linked to, such as going from the Google News web page to an entertainment article listed on Eonline.com.

When the link is external to the site of the referring page, the full or "absolute" web address, including the `http://` part and any other path information that leads visitors to the particular page, needs to be included in the hypertext reference between the quotation marks:

```
<a href="http://www.pandora.com/">Listen to Pandora Radio</a>
<a href="http://www.classondemand.net/media/Instructor.
    aspx?ArtistID=45">Online Adobe Training with Sue Jenkins</a>
```

Global links are generally reserved for linking to resources or other services outside the domain that may benefit site visitors, such as the wonderfully useful list of resources for designers on the Online Graphic Design Degree website at `www.onlinegraphicdesigndegree.com/resources/`, shown in Figure 1-10.

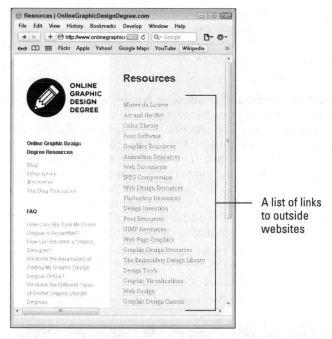

A list of links
to outside
websites

Figure 1-10: Links that lead visitors to other websites are global links.

Linking targets

By default, most browsers automatically open the page or file specified in the hyperlink in the same browser window as the referring page. There is no special code you need to add to your link to make this "open in the same window" feature happen. When links open within the same browser window, that's called "targeting the same window" because the destination browser window is typically referred to as the *target* window. To make the linked file open in a new browser window, specify the target location in the link code by using the `target` attribute.

You can use four general `target` attributes to open links in different locations, depending on your needs:

✔ **Open link in a new window:** To make your link open a new browser window and display inside the new window, use the `"_blank"` target attribute:

```
<a href="http://www.weather.com" target="_blank">Weather</a>
```

✔ **Open link in the same window:** Use the `target` attribute "`_self`" to force the link to open in the same browser window as the referring page. For best standards compliance, you should always specify the target by using the `target` attribute:

```
<a href="http://www.youtube.com" target="_self">YouTube</a>
```

✔ **Open link in a named window or frame:** When your visitors are likely to have more than one window open at the same time while viewing a particular site, you can target one of the open windows using the window's `id` attribute. For example, if the site visitor has launched a pop-up window (given the `id` attribute of `popup` in the code) to view a close-up image of a product and wants to see that product in another color, a link could be set to display the product in a different color in the same pop-up window, as illustrated in the KennethCole.com browser windows in Figure 1-11. This feature also works with a particular frame within a frameset when the web page has been built using HTML frames:

```
<a href="red.html" target="popup">Red</a>
<a href="disclaimer.html" target="main">Read Disclaimer</a>
```

Figure 1-11: Use the target attribute to tell a browser where a hyperlinked page should open.

✔ **(Frames only) Open link in a window or parent:** When working with old-school (not recommended) frames, you can use the `target` attribute to tell the browser where a particular page within the frame should be displayed:

- *Top:* Use the "`_top`" attribute to target the entire browser window and break any preexisting frames.

- *Parent:* Use the "`_parent`" attribute to target the master frame of a nested frameset.

Frames are a deprecated way of constructing web pages, are not supported by HTML5, and are therefore not covered in this book. To find out more about this old-fashioned HTML technique, see `www.w3schools.com/HTML/html_frames.asp`.

As a courtesy, it's good to inform site visitors any time a new browser window will open from a link, especially when the linked file is a PDF, MS Word document, or some other non-HTML file, because some visitors might consider the launching of any new windows annoying. To help ease any possible discomfort, add a custom graphic next to the global link, such as the example next to the Download Our Catalog link shown in Figure 1-12, or insert some text in parentheses, as in (opens new window), so that visitors will know in advance that a new window will open.

**Book III
Chapter 1**

Adding Text,
Images, and Links

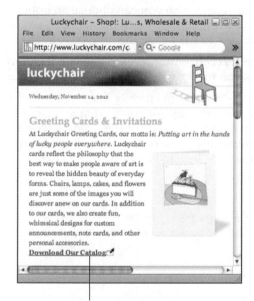

Link to resources that will download

Figure 1-12: A simple illustrative graphic can alert visitors that a page or document will open in a new browser window.

Linking graphics

Linking graphics is as simple as linking text. To convert a regular image on a page into a hyperlinked image, just wrap the right bit of HTML code around the image object. For example, the following code makes the `brochure request.gif` graphic into a clickable link that takes visitors to the `brochure.html` page:

```
<a href="brochure.html"><img src="brochurerequest.gif"></a>
```

To insert an image on your page and convert it into a hyperlink, follow these steps:

1. **Create a working folder on your desktop called `ImageLinkDemo`.**

2. **Inside this folder, create another folder called `images`. Inside this `images` folder, place a copy of one of your optimized web graphics, which you will use for this exercise.**

   To save a copy of a graphic from the website, right-click (Windows) or Control+click (Mac) the image in the browser window. Doing this opens the contextual menu, from which you can choose an option to save a copy of the file. After the image has been downloaded to your computer, move it into the `images` folder inside the new `ImageLinkDemo` folder.

3. **Using your preferred HTML editor, create a new document and save it to the `ImageLinkDemo` folder with the filename `imagelink.html`.**

   Most modern HTML editors automatically insert the structural HTML tags (the bones) of the web page for you so that you can instantly begin adding your own content to the body of the page. However, if you're hand-coding or using an older editor that doesn't insert the bones, add the following HTML5 code by hand to your empty page:

   ```
   <!doctype html>
   <html>
   <head>
   <meta charset="utf-8">
   <title>Untitled Document</title>
   </head>
   <body>
   </body>
   </html>
   ```

4. **Insert a copy of the image you just saved into the `images` folder of your `ImageLinkDemo` folder.**

   To do this, add the image code with the source of your image and alternative text (`alt`) attribute between the opening and closing `<body>` tags, as shown in the following example:

   ```
   <img src="images/filename.gif" alt="alternative text">
   ```

   Be sure that the filename, file extension (`.gif`, `.jpg`, `.png`), and alternative text in your HTML code match the specifics of your selected image. If you happen to know the width and height of the image, feel free to add those as attributes to the image code. For example, your code might look like this:

   ```
   <img src="images/dfddvd.jpg" alt="Dreamweaver for
      Designers DVD" width="100" height="156">
   ```

5. **Turn the image into a hyperlink by wrapping the anchor tag and `href` attribute code around the image tag.**

   For testing purposes, feel free to use Amazon for the "link to" address, as in the following code example:

   ```
   <a href="http://www.amazon.com" target="self"><img
      src="images/dfddvd.jpg" alt="Dreamweaver for
      Designers DVD" width="100" height="156"></a>
   ```

   If desired, feel free to add any additional text and graphics to your page and style everything to your liking.

6. **With all the code now in place, save your file and launch a copy of it in a browser window.**

   To preview the saved file, drag and drop the HTML file by its icon into any open browser window, and the page should display, regardless of whether you have an active Internet connection. If you're using an editor like Dreamweaver, BBEdit, or KompoZer, you should be able to use a shortcut key (like F12) or press a button on the interface to launch the page in a primary browser for local testing purposes. Figure 1-13 shows an example of a simple page with a linked graphic.

7. **To test the accuracy of your code, click the hyperlinked graphic in your browser window. If your browser switches to Amazon, you've coded the link perfectly!**

   If the hyperlink didn't take you to Amazon (or the URL you inserted in the `href` attribute of your code), go back and check the spelling and syntax in your code. Something as small as a missing period, slash, angle bracket, quotation mark, or closing tag can make all the difference in the functionality of your page!

**Book III
Chapter 1**

**Adding Text,
Images, and Links**

A linked image

Figure 1-13: Hyperlinked images should display a hand cursor when the mouse is positioned on top of them in a browser window.

When the image becomes a hyperlink, the image automatically takes on a border with the default blue hyperlink color for unvisited links and the default purple hyperlink color for visited links. You can modify this attribute in one of three ways:

✔ Alter the thickness of the border by adding the `border` attribute with a value of 1 or more, as in the following:

```
<a href="http://www.amazon.com" target="self"><img src="images/dfddvd.
    jpg" alt="Dreamweaver for Designers DVD" width="100" height="156"
    border="10"></a>
```

✔ Remove the border by adding the `border` attribute with a value of `"0"`, as in the following:

```
<a href="http://www.amazon.com" target="self"><img src="images/dfddvd.
    jpg" alt="Dreamweaver for Designers DVD" width="100" height="156"
    border="0"></a>
```

✔ Override the border color and style by creating a custom CSS style and applying it to the image using the `class` attribute, ignoring the `border` attribute in the code, as in this example:

```
<a href="http://www.amazon.com" target="self"><img src="images/dfddvd.
    jpg" alt="Dreamweaver for Designers DVD" width="100" height="156"
    class="borderstyle"></a>
```

The custom border style you add to the head area of your code might be something like this:

```
<style type="text/css">
  <!--
  .borderstyle {
  border: thin dotted #999;
  padding: 10px;
  }
  -->
</style>
```

To preview the changes to the border of your image, save your file and relaunch your test page in a browser using one of the methods I describe in Step 6. If you added the `border` attribute to your image with a value of 1 or more, the image will appear with either a blue (default link color) or purple (default visited-link color) border, and if you added the border attribute with a value of `"0"`, the default link color will be removed. If you added a CSS style to your code, your graphic might look like the example shown in Figure 1-14.

Figure 1-14: Apply a custom CSS style to override the default blue and purple hyperlink border colors.

Creating other link types

In addition to the regular hyperlinks for text and graphics, you can create three other types of HTML links in your files: e-mail links, image map links, and named anchor links.

E-mail links

An e-mail link launches the site visitor's computer or other device's default e-mail program and opens a blank e-mail message with the Mail To field set to the address specified in the e-mail link. E-mail links use the anchor tag and `href` attribute like a regular hyperlink, but they also include a special `mailto:` syntax combined with the actual e-mail address that tells the browser that the link is an e-mail link, as in the following code:

```
<a href="mailto:contact@url.com">contact@url.com</a>
```

For times when you'd like to have the e-mail link automatically populate the Subject line of the outgoing e-mail message, you can do this simply by appending the e-mail address with a question mark, the word *subject*, and the actual line of text to be used as the subject line, as shown here:

```
<a href="mailto:contact@url.com?subject=Brochure Request">Request a brochure</a>
```

This is an urgent warning: HTML e-mail links are extremely vulnerable to spam-bots and other spam-harvesting tools and therefore are a terrible way of adding an e-mail address to your website. What, then, should you do if you need to list an e-mail address on your website? Simple answer: Encrypt all your e-mail addresses by using any of the widely available encryption methods. To find out more about e-mail encryption, read the nearby sidebar, which recommends three websites that provide free e-mail encryption.

Protecting your e-mail addresses from spam

The Internet is an amazing place where information on nearly everything under the sun is readily available. You can communicate rapidly with your friends, families, and strangers through the revolutionary system of e-mails. Like the rest of the world, however, the Internet can also be a place for dishonesty, fraudulence, and unethical business practices. With regard to the privacy and sanctity of your e-mail addresses, this means trying to protect your e-mail address from being harvested for spam.

The main reason you get spam initially is that e-mail addresses listed on web pages (either alone as text or especially when coded with the `<mailto:>` tag) are very vulnerable to being harvested by human-initiated spam-bots, which are e-mail-gathering applications that operate 24 hours a day in search of innocent e-mail addresses. And because the creators and users of these e-mail harvesters have no ethics with regard to your privacy, they're likely to sell your e-mail address, when harvested, to other companies that also profit from these illicit spam lists. Nice, huh?

To combat this rampant Internet crime, the best defense is to encrypt *all* e-mail addresses appearing on every site you create. Protect the e-mail addresses that you display on a web page, first and foremost, by *not* listing them as text or hyperlinked e-mails. Instead, take a few extra minutes to encrypt or otherwise hide the e-mail addresses from those malicious spam-bots and their creators.

Here are two fine recommendations for encrypting and hiding e-mail addresses:

✔ **Encrypt with a JavaScript:** Several freeware and shareware versions of encryption tools are available online, including the following:

DynamicDrive: `www.dynamicdrive.com/emailriddler`

csarven.ca: `www.csarven.ca/hiding-email-addresses`

Address Munger: `www.addressmunger.com/contact_form_generator`

Dan Benjamin's Hivelogic Enkoder Form: `http://hivelogic.com/enkoder`

✔ **Encode using entities:** When typing a regular e-mail address on a web page, use HTML code entities for the special characters instead of regular text, or for the entire e-mail address. For instance, because the entity for @ is `&#64;` and the entity for . is `&#46;`, the code for `contact@myfavoriteshoesonline.com` would change to contact `&#64;` my-favoriteshoesonline `&#46;` com. To convert any e-mail address into HTML code entities, visit the Texas Web Developers website: `www.texaswebdevelopers.com/examples/xmlentities/xml_entities.asp`.

With most JavaScript encryption applications, you usually type your e-mail address, press a button, and get some code back that you can copy and paste into your web page. The code contains the encrypted e-mail address and, when viewed on a web page, looks just like a regular hypertext e-mail address.

For example, if you used the encryption application on Dan Benjamin's website, you'd paste the JavaScript code returned from the Enkoder Form into the place in your page's HTML code where you would like the e-mail address to appear. To illustrate, the encrypted e-mail address you might use to replace the following regular e-mail link

```
<a href="mailto:contact@myfavoriteshoesonline.com">contact@myfavoriteshoesonline.com</
    a>
```

might look like this:

```
<script type="text/javascript">
/* <![CDATA[ */
function hivelogic_enkoder(){var kode=
"kode=\"nrgh@%{@hgrn\\000,f+hgrFudkFprui1jqluwV@.{>;54@.f,3?f+il>60,1+wDhgr"+
"Fudkf1hgrn@f~,..1>kwjqho1hgrn?1>3@l+uri>**@{>_%/--.toup4/.kyxk|kx4/--.zorv"+
"y4kjuqCkjuqA(qujkC(buqkjbb(bC-/.-otpu/4k.xy|kxk/4--z.royvk4ujCqjkqubbbbAjb"+
"b(bius{tk4zx}zo.kbb(bbbbbbbbbbbbbgBn&kxC1bbbbbbbbbbbbbbbbbbb(bbbbbbbbbbbbbg"+
"srouzi@tugzzisF1\\177|gxuzoykunyktuorkti4subbbb&bbbbbbbbbbbbbbbbbbbbbbbb(b&b"+
"bbbozrzCkbbbbbbbbbbbbbbbbbbbb(bbbbbbbbbbbbbbuiztigFz\\177sglu|oxkznykuuyrtto4"+
"kui&sbbbbbbbbbbbbbbbbbbbb(bbbbbbbbbbbbbiDtugzzisF1\\177|gxuzoykunyktuorkti4s"+
"uB&g5bbbbbDbbbbbb(b/bbbbbbbbACbb(bjkquAbb(buqkjqCju4kvyor.z--4/kxk|yx.k4/up"+
```

Book III Chapter 1

Adding Text, Images, and Links

(continued)

(continued)

```
"to-./-(bA~C--Alux.oC6AoB.qujk4rktmzn37/Ao1C8/\\001~1Cqujk4ingxGz.o17/1qujk"+
"4ingxGz.o/333__qujkC~1.oBqujk4rktmznEqujk4ingxGz.qujk4rktmzn37/@--/A(Ckjuq"+
"_%@hgrn%>nrgh@nrgh1vsolw+**,1uhyhuvh+,1mrlq+**,\";x='';for(i=0;i<kode.leng"+
"th;i++){c=kode.charCodeAt(i)-3;if(c<0)c+=128;x+=String.fromCharCode(c)}kod"+
"e=x"
;var i,c,x;while(eval(kode));}hivelogic_enkoder();
/* ]]> */
</script>
```

The only potential drawback to encrypted e-mail addresses is that visitors who have JavaScript disabled in their browsers will not be able to use these links. To prevent that from happening, be sure to add <noscript> tags to your code, directly following the script tags, that include alternative contact information, as in the following example:

```
<noscript>
Send email to info ~at~ company ~dot~ com
</noscript>
```

Image map links

An image map is a graphic that has one or more hotspots defined on it with coordinates in the HTML code that make those hotspots clickable to another page on the Internet like regular hyperlinks. You can also attach behaviors to hotspots to call JavaScript functions, such as displaying another image when the hotspot is moused over or clicked, or creating a link from the hotspot that launches another browser window.

Images can have as many image map hotspots as you need, as long as each hotspot coordinate is specified in the code. For example, a software training school website might have a group photograph of all the in-class instructors who work there. Each instructor in the photograph could then have an associated hotspot that, when clicked, transfers visitors to an individual instructor bio page.

Image map coordinates are fairly time consuming to create when hand-coding but are super easy to make using a WYSIWYG coding program such as Dreamweaver. In Dreamweaver, you can use the Rectangular, Circle, or Polygon Hotspot tool to draw one or more precise hotspot shapes on an image. After the hotspot coordinates are defined in the code, the hyperlink to the desired web page can then be specified along with a target destination for the link to control where the linked page will open. The following HTML code shows an example of how a rectangular hotspot can be mapped onto a graphic:

```
<img src="images/dfddvd.jpg" alt="Dreamweaver for Designers DVD" width="100"
    height="156" class="borderstyle" usemap="#amazon">
<map name="amazon" id="amazon">
<area shape="rect" coords="0,0,100,156" href="http://www.amazon.com/" target="_
    blank" alt="Order today from Amazon.com">
</map>
```

In Dreamweaver, the hotspot area is displayed in Design view by a see-through, light-blue shape, as demonstrated in Figure 1-15.

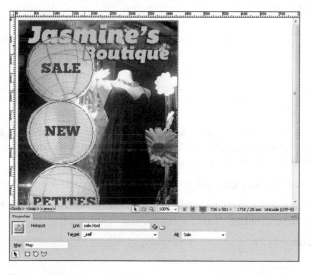

Figure 1-15: Image map hotspots are a snap to create in Dreamweaver.

Named anchor links

These special hyperlinks, which are sometimes referred to simply as *anchor links,* help visitors jump from one part of a web page to another part of that same page when clicked. Anchor links are particularly useful as quick links to sections referred to in a table of contents or the sequence of answers in a list of FAQs. You can also use named anchor links to jump visitors back to the top of the page after long passages of text.

Named anchor links require two parts in the HTML code to function correctly: a) the linked text or graphic that points to the destination elsewhere on the page and b) the anchor, which is located at the destination.

Because all anchors need to be given their own specific name for the anchor link to function correctly, try to name each of your anchors after its usage or purpose. For example, if your table of contents is listed numerically, you could name the anchor by its section, such as a23179 or faq8. Anchor names may include any combination of numbers and letters but cannot contain any spaces or funny characters (such as / or *) or begin with a number. For instance, to make a link at the bottom of a long page take visitors, when clicked, back to the top of the page, you'd need to insert the link that refers to the anchor at the bottom of the page and the anchor itself near the top of the page code:

- **Link:** `<a href="#top">Top</a>`
- **Anchor:** `<a name="top"id="top"></a>`

To better help you digest the concept, the following steps demonstrate how to set up your page with a few named anchor links.

1. **Open your favorite HTML editor, create a new document, and save it with the filename `anchors.html` into the `ImageLinkDemo` folder you created in the last exercise.**

   If you have already deleted that folder, just create a new one.

2. **Inside the `anchors.html` file, type the following content between the opening and closing `<body>` tags:**

   ```
   Table of Contents:

   Document Setup
   Using Fonts
   Text Flow

   Document Setup: Define your page size as the final
   trim size of your document. To create a bleed, extend
   your page elements .125 (one-eighth) inch off the
   document's edge.

   Using Fonts: Computers use screen fonts to display your
   type on the monitor and printer fonts to send to the
   laser printer or for printing.

   Text Flow: Because of kerning, tracking, hyphenation,
   and "target printer" preferences specific to your
   software, your text may reflow if you ask us to make
   type changes.
   ```

3. **To insert the first named anchor, place your cursor in the code right before the paragraph that begins `Document setup: Define...` and type**

   ```
   <a name="docsetup"></a>
   ```

If you're using a code editor, the program may have a way to quickly insert the named anchor for you rather than hand-coding it. Dreamweaver, for instance, has a Named Anchor button in the Common area of the Insert panel that is shaped like a golden anchor. When clicked, this button quickly inserts the appropriate code for the named anchor, after providing the program with the anchor name, in the spot where your cursor is located on the page.

The Document Setup section of your code should now look like this:

```
<p><a name="docsetup"></a>Document Setup: Define your page size as the
    final trim size of your document. To create a bleed, extend your
    page elements .125 (one-eighth) inch off the document's edge.</p>
```

As you can see, the named anchor tags don't surround any content, but rather mark the territory so that an anchor link can jump to this destination. In other words, you don't want to create a regular hyperlink here from surrounding content; you merely want to create a destination hotspot on the page.

4. **Create the link to the new named anchor by inserting a regular hyperlink around the text that will link to the anchor.**

   To do this, rather than adding a filename to the `href` attribute, you add a number symbol (#) along with the name of the anchor.

   ```
   Table of Contents:

   <a href="#docsetup">Document Setup</a>
   Using Fonts
   Text Flow
   ```

5. **To test your new named anchor, save the file and launch the page in a browser window.**

   The words `Document Setup` in the Table of Contents area should appear in the browser as an underlined hyperlink that, when clicked, jump the page to the Document Setup section farther down on the page.

   To test the functionality of the named anchor link in a way that makes more visual sense so that you can see the jump occur, reduce the dimensions of your browser window so that the Document Setup text area is hidden from your view before you click the link.

6. **Repeat Steps 3 and 4 for the `Using Fonts` and `Text Flow` entries.**

   As long as each named anchor has its own unique name, you can have as many of them on the page as you like.

In addition to using named anchor links to jump from one spot to another on the same page, use named anchors to link to a specific spot on another page. For instance, you may want site visitors to be able to click a hyperlink on one page and be taken to the named anchor destination in the middle of another page, such as clicking a link called Sign Up to take visitors to the Dance Workshop section in the middle of a page named `schedule.html`.

To make that happen, just append the regular filename in the `href` hyperlink code with the number symbol and the name of the desired anchor, as shown in the following example:

```
<a href="schedule.html#danceworkshop">Sign up for the next Dance Workshop</a>
```

Now that you see how easy it is to create named anchor links, you might never create a long page without them!

Labeling Content for CSS Markup

Before you get into the nitty-gritty of CSS coding in Book III, Chapter 3, it's a good idea for you to get into the habit now of *labeling,* or assigning an ID name to, all the objects in your pages using the `id` attribute. Doing this is especially important to do for any objects you plan to style with CSS and/or make dynamic with the use of JavaScript or jQuery code.

The W3C (World Wide Web Consortium, www.w3.org) refers to the objects on your page as *elements,* which really just means anything, including text surrounded by paragraph or header tags, that can be added to a web page.

To label an element, add the `id` attribute with a unique name to the element's opening tag. If you take this extra step as you insert each object onto the page, you'll save yourself some time later on when you're ready to style and position your content with CSS as well as add any dynamic functionality to those elements. To add the label, the proper syntax is `id="name"`.

When adding the `id` attribute to your elements, keep the following general usage rules in mind:

- ✔ **No two objects can use the same `id` value in a single HTML file.**
- ✔ **The `id` is case sensitive and must begin with a letter.** It may, however, contain any combination of letters and numbers as well as periods, underscores, hyphens, or colons.
- ✔ **For ease of use and semantic integrity, name your `ids` after their purpose as much as possible.** Although technically, you can call `ids` whatever you want, a descriptive name, such as `sidebar1` or `sale_items`, is more helpful than calling something `bigBlueHeader` or `LeftPad20px`, because certain attributes (such as `Blue` or `20px`) may change as the site is being built.

In addition to using the `id` attribute as CSS selectors and script elements, IDs can also be used as anchors for hypertext links, names of objects, and identifiers for other applications that might be parsing data from your pages, such as when a script extracts data from a form field into a database.

The id attribute can also be added to text blocks, tables, images, <div> tags, plug-ins, media files, form fields, and any other objects or elements you plan to style with CSS and/or make dynamic with JavaScript, jQuery, or other programming languages. The following examples show how and where to add the id labels to a few different tags:

```
<table width="500" cellspacing="0" id="productdetails">
<div id="sidebar2">
<img src="images/1.gif" name="number1" width="50" height="50"
    id="number1">
<p id="highlight">Get 'em while they're hot!</p>
```

In some cases, depending on the browser, the id attribute is used to replace the old name attribute, whereas in other instances the name attribute is still required to display that object correctly. The situation can get even more confusing when you begin dealing with form fields because the id and name attributes function differently, depending on which browser the visitor is using to view the page with! Therefore, to avoid mass confusion and reduce your troubleshooting time, you may want, in certain circumstances, to include both attributes within particular tags, as with images and form fields in the following code examples:

```
<img src="images/greetingcards.gif" alt="Luckychair Greeting Cards"
    name="greetingcards" id="greetingcards" width="220" height="300">
<input type="text" name="textfield" id="textfield">
```

Of course you're not expected to know which ones need both and when. Instead, you can simply code with both attributes, or better yet, when using a code editor like Dreamweaver, the program will automatically know which tags to add both attributes to and do the coding for you!

Making Content Accessible

In earlier chapters, you find out about some of the must-have site Accessibility features to include in your site's design and code. These include HTML footer links, a site map page with simple hypertext links to all the pages on the site, alternative text attributes for all your images, unique page titles for every page, and the use of description and other optional meta tags in the head of the page to help visitors find your site through search engines. You can further improve page accessibility by including additional accessibility tags and tag attributes in the code.

Though some designers might prefer to first get all their content on the page and then go back and improve it for accessibility, you may find that it's more efficient to add the accessibility features to your code during the page-building process. When you add accessibility as you code, you're assured of including all the different tag attributes and other accessibility enhancements to each element, rather than having to second-guess and do double the work by going back and checking everything at a later time to see whether you remembered or forgot to add them.

Table 1-2 lists the most common accessibility coding enhancements. Use them as often as possible on all your web pages.

Table 1-2	Accessibility Improvement Tags	
Name	*Description*	*Sample Usage*

Alternative text attribute in an image tag	Provides descriptive text for images to visitors using assistive devices to access the web, as well as non- human visitors like search engine robots and spiders.	`<img src="images/`
		`search.gif"`
		`width="70"`
		`height="30"`
		`alt="Search">`

Title tag	A unique descriptive page title can be applied to each page on a site. Title tags are scanned by search engine robots and can help improve search engine listings and rankings when peppered with site-relevant descriptive keywords.	`<title>James Graham :`
		`Oil portraits of`
		`animals and pets by`
		`New York painter.</`
		`title>`

Object labels	Use the `id` attribute to label objects on the page that will be styled with CSS or made dynamic with JavaScript. When labeling images for JavaScript, be sure to also include an identical `name` attribute.	`<img src="images/`
		`rainbow.jpg"`
		`width="250"`
		`height="200"`
		`id="rainbow"`
		`alt="Rainbow over`
		`Kansas City">`
		
		or
		
		`<img src="img/icon_`
		`dream.gif" width="80"`
		`height="80"`
		`alt="Dreamweaver"`
		`border="0"`
		`name="dreamweaver"`
		`id="dreamweaver">`

Name	*Description*	*Sample Usage*
Long description	The alternative text (`alt`) attribute can only handle about 70 characters max of text. To provide a longer description for any image, add the long description attribute to the image that links to a separate web page that contains the longer textual description.	```<img src="images/ seattle.jpg" alt="Seattle,WA" width="500" height="400" longdesc="seattle. html">```
Title attribute for hyperlinks	Add the `title` attribute to all hyperlink tags. Title attributes help search engines index pages, provide pop-up screen tips in some browsers, and aid visitors using assistive devices.	```<a href="1040.pdf" title="1040 Form (PDF)" target="_ blank">Download the 1040 Form (PDF)</a>```
Table title attributes	Similar in function to `alt` text for an image, the `title` attribute goes in the opening table tag and provides a title and description for the contents of a table.	```<table width="400" border="1" cell spacing="0" id="earnings" title="Earnings" summary="Projected 3rd Quarter Earnings">```
Link tags in the `<head>` of the page that point back to the home page and site map page	These links help improve accessibility of these all-important pages to visitors using assisted-viewing devices. In addition, they assist search engine robots/spiders in more readily indexing pages in a database. The `rel` part of the link defines the relationship between the current page and the page being linked to.	```<link rel="Index" href="index.html">``` ```<link rel="SiteMap" href="sitemap.html">```

continued

Book III Chapter 1

Adding Text, Images, and Links

Table 1-2 *(continued)*

Name	Description	Sample Usage
Footer links	Add navigational text hyperlinks at the foot of each page to mirror any graphic-only links to the main pages on a site. Footer links may also include links to other important pages such as privacy policy or terms of service pages.	<u>Home</u> - <u>About Us</u> - <u>Contact</u> Each word in the footer should be hyperlinked to its respective page using the standard hyperlink anchor tag with `href` attribute, as in `<a href="about.html" target="_self">About Us</a>`
A site map page	This page includes hyperlinks to all the accessible pages on a site, typically in list format with any sub-pages listed under the relevant main category page listing.	<u>Home</u> <u>About Us</u> <u>Company History</u> <u>Board of Directors</u> <u>Our Mission</u> <u>Contact</u> Each word or phrase is hyperlinked to its respective page, as in: `<a href="board.html" target="_self">Board of Directors</a>`
Contrasting foreground and background colors	One of the most common disabilities for visitors on the Internet is color blindness. To assist these visitors in having a positive experience on your website, use colors with a strong enough color contrast that the difference can be easily detected.	Check out the accessibility color wheel by Giacomo Mazzocato: `http://gmazzocato. altervista.org/color wheel/wheel.php`. Use this tool to assist you with choosing color combinations that can improve page readability for those with partial or full color blindness.

Name	*Description*	*Sample Usage*
Hyperlink targets	Add the `target` attribute to your hyperlinks so that the browser knows where you want the linked page to load, whether that's in the same or a new browser window.	`<a href="index.html" target="_self" title="Home">Home</a>`
Access keys	Add keyboard shortcuts with the `accesskey` attribute that visitors can use (typically in combination with the Alt or Option key, as in Alt+C) to quickly move their cursor to links, form fields, and other accessible objects on a page.	`<a href="index.html" target="_self" accesskey="0" title="Home ">Home</a>`
Tab index	Often used in conjunction with the `access key` attribute, the `tabindex` attribute allows visitors to use the Tab key to advance from one link, form field, or other accessible object on a page to the next. If desired, the order of the tab index need not follow a direct top-to-bottom, left-to-right progression.	`<a href="index.html" target="_self" accesskey="0" title="Home " tabindex="1">Home</a>`

Chapter 2: Organizing Content with Tables and Lists

In This Chapter

- ✓ Using tables to organize content
- ✓ Adding content to tables
- ✓ Formatting tables and table cells
- ✓ Nesting tables
- ✓ Organizing content with lists
- ✓ Setting the list type
- ✓ Nesting lists

*W*hen it comes to keeping your content organized so that visitors can quickly find what they're looking for, consider marking up your data and list information with HTML tables and lists. Tables are useful for displaying tabular data and information with multiple categories, such as financial figures, store locations, and menu offerings. Lists are effective when you need to show things in sequence, such as how items in a set are structured relative to one another (as with links to all the site's pages on a site map page or a set of navigation buttons) or for times when you need your content to display in the order in which a set of items should be accessed or utilized (as with items in a numbered list).

In this chapter, you find out how easy it is to mark up basic content into table and list format. In addition, you read about adding and formatting content in tables, nesting tables for complex page elements, organizing and structuring list content, and list nesting to create multitier lists.

Lunch Menu:

| Lite Fare | Garden Salad |
| | Soup |

Inserting Tables on a Page

Although most modern page layouts rely on layers using `<div>` tags to organize content on the page within the browser instead of tables, which was once the norm, tables themselves are still very useful within the body of the page for organizing data and other content that requires gridlike arrangement. In the following sections, you find out more about the basics of organizing your content in tables.

Discovering what you can do with tables

Tables are the perfect way to organize multi-row and multi-column data and other content within regions of a web page, particularly because anything that can go on a page can be placed inside a table cell. Furthermore, in a table, you can control the alignment, width, and height of the table cells, as well as style the contents of the table and the individual table cells with CSS, providing you with a whole new level of control over the contents of the table.

Tables can have any number of rows and columns, be any width and height, have any colored border, and have any background color or tiling background image. What's more, the cells of the tables can also have unique widths, heights, and background colors and/or background images that sit on top of whatever styling attributes happen to be applied to the table. Not only that, but you can quickly include a row of table headings by adding a row of header cells instead of data cells.

One of the only real drawbacks to working with tables is that they require a lot of code to do the job they do, which can increase the overall size of the HTML file. For example, the table in Figure 2-1 looks fairly straightforward, but on the code level it looks like this:

Winter 2013 Schedule	MON	TUES	WED	THURS
First Class	1/7/13	1/8/13	1/9/13	1/10/13
No Class	2/18/13	2/12/13	2/13/13	2/14/13
Last Class	3/25/13	3/26/13	3/27/13	3/28/13

Figure 2-1: Tables require a lot of HTML coding to display content in an orderly manner.

```
<table id="schedule">
  <tr>
    <th>Winter 2013 Schedule</td>
    <th>MON</td>
    <th>TUES</td>
    <th>WED</td>
    <th>THURS</td>
  </tr>
  <tr>
    <td class="cellstyle">First Class</td>
    <td class="cellstyle">1/7/13</td>
    <td class="cellstyle">1/8/13</td>
    <td class="cellstyle">1/9/13</td>
    <td class="cellstyle">1/10/13</td>
  </tr>
  <tr>
    <td class="cellstyle">No Class</td>
    <td class="cellstyle">2/18/13</td>
    <td class="cellstyle">2/12/13</td>
```

```
      <td class="cellstyle">2/13/13</td>
      <td class="cellstyle">2/14/13</td>
   </tr>
   <tr>
      <td class="cellstyle">Last Class</td>
      <td class="cellstyle">3/25/13</td>
      <td class="cellstyle">3/26/13</td>
      <td class="cellstyle">3/27/13</td>
      <td class="cellstyle">3/28/13></td>
   </tr>
</table>
```

Understanding the structure of a table

To display correctly in a browser, each table requires several components.

The first part is the opening and closing `<table>` tags, which define the table's beginning and end within the HTML. The opening `<table>` tag is where you can add attributes to the code (for things like setting the width of the table, though that too can be set with CSS instead) and apply any special formatting to the table using CSS styles, as in the following example:

```
<table width="300" id="menu">
</table>
```

In between the table tags come the opening and closing table row tags, `<tr>` and `</tr>`, which define a row within the table. To have more than one row, insert another pair of table row tags, as in the following example:

```
<table width="300" id="menu">
<tr></tr>
<tr></tr>
</table>
```

To define individual table cells, which make up the columns across each row in the table, insert a pair of table data tags, `<td>` and `</td>`, between the table row tags. To have more than one column in a row, insert another pair of table data tags between the table row tags, as in the following example:

```
<table width="300" id="menu">
<tr>
    <td></td>
    <td></td>
</tr>
<tr>
    <td></td>
    <td></td>
</tr>
</table>
```

To define table heading cells, which typically make up the columns across the first row in the table, insert a pair of table header tags, `<th>` and `</th>`, between the table row tags, as in the following example:

```
<table width="300" id="menu">
<tr>
    <th></th>
    <th></th>
</tr>
<tr>
    <td></td>
    <td></td>
</tr>
</table>
```

To hold a table cell open so that it doesn't collapse when no content is inside of it, insert the "nonbreaking space" code entity   into the code between the opening and closing table cell tags:

```
<td> </td>
```

The minimum number of rows and columns you can have in a table is one each, which creates a one-celled table using a single pair of <tr> and <td> tags:

```
<table width="300" id="menu">
<tr>
    <td> </td>
</tr>
</table>
```

After you set up the basic table structure of your table using <table>, <tr>, <th>, and <td> tags, you can specify the desired number of rows and columns, insert content in the cells as needed, and style the table, table cells, and cell content using CSS.

That said, you can also still use a number of HTML table and table cell attributes to alter the structure of the table in a manner that meets your needs and ensures that the table will appear as you envisioned in the browser. For instance, you can merge and split table cells to create unusual table layouts and have content span across a series of table cells both vertically and horizontally.

Fortunately, with the advent of HTML editors, coding tables by hand is no longer a necessary evil. Most code editors should allow you to quickly and painlessly split and merge cells, set table and cell widths, and add color to borders and backgrounds with just a few clicks. Nonetheless, even though you'll likely use a code editor to build your tables for you, you should still understand the underlying structure of tables so that you can easily manipulate them at the code level if needed.

The following sections walk you through the steps of adding content to your tables, formatting the table and table cells using HTML attributes, and nesting tables for more complex content organization. As for styling the table and table content with CSS styles, which is the recommended method for styling your tables, Book III, Chapters 3 and 4 tell you more about working with CSS.

Adding content to table cells

Any content that can go elsewhere on the web page can be placed inside a table cell. This means you can add text, graphics, Flash movies, animations, Shockwave movies, applets, plug-ins, audio files, video files, e-mail addresses, JavaScript, hyperlinks, named anchor links, layers, form fields, Spry widgets, tabular data, dynamic data, blog data, PayPal buttons, shopping cart elements, and even hidden elements that reside in the code but do not appear on the web page. Figure 2-2 shows an example of two tables stacked on top of each other, one with a background image and HTML text and the next with two rows and four columns, each cell displaying a linkable graphic and hypertext link to detail pages about each product.

1-celled table with HTML text and background image

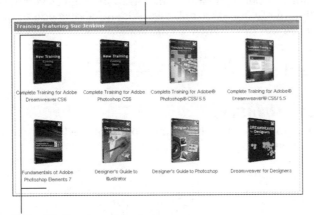

Table with 2 rows and 4 columns

Figure 2-2: Table cells can hold any content that can appear elsewhere on a web page, such as text, graphics, links, animations, and videos.

To add content to a table, place your cursor inside any table cell (between any pair of opening and closing `<th>` or `<td>` tags, if you're hand-coding) and simply add the desired content and necessary HTML code. If you're using an HTML editor, you will likely have special tools, buttons, or menu options within the program that you can use to add the content more quickly and efficiently. For instance, in Dreamweaver, you can use the Insert menu commands or any of the buttons in the Insert panel to quickly add links, graphics, images, and media files. After the data is inserted, you can style and format the table and table content with CSS and continue adding data in the other table cells.

Formatting Tables

When styling your tables and the content within them, do as much as you can with Cascading Style Sheets. Of course, within the code of your tables, you can still set table and cell widths, table and cell alignment, cell padding, and cell spacing. However, try to use CSS exclusively to specify these and any other table and cell attributes that have to do with how the table looks. CSS provides you with greater control of the presentation of the table content as well as make the presentation of the content more easily editable, because all the site's styling is then contained in the CSS rather than on the individual pages of the site.

The id attribute

Anytime you intend to style a part of your table with CSS — whether it's the table background, table border, cell background, cell alignment, or any of the other attributes discussed in the following sections — be sure to add an id attribute to each of your tables in the opening <table> tag. This helps make your tables easier to identify from one another, gives you the opportunity to apply different styling to them if desired, and allows you to quickly apply both CSS and JavaScript to them as needed:

```
<table width="400" border="1" cellspacing="10"
    cellpadding="0" id="storehours">
```

The class attribute

For styles that you'll be applying to multiple table cells, add the class attribute to individual <td> tags:

```
<table id="offices">
<tr>
    <td class="locations">Atlanta</td>
</tr>
</table>
```

Table widths and heights

You can set each of your tables to have specific widths and heights within the page. Those attributes can be specified in the code in the opening <table> tag. However, even though it was once a common practice to specify the height in the table, the height attribute has been deprecated, so if you need to set a height, you must now do that in the CSS.

However, the width can be set in either the CSS (which is best) or within the HTML as an attribute of the opening table tag. Table widths are most often notated in the code in pixels or in a percentage that is relative to the size of the viewing browser window (or other container tag, such as a layer or table). For example, as illustrated in Figure 2-3, a table's width can be fixed at 450 pixels or be set to a width that is equal to 70 percent of the browser window:

```
<table width="70%">
<table width="450">
```

Anytime a percentage is specified in the code (or in the CSS), that number will maintain the same aspect ratio to the browser as the user increases or decreases the size of the browser window on his computer's desktop.

On the other hand, should the width of the table not be specified in the opening table tag or in the CSS, the size of all the table cells within the table will collapse to fit the contents inside them, whatever those contents might be. This means that the contents with the largest width and height in any one cell will determine the width of the entire column and/or the height of an entire row.

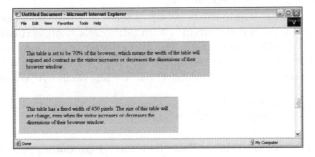

Figure 2-3: You can specify table widths in fixed pixel dimensions or as a percentage relative to the size of the browser window or surrounding container tags.

**Book III
Chapter 2**

**Organizing Content
with Tables and
Lists**

However, when you set the size of the table cell, the contents of a cell have no effect on the width and height of its respective column or row. The only exception to this is when the contents of the cell exceed the preset cell size. Typically, to set the width of an entire column, you only need to add the `width` attribute to the first cell in the first row; all other cells in the column beneath that cell automatically take on the same dimensions. Here's what the code for a 500-pixel-wide, 2-row, 2-column table with a 1-pixel border and set cell widths without CSS looks like:

```
<table width="500" border="1">
  <tr>
    <td width="300">Select Item</td>
    <td width="100">Price</td>
  </tr>
  <tr>
    <td>#TA57694</td>
```

```
      <td>$150.00</td>
   </tr>
</table>
```

Of course, a better method for setting the width of the table and cells is to use CSS, in which case your code might look more like the following:

```
<table id="products">
   <tr>
      <td>Select Item</td>
      <td>Price</td>
   </tr>
   <tr>
      <td>#TA57694</td>
      <td>$150.00</td>
   </tr>
</table>
```

Table and cell alignment

You can align a table within the browser window or within another container, whereas you can align the content within table cells both vertically and horizontally. With table alignment, you can either use CSS for the greatest control or resort to using the old `align` attribute — with a value of `left`, `right`, or `center` — in the opening `<table>` tag, as in the following:

```
<table width="300" align="center" cellpadding="2"
   cellspacing="0">
```

Unfortunately, because this attribute has been deprecated, you might find that adding the `align` attribute to the `<table>` tag produces uneven results in certain browsers.

To resolve that issue, simply create a custom class CSS style such as the following:

```
.tablealign {
   margin-right: auto;
   margin-left: auto;
}
```

When applied to your table using the `class` attribute in the opening table tag, this style horizontally aligns the table within the browser window:

```
<table class="tablealign">
   <tr>
      <td>Select Item</td>
      <td>Price</td>
   </tr>
   <tr>
      <td>#TA57694</td>
```

```
      <td>$150.00</td>
    </tr>
</table>
```

This latter method is more widely supported by different browsers on both Mac and PC platforms, and thus is more likely to display your content accurately with the desired alignment.

To set the alignment of the contents inside any table cell, you could apply the `align` (horizontal alignment) and `valign` (vertical alignment) attributes in the opening `<td>` tag of the cell that requires alignment:

```
<td width="200" rowspan="2" align="left"
    valign="top">Kittens</td>
```

Horizontal alignment options are `left`, `center`, and `right`, and vertical alignment options are `top`, `middle`, `bottom`, and `baseline` (which aligns the image bottom to the baseline of text within the table cell and at times looks no different from the bottom attribute).

When using CSS to set the alignment of content in a table cell, you can replace the old HTML `align` attribute with the CSS `text-align` attribute to create left-, right-, center-, and justify-aligned content within a table cell. Likewise, for vertical alignment within a table cell, you can use the `vertical-align` attribute to vertically align your content to `baseline`, `bottom`, `middle`, `sub`, `super`, `text-bottom`, `text-top`, `top`, and `inherit`.

Figure 2-4 shows an example of the variety of cell alignment options you can create by using the `align` and `valign` attributes for your table cell content, which all mirror the alignment options you can create now with CSS.

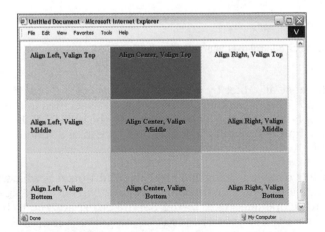

Figure 2-4: Rather than use the old align and valign attributes to align content in your table cells, use CSS!

Table borders

When adding a border to a table with the old HTML `border` attribute, the size you specify in the code refers only to the thickness of the table's outer edge. Any border width larger than 1 pixel creates a beveled table edge, as shown in Figure 2-5.

Figure 2-5: Adding a border larger than 1 pixel on a table using HTML code produces a border with a beveled edge.

If you hate the bevel (which is very old school and can make your table look awkwardly retro), you can create a non-beveled outer table border of any thickness and color, like the one shown in Figure 2-6, by using CSS. See Book III, Chapter 4 for details on border formatting with CSS.

Figure 2-6: For more control over your table borders, use CSS.

Likewise, because all tables by default have 1 pixel of `cellpadding` and `cellspacing` (even when these attributes aren't specified in the code), when you apply a 1-pixel border to a table with the old HTML `border` attribute, the border looks like a double line instead of a solid line, as shown in Figure 2-7.

To remove this default spacing and create a solid 1-pixel border with the HTML `border` attribute, include both `cellpadding` and `cellspacing` attributes in the opening `<table>` tag. Set the `cellpadding` to the desired amount and set the `cellspacing` to 0:

Today's Menu		
Lite Fare:	Garden Salad	$8.00
	Soup	$4.00

Figure 2-7: Tables with a 1-pixel border and no attributes specified for cellpadding and cellspacing display a double-lined border effect.

```
<table width="600" border="1" cellpadding="10"
   cellspacing="0">
  <tr>
    <td width="300">Google</td>
    <td width="300">Yahoo</td>
  </tr>
</table>
```

Better yet, zero-out both the `cellpadding` and `cellspacing` in the HTML and apply a custom border and padding to the table with CSS.

Cellpadding and cellspacing attributes

Because content can sometimes look too cramped within a table cell, you can apply two special HTML table attributes to your table to give the content a little more breathing room. These two attributes, `cellpadding` and `cellspacing`, uniformly apply extra space to all the cells and cell walls, respectively, within a table:

- `cellpadding`: This is the pixel space that can be adjusted between the contents of the table cells and the cell walls. The larger the number of pixels, the more padding is added between the cell walls and the cell contents. Think of this as if you're moving your furniture away from the walls of the room so that you can more freely walk the perimeter of the room unencumbered.
- `cellspacing`: This is the pixel space, or thickness, within the cell walls between the cells. You can think of this as having thick or thin walls between your bedroom and your pretend-brother's; the thicker the walls, the less his loud music will annoy you.

All tables by default have 1 pixel of `cellpadding` and `cellspacing`, even when these attributes aren't specified in the code. Therefore, to remove this default spacing, you must "zero out" these attributes in the code, as follows:

```
<table width="200" border="1" cellpadding="0"
   cellspacing="0">
  <tr>
    <td width="300">Peanuts
     </td>
```

```
    <td width="100">Popcorn
      </td>
   </tr>
</table>
```

You can use the `cellpadding` and `cellspacing` attributes alone or together to achieve the desired results. For example, the four tables shown in Figure 2-8 all have 1-pixel borders, but the first has `cellpadding` and `cellspacing` set to 0, the second has `cellpadding` set to 10 and `cell spacing` set to 0, the third has `cellpadding` set to 0 and `cellspacing` set to 10, and the fourth has both `cellpadding` and `cellspacing` set to 10.

For an alternative method of applying spacing between the content in your table cells and the table cell walls, use the padding and border-spacing style attributes in your CSS.

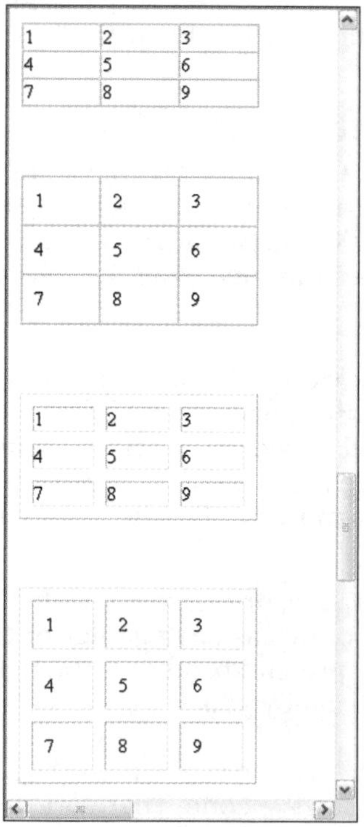

Figure 2-8: Use the cellpadding and cellspacing attributes to structure how content sits within a table, or use CSS styles to control the padding and border-spacing.

Table headers

In the past, when you wanted to format the topmost row and/or leftmost column in the table to be structurally different (typically bolder and one font size bigger) than the rest of the table's content, you'd use the old `<th>`, or table header, tags in place of `<td>` tags.

Several table head attributes (including `width`, `height`, `bgcolor`, and `nowrap`) were deprecated in the XHTML 1.0 Strict DTD and are no longer usable with HTML5. However, some designers still use `<th>` because it has a certain semantic meaning above and beyond `<td>` tags. If your tables need header rows or header columns, use the `<th>` tag. You may then go right to CSS to create and apply custom styles to any table cell, row, or column that requires special formatting.

For example, to create a table header row or column styled with CSS, create a custom style and apply it selectively to the desired table head:

```
<tr>
    <th class="tableheadstyle">Specialty Drinks:</th>
    <td>Iced Cafe Mocha</td>
    <td>$3.75</td>
</tr>
```

The nowrap attribute

Another deprecated tag in XHTML 1.0 Strict code is the `nowrap` attribute, which used to override any specified column width applied to a table cell so that the contents of that cell would display in a complete line without any line breaks or text wrapping:

```
<td nowrap="nowrap">Address, Telephone, and Store Hours</td>
```

To perform the same function today, use the CSS `width` attribute for keeping cells wide enough to display the cell's contents without wrapping. This will ensure that the cell widths are set to the proper size within the CSS to accommodate the content. Alternatively, you can create a custom class style that contains the `white-space: nowrap` style declaration and apply that class to your `<td>`:

```
<td class="nowrap">Address, Telephone, and Store Hours</td>
```

Splitting and merging table cells

Tables need not be totally uniform with an equal number of rows and columns. If your table requires it, you can split any single cell into two or more columns or rows. Likewise, you can merge any two or more contiguous (touching) table cells into a larger rectangular shape. What's more, if you're using a good code editor, the program should handle all of the merging and spanning code for you so that you can focus on the table's layout.

To uniformly merge table cells, whether horizontally or vertically, one of two special attributes, `colspan` or `rowspan`, must be added to the `<td>` tag that initiates the merge. In effect, both of these attributes define a region that spans *n* number of rows or columns.

As shown in the following code example and illustrated in Figure 2-9, when the colspan attribute is used, only one <td> tag is needed for the part of the row being spanned. Likewise, when the rowspan attribute is used, any row or rows after the first cell in the rows being spanned do not need a <td> tag:

```
<table width="450" border="1">
  <tr>
    <td height="23" colspan="3">Overview:</td>
  </tr>
  <tr>
    <td width="126" rowspan="2">Key Features:</td>
    <td width="183">Snowball Maker</td>
    <td width="323">Make round compact snowballs.</td>
  </tr>
  <tr>
    <td>Snow Castle Molds</td>
    <td>Build your own forts!</td>
  </tr>
</table>
```

Overview:		
Key Features:	Snowball Maker	Make round compact snowballs.
	Snow Castle Molds	Build your own forts!

Figure 2-9: Split and merge table cells using the colspan and rowspan attributes.

Background and border colors

Like many of the other attributes for tables, you can create custom styles in CSS that do the same thing, only better. Nonetheless, you should still understand everything that can be done with HTML, in the event you inherit an old site that uses these attributes.

The background color (bgcolor) attribute is one of those attributes that used to be applied to both the table in the opening <table> tag and to individual table cells in the opening <td> table cell tags. Similarly, you could apply a border color (bordercolor) attribute to the entire table as well as to table cells, though the bordercolor attribute for individual table cells is inconsistently supported in browsers and isn't a recommended practice.

To illustrate how you might use these attributes (though, as I mention previously, it would be much better if you applied these styles to your table with CSS instead), you could have an overall background color on the entire table, a border color for the table, and a different background color set for one or more of the table cells, as illustrated in Figure 2-10.

Blue Plate Specials	
Meat Loaf & Mashed Potatoes	$8.95
Old Fashioned Macaroni & Cheese	$7.95

Figure 2-10: Tables can be styled with background colors, border colors, and cell background colors.

When styling with custom styles in CSS, your code might look like the following:

```
<table class="blueplates">
  <tr>
    <td colspan="3" class="specials">Blue Plate Specials</td>
  </tr>
  <tr>
    <td class="menuitems">Meat Loaf &amp; Mashed Potatoes</td>
    <td class="menuitems1">$8.95</td>
  </tr>
  <tr>
    <td class="menuitems">Old Fashioned Macaroni &amp; Cheese</td>
    <td class="menuitems2">$7.95</td>
  </tr>
</table>
```

By contrast, HTML code using the old `bgcolor`, `bordercolor`, and other deprecated table attributes would look something like this:

```
<table width="350" border="1" cellpadding="10" cellspacing="0"
    bordercolor="#000066" bgcolor="#99ccff">
  <tr>
    <td height="23" colspan="3" bgcolor="#99ccff"><strong>Blue Plate Specials</
    strong></td>
  </tr>
  <tr>
    <td width="286" bgcolor="#ffcc99">Meat Loaf &amp; Mashed Potatoes</td>
    <td width="68" bgcolor="#ffcc33">$8.95</td>
  </tr>
  <tr>
    <td bgcolor="#ffcc99">Old Fashioned Macaroni &amp; Cheese</td>
    <td bgcolor="#ff9900">$7.95</td>
  </tr>
</table>
```

To keep your HTML code as light and clean as possible, and to separate form from content, I strongly recommend — no, *urge* — you to use CSS for background and border color styles instead of using the `bgcolor` and `bordercolor` attributes described here.

Tiling background images

In addition to, or instead of, adding a background color to a table or table cell, you can also apply CSS styles that will apply a *tiling* background image to a table or table cell. A tiling image is an image that repeats endlessly both horizontally and vertically, like the one shown in Figure 2-11. You tile a background image by creating a special background style in the CSS and then applying that style to a table or table cell:

```
<td colspan="2" class="pattternbg">Get Connected!</td>
```

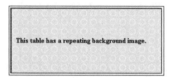

Figure 2-11: Use the background attribute to apply a repeating image to the background of a table or table cell or, better yet, use CSS.

By contrast, the old HTML way of adding a tiling background image involved applying the `background` attribute, which specifies the location and filename of a graphic to tile in the background, to the opening `<table>` tag and/or to any opening table cell (`<td>`) tag within the table:

```
<td colspan="2" background="images/funkypattern.png">Get
    Connected!</td>
```

The two main drawbacks of applying a background image to a table or table cell using the `background` attribute are as follows:

- ✔ The image tiles, giving you no control over how it repeats.
- ✔ CSS does the job much better, including allowing you to set the starting point of the background image relative to the top-left corner of the container, such as the table or an individual table cell, as well as how and where the background image repeats.

Therefore, if you need to tile an image in a table or table cell — or in any other container, for that matter — use CSS.

Nesting tables

When your table data has more complex layout requirements, you can nest tables inside other table cells. For example, you might need to create a section on your page to display product information in such a way that you can organize a product image, product name, description, details, stock number, and price. With a single table, you may not be able to size all the cells exactly as you'd like, but with a table nested inside another table cell, you could, as shown in the Dreamweaver nested table set of Figure 2-12.

You may nest tables as often as you need to create the layout you desire. Each nested table can be formatted and structured to suit your needs, and all the tables and all their respective contents can be styled uniquely using CSS.

Imprintable Invitations!

Each box includes 10 blank
imprintable #10 size invitations
with matching colored envelopes

Stock No #23003

Qty: ☐ @ #12.00 ea

Add to Cart

Figure 2-12: Use nested tables to create customized content layouts for your data.

Inserting Lists on a Page

Lists are one of the best ways to organize content on your web pages because they're easy to implement and can be tiered to create multilevel lists. Better yet, when combined with CSS, you can use list formatting to create dynamic standards-compliant HTML navigation systems that include both text and graphics.

To convert regular text into list format, you must add two tag components to the HTML code. First, the entire list must be surrounded by list tags. Second, each item in the list must be surrounded with list item tags. But, before you start coding, you have to first decide which kind of list you want to add to your page.

Examining the two list types

You can make two different kinds of lists in HTML: ordered lists, which use <ol> tags, and unordered lists, which use <ul> tags. Ordered lists display items in a sequence with an Arabic or Roman numeral or letter next to them, whereas unordered lists simply list items with one of three types of bullets next to them. In both instances, the type of bullet or number is an attribute of the ordered or unordered list tag.

After you choose whether you want to create an ordered or unordered list, you can add individual items to the list using the opening and closing <li> list item tags, as in the following example:

```
<ol>
  <li>Ham & Swiss Cheese</li>
  <li>BLT</li>
  <li>Grilled Cheese</li>
  <li>Egg Salad</li>
```

```
   <li>Tuna Salad</li>
   <li>Chicken Salad</li>
</ol>
```

In addition, you may also specify a list type as an attribute of the ordered or unordered list so that the list displays your items with the desired appearance:

✔ **Ordered lists** may be set to have one of five different appearance types: numbered (1, 2, 3), lowercase lettered (a, b, c), uppercase lettered (A, B, C), lowercase Roman (i, ii, iii), and uppercase Roman (I, II, III). To specify the list type for ordered lists, enter **1**, **a**, **A**, **i**, or **I** in the type attribute of the opening ordered list tag:

```
<ol type="1">
   <li>Crosswords</li>
   <li>Sudoku</li>
   <li>Word Search</li>
</ol>
```

✔ **Unordered lists** are essentially bulleted lists that can be set to display all the items in the list with one of three types of bullets next to it: disc, circle, or square, as shown in Figure 2-13. The type of bullet can be set by adding the type attribute to the opening unordered list tag:

```
<ul type="circle">
   <li>Mercury</li>
   <li>Venus</li>
   <li>Earth</li>
</ul>
```

With both ordered and unordered lists, it's okay to leave off the type attribute. By default, all ordered lists use the numbered type, and all unordered lists use the disc type.

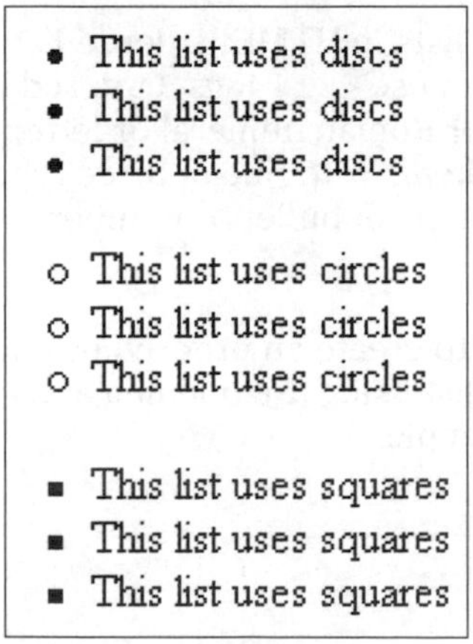

Figure 2-13: Use HTML markup to specify one of three different bullet types in an unordered list.

List item tags: To close or not to close

In some older HTML training materials, both in book form and online, you may occasionally find instruction that says it is okay to omit the closing </li> tag from your list HTML markup. In fact, the W3C openly states that this is fine to do in HTML; however, that doesn't necessarily mean the same closing tag omission is acceptable when coding in XHTML or HTML5. This is especially true when using the XHTML 1.0 Strict DTD, which, among other things, requires that all tags be closed.

Furthermore, if you use any of the XHTML or HTML5 DTDs and fail to close your list items with closing </li> tags, the code in your page may not validate based on accessibility and standards compliance, which you read about in Book IV, Chapters 1 and 2. Therefore, to avoid possible validation issues, make your pages as accessible as possible, and to ensure a clean transition when migrating from HTML to XHTML or HTML5, always close your tags.

If you'd rather use a custom bullet graphic instead of the three HTML list bullet types mentioned here, take heart. You can easily create and use your own custom bullet graphics when you combine your list with special CSS styles. Turn to Book III, Chapter 4 to find out more about styling lists.

Nesting lists

To create a nested list, which is a list that has one or more subsections or sublists in it, just add a full set of list markup tags to the code in line with any of the primary list items. In the following example, an unordered list is nested inside an ordered list:

```
<ol type="A">
  <li>Coffee
    <ul type="disc">
      <li>Regular</li>
      <li>Decaf</li>
    </ul>
  </li>
  <li>Tea</li>
  <li>Juice</li>
</ol>
```

Each of your lists may contain as many nested lists as needed to format your list in the desired configuration. To see how fast and easy it is to create a list, follow these steps:

1. **Enter the following content into a blank web page in your favorite HTML or code editor, making sure to add the following text between the opening and closing body tags:**

```
Digital Cameras - SLR
   Nikon
      12.1 megapixel
      14.0 megapixel
      16.1 megapixel
   Canon
   Panasonic
Digital Cameras - Point & Shoot
   Sony
   Canon
   Fujifilm
   Panasonic
```

Your code editor should have already added the bones of the code to your web page, including the DTD, head, title, and body tags.

2. **Select a list type for the main list, such as unordered, and add the markup for the list type and list items. Repeat for the other two list levels.**

   For instance, you might make Digital Cameras – SLR and Digital Cameras – Point & Shoot into a numbered list and then make the subitems in each list bullets, as in this example:

```
<ol>
   <li>Digital Cameras - SLR
     <ul>
       <li>Nikon
         <ul>
            <li>12.1 megapixel</li>
            <li>14.0 megapixel</li>
            <li>16.1 megapixel</li>
         </ul>
       </li>
       <li>Canon</li>
       <li>Panasonic</li>
     </ul>
   </li>
   <li>Digital Cameras - Point &amp; Shoot
     <ul>
       <li>Sony</li>
       <li>Canon</li>
       <li>Fujifilm</li>
       <li>Panasonic</li>
     </ul>
   </li>
</ol>
```

3. **Save your file with the `.html` extension and select the Preview in Browser option in your editor to view your markup in a browser.**

   Most editors provide the option of viewing the code in a browser of your choice. For example, in Dreamweaver, you'd choose File⇨Preview in Browser and then select one of the browsers from the editable list of installed browsers on your computer. Figure 2-14 shows an example of how this list appears in a browser window.

```
1.  Digital Cameras - SLR
       ◦ Nikon
            ▪ 12.1 megapixel
            ▪ 14.0 megapixel
            ▪ 16.1 megapixel
       ◦ Canon
       ◦ Panasonic
2.  Digital Cameras - Point & Shoot
       ◦ Sony
       ◦ Canon
       • Fujifilm
       ◦ Panasonic
```

Figure 2-14: List markup can be used to create complex multitier and multitype lists.

Adding content and formatting a list

What kinds of content can appear in your list? The sky is the limit. List items can include text, hyperlinks, graphics, tables, layers, Flash movies, and anything else that can appear elsewhere on a web page. In addition, you can use bold and italic tags to add emphasis, turn a list item graphic into a link, add named anchor links to content farther down on the same page, and best of all, select a font face, color, size, custom bullet, and more by creating and applying a custom CSS style to your list. Figure 2-15 illustrates how multiple CSS styles can be applied to different parts of a list. For details about customizing your lists with CSS, see Book III, Chapter 4.

```
1. Digital Cameras - SLR
     • Nikon
          ▪ 12.1 megapixel
          ▪ 14.0 megapixel
          ▪ 16.1 megapixel
     • Canon
     • Panasonic
2. Digital Cameras - Point & Shoot
     ▪ Sony
     ▪ Canon
     ▪ Fujifilm
     ▪ Panasonic
```

Figure 2-15: For best results, use CSS to format the content in your lists.

Some browsers may still support a few deprecated list tag attributes that can alter when a list begins relative to the starting point. For instance, to make an ordered list begin later than the first item, such as starting with the letter *F* in a list with the alphabetical `type` attribute or the number 20 in a numbered list, add the `start` attribute to the opening `<ol>` tag:

```
<ol type="A" start="6">
  <li>Coffee
    <ul type="disc">
      <li>Regular</li>
```

```
      <li>Decaf</li>
    </ul>
  </li>
  <li>Tea</li>
  <li>Juice</li>
</ol>
```

Though in ordered lists you can't break up a list and continue the numbering from one part to another, you can reset the number in a list item by adding the value attribute to the <li> tag. This sets the new starting value for all subsequent list items:

```
<ol type="1">
  <li value="10">Coffee
    <ul type="disc">
      <li>Regular</li>
      <li>Decaf</li>
    </ul>
  </li>
  <li>Tea</li>
  <li>Juice</li>
</ol>
```

Keep in mind that some list attributes have been deprecated and that you may get inconsistent results in different browsers. For instance, the start and type attributes were deprecated in HTML 4.01 and XHTML but reinstated in HTML5. Thus, for best control over the style of your list content, use CSS, as in the following example:

```
<ol id="menu">
  <li class="beverages">Coffee
  <li class="beverages">Tea</li>
  <li class="beverages">Juice</li>
</ol>
```

Chapter 3: Styling with Cascading Style Sheets

In This Chapter

✔ **Getting familiar with the CSS syntax**

✔ **Creating inline, internal, and external CSS**

✔ **Understanding CSS selectors**

*1*n earlier chapters of this book, you discover that Cascading Style Sheets are really the way to go when it comes to styling the content on your pages. Yet until now, I haven't gotten into the nuts and bolts of how to create and apply CSS to your HTML. That's what this chapter is all about.

To make the task of finding out about styling pages with CSS flow as smoothly as possible, this chapter breaks down CSS into several easily digestible parts. First, you read about the anatomy of the CSS style syntax. Then you discover the difference between inline, internal, and external style sheets and find out how to link an external CSS to an HTML file. After that, you find out the basics of creating custom class styles, redefining default tag styles, setting up ID styles, and using compound CSS styles to style several tags at once. Then, you move on to the advanced concept of pseudo-classes and you find out how to create custom link styles for various sections within your web page. To round it all out, at the end you discover how to create a master CSS file.

Normal

Visited

Hover

Active

Understanding CSS Basics

Back in the late 1990s, a tool called Cascading Style Sheets was developed as an enhancement to traditional HTML markup that enabled designers to place all the styling information for an entire website into a single, centralized, external document. This external CSS file served to decrease the file size of all the HTML pages while at the same time reducing the amount of code required for styling in every page of a website.

In addition to keeping the HTML code less cluttered than pages used to be when coding with the old `<font>` and other HTML tags for text formatting, the use of CSS provides several other benefits, including the following:

✔ **Faster page download times:** Both the HTML files and the CSS file load quicker when all the page-styling information is contained in the CSS.

✔ **Improved site access for visitors with disabilities:** Screen readers and other assistive devices can disable or otherwise ignore CSS, providing easier access to the content on a website.

✔ **Improved management of visual presentation:** A single external CSS file means that you can quickly make style modifications to an entire site by modifying the CSS, which is much faster than it would be if you were using the old <font> and other formatting tags.

To illustrate, consider that you were using old HTML tags for styling, which means you'd have to specify the font face, size, and color each time a new paragraph required a different font appearance, on every page of your site:

```
<p><font color="#FF6666" size="2" face=
  "Georgia,Times,serif"><a href="casestudies.html">
  <b>Read our Case Studies</b></a></font></p>
```

Now compare that to working with CSS. When all the font attributes for paragraphs are transferred to the default styling for paragraphs (the <p> tag) in an external Cascading Style Sheet, the HTML code becomes much cleaner:

```
<p><a href="casestudies.html"><strong>Read our Case
  Studies</strong></a></p>
```

✔ **Easier site maintenance after the site is published:** With the old <font> and other HTML style tags and attributes, any time the site's look needed changing, you would have to individually modify each file, and then you'd have to upload *all* the changed files to the server before those changes would take effect for site visitors. With CSS, you need only upload the updated CSS file to the remote server, and then everyone can see the style changes. Fast and simple!

Using CSS as a web standard

You find countless benefits of working with CSS, the most striking of which is that when you place all of your styling information in a single external CSS file, rather than embedding it within the HTML markup of your individual web pages, you get the maximum amount of control over the look of your entire site. This is especially desirable during the design phase as you are constructing the pages for your site, and again later during the maintenance phase when it becomes time to make site-wide style changes.

The World Wide Web Consortium (W3C) strongly recommends CSS for styling web pages because it gives designers and programmers the highest degree of control over how web content is presented in a browser window on a computer, laptop, tablet, smartphone, or some other device. Much like a word processor or page-layout program's style sheets, CSS for the web enables you to set default formatting options so that all the text and other content, such as graphics, forms, animations, and videos, follow the design specifications of the mock-up. CSS also allows you to create customized styles that control the look and position of the objects and elements on your pages. You can then use those custom styles by selectively applying them to the various text, images, lists, tables, and other objects on a page as needed.

As you'll quickly find out, CSS can be used to control nearly everything about your site content's presentation in a browser. Use CSS to apply detailed settings to pretty much any page element, including the following:

- ✔ Font face, size, style, and color
- ✔ Margins, padding, and indenting
- ✔ Line and letter spacing
- ✔ Background colors and background images
- ✔ Border colors, size, and styles
- ✔ Table and list formatting
- ✔ Layer size, style, and positioning
- ✔ Hyperlink formatting

Thankfully, CSS is pretty easy to understand and use. By the end of this chapter, if you diligently read the text and follow along with each of the exercises found here, you should be well on your way to styling your own pages with Cascading Style Sheets.

In the sections that follow, you find out about the structure of a CSS style, the different ways you can add CSS to your pages, setting media types for displaying CSS on different devices, and more.

Taking a look at the anatomy of a style

To understand Cascading Style Sheets, you must first understand the anatomy of a style, which is made up of a *selector* and one or more *declarations* made up of *property/value* pairs, both of which make up the rules for the style and instruct a browser on how to display the content. Figure 3-1 diagrams the anatomy of a CSS style to help you understand how to write styles correctly in your CSS files.

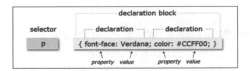

Figure 3-1: Each style in a Cascading Style Sheet has a selector and declaration.

The syntax of a CSS style runs generally as follows, with a selector and one or more declarations, including all the funny punctuation and spacing:

```
selector { property: value; }
```

To explain more precisely, the selector and declaration work together as follows:

- ✓ **Selector:** The selector is the name of the style, which can be a tag name such as p or h1, a custom class name such as .superscript or .tableborder, or the ID of an object preceded by the number symbol (#), such as #sidebar or #menutable. Selectors can also be compound, which specify style attributes for a specific location within the code. The selector tells the browser which tag(s) in the HTML to select and apply the style to, such as all content on the entire site that is surrounded by <h1> tags.

  As you find out later in this chapter, you can use four different types of contextual selectors. Generally, each selector identifies a single element on the site to be styled in a particular way. However, for maximum efficiency of your code, you can also group selectors together, separated with commas without spaces, when you would like certain selectors to share particular style attributes, as in the following example, which sets the default font to Georgia for all paragraphs, heading 1s, and heading 2s:

  ```
  p,h1,h2 {font-family: Georgia, Times New Roman, Times,
      serif; }
  ```

- ✓ **Declaration:** The declaration, which is the part of the style that is listed between opening and closing curly braces ({}), can contain a single style definition or several style definitions in a block, each separated by semicolons. The declaration provides the details of the style, including what should be changed (the *properties*) and to what degree (the *values* of those properties), such as the color of an element being changed to a particular blue. In addition, even though only four types of selectors exist, declarations can include an unlimited number of property-value pairs (style attributes) from any of the eight different style categories, which are outlined in the following section.

In the actual usage, a CSS style might look something like the following code example, where the style selector is h1 and the declaration defines the desired color of any content placed between h1 tags:

```
h1 { color: #CC3333; }
```

Exploring inline, internal, and external CSS

You can place the actual CSS code in three locations relative to the HTML code that it will be styling and formatting: inline, internal, or external. There are benefits and drawbacks to placing CSS code in each location, but most professional designers recommend using external CSS.

Inline CSS

These styles sit right next to the HTML code, typically preceding the content they'll be styling. Though this type of CSS code isn't used much for full website styling (because designers prefer to use either internal or external styles instead), some designers use inline styles for HTML e-mail formatting. The following example shows inline CSS applied to the <p> tag of HTML code using the style attribute:

```
<p style="color: #3399CC; font-size: 18px;">The Solar System</p>
```

Internal CSS

These style definitions (sometimes also called *embedded* styles) must be placed between the opening and closing <head> tags of an individual web page's HTML code for the styles to be applied to the content on that page. To take effect, internal CSS styles must be surrounded by <style> tags so that the browser can identify the content between them as CSS styles. Furthermore, within the <style> tags, the styles must also be surrounded by comment tags (<!-- and -->) to prevent older browsers from displaying the style definitions as text in the body of the web page.

For example, in the following HTML 4.01 code, the internal CSS for the <p> tag appears between the <head> tags so that all instances of text within the <p> tags in the body of the HTML are formatted as 12px with the hexadecimal color value of #003366:

```
<!DOCTYPE HTML PUBLIC "-//W3C//DTD HTML 4.01 Transitional//
    EN" "http://www.w3.org/TR/html4/loose.dtd">
<html>
<head>
<meta http-equiv="Content-Type" content="text/html;
    charset=iso-8859-1">
<title>Web Design All-in-One For Dummies</title>
<style type="text/css">
<!--
p {font-size: 12px; color: #003366;}
-->
</style>
</head>
<body>
<p>Crafting the Elements of Design</p>
</body>
</html>
```

Book III
Chapter 3

Styling with Cascading Style Sheets

Although it is true that internal CSS is far more efficient than styling your content using the old HTML <font> tags, keep in mind that the definitions apply only to the page that includes them, which isn't very useful or economical when dealing with multipage websites.

External CSS

External style sheets, which some people refer to as *linked styles* or *linked style sheets,* are the gold standard for CSS because they truly separate your styles from your content. External CSS files are useful for any size website, from sites as small as just a couple of pages to sites that contain hundreds of pages. External CSS is so fantastic because it keeps all the styling in one centralized file for easy access and easy maintenance.

External style sheets must be saved with the .css file extension. The file can then be placed anywhere within the site relative to the other site files, but most designers place it either at the root level of the site or inside a folder at the root level, such as css/mycssfile.css. Your individual style definitions are then placed inside this external CSS file using the same style syntax of selector and declaration; however, you don't need to wrap the style information in style or comment tags. In other words, the only things in the external CSS file are the individual style definitions, such as

```
p {font-size: 12px; color: #003366;}
```

After you create your external style sheet, to get it to begin styling your pages, just insert a special link back to the CSS file. This link to the external CSS file must be added to all the pages on your site that you want to use it. In the HTML, you add a link to the external CSS file between the opening and closing <head> tags, as shown in the following HTML5 code example:

```
<!doctype html>
<html>
<head>
<meta charset="iso-8859-1">
<title>Web Design All-in-One For Dummies</title>
<link href="mycssfile.css" rel="stylesheet" type="text/css">
</head>
<body>
<p>Crafting the Elements of Design</p>
</body>
</html>
```

You find additional details about linking external CSS files to HTML pages in the next section.

Combining different types of CSS on your site

Although it is certainly more likely that you'll use a single master external CSS file for styling an entire site, nothing is stopping you from incorporating inline, internal, and external CSS in any combination or from using multiple external CSS files to achieve the desired results. For example, you might have one external CSS file, a few internal CSS styles on a couple of pages, and a few instances of inline styles on a particular page of a site.

Should you choose to combine different types of CSS on your site, keep in mind that all style definitions are hierarchical in nature. That's the cascading part of Cascading Style Sheets. This means that any style definitions that sit closest to the content on your pages — your text, graphics, and so on — override any styles that sit farther away. In other words, external CSS is overridden by internal CSS, which is overridden by inline CSS or any other inline styling tags and attributes, including any old <font> tags. To make matters even more interesting, a visitor's browser is truly the closest thing to the content, which means that if his browser has any customized preferences set with regard to the display of CSS, it may override your CSS styles, regardless of whether your styles are inline, internal, or external.

This hierarchical rule also applies to redundant or conflicting CSS within the same document. For instance, if a file contained something like two <body> tags with conflicting font-family declarations, the style definition that sits lower in the list of styles, closer to the content, will be the style applied to the page. In the following example, the body selector that specifies Geneva would be used to style the page, whereas the other style rule would be ignored:

```
body {
  font-family: Georgia, "Times New Roman", Times, serif;
}
body {
  font-family: Geneva, Arial, Helvetica, sans-serif;
}
```

Additionally, as you'll quickly come to realize, after you set certain style attributes in the CSS for particular tags such as the body or paragraph tags, only attributes that differ from those need to be specified for subsequent styles. You could, for example, make Verdana the default font for all paragraph text on all the pages on the entire site by setting that as a style attribute for the selector called p. When this style is applied to your pages, all the paragraph text throughout your site would display in Verdana unless specified differently in subsequent style definitions.

Externalizing CSS

During the site-building process, it's often much faster to develop your CSS when the styles are internal rather than external. The difference in speed isn't much, but it's noticeable to seasoned designers. For this reason, you should work with internal CSS while you create a master page or template in HTML. You then externalize the CSS by moving all the CSS code from inside the page to a linked external CSS file. At that point, you can continue with the development of your site and build any remaining pages based on the master/template.

If you use Dreamweaver, you can take advantage of a tool that externalizes the CSS, as you find out in the later section in this chapter called "Linking CSS with Dreamweaver." If you're using a different program or hand-coding your pages, you can easily externalize your internal CSS manually. Simply select and cut all the CSS styles from within the page, paste the cut styles into a new blank document, save the file with the .css file extension, and add the link tag to that file to the head of your page. You find out about linking external CSS to a page in the next section.

Linking external CSS to a page

To link an HTML page to an external CSS, just insert a single line of code into the head of your page that references the name and location of the external CSS file relative to the root level of the server on which the site resides. The line of code for the link must be placed somewhere between the opening and closing `<head>` tags of every HTML page on your site that you want to be styled with it. When the filename of the CSS is entered accurately in the HTML file using the correct link syntax, the link code provides instructions to the browser about how the CSS style information should be interpreted and applied to the page, which in turn determines how the page appears in the browser.

Here's an example of a link to an external CSS file with the filename `main.css`, where the file that is being sourced uses the `href` attribute of the link tag, which is an unclosed tag in HTML:

```
<link href="main.css" rel="stylesheet" type="text/css">
```

When the link code is added to an XHTML page, the tag must be closed by adding an extra space and forward slash before the end:

```
<link href="main.css" rel="stylesheet" type="text/css" />
```

The other attributes within the `<link>` tag besides the `href` are required to help the browser interpret the data on the linked CSS file:

- The `rel` attribute sets the relationship between the original document and the linked file, and it identifies the linked file as a style sheet.

- The `type` attribute specifies the type of style language being used within the linked file, which in this case identifies that the linked file is written in "text/css" format.

For consistency, try to place the CSS link in your web pages in the same location within the code from page to page. For instance, you might want to add the link tag directly following the last meta tag, or place it right above the closing `</head>` tag. Being consistent can help you quickly find the tag should you ever need to modify it.

Besides the placement of the link within the HTML pages that use the external CSS file, you should also pay some attention to where the CSS file(s) is located relative to the other files within the site.

Most often, each site has just one CSS file, and that file sits at the root level, which is just a fancy way of saying that the CSS file is in the same location as the `index.html` file, which is the home page for your site. The root level refers to the ground floor of your site, whether it's a local copy of your site sitting on your computer in front of you or a copy of the site located on the remote host server. With most sites, the home page sits at the root level along with an `images` folder and all the other main pages of the site. For larger sites, some designers create subfolders at the root level to house other things such as external JavaScript and jQuery files, external CSS files, CGI scripts, or groups of pages that fall into a similar category (for instance, all the pages relating to a company's products or services).

Should your site require two or more Cascading Style Sheets (perhaps one for all the pages and a second for a handful of pages that will be printed; see the next section), it may be beneficial for you to create a separate folder called `css` at the root level of the site and then save those CSS files together inside it. You may then access each CSS from that location, providing that the `href` of your CSS link indicates the new location of the folder along with the filename:

```
<link href="css/main.css" rel="stylesheet" type="text/css">
```

Setting CSS media types

In web-speak, the *media type* is the specification within a Cascading Style Sheet that identifies the device that will be used to access the HTML file being styled. Examples of a media type include a computer screen, printer, tablet, mobile device, smartphone, Braille translator, speech synthesizer, or other type of assistive device. Today, with more than 20 percent of all Internet users accessing the web with smartphones and tablets, the media type is becoming increasingly important to web designers and developers.

Exploring different media types

By default, it is presumed that all web pages should be accessible by any and all devices, or media types, that can access a web page. For that reason, it wasn't even necessary to specify a media type in the tag that links to the external CSS. However, when your pages do require one or more CSS files to style the content for different devices, such as a screen (computer monitor) and a handheld (tablet device), it's a really, really good idea to add the media type attribute to each CSS link tag. Table 3-1 identifies all the media types currently in use.

Table 3-1	CSS Media Types
Media Type	*Definition*
All	Good for all devices, recommended as the default catchall type when multiple cascading style sheets are specified.
Aural	Used with text-to-speech devices.
Braille	Used for Braille tactile feedback devices.
embossed	Used for paged Braille devices.
handheld	Used for web-enabled small-screened devices including e-book readers, tablets, and smartphones, such as the Kindle, iPad, and iPhone.
Print	Best for files intended for print, whether actually printed or viewed only in Print Preview mode.
projection	Used for overhead projectors or documents turned into transparencies for projection.
Screen	Best for color monitors.
Tty	Good for teletype machines, special text terminals, and other "fixed-pitch character grid" devices. Note: When creating CSS for this type, avoid specifying the sizes of any objects on the page in pixels.
Tv	Used for TV-type devices that might have less robust features than a regular color computer monitor.

Creating separate CSS files for different media types

Although many CSS style declarations work across all media types, some are to be used only with specific media, like the speech-rate property that can be used only with aural devices. Likewise, when certain style declarations are shared by two devices, those declarations might need adjusting in the secondary CSS so that those styles look good on both devices. In cases like this, creating two separate CSS files, one for each device, might be necessary to improve the experience of the HTML document on both devices.

Here's an example. Consider that you have a web page that looks good onscreen, but when the content is printed, some of the graphics on the page take up so much room that they force the printer to cut off some of the text along the right edge of the page, as well as push any overflow text onto another page. You can easily solve this problem by creating two separate style sheets: one for all media types and another for printers.

The following steps illustrate how you can set a document to use two CSS files with different media types:

1. **Launch your favorite web browser and open the sample CSS media types demo file** `cssmediatypes.html`.

Find it at this book's web page online. (See the introduction for more information.)

This page, shown in Figure 3-2, contains a `<link>` tag with an `all` media type attribute that specifies a particular external CSS.

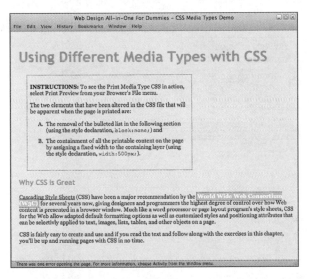

Figure 3-2: A page styled with a linked external CSS file with a media type set to all will display nearly identically in all web-enabled devices.

2. **Under the View menu, look for and select the option that will allow you to view the source code of the page.**

   The exact command varies by browser. For instance, in Firefox the command is View➪Page Source, in Internet Explorer it's View➪Source, and in Safari it's View➪Source.

   Right before the closing `</head>` tag, you can see a second link to an external CSS file that instead uses the `print` media type:

   ```
   <link href="cssdemo.css" rel="stylesheet" type="text/css" media="all" />
   <link href="cssmediatypes.css" rel="stylesheet" type="text/css"
       media="print" />
   ```

3. **To see how the content on the page looks differently when you try to print it, choose File➪Print Preview to open the Print Preview dialog box.**

   Figure 3-3 shows how the `print` media type CSS looks in the Print Preview dialog box. The `cssmediatypes.css` style sheet contains a few attributes that are different from the `cssdemo.css` style sheet. Namely, in the `css mediatypes.css` file, the entire bullet list at the bottom of the page has been styled as a hidden block by using the `block: none;` declaration, and the contents on the entire page have been placed inside a layer that has been styled to have a fixed width of 500 pixels when the page gets printed.

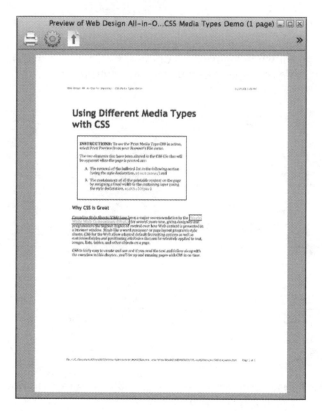

Figure 3-3: A page styled with a linked external CSS file with a media type set to print will not become apparent until the page gets printed.

Adding media-dependent style sheets to your HTML files

You can add external media-dependent style sheets to the head area of your HTML files in two ways: linking and importing. Although both methods can essentially do the same thing for entire external CSS files, importing accommodates style-specific applications for different media types.

Here's an overview of the two CSS attachment methods:

- **Linking:** Use the `<link>` tag to specify both the location and filename of the external CSS and the desired media attribute, such as `screen`, `all`, or `print`, to define the media type:

  ```
  <link rel="stylesheet" type="text/css" media="print" href="forprint.css">
  ```

- **Importing:** Use the `@media` or `@import` at-rules surrounded by `<style>` and comment tags (to hide the style specification from displaying in the body of the page when the page is viewed in older browsers). The syntax is slightly different for `@media` than it is for `@import`, but both methods do essentially the same thing when the specified CSS is applied to the page:

```
<style type="text/css">
<!--
@media print {
 /* printversion.css */
}
-->
</style>
```

or

```
<style type="text/css" media="print,handheld">
<!--
@import url("css/printhandheld.css");
-->
</style>
```

When you want to use internal CSS as opposed to an external CSS file, you can use the @media method to indicate one or more media types as well as include particular style definitions that will remain internal to the HTML page, as in this example:

```
<style type="text/css">
<!--
@media screen, print {
 body { font-family: Georgia, "Times New Roman", Times, serif; }
}
-->
</style>
```

Alternatively, when certain attributes will be different onscreen than they will be for another media type, you can stack the style definitions on top of one another, as shown here, allowing you to apply media-specific rules to specific styles within your page:

```
<style type="text/css" media="all">
<!--
@media screen {
 p { font-size: 10px; }
}
@media print {
 p { font-size: 12px; }
}
-->
</style>
```

If, on the other hand, your CSS files are external to the pages on the site, sitting at the root level or inside a css folder, the @import or <link> method is more useful. For instance, you could use the <link> method to list the all media type for the first linked CSS file, and beneath that, add another link tag to list another media type and CSS file:

```
<link rel="stylesheet" type="text/css"
   media="all" href="mystylesheet.css">
<link rel="stylesheet" type="text/css"
   media="print" href="mystylesheetprint.css">
```

CSS3 media queries

One of the newer ways to handle multiple media types is to use *media queries,* the CSS3 feature that lets you add expressions to your code, which identifies the device type and then applies specific attributes in your CSS. CSS3 is the current Internet standard for style sheet languages used to define how elements look when displayed in a browser.

The CSS3 attributes you can specify in a media query include the width and height of the viewport of the browser or device, the orientation (landscape versus portrait), and the resolution.

To understand how media queries work, take a look at the example of a simple two-column web layout with a `div#wrapper` width of `960px`. To make the page automatically scale downwards to display nicely on a smaller device with a maximum width of `480px`, you'd simply create an `@media` query that specifies style rules for the screen by modifying the `div#wrapper` container width down to `400px`:

```
@media only screen and (max-device-width: 480px) {
   div#wrapper {
   width: 400px;
   }
```

As long as you place this and any additional small device CSS styles you may need toward the bottom of your external CSS file, the cascading part of CSS kicks in beautifully in the correct order. In other words, these later CSS styles automatically overwrite any style rules meant for regular browsers earlier in your CSS. How awesome is that?

Alternatively, you could put these small device-specific styles into their own CSS file, as long as you ensure that the link to this small device CSS file is placed underneath the default CSS file for your site, as shown in the following sample code:

```
<link rel="stylesheet" type="text/css" href="css/main.css"
   media="all">
<link rel="stylesheet" type="text/css" media="only screen and
   (max-device-width: 480px)" href="css/small-device.css" />
```

To make the process of developing the `small-device.css` file go quickly, you can start with a copy of your `main.css` file. Then simply modify any styles that need to be changed for small devices and delete any styles you don't need.

One popular method for adjusting a site is to change multiple columns into a single stacked column by using the `float:none` and `width:auto` styles. Another common change is to replace larger images with smaller images, as with the logo and any background images for certain containers.

Whichever method you use, be sure to also include the viewport meta tag in the head of your code to ensure that your pages load correctly in certain devices, such as the iPhone:

```
<meta name="viewport" content="width=device-width" />
```

For the most up to date information on working with media queries, see www.w3.org/TR/css3-mediaqueries.

Linking CSS with Dreamweaver

Dreamweaver users can easily insert a link tag to an external CSS without having to commit to memory all the required code or the proper syntax. Moreover, when creating links to an external CSS file in Dreamweaver, you can also use that opportunity to select a CSS media type, if desired.

In the following steps, you find out how to link an external CSS file with the `all` media type to an open HTML file in Dreamweaver.

To complete all the steps, you need Dreamweaver along with sample HTML and CSS files. Place both copies of the saved files into a folder on your computer and then proceed with the following steps:

1. **Launch Dreamweaver and set up a managed site by choosing Site⇨New Site.**

   The Site Setup dialog box appears, showing the Site category, which displays fields for the Site Name and Local Site Folder.

2. **In the Site Name field, enter the name of your site.**

   Enter a name that matches the name of the client or indicates your site's purpose is best, such as ABC Company or My Blog.

3. **In the Local Site Folder field, verify that the path points to the folder on your computer that you want to use for this site.**

   For example, if you have a folder on your computer dedicated to local websites and you want to create a folder inside that to house the files for a new ABC Company website, your Local Site Folder path might be something like this:

   ```
   Users\yourusername\Documents\local-sites\ABC Web
   ```

4. **Click Save to close the dialog box.**

Your new managed site opens, displaying all the existing files and folders (if any) in the `root` folder in the Files panel.

5. **From the Files panel, open the HTML file that you will be adding the CSS link to.**

   The file you use should have some type inside of it and be marked up with paragraph, h1, and list tags.

6. **To add the link, click the Attach Style Sheet icon (which looks like a little piece of chain) at the bottom of the CSS Styles panel.**

   Clicking the icon opens the Attach External Style Sheet dialog box, shown in Figure 3-4. If you don't see the CSS Styles panel in the Dreamweaver workspace, choose Window➪CSS Styles to open it.

Figure 3-4: Use Dreamweaver's Attach External Style Sheet dialog box to select the desired CSS file and media type.

7. **In the File/URL text field, type the name of the CSS file you'd like to link to or click the Browse button to find and select the desired CSS file.**

   If you're using the sample files you just downloaded from the web, click the Browse button to navigate to the location where you saved the sample files and select the file `cssdemo.css`.

8. **In the Add As area of the dialog box, click the Link or Import radio button to select the desired method for adding the CSS file to your HTML page.**

   The Link option adds the CSS as an external file by using the `<link>` tag:

   ```
   <head>
   <link href="cssdemo.css" rel="stylesheet" type="text/
       css">
   </head>
   ```

   The Import option specifies the external CSS within a style link inside the head of the page by using the `@import` at-rule. Keep in mind that this method is not recommended for CSS3 media queries:

   ```
   <head>
   <style type="text/css">
   ```

```
<!--
@import url("cssdemo.css");
-->
</style>
</head>
```

9. **In the Media drop-down menu area, type the word** all, **or click the menu's down arrow and select the** all **media type.**

   To specify multiple media types rather than just one, enter the names of each of the desired media types, separated by commas and no spaces, as in screen,print,tty.

10. **If desired, click the dialog box's Preview button to see how the newly linked CSS file styles your sample HTML file.**

11. **Click OK to complete the attachment of the external CSS file.**

   Dreamweaver's CSS Styles panel now displays the newly attached CSS file and lists all the styles inside it, and the sample HTML file is styled with the style rules on the linked CSS.

Working with CSS Style Selectors

Now that you understand the differences between inline, internal, and external CSS styles, you are ready to discover the four different contextual selectors, or CSS selector types:

- Class styles
- Tag redefine styles
- ID styles
- Compound styles, which include customized CSS styles like descendant selectors, advanced combinators, and pseudo-classes

Though they all use roughly the same syntax for the style declarations, each type determines which precise parts of the HTML will be modified. In addition to these four main contextual selectors, web designers are also using the new CSS3 selectors. Browser support for CSS3 continues to improve.

Applying custom class styles

Class styles, which are also sometimes called *custom class styles, custom styles,* or *custom classes,* are for those times when you want to create a special style and then selectively apply it to an unlimited number of elements or objects on a web page. For example, in the sentence "Our Daily Deals newsletter brings you the hottest sales, promotions, and special offers at the most popular stores in one easy-to-read daily e-mail," you could create a custom class style to modify the words *Daily Deals* and then apply that style to those words in the HTML.

When writing the class styles in the CSS file, be sure to include a period (.) directly before the selector name, as shown here:

```
.dailydeals {
  font-family: Georgia, "Times New Roman", Times, serif;
  font-size: 23px;
  font-weight: bold;
  color: #336699;
}
```

The presence of the period performs two functions:

✓ It helps you to quickly identify, at a glance, the class styles from other types of styles when reviewing your CSS code.

✓ Perhaps more importantly, it informs browsers that the style is a custom class that will be selectively applied to content on the page.

When you create a class style, you can name the selector anything you like, as long as it isn't the name of a currently used HTML tag. For example, it would be a really bad idea to create a class style called .body or .p. So, in keeping with the concept of semantic HTML, try to name your class styles after the function they'll be performing, such as .highlight or .imageborder.

When you're finished writing out the style rules in the CSS for your class style, you can apply the style to any object in the HTML document by adding the class attribute to the opening container tag of the object or content being styled:

```
<p class="dailydeals">Our Daily Deals newsletter brings you the hottest sales,
    promotions, and special offers at the most popular stores in one easy-to-
    read daily e-mail.</p>
```

When specifying the class style in the HTML code with the class attribute, the period that is required in the CSS when creating the style definition doesn't need to be placed in front of the style name in between the quotation marks, as shown in the previous code.

If you prefer that the class style be applied only to one or two words or a short phrase instead of all the elements within a container tag, you can selectively apply the class style to your object(s) using the <span> tag with the class attribute:

```
<p>Our <span class="dailydeals">Daily Deals</span> newsletter brings you the
    hottest sales, promotions, and special offers at the most popular stores in
    one easy-to-read daily e-mail.</p>
```

The <span> tag is an inline tag used to apply styling to elements within the flow of document text. This tag is essentially an empty HTML container tag that does nothing until you tell it to do something by applying an attribute to it, such as adding the `class`, `id`, or `style` attribute to style content. Figure 3-5 illustrates the difference between adding a class attribute to a `<p>` tag (top) versus adding it to a `<span>` tag that surrounds specific content (bottom).

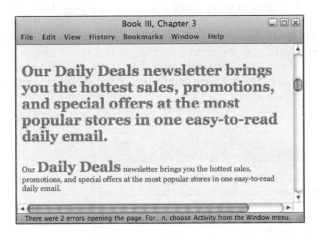

Figure 3-5: Class styles can be added to an existing container, such as a `<p>` tag (top), or wrapped around specific content using the `<span>` tag (bottom).

Making CSS tag redefine styles

By default, all HTML tags are structurally preformatted to look a particular way and perform specific functions. Take the `<h1>` tag, for example. This tag is preformatted to be big, black, and bold, and it is intended to identify the main heading within the text, as opposed to the regular text, which is marked up with `<p>` tags in the content.

When you create a *tag redefine style,* you use the tag name as the selector name to overwrite the preformatted look of any existing HTML tag, such as `<p>` and `<h1>`. The tag redefine style can be changed to anything you like, such as tailoring the default look of all content between `<h1>` tags to match the design and color scheme of your site, whether that be Impact, 28 pixels, bold, italic, and #000000 or Palatino Linotype, 32 pixels, bold, and #FF99FF:

```
h1 {
  font-family: Palatino Linotype, Book Antiqua, Palatino,
    serif;
  font-size: 32px;
  font-weight: bold;
  color: #FF99FF;
}
```

Redefining existing tags is one of the best ways to globally style content on a site without having to selectively apply the styles here and there, as you must with custom class styles. In fact, to streamline the CSS process, most designers at a minimum begin each CSS file by creating tag redefine styles for the `<body>`, `<p>`, `<h1>`, `<h2>`, `<ul>`, `<ol>`, `<li>`, and `<td>` tags. A tag redefine style for the `<body>` tag, for instance, can take on many of the attributes that were formerly applied to the opening `<body>` tag in HTML code, such as the default page margin spacing and page background color.

In addition to modifying a tag's preformatted styles, tag redefine styles can also be used to add new styles to a particular tag. For example, all web pages, unless otherwise specified, have a default 9-pixel margin of space between the edge of the browser window and its contents, as illustrated in Figure 3-6.

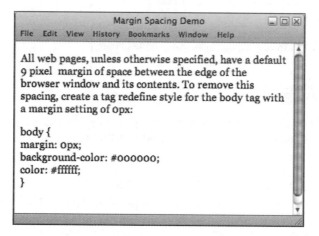

Figure 3-6: All pages have a default 9 pixels of margin spacing around the entire browser.

To remove or change this setting, the margin attribute may be redefined in the body tag. Figure 3-7 shows an example of how a style for the `<body>` tag might be redefined in the CSS, where the margin spacing is set to 0 on all four sides of the browser window, the background color of the page is set to black, and the font color for text within the body is set to white, as in the following style code:

```
body {
 margin: 0px;
 background-color: #000000;
 color: #ffffff;
}
```

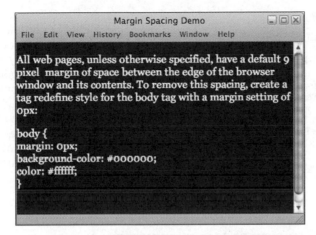

Figure 3-7: Create a tag redefine style for the body to remove any unwanted default margin spacing.

Creating ID styles

An *ID style* is a kind of hybrid CSS style rule that combines certain elements of both custom class and tag redefine styles. With an ID style, the declarations defined in that style are automatically applied to any object on the page that has an `id` attribute that matches the `id` name in the ID style.

To style an object with an `id` attribute, you must first create a selector that includes the number symbol (#) followed by the `id` name, such as `#sidebar`, and then add as many declarations to the style as desired, as in the following example:

```
#sidebar {
  border: 1px dashed #cad0d6;
  margin: 0px 1px 0px 0px;
  padding: 10px;
}
```

After you've created your style in the CSS, add the `id` attribute and style name value to the opening tag of the object or other HTML container tag that uses the style, as in `<div id="sidebar">`. The `<div>` tag is a block-level container. Typically, block-level tags contain inline elements and other block-level elements.

To illustrate this idea further, presume that you have a layer on your page (using the `<div>` tag) that contains a header that says "Popcorn Makers" and below it a listing of five different brands of popcorn makers for sale, such as the one shown in Figure 3-8.

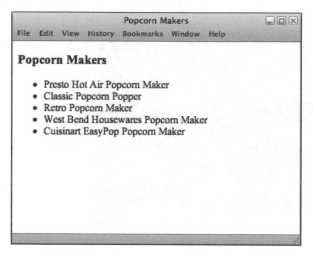

Figure 3-8: To style an object automatically with an ID style, you must first add the id attribute to the object's opening tag.

When you give the `<div>` layer an ID attribute of `popcornmakers`, using the syntax `id="popcornmakers"`, and create a style using the syntax `#popcornmakers`, that ID style is automatically applied to the layer, as shown in Figure 3-9.

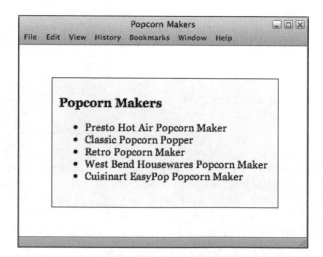

Figure 3-9: ID styles in the CSS are automatically applied to objects on the page with the same ID.

Here's an example how this ID style is written in the CSS:

```css
#popcornmakers {
  font-family: Georgia, "Times New Roman", Times, serif;
  background-color: #FFC;
  border: 1px solid #039;
  position: absolute;
  width: 330px;
  height: 180px;
  z-index: 1;
  left: 50px;
  top: 50px;
  padding: 10px;
}
```

And here is what the HTML markup looks like:

```html
<div id="popcornmakers">
 <h3>Popcorn Makers</h3>
 <ul>
  <li>Presto Hot Air Popcorn Maker</li>
  <li>Classic Popcorn Popper</li>
  <li>Retro Popcorn Maker</li>
  <li>West Bend Housewares Popcorn Maker</li>
  <li>Cuisinart EasyPop Popcorn Maker</li>
 </ul>
</div>
```

Just like the tag redefine selector, which automatically changes how contents surrounded by a particular tag appear, anytime that a style name uses the #id syntax, the style definition is automatically applied to the object with the matching id attribute.

Building compound styles

After you've mastered working with custom class, tag redefines, and ID styles, you can step into the big leagues of compound styles. To understand how to work with compound styles, you must first have an understanding of HTML/CSS document trees, which define the relationships between objects within the document. Just as humans have a family tree, your document and the objects within it can be defined by their relationships. This means you can identify the objects in your documents by their relationship to other objects. Every object can have ancestors, descendants, parents, children, and siblings. For instance, the *footer* (bottom section) of a web page might include an unordered list of linked text. In this scenario, the parent container for the list is the footer, and the individual list items are siblings. Furthermore, if the footer is the child of the <body> tag, the placement of this list within the document tree might look like this:

```html
<body><footer><ul><li></li></ul></footer></body>
```

Compound styles are where a lot of the fancy footwork in CSS happens because selectors can be written in a variety of ways, including the following most popular usages:

- **Pseudo-classes:** A pseudo-class as a special type of selector that lets you format items that are not in the document tree, such as hyperlink states, first and last child elements, and active elements. In other words, they're not used for actual elements but rather conceptual elements, like every other row in a table. The most common usage is to create styles for hyperlinks, which you find out about later in this chapter.

- **Multiple selectors:** Used to apply the same styles to several tags, the advanced selector is divided by commas, either with or without spaces, as in body,th,td {...} or body, th, td {...}.

- **Descendant selectors:** Also called *advanced combinators*, you can use these selectors to style very specific elements on your page, such as descendants of another element in the document tree. For instance, rather than create a tag redefine style for all list items in your site, you can target all list items within an ordered list in the sidebar of your layout with a selector named #sidebar ol li. These styles can be written to include any combination of tags, tag redefines, ID styles, and custom class names.

Understanding pseudo-classes

To reiterate, a pseudo-class represents a type of selector that styles conceptual elements rather than actual objects. There are five categories of pseudo-classes:

- **Input and link:** Use these for any form fields like buttons and text fields, and for the four link states: link, visited, hover, and active.

- **Content-related:** These let you insert content before or after a specified element. For example, you may want to change the color of the first letter in a paragraph.

- **Position/number-based:** Use this any time you need to style the first or last element of a type within any parent element, such as the first item in a list, or when you'd like to modify an element after a specified number, like every other row in a table.

- **Relational:** To use relation pseudo-classes, you must identify in advance the items that need to be styled based on their position in the document tree. For instance, you can use them to select any empty text and child-free elements, as with an empty set of span tags, <span></span>.

- **Text-related:** Use these for any first or last line, first or last letter, or selected text. For example, you may want to style the first line of all paragraphs to be in small caps.

Table 3-2 shows a list of these pseudo-classes by type with definitions.

When written, pseudo-classes are always preceded by a colon, such as the :hover and :before properties. When you pair a pseudo-class with a tag, the tag is always placed before the colon, as with a:hover or p:before. What's more, pseudo-classes can be chained together for even more specific application of styles. For instance, you can style the first letter of the first paragraph of text following a heading 1 element by using the following pseudo-class syntax:

```
h1:first-child:first-letter {...}
```

Sometimes the best way to visualize how these specialized selectors work is to see a working example. A free test and development area for each of these is at www.w3schools.com/cssref/css_selectors.asp. You can also learn more about working with pseudo-classes and other advanced CSS combinators, at www.w3.org/TR/css3-selectors/#pseudo-classes and www.vanseodesign.com/css/combinators-pseudo-classes.

Table 3-2	CSS Pseudo-Classes	
Pseudo-Class Elements	*Type*	*Definition*
:link, :visited, :hover, :active	Input and link-related	Used to create custom styles for the four hyperlink states.
:checked	Input and link-related	Selects checked form check boxes.
:enabled, :disabled	Input and link-related	Lets you select any inputs that have either the default state of enabled or a specified attribute of disabled, as with a disabled form field that is grayed out.
:focus	Input and link-related	Lets you create styles that will select links that are the current focus of the keyboard, especially helpful for those using the keyboard for navigation. Great for hyperlinks, input, and text areas on forms.
:indeterminate	Input and link-related	Selects form radio buttons before a visitor interacts with them, so they are neither selected nor unselected.

continued

Table 3-2 *(continued)*

Pseudo-Class Elements	Type	Definition
`:target`	Input and link-related	This one is tricky and only works when paired with an ID style and anchor link. For example, when the visitor is at `www.mysite.com/#about`, the selector for that location would be `#about:target`.
`:before, :after`	Content-related	Lets you insert content before or after a specified element.
`:first-child, :last-child`	Position and number-related	Lets you select the first or last element of the specified type within a parent element, as with the first or last item in a list.
`:first-of-type, :last-of-type`	Position and number-related	These will choose the first or last element of a type within any parent element. For example, if you have three div tags in a sidebar div that each contain a heading 1, image, paragraph, and image, you could target and style the first or last image within each sidebar div.
`:nth-of-child(N)`	Position and number-related	Using a simple algebraic expression where `(N)` represents a number, you can use these to select odd/even as well as specific numbered elements, like the first three items in an ordered list or every other row in a table.
`:nth-of-type(N)`	Position and number-related	Using a simple algebraic expression where `(N)` represents a number, use this to select different type elements within the same level. For example, in a div containing multiple paragraphs and images, you'd use div `img:nth-of-type(odd)` to select every other image. Similarly, you could use `p:nth-of-type(2)` to select the second paragraph within the body.

Pseudo-Class Elements	Type	Definition
`:nth-last-child(N)`, `:nth-last-of-type(N)`	Position and number-related	These two selectors work exactly like the `:nth-child` and `:nth-of-type` selectors but count upward from the bottom of the HTML document tree rather than from the top down.
`:only-of-type`	Position and number-related	Use this selector to style an element that is the only one of its kind within a parent element, as with a single paragraph inside of a `<div>` tag.
`:root`	Position and number-related	Selects the root of the document, the `<html>` element.
`:empty`	Relational	This selects any empty text and child-free elements, as with an empty set of span tags, `<span></span>`.
`:not(S)`	Relational	Use this selector to get rid of elements from the specified selector inside the parameter of `:not()`, such applying a specific style to all `<span>` tags except those with a Class style of `.magcover`, as in `span:not(.magcover)`.
`:first-line`, `:last-line`	Text-related	Selects the first or last line of an element, such as the first or last line in a paragraph.
`:first-letter`, `:last-letter`	Text-related	Selects the first or last letter in a text block, as with creating dropcaps from the first letter in a paragraph.
`:lang`	Text-related	Used to match any element that has (or is) a descendant of an element with a matching `lang` (language) attribute.
`:selection`	Text-related	When text is selected, this will change the style of that selection.

Creating hyperlink styles with pseudo-classes

One of the most common usages of the compound styles is to create custom hyperlinks with pseudo-classes, which can be used to modify the default color and attributes of hyperlinks. The hyperlink compound pseudo-class style can be written as a two-part selector where the anchor tag is separated by a colon followed by the name of the link state, as in `a:link`, `a:visited`, `a:hover`, and `a:active`.

The appearance of a hyperlink is determined by a visitor's interactivity with it in a browser:

- **Normal links** are unvisited links.

- **Visited links** are links that the visitor has already clicked.

- **Hover links** change their appearance when a visitor hovers the cursor over them.

- **Active links** change their appearance only as a visitor clicks directly on a link, before releasing the mouse button.

As you may well know, all hyperlinks by default display in either blue underlined text (unvisited link) or purple underlined text (visited links). Because these colors are unlikely to match the particular colors in your site's design, you can override the default link styles by creating custom hyperlink styles. Even better, in addition to the unvisited and visited hyperlink states, with CSS, you can add styles for two additional hyperlink states, namely, the hover state, which occurs when a visitor mouses over a link, and the active state, which appears when a visitor clicks a link.

To change just the color of a hyperlink for all four link states, add the following style definitions to your CSS, replacing the hexadecimal values in this example with your desired color values for each of the link styles:

```
a:link {
  color: #CC0000;
}
a:visited {
  color: #339933;
}
a:hover {
  color: #000000;
}
a:active {
  color: #99CC33;
}
```

To further make things interesting, you can add additional style declarations for any of or all the four link states. For instance, you might want to remove the underline, add a background color, or apply a dotted border around the hyperlink, as demonstrated here and shown in Figure 3-10:

```
a:link {
  color: #CC0000;
}
a:visited {
  color: #339933;
  text-decoration: none;
}
a:hover {
  color: #000000;
  background-color: #0CC;
}
a:active {
  color: #ffffff;
  text-decoration: none;
  border: 2px dotted #CCC;
  background-color: #000;
}
```

Figure 3-10: Create four distinct styles for each of the four hyperlink states.

When creating these link styles, you must take care that each style gets added to the CSS in the same order it will be experienced on a website by a site visitor: link, visited, hover, active. If the styles are added to the CSS out of order, the link styles may not work properly when viewed in a browser. Therefore, get in the habit of creating the normal link state first, then add the visited state followed by the hover state, and finally the active state, as shown in the preceding example.

Creating a master CSS file

Other HTML tags that web designers often redefine in the CSS include <html>, <h1> through <h6>, <td>, <li>, and <img>. To tell the truth, many designers create their own version of a master CSS file, which they then adapt to the needs of each individual site, to help speed the process of building a website from scratch.

As you build more and more websites, some styles will become a regular part of your standard design practice. For instance, you might always want to set your page margins to 0, specify a page background color to white, choose a default font for all text content, create redefine styles for paragraphs and headings, specify style attributes for at least two (link and visited) if not all four hyperlink states, and make a custom bullet style for styling lists.

Before you begin creating the master CSS, download a copy of the sample HTML file called sample.html from this book's web page. (See the introduction for more information.)

Use this file to test the styles for your CSS as you create the master css file. The sample HTML file includes paragraph text, a heading 1, a heading 2, an unordered list, and a couple of functioning hyperlinks.

To create your own master CSS file, follow these steps:

1. **Create a new blank document, without any HTML coding, and save it with the filename master.css.**

   Save this CSS file in the same location on your computer as your sample.html file.

2. **Inside the <head> area of your sample.html file, add a link to the new external css file that includes the media type set to all:**

   ```
   <link href="master.css" rel="stylesheet" type="text/css" media="all">
   ```

   This link tells the sample.html file to use the style definitions in the linked external CSS.

3. **Inside the master.css file, create a Tag redefine style for the <body> tag that sets the top, left, bottom, and right page margins to 0px; the padding on all four sides of the page to 10px; and the background to a light peachy orange color with the hexadecimal value of #fc3bb6.**

Your style code should look like this:

```
body {
  margin: 0px;
  padding: 10px;
  background-color: #fc3bb6;
}
```

When all four sides of an object use the same value, as with the margin spacing and padding shown here, the value needs to be specified in the CSS only once. However, when the value is different on one or more sides, you must specify values for each of the sides:

```
body {
  margin: 10px 10px 0px 0px;
  padding: 20px 0px 0px 20px;
  background-color: #fc3bb6;
}
```

4. **Create a tag redefine style in your CSS file for the <p>, <h1>, and <h2> tags by specifying the font, font size, and font color for each.**

Use any font, size, weight, and color you like because you can customize the values later to match any specific project. Here's an example of the code you might use:

```
p {
  font-family: Georgia, "Times New Roman", Times,
    serif;
  font-size: 12px;
  color: #000000;
}
h1 {
  font-family: Arial, Helvetica, sans-serif;
  font-size: 36px;
  font-weight: bold;
  color: #000066;
}
h2
  font-family: Arial, Helvetica, sans-serif;
  font-size: 24px;
  font-weight: bold;
  color: #000066;
}
```

5. **To change the default hyperlink style, you can create pseudo-class element styles for each of the four hyperlink states.**

You may specify any attributes you like for each of the four states, from changing the font or font weight, to modifying the text color or background color, to altering the default text decoration.

Here's an example of the code you might use for the four link states:

```
a:link {
  font-weight: bold;
```

Book III
Chapter 3

Styling with
Cascading Style
Sheets

```
    text-decoration: underline;
    color: #0099cc;
    }
a:visited {
    font-weight: bold;
    text-decoration: underline;
    color: #990000;
    }
a:hover {
    font-weight: normal;
    text-decoration: none;
    color: #ffffff;
    background: #ff9933;
    }
a:active {
    font-weight: normal;
    text-decoration: none;
    color: #ffffff;
    background: #cc0000;
    }
```

6. **To style the unordered list, you can either redefine the `<li>` tag or create a class style that can be selectively applied to any `<li>` tag with the `class` attribute. If desired, specify an image to replace the default bullets.**

   The style definition looks the same whether you redefine the `<li>` tag or create your own custom class style; only the selector is written differently, as either `li` or perhaps as `.bullet`.

   Your code for the bullet `li` tag redefine style might look something like this:

   ```
   li {
       list-style-position: outside;
       list-style-image: url(images/bullet.gif);
       font-family: Arial, Helvetica, sans-serif;
       font-size: 12px;
   }
   ```

7. **Save your HTML and CSS files and launch your HTML file in a browser window.**

   To view the page in a browser, you can either double-click the HTML file or drag and drop the file icon into any open browser window.

   The file should display with all the style attributes you just created in your master CSS file, as shown in Figure 3-11. If it doesn't look quite right or if certain elements aren't displaying properly, reopen the files and check the accuracy of all your code, fix any errors you find, and retest. Be sure you've remembered to add the period (.) before all your custom class names and a number symbol (#) before all your hexadecimal color values.

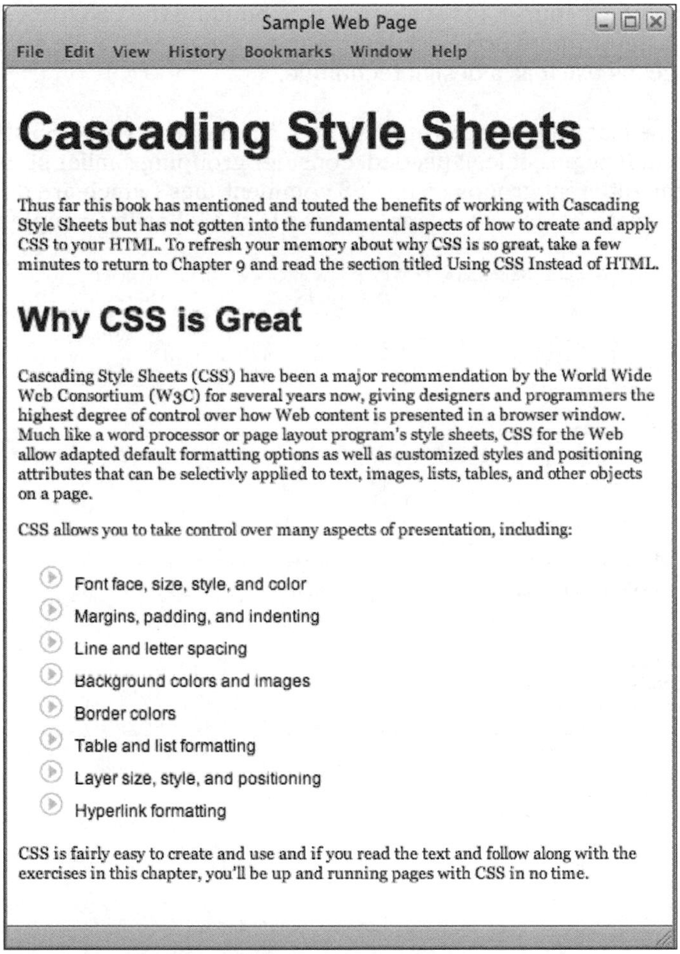

Figure 3-11: Creating a master CSS file, like the one styling this page, can make building each site go much faster.

8. **Test your new hyperlink styles in the browser window by**

   a. Mousing over a link to see the hover style.

   b. Clicking and holding the mouse over a link to see the active style.

   c. Clicking a link and returning to your sample page by clicking the browser's Back button to see how the link changes from the normal to the visited link state.

Now that you have your first master CSS file, rather than reinvent the wheel each time you start a new web project, you can use this file as the starting point. Of course, for some projects, building the CSS from scratch might be easier or more practical, but if having a master CSS file saves you time, by all means use it as a design technique.

One last thing about your CSS files. Try to keep your CSS styles organized as much as possible. If needed, consider grouping similar styles and labeling the different groups using CSS comment tags (which are different than HTML formatting tags, `<!--` and `-->`), as in the following sample master CSS file:

```css
/***** Global Settings *****/

body {
  background-color: #B3D2E1;
  margin: 0px;
  padding: 0px;
}
body,th,td {
  font-family: Georgia, "Georgia Ref", Tahoma, "Palatino Linotype", Palatino,
    serif;
  font-size: 12px;
  color: #26506c;
}

/***** Headings *****/

h1 {
margin: 0px;
padding: 30px 0 20px 0;
font-size: 32px;
font-weight: bold;
}
h2 {
margin: 0px;
padding: 20px 0;
font-size: 18px;
font-weight: bold;
}
h3 {
margin: 0px;
font-size: 14px;
font-weight: bold;
}

/***** Common Formatting *****/

p {
  font-family: Georgia, "Georgia Ref", Tahoma, "Palatino Linotype", Palatino,
    serif;
  font-size: 11px;
  color: #26506c;
  margin: 0px;
  padding: 0px;
}
img {
  border: 1;
  padding-top: 5px;
  padding-right: 5px;
  padding-bottom: 5px;
  padding-left: 5px;
```

```
}

/***** Links *****/

a:link {
  font-weight: bold;
  text-decoration: underline;
  color: #26506c;
}
a:visited {
  font-weight: bold;
  text-decoration: underline;
  color: #26506c;
}
a:hover {
  font-weight: bold;
  text-decoration: none;
  color: #3C474F;
  background: #CAD0D6;
}
a:active {
  font-weight: bold;
  text-decoration: none;
  color: #FFFFFF;
  background: #99CA3C;
}
```

One last point you should know about CSS: Browsers aren't perfect or consistent, which means you'll always have rendering bugs and glitches. This can be a significant source of frustration for beginners because while the code may in fact be technically correct, the browsers themselves are misrendering it. The good news is that you won't be the first person to encounter your particular issue. These resources might offer a solution:

- ✔ www.quirksmode.org/bugreports/

- ✔ http://websitetips.com/css/solutions/

- ✔ www.noupe.com/css/using-css-to-fix-anything-20-common-bugs-and-fixes.html

Dreamweaver users can also use the Browser Compatibility Check (BCC) feature, which identifies and offers solutions to the most common browser rendering issues. To find out more, see the section on checking browser compatibility in Book IV, Chapter 2.

Chapter 4: Understanding CSS Style Properties

In This Chapter

✓ Understanding the CSS box model

✓ Using the eight style categories

✓ Using the new CSS3 style categories

✓ Working with style attributes

✓ Extending your knowledge of CSS with online resources

In earlier chapters of the book, you find out that CSS is the best way to add formatting to the elements on your web pages, from font sizes to image placement to link colors. And, in Chapter 3 of this minibook, you discover the fundamentals of Cascading Style Sheets and how to apply CSS styles to your pages.

As a complement to the previous chapter, this chapter is designed to help you with choosing the right attributes for all of your styles so that you can best style and position your content with CSS. Here you are introduced to the CSS box model concept and the eight style property categories of CSS. A strong understanding of the box model along with these style categories (each has its own special set of CSS style declarations) can help you choose the attributes you need when you create your own style sheets. In addition, you find instructions on formatting the different elements on a page with CSS as well as a helpful list of the best online CSS/CSS3 resources available, should you decide you want to start using the more advanced capabilities of CSS.

Working with the CSS Box Model

When styling and positioning your content with Cascading Style Sheets, it helps to understand the logic behind how CSS handles elements on a web page. Each object or element is treated like a rectangular box that has margin space surrounding it, padding space inside of it, a border around it, and content inside of it, as illustrated in Figure 4-1.

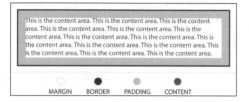

This is the content area. This is the content area. This is the content area. This is the content area. This is the content area. This is the content area. This is the content area. This is the content area. This is the content area. This is the content area. This is the content area. This is the content area. This is the content area. This is the content area. This is the content area.

MARGIN   BORDER   PADDING   CONTENT

Figure 4-1: With the CSS box model, all web page elements have margin, padding, border, and content areas.

When creating styles, the margins, padding, and border attributes are totally optional. If needed, they can be specified in the code, and when not explicitly specified, these areas often have a default width of 0. These three attributes can be set to have any thickness and can be applied both uniformly and nonuniformly to the four individual sides (top, right, bottom, left) of the rectangle. Although padding and borders must be set with 0 or positive values, margins can be assigned either positive or negative values. Margins and padding are always transparent, and borders can be set to any of several different styles.

When calculating the dimensions of the rectangular box surrounding an element, you must always measure by the outer margin box. To illustrate, suppose you have an element that has a specified width and height of 100 x 200 pixels. If you then add a 10-pixel margin, 20 pixels of padding, and 5 pixels of border uniformly to all four sides of that element, the adjusted total width and height of that element would be 170 x 270 pixels.

As you create your web page layouts, keep in mind that each element's rectangular box can contain any number of additional boxes and nested boxes. This simple fact allows for some pretty complex organization and styling, which is especially useful when laying out pages using layers.

Another important fact to remember is that there are two general kinds of boxes in CSS:

- **Block:** These boxes are generated by certain web page elements like paragraphs, headings, layers, lists, and tables. Blocks take up the full width available within the browser or containing (parent) element and add a new line of space both before and after the element. Blocks can also be containers for other block and inline elements — for instance, you can place a paragraph of text inside a `<div>` tag.

- **Inline:** These boxes are generated by other web page elements such as text, images, anchors, and tags (such as `<strong>`, `<em>`, and `<span>`) and take up only as much space as is needed to display the element with its CSS styling. Inline boxes don't force elements onto new lines, but rather allow them to sit next to one another, side by side.

With CSS, however, you can override these default boxes and apply styling that forces certain elements to appear in the browser in precise ways. For example, lists are typically block elements that display in a vertically stacked list, like the one shown in Figure 4-2. Here's how the code for that illustration might look when the <li> tag has been styled to have a yellow background and a 5px bottom margin:

```
<ul>
  <li><a href="#">Home</a></li>
  <li><a href="#">About</a></li>
  <li><a href="#">Services</a></li>
  <li><a href="#">News</a></li>
  <li><a href="#">Contact</a></li>
</ul>
```

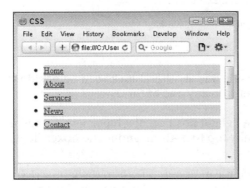

Figure 4-2: Lists are block elements that take up the full width of the browser or parent container.

By applying the display:inline; attribute to the <li> tag redefine in the CSS and adding the class navbar to the <ul> tag as shown in the following code, you can force the list items to appear in a horizontal row like a set of navigation links, as shown in the example in Figure 4-3:

```
<style type="text/css">
 .navbar li {
  display: inline;
  background-color: #ff9933;
  border: 1px solid;
  border-color: #ff3333 #990000 #990000 #ff3333;
  margin-bottom: 5px;
  padding: 4px;
 }
</style>

<ul class="navbar">
  <li><a href="#">Home</a></li>
```

```
    <li><a href="#">About</a></li>
    <li><a href="#">Services</a></li>
    <li><a href="#">News</a></li>
    <li><a href="#">Contact</a></li>
</ul>
```

Figure 4-3: You can convert lists into horizontal menu bars with CSS.

In addition to sitting inside one another, blocks can be positioned relative to other blocks and elements in any one of three ways:

- **Normal:** This is the default position of a block level element. Block boxes always flow vertically top to bottom, and inline boxes flow horizontally from left to right.

- **Float:** A block element can be set to float to the left or right of another element using the float property. For example, floats are often used to make text wrap around a left- or right-aligned image.

- **Absolute:** Block elements using absolute or fixed positioning are removed from the normal flow of a web page and will appear in the exact position on a web page as specified in the CSS.

Now that you have a general understanding about working with the CSS box model, you are ready to find out more about the different style properties available in CSS, as described in the next section.

Exploring the Eight Style Property Categories

To help you with choosing the right declarations for your styles, whether creating custom class, tag redefine, ID, or compound style, you should become familiar with the eight CSS style categories in use before CSS3. Then, when you know the category you need, choosing the style values from within it will be much more intuitive and easy.

The eight style categories in CSS are as follows:

- ✔ Type
- ✔ Background
- ✔ Block
- ✔ Box
- ✔ Border
- ✔ List
- ✔ Positioning
- ✔ Extensions

For each of these eight categories, your styles take the same general format, with a selector providing the name of the style and a declaration outlining the property-value pairs that make up the style. To see a diagram of a style, refer to Figure 3-1 in Book III, Chapter 3.

The following sections describe the specific style rules in each of the eight style categories.

The type properties

The type properties include attributes that can modify the way text appears on a web page. Attributes include font face, font size, font style, font color, font decoration, font weight, font variant, font case, and line height. Keep in mind that these properties can also be applied to most third-party fonts such as Typekit and Google fonts, which you find out about in Book II, Chapter 1.

`font-family`: Specify a font or font set that you are confident your visitors will have installed on their computers, regardless of whether they are visiting on a Mac or a PC. The set of "web-safe fonts" that you can confidently choose from include, in no particular order, Arial, Verdana, Helvetica, Geneva, Georgia, Georgia Ref, Tahoma, Century Gothic, Courier, Courier New, Times, Times New Roman, Lucida Sans, Lucida Console, Copperplate Gothic, Gill Sans, Palatino, Palatino Linotype, Trebuchet, Impact, serif, and sans serif.

For maximum control over the display of fonts on your website, select a *font set* or, in CSS terms, a `font-family`, rather than a single font. Font sets identify the preferred font face followed by one or more alternative font choices should the first font be unavailable on the visitor's computer. A typical font set might include Georgia, Times New Roman, and a serif, and would be written in the CSS code as follows:

```
p { font-family: Georgia, "Times New Roman", Times, serif; }
```

`font-size`: Fonts can be specified to display in any numerical size in a variety of units, such as 1.5em or 12px. Standard font sizes include 10, 12, 14, 15, 18, 20, 24, and 36 pixels. However, you may set them to any size and unit desired, including `px` (pixels), `pc` (picas), `pt` (points), `in` (inches), `mm` (millimeters), `cm` (centimeters), `em` (ems), `ex` (exs), or `%` (percentage). Because precise sizes can override a browser's capability of increasing or decreasing font sizes, consider using ems or percentages instead of pixels or points.

```
p { font-size: 1.5em; }
td { font-size: 12px; }
```

`font-style`: The style refers to an attribute of the font's face. The default style for most fonts is `normal`, which doesn't need to be specified in the CSS. Other options available in most fonts for the `font-style` include `italic` or `oblique`.

```
p { font-style: italic; }
```

`color`: The color of a font can be any one of the 16.7 million colors that you can see on a 24-bit computer monitor, including the 216 web-safe colors you find out about in Book I, Chapter 4. As long as the desired color has a hexadecimal value for onscreen rendering, the font can be that color. When specifying color for fonts or any other attributes, be sure to include the number symbol (#) before the hex number, such as `#ffffff`, so that the color will display correctly. Without the number symbol, the color attribute may be ignored in some browsers.

```
p { color: #66ccdd; }
```

If the values in each pair are identical, you can write the hex value in shorthand:

```
p { color: #6cd; }
```

Alternatively, you can specify colors using RGB, RGBA (rgb+alpha), HSL (hue, saturation, lightness), or HSLA (hsla+alpha) values, as well as predefined cross-browser color names such as `lemonchiffon` and `seashell`:

```
p { color: rgb(153,0,0); }
p { color: rgba(153,0,0,0.5) }
p { color: hsl(0,100%,60%) }
p { color: hsla(0,100%,60%,0.3) }
p { color: darkred; }
```

`line-height`: Line height is what print designers often refer to as *leading*. Leading refers to the space between lines of type from the baseline of letters on one line to the baseline of letters on another line. The word comes from old printing-press days when strips of lead were used to create the spacing between lines and blocks of metal type. The default line height (normal) automatically calculates a standard line height based on a ratio of font size to line height. To adjust the setting precisely, include this attribute with a numeric value in px (pixels), pc (picas), pt (points), in (inches), mm (millimeters), cm (centimeters), em (ems), ex (exs), or % (percentage).

```
p { line-height: 18px; }
```

font-weight: By default, all fonts use a normal font weight. Other weight options include bold, bolder, lighter, and bold settings in increments between 100 and 900, with 400 being roughly equivalent to normal and 700 equal to bold.

```
p { font-weight: bold; }
```

font-variant: The variant refers to whether the font displays in normal (uppercase and lowercase) font characters or in small caps.

```
p { font-variant: small-caps; }
```

text-transform: Regardless of how text has been entered into a web page, the case in which it displays in a browser can be modified with CSS using the text-transform attribute. Options include capitalize, uppercase, lowercase, and none. Choosing capitalize, for example, changes the text to display all words with initial capitals letters.

```
p { text-transform: capitalize; }
```

text-decoration: This attribute specifies how text can be decorated. Most of the attributes, however, either aren't useful for the web (line-through and overline) or aren't supported by all the different browsers (blink). The two decorations that are often useful, especially when creating styles for custom link states, are underline and none.

```
p { text-decoration: underline; }
```

Here's a brief overview of the five text-decoration styles:

- ✔ underline: This option, which is the default decoration for hyperlinks, displays an underline beneath the text.

- ✔ overline: This option adds an overline above the text.

- ✔ line-through: Choose this option to make text look like it's been struck through with a line.

- ✔ blink: This attribute makes styled text blink in the browser window. This attribute isn't supported in all browsers.

- ✔ none: Use this option to remove any default type decoration, such as removing the underline on a hyperlink.

**Book III
Chapter 4**

**Understanding CSS
Style Properties**

The background properties

You can apply background properties to a number of different objects on a Web page, including the whole page, a particular layer, a table, a table cell, and even text.

background-color: A background color can be applied to most objects on a page, including text, tables, table cells, layers, and the body of a page using a hexadecimal value. When specifying hexadecimal color for any style, remember to add the number symbol (#) before the hex value, as in #cc9900, for best browser display results.

```
p { background-color: #33ff00; }
```

background-image: You can apply images, such as a background color, to the background of many different objects on a web page, including the body of a page, tables, table cells, and layers. You can control how the image tiles (repeats) by using the repeat attribute.

```
.mylayer { background-image: url(images/car.gif); }
```

background-repeat: The repeat attribute tells a browser how the background image should be repeated in the area it's filling. By default, and unless otherwise specified, all backgrounds will tile vertically and horizontally to fill the entire background space of the styled tag or object.

```
body {
background-image: url(images/zigzag.gif);
background-repeat: repeat-x;
}
```

The repeat attribute has four variables, each of which is illustrated in Figure 4-4:

- repeat: This option is the same as the default setting for background images and tiles the background image both horizontally and vertically.
- repeat-x: Use this option when you want the background image to tile only along the horizontal axis. If desired, use it in conjunction with the horizontal and/or vertical background-position attribute.
- repeat-y: Use this option when you want the background image to tile only along the vertical axis. If desired, use it in conjunction with the horizontal and/or vertical background-position attribute.
- no-repeat: This setting displays the background image as a single static image with no repeating in either direction.

background-attachment: This attribute refers to how the background image interacts with the content above it. The background image can behave in three different ways — scroll, fixed, and inherit — but not all three are consistently supported by all browsers, so be sure to test whichever option you select in a variety of browsers and browser versions on both Mac and PC platforms.

```
body {
background-image: url(images/biodiesel.gif);
background-attachment: fixed;
background-repeat: repeat-y;
}
```

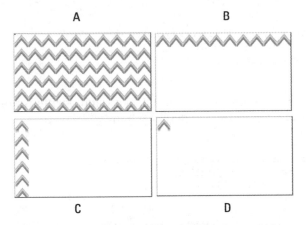

Figure 4-4: Use CSS to control how images repeat within a container. A. repeat, B. repeat-x, C. repeat-y, D. no-repeat.

Here is an explanation of the different background attachment styles:

✔ scroll: This is the default option for how the background image is attached to the page, which works the same whether the attribute is specified or unspecified in the CSS. With this option, the background image scrolls along with any text and other objects on the page.

✔ fixed: The fixed attribute keeps the background image fixed to the browser window while text and other objects on the page scroll past it.

✔ inherit: When you specify this option, the background image inherits the attachment rule, whether scroll or fixed, from its parent container, as with a table cell inside a table.

background-position (X): Set the horizontal background-position attribute to control where in the browser window the background image displays and repeats. Choose left, center, or right or type any value in px (pixels), pc (picas), pt (points), in (inches), mm (millimeters), cm (centimeters), em (ems), ex (exs), or % (percentage).

```
p {
background-image: url(images/recycle.gif);
background-repeat: repeat-x;
background-position: left;
}
```

background-position (Y): Set the vertical background-position attribute to control where in the browser window the background image displays and repeats. Choose top, center, or bottom or type any value in px (pixels), pc (picas), pt (points), in (inches), mm (millimeters), cm (centimeters), em (ems), ex (exs), or % (percentage).

```
p {
background-image: url(images/gogreen.png);
background-repeat: repeat-y;
background-position: center;
}
```

When both the horizontal and vertical background positions need to be specified in the CSS, list them together separated by a space:

```
p {
background-image: url(images/earthsafe.jpg);
background-repeat: repeat-x;
background-position: left center;
}
```

The horizontal position always goes before the vertical position when the two are combined. If this order is not followed, the element may not render properly, resulting in unexpected display issues when viewed in different browsers.

The block properties

Block properties control the alignment and spacing of objects on a page through their tags and attributes. Blocks, which you are introduced to in the first section of this chapter, include text, content inside <div> tags (both with and without positions specified), tags using the display:block style, and images or paragraphs set with absolute or relative positions.

word-spacing: To adjust the spacing between individual words, use any positive or negative number in px (pixels), pc (picas), pt (points), in (inches), mm (millimeters), cm (centimeters), em (ems), ex (exs), or % (percentage), such as word-spacing: 2px;.

```
p { word-spacing: 2px; }
```

letter-spacing: With this attribute, you can uniformly increase or decrease the space between characters by specifying a positive or negative value in px (pixels), pc (picas), pt (points), in (inches), mm (millimeters), cm (centimeters), em (ems), ex (exs), or % (percentage), such as letter-spacing:1em;. Note that changing the letter-spacing attribute overrides any preexisting text justification.

```
p { letter-spacing: 1.5em; }
```

vertical-align: You can vertically align text along the text baseline, sub (subscript), super (superscript), top, text-top, middle, bottom, and text-bottom, or by any value, positive or negative, in px (pixels), pc (picas), pt (points), in (inches), mm (millimeters), cm (centimeters), em (ems), ex (exs), or % (percentage), such as vertical-align: top;.

```
p { vertical-align: top; }
```

text-align: This option can be applied only to text. Alignment options include left, right, center, or justify.

```
p { text-align: center; }
```

text-indent: Also to be used only with text, this style rule creates a first-line indent that can be set to any positive or negative value in px (pixels), pc (picas), pt (points), in (inches), mm (millimeters), cm (centimeters), em (ems), ex (exs), or % (percentage), such as text-indent:12px;.

To indent nontext objects on a page, it is no longer recommended that you use the <blockquote> tag, because this tag has been deprecated. Instead, add an indent using margin and/or padding style attributes.

```
p { text-indent: 10px; }
```

white-space: White space inside or around text in any block-level element can be displayed in three different ways: normal, pre, and nowrap. Choose normal to ignore any white space, pre to leave the white space in with the text as it was coded, or nowrap to force any text to wrap only if the code has line break (<br>) tags.

```
p { white-space: pre; }
```

display: This attribute controls how the styled object displays in the browser. Value options are block, compact, inline, list-item, marker, none, run-in, and table.

```
p { display: none; }
```

Choose from any of the following settings:

✔ none: Use this option to hide a styled element from displaying in the browser. This option is extremely useful when creating multiple style sheets so that some elements can be hidden from view on one device but not another, as with a secondary CSS for the print media type.

Book III
Chapter 4

Understanding CSS
Style Properties

✔ `inline`: Use this option to display the object styled inline with other elements, often in the same block, as with making list items display in a single row.

✔ `block`: This turns any styled element into a block, after which further block-styling attributes may be applied. Block-level elements take up the full width of available space, including line space above and below the element, similar to the way paragraphs have space above and below them.

✔ `list-item`: This option converts styled text into an unbulleted list, similar to `<ul>` and `<ol>` tags.

✔ `run-in`: This feature is either unsupported, incompletely supported, or fully supported, depending on the browser. Currently the browsers that provide full support include Safari, Chrome, IE 8+, and Opera 5+. Add the `run-in` attribute to force a block box following a run-in box to become an inline box of the block box. One interesting usage is to make a header's baseline share the same baseline as the first line of a following block of paragraph text.

✔ `inline-block`: Use this option to make a block behave as an inline block with a specified width.

✔ `compact`: This option is a still quite buggy and is currently only haphazardly supported. In fact, it may already be deprecated, but that cannot be confirmed at this time. When specified, this attribute forces other blocks in the code after it to display along its side.

✔ `marker`: This converts content in a display block into a marker box, using the `:before` or `:after` pseudo-element, inside which you can further style the content.

✔ `table`: Use this attribute to display elements inside a table without having to use HTML tables. In theory, any nested elements would display as if they were `table-row` and `table-cell` elements. Additional display table values for this property are `inline-table`, `table-row-group`, `table-header-group`, `table-footer-group`, `table-row`, `table-column-group`, `table-column`, `table-cell`, and `table-caption`. This property is now supported in all major browsers including IE 9+ and IE 8, but only in IE 8 when `<!doctype html>` is not present.

✔ `inherit`: When you specify this option, the styled object inherits the display value from its parent element.

Blocks are one of the property categories that have a lot of capabilities beyond the basic ones described here. Not all properties are consistently supported by all browsers, but depending on the target audience, some of them might be perfectly suited for a particular web project. To find out more about display properties, review the block information pages at the W3C website. For further discussion of block display attributes, visit the W3C website:

✔ www.w3.org/TR/REC-CSS2/visuren.html#display-prop

✔ www.w3.org/TR/REC-CSS2/tables.html#value-def-table-column

✔ www.w3.org/TR/REC-CSS2/generate.html#markers

The box properties

With the box properties (refer to Figure 4-1), you can position styled objects anywhere in a browser window, position objects relative to the other objects on the page, and apply the padding and margin box style rules selectively to any of or all the four sides of the styled object, such as left and bottom or top, left, and right. When styling less than all four sides, be sure to add 0 values to the sides that should not contain values, rather than leaving them blank.

width/height: Use the width and height attributes to set the dimensions of an object or container such as a table, table cell, or layer. Set the attributes to auto to force the size of the object to match the contents of the object, or enter any value, positive or negative, in px (pixels), pc (picas), pt (points), in (inches), mm (millimeters), cm (centimeters), em (ems), ex (exs), or % (percentage).

```
#rings { height: auto; width: 475px; }
```

float: Use this style to control the side (left, right, or none) on which other objects will float around the styled object.

```
.saleitems { float: right; }
```

clear: Often used in conjunction with the float property, this style attribute controls whether other objects can appear next to the styled object. Variables for this attribute include left, right, both, and none. For example, when a layer appears on the side of an object with the clear side specified, that object is bumped to the area below the layer.

```
.news { clear: both; }
```

padding: This property is like the margin, only with padding you apply extra space between the styled object and any border surrounding it, as with a sentence or a word inside a table cell. Set the padding size on the left, right, top, and/or bottom sides using any value, positive or negative, in px (pixels), pc (picas), pt (points), in (inches), mm (millimeters), cm (centimeters), em (ems), ex (exs), or % (percentage). When uniform sizes are applied to all four sides of the styled object, only one value, as in padding:10px;, needs to be listed in the declaration. Otherwise, specify values for all four sides:

```
.sidebarimage { padding: 10px 0px 10px 0px; }
```

margin: Use the margin property to add or subtract additional space between the page edge (or parent container) and the object being styled, such as the area surrounding a word or layer. Set the margin size on the left, right, top, and/or bottom sides using any value, positive or negative, in px (pixels), pc (picas), pt (points), in (inches), mm (millimeters), cm (centimeters), em (ems), ex (exs), or % (percentage). You may also use the auto value on both sides of a styled object to center the object within its parent container. When uniform values are applied to all four sides, only one value needs to be listed in the declaration. Otherwise, specify values for all four sides:

```
#contact { margin: 0px auto 0px auto; }
```

The border properties

Border properties define the color, style, and width of borders around any styled object. Because borders can go on all four sides of an object, each side can have totally different border attributes! For best results, as with margins and padding, be sure to add a 0 or none to any side property not being styled:

```
.tablecell {
  border-top: 0px none;
  border-right: 2px dotted #069;
  border-bottom: 1px solid #09C;
  border-left: 2px dotted #069;
}
```

style: You can specify borders in any of the following styles: solid, dotted, dashed, double, groove, ridge, inset, outset, or none. Style must be specified in conjunction with the color and width.

```
.tablecell { border: 2px dashed #330066; }
```

width: You can set options for the thickness of the border to thin, medium, or thick. Or, for more precise measurements, use as any value in px (pixels), pc (picas), pt (points), in (inches), mm (millimeters), cm (centimeters), em (ems), ex (exs), or % (percentage. Specify the width along with the color and border style.

```
.tablecell { border: 1px dotted #660033; }
```

color: To colorize the border attribute, specify the hexadecimal value of the desired color and be sure to include the number symbol (#) before the hex value. Also include a style type and width for the border.

```
.tablecell { border: 5px solid #003366; }
```

Figure 4-5 shows examples of each of the different border styles.

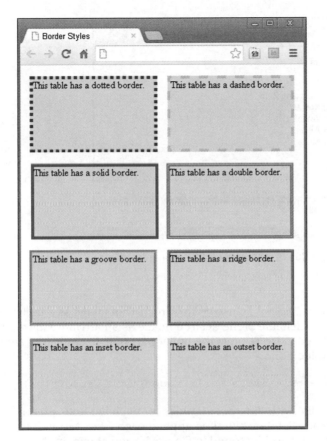

Figure 4-5: Borders come in eight flavors and can be selectively applied to any of or all the sides of a container.

The list properties

Lists styled with CSS are much more robust than lists styled with standard list HTML formatting. With CSS, you can easily select the list type for both numbered and bulleted lists, set the position of the bullets relative to the contents within the list, and even choose to use your own graphic for the bullet image.

`list-style-type`: For ordered lists, set the list type to `decimal`, `lower-roman`, `upper-roman`, `lower-alpha`, `upper-alpha`, or `none`. When creating unordered lists, choose the `disc`, `circle`, or `square` list type. Figure 4-6 shows examples of each of these list types.

```
li { list-style-type: circle; }
```

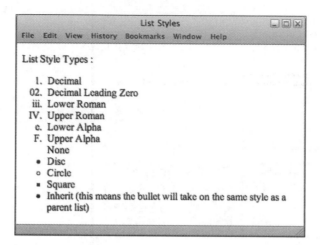

Figure 4-6: Use CSS to set the list type for your ordered and unordered lists.

list-style-image: To use your own custom image as a bullet, enter the location and filename of the desired image as an attribute for the unordered list tag. You can also remove the bullet part of list styling by using the property value none.

```
ul { list-style-image: url(images/mybullet.gif); }
```

To create a list with different graphics for each list item, create custom styles for each list item and then append each <li> tag with the matching class attribute, as illustrated in Figure 4-7 and shown in the following code example, which also makes each item in the list a hyperlink:

```
.redarrow {
list-style-image: url(redarrow.gif);
}
.bluearrow {
list-style-image: url(bluearrow.gif);
}

<ul>
<li class="redarrow"><a href="http://www.thiswebsite.com"
   />Go to This Site</a></li>
<li class="bluearrow"><a href="http://www.thatwebsite.com"
   />Go to That Site</a></li>
</ul>
```

list-style-position: With the position property, you can position the bullet relative to content inside each list item. The position can be located either inside or outside the text. As illustrated in Figure 4-8, when set to inside, the text wraps beneath the bullet along the left margin, and when set to outside, the bullet stays outside any wrapped text, like a hanging indent.

```
li { list-style-position: outside; }
```

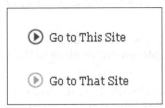

Figure 4-7: For customized unordered lists, use your own bullet graphics.

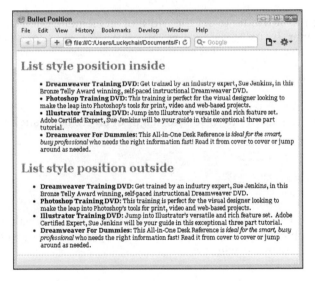

Figure 4-8: Bullets may be positioned inside (top) or outside (bottom) list item content.

The positioning properties

The positioning attributes are used primarily to style layers using the `<div>` tag, though you can also use them to style the position of an image, container, or block-level element within the browser. For layers, both the contents as well as the container can be styled with attributes in this category.

`position`: Determines how a styled element should be positioned in a browser window. Specify whether the position is `absolute`, `fixed`, `relative`, or `static`.

```
#footer { position: relative; }
```

When setting the position, use one of the following style values:

✔ `absolute`: Sets the element's position absolutely based on the numeric values entered for the element's placement relative to the upper-left edge of the browser window, or to the closest absolutely or relatively positioned parent element.

✔ `fixed`: Sets the element's position absolutely based on the numeric values entered for the element's placement relative to the upper-left edge of the browser window.

✔ `relative`: Sets the element's position by the numeric values entered for the object's placement relative to the styled element's position in the file's text flow.

✔ `static`: Sets the element in an exact location within the text flow.

`width`: Use this attribute to set the width of an element, such as a layer or other container, by using `px`, `pt`, `in`, `cm`, `mm`, `pc`, `em`, `ex`, `%`, or `auto`.

```
#layer1 {
width: 760px;
}
```

`height`: Use this attribute to set the height of an element, such as a layer, by using `px`, `pt`, `in`, `cm`, `mm`, `pc`, `em`, `ex`, `%`, or `auto`.

```
#layer1 {
height: 100px;
}
```

`visibility`: This attribute determines the initial visibility value of an element, which can be set to `hidden`, `inherit`, or `visible`, when the page first opens in a browser window.

```
#layer1 {
visibility: hidden;
}
```

Visibility should not be confused with the `display` attribute, which determines whether an element should be treated as a block or an inline element or be completely ignored by the browser with the `display:none;` attribute. With visibility, you're dealing with the initial visibility state of an element, such as a layer, when the page first loads in the browser. This attribute can also be toggled on and off by using JavaScript to hide and show elements on the page, thereby lending a bit of interactivity to the page for the visitor.

To modify the visibility of your element, add the visibility property to your CSS selector with one of the following values:

✔ `hidden`: This option hides a layer from displaying when a page initially opens in a browser.

✔ `inherit`: This option causes any layer to inherit the visibility of a parent layer; if a parent doesn't exist, the layer will be visible. When the visibility is unspecified, `inherit` is the default attribute.

✔ `visible`: Choose this option to force the layer to be visible, regardless of any parent layer's visibility setting, when the page first opens in a browser window.

`z-index`: This attribute specifies a layer's stacking order relative to any other layers on the page as they are viewed in a browser. Set the z-index to `auto` when the number is noncritical, set it to `inherit` to make the layer inherit a parent layer's z-index value, or enter a specific positive or negative number, such as 1, 15, or 100, when the number is important relative to the other layers on the page. The higher the number, the closer the layer appears to the front or top of the page closest to the visitor; the lower the number, the closer the layer appears to the browser's background.

```
#lastchance {
z-index: 4;
}
```

Figure 4-9 shows an example of several layers on a page with different `z-index` values.

**Book III
Chapter 4**

**Understanding CSS
Style Properties**

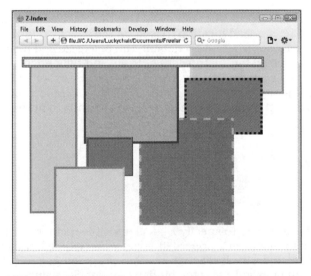

Figure 4-9: Each layer on a page may have its own z-index to represent the stacking order of the layers on the page.

`overflow`: The overflow setting can be used to specify what happens to any contents within a layer that exceed the size of the layer as defined within the CSS. For instance, if a layer is 200px by 200px in size but contains a full page of text, the overflow setting determines how the text will fill the layer. Set the overflow attribute to auto, hidden, scroll, or visible.

```
#aboutus {
overflow: scroll;
}
```

Here is a description of each of the overflow values you can use:

- ✔ auto: Choose this option to have the browser automatically add scroll bars to the layer if and only if the contents exceed the layer's defined width and height.

- ✔ hidden: When this option is selected, the size of a layer is maintained and any content exceeding that size is cut off or clipped from view in a browser window.

- ✔ scroll: Choose scroll to add scroll bars to the layer, regardless of whether the content fits or exceeds the layer's width and height. This attribute isn't uniformly supported by all browsers, so be sure to test it before publishing.

- ✔ visible: Choose this option to have the layer expand vertically and then horizontally, if needed, to fit any contents that exceed the specified layer width and height so that all the contents are visible.

Placement (left, top, right, bottom): Use the placement attribute to specify the exact size and location (based on the specified type) of a styled element in a browser window. By default, the pixel size and placement of an element are specified for the top, left, bottom, and right edges. However, you can use other units (including pt, in, cm, mm, pc, em, ex, or %) if desired or set the value for any of the sides to auto. For layers, if the contents within that layer exceed the specified size, the layer expands to fit the contents.

```
#specialitems {
left: 500px;
top: 300px;
right: 0;
bottom: 0;
}
```

clip: Use this attribute to specify a smaller visible rectangular area within a layer relative to that layer's upper-left edge. When clipped, the hidden area can be manipulated with JavaScript or other programming to create special effects that can hide and show the hidden content. Set values for the clipped area to the top, left, right, and bottom edges of the layer by using px (pixels), pc (picas), pt (points), in (inches), mm (millimeters), cm (centimeters), em (ems), ex (exs), or % (percentage), or a value of auto.

```
#bunnygame {
clip: rect(10px,100px,0px,60px);
}
```

The extension properties

With extension properties, you can change the way the cursor displays in different circumstances, create page breaks, and add special-effect filters to certain elements on the page. Unfortunately, since their inception, very few of them are supported by the most popular browsers. If you'd like to use any of these attributes, test them in as many browsers as you can on both Mac and PC platforms to make sure that they work and/or fail in an acceptable way.

`page-break-before/-after`: This attribute forces a page break when printing a page, either before or after the object styled with this attribute. Choose `left`, `right`, `always`, or `auto` values for before and/or after the desired styled object, as in the following:

```
#sidebar3 {
page-break-before: always;
page-break-after: left;
}
```

`cursor`: You can specify a different cursor to appear when a visitor mouses over an object that is styled with this attribute. Choose from `crosshair`, `text`, `wait`, `default`, `help`, `e-resize`, `ne-resize`, `n-resize`, `nw-resize`, `w-resize`, `sw-resize`, `s-resize`, `se-resize`, and `auto`. There are also 15 new CSS3 cursor options, all of which work in the latest version of Firefox, Chrome, Safari, Opera, and IE9+: `none`, `context-menu`, `cell`, `vertical-text`, `alias`, `copy`, `no-drop`, `not-allowed`, `ew-resize`, `ns-resize`, `news-resize`, `nwse-resize`, `col-resize`, `row-resize`, and `all-scroll`. To see examples of these cursors in action, visit www. sitepoint.com/css3-cursor-styles/.

```
#helpmenu {
cursor: help;
}
```

`filter`: You can choose from several special-effect filters, including Alpha, BlendTrans, Blur, Chroma, DropShadow, FlipH (flip horizontal), FlipV (flip vertical), Glow, Gray, Invert, Light, Mask, RevealTrans, Shadow, Wave, and Xray. Most filters require numeric input such as the mask filter, which must contain the hexadecimal value of the color for the mask, as in `filter:Mask(Color=#ffcc33);`.

```
#details {
filter: invert;
}
```

Although it's true that these filters can do some cool and unusual things, for the longest time they haven't worked in any browsers other than IE. To see an example of a few of these filters, open the following link within an IE browser: www.xentrik.net/css/filters.php. Thankfully, many of these filters have been reinvented as new CSS3 styles that have much better browser support.

Exploring the CSS3 Categories

CSS has several style categories, each with its own set of individual style attributes and capabilities. Similarly, CSS3 has two parts, modules and property sets. In fact, the property sets are really the style attributes available within each module. Although some of the modules overlap or extend capabilities of regular CSS (which is the combination of CSS1 and CSS2), many of them are new and amazing, giving you the power to include features on your sites that were previously possible only with graphics, code hacks, Flash, JavaScript, jQuery, or other programming languages. In the next sections, you can explore the modules and then get into some examples for working with CSS3.

Working with CSS3 modules

For simplicity, I've separated the CSS3 modules into ten categories: borders, backgrounds, fonts, text effects, multiple columns, transitions, 2D transitions, 3D transitions, animations, and user interface. Take a brief look at each module to see what it can do.

Borders: The border module extends the capabilities of the borders category by adding options for setting the border radius to make curved corners, the box shadow for adding drop shadows, and the border image for using graphics to style borders rather than using a single color per edge.

Backgrounds: There are currently three new additions to the background category with CSS3. The background size is especially handy for creating scalable graphics, the background origin offers three locations to position background images relative to the box model, and the background clip allows background colors to be clipped to the contents of a box rather than to the edges of a box. In addition, as I detail in Book III, Chapter 3, CSS3 now allows you to use multiple background images for any container.

Fonts: Instead of being stuck using web-safe fonts for all your designs, the new @font-face property lets you choose and use any font hosted on your web server. What happens is a .ttf (True Type Fonts) or .otf (OpenType Fonts) font file gets automatically downloaded to the user's device if and when that font is not detected. You may have already seen a similar feature in action with sites using Google fonts and Typekit fonts. This style rule extends that capability by allowing you to use your own system fonts.

However, be sure not to break any copyright laws by specifying copyright protected fonts!

Text Effects: There are actually 11 new properties in this module, but not all of them have major browser support. The properties that do currently have support are justify, overflow, shadow, word break, and word wrap. Refer to the section "Discovering useful CSS3 tricks" later in this chapter for an example.

Multiple Columns: Without having to use extra containers or floats, you can now create multiple text columns with the ten different multiple column properties. Although most of them work now, some still do require browser-specific style prefixes. Even so, they're still pretty darn neat. For best results, set the column count and gap width. Read about this technique in the later section "Discovering useful CSS3 tricks."

Transitions: Hold onto your hat, you can now create movement on the page without animated gifs, Flash, or JavaScript! Transitions come in three flavors, regular, 2D, and 3D. With the regular transition, you can modify any one or more properties of an element, such as altering the width of an object over a specified number of seconds, when combined with the :hover pseudo-class. You find an example of this technique later in this chapter.

2D Transitions: The items in this module allow you to manipulate the 2D properties of an element. Use them separately or combined to move, scale, skew, spin, stretch, and turn elements along a horizontal or vertical plane. For instance, you can make a box grow and spin while moving from left to right.

3D Transitions: As if 2D transitions weren't cool enough, wait until you see what the 3D transitions do! Using a method that transforms the object along the X and/or Y axis, you can make your objects appear to rotate in 3D space, providing viewers with a chance to see the reversed "back" side of an object. Though browser support is limited for more advanced transformations, eventually you'll be able to rotate, scale, and move along the X, Y, and Z axes, among other things. Simply powerful.

Animations: Okay, what happens when we put all these new transformation techniques together? CSS3 animations, baby — the kind that can replace animated GIFs, Flash, and even some JavaScript. All the magic happens by way of binding the new @keyframes property to a selector by using the animation property with a specified name and duration. For example, you could change the position and background color of an object so that the object has the appearance of morphing through space, and then you could include the code to make the animation reverse order and continue looping endlessly.

User Interface: With these new properties, you can add properties to different objects that convert them into interactive elements for site visitors. For instance, you can resize layers and textarea form fields, invoke the tab and arrow keys on a keyboard, and create an offset outline that extends beyond the border edge.

Now that you have an overview of the new modules, you can find out more about what they can do. For example, you can create shadows on shapes and text, apply background gradient effects, and move your objects from here to there.

Working with CSS3 selectors

In mid-2010, web designers and developers rejoiced as CSS3 began to make its way into the mainstream. Since that time, browser support for CSS3 has steadily increased and improved, even though CSS3 isn't officially a W3C standard yet. In fact, the only drawback (if you even want to call it that) to using these selectors today is that you may occasionally still need to add some browser-specific prefixes to your CSS to ensure that all the CSS3 styles appear correctly in the older versions of the most popular browsers.

To illustrate, if all browsers supported the CSS3 `columns` selector, you'd only need to specify a single `columns` declaration in your style like this:

```
div {
    columns:100px 3;
    }
```

However, because this selector isn't supported in the same way by all the popular browsers, the workaround is to write your single CSS3 declaration first, and then directly below it you'll include duplicate declarations with browser-specific prefixes. Note how CSS comments are added to the CSS to identify the browsers associated with each prefix:

```
div {
    columns:100px 3;
    -webkit-columns:100px 3; /* Safari and Chrome */
    -moz-columns:100px 3; /* Firefox */
    }
```

Here is a list of CSS3 prefixes by browser:

Browser	Prefix
Internet Explorer	-ms-
Firefox	-moz-
Google Chrome	-webkit-
Safari	-webkit-
Opera	-o- or -xv-

For an up-to-date listing of browser support for all the CSS3 properties, check out the chart at `www.w3schools.com/cssref/css3_browser support.asp`.

Also be sure to download a free copy of the Smashing Magazine *CSS3 Cheat Sheet* PDF, which can help you discover how to use CSS3 in your web designs: `http://coding.smashingmagazine.com/2009/07/13/ css-3-cheat-sheet-pdf/`.

Discovering useful CSS3 tricks

You can do literally hundreds of tricks with CSS3. In fact, CSS3 tricks could make up an entire book! Still, until all the major browsers support every CSS3 module completely, it makes sense to focus here on topics that you can actually use today to help you make your web designs unique. Therefore, I've selected ten of the most popular and useful CSS3 techniques.

Adding multiple background images

Before CSS3 came along, you could specify only one background image per container. If you needed a second background image, you'd have to add another container to your code. Now, with CSS3, you can easily add as many background images to any one element as you please. Figure 4-10 shows an example of a container with three background images, a pattern, and two PNG files with transparency.

Figure 4-10: Use CSS3 to set multiple background images for any container.

The simplest way to add multiple images is to separate each by a comma, making sure to place the image you want to be in the topmost position first and any additional images below it in the desired stacking order:

```
.box {
/* fallback */
background: url(bg-full.png) top left no-repeat;
/* modern browsers */
background:
```

```
url(bg-top.png) top left no-repeat,
url(bg-bottom.png) bottom right no-repeat,
url(bg-middle.png) left repeat-x;
}
```

As a fallback for older browsers, you can include a single image that has all the combined elements of your separate images at the top of the style block, as noted here by the `/* fallback */` comments. This method ensures that older browsers display the first image and ignore the rest.

Rotating objects

As a web designer, one of the ways you can add some interest to your 2D design is to break away from the linear structure of the grid by rotating an object in space. With CSS3, you can effortlessly rotate an object by applying the `transform: rotate` style to any object:

```
.rotate {
    transform:rotate(-4deg);
    -webkit-transform:rotate(-4deg); /* Safari and Chrome */
    -moz-transform:rotate(-4deg); /* Firefox */
    -o-transform:rotate(-4deg); /* Opera */
}
```

Objects can be rotated clockwise (4deg) or counterclockwise (-4deg). You may also scale and skew an object with the `scale()` and `skew()` transform methods by specifying numerical values or degrees for the X-axis and Y-axis:

```
div {
    transform: scale(3,6);
    -ms-transform: scale(3,6); /* IE 9 */
    -webkit-transform: scale(3,6); /* Safari and Chrome */
    -o-transform: scale(3,6); /* Opera */
    -moz-transform: scale(3,6); /* Firefox */
    }
div {

    transform: skew(10deg,20deg);

    -ms-transform: skew(10deg,20deg); /* IE 9 */

    -webkit-transform: skew(10deg,20deg); /* Safari and Chrome
    */

    -o-transform: skew(10deg,20deg); /* Opera */

    -moz-transform: skew(10deg,20deg); /* Firefox */

    }
```

Rounding edges

Hallelujah! Instead of having to use one image or up to four separate images to give the illusion of a curved shape, with CSS3 you can now create containers with curved corners! Here's the code, which has the fully supported CSS3 declaration at the top followed by prefixed duplicates for other browsers:

```
#box {
    border-radius: 20px;
    /* for Mozilla Firefox */
    -moz-border-radius: 20px;
    /* for Safari & Google Chrome */
    -webkit-border-radius: 20px;
}
```

You can use the `border-radius` style on any object including rectangular images. The bigger the number of pixels, the rounder the edge.

Creating multiple columns

Before CSS3, if you wanted to have multiple columns on your page you'd need to either float elements within containers or position them absolutely relative to a parent container. Now, with CSS3, you can easily create multiple columns within a single container using the column property by setting the values for column number and gap width, either with or without a vertical rule between them.

```
#box1 {
    /* for browsers not requiring a prefix */
    column-count: 4;
    column-gap: 30px;
    column-rule: 3px solid #fff;
    /* for Mozilla Firefox */
    -moz-column-count: 4;
    -moz-column-gap: 30px;
    -moz-column-rule: 3px solid #fff;
    /* for Safari & Google Chrome */
    -webkit-column-count: 4;
    -webkit-column-gap: 30px;
    -webkit-column-rule: 3px solid #fff;
}
```

Figure 4-11 shows a comparison of one layer using the multicolumn style and another layout without columns. For more information about how you can further control the look of your multiple columns, see www.quirksmode. org/css/multicolumn.html.

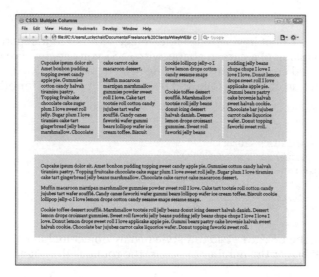

Figure 4-11: Create containers with multiple columns of text by using CSS3.

Creating a box shadow

Imagine being able to create a shadow without the use of a graphic. With the CSS box shadow style in CSS3, you can! The only catch with this fine style is that IE 8 and IE 5.5–7 require a workaround to display it properly. Thankfully, you don't need to worry about finding that hack, because I've included it here for you:

```
.boxshadow {
-moz-box-shadow: 3px 3px 4px #6f6f6b; /* Firefox 3.5+ */
-webkit-box-shadow: 3px 3px 4px #6f6f6b; /* Safari 3.0+,
Chrome */
box-shadow: 3px 3px 4px #6f6f6b; /* Opera 10.5, IE 9,
Chrome 10+ */
/* For IE 8 */
-ms-filter: "progid:DXImageTransform.Microsoft.
Shadow(Strength=4, Direction=135, Color='#000000')";
/* For IE 5.5 - 7 */
filter: progid:DXImageTransform.Microsoft.
Shadow(Strength=4, Direction=135, Color='#000000');
}
```

You may use this feature alone or pair it with any other CSS styles. For example, Figure 4-12 shows the box shadow paired with a border and rotation.

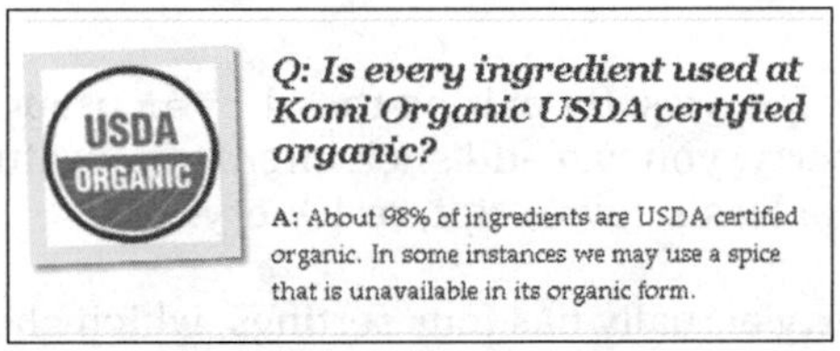

Q: *Is every ingredient used at Komi Organic USDA certified organic?*

A: About 98% of ingredients are USDA certified organic. In some instances we may use a spice that is unavailable in its organic form.

Figure 4-12: Add the Box Shadow style to your images to make them pop. This image also uses the border and rotate styles.

Adding a text shadow

Similar to adding a drop shadow to a container or other object, you may also give your text the drop shadow treatment by using the text-shadow CSS3 declaration. Values for this declaration include the horizontal and vertical shadow distance, and an optional blur and color.

In the following code example, the first and second values represent the horizontal and vertical offset, the third number is the blur distance, and the hexadecimal value sets the shadow color:

```
.textshadow {
    text-shadow:5px 5px 10px #000000;
    }
```

Try it yourself to see how it looks and play around with the values to achieve different effects.

Using transparency

Another fantastic feature of CSS3 is the ability to apply transparency to an object by using the opacity declaration. In fact, depending on which element you apply this style to, the transparency can change the entire contents (such as a `<div>` filled with content) or a single element, such as paragraph text or an image. IE 8 and earlier require an alternative declaration for the alpha filter as follows:

```
div {
    background-color:#CCC;
    opacity:0.5;
    /* IE8 and earlier */
    filter:Alpha(opacity=50);
    }
```

The default value for opacity is 1, which is the same as full opacity. Decrease the number to less than one to add transparency. The alpha opacity values range from 0–100 percent.

Making transitions

Talk about powerful new features: By pairing the :hover pseudo-class with the CSS3 transition property, you can add slick interactive features to your objects without the use of Flash, JavaScript, or jQuery!

The transition property actually has four settings, which should be written in the CSS in the following order: property, duration, timing-function, delay.

The following list describes the settings:

- transition-property: Identifies which CSS property will alter, such as the width or height, as in transition-property:width;.

- transition-duration: Sets the value in seconds for the transition to complete, as in transition-duration: 5s;.

- transition-timing-function: Specifies the speed curve of the effect. Values may be set to linear, ease, ease-in, ease-out, ease-in-out, or cubic-bezier(n,n,n,n), as in this example: transition-timing-function: linear;, which is equivalent to cubic-bezier(0,0,1,1).

- transition-delay: Determines how many seconds will elapse before the effect begins, as in transition-delay: 2s;.

In the following code example, after a 2-second delay, an orange box smoothly changes over 5 seconds from 100px to 500px wide when a visitor hovers the mouse over the <div> container:

```
<!DOCTYPE html>
<html>
<head>
<style type="text/css">
div {
    width:100px;
    height:100px;
    background-color: #F90;
    transition: width 5s linear 2s;
    -moz-transition: width 5s linear 2s; /* Firefox 4 */
    -webkit-transition: width 5s linear 2s; /* Safari & Chrome
    */
    -o-transition: width 5s linear 2s; /* Opera */
}

div:hover { width:500px; }
</style>
</head>
<body>
<div></div>
</body>
</html>
```

Resizing elements

You've no doubt heard of resizing a browser window. With CSS3, you can now give visitors the ability to resize any `<div>` tag or form `textarea` element by using the `resize` property. The `resize` value can be set to `none`, `both`, `horizontal` or `vertical`, and it is typically paired with the `overflow` property set to `auto`.

In the following example, a 300px wide container can be resized both horizontally and vertically, and any overflow content automatically reflows to fit the container's changing dimensions, adding scrollbars when applicable:

```
div {
    width:300px;
    resize:both;
    overflow:auto;
}
```

Creating gradients

In the past, when designers wanted a gradient background for an element, they'd create a graphic and then repeat it along the X- or Y-axis to fill the space. Using CSS3, you can create your own faster-loading gradients.

Believe it or not, you can create the gradient effect using the `background-image` property paired with values for the gradient type, position, color stop, and color value. Though the syntax for the CSS is slightly different for WebKit than Mozilla, the results are identical, as illustrated in Figure 4-13:

```
.gradient {
    /* Safari & Chrome */
    background-image:
    -webkit-gradient(linear,left bottom,left top,color-stop(0,
    #74B4DB),color-stop(1, #F7ECCA));
    /* Firefox */
    background-image:
    -moz-linear-gradient(center bottom, #74B4DB 0pt, #F7ECCA
    100%);
    height: 200px;
}
```

Figure 4-13: Create beautiful gradient backgrounds with CSS3.

In addition to the technique shown here, you can also create more complex gradient effects by using the free online gradient editor on the ColorZilla website at www.colorzilla.com/gradient-editor/.

To find out even more about these ten techniques and working with CSS3 in general, visit www.css3.info and www.w3.org/TR/css3-selectors/.

Styling the Content on Your Pages

Now that you know all about CSS styles and style sheets, you should be able to figure out how to style the content on your pages. In the following sections, you find out about styling the different areas of your pages as well as how to perform a few advanced CSS techniques.

Styling paragraphs, headings, and footers

When you are styling paragraphs, headings, and footers, most of the work can be automatically accomplished by creating tag redefine styles for the <p> tag and however many heading tags you intend to use, such as <h1>, <h2>, and <h3>:

```
p {
    font-family: Georgia, "Times New Roman", Times, serif;
    font-size: 12px;
    color: #039;
    background-color: #FCEBB6;
}
```

In some circumstances, you may want to create a custom style and apply that selectively to individual words or phrases throughout your text by using the class="stylename" attribute as part of the opening tag that surrounds the content, whether that be a paragraph, heading, or span tag:

```
.stylename {
    font-family: Georgia, "Times New Roman", Times, serif;
    font-size: 10px;
    font-style: italic;
    font-weight: bold;
    font-variant: small-caps;
    color: #006;
}
```

```
<p class="stylename">This entire paragraph will be styled
    using the stylename class, which overrides the redefined
    paragraph style.</p>
```

When styling footer content, you may want to create styles to format all the content that goes there. To start, many designers isolate the footer content into its own layer. If you'll be coding with HTML5, you can use the `<footer>` tag for your footer content. Otherwise, when using HTML 4.01 or XHTML you can style that layer using an id style:

```
<div id="footer">
<a href="index.html" target="_self">Home</a> | <a
   href="about.html" target="_self">About</a> | <a
   href="services.html" target="_self">Services</a> | <a
   href="contact.html" target="_self">Contact</a><br />
&copy; 2009 CompanyName.com. All Rights Reserved.
</div>
```

Within that `<footer>` or id style, you could set the font family, size, weight, and color for the layer's contents; apply a background color and border attributes to the layer; and set the layer's width, height, z-index, and visibility.

```
#footer {
   font-family: Verdana, Geneva, sans-serif;
   font-size: 0.7em;
   font-weight: bold;
   color: #FFF;
   background-color: #666;
   padding: 10px;
   margin: 20px;
   height: auto;
   width: 90%;

}
```

After that's done, you can begin to create individual custom styles, ID styles, custom hyperlinks, and advanced combinators to style the various parts of the footer content. For instance, you could create a set of hyperlink styles that would only be applied to the links within the footer:

```
#footer a:link {
   color: #CC0;
}
#footer a:visited {
   color: #0C6;
}
#footer a:hover {
   color: #FFF;
   background-color: #CC0;
   text-decoration: none;
}
#footer a:active {
   color: #FFF;
```

```
    background-color: #0C6;
    text-decoration: none;
}
```

Figure 4-14 demonstrates how a layer styled with the `#footer` and `link` CSS styles shown here would look in a browser.

Figure 4-14: Use CSS to create custom styles for the links and other text in the page footer.

Styling lists and tables

Styling lists and tables is a bit different from styling content out in the body of the page, because both lists and tables have specific tags that can be redefined to control how content sits within those structures.

Lists

With lists, you can select type attributes, such as font, size, and alignment, and apply a background color and border to each list item. In addition, you can select the desired list style type, select the bullet's position relative to the list item content, and choose to use your own custom bullet graphic.

The secret to keeping all the list styles in order is to wrap your list between `<div>` tags with an `id` attribute, and then create styles for the `<div>`, `<ul>`, and `<li>` tags. This is especially useful when creating navigation systems with list formatting:

```
<div id="nav">
  <ul>
   <li><a href="#">Home</a></li>
   <li><a href="#">About</a></li>
   <li><a href="#">Services</a></li>
   <li><a href="#">Contact</a></li>
  </ul>
</div>
```

Here are the styles you might create for your list in the CSS. This code includes styles for normal and hover link states:

```
#nav {
   position:absolute;
   width:539px;
   height:57px;
   z-index:4;
   right: 30px;
}
#nav ul {
   list-style-type: none;
   margin: 0px;
   padding-top: 31px;
   padding-right: 0px;
   padding-bottom: 0px;
   padding-left: 8px;
}
#nav ul li {
   display: inline;
   font-family: Arial, Helvetica, sans-serif;
   font-size: 14px;
   font-weight: bold;
   color: #4e2d17;
   padding: 0px;
   margin: 0px;
}

#nav ul li a:link, #nav ul li a:visited {
   text-decoration: none;
   color: #4e2d17;
   background-color: #FAF8ED;
   padding-top: 57px;
   padding-right: 6px;
   padding-bottom: 10px;
   padding-left: 6px;
}
#nav ul li a:hover {
   color: #FFF;
   background-color: #E51B24;
}
```

Figure 4-15 illustrates how this navigation menu looks in a browser when a visitor mouses over one of the links. To find out more about building navigation systems with HTML and CSS, turn to Book III, Chapter 6.

Book III
Chapter 4

Understanding CSS
Style Properties

Figure 4-15: Create custom list styles, including simple navigation menus, with CSS.

Styling all four sides

For any styles you create that include declarations from the box, border, or positioning property categories, pay special attention to the rules that are applied to container tags (such as a layer, table, or table cell) that include top, bottom, left, and right sides. Rather than adding a rule to only the sides you want to style, you should enter values for all four sides to improve the way the page is rendered in a variety of browsers.

Typically your options are to style the unused sides with a zero value or a value of None. For example, the `padding` attribute in the box properties category can take on values for `top`, `bottom`, `left`, and `right`. To add padding only on the top and left sides of an object, be sure to enter 0 as the unit for the right and bottom sides of the style definition:

```
.mystyle {
  padding-top: 5px;
  padding-right: 0px;
  padding-bottom: 0px;
  padding-left: 5px;
}
```

Likewise, the `border` style attribute in the border properties category has four sides. However, to specify that you don't want a particular side styled, use the `none` property value:

```
.test {
  border-top: 0px none;
  border-right: 1px solid #039;
  border-bottom: 0px none;
  border-left: 1px solid #039;
}
```

Tables

With tables and CSS, you can style the entire table, individual table cells, whole rows or columns, and the contents of each cell. Begin by inserting a table and adding the desired content to each of the table cells. Apply any cell padding and cell spacing to the table as desired. Then, to make the process of styling your table easier, be sure to add an `id` attribute to the opening table tag and the `class` attribute to the first opening table row tag:

```
<table id="longjohns" width="300" border="0" cellpadding="10"
    cellspacing="0">
 <tr class="longjohnsth">
  <td width="220">Children's Silk Long Johns</td>
  <td width="80">Price</td>
 </tr>
 <tr>
  <td>Crewneck Long Underwear Top</td>
  <td>$17.95</td>
 </tr>
 <tr>
  <td> Long Underwear Pant</td>
  <td>$17.95</td>
 </tr>
</table>
```

Next create a style for that `id`, which you can use to format the main parts of the table, such as the table's size, background color, and border:

```css
#longjohns {
  background-color: #996;
  height: 200px;
  width: 300px;
  color: #FFF;
}
```

After you complete the table's main formatting, you can create advanced combinators (also called *dependent selectors*) and custom styles for the different table cells, as illustrated in Figure 4-16.

```css
#longjohns tr td {
  border-top-width: 0px;
  border-right-width: 0px;
  border-bottom-width: 1px;
  border-left-width: 0px;
  border-top-style: none;
  border-right-style: none;
  border-bottom-style: dotted;
  border-left-style: none;
  border-bottom-color: #FFF;
}
.longjohnsth {
  font-weight: bold;
  background-color: #C9C9AD;
  color: #000;
}
```

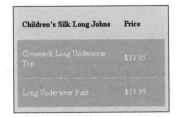

Figure 4-16: Use CSS to create custom styles for the individual cells within your table.

Book III
Chapter 4

Understanding CSS
Style Properties

Styling images and layers

Images need not just sit on your page exactly where you stick them. Instead, use CSS with your images to position them relative to other content, and add padding and border attributes to one or more sides.

To style an image, you have three options:

✔ Create a tag redefine style for the `<img>` tag to create a style that applies to all images on your page(s).

```
img { border: 2px dotted #069; }
```

✔ Create a custom class style that can be selectively applied to individual images as needed.

```
.myimg { border: 2px dotted #069; }

<img src="mygraphic.gif" alt="My Graphic" width="130"
    height="95" class="myimg">
```

✔ Create an ID style that automatically styles the image with a matching `id` attribute.

```
#mystyle { padding: 5px; border: 5px dashed #F90; }

<img src="mygraphic.gif" alt="My Graphic" width="130"
    height="95" id="mystyle" name="mystyle">
```

In addition to these general image-formatting options, you may also add CSS style rules to your images that control how other objects sit on the page relative to the styled image. Using the `float` and `clear` style attributes, you can control whether other objects will float to the left or right of the styled object. In addition, you can use these attributes to force other elements to move into the area below the styled object. For example, to make a series of images `float` and `clear` to the right of a block of text, as shown in Figure 4-17, create a custom style with the `float` and `clear` attributes:

```
.imgfloatright {
  margin: 0 0 10px 10px;
  float: right;
  clear: right;
  }
```

Then apply that style selectively to each image within the text block. The images should sit at the top of the block of text, as shown here:

```
<img class="imgfloatright" src="images/image.gif" width="100" height="100"
    alt="">
<img class="imgfloatright" src="images/image.gif" width="100" height="100"
    alt="">
<img class="imgfloatright" src="images/image.gif" width="100" height="100"
    alt="">
<p>&#8220;Any intelligent fool can make things bigger, more complex, and more
    violent. It takes a touch of genius -- and a lot of courage -- to move in
    the opposite direction.&#8221; &#8212;Albert Einstein </p>
<p>&#8220;Any people anywhere, being inclined and having the power, have the
    right to rise up, and shake off the existing government, and form a new
    one that suits them better. This is a most valuable - a most sacred right
    - a right, which we hope and believe, is to liberate the world.&#8221;
    &#8212;Abraham Lincoln </p>
```

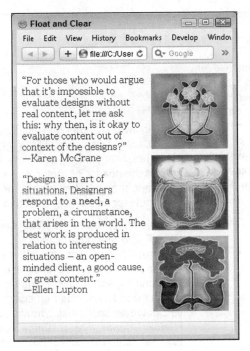

Figure 4-17: The float and clear styles can make objects float beside other content.

Formatting `<div>` layers with CSS is a complex affair because you can pretty much control everything related to the style and positioning of a layer. In most instances, designers begin by giving each of their layers a unique ID, such as `id="sidebar"`. After the layer has been named in the HTML, an ID style can be created to control the positioning, width, height, z-index, font family, font size, font color, background color, padding, and border of the layer.

The following declaration shows example CSS for an ID style:

```
#sidebar {
  position: relative;
  width: 350px;
  height: 200px;
  z-index: 1;
  font-family: Arial, Helvetica, sans-serif;
  font-size: 16px;
  background-color: #F5F5F5;
  color: #666;
  border: 5px double #999;
  padding: 20px;
  }
```

Beyond that, the layer contents can be further styled with any combination of tag redefines, ID styles, custom class styles, and advanced combinators.

Using CSS with HTML5

If you'll be coding using HTML5 instead of HTML 4.01 or XHTML, rest assured you can use any CSS or CSS3 style with your HTML5 code elements. The only significant changes with regard to CSS, in fact, are with the HTML5 code itself, because HTML5 includes several new content specific tags to simplify your HTML code. To illustrate, here's an example of how you might code the bones of your HTML5 page by using the `<header>`, `<nav>`, `<section>`, `<aside>`, and `<footer>` tags:

```
<!doctype html>
<html>
<head>
<meta charset="utf-8">
<title>Page title</title>
</head>
<body>
  <!-- Header -->
  <header></header>
  <!-- Navigation -->
  <nav></nav>
  <!-- Introduction -->
  <section id="intro"></section>
  <!-- Main content area -->
  <section id="main"></section>
  <!-- Sidebar -->
  <aside></aside>
```

```
  <!-- Footer -->
  <footer></footer>
</body>
</html>
```

You can style any content specific tag like the `<aside>` just as you would any regular tag by either redefining the tag itself, which would be fine for the header or footer, or giving the tag an ID and then creating a style for that ID, as you would for an aside or a section.

In addition to these content specific tags, HTML5 also introduces some super cool features such as new form controls, a `<canvas>` tag for 2D drawing, `<video>` and `<audio>` tags, and support for local data storage. Keep in mind that HTML5 isn't officially a standard yet. However, most major browsers, such as Firefox, Chrome, Safari, Opera, and Internet Explorer, support some HTML5 features, and support continues to grow with each new browser version release.

For a complete listing of HTML5 tags and an explanation about their usage, visit `www.w3schools.com/html5/html5_reference.asp` and `www.w3schools.com/html5/default.asp`.

Finding CSS Resources Online

One of the best ways to discover more about CSS is to look at the code developed by others. By reverse-engineering the CSS and HTML code, you can really get an in-depth understanding of how positioning and styling of content with CSS works. Then you can implement the same or similar methods in your own web pages.

Several amazing websites showcase innovative and unique CSS styling, some of which also allow you to view the source code behind the work. My long-time favorite resource is Dave Shea's `www.csszengarden.com`, shown in Figure 4-18, but you can easily find many others by searching for "CSS," "CSS tutorials," "CSS tips," and so on. Table 4-1 lists some great sites you should definitely visit and bookmark.

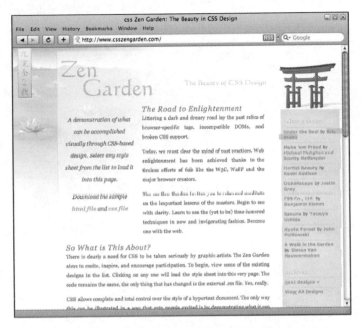

Figure 4-18: Check out other designers' CSS at CSS Zen Garden.

Table 4-1	CSS Online Resources
CSS Resource Name	*CSS Resource Web Address*
W3Schools Tutorial	`www.w3schools.com/css/default.asp` and `www.w3schools.com/css3/default.asp`
W3C Tutorial	`www.w3.org/MarkUp/Guide/Style` (a bit dated, but still a nice resource)
W3C's CSS	`www.w3.org/Style/CSS`
CSS Zen Garden	`www.csszengarden.com`
CSS3 Files	`www.css3files.com`
CSS-Tricks	`http://css-tricks.com`
Max Design	`http://maxdesign.com.au`
SitePoint	`http://reference.sitepoint.com/css`
CSS play	`www.cssplay.co.uk`
A List Apart	`www.alistapart.com/topics/code/css`

Finally, having a reference guide at your fingertips is also extremely useful. You can find a number of more-detailed CSS references by searching for titles at `www.wiley.com`.

Chapter 5: Creating Web Layouts

In This Chapter

✓ Discovering the benefits of standards-compliant, accessible layouts

✓ Exploring mobile first and responsive web concepts

✓ Understanding the difference between layouts using tables and layers

✓ Finding out how to create a simple layers-only layout

✓ Creating tables-based layouts for HTML e-mails

✓ Finding and using free online layers-based layouts

I n this chapter, you start by finding out about the benefits of creating standards-compliant, accessible layouts and get a primer on how to work successfully with layers. Then you explore two new concepts to web design, namely responsive web and mobile first. Following that, you discover how to create a simple CSS-styled, layers-based layout on your own and how to use the old-school HTML tables-based layout in case any of your clients ask you to create an HTML e-mail or HTML newsletter for them. At the end of the chapter, you find a helpful list of resources for finding excellent, free CSS layers-based layouts on the web.

Creating Standards-Compliant, Accessible Layouts

The World Wide Web Consortium (www.w3.org), or W3C, is an international vendor-neutral organization that defines standards on the web to improve web accessibility and hardware/software interoperability. By following the recommendations of the W3C, designers, programmers, and web developers can design and build interoperable websites that are coded semantically, look great, and function efficiently. Thus, to build a standards-compliant website means to use the recommended standards and guidelines put forth by the W3C.

HEADLINE GOES HERE

by Human Resources Department

Dear Employees, Families, and Friends,

Lorem ipsum dolor sit amet, consectetuer diam nonummy nibh euismod tincidunt ut magna aliquam erat volutpat. Ut wisi enim quis nostrud exerci tation ullamcorper sus ut aliquip ex ea commodo consequat. Duis iriure dolor in hendrerit in vulputate velit consequat, vel illum dolore eu feugiat null eros et accumsan et iusto odio digni

◄ Bullet 1

What, then, is *semantic HTML*? Simply put, it's the use of HTML tags and coding that match either what the content is, like using <p> tags for paragraph text, or what the content is for, like using the <label> tag for form controls such as text fields and radio buttons, which don't have implicit labels. In other words, by following a few simple rules of the HTML road, you can quickly be on your way to developing sites that make everyone happy.

By the way, that "everyone" includes making your pages accessible to the widest-possible human and nonhuman audience. Think of *accessibility* as a fancy way of saying that you can make code enhancements to your website to improve how visitors with disabilities and search engine robots/spiders access the information on your site's pages. Common coding enhancements include adding alternative text for images, titles and targets for links, access and tab index keys, form input labels, object labels, footer links, a site map page, page titles, meta tags, and link tags to the home and site map pages in the <head>.

In addition to semantic coding, standards compliance also means exclusively (or nearly exclusively!) using layers-based layouts, which is another great way of making your pages accessible to the widest possible audience. Remember, you have no control over what computer, device, and browsing tools your target audience will be using to access your website. As shown in Figure 5-1, those tools likely include all the different browsers and browser versions on both Mac and PC, handheld devices like smartphones and tablets, speech synthesizers, video game consoles, and web spiders or robots, to name a few.

Sadly, though standards compliance has been a hot issue in the web design world for the last ten or so years, many sites today still barely comply with web standards, especially the older sites that were built using table-based layouts and sites that are built by the less informed and non-designers. That's where you come in.

As a designer today, you can help make the future of the WWW a better place by following the HTML standards recommended by the W3C when building any new site or redesigning an existing site. Working with layers fits right into the W3C's overall mission of standards compliancy by allowing you to precisely position and style content using CSS instead of HTML. What's more, standards-compliant code is lighter, pages load faster, pages are easier to maintain, and more visitors (whether they're humans using a browser or other device or nonhumans such as search engine robots) can access the content on those pages.

Figure 5-1: Web visitors will likely use a variety of devices to access your site.

Building Sites with Mobile First and Responsive Design

In addition to the standards set forth by the W3C, web designers, web developers, UI (user interface) designers, and UX (user experience) designers are playing a major role in helping to define new standards.

Recently, there has been a major push by professional web designers, web developers, and web standards advocates for all designers to use two important workflow strategies: *mobile first* and *responsive web*. Essentially, these design recommendations promote the user's experience no matter what device is being used to access the web. In fact, with the explosion of new capabilities brought forth by the ever-increasing support of CSS3 and HTML5 in major browsers, everyone seems to be jumping onto the responsive web bandwagon, including major smart software developers like Adobe. For example, mobile first and responsive web have been (and continue to be) a driving force in Adobe's development of improved support for fluid grid layouts, CSS3, and HTML5 in Dreamweaver. Clearly, web designers may well be on the cusp, if not smack in the middle of, some major exciting changes in the world of web technology!

So, what do mobile first and responsive web actually mean? These ideas might seem radical for the seasoned designer yet perfectly logical to anyone new to web design. One thing for sure, however, is these concepts are already changing the way people design and build websites. In the following sections, I examine both concepts in more detail.

Mobile first

Mobile first is a concept promoted by Luke Wroblewski in 2009, when he urged designers and developers to develop the mobile version of a website first, before the desktop version. This approach turns seasoned designers upside down. You see, the norm for years has been to develop the desktop version first and then maybe create a modified mobile version afterwards. Wroblewski's reasoning for this change has three main points to consider:

- Mobile usage is exploding.
- Mobile also has more capabilities to engage visitors with interactivity such as GPS and touch input.
- Mobile forces a site to simplify the delivery of content by displaying only the most important information for a focused user experience.

The last idea, to focus on user experience, is more important than you might think. Typically, when a customer hires a designer to build a website, the customer already has a good idea about what content should go onto the site. This approach, where the customer chooses what to share with site visitors, doesn't always take those visitors' needs into account. Ideally, a site should be designed to allow visitors to quickly and efficiently find what they need. If you follow Wroblewski's lead and build sites that provide visitors with focused content and an easy-to-use interface, that's smart business.

To find out more about Wroblewski's ideas about mobile first, I highly recommend watching his *MobileFirst! LinkedIn 2010 TechTalk* video at www.lukew.com/ff/entry.asp?1137.

Responsive web

Responsive web is based on the concept of *responsive architecture,* where a physical space is programmed to respond to the presence of people and adjust certain parameters accordingly, such as walls moving to alter the size of the room or smart glass that changes opacity. When you apply this same idea to web design, you can shift from creating static fixed-width sites for specific devices (like a browser only) to creating *flexible experiences* where websites are designed with fluid grids and flexible images that adapt to a variety of devices, such as browsers, tablets, and smartphones.

One of the fastest ways toward achieving a responsive web today is to build sites using a fluid grid combined with CSS3 media queries to automatically detect which device is accessing a site and then assign a corresponding CSS style sheet with device-specific styles. For example, image sizes can be set to a percentage of a containing column rather than having specific fixed widths. What's more, you could even start using ems (a more flexible unit of measure) instead of pixels in your media queries for truly proportional font sizes, as outlined on the Cloudfour blog at `http://blog.cloudfour.com/the-ems-have-it-proportional-media-queries-ftw/`.

Another popular technique is to *linearize* the page when the viewports of the devices accessing the page are smaller than a specified size, forcing all the containers to fall in a single vertical stack rather than side by side. You can view a nice example of this concept in a test site created by Ethan Marcotte at `www.alistapart.com/d/responsive-web-design/ex/ex-site-larger.html`.

Likewise, you can tie the number of columns within the layout to a specific device's style sheet, which gives you the freedom to design custom display solutions for different sections of a site, like how a menu looks and functions, to accommodate the varying screen sizes.

In addition to creating sites for a variety of devices, designers need to embrace new technologies and developments to existing technologies, such as HTML5 and CSS3, as well as a new breed of preprocessors and CSS authoring frameworks such as Compass, Foundation, and Susy, which can help developers and designers deploy standards-compliant, responsive sites from a predefined framework. If you're ready to start designing and building the responsive grid sites of the future today, I highly recommend exploring and absorbing the information on the following sites:

- ✔ `http://beta.theexpressiveweb.com` Get the latest expressive features of CSS3 and HTML5 from this awesome showcase site made by the folks at Adobe.

- ✔ `http://html.adobe.com` This is Adobe's site on HTML. Here you can find information on web standards, open-source coding, upcoming events, and more.

- ✔ `http://docs.webplatform.org` If you're seeking a wiki on all things web, check out this site, which is filled with Q&A, Chats, Blogs, and Tutorials.

✔ www.css3files.com This fun blog site by Christian Krammer features clear examples of several new CSS3 techniques.

✔ http://tv.adobe.com/watch/learn-dreamweaver-cs6/using-fluid-grid-layouts/ Watch this video on Adobe TV to get started using fluid grid layouts.

✔ www.scoop.it/t/gonzodesign Gonzodesign is the pseudonym for web expert Jan Rajtoral, who curates this Scoop.it site on the topic of responsive web design.

✔ http://webdesign.tutsplus.com/tutorials/applications/getting-started-with-dreamweaver-cs6-fluid-grids/ When you're ready to jump into fluid grid design, check out the "Getting Started With Dreamweaver CS6 Fluid Grids" tutorial from Tom Green at webdesign.tutsplus.com.

✔ http://foundation.zurb.com/docs/index.php Foundation is one of the hot new development tools for generating front-end code faster and better.

✔ http://compass-style.org Compass is an open-source CSS Authoring Framework that can help you create cleaner markup.

✔ http://susy.oddbird.net This site is a great source for creating responsive grids for Compass.

Working with Layers

If you're brand-new to the world of web design, finding out how to build layers-based layouts from the start is easy enough to do. However, if you've been doing a bit of web design on your own and have been working with tables-based layouts, you'll probably need to unlearn a few habits you might have developed from working with tables.

Discovering the benefits of layers-based layouts

To be sure, some web design purists will tell you unequivocally to create only layers-based layouts, whereas the more old-school designers might say that working with a hybrid table/layers layout is also fine. Because you want to do the right thing, your goal should be to try to use layers-based layouts whenever possible. Nonetheless, rules are made to sometimes be broken, so if parts of your design really do require tables, feel free to use them and don't feel guilty about it. A hybrid tables/layers layout is far more user friendly than a tables-only layout.

Before launching into how wonderful layers are, rest assured that using tables is not a bad thing and that if you choose to occasionally use tables in your pages, no Layers Police will come in the dead of night and take you to Table User's Prison. Layers are simply the more politically correct technique to use because they make pages that are more accessible, especially if you design and build your site with responsive web and mobile first in mind. In addition, layers are more flexible than tables because when combined with CSS, they can be positioned relatively or absolutely anywhere on a Web page. In addition to making pages more accessible, you find several wonderful benefits of creating layouts with layers:

- The code is cleaner because it uses less HTML markup.

- Layers free you from having to design within the traditional rows-and-columns framework of tables.

- You can stack layers directly on top of other layers using the z-index style attribute. The larger the z-index number, the closer the object appears to the viewer in the browser window.

- You can control layer visibility in a browser window with JavaScript.

- You can position layers anywhere on a page, including overlapping with other layers.

- Layers can be nested inside other layers.

- Layers can be styled and positioned on the page with CSS using #layer ID as the selector name.

- Layers can contain any content that can be placed elsewhere on a page, just like tables, and that content can be styled with CSS.

- The position of layers can be easily adjusted on the fly with CSS3 media queries, allowing you to style the elements on the page to fit the viewports of a variety of devices.

- By modifying the CSS alone, you can completely change the look and position of the layer's contents.

Understanding what layers are

Think of layers as a cousin to the single-celled table or as a boxlike container that can be placed anywhere on a web page, including alongside, above, below, and nested inside other layers.

The code for a layer that can be easily styled with a CSS id attribute is very simple:

```
<div id="LayerName">Here is a sentence inside a layer.</div>
```

When a layer tag (the <div> tag) includes an id attribute, simply create an ID or class CSS style for it to style and position the layer and its contents. Here's an example of the CSS for the id of a <div> tag:

```
<style type="text/css">
<!--
#LayerName {
```

```
     position: absolute;
     left: 200px;
     top: 100px;
     width: 500px;
     height: 400px;
     z-index: 1;
     font-family: Verdana, Arial, Helvetica, sans-serif;
     font-size: 1.2em;
     font-weight: bold;
     color: #FFF;
     background-color: #99cc66;
     margin: 0px;
     padding: 10px;
     border: 10px solid #000000;
}
-->
</style>
```

Figure 5-2 illustrates the difference between an unstyled layer and a layer in Dreamweaver using the #LayerName CSS style.

Each layer on your page can have its own CSS style, and that style can include as many different style and positioning attributes as you like. You can also create custom CSS styles to control the style and positioning of any part of the contents of a layer, including text, graphics, media, and other file types. While at first working with layers and CSS may not feel as intuitive as you'd like it to — especially if you've already worked with tables — with a little practice you'll soon come to appreciate and respect the vast customization capabilities of working with layers.

Furthermore, as you see in the next section, with the knowledge of a few simple techniques, you can soon be on your way to creating your own simple layers-based layouts.

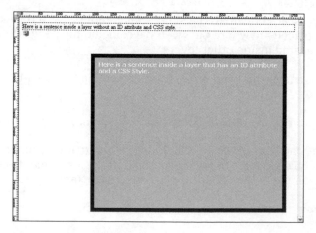

Figure 5-2: Add a CSS style to your layer to control the layer's look and position.

Creating a Layers-Only Layout

All HTML tags are like containers that each have specialized functions. Paragraph tags, for instance, surround paragraph text, and image tags display images. Regarding layers, think of them as free-spirited, single-celled tables. Layers can hold any kind of content, including text, graphics, Flash movies, and other media, and both the layer and its contents can be styled and positioned within a web page. In fact, using CSS for positioning, you can place layers next to other layers as well as nest them inside, above, below, and on top of other layers. Furthermore, with CSS, you can even style and position a series of layers to look similar to tables without all the extraneous code that tables require.

In the sections that follow, you find out how to add layers to your pages and how to build and style a simple CSS layers-based layout.

Adding a layer to a page

Adding a layer to a page is quite simple because it requires only the `<div>` tag with an `id` or `class` attribute for attaching a CSS style. You can then place any content inside the layer, such as a graphic:

```
<div id="header"><img src="images/logo.gif" width="200"
    height="150" alt="Company Name Here"></div>
```

When the `<div>` tag is assigned an `id` or `class` attribute, you can create a CSS style for the layer, such as in the following example, and place that style either in an internal style sheet in the `<head>` area of the page or (preferably) in a linked external CSS file:

```
<style type="text/css">
<!--
#header {
  position:absolute;
  left: 0px;
  top: 0px;
  width: 760px;
  height: 200px;
  z-index: 1;
  font-family: Georgia, Times New Roman, Times, serif;
  font-size: 12px;
  color: #43BFC7;
  background-color: #2B3856;
  margin: 0px;
  padding: 10px;
  border: 10px solid #000000;
}
-->
</style>
```

The z-index of a layer sets the stacking order, where the position sets the layer's position relative to other containers on the page.

To nest a layer inside another layer, simply add a new set of <div> tags inside another set. To help keep track of where each layer starts and ends, include comment tags in your HTML:

```
<!-- header layer start -->
<div id="header">
  <!-- navigation layer start -->
  <div id="navigation">
  </div><!-- navigation layer end  -->
</div><!-- header layer end  -->
```

One of the most wonderful things about layers is that when combined with CSS styling, you can create unlimited variations with essentially the same HTML markup. This means that you can change the entire look of a website by modifying the CSS and changing some of the graphics. This concept is expertly demonstrated by the various CSS layout designs submitted to CSS Zen Garden (www.csszengarden.com).

Building a CSS layers-based layout

To illustrate how easily a page layout can be completely transformed with a few minor changes to the CSS, the following steps show you how to create a simple, fixed-width, two-column page layout with layers. Then, in the section that follows, you find out how to apply CSS to control the look of the page.

The page you're about to build will have a three-part layout that consists of a header, a two-column main content area, and a footer. The header will contain a logo, navigation bar, and photographic banner. Within the two-column main content area, both the left and right columns will be fixed in width, and the entire layout will be centered within the browser window.

For this layout to function properly, you must add a series of layers to the page in the proper order. The id attributes of each of the layers are named semantically to match the function they'll perform, such as navbar and footer.

To create this CSS layers-based layout, follow these steps:

1. **Create a folder on your computer to save the files associated with this project.**

   For example, you could create a folder on your desktop called WebLayout and then make sure that you save the HTML, images, and other files to this folder.

2. **Using your favorite HTML editor, open a new blank HTML document, select the HTML5 DTD (this is a line of code that tells the browser how**

to interpret the HTML, whether that's HTML 4.01, XHTML, or HTML5), and save the file with the name `mypage.html` to the `WebLayout` folder you just created.

3. **In your code, between the opening and closing `<body>` tags, insert six layers using the `<div>` tag and give each one its own `id` attribute:**

```
<div id="wrapper">
  <div id="header">
  </div>
  <div id="main">
    <div id="content">
    </div>
    <div id="sidebar">
    </div>
  </div>
  <div id="footer">
  </div>
</div>
```

4. **Add placeholder content to identify each part.**

This step helps you easily identify each layer and further understand how the layers are organized on the page.

```
<div id="wrapper">
  <div id="header"><p>Insert Header</p>
  </div>
  <div id="main">
    <div id="content"><p>Insert Main Content</p>
    </div>
    <div id="sidebar"><p>Insert Sidebar Content</p>
    </div>
  </div>
  <div id="footer"><p>Insert Footer</p>
  </div>
</div>
```

You can go back into each section later and replace the placeholder text with real content. When inserting text, be sure to use semantic HTML by wrapping the correct tags around the content, such as `<p>` tags for paragraph text and `<h1>` to `<h6>` tags for headings.

5. **Inside the layer with the `id="header"`, insert three nested `<div>` tags for the `logo`, `navbar`, and `banner`.**

```
<div id="header"
  <div id="logo">
  </div>
  <div id="navbar">
  </div>
  <div id="banner">
  </div>
</div>
```

6. **Between the opening and closing logo `<div>` tags, insert your logo graphic and convert it into a hyperlink to a file named `index.html`.**

   Ideally, the logo should be a clickable link that returns visitors to the homepage. Your code for this area should now look something like this:

   ```
   <div id="header">
     <div id="logo"><a href="index.html"><img src="images/
       springfield.png" width="303" height="100"
       alt="Springfield Design Studio"></a>
     </div>
     <div id="navbar">
     </div>
     <div id="banner">
     </div>
   </div>
   ```

7. **Inside the layer with the `id="content"`, type a heading and a few paragraphs of text. Wrap the heading in `<h1>` tags and the paragraph text in `<p>` tags:**

   ```
   <div id="content"><h1>Heading For Text Below</h1>
   <p>Sample paragraph text. Sample paragraph text sample
       paragraph text.</p>
   <p>Sample paragraph text. Sample paragraph text sample
       paragraph text.</p>
   </div>
   ```

8. **Inside the layer with the `id="navbar"`, create an unordered list with the following null hyperlinked list items:**

   ```
   <div id="navbar">
     <ul>
       <li><a href="#">Link 1</a></li>
       <li><a href="#">Link 2</a></li>
       <li><a href="#">Link 3</a></li>
       <li><a href="#">Link 4</a></li>
     </ul>
   </div>
   ```

   You'll style the `<ul>` and `<li>` tags with CSS later in the chapter to make the links sit horizontally in a row. For more information about creating navigation systems and styling list items with CSS, see Book III, Chapter 6.

9. **Inside the layer with the `id="banner"`, insert a graphic:**

   ```
   <div id="banner">
     <img src="images/banner1.jpg" width="960"
       height="300" alt="Creative Design Solutions">
   </div>
   ```

10. **Inside the layer with the `id="sidebar"`, insert dummy content or notation for what you plan to include in that section.**

How'd they do that?

One of the best ways to find out more about CSS is to take a look at what others have done before you. Beyond the basics of CSS, you can do quite a few unusual and wonderful things with CSS. One of those more advanced techniques is to create what's called a *descendant selector style,* which uses a unique form of CSS syntax to apply a style to the set of tags specified in the style's selector, such as a `border` attribute for an image inside a table cell inside a sidebar layer that sits inside another layer:

```
#container #sidebar td img {
   border: 1px solid #000000;
}
```

Descendant selector styles can be used for all kinds of styling tasks, including combining them with pseudo-class selectors to create custom link states for specific parts of a web page. Here's an example of a selector for the hover state of a hypertext link that applies only to links inside a layer called `#sidebar`:

```
#sidebar a:hover {
   padding: 10px;
   border: 1px solid #6699CC;
   background-color: # 336699;
   color: #fff;
}
```

Here's another example of a descendant selector style that modifies the hover state of any linked item in an unordered list that sits inside a layer called `linklist`:

```
#linklist ul li a:hover {
   color: #990033;
}
```

Descendant selector styles can even help you to control how an image or text sits inside a layer. For instance, rather than apply a style that would add padding to an entire layer, you could selectively apply padding to the contents of that layer by using a special descendant selector style that only applies to specified tags nested inside the layer, such as the `<h1>` tag, as in the following code:

```
<div id="sidebar"><h1>Today's Specials<img src="images/20percent.gif" alt="20% Off! "
        width="250" height="165" border="0"></h1>
</div>
```

To apply a style to the contents of that `<h1>` tag, your descendant selector style would look something like this:

```
#sidebar h1 {
   margin: 0;
   padding: .75em;
}
```

In this scenario, this new style is automatically applied to the `<h1>` tag inside that layer, but not to any other `<h1>` tags on the page.

Create descendant selectors for any set of tags and preexisting styles, including links in a footer, images in a navigation bar, and text in a sidebar layer or any other location on your page.

**Book III
Chapter 5**

**Creating Web
Layouts**

For example, you might include a heading 1, some graphics, and some text:

```
<div id="sidebar">
  <h1>Featured projects </h1>
  <p><img src="images/project1.jpg" width="300"
   height="100" alt=""><br>
     Web Design &amp; Production</p>
  <p><img src="images/project2.jpg" width="300"
   height="100" alt=""><br>
     Branding, Web &amp; Graphic Design</p></div>
```

11. **In the footer layer, repeat the main navigation links and add any additional footer copy.**

    You might add social media links and a copyright notice, as shown here:

```
<div id="footer"><a href="#">Home</a> | <a
    href="#">Link 1</a> | <a href="#">Link 2</a> | <a
    href="#">Link 3</a> | <a href="#">Link 4</a> |
    <a href="#">Follow us on Facebook</a> | Copyright
    &copy; Springfield Design Studio</div>
```

The HTML code © is the special HTML entity used for the copyright symbol. Use this entity instead of the regular copyright symbol (©) to ensure that the copyright symbol displays more accurately in the widest variety of browsers, tablets, and smartphones and reads properly by screen readers and other assistive devices.

When previewed in a browser, your code should create a page that looks like the example shown in Figure 5-3.

Styling a CSS layers-based layout

In the steps that follow, you'll create the CSS that controls how the page content you just coded is styled, positioned, and presented in a web browser.

When styling content with CSS, it is often best to style the page from the top to bottom, or outside in, by starting with redefining the <body> tag, then adding styles for various layers, and finally creating any *descendant selectors* (see the nearby sidebar) to style the content within the layers, including any <p> and <h1> through <h6> tags.

For demonstration purposes, the CSS in the following steps is placed inside the page between the <head> tags rather than on an external style sheet. However, if this layout were to be used for a real website, move the CSS into an external CSS file before you create any additional pages for your site, because an external CSS file makes site management vastly easier.

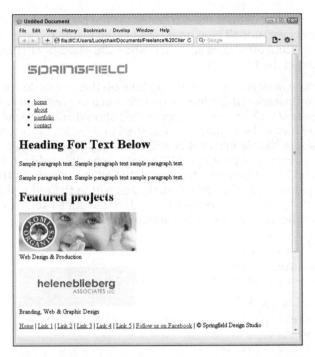

Figure 5-3: With no CSS styling, the HTML on the page has limited formatting.

Follow these steps to apply CSS the layers-based layout you created in the preceding section:

1. **Begin by adding an internal style area between the `<head>` tags on the page using the style tags with comments:**

   ```
   <style type="text/css">
   <!--
   -->
   </style>
   ```

2. **Between the comment tags (`<!--` and `-->`), add two tag redefine styles, one for setting page size for the `<html>` and one for the `<body>` tag to set the page margins to 0, which makes the site layout begin at the upper-left edge of the browser. If desired, include a style declaration for the page background color.**

   ```
   html {
       height: 100%;
       width: 100%;
       }
   body {
     margin: 0px;
     background-color: #3E4440;
       }
   ```

The <body> tag defines the attributes for the body of the entire web page. However, not all container tags nested inside the <body> tag inherit the font attributes specified when the <body> attributes are redefined in the CSS.

In CSS, to *inherit* is to automatically take on the properties of a *parent* class. For instance, if the font is specified in a tag redefine style for the body (parent), all paragraph tags (child) should automatically inherit the same font unless otherwise specified in the CSS. Unfortunately, not all browsers handle inheritance the same way (see www.ericmeyeron css.com/bonus/render-mode.html), especially when it comes to tables and lists. Therefore, to ensure that all containers on the page use the same font and other global attributes within the redefined body style declaration, you could create a secondary advanced selector style that specifies the <body> and other subcontainer tags:

```
body {
   margin: 0px;
   padding: 0px;
   background-color: #ffffff;
   }
body,th,td {
   font: 1.1em "Trebuchet MS", Arial, Helvetica, sans-
     serif;
   text-align: left;
   color: #5e6961;
   }
```

Alternatively, you could simply create a tag redefine style for your paragraphs and headings, and custom styles for your tables and table cells.

Note the unit of measure for the font size. An em is one of the units of measure acceptable on the web that also makes pages more accessible to a wider audience. What makes the em different from pixels and percentages is that each em unit varies because its size is equal to the point size of the specified font face. For instance, if the font for a page is set to 10px, one em is exactly 10px.

In the next step, you create styles for each of the <div> tags so that the individual layers are styled and positioned accurately on the page.

3. **Create a style for the layer with the id="wrapper" to set the background to white (#FFFFFF), the width to 960px, the height to auto, the padding to 0, and the margins to auto:**

```
#wrapper {
   background-color: #FFFFFF;
   width: 960px;
   height: auto;
   padding: 0px;
   margin: auto;
   }
```

The wrapper layer holds all the content together in the center of the browser.

4. **Create the default link styles to control the look of all hyperlinks on the page, including unvisited, visited, and hover states:**

```
a:link, a:visited {
    color: #0bb38d;
    text-decoration: underline;
    margin-right: 2px;
}
a:hover {
    color: #FFF;
    background-color: #5e6961;
}
```

5. **Make a new style for the header layer by using the #layerid syntax and setting the position to relative:**

```
#header {
    margin-right: auto;
    margin-left: auto;
    padding: 0px;
    height: 400px;
    position: relative;  }
```

Setting the layer's position to relative allows you to absolutely position any nested layers inside of it.

To see for yourself how relative positioning affects the layout, change the position to absolute, save the changes, and preview the web page in a browser. What you'll see is that the child element becomes absolutely positioned relative to the page (<body>) rather than the parent container (<div id="#wrapper">). Big difference! When you're done with this test, be sure to return the position to relative.

6. **Create three dependent selector styles for the header content, namely, the three nested layers for the logo, navbar, and banner:**

```
#wrapper #header #logo {
    background-image: url(images/springfield.png);
    background-repeat: no-repeat;
    height: 100px;
    width: 303px;
    position: absolute;
}
#wrapper #header #navbar {
    position: absolute;
    height: 100px;
    width: 380px;
    left: 582px;
}
#wrapper #header #banner {
```

```
    position: absolute;
    height: 300px;
    width: 960px;
    top: 100px;
    background-image: url(images/banner.jpg);
    background-repeat: no-repeat;
}
```

Notice that each of these styles includes a declaration that sets the position to absolute. This allows the nested layer to sit in a fixed location relative to the parent layer's (#header) top-left corner.

At this point, the logo and banner look right and the navbar container appears to be positioned correctly, but the navigation links still look like a bulleted list. You tackle that next.

7. **To style the list of navigation links, develop a style for the `<ul>` and `<li>` tags, as in this example:**

```
#navbar ul {
    list-style-type: none;
    margin: 0px;
    padding-top: 34px;
    padding-right: 0px;
    padding-bottom: 0px;
    padding-left: 0px;
}
#navbar ul li {
    display: inline;
    font-family: "Century Gothic", Century;
    color: #959f9f;
    font-size: 18px;
    padding-top: 0px;
    padding-right: 0px;
    padding-bottom: 0px;
    padding-left: 18px;
    margin: 0px;
}
```

8. **(Optional) Create special styles for each of the different link states.**

```
#wrapper #header #navbar ul li a, #wrapper #header
    #navbar ul li a:link, #wrapper #header #navbar ul li
    a:visited{
    color: #5E6961;
    background-color: #FFF;
    text-decoration: none;
    padding-right: 2px;
    padding-left: 2px;
}
#wrapper #header #navbar ul li a:hover {
    color: #FFF;
    background-color: #5E6961;
}
```

By listing the styles in the selector name separated by commas, as with the a, a:link, and a:visited styles shown here, several locations (even virtual ones!) within the code can share the same style.

If you're using a hexadecimal value that has the same number or letter for each pair of the three-pair number, you can use a shorthand syntax where only the first number or letter of the pair needs to be specified, such as #FFF for #FFFFFF or #F36 for #FF3366.

9. **Create an ID style for the main layer and dependent selector styles for the content and sidebar layers:**

   ```
   #main {
       margin-right: auto;
       margin-left: auto;
       margin-top: 40px;
       margin-bottom: auto;
       padding: 0px;
       min-height: 340px;
       height: auto;
       position: relative;
   }
   #wrapper #main #content {
       width: 540px;
       padding-right: 30px;
       padding-left: 30px;
       clear: left;
       float: left;
       height: 300px;
   }
   #wrapper #main #sidebar {
       height: 300px;
       width: 300px;
       clear: right;
       float: right;
       margin-right: 20px;
       color: #5E6961;
       padding-right: 0px;
       padding-left: 0px;
       font-size: 0.9em;
       font-style: italic;
   }
   ```

   The float attribute tells the browser to keep that layer always positioned on a particular side of the page. You can set the float attribute to left, right, none, or inherit. Adding the float:left; or float:right; attribute to a style tells the browser that the layer must float to the left or right of the other layers within the same container.

10. **Define three styles for the footer area.**

    One for the footer layer, one for any unvisited and visited hyperlinked text within the footer, and a third for the hyperlink hover state within the footer, which can be different from hyperlink styles found elsewhere on the page:

**Book III
Chapter 5**

**Creating Web
Layouts**

```
#footer {
    height: 40px;
    font-family: Arial, Helvetica, sans-serif;
    font-size: .75em;
    text-align: center;
    position: relative;
    padding-top: 40px;
    background-image: url(images/footerbg.png);
    background-repeat: no-repeat;
    background-position: center top;
}
a.footer:link, a.footer:visited {
    color: #5e6961;
    text-decoration: none;
    padding-right: 5px;
    padding-left: 5px;
    background-color: #FFF;
}
a.footer:hover {
    color: #FFF;
    background-color: #5e6961;
    text-decoration: none;
}
```

When you create specialty link styles like these for the footer, the styles must be applied to each of the links within the footer.

To apply the style to links the footer, do one of the following:

Dreamweaver: Select a link in Design view and then apply the style to it by selecting the style name from the Class menu in the Properties inspector. Dreamweaver automatically adds the class attribute to the link for you.

Hand-coding: Apply the custom `class` attribute to the opening tag for each of the links:

```
<a href="#" class="footer">Link 1</a>
```

11. **Save the code changes you have made to your web page and preview your layers-based layout in a browser.**

    You can preview the file by double-clicking the HTML file icon or by dragging and dropping the HTML file into an open browser window.

    Feel free to create any additional styles for your page as desired. When finished, your layout should look similar to the example shown in Figure 5-4.

12. **To see how the CSS can be easily modified, go back into the code and make a change or two, such as customizing the page title, changing the background color of the page, and creating a style for the <h1> text appearing in the main content area.**

    The more you play around with CSS, the better you begin to understand how to use this powerful tool.

Figure 5-4: Test your CSS for display accuracy by previewing your page in a variety of different browsers and devices.

Finding Online Resources for Layers-Based Layouts

One of the best ways to find out about CSS and really understand the power of layers-based layouts is to begin the design process using a predefined CSS layers-based design template. Several resources are available online where you can obtain free, cleanly coded, standards-compliant templates, including responsive web templates. You can then use them as they are or modify the templates to match your site design by tweaking and adding your own CSS styles.

Dreamweaver users can use any of the 18 beautifully commented CSS layers-based page layouts that come built into Dreamweaver. These page-design guides are accessible from the New Document dialog box in the Blank Page category under HTML in the Page Type column, as shown in Figure 5-5, and in the Blank Template category under HTML Template in the Template Type column. You also have access to the Fluid Grid Layout (new in CS6), also accessible from the New Document dialog box, as shown in Figure 5-5.

The layout shown in Figure 5-6 uses the option *2 Column Liquid, Right Sidebar, Header and Footer,* for example (liquid meaning it's a fluid layout). It comes with its own CSS file (which can be placed internal or external to the file) and has a header for the site's branding, a main area with a liquid two-column design for the site's main and sidebar content, and a footer, all of which can be customized through Dreamweaver's CSS Styles panel.

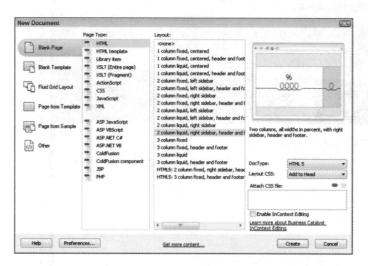

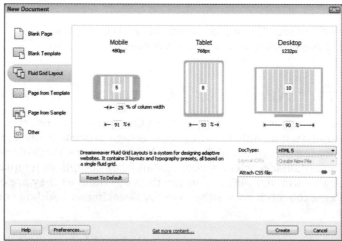

Figure 5-5: Dreamweaver includes 18 prewritten CSS layers-based layouts and 1 fluid grid layout that you can use as a starting point to build a website.

The more time you take to explore all the wonderful things you can do with CSS, the more all of it will start to make sense to you. Visit as many of the sites listed (in no particular order) in Table 5-1 as you can, and be sure to also do a search for *"free CSS3 layouts"*, *"free html5 templates"*, and *"free responsive html5 templates"* in your favorite search engine to find additional CSS page-layout resources on the web.

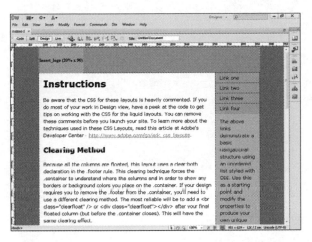

Figure 5-6: This particular layout in Dreamweaver includes areas for a general page layout.

Table 5-1	Free CSS Page Layout Templates
Site Address	*Freebies, Tutorials, Tips, and More*
`www.noupe.com/design/html5-and-css3-collection-fresh-free-web-templates.html`	Free HTML5 and CSS3 templates from the folks at smashing magazine.com
`www.freecsstemplates.org`	Free CSS layouts and templates for websites and blogs
`http://cssr.ru/simpliste/`	Free open-source responsive web template
`www.egrappler.com/free-responsive-html5-portfolio-business-website-template-brownie/`	Free responsive HTML5 Portfolio/Business website template called "Brownie"
`www.cssjunction.com/freebies/html5-css3-responsive-web-template/`	Free responsive HTML5 website template called "It Fits"
`http://webcodebuilder.com/examples/responsive-html5css3-template/index.html`	Free responsive HTML5 website template from WebCodeBuilder.com
`www.adobe.com/devnet/dreamweaver/articles/dreamweaver_custom_templates_pt2.html`	Dreamweaver customizable starter designs for web designers

Chapter 6: Constructing Navigation Systems

In This Chapter

✓ Considering the site's organization and target audience

✓ Finding out about navigation systems

✓ Creating text navigation menus

✓ Making rollover buttons with JavaScript

✓ Creating CSS list navigation menus without graphics

✓ Making CSS list navigation menus with graphics

✓ Building multitier Spry menus in Dreamweaver

A rchitecturally, the single most important element of a website is its navigation system. That's because it is the one unifying feature of a site that enables visitors to quickly survey a site's structure and access the desired information. Think about your own habits when you go to a new site. Most visitors, unconsciously or not, expect to be able to find what they're seeking within one to three clicks. If they can't find what they're looking for — or worse yet, if the links they click mislead them in some way — they will promptly leave that site and go search somewhere else, unless of course they know that it's the only online resource that has what they're looking for. For these reasons alone, a site's navigation system must be easy to find and easy to use. Better yet, make it visually appealing too, and you have yourself a great navigation system.

In this chapter, you find out how to choose and then create the right navigation system for a website. You start by discovering some basics about matching a site to the right navigation system based on its target audience. Then you follow along with steps that show you how to build text menus and rollover buttons, as well as CSS list menus both with and without graphics, and multitier Spry navigation menus.

Assessing the Navigational Needs of Your Site

To select the right navigation system for a site, you need to go back to the site architecture — the site map — which you find out how to create in Book I, Chapter 3. With a strong understanding of the site's structure and organization, you can then choose the right type of navigation for the site. For example, if the site is small and will have only five main navigation links, you can be more creative with your selection of a navigation system. By contrast, if you're building a site that has ten main navigation links, each of which includes subnavigation menus that may also include additional levels of subnavigation links — in other words, a big site that requires a multitier navigation system — you need to understand quite a bit about HTML, CSS, and JavaScript *before* you convert the navigation in your mock-up into a working navigation system on your website.

Having a good idea of the organization and structure of all the pages on any particular site provides you with the best understanding of the type of navigation that you need. By reviewing the architecture, you can easily identify the labels for each page and the order of all the main navigation links and subpages of the site. Each of the site's pages should fit into one of three categories for the navigation:

- **Main navigation links:** These pages represent the main pages on the site, such as About and Contact, which should be easily accessible from any other page on the site through the navigation system.

- **Subnavigation links:** These links are menu links to subpages that are accessible through some kind of submenu off the main navigation. In other words, subpages are pages that fall logically into a category beneath one of the main pages, such as a Directions page in a submenu under a Contact Us page that provides visitors with information on how to get to a company's facility. A subnavigation menu can be a pop-up menu from the main navigation link, a second row of links that appears below the first row when activated by the main navigation link for that group, or even a sidebar area that appears somewhere on the page when activated by the main navigation link of that group.

- **Non-navigational links:** Many websites have pages that don't need to be included within the main navigation or subnavigation areas but must still be accessible to visitors through hyperlinks located in various spots throughout the site, such as in the footer of all the pages on a site or in the body text area of a particular page. Links like these might include Privacy Policy, Site Credits, or Site Map pages.

In addition to the site organization, four other factors may further influence which type of navigation works best for a website:

- **General usability:** Consider the general usability of the navigation system. The menu must be intuitively easy to read and use, include concisely written and meaningful labels, and be in the same location on every page of the site so that visitors don't need to go searching on different areas of the page to find it.

✔ **Target audience:** The target audience can often help determine the relative complexity or simplicity of the navigation menu type. For instance, a target audience comprised mostly of seniors and visitors with disabilities might require larger fonts for menu buttons than an audience made up primarily of high school and college students. Likewise, the navigation for an indie electropop band website could be far more obscure and unusual than the navigation system for a site that sells MP3 downloads.

✔ **Expandability:** Find out in advance whether the site's navigation is anticipated to grow with additional pages and/or subcategories. If the site will be growing at some time in the near or foreseeable future, make sure that you choose a navigation system that will be easy to update and expand, because some navigation systems take less time to reconfigure than others do. For instance, text and CSS-styled list menus are far more readily expandable than menus that rely on precisely sized rollover graphics powered with JavaScript or jQuery.

✔ **Technology:** Touch-based devices don't support rollovers. If a navigation system is designed using rollovers, site visitors might not be able to access subpages on a site. To make sites as accessible as possible, consider using HTML list menus styled with CSS.

Discovering the Basic Principles of Navigation Systems

Whether they contain two pages or 200, all websites must supply a method that allows visitors to move freely among all the pages on the site. The simplest form of page navigation is the hypertext link, which requires only that the destination filename be specified in the link code. Although extremely functional and accessible to the widest possible audience on nearly any web-enabled device, a text-only navigation menu can tend to look kind of, well, boring. To spiff things up a bit, consider giving your site a more complex-looking menu that uses some combination of text, CSS, graphics, and possibly even JavaScript or some other programming language to handle its dynamic functionality, such as giving the menu cool details such as bevels, gradients, and borders or adding smoothly gliding flyout subnavigation menus.

The navigation on a site needs to provide a simple route to all the most important pages on the site. How that route looks and functions is the key role of the navigation system. Discuss with your client where on the page the navigation menu area will be placed relative to the other content. If the navigation menu also requires subnavigation, be sure you discuss with your client how and where the subnavigation items should be displayed.

Wide versus deep menus

To further guide you in the selection and implementation of your navigation system, take to heart the following important principle in web design navigation:

> *The visitor should be able to find what he or she is looking for in the fewest number of clicks possible.*

To help realize this standard, you may choose to design a navigation menu that is either wide or deep, depending on the number of main navigation links in the menu:

- **Wide:** A *wide* menu refers to a navigation system that lists links to all the main pages on a site, often in a single horizontal row, as shown in Figure 6-1. If the site is small, having four to seven main navigation links across the page might be a suitable solution. On the other hand, for a site that has 14 main pages, there is probably no visually appealing way to list all 14 links in a single horizontal row. You could try breaking the links into two rows of seven, but that might confuse site visitors unless you paid careful attention to the design and layout. Alternatively, you could present the wide menu to visitors as a single vertical list of navigation buttons, as is done with the Shop By Department links along the left side of www.homedepot.com. If, however, the large number of main pages is simply the result of the client's failure to organize content, help your client rethink the architecture in terms of a deep navigation menu system instead.

Figure 6-1: Wide navigation menus are best for sites with a small number of main pages and few or no subpages.

✔ **Deep:** In a *deep* menu, all the web pages are grouped into categories of similar interest to reduce the total number of main navigation links, which can be displayed either horizontally or vertically on the pages of the site. Each category has a main page (such as About Us) and one or more subpages (such as Company History, Board of Directors, and Our Sponsors) that visitors can access through some kind of customized subnavigation menu system, like the one shown in Figure 6-2.

Depending on the orientation of the main navigation menu on the page, the subnavigation menus can either pop up, drop down, or fly out from the main menu. For instance, the subnavigation might be displayed as a second row of links that appears below the first row of links when activated by the main navigation link for that group, or perhaps it might be displayed as a sidebar area that appears somewhere on the page only when activated by the main navigation link of that category.

Figure 6-2: Deep navigation menus are suitable for sites with multiple pages and subpages.

Single-tier menus

Single-tier, or single-level, menus are always wide menus, regardless of whether the navigation links are displayed horizontally or vertically on the page. Because single-tier menus don't have many links, they provide you with the most freedom when it comes to choosing a method to construct them. For instance, you might want to style the entire menu with background graphics and Google fonts to give it a totally unique look. You may even want to use JavaScript or some other programming language to dynamically create rollover effects or some other kind of unique interactive menu features on the page. Whether you're using HTML text, CSS, JavaScript, or any combination of these tools to create your single-tier menu, the sky really is the limit.

Multitier menus

Multitier menus use links with submenus to create tiers of navigation. Each tier may include additional submenus, and every link, no matter where it lies within the tiered navigation scheme, provides visitors access to any page on the menu with a single click.

With multitier menus, you must have a firm understanding of how to construct this type of menu before you design it in your mockup and get approval on it from the client. New designers often design a menu and sell their clients on its functionality before they know whether they have the skills to build it! To avoid putting yourself in an awkward situation like that, familiarize yourself with all the different kinds of menus that you can easily replicate. Better yet, try to build the menu before you show your mockup to the client so you're 100 percent sure that you can include it in your design.

Choosing the Right Menu for Your Site

To build a deep or wide single-tier or multitier navigation system, you can choose from several kinds of different coding solutions, depending on the site's specific needs:

- **Text-only:** These horizontal or vertical navigation menus are made up of plain hyperlinks that are often separated by some kind of character (such as a dash or other symbol) or small graphic (such as a horizontal or vertical divider). Craigslist is a perfect example of this type of total minimalization.

- **CSS list:** The most user-friendly and accessible form of navigation system is built with HTML text links and CSS styling. Using CSS list formatting, CSS list menus can be either single-tier or multitier and can be made to sit horizontally or vertically across the page. With a more enhanced understanding of CSS, you can even understand how to build CSS list menus using your own custom graphics and CSS styles to create rollover type menus.

- **Rollover buttons:** Rollover buttons can be created by combining HTML, CSS, and graphics either with or without JavaScript. If you prefer to use graphics that include text instead of HTML text links, create your own custom button graphics and combine them with JavaScript to create interactive buttons. When a visitor moves her cursor over the button graphic, the JavaScript can temporarily display an "over state" graphic there instead. When the visitor moves her mouse off the graphic, the "over state" graphic disappears and the original "normal state" graphic is restored. You can also create rollover buttons without JavaScript by building a CSS list menu with HTML text and styling the individual buttons with CSS.

To make your sites as accessible as possible, try to minimize the use of traditional JavaScript rollover buttons and instead use the CSS list menus. You can even use background graphics with the CSS if you like. Whichever style you choose, remember that visitors using tablets or smartphones will not be able to access any CSS hover states.

- **Form menu (jump menu):** Form-style menus, known also as *jump menus*, let visitors select a destination page from a predetermined set of link options listed on a drop-down menu. Upon their selection of an option from a jump menu, the form can force the browser to automatically redirect the visitor to the selected page, or the visitor may be required to click an attending Go or Submit button before the page redirect occurs. You can style your jump menus with CSS, though keep in mind that not every browser displays the CSS styling in exactly the same way. Without CSS, the menus will use the browser's default form field styling.

✔ **JavaScript multitier:** Like the text-only navigation menu, a JavaScript multitier menu uses JavaScript to create and display the different levels of subnavigation. Though typically built using only HTML text hyperlinks, these menus can also use rollover menu buttons in both the main and submenu areas. More often than not, however, the main menu is created with rollover buttons, whereas the subnavigation uses HTML text hyperlinks. Note that this menu type is no longer a recommended solution, because CSS list style menus use far less coding and are considered far more standards-compliant.

✔ **Flash:** Flash menus can be created using Adobe Flash, which uses its own form of interactive scripting language called *ActionScript*. Flash menus may contain text, graphics, rollover effects, sound, and other types of animation and special effects, but bear in mind that they may not always be search engine friendly. After you build the menu in Flash, you can export and save it as an `.swf` file. You can then insert the `.swf` file into a web page as a multimedia file that automatically plays when the page first loads inside a browser window.

For examples of what you can do with a Flash menu, like the sample shown in Figure 6-3, visit `www.flashmenus.net`.

Figure 6-3: Flash menus can include text, graphics, rollovers, sound, and more.

✔ **Tree-style:** Similar in layout to the Explore feature on PCs running the Windows OS, tree-style menus list directories (main menus) and subdirectories (submenus) using tiny icons for folders and files along with little plus (+) or minus (–) symbols to indicate whether any of the items in the menu are expanded or collapsed. Because these menus appear more as application oriented than they do as navigation systems for a website, tree-style menus are used rather infrequently and typically only on technically oriented sites.

✔ **Web application:** Like JavaScript menus, these menus make use of a server-side programming language (such as PHP, Perl, ASP.NET, C#, VB.NET, Ruby, and so on) to create interactive menu systems that use a combination of HTML text, CSS styling, and optimized web graphics.

With so many options to choose from, it may seem like a difficult task to select the right navigation system (or blend of them) for a website. But truly, the answer should be quite clear based on several factors, including your skills as a designer plus the number of navigation and subnavigation links on the site map, the target audience profile, and the client's preferences. For instance, your client may come to you with a particular preference that simply must be catered to, such as "I want the navigation menu to sit across the top of the page, below the logo, and have the subnavigation display in a row directly below it."

After creating a few of the different types yourself, you're likely to develop a personal preference for one or two of the menu styles over the others, and you can then propose these menu styles to your clients before you even begin your mock-ups. Alternatively, you may be the kind of person who loves to figure things out as you go, and you are willing to discover new skills and do whatever it takes to make the best navigation system for the site. No matter how it functions or what it looks like, as long as the menu is easy to find, easy to read, easy to use, and always in the same spot on every page, the one you decide upon can be the right choice for your site.

In the remaining sections of this chapter, you find out how to create a few of the most popular types of navigation systems.

Creating Text Navigation Menus

The most accessible, user-friendly, search engine–friendly, easy-to-build navigation system is the text navigation menu. Text-only menus generally consist of a series of HTML hypertext links to the main pages of the site.

Text navigation menus can be presented on a web page in one of three ways, as illustrated in Figure 6-4:

✔ **Horizontal row or vertical column:** Similar to an HTML footer menu, the text navigation menu can include all the HTML hypertext links in a single row or column with each link separated by a character of some kind, such as a bullet (•), dash (-), or vertical line (|) when listed horizontally, or by a line break (`<br>`) when listed vertically.

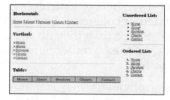

Figure 6-4: Text navigation menus can be displayed vertically or horizontally, inside table cells, or in an ordered or unordered list.

✔ **Table cells:** The second way to display a text menu is to isolate and separate each of the links by placing them inside individual table cells. This technique allows a little more styling pizzazz with CSS and tends to render more uniformly in browsers, even though it does make use of HTML table tags, which some purist CSS designers frown upon, especially because you can re-create the same look using HTML lists styled with CSS.

✔ **Ordered or unordered list:** This is probably the best of the three ways because you have the option of creating numbered lists, bulleted lists, or custom styled lists either with or without bullets or other graphics.

Whichever option you choose, by applying CSS styling to your hyperlinks you can give them more of a button appearance by changing the look of the normal, visited, hover, and active states.

Creating Rollover Buttons

A traditional rollover button is a graphic that changes its appearance when a visitor rolls the cursor over it. JavaScript controls the visibility of two same-sized button graphics in the browser: One graphic shows the button's normal state, and the other graphic shows the button's "over" state, as illustrated in Figure 6-5.

You might not want to use traditional rollover buttons for an entire menu because they rely on JavaScript for their functionality and are considered code heavy compared with their *pure CSS* (just HTML and CSS) counterparts. However, you might occasionally want to use them for special purposes, such as a signup button that requires the use of a particular font or other graphic image. Therefore, knowing how to make a rollover button with graphics and JavaScript is a skill you should have just in case you ever need to use it.

You can code rollover buttons by hand, but it's much faster to add them to your pages if you're using an HTML editor such as Dreamweaver that lets you quickly add them to your pages. In the following sections, you find out how to hand-code a rollover button, output rollover buttons in Fireworks, and create rollover buttons in Dreamweaver.

Book III
Chapter 6

Constructing
Navigation Systems

Figure 6-5: Rollover buttons need two graphics: one for the normal state (top) and another for the over state (bottom).

Understanding how to build rollovers

To build a rollover, you need two button graphics that are exactly the same width and height so that the JavaScript rollover effect displays both graphics smoothly. Otherwise, if one of the graphics is different in size than the other, the over state graphic will be stretched or squashed to match the same dimensions as the normal state graphic, giving the over state graphic a skewed effect. Not good.

The JavaScript for rollovers usually requires up to three different script parts (depending on how the script was written), and those parts must be placed in specific locations within the HTML code for the JavaScript to function properly in a browser:

- ✔ **Preload script:** This part of the script must be placed in the `<head>` area of the code. When the page is loaded into a browser window, this bit of script is what preloads the rollover state graphics into the visitor's browser's cache so that by the time the visitor mouses over a button, the over state button graphic is ready to appear. Without the preload script, a delay would likely occur in the rollover functionality.

- ✔ **Event handler script:** This part of the script gets added to the opening body tag and tells the browser when to process a preload script. With a preload script that uses the `onload` event handler, the "when" means right as the page initially loads in the browser. Common event handlers include `onmouseover`, `onclick`, and `onload`.

- ✔ **Rollover script:** This part of the JavaScript is added to your HTML between the opening and closing `<body>` tags in the location you'd like the rollover to appear. This script contains the instructions to the browser on how to handle the rollover functionality for the normal and over mouse states.

These aren't the only locations for JavaScript within a web page. For instance, when flanked by `<script>` tags and placed between the opening and closing `<body>` tags of the page, JavaScript code executes immediately as the page loads in a browser. To have the script load at other times, it must be moved elsewhere in the code and then called upon to execute when a visitor's mouse movement triggers a particular event.

Hand-coding a rollover button

Although most JavaScript button scripts perform the same task of swapping one image for another, the script itself can be written in several different ways. For the example rollover button, the JavaScript must be added to all three of the following locations:

✔ **Between the opening and closing `<head>` tags:** These function scripts must be placed between two `<script>` tags somewhere inside the head of the code. For rollovers, this script contains parameters for a preload function.

```
<head>
<script type="text/JavaScript">
<!--
function MM_swapImgRestore() { //v3.0
  var i,x,a=document.MM_sr; for(i=0;a&&i<a.
    length&&(x=a[i])&&x.oSrc;i++) x.src=x.oSrc;
}
function MM_preloadImages() { //v3.0
  var d=document; if(d.images){ if(!d.MM_p) d.MM_p=new
    Array();
    var i,j=d.MM_p.length,a=MM_preloadImages.arguments;
    for(i=0; i<a.length; i++)
    if (a[i].indexOf("#")!=0){ d.MM_p[j]=new Image;
    d.MM_p[j++].src=a[i];}}
}

function MM_findObj(n, d) { //v4.01
  var p,i,x;  if(!d) d=document; if((p=n.
    indexOf("?"))>0&&parent.frames.length) {
    d=parent.frames[n.substring(p+1)].document; n=n.
    substring(0,p);}
  if(!(x=d[n])&&d.all) x=d.all[n]; for (i=0;!x&&i<d.
    forms.length;i++) x=d.forms[i][n];
  for(i=0;!x&&d.layers&&i<d.layers.length;i++) x=MM_
    findObj(n,d.layers[i].document);
  if(!x && d.getElementById) x=d.getElementById(n);
  return x;
}

function MM_swapImage() { //v3.0
  var i,j=0,x,a=MM_swapImage.arguments; document.MM_
    sr=new Array; for(i=0;i<(a.length-2);i+=3)
  if ((x=MM_findObj(a[i]))!=null){document.MM_
    sr[j++]=x; if(!x.oSrc) x.oSrc=x.src; x.src=a[i+2];}
}
-->
</script>
</head>
```

✔ **Inside the opening `<body>` tag:** The event handler part of the script instructs the browser on how and when to execute any scripts coded in the `<head>` of the page, often using the `onload` attribute, as in

```
<body onload="preloadImages();">
```

or

```
<body onload="MM_preloadImages('images/button1-over.
  gif')">
```

✔ **In the code, between the `<body>` tags:** JavaScript placed in line with the rest of the HTML code is executed in the browser based on the parameters and instructions contained within the JavaScript in the `<head>` and opening `<body>` tag. For example, a JavaScript for a rollover button contains instructions for swapping two images based on two mouse events, `onmouseover` and `onmouseout`:

```
<a href="contact.html" onmouseout="MM_swapImgRestore()"
   onmouseover="MM_swapImage('Image1','','images/
   button-contact-over.gif',1)"><img src="images/
   button-contact.gif" alt="Contact Us" width="100"
   height="30" border="0" id="Contact"></a>
```

Feel free to use this script as often as you like. Or, to find an alternative script for your rollover button, you have two options: You can use the JavaScript supplied by your HTML/code editor or image optimization program (such as Dreamweaver or Fireworks), or you can search the Internet for free JavaScript that can handle the rollover effect. Two sites that provide quite a few free rollover buttons and other JavaScript scripts include `http://javascript.internet.com` and `www.javascript.com`.

Outputting rollovers in Fireworks

If you're interested in working with Fireworks, use the following steps to create a simple button with normal and rollover states and then output the optimized graphics along with an HTML file loaded with JavaScript:

1. **Open a new document in Fireworks by choosing File➪New.**

2. **When the New Document dialog box appears, set the canvas size to 100 pixels wide and 30 pixels high, leave the resolution at 72 pixels/inch, and set the canvas color to white. Then click OK.**

   A new untitled Fireworks `.png` document window appears in the workspace.

3. **Draw a rectangle on the artboard by using the Rectangle tool found in the Vector shapes area of the toolbar.**

   The button needs to have two parts for the normal and over button states. To draw the rectangle, drag a rectangular shape on top of the artboard and release your mouse button. The shape remains selected, allowing you to modify that shape's properties in the Properties panel.

4. **In the Properties panel, set the width and height of the rectangle to 100x30 and the X/Y coordinates to 0/0.**

   This positions your rectangle directly on top of the artboard space. The rectangle will be filled with the last color used. If desired, select a different color through the fill color box in the Properties panel or by clicking a swatch in the Swatches panel. For example, you may want to select a bright green with the hex value of `#99CC00`.

5. **To add text to the button, select the Text tool from the toolbar and specify the desired font attributes in the Properties panel before adding the text.**

   To type, simply click once to set the insertion point with your cursor and begin typing a word, such as **SALE**.

   For example, you could select Arial, Bold, 24 pixels, and white as the font. Although the text can be any color, the stroke color should be set to None.

   To reposition the word in the center of your rectangle, select the Pointer tool (the black arrow) from the toolbar and then click and drag the word into the desired location. If desired, feel free to add a bevel and emboss style to your rectangle shape through the Filters menu on the Properties Inspector.

6. **Create the second state or frame for the rollover state of the button graphic.**

   In the upper-right corner of the States panel (previously referred to as the Frames and History panel if using Fireworks CS3 or earlier), click the options menu and choose Duplicate State (or Duplicate Frame). If the Duplicate State dialog box appears, select After Current State and click OK to continue.

   This creates a duplicate of the current state (frame) with the same panel, with the same colored rectangle and text.

7. **With the second state (frame) still selected in the States (Frames and History) panel, select the second state rectangle and change its color in the Properties panel.**

   If desired, you may also change the color of the button text in State 2, as illustrated in Figure 6-6.

8. **Select the outer rectangle shape on State 1 (Frame 1 in earlier versions of Fireworks) and choose Edit⇨Insert⇨Rectangular Slice.**

   This step is necessary to apply the JavaScript behavior and create the rollover button effect.

9. **Open the Behaviors panel by choosing Window⇨Behaviors, click the plus sign in that panel, and choose Simple Rollover.**

   Upon selecting this option, the `onMouseOver` simple rollover action is added to the Behaviors panel. This is the JavaScript.

10. **To preview your rollover button in Fireworks, click the Preview button at the top of the document window and move your cursor over the button graphic.**

    When you move your cursor over the button graphic, the normal state button is replaced with the over state button, and when you move your cursor off the button, the normal state reappears.

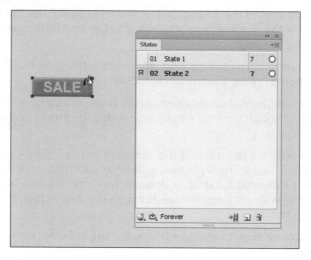

Figure 6-6: When creating buttons in Fireworks, you can modify the colors and other attributes for the rollover state.

11. **To add a filename or URL to the button graphic, enter the filename in the Link field in the Properties panel.**

    You may also add alternative text for the button in the Alt field and set a link target on the Target menu in the Properties panel. For example, if you wanted your button to take visitors to the Sale page, you'd enter **sale.html** in the Link field, **Now on Sale** in the Alt field, and **_self** in the Target field.

12. **Open the Optimize panel (Window⇨Optimize) and choose the GIF Adaptive 256 option from the Export File Format drop-down menu.**

    When you're ready to save your rollover button, you must select an appropriate output option.

    If your graphic contains gradients or photos, the PNG24, PNG32, or JPEG format might work better. Alternatively, like the GIF setting, the PNG 8 option also works well for button graphics with large, flat areas of color.

13. **To export your rollover button, choose File⇨Export.**

14. **When the Export dialog box opens, enter the desired filename (such as `rollover.html`) and set the Export option to HTML and Images, the HTML option to Export HTML File, and the Slices option to Export Slices. When ready, click the Save button.**

    Upon clicking the Save button, Fireworks exports button graphics for each of the two button states and an HTML file that includes the JavaScript for the rollover functionality.

15. **To test the button within the HTML file, drag and drop the HTML file into an open browser window.**

    Figure 6-7 shows an example of how your rollover button might look in a browser.

Figure 6-7: Test your graphic rollover buttons in a browser window.

16. **Save your Fireworks button graphic file for future use as a Fireworks PNG file by choosing File⇨Save.**

    The HTML file contains all the HTML and JavaScript code needed to make your two saved rollover button graphics function.

Creating rollover buttons in Dreamweaver

Dreamweaver users can create rollover buttons by two methods, both of which use different JavaScript code. The first method involves attaching the Swap Image and Go to URL *behaviors* to already inserted normal state graphics on the page. The second method, described in the following steps, allows you to choose both the normal and rollover graphics, specify the web page the rollover button will hyperlink to, and enter alternative text for the button link, all using the Insert Rollover Button option.

A *behavior,* in this context, is any interactive JavaScript that Dreamweaver can insert into the code of your page. Behaviors can pair an event with an action that is triggered by the event, such as changing the normal state button graphic to the over state button graphic (the action) when a visitor hovers the cursor above it (the event). Dreamweaver comes preinstalled with about 20-odd behaviors to help designers quickly configure the interactive features on their web pages.

To complete the following steps, you need two optimized button graphics of the same width and height: one for the normal state and the other for the mouseover state of the rollover button. Your button graphics can be any color and size and include any special effects and styles as desired. For example, you might create a graphic that is 80 x 20 pixels in size, includes the text SHOP in the center, has a smooth, beveled edge, and has a blue background for the normal state and a green background for the mouseover state. If you've already completed the Fireworks steps in the preceding section, feel free to reuse your two button graphics for the Dreamweaver steps here.

Follow these steps to make Dreamweaver insert a rollover button on your page and automatically write all the necessary JavaScript in your code:

1. **Launch Dreamweaver and choose File⇨New to open a new document in the Dreamweaver workspace.**

2. **Save the file with the filename `rollover.html` to the folder of your choice. Within that folder, create another folder called `images` and place a copy of your two optimized button graphics inside it.**

   For best results, define a managed site in Dreamweaver with the root-level directory set to the folder you just saved the `rollover.html` file in.

   For a tutorial on defining a Dreamweaver site, see `http://tv.adobe.com/watch/digital-design-cs5/gs01-defining-a-new-site`.

3. **In Design view, click once to place the insertion point inside the `rollover.html` file so the rollover button can be added to the page.**

   You must always specify the location on the page before adding the graphics so that Dreamweaver knows where to insert the JavaScript and images. That location can be anywhere inside the body, including nested inside a `<div>` layer or any other container.

4. **To add your rollover button to the page, choose Insert⇨Image Objects⇨Rollover Image.**

   This step opens the Insert Rollover Image dialog box, shown in Figure 6-8.

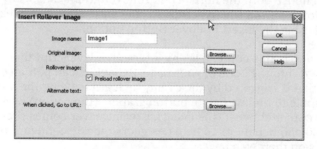

Figure 6-8: Use Dreamweaver's Insert Rollover Image dialog box to quickly add rollover buttons to your pages.

5. **In the dialog box, type a name for the rollover button, browse to and select the graphics to use for both the original and rollover image states, and add alternative text to mirror any text on the button graphic. Then add a filename, URL, or null link for the hyperlink.**

   The image name that you provide acts as an `id` attribute for the image that the JavaScript attaches to. The Preload Rollover Image option is enabled by default to add the preload script to the HTML. Leave that option enabled. If you don't give the image an image name, Dreamweaver will use a default name such as Image1.

6. **Click OK to close the dialog box.**

   Upon closing the dialog box, Dreamweaver inserts the rollover button normal state graphic and JavaScript onto the page at the insertion point.

   Take a peek at the code so that you can see that JavaScript has been placed between the `<head>` tags and in the opening `<body>` tag, as well as at the insertion point in the body of the page inside the `<a href>` tag that controls the hyperlink for the normal state button graphic.

7. **Save the page and preview it in a browser by selecting any of the browsers listed on Dreamweaver's File⇨Preview in Browser menu, or click the Live (or Live View) button to preview the button within the Dreamweaver workspace.**

   To test the rollover button functionality, move your cursor over the button graphic.

Creating CSS List Navigation Menus without Graphics

**Book III
Chapter 6**

**Constructing
Navigation Systems**

As I described briefly in Book III, Chapter 4, lists are currently the most standards-compliant way to build accessible navigation on your websites. What makes CSS list navigation menus so great is their ability to take on whatever style attributes you throw at them. For instance, you can choose the font, size, color, alignment, border, and background for each list item, as well as choosing a specific list type, using your own bullet graphics, or removing the bullet completely from each list item.

To keep your navigation menu in order, be sure to wrap your list code between `<div>` tags with an `id` or a `class` attribute. You can then set up styles for the `<div>`, `<ul>`, and `<li>` tags to position and style the list however you like. Here's an example of how you might write the HTML:

```
<div id="nav">
  <ul>
    <li><a href="#">Home</a></li>
    <li><a href="#">Work</a></li>
    <li><a href="#">About</a></li>
```

```
    <li><a href="#">News</a></li>
  </ul>
</div>
```

Then, for the CSS, you might create styles for the <div> layer, <ul>, and <li> tags and the link, visited, and hover states for the links:

```
#nav {
    position:absolute;
    width:300px;
    height:50px;
    z-index:1;
    right: 45px;
    top: 0px;
}
#nav ul {
    list-style-type: none;
    margin: 0px;
    padding-top: 12px;
    padding-right: 0px;
    padding-bottom: 0px;
    padding-left: 8px;
}
#nav ul li {
    display: inline;
    font-family: "Courier New", Courier, monospace;
    font-size: 1.4em;
    color: #006699;
    padding: 0px;
    margin: 0px;
    font-weight: bold;
}

#nav ul li a:link, #nav ul li a:visited {
    text-decoration: none;
    color: #FFFFFF;
    background-color: #006699;
    padding-top: 20px;
    padding-right: 6px;
    padding-bottom: 10px;
    padding-left: 6px;
}
#nav ul li a:hover {
    color: #FFF;
    background-color: #E51B24;
}
```

Figure 6-9 shows how this particular list looks in a browser window when the cursor hovers over one of the links. As you can see, each item in the menu has a simple button appearance and functionality.

Figure 6-9: CSS list navigation menus are easy to code and easy to style.

Creating CSS List Navigation Menus with Graphics

Another one of the cleanest ways to create a navigation menu is to combine HTML list formatting with CSS and a couple of graphics. This method allows you to use text and graphics while keeping the code uncluttered. It also produces the fastest-loading and most accessible type of navigation system when compared to any of the JavaScript navigation methods.

As with CSS list navigation menus without graphics, you'll want to nest an unordered list inside a <div> container tag with an id attribute and then create CSS styles for that id as well as for the <ul> and <li> tags and all the hyperlinks on the menu. You can then style each hyperlink with two graphics.

How you style the HTML is another story because you have several ways to do it. One method is to use two near identical graphics for the normal and over states, which are toggled on and off through the :hover pseudo-class. Another method is to create a set of graphics that can be used to create the expandable buttons with text inside them. Essentially, one of the graphics forms the left side of the menu buttons, and the other forms the buttons' right sides. What's unique about this option is that the normal and over states are stacked into two separate images. In other words, in the left-side button graphic, you stack the normal state left button edge directly on top of the over state left button edge. Then you do the same thing for the right button, as shown in Figure 6-10.

**Book III
Chapter 6**

Figure 6-10: This button has two sides, a thin sliver for the left and a larger block for the right.

In the following steps, you discover how to build a list navigation menu using CSS and the green and blue rounded tab graphics from Figure 6-10. To do this, you can either create and use your own similar graphics or go to this book's website to download a copy of the images shown here.

As you can see, these images are a lot larger than the menu list buttons they'll be styling. This is because the images are styled in the list as background images, aligned to the upper-left and upper-right corners for both the regular link and hover link states, and they are deliberately big enough to accommodate both short and long buttons.

If you're creating your own graphics with different dimensions than the ones shown here, you need to adjust the code — specifically the offset in the hover — so that the mouseover effect functions properly. What is essentially happening here in this example is that you're creating CSS that toggles between the top half and the bottom half of the graphic so that the rollover button displays both normal and over states.

Follow these steps to build a CSS-styled list navigation menu:

1. **In your favorite HTML editor, open a new blank HTML page and save it with the name `csslistmenu.html`.**

   To help keep things organized, set up a folder on your computer called `ListMenu` and save your `csslistmenu.html` file to that folder. Also inside that folder, create another folder called `images`, and inside that `images` folder, place a copy of the two button graphics.

2. **Within the body of the page, create an unordered list with the following six list items: About Us, Our Services, Our Clients, Press Releases, Employment Opportunities, and Contact Us.**

   You don't have to include a list type attribute on your `<ul>` tag to specify which bullet type to use for this particular unordered list because you'll be styling the list with graphics in the CSS.

3. **Wrap the entire list with a pair of `<div>` tags and give the opening `<div>` the ID of `id="tablistmenu"`.**

   Your code should look like this:

   ```
   <div id="tablistmenu">
    <ul>
     <li>About Us</li>
     <li>Our Services</li>
     <li>Our Clients</li>
     <li>Press Releases</li>
     <li>Employment Opportunities</li>
     <li>Contact Us</li>
    </ul>
   </div>
   ```

4. **Convert each item in the list into a hyperlink, either by adding a filename with extension, such as `contact.html`, or using the null link number symbol (#). Be sure to also include a title attribute for each of the `<a>` tags to make the links accessible, as in the following example:**

   ```
   <li><a href="#" title="Contact Us">Contact Us</a></li>
   ```

   Null links are great to use as stand-ins for real links when building components of a page like navigation menus. Later, when the whole component or page is complete, you can replace the null links with the real links.

Figure 6-11 shows an example of what your unordered navigation list may look like at this point when launched in a browser window.

- About Us
- Our Services
- Our Clients
- Press Releases
- Employment Opportunities
- Contact Us

Figure 6-11: This type of CSS navigation system starts as a simple unstyled list.

5. **Add a pair of `<span>` tags around each link item, close to the content between the link `<a>` tags, as in the following sample code:**

```
<li><a href="#" title="Contact Us"><span>Contact Us</
    span></a></li>
```

Each button on the menu needs a background image with curved corners. However, because the width of each menu item is determined by the length of the text within each link item, you must use two graphics to build the button background: one graphic for the left side and another for the right side. The left side of the button is applied by creating a style for the `<li>` tags, and the right side of the button is applied by using these `<span>` tags. When combined, they give the illusion of a single background image. Pretty smart, right?

6. **To style the list, create an internal CSS and make a tag redefine style for the `<body>` with the font set to Verdana, bold, 11px, with a 1.5em line height:**

```
<style type="text/CSS">
<!--
body {
  font-family: Verdana, Geneva, sans-serif;
  font-size: 0.6em;
  line-height: 1.5em;
}
-->
</style>
```

Later, when the navigation is complete, you can move the CSS (on your own) to an external CSS file.

7. **To separate the body style from the menu styles you're about to create, add a Menu Styles comment to the internal CSS, right after the `<body>` redefine style definition:**

```
<style type="text/CSS">
<!--
body {
  font-size: 0.6em;
  line-height: 1.5em;
}
/* :::MENU STYLES::: */
-->
</style>
```

See the nearby sidebar for more about the benefits of adding comments to CSS files.

8. **Create a new style for the `<div>` tag with the ID of `tablistmenu` with the following style attributes:**

```
#tablistmenu {
  float: left;
  width: 100%;
  background: #cae4ef;
  border-bottom: 1px solid #0e5d7e;
  line-height: normal;
}
```

This style defines a space behind the navigation buttons that stretches across the full width of the browser window, has a blue background color, and includes a 1-pixel solid navy blue border along the bottom edge of the `<div>` container.

9. **To style the list, create a compound style for the `<ul>` inside the `#tablistmenu`.**

However, rather than simply list `<ul>` as the selector, use compound CSS syntax to write a contextual descendant selector that identifies the `<div>` with the ID of `tablistmenu` as the sole location for the `<ul>` styles, like this:

```
#tablistmenu ul {
  margin: 0px;
  padding: 10px 10px 0px 50px;
  list-style: none;
}
```

This `<ul>` style sets the margin for the entire list to 0px; adds padding on the top, right, and left sides of the list; and sets the list style (where a customized bullet graphic might go) to none.

10. **Create a style for the `<li>` tags so that each item will display in line (in a row) with no margin or padding:**

```
#tablistmenu li {
  margin: 0px;
  padding: 0px;
  display: inline;
}
```

If your code editor doesn't have a preview or design pane, launch your page in a browser to see the list displaying in line. At this stage, your list should look something like the example in Figure 6-12.

About Us Our Services Our Clients Press Releases Employment Opportunities Contact Us

Figure 6-12: Styling the <li> tags gives your CSS navigation system a horizontal layout.

11. **To add the left side of the background image to each linked item in the list, create a compound ID style that will be automatically applied to each link inside the list.**

    This style specifies the background image and a few other important CSS attributes:

    ```
    #tablistmenu a {
      float: left;
      background: url(images/cssmenuleft.gif) no-repeat
       left top;
      margin: 0px;
      padding: 0px 0px 0px 4px;
      text-decoration: none;
    }
    ```

    Note that the background image is set to no-repeat with an orientation relative to the upper-left corner of the list item link. This image handles creating the look for the left side of each button on the navigation menu. To style the other half of the buttons, you must create a second style that wraps around the link text using the <span> tag.

12. **To add the right side of the background image to each linked item in the list, create a new compound style that will be applied automatically to the <span> tags that surround each link in the list:**

    ```
    #tablistmenu a span {
      float: left;
      display: block;
      background: url("images/cssmenuright.gif") no-repeat
        right top;
      padding: 5px 10px 4px 6px;
      color: #036;
    }
    ```

    This background image is also set to no-repeat but has an orientation relative to the upper-right corner of the list item link. In addition, this style specifies the color of the text on each link — in this case, navy blue using the hex value of #003366, or simply #036.

13. **Create three styles in the CSS to control the position of the background graphics on the left and right side of the navigation menu buttons when a visitor hovers his or her mouse over the buttons.**

This part requires three new CSS styles, which work as follows:

- The first style sets the color that the link text will change to for the hover state of each link.

- The second style handles the position of the left background image when a visitor hovers his cursor over the buttons. In the case of this menu, the background position of the over state part of the graphic begins at exactly –42 pixels down from the upper-left edge of each graphic.

- The third style does the same thing for the background image on the right side of the button. The horizontal and vertical background positioning attributes must be adjusted for both the list link and link span hover states to function accurately:

```
#tablistmenu a:hover span {
  color: #0e5d7e;
}
#tablistmenu a:hover {
  background-position: 0% -42px;
}
#tablistmenu a:hover span {
  background-position: 100% -42px;
}
```

14. **Save the page and preview it in a browser by selecting any of the browsers listed on the File⇨Preview in Browser menu.**

With the page open in your browser, move your cursor over the list items to see how each of the button graphics changes. Your completed navigation menu should look like the example in Figure 6-13.

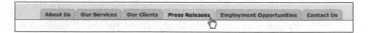

Figure 6-13: CSS List Navigation menus with graphics help add pizzazz to your HTML lists.

The beauty of this particular CSS list menu is its simplicity. Each button uses HTML list item text styled with CSS, and the same two graphics are used repeatedly for the background of each button. As with all web graphics, after the image is loaded into the visitor's browser cache, the reuse of that image no longer requires downloading and re-caching. This menu also saves tons of file space, which translates into faster page download times in the browser. Better still, when visitors using assistive devices — which often ignore CSS — come to the page, as well as any visitors who may have turned off their browsers' CSS functionality, the links in this particular menu will still be organized and accessible.

Adding comments to CSS files

To help you keep track of where certain styles begin and end in the CSS, add special comments between CSS comment tags whenever different style sets, like the menu list styles or link states, are introduced. In addition to being helpful to anyone else viewing your CSS, they also give your CSS a more organized, polished look.

Comment tags within a CSS use the `/*text*/` syntax (which is different from HTML comment tags, `<!-- like this -->`), where the `text` part can contain any text you like, spanning as many lines in the code as needed. When written correctly, these comments are not displayed on the web page.

To illustrate, you might add the following comment and comment tags to your CSS code to mark the beginning of the menu button styles:

```
/* :::MENU STYLES::: */
```

The semicolons (`:`) in this example help the eye identify the comment tag more readily. Certainly, however, you can add other special characters or use none, leaving only descriptive text between the comment tags, in normal uppercase and lowercase lettering (Menu Styles) or in all caps, as shown here.

When any section of styles is fairly long, you might also want to include ending comments and comment tags for the section, such as

```
/* :::END MENU STYLES::: */
```

In external CSS files, these CSS comment tags (and the contents inside of them) can stand alone between the style rules. However, when including CSS comment tags on an internal CSS, you must make sure that the special CSS comment tags fall between the regular HTML comment tags (`<!--` and `-->`) in the code:

```
<!-- /* .....MENU STYLES..... */ -->
```

If you forget to include the regular HTML tags, both the style declarations and the comments will appear in the body of the page! Therefore, for simplicity's sake, try to put all your CSS into an external CSS file.

Creating Multitier Spry Menus in Dreamweaver

When it comes to multitier JavaScript menus, many of them can look and function well even without the use of button graphics. In fact, you can create an entire menu with any number of fly-out submenus, all with the use of JavaScript and a little CSS styling. Like any JavaScript function, you can write the code in a variety of ways — or simply use scripts that are free or cost a fee. Some free scripts come preinstalled in code editors such as Dreamweaver, and others are shared openly online. Specialty scripts that are for sale often incorporate interesting effects such as fades, swipes, and other unusual dynamic transitions, many of which can now be performed with HTML5 and CSS3.

Up until a couple of years ago, adding JavaScript menus through Dreamweaver's Behaviors panel was one of the fastest and easiest ways to create a multitier navigation menu. Then, starting with Dreamweaver CS3, a new JavaScript menu system was introduced using the Spry framework (a robust combo of HTML, CSS, and JavaScript) to replace the old Dreamweaver Show Pop-Up menu. This new menu system, which uses the Spry Menu Bar widget, can be easily inserted, configured, and customized through the Property inspector and CSS Styles panels. Dreamweaver Spry menus support an unlimited number of submenus for each main menu item and are comprised of list item HTML tags (<ul>, <li>, and <a>) with CSS styling.

To use the Spry Menu Bar widget, just insert the widget onto your page and use the Property inspector to specify the name and order of each of the main links and subnavigation menus. When the structure is in place, you can further customize the presentation features of the menu by changing such things as the font face, font color, background color, border properties, and position through the CSS Styles panel. Best of all, Dreamweaver handles all the code writing for you! Figure 6-14 shows an example of a completed Spry Menu Bar as it appears in Design view in the Dreamweaver workspace.

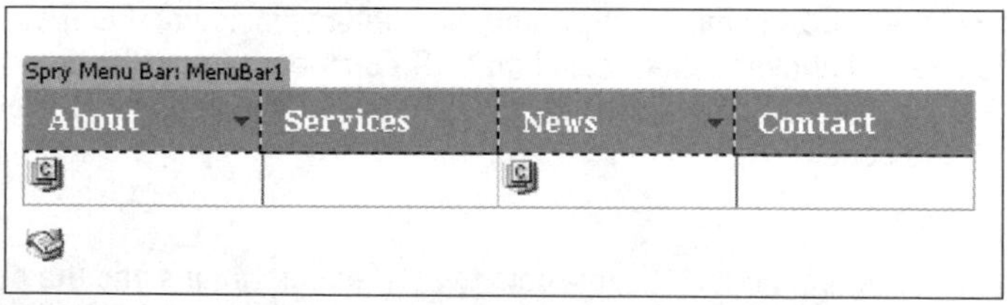

![Spry Menu Bar: MenuBar1 with menu items About, Services, News, and Contact]

Figure 6-14: Dreamweaver's Spry Menu Bar uses HTML, CSS, and JavaScript.

Spry Menu Bars are just one of several Spry widgets you can add to your pages in Dreamweaver. Each time you insert a Spry widget into your page, a corresponding CSS file (such as `SpryAssets/SpryTabbedPanels.css`) and JavaScript file (such as `SpryAssets/SpryTabbedPanels.js`) are added to the root level of your managed site inside a folder called `SpryAssets`. Sometimes, the widget may include graphics too, and those are also automatically added to the `SpryAssets` folder. You must upload this folder and its entire contents, along with any pages that contain a Spry widget, to the host server for the widget to function properly.

Follow these steps to insert a Dreamweaver Spry Menu Bar on your page:

1. **Choose File⇨New to open a new document in the Dreamweaver workspace. Name the file `sprymenu.html` and save it to the folder of your choice.**

   For best results, define a managed site to the folder in which you saved the `sprymenu.html` file. For a reminder about how to create a managed site, watch the free tutorial video at `http://tv.adobe.com/watch/ learn-dreamweaver cs5/simplified-site-setup-in- dreamweaver-cs5/`.

2. **Place your cursor inside the area on your page where you want to insert the Spry widget and click the Spry Menu Bar widget button in the Spry category of the Insert panel.**

   When inserting the Spry Menu Bar, you're prompted to select either a horizontal or vertical layout before Dreamweaver adds the code to the page. For this example, choose horizontal.

   By default, the widget is generically named something like `MenuBar1`.

3. **To change the name of the widget, modify the widget's `id` attribute in the Menu Bar name field on the far left side of the Property inspector.**

   After the name change has been made, Dreamweaver automatically updates all instances of the widget's ID within the corresponding JavaScript and CSS files in the `SpryAssets` folder.

4. **To customize the items on the menu, select the Item 1 menu link in the Property inspector and adjust that button's settings in the Property inspector Text, Link, and Title fields.**

   To help you understand how to customize the Spry menu, Dreamweaver automatically configures each inserted Spry Menu Bar with a default set of four menu buttons that include submenus for menu buttons 1 and 4.

   When modifying the Spry menu's items through the Property inspector, you must select the entire menu by its blue Spry Menu Bar tab in Design view to see the Menu Bar properties. If you accidentally try to select a button in Design view instead, which changes what's displaying in the Property inspector, simply reselect the Spry menu in Design view by its blue tab.

5. **Using the tools on the Property inspector, customize your menu by adding, removing, labeling, and reordering the menu and submenu items, and by applying links, link titles, and link targets.**

   Use the following fields on the Property inspector to assist you in customizing your menu:

Book III
Chapter 6

Constructing
Navigation Systems

- *Text:* Type a text label for each menu item, such as About or Contact Us.

- *Add Item:* Click the Add Menu Item (+) button above the first menu box to add another menu item. To add a submenu item, select the desired main menu item and then click the Add Menu Item (+) button above the second or subsequent menu boxes. This ensures that the main menu includes the correct corresponding submenu item(s). Repeat as needed to create further sub- and sub-subnavigation menu items.

- *Remove Item:* To delete an item from the main menu or from any of the submenus, select the menu item within the desired menu box and click the Minus (–) button.

- *Link:* Type the filename with extension or the entire URL of the target link destination, as in `about.html` or `http://www.adobe.com`. If desired, use the folder icon to browse for and select an existing file on your computer or from within your managed site.

- *Target:* To improve code accessibility, select a target for the link that will determine where the link opens relative to the linking browser window. To find out more about link targets, turn to Book III, Chapter 1.

- *Move Item Up/Down:* Adjust the order of any menu or submenu items by selecting the item that needs to be moved and clicking the up or down arrow until the item is positioned in the desired location.

6. **To modify the appearance of your menu buttons, you must modify the CSS through the linked `SpryMenuBarHorizontal.css` file listed in the CSS Styles panel.**

   Use the following guide to assist you with editing specific styles:

   - *Submenu Border style:* To change the border attribute for submenus, modify the CSS for the style called `ul.MenuBarHorizontalul`.

   - *Normal button style:* To change the text color and background color for the buttons on the menu, modify the CSS for the style called `ul.MenuBarHorizontal a`.

   - *Menu Over button style:* To edit the text color and background color for the over state of the menu buttons, modify the CSS for the style called `ul.MenuBarHorizontal a:hover,ul.MenuBarHorizontal a:focus`.

   - *Submenu Over button style:* To edit the text color and background color for the over state of the submenu items, modify the CSS for the style called `ul.MenuBarHorizontala.MenuBarItemHover,ul.MenuBarHorizontala.MenuBarItemSubmenuHover,ul.MenuBarHorizontala.MenuBarSubmenuVisible`.

To find out more about customizing your Spry menus through the CSS Styles panel, select the Spry menu by its tab in Design view and click the Customize This Widget link on the Property inspector or visit www.adobe.com/go/learn_dw_sprymenubar_custom.

7. **Save the HTML page with your Spry menu by choosing File➪Save.**

Dreamweaver alerts you with a dialog box reminder, like the one shown in Figure 6-15, about the SpryAssets folder being added to your managed site that must be uploaded to the server for your Spry menu to function properly in a browser.

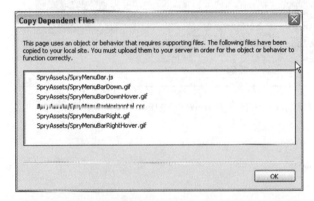

Figure 6-15: Be sure to upload the special SpryAssets folder to the server along with your Spry menu pages to ensure that your menu functions properly.

8. **To preview your Spry menu in a browser window, select one of the browsers listed on the File➪Preview in Browser menu.**

To experience the Spry menu dynamic functionality, move your cursor over any of the menu buttons. Figure 6-16 shows an example of what the menu might look like when you move your mouse over one of the Spry menu buttons.

To make changes to the contents or style of your Spry menu, reselect the menu by its blue tab in Design view, modify the menu items through the Properties inspector, and alter any of the styles in the CSS Styles panel.

Figure 6-16: Spry menus display dynamic rollovers and submenus.

Chapter 7: Building Web Forms

In This Chapter

- Determining which data to request from visitors
- Encrypting collected form data
- Building validating web forms
- Using Dreamweaver's Spry Form fields
- Testing and publishing web forms
- Using online web form services

If you've ever filled out an online survey, signed up for a website's newsletter, or purchased something on the Internet, you've probably used a form. Forms can be short or long, and they come in many shapes and sizes, but they all use similar HTML tags combined with JavaScript or some other programming language to validate and collect data. Forms allow sites to collect information from visitors for a variety of different reasons, including to sign up for services, request information, join a mailing list, purchase products, register for events, pay bills, handle online banking, and much more. Though not every website includes a form, as a designer you should understand what forms are and how they work so that you're poised to build one when the need arises. Furthermore, despite its somewhat complicated-sounding functionality, building a form in HTML is pretty easy because you only need to use a handful of tags to create the individual form fields. After you determine which information you'd like to collect from visitors, you can begin to organize the various parts of the form into a neat table format, complete with labels on one side and fields for user input on the other.

After building the form in HTML, the next thing you have to contend with is how to process that data. Unfortunately, by default, all forms are unsecure. This means that any data collected could be easily pilfered — unless you take certain security measures. Though you might think that security shouldn't matter much unless you're collecting personal information like someone's name and address or credit card number, it does. Everything you collect is personal and requires protecting, from an e-mail address, account number, and username to whether someone reads magazines about fly-fishing or is interested in receiving further information about debt consolidation.

In this chapter, you find out how to build a web form in HTML, add JavaScript validation to the form so that visitors will be assisted in completing the form accurately, and submit the data collected from a valid completed form to a remote location for secure processing. You'll also find out how to insert and use self-validating Spry Form fields in Dreamweaver, which provide more detailed prompts to visitors when completing forms. In addition, I briefly discuss form encryption and other security measures you can take to help keep that collected information safe. You also find out about online form services that can process form data securely for you.

Deciding What Visitor Information to Collect

To organize the layout of your web form, take your cues from the information you'll be collecting from visitors. You may request any kind of data you need, within reason, including the following:

- Personal information, such as a visitor's name, address, phone number, fax number, and e-mail address

- Purchasing information, such as items ordered, a credit card, a billing address, and a shipping address

- Private account information, such as a username, account number, password, and password hint question

- Miscellaneous information, such as visitor feedback and opinions, visitor interests about a particular topic, or even something silly like the visitor's food preferences or favorite contestant on *American Idol*

Form information can be gathered from visitors using a variety of form fields, including single-line and multiline text boxes, check boxes, radio buttons, drop-down menus, and buttons. Figure 7-1 shows an example of a typical form that includes several of the more common form fields.

Online transactions, as with transactions made in person, often require the collection and sending of secure and personal data from one party to another. By federal law, this data — whether collected online or not — provides consumers and individuals with certain legal and ethical rights. For instance, a gaming site may not legally collect information from minors without a parent's consent. Furthermore, every website has a moral and legal obligation to inform visitors of how collected data may be used. Many sites include a link to a privacy statement or similar policy that outlines what specific data the site owner is collecting and how that owner may use that data or disclose it to other parties, affiliates, and subsidiaries. To find out more about federal privacy laws in the United States, visit www.ftc.gov/privacy and www.justice.gov/privacy-file.htm.

'Name:	
'Telephone:		Ext:	
'Email:	
Username:	
Password:	
Reenter password:	
Password Hint:	Select a question ▼
I am interested in: (check all that apply)	☐ Web Design ☐ Illustration ☐ Print Design ☐ Other
Join Mailing List:	◉ Yes ○ No
* Required fields	Submit

Figure 7-1: Use forms to collect personal, purchasing, and account data from visitors.

Try not to be too intrusive in your request for visitor information. Collect only the information that you (or your client) really need and nothing more. For instance, if the site plans to send regularly scheduled e-newsletters to registered visitors, is it really necessary to collect the visitor's complete name, mailing address, phone number, fax number, and cellphone number along with the e-mail address? Maybe, but maybe not. Collect only the information that has relevant usage for the site, because requesting too much information might deter people from completing the form at all. Some websites get around the issue of wanting and needing information by including all the desired fields in the form but making only certain form fields required, rather than all the fields, for the form to be successfully submitted.

To simplify the process of collecting information from visitors, make your web forms as user-friendly as possible. Forms should be easy to navigate with a mouse or with the Tab key, be easy to read, and not be too long. For example, you can set form fields to move automatically to the next box, as with the area code and phone number. If you do have a lot of information to collect, consider breaking the form up into two or more pages. Forms should also be clear in their request of specific information, including providing hints about how the collected data should be formatted in the form input fields, such as omitting dashes and spaces from a phone number (2125551212) or making sure to include them (212-555-1212). Providing hints that instruct visitors how to fill in form fields, as well as indicators (such as an asterisk, *) that identify which fields are required and must be completed before the form can be successfully submitted, are great additions to enhance form usability and improve conversion rates. In other words, the easier the form is to complete, the more likely it is that visitors will complete and submit the form.

The easiest way to build a form is to set up all the form labels first, such as Name, Address, and Telephone Number. Many designers use tables and other HTML formatting code, such as paragraphs and line breaks, to organize their form labels and form input fields. Most forms can fit nicely inside a multi-row, two-column table. Along the left column of the table, you'd add the form labels to individual table cells. Along the right column, you'd add the form fields to collect the data inside the cells next to each label. When those steps are complete, you can add any field input hints (such as instructions to enter a six- to eight-digit passcode) and required field indicators (* required).

After you build the form, you can then apply CSS styling to make the form match the look of the rest of the site. For unusual layouts, feel free to use nested tables to organize the fields and labels. As long as all the form fields reside inside a single set of <form> tags, whether or not those fields sit inside tables or in nested table cells will not affect form functionality.

Your main goal is to keep the information neat and organized so that the visitor knows intuitively how to navigate through the form and submit it.

Encrypting and Processing Collected Form Data

All web pages, on their own, are unsecure documents. Therefore, when transmitting files and collected data over the Internet, you must take special precautions to protect the information you're collecting, especially when that information is private and confidential, such as a credit card number, account number, username, password, Facebook or Twitter login credentials, or other personal information that a visitor might feel uneasy about sharing online. This online security is the full responsibility of the website owner, or of the service provider performing the form data collection, such as online form processing services. When visitors come to your site, they need to be assured in some way that a dishonest outsider can't hack the information they're transmitting to your site online, which could result in some form of identity theft.

In the following sections, you find out more about what data encryption is and how you can secure your site.

Deciding whether to purchase an SSL digital security certificate

The ultimate type of website security is the SSL (Secure Sockets Layer) digital security certificate. SSL helps provide secure connections between the visitors and the host server computer by encrypting all the collected and transmitted data. When an SSL certificate is detected, the browser or device alerts visitors of the site's security in the following ways:

✔ Most browsers display the URL with an `https://` instead of the normal `http://`.

✔ Some kind of icon appears to inform the visitor of that site's security. Most browsers today indicate to the visitor that a site uses SSL by displaying a small lock icon in the very left of the address bar. Older browsers may instead display a lock icon at the upper-right edge of the browser window or at the bottom of the browser window, or they might display the entire address bar in another color.

All these visual indicators provide the visitor with a sense of security about submitting personal information to a site. Figure 7-2 shows a few of the SSL secure lock icons you might see in your browser when visiting a secure website.

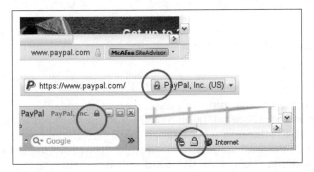

Figure 7-2: Secure sites that have SSL certificates display a lock icon somewhere within the browser to alert visitors of the site's security.

Don't forget to factor in the cost. You can purchase SSL certificates from several agencies, but before you do, be sure to check with your site host provider first to see whether its servers support the SSL company you'd like to use. The most popular (and most expensive) SSL providers are VeriSign (www.verisign.com), Thawte (www.thawte.com), and GeoTrust (www.geotrust.com), but a few others exist, too. SSL certificates range in price from affordable to the more expensive. Expect to pay an annual rate between $149 and $2,998 for the certificate. The low end would be for smaller sites with fewer than 100 products, and the high end would encompass large sites with thousands of products, better organization validation, stronger encryption methods, and significantly higher warranty rates. Your host provider can often handle the procurement and installation of the certificate for you, either with or without an added installation fee.

In many cases, purchasing an SSL certificate simply won't be cost effective. If your site falls in that category, you have four possible options for making the form data you collect from visitors as secure as possible:

✔ **Shared SSL:** Check with your host provider to see whether it offers some kind of less expensive, shared SSL certificate, where you buy into a group license that is installed on the server hosting your domain.

✔ **Data encryption:** Look into using alternative encryption solutions for the collected data, such as using a combination of JavaScript, jQuery, or PHP and browser cookies or creating a secure login script (all of which fall beyond the scope of this book). At a minimum, you should use simple data encryption at the host end.

✔ **Third-party form processing:** Find a reputable form-processing site and pay it to host your forms and process the data securely for you. To find out more about this option, read the "Using Online Web Form Services" section at the end of this chapter.

✔ **Third-party payment processing services:** When collecting payment on your forms, consider using a third-party, online credit card processing service, such as PayPal or Authorize.net. For a minimal transaction fee, such services can take on the risks of liability and information security that comes with credit card processing.

Understanding how data encryption works

If you don't quite understand what data encryption means, here's a simple analogy: When you submit data on a web form, the data passes from your browser to the destination server, much like a letter might pass through several post offices and mail carriers en route from your mailbox to the recipient's mailbox. Also much like a letter, it is possible that while the data is traveling, someone could open it up and look at it. On the web, if your data (or letter) is unencrypted, anyone who intercepts it can see exactly what your data is. When your data (or letter) is encrypted, however, if someone opens it, the text is like a secret code that only the recipient can understand.

Data encryption, then, is a process whereby information submitted to a server from a completed web form is scrambled during the data transfer by an application or some kind of server-side script written in PHP, CGI, ASP, JSP, ColdFusion, or Perl.

In addition to transmitting the data securely to the site owner, most scripts also include instructions for returning information to the visitor after completing the form. For example, some forms forward the visitor to a Thank You page (see the nearby sidebar, "Form-forwarding thank-you scripts"), whereas others stay on the page but replace the form with a Thank You message. Most forms also send notification of the completed submission to a specified e-mail recipient, such as the webmaster and the visitor who completed the form.

When using the Thank You page method, you can include as much or as little information on the page as desired. For example, the Thank You page might include a thank-you message, links to popular product categories, and a link back to the site's home page. Alternatively, the Thank You page may just contain the company logo, navigation, and simple thank-you message, like the example shown in Figure 7-3.

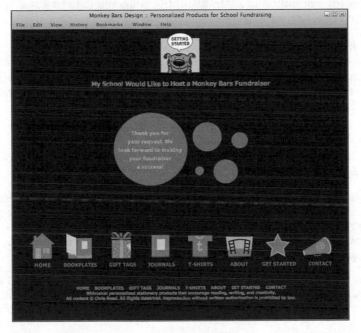

Figure 7-3: Create a Thank You page that visitors can see after submitting a form.

Check with your host provider to see what it offers in the way of form-encryption services, as many different technologies are available. Most host providers have some kind of uncomplicated form-processing services to handle simple form data transmission and encryption with a Perl, ASP, PHP, or CGI script. CGI (which stands for Common Gateway Interface), for instance, is a web interface that lets web pages communicate securely with server-side web applications for both data collection and data feedback. Perl (Practical Extraction and Reporting Language) is a programming language used for building CGI programs that perform server-side information processing such as encrypting data submitted to a server from a form. Perl scripts can also be configured to output data securely to another source, such as an e-mail address or database.

Typically, the form processing script comes preinstalled with the hosting plan, or the host provider can install it for the domain upon request. Two of the most popular scripts are the `formmail.pl` script created by Matt Wright at www.scriptarchive.com/formmail.html and the PHP

Huggins Email Form Script at www.jamesshuggins.com/h/hefs/ huggins-email-form-script.htm. To make these form-processing scripts function properly, some files must be installed on the server hosting the site. In addition, you must also do a tiny bit of code customization so that the script forwards the visitor to a particular page (thankyou.html) in the browser and securely transmit the collected data to a specified e-mail form collection address (sales@yoursite.com).

Scripts like these are extremely straightforward to use if you're willing to put in a little time. You need to read any accompanying README file that comes with the script, as well as to perform the necessary testing before publishing the form to site visitors to ensure that the form is processing collected data as desired.

Form-forwarding thank-you scripts

When visitors submit a form online, most of them like to see some kind of acknowledgment of their submission, such as a sentence that appears automatically on the page that says something like "We received your submission." Another popular indication of the form submission is having the browser automatically transfer visitors to a special "Thank You page" that tells them more about how their submission will be processed.

In most cases, creating and configuring a special forwarding Thank You page is as simple as creating a web page, adding a hidden field or two to the form, and inserting the URL of the forwarding page in a specific location inside the script that encrypts and processes the collected form data.

A good Thank You page looks structurally and graphically like the rest of the pages on the site, including navigation buttons and branding. It also contains text that acknowledges the visitor's submission. How that particular text will be worded is completely up to the site owner. The rest of the space on the Thank You page can include other information that might be helpful to the visitor, such as shipping policy information for a retail purchase, store hours, sale information, additional products the consumer might be interested in purchasing, or other special news that the visitor might not otherwise be aware of.

Because every script or program is different, your particular site and hosting account may require a different configuration. That said, most host forwarding options are fairly similar, and the following instructions can tell you generally what to do and where to do it on your host account:

1. **Create the Thank You page based on the existing look and feel of the site. Save the thank-you file with a name like thankyou.html so that it will be easy to remember.**

2. **Add a redirecting hidden form field at the top of the form in the HTML code, directly following the opening <form> tag.**

The particular script you're using might instruct you to add recipient and subject hidden fields to the form, too:

```
<form action="cgi-bin/email.pl" method="post" name="MyForm" id="MyForm">
<input type="hidden" name="redirect" value="http://www.mysite.com/thankyou.html">
<input type="hidden" name="recipient" value="info@mysite.com">
<input type="hidden" name="subject" value="Company Info Request">
```

3. **Specify the SMTP server, domain name, recipient e-mail address, and forwarding URL inside the data processing script file.**

   Good scripts include comment tags that clearly indicate what needs to be customized in the script and exactly where to make those changes.

   The SMTP server is your domain or the domain of the host provider, such as `$smtp_server="smtp.hostdomainname.com";`.

   The recipient address should be the address at the website that will receive notification of a form submission, such as `@recipient_addresses=('info@mydomain.com');`.

   The recipient domain name is the address of the website that will be submitting the form data, such as `@recipient_domains=('mydomain.com');`.

4. **Upload the customized script to the domain host's `cgi-bin` folder (which the host provider should have already installed on the domain) and upload the form and Thank You pages to the root level of the live server for testing.**

   You must test the form and script in a live server environment to ensure that everything is functioning properly. To assist with the testing process, you can modify the form filename, SMTP server (Simple Mail Transfer Protocol is the protocol used on the Internet to send e-mail messages), and recipient e-mail address and then change that information to the correct names when the form is ready for publishing. For example, you could use your own e-mail address while configuring and testing the form and then change the e-mail address to the client's address right before the form page gets published.

   Correct any errors that you find as quickly as possible once the form page is live. Many times you won't know about an error or processing issue until the form is published. When the form is error free, you may begin collecting data from visitors.

Understanding the Structure of Web Forms

Building forms on your web pages requires only a small number of HTML tags. Because each is tag is fully customizable, however, you can use them to create an infinite number of form layouts. The main HTML form tags are `<form>`, `<input>`, `<select>`, `<textarea>`, `<label>`, `<fieldset>`, and `<legend>`. With the addition of specific tag attributes, such as `type`, `id`, and `value`, you can customize each of these tags to create all the different types of form fields, such as hidden fields, text fields, text areas, check boxes, radio buttons, lists, menus, and buttons.

Structurally, you can add the HTML form fields to the page in any configuration you need, as long as the entire form is encased in `<form>` tags. The opening `<form>` tag is where you provide processing instructions and other information to the server. Without these tags, the browser and server cannot collect, encrypt, and process data from site visitors.

If you forget to add the tag, the form won't work. Establish a great habit right now by always remembering to build your forms starting with the insertion of a pair of `<form>` tags, along with the `name`, `id`, `method`, and `action` attributes:

```
<form id="form1" name="form1" method="post" action=""></form>
```

In between these `<form>` tags you may insert a table with any number of rows and columns to house the labels and form fields for the information being collected. For instance, you may need to collect visitors' first names, last names, and e-mail addresses. This would only require a two-column table with four rows: three rows for the labels and form input fields and the fourth row to insert a Submit button to process the collected data, as illustrated in Figure 7-4.

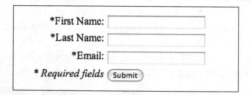

Figure 7-4: A simple web form.

Although the `<input>`, `<select>`, and `<textarea>` tags insert form elements on the page for straightforward data collection, the last three form elements in the preceding list, `<label>`, `<fieldset>`, and `<legend>`, along with the tag attributes `accesskey` (which assigns keyboard shortcuts to particular form fields) and `tabindex` (which advances a visitor through form fields using the Tab key), are accessibility-enhancement features. Use these in conjunction with other form tags to facilitate assistive devices like screen readers with accessing the information on the form, as in the following code examples:

```
<input type="checkbox" value="checkbox" name="checkbox" id="checkbox"
    accesskey="e" tabindex="5">
<label for="checkbox">Chocolate</label>
```

```
<fieldset><legend>The legend assigns a caption to a fieldset, which is used to
        group related items in a form.</legend></fieldset>
```

You use the `<label>` element to help screen readers find control fields like radio buttons and check boxes, the `<fieldset>` element to group sets of related controls, and the `<legend>` element to include a caption with any `<fieldset>`.

Creating a Web Form

It's easy to build a web form on your own. The following steps show you how to create a simple web form in Dreamweaver that is configured to process collected data using a dummy Perl script installed on a mock server. If you're not using Dreamweaver, you can still follow along to see the code elements and general structure of the form-processing component.

In the following sections, you first create the structure of a form and then add text fields, check boxes, menus, radio buttons, and a Submit button.

Creating the structure of the form

Follow these steps to create the general structure of the form in Dreamweaver. If you are using another code editor, you can easily adapt the steps by using your editor's form tools and commands to perform the same tasks.

**Book III
Chapter 7**

Building Web Forms

1. **In Dreamweaver, choose File⇨New to open a new blank HTML document in your workspace, and save it with the filename myform. html.**

   To help keep track of things while you're working, save the HTML file to a new folder on your desktop called Forms. Then manage a site to that Forms folder before proceeding to Step 2.

   To create a managed site, choose Site⇨New Site. When the Site Setup dialog box opens, enter a name for the site in the Site Name field, and in the Local Site Folder field, browse to and select the Forms folder you just created on your desktop. Exit the Site Setup dialog box when finished to resume work on your myform.html file. Note: In older versions of Dreamweaver, the Site Setup dialog box is called Site Definition, and the Local Info category is listed on the Advanced tab.

2. **With your insertion point positioned in Design view at the top of the open HTML page, choose Insert⇨Form⇨Form to insert a set of <form> tags on the page.**

   You can also click the Form button (which looks like a little square with a dotted red outline) in the Forms category of the Insert panel.

If the Input Tag Accessibility Attributes dialog box appears, input an ID, a label, an access key (to assign a keyboard shortcut to any element on the page), and a tab index number (to set the tab order of that tag relative to other form fields or objects on the page).

In Design view, the <form> tags create a bounding area with a red 1-pixel, dashed, rectangular border, like the one shown in Figure 7-5. Within this border, you can add *form objects,* such as text fields, check boxes, radio buttons, lists, menus, and buttons. The dashed line is meant to help you visually define the bounds of the form data within the Dreamweaver workspace, and it isn't visible in a browser window. If the line doesn't appear for you in Design view, you can enable this feature by choosing View⇨Visual Aids⇨Invisible Elements.

Figure 7-5: Dreamweaver marks the boundaries of a form with a dotted red line.

In Code view, the inserted <form> tags automatically contain several tag attributes, including the id and name, which should be identical to one another and will be used later to assign JavaScript and apply CSS styles to the form:

```
<form id="form1" name="form1" method="post" action=""></form>
```

The code also includes the method attribute, which tells the server whether this form will collect or transmit data, and the action attribute, which instructs the browser on where to send the collected information.

By default, all newly inserted forms use the post method of data transmission, but you may change that to default or get, if desired. For this example, leave the method set to post, but read the following descriptions of all three methods so that you'll know for future use what each one does:

- `post`: This method hides collected data during the HTTP request between the visitor's computer and the remote server but doesn't encrypt it. Therefore, whenever possible, try to use a secure server connection (using SSL) when transmitting private information, or at least use a script or program to encrypt the data from transmission to receipt.

- `get`: This method appends the URL of the form page with the actual value of the collected information when the data is sent. When the form is gathering simple data, this is usually okay, but this method has some serious drawbacks. The main disadvantage is that the `get` method makes the URL bookmarkable, making the page data vulnerable to spybots and hackers. Also, the URL can contain only a maximum of 8,192 characters, which limits the length of form data you can process with this method.

- `default`: This setting relies on the visitor's browser's default settings to choose the transmission method. Because the `default` form data transmission method can differ from one browser to another, however, it's much better to choose either `post` or `get` instead.

3. **Customize your form by adding form-processing details to your `<form>` tag, starting by replacing the default identical form `name` and `id` (form1) attributes with a unique form `name` and `id` of your choice.**

   For instance, you could use a custom name/id of `reqinfo`, short for Request Info, as in the following code example:

   ```
   <form id="reqinfo" name="reqinfo" method="post" action=""></form>
   ```

   Naming your forms does two things. First, it identifies the particular form on your page so that the processing script can be easily attached to it. Second, it helps you more readily identify a particular form when a site includes more than one form.

4. **In the Action field in Dreamweaver's Property inspector (or in the code, if you prefer to hand-code your HTML edits), type the filename and location (relative to the root level of the host server) of the script that will process the collected form data.**

   For instance, if you're using a CGI script stored in a `cgi-bin` folder on your remote host, type in the path to the script along with the filename, such as `cgi-bin/email.pl`. Your HTML code should now look something like this:

   ```
   <form id="reqinfo" name="reqinfo" method="post" action="cgi-bin/email.
      pl"></form>
   ```

   Both CGI and Perl scripts must be placed inside the host server's `cgi-bin` folder, which the host provider should have already installed on the server when the hosting package was purchased. If you don't see this folder, contact your host provider.

If you plan to use some other type of form-processing system (such as sending the collected data to an application on the same or on another server), check with your system administrator and/or host provider about how to properly configure the `action` attribute of the `<form>` tag.

5. **(Optional) In the Enctype (short for Encoding Type) drop-down menu in the Property inspector, choose the application/x-www-form-urlencode encoding type for the data being sent to the server.**

   By default, this field is blank. If you'd like to change it to the default type for the post method, select application/x-www-form-urlencode. Or when adding a file-upload field to a form, select the multipart/form-data type.

   If you're unsure of what to select here, leave the field blank and check with your host provider or system administrator.

6. **(Optional) Set the target browser location for any returned data or documents in the Target drop-down list:**

   - `_blank`: Displays the returned document or data in a new browser window

   - `_self`: Displays the returned data in the same window

   - `_top`: Uses the current open window even if other windows are open

   - `_parent`: Uses the parent window of the current file

   Your opening `<form>` tag should now look like the following code:

   ```
   <form action="cgi-bin/email.pl" method="post" enctype="application/x-www-
       form-urlencoded" name="reqinfo" target="_self" id="reqinfo">
   ```

   Figure 7-6 shows an example of this same data when listed in your Property inspector.

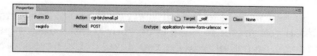

Figure 7-6: View the form field data in the Dreamweaver Property inspector.

7. **With your insertion point inside the dashed red line of the form in Design view (or in Code view, with your cursor between the opening and closing `<form>` tags), choose Insert⇨Form⇨Hidden Field to add a hidden field to the form.**

   See the nearby sidebar for more on hidden form fields.

8. **Using the Property inspector, change the name/ID of this field from "hiddenField" to "subject" and apply a value attribute with the label of "InfoRequest".**

   ```
   <form><input type="hidden" name="subject" id="subject" value="Info
       Request"></form>
   ```

9. **With the insertion point between the opening and closing <form> tags directly following the hidden tag you just inserted, choose Insert⇨ Table to insert a seven-row, two-column table with cellpadding=0, cellspacing=4, and border=0.**

   The table provides the structure to organize the form fields and labels.

10. **Along the left side of the table, enter the following text in each of the cells starting from the top:** *Name, *Telephone, *Email, I am a, I am interested in (check all that apply), Join Mailing List, and *Required fields.

Labeling the form before inputting the different form fields can assist you in selecting the right form fields for the data being requested.

Hidden form fields

Book III
Chapter 7

Building Web Forms

Hidden fields are special form fields that do not appear anywhere in the browser window but allow you to store and send information on the form along with the information the visitor inputs and submits. Hidden fields are often needed to assist scripts with processing the form data. The name/ID of the hidden form field can be used for things such as Redirect, Recipient, Subject, and Title to apply or include a sentence, e-mail address, URL, or other information to the form data being collected.

Here are some examples of how you can use hidden fields:

As a redirect to another page after form submission:

```
<input type="hidden" name="redirect" value="http://www.mysite.com/thankyou.html">
```

As an identifier of the e-mail address to receive notice of a form submission:

```
<input type="hidden" name="recipient" value="contact@mysite.com">
```

As an e-mail subject line prescript for the recipient hidden form field:

```
<input type="hidden" name="subject" value="Info Request">
```

As a title for the collected data to be sent along with the data:

```
<input type="hidden" name="title" value="Website Info Request">
```

The only downside to hidden fields is that anyone (including spambots) can view hidden fields by looking at the HTML source code in the browser, so be careful about using hidden fields for private information such as e-mail addresses and secret passwords.

Adding individual form fields

Next, you add individual form fields along the right column of the table in the cells next to each of the labels:

1. **Add a text field by placing your insertion point in the upper-right table cell and choosing Insert⇨Form⇨Text Field.**

   Text fields are used to collect text or numerical data, such as a name, address, telephone number, e-mail address, or password.

   If the Input Tag Accessibility Attributes dialog box appears for this or any of the following form fields, input an ID, a label, an access key (to assign a keyboard shortcut to any element on the page), and a tab index number (to set the tab order of that tag relative to other form fields or objects on the page). To skip adding any accessibility attributes, click the Cancel button to close the dialog box and insert the form field without them.

2. **Select the newly inserted text field and use the Property inspector to change the `name` attribute of the `TextField` from `"textfield"` to `"Name"`.**

   When you give each text field a unique name, or ID, you're identifying the input to be collected. Names can contain numbers and letters as well as the underscore character but can't include any spaces or special characters.

   When you modify the default text field name to something else, Dreamweaver automatically inserts both the `name` and `id` attributes into the tag with the new name provided. Both fields are inserted so that CSS and JavaScript can be easily applied to the field. Text fields can be set to be single line, multiline, or password fields:

   - *Single line* uses the `<input>` tag with the `type=text` attribute.

   - *Multiline* creates multiline text input fields and uses the same HTML code as a text area form field. Multiline fields use the `<textarea>` tag with the `cols` attribute for character width and the `rows` attribute for number of lines. Enter the number of lines desired in the Property inspector.

   - *Password,* which uses the `<input>` tag with the `type=password` attribute, makes asterisks or bullets appear when typing inside the form field in a browser. The data, however, is not encrypted; you must use some kind a data encryption with the form to secure the data.

   Figure 7-7 shows an example of single line, multiline, and password text fields.

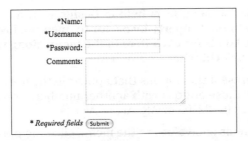

Figure 7-7: Text fields can be configured as single line, multiline, or password fields.

In addition, you can set the text field to display a word or phrase when the page loads in the browser by entering text into the Init Val box. This text can then be replaced with information from the visitor.

3. **In the next two table cells down, insert two additional text fields and use the Property inspector to rename them. Name the text field next to Telephone "Telephone" and the text field next to Email "Email".**

   To fix the width of the form field to a precise size, you could select the form field and add a number in pixels, such as 23, to the Char width field in the Property inspector. However, controlling the width of any input field with CSS is a better option because different browsers interpret this HTML attribute in different ways. To apply a custom class CSS style to a form field through the Property inspector, choose the desired style from the Class drop-down menu.

   If desired, enter a number in the Max Chars field to set the maximum number of characters allowable for the specified form field. This is especially useful for limiting phone numbers to ten digits, zip codes to five digits, or other data that requires a limited number of character input. If a visitor enters more characters than defined by this field, the browser tells the visitor's computer to make an alert sound.

4. **To add a menu, with your insertion point in the empty cell to the right of I am a, choose Insert⇨Form⇨List/Menu.**

   This inserts a blank List/Menu field, which can display on the form as either a list or a menu, depending on which type you select in the Property inspector. Use this form field to provide a list or menu to visitors that allows users to make a selection from a set of items, such as a state or country.

   For this example, leave the type set to Menu, and next you'll enter a series of options that the visitors can choose from and select.

5. **Select the new list/menu form field in Design view and click the List Values button in the Property inspector to open the List Values dialog box. Enter the labels for each item in the menu along with values for those items. Click OK when you're done.**

The labels represent the options that appear in the menus, whereas the values identify those options with another number, word, abbreviation, or code, such as 01, 02, 03 or AR, AL, or AK.

To add more items and values to the menu, click the plus (+) button. To delete an item, select it and click the minus (—) button. You may also reposition items relative to one another by selecting an item and clicking the up or down arrows.

As shown in Figure 7-8, the first item in the menu can be instructional. For instance, by entering the words **Select one**, you're informing visitors on how to use the menu field on the form. With instruction fields, you may enter a value or leave the value field blank (`value=""`). The rest of the list items in the menu correspond to options the visitor can select.

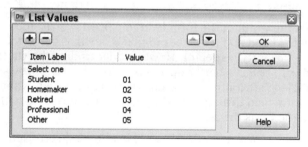

Figure 7-8: Use the List Values dialog box to input items that will appear in the List/Menu form field.

Next, you add check boxes to the form that allow visitors to select as many options as desired within a particular category. To help keep the information neat and organized, insert a nested table.

6. **To the right of the cell containing `I am interested in`, insert a table (choose Insert⇨Table) with two rows and two columns.**

You'll be entering a set of check boxes into each of the nested table cells.

7. **With your cursor inside the upper-left cell of the new, nested table, choose Insert⇨Form⇨Checkbox.**

This step opens the Input Tag Accessibility Attributes dialog box, as shown in Figure 7-9. Don't close this dialog box; you will enter specific data inside of it in the next step.

Check box fields allow users to specify multiple responses when presented with a single question, such as the responses to the statement I enjoy learning about:. You can add as many check boxes to the form as you want to support the question being asked.

8. **Enter the word** Interests **in the ID field and the words** Web Design **in the Label field, select Wrap with Label Tag for the style, choose After Form Item as the position, and if desired, enter an access key and tab index number. When you're finished, click OK.**

   This inserts a check box with a text label of Web Design directly following it, along with the id and name attributes set to "Interests":

   ```
   <label>
   <input type="checkbox" name="Interests" id="Interests"
       accesskey="w" tabindex="6">
   Web Design</label>
   ```

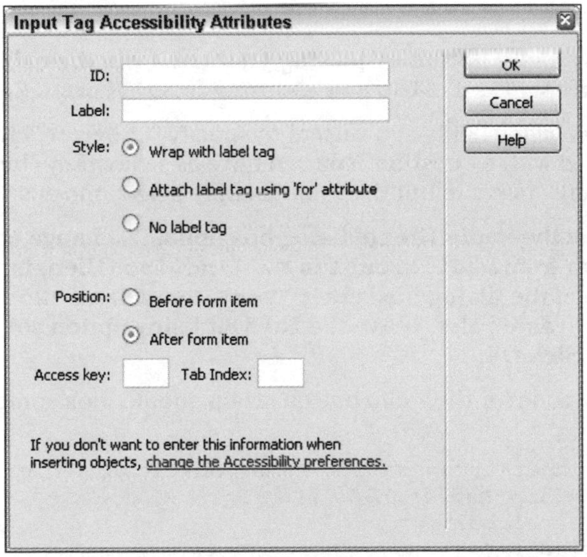

Figure 7-9: Insert check boxes with labels in your forms using Dreamweaver's Input Tag Accessibility Attributes dialog box.

9. **Select the check box and use the Property inspector to set the Checked value to "Web":**

   ```
   <label>
   <input type="checkbox" name="Interests" id="Interests"
       accesskey="w" tabindex="6" value="Web">
   Web Design</label>
   ```

The checked value helps to identify the collected data with the visitor's specific selection. In this case, the value of "Web" indicates the visitor is specifically interested in web design.

10. **Repeat Step 5 to insert check boxes inside each of the remaining three cells in the nested table. Leave the name set to "Interests" for all of them, but change the individual Checked Values to "Print", "Illustration", and "Other", respectively.**

Giving all the check boxes the same name of "Interests" instructs the browser that all the check boxes belong to the same group.

For visitors who select the Other option, insert a text field to the right of the word "Other" with the name/id attribute of "Interests".

If desired, set the initial state of one or more of the check boxes to be checked (selected). For instance, if you'd like to prompt visitors to join a mailing list, one of the check boxes can have that option preselected. Visitors can then select and deselect the check boxes before submitting the form.

11. **Add a radio button by placing your cursor in the cell to the right of Join Mailing List and choosing Insert⇨Form⇨Radio Group.**

Radio button fields allow users to specify "either/or" choices when presented with a question. You can have as many radio buttons as you want for any question, but the user can only select one answer.

12. **When the Radio Group dialog box appears, change the name of the group from RadioGroup1 to MailingList. Then, in the Label/Value area of the dialog box, enter "Yes","yes" and "No","no" as the label/value pairs. Leave the Lay Out Using option set to Line Breaks and click OK.**

Your code for the radio button group should look something like this:

```
<label>
<input type="radio" name="MailingList" value="yes"
    id="MailingList_0">
Yes</label>
<label>
<input type="radio" name="MailingList" value="no"
    id="MailingList_1">
No</label>
```

In a radio group, both buttons use the same name so that a visitor can make an either/or selection only as defined by the different value attributes, yes or no.

If desired, you may also set the initial state of the Yes button to checked using the Property inspector, which adds the following initial state code to the input field:

```
<input type="radio" name="MailingList" value="yes"
    id="MailingList_0" checked="checked">
```

Replacing form buttons with graphics

Forms need not look boring! You can spruce them up with CSS and even use your own graphics instead of the default form buttons by using the Image Field option. For instance, you might want to replace the regular old Submit button with a graphic button that says "SIGN ME UP!" When you replace the Submit button with an image, the image buttons become clickable by default, unless you apply a different JavaScript to the image.

To add an custom button graphic to your form, follow these steps:

1. **Place your cursor inside the form area on your page where you want to insert your custom button graphic.**

2. **Choose Insert⇨Form⇨Image Field.**

   You can also click the Image Field button in the Forms category of the Insert panel.

3. **When the Select Image Source dialog box appears, browse to and select the button image you want to add to the form.**

If you enabled accessibility features, the Input Tag Accessibility Attributes dialog box opens. Complete the dialog box and click OK to insert your image or click the Cancel button to insert your button without accessibility attributes.

Your code for a graphic form button should look similar to the following:

```
<input type="image" name="signup"
       id="signup" src="images/
       signup.gif" />
```

If you'd like to make your button perform another function besides submitting form data, apply the desired JavaScript behavior to it. For example, your button could run a script that launches a pop-up browser window with technical specifications about a particular product.

**Book III
Chapter 7**

Building Web Forms

In form fields that have a default selection enabled, that selection will remain in effect unless the visitor notices and changes it.

13. **In the last cell in the lower-right corner of the table, insert a Submit button by choosing Insert⇨Form⇨Button.**

    Submit buttons are the default button type for forms.

14. **If you want to change the label that displays on the button, modify the Value field from "Submit" to anything else, such as "Send".**

    Et voilà, your form is now complete! Figure 7-10 shows the finished example form in Dreamweaver's Design view.

When you're finished entering fields for your form, save the file and preview it in a browser to see how each of the form fields functions. If you like what you see, you can then style the form with CSS, add a validation script, test it, and publish it.

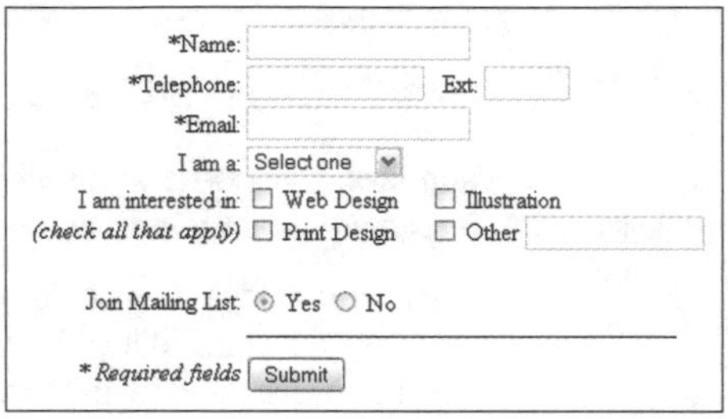

Figure 7-10: Preview your form in a browser to ensure that you like the way it looks, and be sure to upload the form to a server for testing before publishing it on the web.

Validating Web Forms

A web form by itself is a nice way to collect data, but it doesn't do everything it could to help the visitor in filling out the form fields and submitting the correct information accurately the first time. By contrast, a *self-validating* web form can alert visitors when they've missed information or have entered their data in the wrong format.

In the following sections, you find out what a validating form is and how to add validating behavior to your form.

Understanding what a validating form is

A *validating form* refers to a form that includes JavaScript that can verify whether the visitor has correctly completed all required fields on the form before the data gets transmitted over the web. That way, should a visitor try to submit incorrect or incomplete information, an error message appears either somewhere on the page or in a special pop-up alert message window above the open browser, identifying the problem or omission. These error messages help the visitor locate and fix the problem before resubmitting the form.

On *dynamic* websites (sites that use programming to dynamically display content from a database), validation is typically done with a programming language such as PHP, ASP, JSP, or ColdFusion. However, for small, non-dynamic sites, more often than not form validation is accomplished with JavaScript.

If you're using Dreamweaver, you can automate the task of adding a JavaScript validation script to any <form> tag by using the special Validate Form behavior in the Behaviors panel.

After inserting the script, you can customize it to validate the various form fields to help make sure that the user fills in all the fields correctly. The validation script is made up of a series of validation events that you can add to some of or all the fields on the web form. By selectively configuring each form field, you can choose whether an error/alert message appears to the visitor either as the visitor completes individual fields (so that he can correct mistakes as he goes from form field to form field) or after the visitor clicks the Submit button (so that he can correct all his mistakes at once).

Regardless of which option you select, the validation is performed on the client side, before the form is submitted to the server to ensure that the server won't collect any data until the form passes validation.

Of course, non-Dreamweaver users can hand-code validation scripts into any form, but that can be a lengthy process that requires some knowledge of JavaScript, especially if you intend to configure a validation rule for each field in the form. The easier and faster method of validation is the aforementioned Dreamweaver validation behavior, which thankfully doesn't presuppose any knowledge of JavaScript.

Adding a Validate Form behavior to a form in Dreamweaver

Follow these steps to apply the Validate Form behavior to an existing form on a web page:

1. **Open your web page that contains the form inside the Dreamweaver workspace.**

   Your form should include several fields, including a place for the visitor's name, phone, and e-mail address. If desired, feel free to use the `myform.html` page you created earlier in the chapter.

2. **To validate the entire form, select the opening `<form>` tag. Otherwise, to validate individual form fields, select the first form field that needs validation.**

   To select the opening `<form>` tag, click the upper-left corner of the form's red, dashed line border in Design view. You can tell that the tag is selected if the Property inspector displays the form properties.

3. **In the Behaviors panel (choose Window➪Behaviors), click the Add Behavior plus (+) button and select the Validate Form option from the resulting drop-down menu.**

   The Validate Form option is located near the bottom of the menu. Upon selecting this behavior, a Validate Form dialog box like the one shown in Figure 7-11 appears, listing all the named form fields in the form.

   Any form fields that you forgot to provide customized names to through the Property inspector will be listed with a default form field name, such as `input "textfield"`. If you see any fields that are unnamed, click the dialog box's Cancel button, update the form fields with custom names through the Properties inspector, and reselect the Validate Form option from the Behaviors panel.

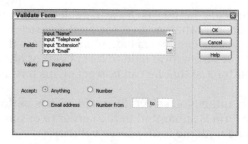

Figure 7-11: Dreamweaver's Validate Form behavior lets you apply an easy-to-use JavaScript validation script to your form.

4. **According to how you'd like to validate form fields, select one of the following options:**

When validating a single form field:

From the Fields list, select the form field by its label, such as `input "Name"`, and configure the rest of the dialog box as desired. For example, make that field required or specify that only a numeric value or e-mail address may be entered in the field.

When validating the entire form:

One by one, select each form field from the Fields listing and specify the Value and Accept fields:

- *Fields:* All the fields on the form are listed here. Select each form field by name and assign validation preferences using the rest of the dialog box options.

- *Value:* Select the Required check box when the field selected in the Fields list must be completed by the visitor.

- *Accept Anything:* When this option is selected, the field in the Fields list will accept any type of input.

- *Accept Number:* With this option selected, the field in the Fields list will accept only a numeric value.

- *Accept Email Address:* Choose this option to have the validation script check for proper e-mail address syntax. This part of the script cannot verify that the entered address is valid, but it can check that it meets the `name@sitename.extension` e-mail format.

- *Accept Number From/To:* Select this option to allow visitors to input a range of numbers predetermined by you, such as any number between 1 and 5.

5. **Repeat Step 4 for each form field in the Fields listing. When you finish, click OK.**

Whether you chose to validate individual form fields or all the fields in the entire form, Dreamweaver automatically adds the appropriate JavaScript validation code to the <head> of the page, along with additional script, either in-line with the form field or within the opening <form> tag at the top of the form.

When validating single fields, Dreamweaver uses the onblur or onchange validation event in-line with the code so that visitors can see any error message as they input data.

```
<input namo="Name" type="text" ld="Name" onblur="MM_validateForm('Name',
    '', 'R');return document.MM_returnValue">
```

By contrast, when validating the entire form, the onsubmit validation event handler is used, and any error messages appear to the visitor after he or she clicks the Submit button.

```
<form action="cgi-bin/email.pl" method="post" name="myform" id="myform"
    onsubmit="MM_validateForm('Name', '', 'R', 'Telephone', '','NisNum
    ', 'Extension', '', 'NisNum', 'Email', '', 'RisEmail');return
    document.MM_returnValue">
```

To test the validation behavior, launch the page in a browser and try entering incorrect data in each of the form fields before submitting the form. Because the validation script processes data on the client side (not the server side), the form doesn't need to be uploaded to a server to be tested. It does, however, need to be on a working server to test the form-processing script.

Building Spry Web Forms in Dreamweaver

Spry validation is the newer, cooler way to validate your forms in Dreamweaver because it uses the more advanced tools in the Spry framework. Using HTML, CSS, and JavaScript, the Spry framework helps designers build XML-rich web pages that provide more interactive experiences for site visitors. If you want interactive experiences for your visitors, use Spry form fields in your forms instead of regular form fields.

Taking a look at the Spry validation widgets

All of Dreamweaver's Spry validation form fields, or *widgets,* mirror the regular form fields. There are Spry form widgets for the Text Field, Text Area, Checkbox, Select (Menu), Password, Confirm, and Radio Group form fields. To use any of these widgets, just insert the desired Spry fields into your form instead of inserting the regular HTML form field tags. The Spry validation widgets are accessible when you choose Insert➪Spry or by clicking one of the Spry Validation buttons in the Spry category of the Insert panel, as shown in Figure 7-12. The main difference between the Spry widgets is how they are styled with CSS and the kind of interactive opportunities they offer to site visitors. For example, with the Spry Validation Text field, visitors can be prompted to enter the correct telephone number format. That way, when the format entered doesn't match the formatting hint (800-555-1212) you provided or when no input is made to the field, visitors see an error message ("Invalid format" or "A value is required").

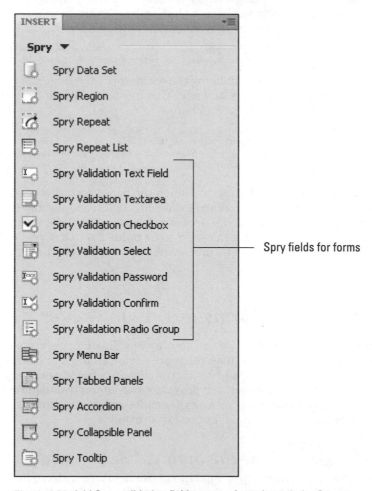

Spry fields for forms

Figure 7-12: Add Spry validation fields to your form through the Spry category of the Insert panel.

After you insert the Spry validation widgets in your form, you may customize how each field validates data, as well as modify how the field appears in the browser using CSS. In fact, when you insert even one Spry widget onto your page, Dreamweaver automatically adds a special `SpryAssets` folder to your managed site that includes an external CSS file (`SpryAssets/ SpryValidationTextField.css`) to help you further customize the look of your Spry validation widgets. In addition to this CSS file, Dreamweaver also adds a JavaScript file (`SpryAssets/SpryValidationTextField.js`) to the `SpryAssets` folder, which helps to manage the interactive dynamic features of the Spry validation widgets.

You must upload the entire `SpryAssets` folder to the server, along with the file(s) that contain the Spry forms, for the Spry validation widgets to function properly.

Adding Spry validation fields to a form

To add Dreamweaver's Spry validation fields to your form, follow these steps:

1. **With your cursor inside the area in your form where you would like to insert a Spry Validation field, click the desired Spry Validation field button in the Spry category of the Insert panel.**

   You may also insert Spry validation widgets by choosing Insert➪Spry and choosing the desired option from the submenu that appears.

   If, after selecting your Spry field, the Input Tag Accessibility Attributes dialog box opens, complete the fields and click OK to add the Spry field to your page.

   Spry Validation form fields look just like regular HTML form fields, only when selected in Design view, they are surrounded by a blue tab and outline that identify the form field as a Spry Validation form field, like the one shown in Figure 7-13.

2. **Select the new Spry Validation field in Design view by clicking the field, and then customize the field in the Property inspector.**

   Set any desired parameters for the Spry field, as you would for a regular form field.

Spry TextField: sprytextfield1	
*Spry Text Field:	A value is required.Invalid format.

Figure 7-13: In Dreamweaver, selected Spry Validation fields display with a blue outline and tab in Design view.

3. **Select the Validation field's blue tab in Design view to set the validation type and format in the Property inspector.**

When you click the Validation field's blue tab, a different set of information appears in the Property inspector. You need to select the right type and format to match the data you intend to collect from site visitors, such as a phone number, currency, date, or credit card.

For a full listing of all the Spry types and formats, go to:

```
http://help.adobe.com/en_US/dreamweaver/cs/using/
    WS2442184F-3DF4-4240-96AF-CC6D792E2A62a.html
```

4. **In the Validate On field listed in the Properties inspector, select an option to set when the validation event will occur.**

   Choose from Blur, Change, and/or Submit. You can choose as many as you like, or disable them all.

   • *Blur:* The field validates when the user clicks outside the field.

   • *Change:* The field validates while the user enters text inside the field.

   • *Submit:* The field validates when the user submits the form.

5. **(Optional) Continue using the Property inspector for the selected Spry widget to set other options as required by the Validation field.**

   For example, when you select the Spry Validation Text Field tab, other settings for this widget include setting the minimum and maximum number of characters, displaying a character counter and/or preview states, changing the required status of a field, creating a customized form field text hint, and blocking extra characters.

After setting the Spry widget's properties in the Property inspector, the field's style and error message (if any) can be further customized in the CSS. Finding the right field, however, can sometimes be tough, so be sure to consult the online help files to ensure that you're editing the correct CSS style.

For more tips about working with Spry and styling your Spry menu with CSS, visit `http://labs.adobe.com/technologies/spry/home.html?promoid=GYUQB`.

Testing Validated Web Forms

Whether you're using regular or Spry validation form fields in your form, the next step before making the form available to the public is to test it for accuracy in validation and processing. In most instances, the validation script won't affect how the form gets processed, but rather it helps to determine whether visitor input is properly entered and formatted before the collected data is submitted to the server for actual processing.

For your testing, you get the best results when you upload the file that contains the form to the root level of the intended host or test server. This is especially critical when the encryption of the collected form data is performed by a Perl or CGI script specified in a particular directory (cgi-bin\filename) on the host server. If you don't perform testing in the intended live environment, you might encounter issues later after the form gets published. To avoid that scenario, test in a live environment so that you can be 100 percent certain that your form passes validation and encryption.

To help keep the form away from potential visitors during the testing phase on the host server, change the filename on the page to something else until you're ready to officially publish it. For example, if the form page will ultimately be called contact.html when you publish it, consider changing the filename to testcontact.html during the testing phase. You can rename the file to contact.html when the page is ready for visitors to use.

To test the accuracy of your form's validation script and data processing capabilities, follow these steps:

1. **Upload the form (via FTP or another access method) to a testing server or to the live host server using a testing filename.**

   The testing server can either be the server hosting the site or another server that mimics the hosting environment of the hosting server. For simplicity's sake, if you're unsure which route to take, test the form directly on the hosting server to ensure that the form will work without error when the site is published. Although this does mean that you need to upload the form page to the host server for testing, no one should be able to access it during the testing unless they happen to know the direct URL to that test page.

   To find out more about File Transfer Protocol (FTP) and how to transfer files to a remote server, turn to Book V, Chapter 2.

2. **To ensure that the form can handle correct input, enter test data in each field on your form and click the Submit button.**

   When you're satisfied that all the validation fields function as intended, submit correctly formatted dummy data. Then, after the collected data has been transmitted over the web, verify that the data is being sent to the proper recipient e-mail address (which can be your own, for testing purposes) when using an e-mail recipient, or to a database at the website collecting the data. Also check to see that any return information to the visitor is functioning (such as a thank-you message within the page or a forwarding script that sends visitors to a Thank You page) and that all other parts of the script are working as planned. For example, your script may automatically send visitors a confirmation e-mail upon submitting the form. Check everything you can possibly check.

Should you encounter any issues processing the collected data after uploading the form to a test server, the trouble will most likely be with the script or programming code being used to process the data. Reread any configuration files that came with the script and continue testing until you get the form to work. If you still continue to have trouble with the form, contact the host provider or system administrator for assistance. Often the script doesn't function properly because a part of the script was not configured accurately or some kind of software still needs to be installed or enabled on the host end. If, after enlisting the help of your host provider or system administrator, you still can't fix the problem, you may need to hire a programmer to assist you.

3. **To see how your form handles bad input, enter incorrect data in each form field and click the Submit button.**

   Be sure to test for every scenario you can think of (letters in number fields, too many characters, not enough characters, wrong input, missing input, incorrectly formatted e-mail addresses, and so on) and make any changes to the form fields, validation widgets, and validation script as needed to correct potential coding errors before publishing the page.

   For example, with the Spry validation widgets, visitors can be prompted with screen hints to fill in form fields accurately, but if you've misspelled a word in the hint or the hint doesn't make sense, now is the time to fix it. Figure 7-14 illustrates how visitors might be prompted with screen hints in a Spry form when entering incorrect or incomplete data. (The top figure shows Hint activated; the second figure shows correctly entered data; the third figure shows incorrect data entered; the bottom figure shows missing data in required field.)

   To make adjustments to an existing regular form-validation script in Dreamweaver, select the form by its opening <form> tag and reopen the Validation Form behavior dialog box by double-clicking the yellow spoke icon for the Validate Form behavior in the Behaviors panel.

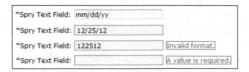

Figure 7-14: Visitors are prompted to enter data correctly on a Spry form.

Whatever you do, do not publish a nonworking form. It is far better to offer visitors the option of sending a simple e-mail to a site than to display a broken form. Take the time to work out the kinks; then publish the form.

Using Online Web Form Services

Creating your own web forms is just one of the ways to collect information from visitors on your site. Another popular method is to use an online web form service to host and securely process your form data for you.

Depending on the type of data you'd like to collect, you may lean toward one web form service over another. Here is a list of popular options by type:

- **E-mail marketing service:** If you want to create a mailing list and collect visitor contact information, consider a service such as Constant Contact (www.constantcontact.com), Mail Chimp (http://mailchimp.com), Vertical Response (www.verticalresponse.com), or Campaign Monitor (www.campaignmonitor.com).

- **Surveys:** To gather feedback from visitors in the form of a survey, consider using Webform (http://webform.com) or SurveyMonkey (www.surveymonkey.com). Not only can survey sites like these help you collect data, but they also can help you analyze it when the survey ends.

- **General forms:** For all other types of forms, such as contact forms, registration forms, and order forms, you might try a form service like Adobe FormsCentral (https://formscentral.acrobat.com), Wufoo (http://wufoo.com), or EmailMeForm (www.emailmeform.com). These services can help you build and format your forms, host them, analyze the data, and more.

These services can cost anywhere from free to monthly fees ranging from $10 to $250 (and higher) depending on the number of forms you process each month. Research the services that appeal to you and give them a whirl. Whichever service you pick, you'll likely be happy with the results.

Chapter 8: Making Your Pages Interactive

In This Chapter

✓ Adding interactivity with JavaScript

✓ Creating customized rollover effects

✓ Launching browser windows

✓ Creating jQuery accordion panels

✓ Adding a jQuery slide show

✓ Building a Lightbox image viewer

✓ Inserting multimedia such as Flash and MP3s

✓ Adding content that changes daily

✓ Using AddThis share buttons

*H*ands down, one of the most interesting aspects of using the Internet is the fact that visitors can interact in a variety of ways with websites. Popular activities include listening to music, watching videos and movies, staying in touch with friends on Facebook, checking Twitter feeds, pinning stuff on Pinterest, playing games, sharing links, reading the news, looking up the local weather, participating in forums, browsing on eBay, researching school topics, blogging, and more.

There are many different ways to make websites interactive, from the very simple to the very complex. For instance, with HTML, CSS, and a sprinkling of JavaScript or jQuery, you can create interactive navigation menus, rollover buttons, accordion panels, tab panels, animated sliders, and image galleries, just to name a few. For many of these functions, you can easily find free JavaScript and jQuery code online to add to your pages without even knowing anything about JavaScript. Similarly, if you have the right multimedia components and their attending browser extensions or plug-ins (many of which are free), you can add different media files to your pages, such as Flash animations, sound files, and interactive games. Another thing that's very popular right now is sharing content through social media links. Giving visitors the tools to share your pages helps improve the odds that they'll do it.

In this chapter, you're introduced to ways of using JavaScript to make your websites more interactive — such as creating multi-image rollover effects, making an image appear to shake, and opening new browser windows. You then advance to working with some simple jQuery scripts to create an accordion panel, a slide show, and a Lightbox image viewer. You also discover how easy it is to insert multimedia files on a page. Finally, I show you how to add a daily tip on your site on the topic of your choice and use social media share icons from AddThis to encourage visitors to share your content with their social networks.

Getting to Know JavaScript

JavaScript is one of the quickest and easiest ways to add pizzazz to your web pages by turning static, regular web pages into dynamic, interactive, interesting — and sometimes extraordinary — web pages.

Without even knowing how JavaScript works, you can use free scripts on your site to do things like making rollover buttons, launching new browser windows, turning the browser's status bar into a message ticker, displaying the current date and time on the site, creating simple interactive games, and turning static images into slide shows. You can use other scripts to generate browser cookies and build dynamic navigation bars, create special effects with images and sounds, add computer utilities and perform math functions, apply password protection to a page, validate forms and e-mails, and even play interesting background and cursor animations within the browser window. Figure 8-1 shows an example of a script from `www.javascript kit.com` that displays the current full date on your site, such as Monday, October 22, 2012. Table 8-1 lists some great JavaScript resources available online.

Figure 8-1: JavaScript, like this date script, can enhance a visitor's web experience.

Table 8-1	Free JavaScript Resources
JavaScript Resource	*Web Address*
W3Schools.com	www.w3schools.com/jS/default.asp
Dynamic Drive	www.dynamicdrive.com
Webdeveloper.com	www.webdeveloper.com/javascript/
The JavaScript Source	www.javascript.com
IRT.org	www.irt.org/articles/script.htm
JavaScript Kit	www.javascriptkit.com/cutpastejava.shtml
HTML Source	www.yourhtmlsource.com/javascript
QuirksMode	www.quirksmode.org/js/intro.html

Keep in mind, however, that not everyone can or chooses to experience the coolness of JavaScript. Roughly 1–2 percent of all Internet traffic comes from visitors who use assistive devices that don't understand JavaScript and from visitors who have purposefully disabled the JavaScript in their browsers and devices. These visitors simply can't experience JavaScript's neat effects or, as is sometimes the case, even access the information that the JavaScript reveals. For those visitors, you must always try to provide alternate access to the same content through different techniques, such as placing relevant content inside a pair of `<noscript>` tags or making plain-text content available on another page. See Book IV, Chapter 2 for more on accessibility improvements.

For the other 98 to 99 percent of visitors who do have JavaScript-enabled browsers and devices, take advantage of this fact and use JavaScript (and jQuery) to make your site more robust, appealing, interactive, and easy to use.

If you're using Dreamweaver, you automatically have access to about 20 or so of the more common JavaScript effects through the Behaviors panel. For instance, you'll find Swap Image and Validate Form behaviors, discussed in previous chapters, plus other cool scripts that open new browser windows, show pop-up messages, insert jump menus, and more.

In addition to Dreamweaver's scripts, you can find tons of free scripts online by doing a search for *"free JavaScript"* in your favorite search engine. Table 8-1 lists the most popular JavaScript resources, though the longer you search, the more you'll find, especially if you refine your search with keywords when looking for specific scripts, such as *"free JavaScript menus"* or *"free JavaScript clock."* In exchange for the free scripts, often the only thing you need to do is leave the script author's contact information and script comment tags inside the script on your page. For example, the following comments appear in one of the digital clock scripts at www. javascriptkit.com:

```
//LCD Clock script- by javascriptkit.com
//Visit JavaScript Kit (http://javascriptkit.com) for script
//Credit must stay intact for use
```

Like many Internet technologies, JavaScript can be used for good reasons, for really annoying reasons (creating unsolicited pop-up browser windows), and sometimes even for computer-damaging (installing adware on a visitor's computer) purposes. Some of the bad reasons have actually prompted some browser developers to create pop-up blockers for your computer, which unfortunately can prevent your honest JavaScript windows from being displayed too. To make sure that you're getting your scripts from reputable sources and not from sites with corrupt hidden agendas, start your script searches with the sites listed in Table 8-1.

Because JavaScript is a scripting language and not a programming language, it is relatively easy to learn after you understand its basic syntax and structure. W3Schools.com has a great, easy-to-follow tutorial at www. w3schools.com/js/. In addition, you can find many fantastic free online JavaScript tutorials with a quick search for *"JavaScript tutorial,"* some of which can be found at the sites listed in Table 8-1.

So that you can see for yourself just how easy it is to use JavaScript, the next part of this chapter introduces you to creating multiple rollover effects, opening new browser windows, and setting up complex image maps. After that, I introduce you to jQuery.

Creating Multipart Rollover Effects

In Book III, Chapter 6, you find out about creating simple rollover buttons through Dreamweaver's Insert menu. The rollover button uses JavaScript and two same-size graphics, one for the button's normal state and the other for the button's over state. When viewed in a browser, the normal graphic appears until a visitor moves the cursor over it. At that moment, the rollover state graphic appears in its place. Then, as soon as the visitor moves the cursor off the button, the original graphic returns to view. This kind of rollover button is super easy to set up, providing an effective way of adding a dynamic vibe to a site.

Although a rollover button is admittedly great, it's not the only way to use JavaScript and graphics to achieve dynamic effects with images on your page. You can actually make multiple parts of a web page change in response to a single visitor action, all with the magic of JavaScript! For instance, you might simultaneously change the color of the layout, play a GIF animation, and display a special message to visitors in the browser's status bar.

With a little bit more code than the simple rollover button — and a few more graphics for the additional rollover states of all the graphics that will be swapped — you can make a single mouseover movement control several image or page property changes at once. What's more, if any of those images are animated GIFs, the animation can be played for either or both the normal and rollover graphic states.

Of course, all this fancy stuff might be for naught, because touch-based devices don't support rollovers or hover states. In other words, if a webpage is designed using rollovers, site visitors on tablets and smartphones might not be able to access content on that page.

To create a multipart rollover effect in Dreamweaver, you need at least four to eight graphics, preferably one pair of graphics for a rollover button and a couple more that can be used to replace existing graphics on your page during the mouseover part of the multipart rollover. For each multipart rollover effect you conceive of, you will need to create and optimize all the necessary graphics yourself. Also, keep in mind that each rollover requires two graphics, one for the normal state and one for the over state.

If you'd like, you may create and use your own graphics with the following steps. Otherwise, download and use the set of graphics and HTML files in the Rollovers demo file at the web page for this book, as described in the introduction. The Rollovers file contains a folder that includes two HTML files — one you can use for this step list and another that shows the completed file (in case you want to peek at the results before starting) — along with an images folder full of graphics.

Non-Dreamweaver users can examine the JavaScript and HTML code in the completed sample file that comes with the free download.

To create a multiple graphic rollover effect using Dreamweaver, where the Swap Image JavaScript behavior alters two graphics at once, follow these steps:

1. **Save your rollover images to a folder on your desktop called Rollovers.**

   The Rollovers file contains a folder that includes two HTML files — one you can use for this step list and another that shows the completed file (in case you want to peek at the results before starting) — along with an images folder full of graphics.

2. **Create a managed site in the new `Rollovers` folder.**

   Choose Site➪New Site to create a managed site. Select the folder created in previous step for managed site.

3. **Open the `rollovers.html` file in the Dreamweaver workspace and select the graphic, in Design view, that says "MAC".**

   The `rollovers.html` file consists of a table with five graphics, each of which is sitting inside its own table cell, as shown in Figure 8-2. In the images folder, you find additional graphics that can be used to create the multi-image rollover effect.

4. **Open the Dreamweaver Behaviors panel (choose Window➪Behaviors), click the Add Behavior (+) button, and choose Swap Image.**

   The Swap Image dialog box opens, listing (by name or id attribute) all images in the open file. Unfortunately, none of the images (except for the one called Services) have been given identical name and id attributes, either by hand-coding or applying that attribute with the Property inspector. Without names to identify each image, it would be difficult to know which images are the right ones to "call" with the JavaScript and create the desired rollover effect.

Figure 8-2: Rollover graphics can be located anywhere on a page, including inside table cells.

5. **Click the Cancel button to close the Swap Image dialog box.**

   For the multipart rollover JavaScript technique to work, you must go back into the HTML code to name all images before applying any behaviors to them.

6. **Select the image at the top of the table that says** `Computer Superstore`, **and in the ID field in the upper-left corner of the Property inspector, enter** superstore, **as shown in Figure 8-3.**

   While you're at it, use the Property inspector to give the graphic some descriptive alt text, such as `Computer Superstore`, to make the graphic more accessible to visitors.

Figure 8-3: Label all the images with the id attribute before applying JavaScript.

7. **Repeat Steps 2 through 5 for the rest of the graphics in the HTML file, providing each with an ID and alt text. Name the images** dell, mac, sony, **and** main **using all lowercase letters, and for the alt text, add** Dell, Mac, Sony, **and** <empty>.

   The <empty> alt text entry in Dreamweaver inserts an empty alt attribute (<alt="">) to the image tag, making the image compliant with accessibility standards.

Now you're ready to add the JavaScript.

8. **In Design view, select the MAC graphic, click the Add Behavior (+) button in the Behaviors panel, and choose Swap Image.**

The Swap Image dialog box neatly displays a list of each of the images with the names you just gave them with the Property inspector, as shown in Figure 8-4.

Next you'll use this dialog box to set the rollover state for all the graphics that will be changing for this multipart rollover — all of which will be triggered by the visitor with a single mouseover event.

9. **With the graphic named `image "mac"` selected in the Images area of the Swap Image dialog box, click the Browse button next to the Set Source To field, navigate to the `Rollover` folder's `images` folder, and select the graphic called `b_mac_over.gif`.**

After selecting this overstate graphic, Dreamweaver places an asterisk (*) next to the words `image "mac"` in the Images field. This is your visual indication that the `b_mac_over.gif` graphic will appear when a visitor moves the cursor over the normal state `b_mac.gif` graphic in a web browser.

Leave the Preload Images and Restore Images onMouseOut options enabled in the dialog box, because both elements are a necessary part of the JavaScript that Dreamweaver adds to the page.

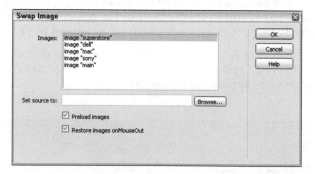

Figure 8-4: Labeled images are neatly listed in the Swap Image dialog box.

10. **Click OK to close the dialog box and save the Swap Image setting. Then save the HTML page (choose File⇨Save) and preview the page in a browser window (choose File⇨Preview in Browser) to test the rollover effect.**

Moving your cursor over the MAC graphic in the browser should make the button's rollover state appear, showing the word MAC with a blue, rounded rectangular outline. Moving your cursor away from the MAC graphic makes the graphic return to its normal state.

11. **Back in the open `rollovers.html` file in Dreamweaver, reselect the MAC graphic in Design view, and then in the Behaviors panel, double-click the yellow gear icon next to the action called Swap Image.**

    Clicking the gear icon reopens the Swap Image dialog box for the MAC swap image behavior.

    Make sure that you have selected the Swap Image and not the Swap Image Restore icon in the Behaviors panel. If you accidentally try to open the Swap Image Restore behavior, you'll see the Swap Image Restore dialog box instead of the Swap Image dialog box.

    Now comes the cool multipart stuff!

12. **In the Images area of the open dialog box, select the image called `superstore` and click the Browse button to set the source for that image's rollover state to `new.gif`. Then select the `image "main"` image and set its source for the rollover state to `mac.jpg`. Click OK.**

    The JavaScript that Dreamweaver has inserted into the code now has instructions to change three different graphics when a visitor mouses over the single MAC graphic, the main button, the Computer Superstore header, and the main area where it says Choose a Computer.

    However, you're not finished yet. Even though the mouseover effect now works, clicking the MAC graphic won't yet take a visitor to an adjoining Mac page. To do that, you have to also assign a hyperlink behavior to that graphic.

13. **To add a hyperlink, select the MAC graphic again in Design view, click the Add Behavior (+) button in the Behaviors panel, and select Go to URL.**

    In the Go to URL dialog box that opens, you find two areas: the Open In box (that lists the Main window) and the URL field.

    Because this page is not part of a larger frameset, only the Main window option is listed in the box. Were the page instead part of a frameset, the individual frame names would be listed here, from which the target destination within the frameset could be selected. Frames is an old, deprecated HTML technique, rarely used anymore, that uses `<frame set>` and `<frame>` tags instead of `<body>` tags to make two or more pages display in a single browser window.

14. **In the URL field, type (or browse to) the destination page URL. For demonstration purposes, type** http://www.apple.com **and click OK.**

    When the URL is local (such as `mac.html`), only the filename and extension are needed. However, when the file resides in a subfolder off the root level or is external to the site, type the full path and filename (for example, `computers/mac.html`) or the complete URL (for example, `http://www.apple.com/macbookpro`).

15. **That's it! Save the file, preview it in a browser, and move your cursor over the MAC button to watch the multipart magic.**

You should observe these results, as shown in Figure 8-5:

- Upon mouseover, the MAC, Computer Superstore, and Choose a Computer graphics all change — and you see a flashing "NEW" animation within the Computer Superstore graphic.

- Upon mouseoff, all the graphics return to their normal states.

- When you click the MAC link, the page transfers to Apple.com.

Figure 8-5: With multipart rollovers, you can make several graphics change with a single mouseover event.

If, for some reason, your page doesn't function as expected, you might have missed a step or accidentally typed the wrong character somewhere along the way. Go back into the code of your page to see whether you can identify and correct any errors; then retest the page in the browser. After that, if you're still having trouble, take a look at the `rollovers_complete.html` file. To isolate the problem in your code, compare your page side by side with the code in the `rollovers_complete.html` file. Look carefully — the problem may be as tiny as the omission of a period or a quotation mark.

Feel free to use this multipart graphic rollover technique on any series of graphics within the same page. This is a fantastic way to showcase your creativity while enhancing the visitor's experience on the site, except if the visitor is using a touch-based device such as an iPad or iPhone, in which case this feature won't work.

Making an Image Shake

No, the Shake effect doesn't include any ice cream or a blender, but it will make an image shake back and forth a few times in the browser, which is a pretty simple way of attracting attention.

A Shake event goes with an object. Dreamweaver users, as mentioned earlier, have access to about 20 different behaviors, which can each be easily added to selected objects through the Behaviors panel. Within the list of Behaviors you'll find a subsection that includes seven special effects that can alter the way a selected element appears in the browser including making an object appear or fade, grow or shrink, shake, slide, or squish.

Now keep in mind that with all effects, the action (in this case, the shaking) is called when a specified event occurs (such as clicking). The default event handler for this particular behavior is `onClick`, but you could change it to `onFocus`, `onBlur`, or one of several other options available for this effect.

Dreamweaver's behaviors work best when you manage a site prior to adding any to a page. To manage a site and then add the JavaScript Shake effect to a selected image in Dreamweaver, follow these steps:

1. **Choose Site➪New Site.**

   The Site Setup dialog box appears to the Site category, which displays fields for the Site Name and Local Site Folder.

2. **In the Site Name field, enter the name of your site.**

   Choose a name that matches the name of the client or indicates your site's purpose, such as ABC Company or My Blog.

3. **In the Local Site Folder field, verify that the path points to the folder on your computer that you want to use for this site.**

   For example, your Local Site Folder path might be something like this:

   ```
   Users\YOURUSERNAME\Documents\local_sites\ABC Web
   ```

4. **Click Save to close the dialog box.**

   Your new managed site opens, displaying all the existing files and folders (if any) in the root folder in the Files panel.

5. **Open any new or existing file and insert a graphic of your choice.**

   The graphic can be anything you like such as a photo or icon.

6. **In Design view, select the graphic, click the Add Behavior (+) button in the Behaviors panel, and select Effects➪Shake.**

   This opens the Shake dialog box with the Target Element set to <Current Selection>.

7. **Click OK to close the Shake dialog box and add the effect to your object.**

   Notice that onClick Shake effect is now listed in the Behaviors panel.

8. **Save your file and launch the page in your preferred browser to view the shake effect.**

   When you click the graphic, the graphic shimmies from left to right four or five times before returning to its original location.

Launching a New Browser Window

On most websites, the visitor is taken from page to page within the same browser window. By contrast, some sites open additional browser windows, browser tabs, or pop-up windows for a variety of reasons, such as giving visitors a close-up view of a product or displaying a printable version of a receipt. A new tab is by far the "nicest" way to view another page, whereas new windows and pop-up windows are increasingly more jarring and distracting. In addition, you must now consider your touchscreen and mobile visitors and the various ways that new pages open on those devices.

The following sections give you some general guidelines for opening new browser windows and tabs as well as explain how to add pop-up windows to a page using an HTML code editor as well as one of Dreamweaver's built-in behaviors.

Deciding when to launch a new browser window or tab

Designers open browser windows or tabs for many of the following reasons:

- To display a close-up image or detailed views of a product or item
- To provide a special logon area for registered visitors
- To open a secure window or tab inside which registered members can access their account information
- To view an Adobe Acrobat PDF file within the browser
- To display special notices, sale information, or shipping details
- To open a resource page on another website
- To provide technical data or other information in a printable format

These diverse uses are all good reasons to open new browser windows or tabs while leaving the original window intact; however, not all web designers feel the same way about launching new browser windows and tabs.

Some designers think that new browser windows and tabs should be launched anytime a link takes visitors away from the main domain they're visiting, as well as when any non-HTML file, such as a PDF, is opened. Other designers take a more firm and limiting approach, with the view that new browsers and tabs should never be opened without the express consent of the visitor. These designers believe additional windows/tabs are a nuisance, like those spamlike pop-up advertising windows that appear automatically when you visit certain websites (or even worse, the pop-up windows spawned by other pop-ups that plaster the screen, against the visitor's will, and sometimes can be stopped only by shutting down the computer).

Whatever your personal view, here are general guidelines for you to follow regarding when (and when not) to open new browser windows or tabs on your site:

- Do open new browser windows or tabs for links to external websites.

- Do open new browser windows or tabs for links to non-HTML documents, such as PDFs.

- Do notify site visitors, either visually or with text, when a new window or tab will be opened. You can do this by using an icon, like the example shown in Figure 8-6, or screen tip of some kind, such as the words "View close-up" or "Page opens in new window/tab."

- Do understand that users may have customized their browsers to treat pop-ups differently than you intend. For instance, you may have visitors who allow pop-ups but use the Tab Mix Plus browser add-on to force pop-ups to open in another tab rather than in their main browser window or as a regular pop-up window.

- Never launch an advertising window. Visitors don't want to be forced to see anything, let alone have to close an annoying advertisement window. Unless it's an emergency or you have a really good reason to launch a pop-up, keep general information within the same browser window.

As with all JavaScript, remember that pop-up windows may be inaccessible to visitors who use screen readers and other assistive devices. To ensure that all content in a pop-up window is accessible to the widest possible audience, make sure that you include special `<noscript>` tags in the code directly following the script to launch the pop-up. Between the `<noscript>` tags, you can include the content you would like these visitors to access, or include a regular hypertext link to the pop-up page so that visitors can access that page directly. Additional enhancements to accessibility include placing the notification of a new window opening in the `alt` text attribute for linking images, adding the `title` attribute to text hyperlinks, and ensuring that all pop-up windows include a Close button or Close hypertext link to make closing the window as easy as possible.

Figure 8-6: Alert visitors with a graphic or screen tip when a link will open a new window, tab, or pop-up window.

Hand-coding the script to launch a pop-up window

Opening another browser window, as you discover in Book III, Chapter 1, can be easily accomplished by including the target attribute (target="_blank") within a hyperlink, as in the following code:

```
<a href="http://www.wiley.com" title="Search For Books"
   target="_blank">Search For Books</a>
```

The target URL opens inside a new browser window, and that new window has the same attributes and dimensions as the parent window that spawned it. In other words, if the parent window (the page with the link) has a navigation toolbar, bookmark toolbar, and status bar, the child pop-up window (the linked page or document) has those features too.

Sometimes, however, you may want the child browser window to be precisely sized and stripped of some of its "*browser chrome*," which includes the window attributes such as scrollbars and menus. That's where the JavaScript comes in. To control the size, browser chrome, and screen position of your pop-up browser window, follow these steps:

1. **Open a new file in your favorite HTML code editor, type** Popup **and select it, and then convert the selection into a null link.**

   Though you could use the hashtag (#) to create the null link, in this example you'll be applying a JavaScript behavior to the link. To do that, apply a JavaScript null link to the code instead, as in this example:

   ```
   <a href="javascript:void(0);">Popup</a>
   ```

   See the nearby sidebar for more on null links.

2. **In the code of the page, between the opening and closing `<head>` tags, insert the following script:**

```
<script type="text/JavaScript">
<!--
function MM_openBrWindow(theURL,winName,features) { //v2.0
 window.open(theURL,winName,features);
}
//-->
</script>
```

This script informs the browser how to handle a JavaScript request, which you add to the code in the next step.

3. **Add the additional JavaScript to the hyperlink HTML:**

```
<a href="javascript:void(0);" onClick="MM_openBrWindow('http://www.
   google.com', 'MyWindow', 'toolbar=yes,location=yes,status=yes,menuba
   r=yes,scrollbars=yes,resizable=yes,width=200,height=200')">Popup</a>
```

The browser opens the linked page in a resizable pop-up window named `MyWindow`, 200 x 200 pixels in size, and includes a toolbar, location bar, status bar, menu bar, and scroll bars.

The browser window chrome, such as the toolbar and menu bar, can be easily removed from the pop-up window by omitting those attributes from the JavaScript. For example, to launch a 500-pixel square pop-up window with no browser attributes, the code would look like this:

```
<a href="javascript:void(0);" onClick="MM_openBrWindow('http://www.
   google.com', 'MyWindow', 'width=500,height=500')">Popup</a>
```

4. **To see how this script functions, save the page and open it in a browser window.**

When you click the Popup link, your custom-sized browser window pop-up opens above the parent window and displays the Google web page. Figure 8-7 shows an example of the link page (parent) and resulting pop-up (child) window.

5. **If you'd like to also control where on the visitor's screen the new pop-up window appears (relative to the upper-left corner of the parent browser window), hand-code the `top` and `left` attributes into the JavaScript:**

```
<a href="javascript:void(0);" onClick="MM_openBrWindow('http://www.
   google.com', 'MyWindow', 'width=200,height=200,top=80,left=200')">Po
   pup</a>
```

Most browsers may not launch a pop-up and will instead open the new page in another tab. Therefore, if you don't see the pop-up result in your preferred testing browser, try another browser or be satisfied with the tab approach preferred by the browser.

Pay close attention to the JavaScript syntax used here. You see no quotation marks around the `top` and `left` pixel attributes (as you'd normally use in HTML code), and the entire sizing area is enclosed between two apostrophes. If you happen to use the wrong characters, such as double quotes, the JavaScript will not function in a browser.

Book III
Chapter 8

Making Your Pages Interactive

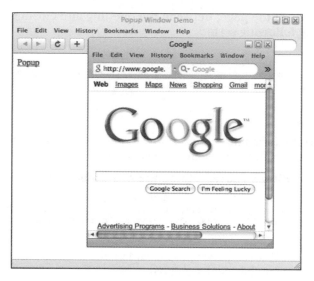

Figure 8-7: Launch a new pop-up window with a tiny bit of simple JavaScript.

Adding a pop-up window to your page with Dreamweaver

If you're a Dreamweaver user, you can add the script for launching a pop-up window through the Behaviors panel and not have to fuss with any hand-coding.

To add a pop-up window to your page in Dreamweaver, follow these steps:

1. **Open a new file in the Dreamweaver workspace and type the words you want to use for the link. Then select the words and convert the selection into a null link by typing** javascript:void(0); **into the Link field of the Property inspector.**

   For example, if you type **Get Directions** and add the null link, your code would look like this:

   ```
   <a href="javascript:void(0);">Get Directions</a>
   ```

2. **With your cursor between any of the letters in the null link (for example, between the *D* and the *i* in Directions), click the Add Behavior (+) button in the Behaviors panel (choose Window⇨Behaviors) and select Open Browser Window.**

   The Open Browser Window dialog box opens, as shown in Figure 8-8.

3. **Enter a URL to display in the pop-up, input the pixels for the window's width and height, select any of the desired window attributes, and type a unique window name for the pop-up.**

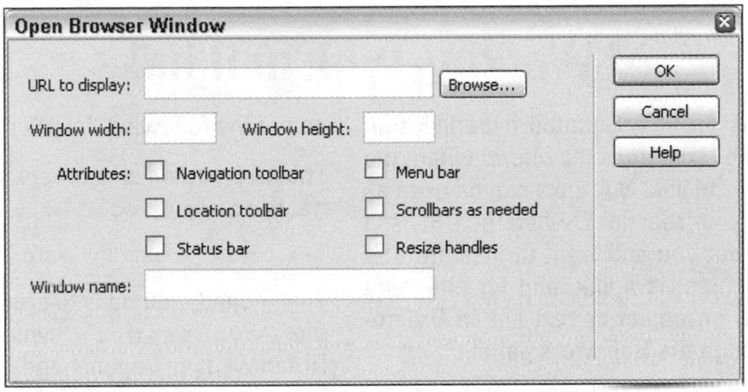

Figure 8-8: Use the Open Browser Window dialog box in Dreamweaver to set the URL and browser window attributes for a new browser window.

Select only the browser window attributes or *chrome* you want to include in the pop-up. If you do not want a particular attribute, leave that check box deselected, and those attributes will be automatically omitted from the pop-up window. For example, to create a 400-x-400-pixel chromeless pop-up window linked to the Google Maps website, enter **http://maps.google.com** in the URL to Display field, **400** and **400** in the Window Width and Window Height fields, and **GoogleMaps** in the Window Name field.

4. **Click OK.**

Upon closing the dialog box, Dreamweaver automatically inserts the JavaScript code to make the pop-up window work. If you look at the code, you can see parts of the JavaScript both in the <head> area and as part of the hyperlink tag within the body of the page. Here's the script you see for the example:

```
<!doctype html>
<html>
<head>
<meta charset="utf-8" />
<title>Open Browser Window Demo</title>
<script type="text/JavaScript">
function MM_openBrWindow(theURL,winName,features) { //v2.0
 window.open(theURL,winName,features);
}
</script>
</head>

<body><a href="javascript:void(0);" onclick="MM_openBrWindow('http://
    maps.google.com ','GoogleMaps', 'width=400,height=400')">Get
    Directions</a>
</body>
</html>
```

Working with null links

A *null link* is an undesignated hyperlink that does nothing and goes nowhere when the visitor clicks the link. Null links can be used as placeholders for real links, when the URL isn't yet known, but you still want to indicate that the text or object is a link, and for attaching behaviors to an object or text link in Dreamweaver through the Behaviors panel.

The simplest way to create a null link is by using a hashtag (#) as a placeholder for the filename or URL of the link, as in this example:

```
<a href="#">Google</a>
```

Unfortunately, because named anchor links are also preceded by the hashtag (#), the browser becomes confused when encountering null links like this. In other words, when the browser can't find the name after the hashtag, as it would with a regular named anchor link, the browser "jumps" the visitor back to the top of the current page, abandoning the visitor's former location within the file.

To avoid having the browser jump to the top of page when it encounters a null link, use either one of the following JavaScript alternatives:

The first method is to create a null link with the `javascript:void(0);` syntax, like this:

```
<a href="javascript:void(0); ">Google</a>
```

The second method is to create a null link with the `JavaScript:;` syntax, which Adobe Dreamweaver recommends when attaching behaviors to text or object links, like this:

```
<a href="JavaScript:; ">Google</a>
```

As an alternative, you could create a null JavaScript link using the following function:

```
<a href="#" onclick="aFunction();return
          false; ">Google</a>
```

The `return false` part of this bit of JavaScript (which must be the final function call) tells the browser that the action of returning a reference to a URL (including internal links) should return as false. Therefore, the link does nothing and goes nowhere.

5. **To control the position of the pop-up window relative to the visitor's parent browser window, go into the code and hand-apply the top and left attributes to the JavaScript:**

```
<a href="javascript:void(0);" onclick="MM_openBrWindow('http://maps.
    google.com ','GoogleMaps ', 'width=400,height=400,top=450,left=150')
    ">Get Directions</a>
```

You may need to test the pop-up script a few times to get the exact positioning the way you want it. Without the addition of the `top` and `left` attributes, the pop-up window will open directly on top of the parent, starting at the parent window's upper-left corner.

Getting to Know jQuery

As anyone who writes JavaScript can tell you, some scripts are used so often that it makes sense to create a personal library to pull from rather than recreating them each time they are needed. In fact, this practice was so prevalent that around 2006 a developer named John Resig created an official open-source cross-browser JavaScript library called *jQuery*. Licensed under the MIT License and the GNU General Public License, this incredible free library is available for public use to help designers and developers quickly add interactive features to web pages without the use of Flash or animated GIFs.

The official jQuery website at `http://jquery.com` offers documentation, tutorials, free downloads, and demos to help you learn to work with jQuery. As you will see, when paired with HTML and CSS, jQuery modules or widgets can transform how visitors interact with websites. Here are just a handful of the things you can do with jQuery:

- Create objects that are draggable, droppable, sortable, selectable, and resizable.
- Add dynamic widgets such as accordion and tab panels, date pickers, dialog boxes, progress bars, and sliders.
- Include special effects into the page such as color animations and explosions (yes!), class transitions, hiding and showing elements, and easing movement from one part of a page to another.
- Build custom themes for jQuery UI with the jQuery UI ThemeRoller.

To get you started on your jQuery learning journey, take a look of the resources and tutorial sites listed in Table 8-2.

Table 8-2	Free jQuery Resources
jQuery Resource	*jQuery Resource Web Address*
jQuery (official site)	`http://jquery.com`
W3Schools.com	`www.w3schools.com/jquery/`
jQuery UI	`http://jqueryui.com`
jQuery Mobile	`http://jquerymobile.com`
jQuery Project	`http://jquery.org`
jQuery Tools	`www.jquerytools.org`
Visual jQuery	`www.visualjquery.com`
jQuery Tutorial	`www.jquery-tutorial.net`
Learn jQuery in 30 days	`http://learnjquery.tutsplus.com`

Book III
Chapter 8

Making Your Pages Interactive

With most jQuery modules, widgets, and plug-ins, you need to modify your HTML code by adding a link to the jQuery library in the `<head>` of your code. Library pages can be located on your host server or called from a trusted remote location such as Google. In addition, you may need to host some JavaScript, CSS, and image files for any particular jQuery script to function properly. To illustrate, the following two sections will show you how to create an accordion panel and a pop-up image viewer using jQuery.

Creating accordion panels

An *accordion panel* is a container on a web page with multiple sections that visitors can expand and collapse, one at a time, by clicking each section's header. You can view an example of an accordion panel here in the demo section of the jQueryUI website at `http://jqueryui.com/demos/accordion/`.

An accordion panel may contain as many sections as needed, and the panel's behavior can be configured to meet specific needs, such as having the panel load in the browser with all sections collapsed or allowing the panels to open on mouseover.

The HTML markup for an accordion panel is quite simple, using a parent `<div>` container filled with nested `<div>` tags for each of the sections:

```
<div id="parent">

<h3><a href="#">Section 1</a></h3>
<div id="sec1">
Section 1 content
</div>
<h3><a href="#">Section 2</a></h3>
<div id="sec2">
Section 2 content
</div>
<h3><a href="#">Section 3</a></h3>
<div id="sec3">
Section 3 content
</div>
</div>
```

Then, to make the code function, you'd need to call a script and add links to several JavaScript and CSS files in the `<head>` of your code, similar to these:

```
<head>
    <meta charset="utf-8">
    <title>Page Title</title>
```

```
 <script type="text/javascript" src="js/jquery-1.7.2.min.
 js"></script>
 <script type="text/javascript" src="js/jquery-ui-1.8.22.
 custom.min.js"></script>
 <link rel="stylesheet" href="css/jquery.ui.all.css">
 <link rel="stylesheet" href="css/mycss.css">
 <script>
 $(function() {
 $( "#accordion" ).accordion();
 });
 </script>
</head>
```

To get copies of all the necessary JavaScript and CSS files and to simplify the process of creating your accordion, you can "roll your own" at the JQueryUI ThemeRoller site, `http://jqueryui.com/themeroller/`, shown in Figure 8-9.

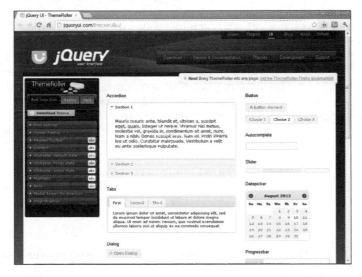

Figure 8-9: Create custom styled jQuery Accordion panels with the ThemeRoller.

Book III
Chapter 8

Making Your Pages Interactive

There you can quickly set visual styles including fonts, corner radius size, and link states, and then download the theme with all the needed HTML, CSS, and JavaScript files and folders for your site. Even better, each download comes with a sample `index.html` file to show you where all the links should go in the head. Figure 8-10 shows an example of how your finished accordion panel might look.

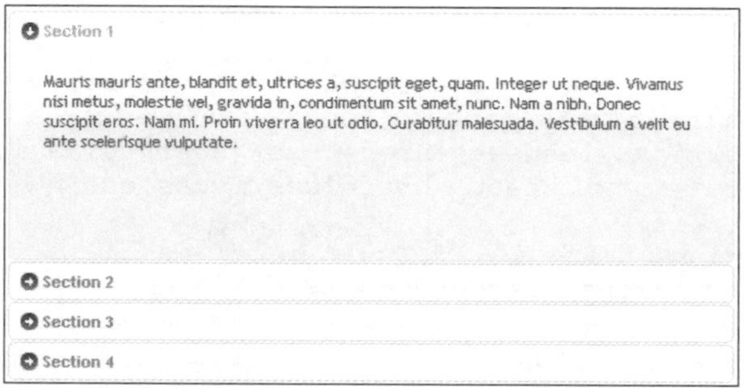

Figure 8-10: Your jQuery Accordion panel can be filled with any content and be custom styled with CSS.

Creating jQuery slide shows

You have several different ways to create a slide show on your site. Some slide shows pair images with JavaScript in a variety of layouts with different functionality, while others combine Flash with text, animation, and graphics. There are many free and wonderful jQuery sliders available today, including the Wow Slider, Nivo Slider, and Lemmon Slider, to name just a few. Nearly all of the galleries, like the super simple jQuery slideViewer shown in Figure 8-11, use the jQuery plug-in (a JavaScript library; see http://jquery.com), which allows you to quickly create an image gallery with just a few lines of HTML code, as in this example:

```
<div id="mySlideViewer" class="svw">
 <ul>
  <li><img src="images/01.jpg" alt="Empire State"></li>
  <li><img src="images/02.jpg" alt="Chinatown"></li>
  <li><img src="images/03.jpg" alt="Statue of Liberty"></li>
 </ul>
</div>
```

To add the jQuery slideViewer to your page in Dreamweaver, follow these steps:

1. **Download the free jQuery slideViewer 1.2 JavaScript file named `jquery.slideviewer.1.2.js` from the following website, and save the file to the root level of a managed site in Dreamweaver:**

   www.gcmingati.net/wordpress/wp-content/lab/jquery/imagestrip/imageslide-plugin.html

   Choose Site➪New Site to create a managed site for this example. In the Local Site Folder field, browse to and select the folder you'll use for this exercise.

2. **Download the latest version of the free jQuery JavaScript file from** `http://jquery.com`.

   The file will likely be called something like `jquery-1.7.2.min.js`. Save the file to the root level of the managed site.

Figure 8-11: The jQuery slideViewer presents your images in a gallery format.

**Book III
Chapter 8**

**Making Your Pages
Interactive**

3. **Download the latest version of the free jQuery Easing plug-in from** `http://gsgd.co.uk/sandbox/jquery/easing`.

   The filename should be something like `jquery.easing.1.3.js`. Also, save this file to the root level of the managed site.

4. **Add the following code to the `<head>` area of your page, which calls each of these JavaScript files when the page with the jQuery slideViewer gallery is viewed in a browser:**

```
<script src="jquery-1.7.2.min.js" type="text/JavaScript"></script>
<script src="jquery.easing.1.3.js" type="text/JavaScript"></script>
<script src="jquery.slideviewer.1.2.js" type="text/JavaScript"></script>
```

Take extra care to ensure that the version numbers of the script source match the version numbers of the files you just downloaded. The gallery will only function when the numbers match.

5. **Place all your gallery images into a folder called `images` on the root level of your managed site. If you don't have an `images` folder yet, create one.**

All the images in your gallery must have the same width and height. If they aren't the same, some images may be stretched or scrunched to match the size of the first image.

6. **Select and copy all the slideViewer's basic CSS from the following website, paste it into a blank new file, and save the CSS in an external file called** `gallery.css`:

   www.gcmingati.net/wordpress/wp-content/lab/jquery/imagestrip/image
       slide-plugin.html

7. **Add a link to the new external CSS file in the head of the page.**

   The link code should look like this:

   ```
   <link href="gallery.css" rel="stylesheet" type="text/css" media="all" />
   ```

8. **In the body of your page, insert a `<div>` with a unique ID (such as `mySlideViewer`) and the `class="svw"` CSS attribute. Inside the `<div>`, type in an unordered list of images, as in the following code:**

   ```
   <div id="mySlideViewer" class="svw">
    <ul>
     <li><img src="images/01.jpg" alt="Purple"></li>
     <li><img src="images/02.jpg" alt="White"></li>
     <li><img src="images/03.jpg" alt="Orange"></li>
    </ul>
   </div>
   ```

   You may use as many images as you like in this slider. The `alt` text, as with any image on your page, will be used to make the images more accessible to visitors with disabilities and to search engine spiders and crawlers.

9. **Directly below the link to the external CSS file in the head of the page, insert the following JavaScript code, which controls how one image slides into the next in the gallery:**

   ```
   <script type="text/JavaScript">
     $(window).bind("load", function() {
     $("div#mySlideViewer").slideView( {
     easeFunc: "easeInOutBack",
     easeTime: 1200
   });
   });
   </script>
   ```

   The timing of the slide animation from one slide to the next is counted in milliseconds. To change the speed, edit the `easeTime` number. The smaller the number, the faster the transition.

10. **Save any open files and preview your new jQuery slideViewer in a browser.**

    To change the border and number indicators from red to another color, modify the styles in the CSS.

    For additional enhancements to the jQuery slideViewer, read the documentation at www.gcmingati.net/wordpress/wp-content/lab/jquery/imagestrip/imageslide-plugin.html.

This slide show uses HTML, JavaScript, and CSS to display your same-sized images in a unified layout with side-swiping transitions and easy-to-use navigation buttons — all without you having to understand a lick of JavaScript or jQuery. Although it isn't necessary that you understand all the code that makes this script function, what does matter is that you like the end results and can easily re-create it with your own color scheme and graphics.

Creating an image viewer with Lightbox2

Groups of images can be presented on the web in a variety of different ways. There are galleries, sliders, and Lightbox image viewers, all of which can be constructed in an unlimited number of ways. For instance, image viewers can be built using some combination of HTML, CSS, JavaScript, jQuery, or even Flash. Although the best solution will be standards compliant and have a small footprint of roughly 25K or less, the right solution often depends on the specific needs of the website.

To illustrate, suppose you're designing a site for an artist who wants to have a portfolio page with eight small images organized into a grid, and when you click any of the smaller images, a larger version will display onscreen. One of the best solutions for this kind of need is the Lightbox2 image viewer. In addition to being one of the most popular image viewers today, it's also lightweight and super easy to install.

If you'd like, you may create and use your own graphics with the following steps. Otherwise, download and use the set of graphics and HTML files in the Lightbox demo file at the book's web page, as described in the introduction.

The Lightbox file contains two HTML files — one you can use for this step list and another that shows the completed file (in case you want to peek at the results before starting) — along with an `images` folder full of graphics.

Book III
Chapter 8

Making Your Pages Interactive

The Lightbox2 image viewer works best when you have two sets of images. The first set is the smaller thumbnail pictures that appear when the page opens in the browser, and the second set is the larger images viewable through the Lightbox2 widget.

The following steps show how easy it is to add the Lightbox2 image viewer to a web page:

1. **Visit the Lightbox2 website and download a copy of the Lightbox2 files:** `http://lokeshdhakar.com/projects/lightbox2/`.

   The Lightbox Zip file contains several files, including a sample file named `index.html`, a folder with two JavaScript files, a folder with a CSS file, and an `images` folder with all the images used in the Lightbox2 image viewer. Copy the extracted contents of this Zip file into your `Lightbox` managed site folder.

2. **(Optional) If you're using Dreamweaver, create a managed site to a new folder on your computer called Lightbox.**

   Choose Site⇨New Site to create a new managed site to the new Lightbox folder. In the Site Name field enter the name Lightbox and in the Local Site Folder field, browse to and select the new Lightbox folder.

3. **Open the file called lightbox.html in Dreamweaver or in your preferred web editor.**

   The layout of this file includes a table filled with eight thumbnail images, ready for you to add the Lightbox2 code, as shown in Figure 8-12.

Figure 8-12: To add a Lightbox2 image viewer to your page, organize your thumbnails in a table or other container on the page.

4. **Add the following links to the JavaScript and CSS files to the `<head>` of your code:**

   ```
   <script src="js/jquery-1.7.2.min.js"></script>
   <script src="js/lightbox.js"></script>
   <link href="css/lightbox.css" rel="stylesheet" />
   ```

   These links call the appropriate files that help make the Lightbox function.

5. **Convert each of the thumbnail images into hyperlinks that point to their respective close-up images and include the `rel="lightbox[mygroup]"` attribute that activates Lightbox.**

TIP

Make sure to replace `mygroup` with a descriptive name for your particular group of images.

For example, change the code for the first image from this:

```
<img src="images/1_thumb.jpg" width="180" height="180"
   alt="Image Title">
```

To this, where the thumbnail image links to the closeup:

```
<a href="images/1.jpg" rel="lightbox[vacation]"><img
   src="images/1_thumb.jpg" width="180" height="180"
   alt="Image Title"></a>
```

6. **(Optional) If you'd like your images to include a caption, add the `title` attribute to the link tag, as show here:**

```
<a href="images/1.jpg" rel="lightbox[vacation]"
   title="City at Night"><img src="images/1_thumb.jpg"
   width="180" height="180" alt="City at Night"></a>
```

7. **Repeat Steps 5 and 6 for the remaining images in the table.**

If desired, match the titles of your closeup images with the alternative text of their respective thumbnail images.

8. **Save your file and preview the Lightbox2 image viewer by launching the page in your preferred browser.**

Click any of the thumbnail images to see how the Lightbox2 works. You should see the browser page dim as a pop-up window appears above it displaying the close-up image of the thumbnail you clicked.

9. **With the close-up image on your screen, hover your mouse over it to see a left or white navigation arrow appear on top of the close-up image.**

Clicking the left or right side of the picture advances you from one close-up image to the next. Below the close-up, you should also see the title of the image along with the current and total number of images in the set (such as Not in Kansas, Image 5 of 8) and a big X you can click to close the Lightbox and return to the parent browser window. Figure 8-13 shows an example of how the sample page looks when the Lightbox is displaying a close-up image.

If for some reason your Lightbox image viewer isn't functioning properly, go back through the steps to check that you've added all the links properly. For additional help, visit the Lightbox2 Forum at `http://lokeshdhakar.com/forums/`.

Book III
Chapter 8

Making Your Pages Interactive

Figure 8-13: The Lightbox2 image viewer lets visitors easily navigate through a series of close-up images.

Adding Multimedia Files

A *multimedia file* is any kind of file that can be viewed, listened to, and interacted with on the Internet, including music, videos, puzzles, QuickTime movies, quizzes, animations, and games.

Unfortunately, because all the different Internet browsers have been developed by different companies over time, not every browser — or even browser version — is equipped to handle media files in quite the same way. For example, some browsers automatically play certain media files, but other browsers require the installation of special plug-ins, applets, or ActiveX controls (specified in the code along with the media file) before those media files will work. To make matters even more complicated, every media file has its own format, as indicated by its file extension — and not all formats are playable in all browsers or all operating systems.

There is good news, however. As Internet users have gotten savvier, so have all the major browser developers. In addition, over the past several years, certain media formats have become more standard than others. For instance, MP3, WAV, and RAM are the most popular formats for sound, and FLV, SWF, QuickTime, Shockwave, and MPEG are the most popular formats for video. What's more, all the newest versions of the most popular browsers (Firefox, Chrome, Safari, and Internet Explorer) automatically have these popular media-file readers preinstalled in them so that visitors can experience the multimedia files in their browsers without having to download any special files from third-party vendors, which even when they're free, are somewhat of a hassle to install. Of course, you'll still occasionally need to update the plug-ins or special files (such as Adobe's free Flash Player), but at least you won't have to go searching for them from the start.

Making pages dynamic with multimedia files

The quickest way to add multimedia files to a web page is to use an HTML editor that can automatically insert the appropriate code for each file type. For example, with the click of a button, Dreamweaver can add Flash animations, Flash video, QuickTime movies, Shockwave movies, Java applets, ActiveX controls, and other plug-ins to your web pages. The only exception is when you plan to add YouTube or Vimeo videos. For details about embedding YouTube or Vimeo video files, see the nearby sidebar.

To add a multimedia file to your page in Dreamweaver, follow these steps:

1. **Create a managed site to a new folder on your computer called** `Multimedia`.

   Choose Site⇨New Site to create a managed site. In the Local Root Folder field, browse to and select the new `Multimedia` folder.

2. **Inside the `Multimedia` folder, put a copy of all the media file(s) you'd like to insert onto your page.**

   If you'll be working with multiple files, you may want to place all the media files inside a media folder at the root level of your site.

3. **Create a new blank page, or open the page you want to add the media file to, and place your cursor at the spot on the page where you'd like to insert the media file.**

   Setting the insertion point tells Dreamweaver where to drop in the appropriate code.

4. **Choose Insert⇨Media and then select the desired media type.**

   The Insert Media dialog box opens for your media type. Alternatively, you can click the desired Media button in the Common category of the Insert panel (shown in Figure 8-14) to access the same list with helpful icons next to each media type. Options in this menu include SWF, FlashPaper, FLV, Shockwave, Applet, param, ActiveX, and Plugin (for QuickTime).

   To view your icons in color, select the Color Icons option from the Insert panel's Options menu located in the top-right corner of the panel.

   To find out how to add sound to your page, see the section later in this chapter called "Adding sound with Dreamweaver."

   After you select the desired media type, Dreamweaver opens the Select File dialog box.

5. **In the Media dialog box, browse to and select the media file in your managed site that you want to insert on the page. Then click OK.**

   Dreamweaver uses the filename and location of the selected file to ensure that the appropriate path to the file gets added to the inserted code. For example, when inserting a Flash SWF animation file,

Book III
Chapter 8

Making Your Pages Interactive

Dreamweaver adds a ton of code that enables the visitor to view the animation in most browsers, replete with comment tags and conditional rules, depending on the visitor's browser scenario:

```
<object classid="clsid:D27CDB6E-AE6D-11cf-96B8-444553540000"
  width="210" height="180" id="FlashID2" accesskey="a" tabindex="1"
  title="MySWF">
<param name="movie" value="media/sample.swf" />
<param name="quality" value="high" />
<param name="wmode" value="opaque" />
<param name="swfversion" value="6.0.65.0" />
<!-- This param tag prompts users with Flash Player 6.0 r65 and
higher to download the latest version of Flash Player. Delete it if
you don't want users to see the prompt. -->
<param name="expressinstall" value="Scripts/expressInstall.swf" />
<!-- Next object tag is for non-IE browsers. So hide it from IE using
IECC. -->
<!--[if !IE]>-->
<object type="application/x-shockwave-flash" data="media/sample.swf"
width="210" height="180">
  <!--<![endif]-->
  <param name="quality" value="high" />
  <param name="wmode" value="opaque" />
  <param name="swfversion" value="6.0.65.0" />
  <param name="expressinstall" value="Scripts/expressInstall.swf" />
  <!-- The browser displays the following alternative content for
users with Flash Player 6.0 and older. -->
  <div>
    <h4>Content on this page requires a newer version of Adobe Flash
Player.</h4>
    <p><a href="http://www.adobe.com/go/getflashplayer"><img
src="http://www.adobe.com/images/shared/download_buttons/get_flash_
player.gif" alt="Get Adobe Flash player" width="112" height="33"
/></a></p>
  </div>
  <!--[if !IE]>-->
</object>
<!--<![endif]-->
</object>
```

In addition to adding the code, Dreamweaver also installs special dependent files in a `Scripts` folder in your local root folder. This folder, which includes an SWF file and a JavaScript file, must be uploaded to the server for the object or behavior to function properly in a browser.

Depending on which media type you select, you may encounter the Object Tag Accessibility Attributes dialog box. If you see that dialog box, enter the requested accessibility information (if desired) and click OK to proceed.

6. **With the media file still selected in Design view, enter any desired additional parameters, attributes, and dimensions for the media file.**

For example, with an inserted Flash video, you can set the width and height of the FLV player, select a skin, apply a CSS style, and choose whether the video will auto-play and/or auto-rewind.

Figure 8-14: Add multimedia files to your page with
Dreamweaver's Insert⇨Media command.

Book III
Chapter 8

Making Your Pages
Interactive

To find out more about adding media files to your web pages, check out the
free online tutorial at www.w3schools.com/media/default.asp.

Embedding YouTube and Vimeo videos

Sites like YouTube and Vimeo are wonderful places to watch and explore
videos. Not only do they allow registered users to upload and share their
own videos, but anyone can grab the code to embed a video they like into a
web page.

To embed a video from YouTube, follow these steps

1. **Navigate to the page on YouTube that has the video you'd like to share.**

2. **Click the Share button located below the video. This opens a share panel with the code you'll need to embed the video into your web page.**

3. **Click the Embed button to open a hidden embed code panel. If desired, you can modify the size and other features of the video player by making selections in the area listed after the embed code box.**

4. **Copy the embed code and paste it into the code of your web page in the location on the page you'd like the video to appear.**

5. **Launch your page in a browser to ensure the video plays.**

To embed a video from Vimeo, follow these steps:

1. **Navigate to the page on Vimeo that has the video you'd like to share.**

2. **Click the white Share icon located in the top-right corner of the video. This opens a Share This Video pop-up panel with the code you'll need to embed the video into your web page.**

3. **To customize the embed options, click the Customize Embed Options link at the bottom of the pop-up panel. Clicking the link opens a hidden panel with settings that let you edit the size, text color, and other features of the video player.**

4. **Copy the embed code and paste it into the code of your web page in the location on the page you'd like the video to appear.**

5. **Launch your page in a browser to ensure the video plays.**

Adding sound with Dreamweaver

Adding sound to your pages with Dreamweaver is as simple as choosing the right media file format and then configuring that object's properties so that the visitor can experience and interact with the file. With the exception of inserting a Flash media type for SWF sound files, you can insert most other media files onto a page with the ActiveX media type.

After inserting the sound file on your page (using the steps described in the earlier section "Adding multimedia files"), follow these steps to configure the sound object's properties using Dreamweaver's Property inspector:

1. **After inserting the sound file on your page through the Insert⇨Media menu, set any desired properties for the inserted object in the Property inspector, such as Width, Height, and Embed. Be sure to also enter the appropriate class ID to identify the file type to the browser.**

Table 8-3 contains a listing of common media type class IDs.

Table 8-3	Class ID Types for Sound Media Files
Media Type	*Class ID*
QuickTime Player	clsid:02BF25D5-8C17-4B23-BC80-D3488ABDDC6B
RealPlayer	clsid:CFCDAA03-8BE4-11cf-B84B-0020AFBBCCFA
Shockwave for Director 6	clsid:166D1DCA-3F9C-11CF-8075-444553540000
Shockwave for Flash	clsid:D27CDB6E-AE6D-11cf-96B8-444553540000
Windows Media Player	clsid:02BF25D5-8C17-4B23-BC80-D3488ABDDC6B

2. **(Optional) Set the parameters of an embedded ActiveX sound file.**

   To do so, first select the sound object in Design view and click the Parameters button in the Property inspector. You must select the sound file before the button appears on the Property inspector. Once clicked, the Parameters dialog box opens. Then click the plus (+) button to add the appropriate parameters and values, as described in Tables 8-4 through 8-6. When finished, click OK.

3. **In the ID text field or Base text field in the Property inspector, fill in the following field for your chosen media type:**

   - *QuickTime:* Enter **http://www.apple.com/qtactivex/qtplugin.cab** in the Base text field.

   - *Shockwave Director 6:* Enter **swd6** in the ID text field.

   - *Shockwave Flash:* Enter **swfl** in the ID text field.

   - *RealPlayer:* Enter **rvocx** in the ID text field.

   - *Media Player:* Enter **mediaplayer2** in the ID text field.

To preview your media file, save any changes and then launch the page in a browser window. If you've entered true as the autostart value, your file should begin to play immediately when the page loads in the browser.

In some cases, your file may not play until you upload the files to your server, so be sure to test both locally and on a remote server before making the page available to visitors.

Table 8-4	QuickTime Player Parameters and Values
Parameter	*Value*
autoplay	false
controller	true
pluginspage	http://www.apple.com/quicktime/download/indext.html
target	myself
type	video/audio
src	(Enter the path and filename to your file)

Table 8-5	RealPlayer Parameters and Values
Parameter	*Value*
src	myfilename.rm
autostart	false
controls	ControlPanel
console	audio
type	audio/x-pn-realaudio-plugin

Table 8-6	Windows Media Player Parameters and Values
Parameter	*Value*
src	(Enter the path and filename to your file)
autostart	false
Showcontrols	true
Showstatusbar	false
Showdisplay	false
Autorewind	true
Type	application/x-mplayer-w
Pluginspage	http://www.microsoft.com/Windows/Downloads/Contents/MediaPlayer

Providing Visitors with Fresh Content

One of the best ways to keep visitors coming back to a site regularly is to entice them with fresh, daily content. The content can be anything you like, as long as it's appealing and relevant to the target audience. For example, you might add daily entries in a blog, insert daily Flash movies and games, offer visitors polls and poll results on popular topics of interest, request feedback from visitors using forms, include free online tools for visitors such as calculators and converters, publish regular site-related articles and tips, offer free printable coupons for products and services, host special contests and sweepstakes, and send out daily, weekly, or monthly newsletters with links back to the site.

Although each of these ideas may not be suitable to every website, some of them function quite well on nearly any site. For example, you can offer daily tips, coupons, information about new products or sale items, or featured news items.

Daily tip or news item

Giving visitors a reason to return to your site each day can increase the chance of them wanting to learn more about the site's products and services. That, in turn, can result in increased web traffic and improved sales!

Aside from daily blog entries, one of the quickest ways to entice visitors to your site is to provide them with some kind of relevant information each day. This could be in the form of a daily tip or suggestion, a horoscope or fortune, a poem, a joke, a famous quote, a photograph, a coupon, or details about a new product or service. The daily item can truly be anything you like, as long as you customize the JavaScript to accurately display the desired information.

The JavaScript used in the following steps can be found in its entirety on the JavaScriptKit site (`www.javascriptkit.com`). The script contains two parts: One part must be placed in the <head> of the code; the other goes inline, between the <body> tags of the code, at the location on the page where the daily tip content should appear.

Searching with Google

Make visitors feel in control over their experience on your site by providing them with a site search tool. You can add the free Google search bar to your site by inserting a tiny bit of code on your page.

To install the Google free search tool with Site Search, follow these steps:

1. **Type the following code at the spot on your page where you'd like the search bar to appear:**

```
<!-- SiteSearch Google -->
<FORM method=GET action="http://www.
        google.com/search">
<input type=hidden name=ie
        value=UTF-8>
<input type=hidden name=oe
        value=UTF-8>
<TABLE bgcolor="#ffffff"><tr><td>
<A HREF="http://www.google.com/">
<IMG SRC="http://www.google.com/
        logos/Logo_40wht.gif"
border="0" ALT="Google"></A>
</td>
<td>
<INPUT TYPE=text name=q size=31
        maxlength=255 value="">
<INPUT type=submit name=btnG
        VALUE="Google Search">
```

```
<font size=-1>
<input type=hidden name=domains
        value="YOUR DOMAIN
NAME"><br><input type=radio
        name=sitesearch value="">
        WWW
  <input type=radio name=sitesearch
        value="YOUR DOMAIN NAME"
checked>YOUR DOMAIN NAME<br>
</font>
</td></tr></TABLE>
</FORM>
<!-- SiteSearch Google -->
```

2. **Replace the words YOUR DOMAIN NAME in the code (in all three locations) with the full URL of your website's home page, such as http://www.*mydomain*.com.**

To have the search feature appear on all the pages of your site, include this code on each page in the same location for consistency.

Businesses can also harness the power of the Google Custom Search Engine. Google searches can help increase web traffic, which can result in increased sales. For more information about Google Site Search, visit www.google.com/cse/.

Adding a daily tip or news item to your page

To add a daily tip or news item to a page on your website, follow these steps:

1. **Open an HTML file in your favorite code editor and place your cursor in the location on the page you'd like the Tip to appear.**

   If needed, create a layer or other container with HTML and position it with CSS before you set the insertion point for the daily tip.

2. **Add the following script to the page at the insertion point:**

```
<script>
<!--

/*
Tip of the day script
By JavaScript Kit (http://javascriptkit.com)
Over 200+ free scripts here!
```

```
*/

var today_obj=new Date()
var today_date=today_obj.getDate()

var tips=new Array()
//Configure the below variable to contain the "header" of the tip
var tiptitle='<img src="../../tip.gif"> <b>JavaScript Tip of the day</
b><br />'

//Configure the below array to hold the 31 possible tips of the month
tips[1]='Tip 1 goes here'
tips[2]='Tip 2 goes here'
tips[3]='Tip 3 goes here'
tips[4]='Tip 4 goes here'
tips[5]='Tip 5 goes here'
tips[6]='Tip 6 goes here'
tips[7]='Tip 7 goes here'
tips[8]='Tip 8 goes here'
tips[9]='Tip 9 goes here'
tips[10]='Tip 10 goes here'
tips[11]='Tip 11 goes here'
tips[12]='Tip 12 goes here'
tips[13]='Tip 13 goes here'
tips[14]='Tip 14 goes here'
tips[15]='Tip 15 goes here'
tips[16]='Tip 16 goes here'
tips[17]='Tip 17 goes here'
tips[18]='Tip 18 goes here'
tips[19]='Tip 19 goes here'
tips[20]='Tip 20 goes here'
tips[21]='Tip 21 goes here'
tips[22]='Tip 22 goes here'
tips[23]='Tip 23 goes here'
tips[24]='Tip 24 goes here'
tips[25]='Tip 25 goes here'
tips[26]='Tip 26 goes here'
tips[27]='Tip 27 goes here'
tips[28]='Tip 28 goes here'
tips[29]='Tip 29 goes here'
tips[30]='Tip 30 goes here'
tips[31]='Tip 31 goes here'

document.write(tiptitle)
document.write(tips[today_date])

//-->
</script>
```

You can also grab a copy of the code from `www.javascriptkit.com/script/script2/tipday.shtml`.

To use this free script, you must leave the comment tags (`<!--` like this `-->`) at the beginning of the code that identify the script's source location; if you remove them, you will be in breach of the author's copyright.

This script "calls" the JavaScript in the page and returns the results of the script on the page in the browser. For example, if today is the seventh day of the month, the daily tip named `tips[7]` (which is currently uncustomized and will say `"Tip 7 goes here"`) will automatically be displayed on the page when viewed in a browser.

If you're working in Dreamweaver, be sure that you add this JavaScript to the HTML code in Code view rather than paste it in Design view.

3. **In Code view, customize the title you'd like to use on your page.**

For example, to use the title Your Daily Tip, you'd change the title text between the `<strong>` tags as follows:

```
var tiptitle='<img src="../../tip.gif"> <strong>Your
Daily Tip</strong><br />'
```

Note that right before the tip title is code for an image. You can either remove that image tag or edit the code to use a custom tip graphic to appear before your tip title. For example, you might update the code look something like this:

```
var tiptitle='<img src="images/dailytip.
png"><strong>Your Daily Tip</strong><br />'
```

4. **Customize each tip between the opening and closing single quotes.**

   For example, to customize the first tip, you'd change

   ```
   tips[1]='Tip 1 goes here'
   ```

   to

   ```
   tips[1]='Be the change you want to see in the world.
       &#8212; Mahatma Gandhi'
   ```

After you've updated all the tips in your code, update the list of tips monthly.

Converting a daily tip JavaScript into an external .js file

JavaScript, like CSS, can be placed in an external JavaScript file to help to reduce the code on the web page. Using an external JavaScript files also centralizes the JavaScript into one location that an unlimited number of HTML files can access and use via a link in the HTML code to the external file, like this one:

```
<script src="dailytip.js" type="text/JavaScript"></script>
```

When multiple JavaScript files are used on a site, all the `.js` files can be housed in a single `scripts` or `js` folder at the root level of the site, which further helps keep your site tidy and organized:

```
<script src="js/dailytip.js" type="text/JavaScript"></script>
```

To convert the daily tip JavaScript into an external `.js` file, follow these steps:

1. **Cut the JavaScript code from the `<head>` of the page, paste it into a blank file, and save it with the `.js` extension at the root level (or in a folder named `js` at the root level) of the website it will be used in.**

   To keep things easy to remember and in the spirit of semantic HTML, name the external file after the function in the script. In this case, you might name the external file `dailytip.js`.

2. **Inside the new external `dailytip.js` file, delete the opening and closing `<script>` tags. Then, save the file, close it, and return to the open HTML file that will display the tip.**

   The comment tags should stay in and will not affect the functionality of the script.

3. **Between the opening and closing `<head>` tags, insert a link to the external `dailytip.js` file, like this:**

```
<head>
<script language="JavaScript" type="text/JavaScript" src="js/dailytip.
    js"></script>
<noscript>
This page includes a daily tip generated with JavaScript. To see a
    complete listing of this month's tips, visit our <a href="http://
    www.mysite.com/dailytips.html">Monthly Tips</a> page.
</noscript>
</head>
```

   To make the script more accessible, the example includes a set of `<noscript>` tags with descriptive information about what the JavaScript does and (when applicable) how visitors can access that information.

After you've updated all 31 Daily Tips in the JavaScript, and presuming that you installed the script near the first of the month, you can virtually forget about it for about 27 days or so — until it's time to change all the tips again for the following month. Keeping your site fresh keeps your visitors interested.

Daily blog entries

If your site includes a blog created with WordPress, Blogger, or Tumblr, making daily, weekly, or monthly entries is a must. In fact, the more content you make regularly available to visitors, the more visitors you will get. Entries can be as simple as a new photo with a caption, a tip of the day, or a recipe, or they can be as complex as a tutorial with screen shots, an opinion piece about a current news item, or proposed change to public policy.

You have several ways to add a blog to your website. For a refresher on working with blogs, see Book I, Chapter 1. To find out about creating a free blog with Tumblr, see *Tumblr For Dummies,* Portable Edition by Sue Jenkins.

If you use social media, you might also want to link up your blog with your Facebook and Twitter accounts, just to name a few. That way, each time you update your blog, a post will be made to your social media account with the blog's title and a link.

Making Your Pages Sharable

One of the fastest ways of growing an audience organically is to offer free content on your site that visitors will feel compelled to share with friends in their own social networks. To help make that possible, you might want to consider adding share buttons to all or at least the most important pages of your site.

ShareThis (`http://sharethis.com`) and AddThis (`www.addthis.com`) are the two most popular services you can use to help you accomplish this task. Both offer free buttons, but they're formatted differently, so check out both sites and choose the one that you think will look best with your site's design.

To illustrate how easy it is to add share buttons on a page, the following steps show you how use the free share buttons from AddThis:

1. **In your preferred HTML or web editor, open the page you would like to add the share buttons to and place your cursor in the location you'd like the buttons to appear.**

   If needed, create a layer or other container to house the share buttons.

2. **Go to the AddThis website at** `www.addthis.com` **and register for a free account.**

   Free accounts give you access to features such as e-mail reports, real-time analytics, and alerts. You can sign up via your Facebook, Twitter, Google, or OpenID account, or you can simply enter in an e-mail address and password.

   After you sign up, the page automatically redirects to the page where you can get the code for your share buttons. Along the left side of the screen are options for the type of code you'll be grabbing.

3. **Choose an option from the Get AddThis For and Style areas.**

   The Get AddThis For section lets you choose the type of site you'll be adding your code to, such as "a website" or "tumblr," whereas the Style option determines how the social media icons will appear on your pages.

   Changing these options changes the preview window as well as the code that appears on the right side of the screen.

4. **Copy the code listed in the Add to Your Site section.**

   To quickly select the code, click once inside the code box and then use your browser or keyboard shortcut to copy the selection.

5. **Switch back to your HTML/web editor and paste the copied code into the code of your page.**

   Your new free share buttons appear on the page wherever you paste them.

6. **Save your file and upload the page to your host server to view the buttons.**

   If desired, explore the AddThis site to find out more about adding additional share buttons and making other changes. Figure 8-15 shows an example of how one set of share buttons might look on a web page.

Figure 8-15: Help encourage visitors to share your site by adding free share buttons.

Chapter 9: Making Websites with Templates and Server-Side Includes

In This Chapter

- ✔ Organizing your site's assets
- ✔ Understanding the benefits of using templates
- ✔ Creating and using templates
- ✔ Working with Server-Side Includes
- ✔ Understanding site-root and document relative paths
- ✔ Comparing templates and SSIs

*A*t this stage, you've probably already designed your mock-up for the site, optimized all the graphics, and chosen how to lay out your pages using layers and tables, and you have a basic understanding about how to position and style the content with CSS. The next step you take in building your website is to create a master page from which you generate all the other pages on the site. Though each page will have different content, the general layout for every page will likely be the same, with the logo, navigation, and other elements in the same location throughout the site. Although it really doesn't matter which page you decide to use to build the site's master page, the home page is usually a good choice, unless for some reason it's drastically different in look and layout from the rest of the site.

Saving time, eliminating busywork, and leveraging browser (and ISP) caching to improve the speed of your site are three of the main reasons why you use a master page to build your site. A fourth reason has to do with managing future site updates after your site is finished. In particular, you have two site-construction solutions for the non-dynamic website that work beautifully: templates and Server-Side Includes, or simply SSIs. These tools, whether used singly or in conjunction with one another, enable you to change every page on a site simply by making the changes once to your master page or master SSI.

In this chapter, after you discover the benefits of organizing your site's assets, you find an overview about working with templates and Server-Side Includes (SSIs). Both techniques, which work in markedly different ways and are suited for different purposes, can help you make global updates to a site with the least amount of effort. In addition, this chapter shows you how to work with both methods, plus it gives you a comparison chart to assist you in determining which solution will work best for any site you happen to create.

Organizing Your Site's Assets

Before you find out about constructing your site, it's important to first consider how you'll organize all your site's assets. Assets are any HTML, CSS, JavaScript, Perl or CGI scripts, PDFs, images, media files, and any other downloadable files you'll use and include on the pages of your site.

To help with the organization of that information, keep these three key tasks in mind: following standard naming conventions, externalizing support code like CSS and JavaScript, and using folders to organize files by type. Not only does following these recommendations help ensure your files are easy to find, but they also help with search engine optimization.

Following standard naming conventions

When creating and naming your files, try to follow the current web standard naming conventions to help ensure your pages and assets display correctly:

- ✔ **Lowercase:** Use only lowercase letters for your filenames, as in `logo.gif`, `intro.swf`, or `index.html` but not `ABOUT.HTML`, `SideBar.Jpg`, or `left.PNG`.

- ✔ **Context:** Name your files after their contents or purpose, such as `bullet.png`, `orderform.pdf`, or `contact.html`, but not `page1.html`, `alp001.pdf`, or `image6.jpg`.

- ✔ **Length:** Keep your filenames short and sweet. Overly long filenames are harder for visitors to remember, so think `summer-ladies-sale.html` rather than `summer-ladies-fashion-sale-items.html`.

- ✔ **Characters:** Other than letters, numbers, dashes, and underscores (though some designers recommend against using them), do not include any spaces, periods, or other odd characters in filenames, as in `registration-2012.html` and `banner_1.png` but not `Tina.Jones#/board photo.jpg`.

- ✔ **URLs:** When naming URLs, separate keywords with dashes, as in `customer-service.html` and `mobile-first.html`.

✔ **Leading zeros:** If you need to create numbered files, be sure to include a leading zero for all numbers under 10. This makes your leading zero fall first in an alphabetical list, such as `01cards.html`, `02cards.html`, and so on.

✔ **Keywords:** If it makes sense to include them, use keywords in your filenames that help visitors find your content, as in `design-services.html` and `golden-gate-bridge.jpg`.

✔ **File extensions:** Be sure to use the correct file extensions. Acceptable HTML files extensions include `.html`, `.htm`, `.shtml`, `.shtm`, `.asp`, and `.php`. Graphics for the web can be `.jpg`, `.png`, and `.gif`. CSS files end with `.css`, and JavaScript files end with `.js`.

Externalizing support code

A major part of the evolution of the web began with the development of external CSS to help separate HTML markup from the styling and positioning information contained in the CSS code. Similarly, JavaScript code that was often contained within the HTML file is now often stored outside the HTML in one or more separate linked files.

Shifting from inside to outside the web page is "externalizing" the code. Not only do externalized CSS and JavaScript files make your pages smaller in file size, but they also help you keep all your site files organized and often make your pages load faster in a browser window, and that's good for search engine optimization (SEO). See Book V, Chapter 2 for more information on SEO.

Using folders to organize by type

If your website offers products or services, or happens to have any deep submenus under any of the main navigation categories, consider creating special directories (folders) in your site structure to group similar assets. This will allow you to place all the relevant files for a particular topic into a single folder, which also makes those assets easy to find and easy to manage.

For example, your `images` folder is the place where you'll put all your images. However, if, in addition to all the images used to create the look of your site you also have one set of images for customer logos, another for photos of your products, and yet another for pictures of board members, you might want to create separate subfolders inside your `images` folder for each of those categories:

`/images` (for regular site images)

`/images/client-logos` (for client logos)

`/images/board-members` (for photos of board members)

Create directories (and subdirectories) for any of the following site assets:

- ✔ Images
- ✔ Downloadable files (such as PDFs, DOCs, and so on)
- ✔ CSS files
- ✔ JavaScript files
- ✔ Media files like Flash animations, videos, and MP3s
- ✔ Server-Side Include (SSI) files
- ✔ Web fonts
- ✔ Any other files that need to be organized by type

In addition to these categories, you may also want to create directories for any HTML files sharing a topic. For example, you might want to make a directory called members to house any pages related to membership benefits. Another example would be to create subdirectories for all products within a particular category, such as t-shirts, hats, and shoes.

When you do make subdirectories for HTML files, name the main file in each folder index.html. This technique allows visitors to access that directory by typing only the domain and directory without the filename itself, such as http://www.nobledesktop.com/seminars/, which is the equivalent of http://www.nobledesktop.com/seminars/index.html.

Comparing Templates and SSIs

Both Dreamweaver templates and SSIs are great solutions to building sites that need regular updating, and they each have different benefits and drawbacks. Templates are good for smaller sites managed by only one or two people, whereas SSIs are good for large sites that may be making regular updates to certain pages. For instance, if you're building a 5–10-page site, templates would be the logical choice. On the other hand, if your site will have 30 or more pages or might be managed by more than one person, SSIs may be the better choice.

Choosing which method to use to build your site can be accomplished by answering a few questions about the site's size, functionality, server type, and future management plans. If you're unsure whether to use templates or SSIs on your site, use the suggestions in Table 9-1 to help you decide.

Table 9-1	Building Websites: Templates versus SSIs	
Use Templates If . . .	*Use SSIs If . . .*
The site is small (under 30 pages).	The site is large (over 30 pages).
The site will be managed by only one or two people.	The site will be managed by three or more people.
Site updates will be made on a regular or semi-regular basis.	The site will require regular or frequent global and partial updates.
Any time changes are made to the template, all the updated template-based pages must be uploaded to the site's server before visitors can see those changes.	Any time changes are made to any SSI files, only those updated SSI files need to be uploaded to the site's server before visitors can see the changes.

Keep in mind that these two options are best for regular, non-blog websites. If you think you'll be adding a lot of new content to your site and would like that content to be archived and always accessible to site visitors, you may want to build your site with a Content Management System (CMS) such as WordPress, Joomla, or Drupal. These systems use their own form of templates and have the added benefit of a built-in database.

Building the Master Page

Building a master page to start your website construction process can help you set the structure of your pages, validate and refine the code, and ensure that all the remaining files are built upon a solid foundation. To build this master page, you should have certain tools at your disposal, such as a good web editing program like Adobe Dreamweaver, a vector program such as Adobe Illustrator, and a photo-editing program such as Adobe Photoshop, so that starting a new page with the master requires the least amount of redundant work. You also want a master file that enables you to quickly and efficiently make updates to the pages at a later time. You might not think you need to consider site updates until after you build the site, but in fact the projected frequency of the updates can be a major determinant for how you create the site's pages from the start. For example, small sites might be better served by using templates, whereas larger sites may be easier to update by using SSIs.

Though most designers create the master page from the home page, you needn't follow that convention. Just remember that whichever page you do choose to develop as the master, it includes all the features that are common to all pages on the site. For instance, if a navigation bar appears across the top of the layout and a set of footer links appears across the bottom of the pages, the code for these elements won't need to be rebuilt for each of the remaining pages on the site. For that matter, even copying and pasting the code from one page to another is too much work.

The two most effective ways for creating a master site page and building your site are templates and SSIs, which are described in the remaining sections of this chapter. Both methods enable you to make sitewide changes to your pages quickly and efficiently.

When you build a master page from the site's home page, an added benefit is that it can provide your clients with a peek into the site-building process and get them even more excited about seeing the finished product. It also gives them an opportunity to review a sample HTML page for layout accuracy and functionality. That way, should the client raise any issues regarding the layout or navigation, you can correct those concerns before generating any of the other pages on the site.

Building Websites with Templates

If you're using a code editor such as Adobe Dreamweaver or Microsoft Expression Web, your application probably contains some kind of system for creating and using templates. A template establishes visual consistency between the pages. It also significantly reduces the time it takes to build the rest of the pages on the site and make changes to those pages anytime the site needs global modifications, both during the site-building process and for any post-launch site maintenance.

Templates are a great solution for most small- to medium-sized websites (under about 30 pages) that use little to no dynamic capabilities because template-based pages can be updated by the code editing application rather quickly with minimal effort on the part of the designer.

After you create the template file, you can specify which areas on that master page will be editable in any *template-based pages*. For example, you might want to create an editable area for the main content on the page and another area for the sidebar content. With the editable areas established, anytime a new template-based page is created, only the content in those editable areas can be altered, whereas the rest of the content is locked down and remains uneditable.

In the following sections, you find out how to create Dreamweaver templates, set up editable regions, and create and manage template-based files. If you're using another code editor, you should be able to easily adapt the examples found here to build your site using your program's template solution.

Using Dreamweaver templates

The true beauty of a template-based web design is that, should any part of the locked, uneditable part of the template need altering (like a navigation button that is no longer needed on the site or sidebar content that needs to be added in), rather than having to individually update all the pages, only the template would need adjustment. The code editor then automatically updates the changed, locked code on all the template-based pages.

Although most sites have only one master template, you're free to create as many templates for a site as you need to; there is no limit to the number or complexity of the templates you create for each web project. Templates can have more than editable regions, too. Designers working with Dreamweaver can create nested templates, optional editable regions, and repeating regions within the template:

- ✔ **Nested templates:** These special templates are created by embedding a template inside another template, such as when one section of the site uses a special layout that requires its own set of editable regions and that layout falls within the editable area of the parent template, as with a product details page on an e-commerce site.

- ✔ **Optional editable regions:** An editable region is an area you specify on a template that can be shown or hidden in a template-based page, such as a link back to the top of a page on pages with lots of content. You set the default visibility of the editable region for when the page opens in a browser. These regions are editable through the template-based page.

- ✔ **Repeating regions:** This type of editable region in a template can be used to create areas that need to be repeated on a template-based page, such as `<div>` layers on a sidebar, items in a list, or an entire table row. Repeating regions are not typically editable unless you add editable regions to them. For instance, you can create a repeating table row and then add a set of editable regions within each table cell.

TIP

Another really useful aspect of working with Dreamweaver's templates is the fact that you can integrate them with Adobe Contribute software. You can manage sites built with Dreamweaver templates through Dreamweaver, whereas the site owner can modify the editable regions of that site without needing to know anything about web design. Contribute is extremely easy to learn and use and puts the client in control of some of his or her site's editability. To find out more about Adobe Contribute, visit www.adobe. com/products/contribute.html.

This chapter only skims the surface of the amazing things you can do with Dreamweaver templates. As your skills grow, you can experiment more with advanced techniques, such as nested templates and so on. To discover everything there is to know about working with Dreamweaver templates as well as how to create a Dreamweaver site and manage it with Contribute, try my book *Dreamweaver CS5 All-in-One For Dummies*.

Preparing a page to become a template

You can build a Dreamweaver template in two ways. You can build templates from scratch with a blank HTML template page, or you can convert any existing HTML/HTML5/XHTML page into a Dreamweaver template by choosing File⇨Save as Template.

Because you're new to web design and presumably new to Dreamweaver too, building a sample page in HTML, HTML5, or XHTML first and then converting it into a template file will probably make more sense than building a template file. Furthermore, by creating the HTML file first, you will have a chance to work out any kinks in the HTML, CSS, and any other type of code and script you're using in the document before it becomes the master template you use to create all the other pages on your site.

To prepare your page for becoming a Dreamweaver template, follow these steps:

1. **Create a new folder on your desktop (`TemplateDemo`, for example), create a managed site pointing to this folder, and place an empty folder named `images` at the root level of the managed site.**

   Managing a site provides access to Dreamweaver's advanced site-management features, and you must perform this step when working with templates so that Dreamweaver can appropriately write code to manage template-based file updates.

   To create a managed site, choose Site⇨New Site, and in the Local Site Folder field, browse to and select the folder (`TemplateDemo`) you just created on your desktop.

2. **Create a new blank HTML, HTML5, or XHTML page with the desired DTD (Document Type Definition) and save the file with any name you like, such as `master.html`, at the root level of your managed site.**

3. **Build the sample page. Set up the layout using `<div>` tags and CSS. Add the content and insert graphics with `alt` text attributes. Create hyperlinks and add footer links at the bottom of the page.**

4. **Style and position all the content with CSS.**

   See Book III, Chapter 3 for the lowdown on CSS.

5. **Insert `<meta>` tags in the `<head>` of the code and any of the other accessibility attributes to the code you can think of to make the page as accessible as possible.**

6. **Add dynamic functionality to your page where desired, such as linking to a database or adding JavaScript and jQuery modules.**

   See Book III, Chapter 8 for more on making your site interactive.

7. **Externalize any CSS and JavaScript.**

   Centralizing CSS and JavaScript code into linked external files helps your pages load faster, as well as help you keep your assets organized.

8. **Run a spell check, read through the code looking for errors, and make corrections where necessary.**

9. **Test the page in as many browsers and browser versions as possible on Mac, PC, and Linux platforms and on any other devices you can test, including smartphones and tablets. Fix anything that needs fixing.**

   Also be sure to test for code accuracy using Dreamweaver's Validation and Browser Compatibility reports in the Results panel. If desired, validate the page using an online validator like the one at http://validator.w3.org.

10. **When the page looks good and functions acceptably on every browser and device, and you are happy with the results, show the page to your client to get feedback and input.**

    If the site is for yourself instead of a client, show it to family or friends for a second opinion. Getting help at this stage is much smarter than waiting until after the site is live on the Internet.

11. **Make any adjustments to the site's code and content if needed and get the client's approval again, in writing, before you build more pages.**

The reason it says "get the client's approval again, in writing" is that clients may sometimes have "brilliant ideas" at this stage. They might think of another page to squeeze into the navigation, want to move something over (even though they've already seen the design and approved it), or add a whole new section to the layout. If your contract states that no modifications can be made at this stage without an addendum to the contract (and it should!), remind your client of this clause and tell him you'd be delighted to make any changes he'd like for an additional fee. If the client is serious about the change, he'll agree to the addendum. But if his brilliant idea was just whimsy or, more often than not, just a natural inclination to want to feel like he's a part of this process, he'll change his mind about wanting to make any modifications to the design and give you his signed approval to continue.

Creating a Dreamweaver template

When you and your client are fully confident in the layout and styling of your sample web page, you're ready to convert that page into a Dreamweaver template. Use your own file if you have one prepared, or use the sample file called `createtemplate.html`, which you can find at this book's web page (as described in the Introduction).

Follow these steps to convert an HTML, HTML5, or XHTML file into a Dreamweaver template:

1. **Using the `master.html` sample web page you created in the previous steps, open the file in Dreamweaver's workspace, choose File⇨Save as Template.**

   The Save As Template dialog box opens, as shown in Figure 9-1.The name of your managed site (Template Demo, for example) should appear in the Site drop-down menu.

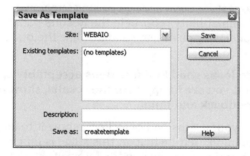

Figure 9-1: Use the Save As Template dialog box to save your file as a template.

   If you've defined a site but that site name isn't showing on the drop-down menu, click the menu's down arrow to select the name of the site for this project.

   Unless you or someone else has already created a template for this managed site, the Existing Templates field should be empty with the message `(no templates)` displayed inside it.

2. **(Optional) In the Description text field, type a short description for the template you're about to create.**

   This description can be a word or sentence that describes the web project or a short phrase about what this template will be used for.

   For example, if the template is for a photographer's portfolio website, the description might read something like **SmoothPortraits.com**. If you're using the example page, you might enter **Springfield** or **Template Demo**.

3. **In the Save As field, enter a filename for the template.**

   A good naming convention for templates is to use the client's name or something similar. For instance, if the client's company is called Home Design Consultation, you might name the template **homedesign** or **HDC**.

4. **Click the Save button to keep your template settings, and when the Update Links dialog box appears, as shown in Figure 9-2, be sure to click the Yes button, as clicking No will break all the links.**

   After you click Yes, Dreamweaver converts the HTML file into a template with the `.dwt` file extension. At the same time the template is being created, Dreamweaver also creates a new `Templates` folder in the root directory of the managed site and saves your new template file inside it. Any additional template files you create will also be stored in this `Templates` folder.

Figure 9-2: Click the Yes button when the Update Links dialog box appears.

Take a moment to examine in more detail why you clicked Yes instead of No. Clicking the Yes button in the Update Links dialog box allows Dreamweaver to automatically update links to graphics and other files within your HTML file with the appropriate document relative path syntax (which you find out about in the later section "Editing Paths to Work with SSIs") to match the new location of the template file inside the `Templates` folder. Saying Yes ensures that any template-based files created from the template will use accurately syntaxed paths.

For example, a link to `about.html` in the original HTML file will be updated to `../about.html` inside the new template file. Likewise, a link to an image such as `<img src="images/snowman.jpg">` would be changed to `<img src="../images/snowman.jpg">`. The dot-dot-slash (`../`) before the link location tells a browser to go up a level in the server's directory to find the specified file.

If you accidentally click the No button in the Update Links dialog box, the links in the template won't function properly. Should that happen, close the new template file, delete it from the new `Templates` folder, and begin again at Step 1. Then make sure you click the Yes button when the Update Links dialog box appears again.

Creating templates with editable regions

By default, the entire Dreamweaver template is locked, which means that any pages generated from it at this point can't be edited unless you want to make global changes to all the pages by editing the template itself or unless you specify one or more editable regions. Editable regions define areas within the template-based pages that you can edit.

Follow the next steps to create an editable region in the template:

1. **With the template file open in the Dreamweaver workspace, place your insertion point inside the document, preferably in Design view, and select all the text in the main content area of the page.**

   If you're using the `createtemplate.html` file (which you may have downloaded while completing the "Creating a Dreamweaver template" section earlier in this chapter), select the contents in the left main area below the banner. If you're using your own template file, select a region within the file that you would like to be editable in your template-based pages.

   The selected content will define the first area on the template that will be converted into an editable region in any template-based files.

2. **Choose Insert⇨Template Objects⇨Editable Region. When the New Editable Region dialog box appears, enter a name to identify the region, such as** Main**, and click OK.**

   The editable region name, as shown in Figure 9-3, identifies the region inside the template as well as inside any template-based pages you create from it. Editable regions have a blue tab and outline to visually separate them from the rest of the content.

3. **Select the next area in your document that you'd like to convert to an editable region by selecting content, choosing Insert⇨Template Objects⇨Editable Region, and giving each new region a unique name.**

   Templates may contain an unlimited number of editable regions, but editable regions may not be nested inside other editable regions.

4. **Save and close the template file.**

   You find out how to create a template-based page in the next section of this chapter.

5. **To modify the template at any time, and thereby update any locked areas in any template-based files, reopen the template file, make the changes to the code, and save the page.**

Upon saving any changes to a template, Dreamweaver asks whether you want to automatically update all the template-based pages. As long as you're in a managed Dreamweaver site and you say Yes, Dreamweaver will handle rewriting all the changed code to any template-based file within that managed site. That's pretty remarkable and a huge time-saver for you!

An editable region

Figure 9-3: Editable regions display with a blue, named tab and an outline.

All Dreamweaver template files contain special template comment tags that identify the beginning and end of each editable region within the file. *Do not* modify these comment tags; without them, Dreamweaver cannot understand how and where to make global modifications to template-based page code. Here's an example of what these special comment tags might look like in your template file:

```
<!-- TemplateBeginEditable name="Main" -->
<h2><a href="#" title="Heading Title">Heading here</a></h2>
<h3>Subheading here</h3>
<p>Lorem ipsum dolor sit amet, consectetuer adipiscing elit,
   sed diam nonummy nibh euismod tincidunt ut laoreet dolore
   magna aliquam erat volutpat...</p>
<!-- TemplateEndEditable -->
```

In addition to the beginnings and endings of editable regions, Dreamweaver templates also include an editable area in the `<head>` of the HTML code, which can be used for inserting JavaScript, CSS, and other `<head>` area elements that need to be placed inside the head of a template-based file. These tags have the `name` attribute of `head`:

```
<!-- TemplateBeginEditable name="head" -->
...
<!-- TemplateEndEditable -->
```

As with the editable region comment tags, *do not* modify these `<head>` comment tags either. They're used to help you manage site content.

Creating and editing template-based files

Template-based files are easy to create and use because the pages behave just like any other HTML page except that they have locked-down, uneditable regions that are controlled by the template.

To create a template-based page in Dreamweaver, follow these steps:

1. **Choose File⇨New to open the New Document dialog box, click the Page from Template category, select the name of your managed site from the Site listing, and select a template from the list of available templates for that site.**

   A preview of the selected template appears in the Preview panel, as shown in Figure 9-4.

Figure 9-4: Create a new template-based document from your existing template with the New Document dialog box.

2. **Click the Create button to open a new, untitled, template-based page in the Dreamweaver workspace window.**

3. **Choose File➪Save to save the new template-based file with a filename and extension of your choice (like `index.html` for the home page or `services.html` for a Services page) to the same managed site.**

   For best results, save the untitled file before you begin adding content to the editable regions.

   The editable regions in the template-based file are outlined in blue and display a blue tab with the region name at the upper-left corner of each editable area. Uneditable regions will be inaccessible (neither clickable nor selectable) both in Design view and in Code view.

4. **Edit the content as needed in the editable regions of the template-based file.**

   Add text, create hyperlinks, and insert images, layers, tables, and other content. Style your content with CSS and add any behaviors or other dynamic features to enhance the page.

5. **Choose File➪Save to save your template-based page after making changes.**

6. **Repeat Steps 1–3 to create additional template-based files.**

   You may also create additional template-based files by taking an existing template-based file by choosing File➪Save As to create a duplicate copy of that file with a new filename.

Working with Server-Side Includes (SSIs)

Another way to manage sites — which may be a better solution than using Dreamweaver templates for larger sites, sites that use programming to control dynamic content, and sites that will need frequent updating — involves using a process called Server-Side Includes (SSIs).

Understanding what SSIs are

Unlike templates, which hard-code all the pages on a site and require you to set editable regions for template-based pages, SSIs break web pages into components, kind of like pieces of a puzzle that are joined together. To assemble the whole page, you pair the main page content, which is unique to the individual page, with the different SSI pieces, which will be the same on every page throughout the site:

✔ The main page contains the general HTML structure and perhaps a few layout elements on the page that never change.

✔ The pieces, composed of HTML, are actually external HTML files that are plugged into the main page with a single line of code where the content should appear.

When the pieces are assembled, the browser that displays the page seamlessly integrates any SSI content with the main content by grabbing the information inside the SSI files from the server and displaying that content as if it were hard-coded into the main page.

SSI files are best for repeating page elements like headers, navigation bars, and footer links, as well as other components or content on pages that require frequent updating, such as sponsor listings and promotions. SSI files can be composed of text, graphics, JavaScript, Flash movies, and anything else that might go on a regular web page. In fact, the only HTML code the SSI files shouldn't contain are the "bones" of the web page, namely the `<html>`, `<head>`, `<meta>`, `<title>`, and `<body>` tags. SSI files do not need those structural code elements because those tags are already provided by the main HTML page where the SSI content is included.

Including an SSI file inside a page

Say, for example, that you have decided to put a site's footer content into an SSI file called `footer.html` partially because it is a repeating element on every page and partially because you know the site will be growing and the footer's navigation links will need updating before too long. That `footer.html` page might include links to all the current main pages on the site, some descriptive text, a link to an RSS feed, follow links to social media sites such as Facebook and Twitter, and copyright information, as shown in Figure 9-5.

Figure 9-5: SSI content, such as this footer area, can include anything found elsewhere on a site, including text, hyperlinks, and images.

To include the `footer.html` SSI file's content inside another page, you must add a special `include` link to your page in the location the SSI's content should be displayed. The link uses comment tags to identify the link as an SSI and contains the filename and path to the external SSI file, as in the following code example where the `footer.html` file is located inside a folder named `includes`:

```
<!--#include file="includes/footer.html"-->
```

By using that same `include` link, presumably in the same location on every page, you can include the `footer.html` SSI content on as many pages of a site as desired. And because the content is pulled from the SSI file and displayed within the page by the browser on the fly as the visitor views the page, the visitor can't tell the difference between actual hard-coded content and content *parsed* in an SSI file. In fact, if visitors were to view the source code of a page that had an SSI link inside it, they wouldn't see the `include` link tag in the code; instead, they would see the actual content from the SSI file, in-line with the rest of the code, as if you had written the page without SSIs. The server and the browser do all the work to ensure that visitors see the parsed SSI content presented seamlessly as part of the page in the browser.

Parsing, by the way, refers to the browser's ability to extract information from one file and apply it to another file. With regard to SSIs, the parsing process involves the browser requesting information from the server and then embedding the returned data into the page that displays in the browser at the specified location in the code.

After you've inserted the SSI `include` link on a page, nothing else needs to be done with the page to ensure that content displays in the specified location. Later, when the SSI content needs updating (such as updating the year in the copyright or adding a new button to a navigation bar), the only file you'll need to edit and re-upload to the remote server hosting the site is the external HTML SSI file (in this example, `footer.html`). After the updated SSI file has been uploaded to the server, all the pages on the site that use that `include` will automatically display the updated version of the external SSI file's content.

You can use as many SSI files as you like to construct the pages on your site. For instance, you might use one for the header, one for the footer, and another for the sidebar.

Editing an SSI file

Editing an SSI file is just like making changes to any other HTML file. Simply open the SSI file in your favorite HTML code editor, as illustrated in Figure 9-6, make the changes, and save the file. As long as you remember to upload the updated version of the SSI file to the remote host server, the changes will automatically appear on any page that includes a link to that particular SSI file.

**Book III
Chapter 9**

**Making Websites
with Templates and
Server-Side Includes**

Figure 9-6: SSI files can be updated in an HTML editor just like regular HTML files.

Ensuring success with SSIs

Although SSIs might seem like a perfect solution for creating easily updatable websites, you need to do a few things beforehand to ensure that you can use them successfully:

- ✔ **The remote host server must be capable of parsing the SSI data.** Before you do any work with SSIs, contact your host provider or system administrator to find out whether the host server is capable of this function. Some servers can do the work but must have special software installed to do it, but others simply can't be configured to perform the task.

- ✔ **The extension on files including any SSIs may need to be changed from `.html` to `.shtml`.** This means that visitors trying to reach a particular page, such as www.*yoursite*.com/contact.shtml, won't be able to access that page if they directly type in the address as **www.*yoursite*.com/contact.html**, unless your host provider offers some kind of redirect feature to ensure visitors will reach the correct page regardless of extension. You can usually find out if this is possible by asking your host provider.

- ✔ **The SSI link code must be accurate.** The link to the SSI file can contain a couple different variables. If these variables are incorrect, the server hosting the pages won't be able to understand how to parse the data contained in the SSI file. The syntax of an SSI link is also slightly peculiar and must be accurate to ensure that the browser parses the SSI file.

- ✔ **You must alter the paths to any links and graphics inside the SSI file.** SSI files require *site-root relative paths* to function properly. You find out how to do that in the next section.

- ✔ **Files that require parsing place greater demands on the server, which can translate into slightly longer page download times.** The delay might be only a fraction of a second longer, but it's there and in some cases might be very noticeable. Any perceived delay could affect visitor loyalty.

If your server can handle SSIs and you determine that this is the right solution for you, read on to find out how to create, insert, and test your SSI files.

Creating, Including, and Testing SSIs

After you've ensured that your host server can process SSIs, find out whether you'll need to change the file extension on pages *that contain* SSIs (not the SSI include files). The host provider should be able to tell you the answer, yes or no:

  ✔ **Yes:** If yes, the change would require you to add an *s* before the normal file extension, such as changing `index.html` to `index.shtml` (or from `index.htm` to `index.shtm`). The *s* in front of the `.html` or `.htm` extension tells the server that SSIs are included in the file and that the server needs to do a little extra work to parse the included SSI content.

  ✔ **No:** If no, that's great news, meaning you may use the regular `.html` or `.htm` extensions for all your files, including those containing SSIs.

After that's sorted out, your next step is to ensure that the SSI include link code within the body of your page is accurate. Depending on the host server's type, you'll use either the word *file* or the word *virtual* in the SSI link, as in the following examples:

```
<!--#include file="footer.html"-->
<!--#include virtual="footer.html"-->
```

Notice how the include link begins and ends with comment tags. Pay particular attention to the lack of space between the opening comment tag, the hashtag, and the word *include*. This entire SSI include link must be typed accurately for the server to provide the data to the browser when the page is viewed in the browser.

The name of your SSI file can be anything you like, but in keeping with the goal of semantic HTML, try to name your SSI files after the function they serve or the content they contain, such as `header.html` or `copyright.html`. When saving your SSIs, you can save them to any location on the host server as long as that path is referenced in the link to it. For instance, the SSI can reside at the root level of your site, or if you plan on having multiple include files, they can all be stored in a folder called `ssi`, `inc`, or `includes`, as in the following example:

```
<!--#include file="ssi/footer.html"-->
```

If your SSIs reside in a folder on a completely different URL on a different server, just be sure to specify the full path to the SSI file:

```
<!--#include file="http://www.mysite.com/ssi/footer.html"-->
```

The last step to using SSIs successfully is to update any paths to graphics or other files in the HTML of the SSI `include` files from *document relative* to *site-root relative*. In other words, any hypertext links or references to objects or images that appear on the page must use the site-root relative paths. You find out how to do this in the "Editing Paths to Work with SSIs" section, later in this chapter.

In the following steps, you convert part of a web page — the footer — into an external SSI and then include that external SSI back into the page it was removed from:

1. **Open a completed HTML file in your favorite HTML editor.**

   If you need a sample file to work with, use the `createssi.html` file, which you can download from this book's web page (as described in the introduction). This page contains a header with a graphic, a navigation bar styled with CSS, a page heading and subheading, body text, a sidebar, and a footer.

2. **With your cursor in the code, select and cut all the footer content, from the opening `<p>` tag below the `<div>` tag with the `id` of `footer` to the closing `</p>` tag right before the closing footer `<div>` tag, as shown in Figure 9-7.**

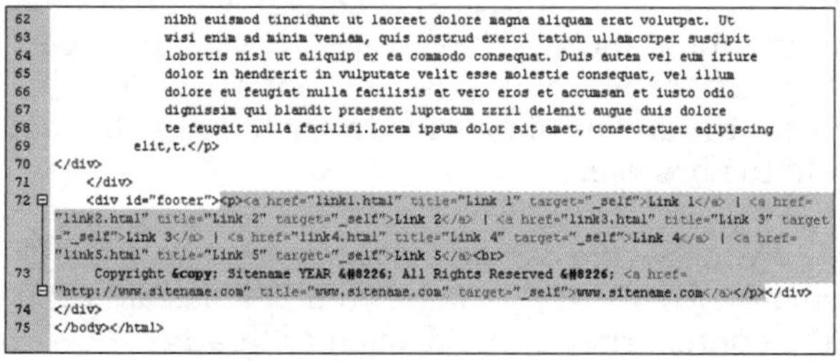

Figure 9-7: An SSI can be created from existing content within an HTML page.

If you are using the `createssi.html` file, the footer code you select and cut from the page should look like this:

```
<p><a href="link1.html" title="Link 1" target="_self">Link 1</a> | <a
    href="link2.html" title="Link 2" target="_self">Link 2</a> | <a
    href="link3.html" title="Link 3" target="_self">Link 3</a> | <a
    href="link4.html" title="Link 4" target="_self">Link 4</a> | <a
    href="link5.html" title="Link 5" target="_self">Link 5</a><br>
Copyright &copy; Sitename YEAR &#8226; All Rights Reserved &#8226; <a
    href="http://www.sitename.com" title="www.sitename.com" target="_
    self">www.sitename.com</a></p>
```

After you select and cut the code from the page, the only tags remaining in that part of the code should be the opening and closing `<div>` tags for the footer.

The cursor should now be flashing in the code in the space between the footer `<div>` tags. Leave your cursor there.

3. **Open a blank HTML file and delete all the HTML code that your code editor might have automatically placed in the file, such as the `<dtd>`, `<html>`, `<head>`, `<meta>`, `<title>`, and `<body>` tags.**

The document should be completely blank, with no HTML tags, markup, or other content inside it.

4. **Place your cursor at the top of the blank file's Code view and paste the footer content you just cut from your original file (createssi.html, for example).**

The pasted code should be exactly the same as what you cut from the other file, as shown in the code example. If the code has any extra line spaces, remove them. Figure 9-8 shows how the code should look in your new file, with none of the structural HTML tags.

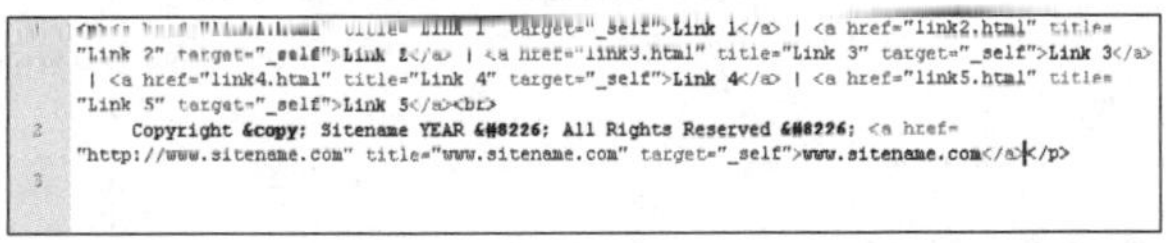

Figure 9-8: The web content saved in an SSI file doesn't need to be surrounded by any structural HTML tags.

5. **Create a new folder at the root level of your project folder called ssi and save this new file with the pasted code as footer.html. Then close the footer.html file.**

The root level of the project folder you're working in should now contain three items: the original file (createssi.html, for example), a folder called ssi, the new footer.html file inside the new ssi folder.

6. **Back in the original file, between the footer <div> tags where you previously cut the code, type the include link to the new external SSI file inside the new ssi folder:**

```
<div id="footer">
<!--#include file="ssi/footer.html" -->
</div>
```

Dreamweaver users can use the Insert⇨Server-Side Include command to select the SSI file and have the link automatically inserted in the code. Upon adding the code, you may even suddenly see the SSI content magically appear in Design view, in-line with the rest of the page content, while still seeing the include link only in Code view, like in the example shown in Figure 9-9.

Note that the word *file* is used here as the type of SSI in the include link. In some servers, the SSI won't appear unless you change the type to *virtual*. Either way, you have a 50/50 chance of being right the first time, so if *file* doesn't make the SSI appear on the page when viewed in a browser and the server is SSI capable, *virtual* should do the trick.

**Book III
Chapter 9**

Making Websites with Templates and Server-Side Includes

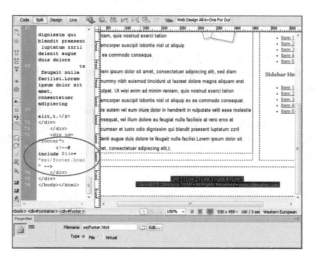

Figure 9-9: Dreamweaver users can see the include link in the code while viewing the parsed content in Design view.

7. Save the page and preview it in a browser to see the results.

The SSI content should appear at the bottom of the page, just as it would in a regular HTML file.

Dreamweaver users who don't see the SSI content in their browsers may need to enable the Preview Using Temporary File option in the Preview in Browser category of the Preferences panel. Non-Dreamweaver users need to upload the sample files to a live server that can parse SSI files to see the SSI in action.

If you still can't see the SSI file, be sure to also test whether the file extension needs to be altered. To get the test file working, you might need to change the file extension on the page that has the SSI link in it from .html to .shtml. You might even need to modify the include type attribute from file to virtual.

If you do see the SSI file on your page, you're about 90 percent finished with the SSI configuration. To make your SSIs fully functional, you must ensure that any links inside the SSI file use site-root relative paths. In the later section "Adjusting paths in an SSI file from document relative to site-root relative," you modify the paths to work properly and test them in a continuation of the preceding steps.

Editing Paths to Work with SSIs

In web design, two types of paths can be used in HTML when referring to files, graphics, and other assets: document relative paths and site-root relative paths. On most websites, you use document relative paths, which have been used thus far in this book. For SSIs to work, however, the paths inside any external SSI files must be changed to site-root relative paths.

The following sections explain more about the two path types and show you how to adjust the paths in an SSI file from document relative to site-root relative.

Understanding the different path types

The following two sections outline the major differences between document relative and site-root relative paths.

Document relative paths

Document relative paths are the default type of path system in web pages. With document relative paths, the path code is always relative from starting point A to destination point B, and the full URL is generally omitted from the path reference. For example, a document relative path from the home page to a subpage of a Contact Us section called Directions might look like the following code example, where the href specifies a file called directions. html that sits inside a folder named contact that resides at the root level of the website's server:

```
<a href="contact/directions.html"><img src="images/arrow.gif">Directions</a>
```

Because the Directions page sits in a directory (folder) called contact, both the directory and filename must be declared in the path. If you were to turn the path into a sentence, you might read it as, "Starting from here, go to the contact folder and open the page called directions.html." When that page is displaying in the browser window, a link on that page back to the home page would need a path that tells the server how to get to the home page from its present location by using the ../ syntax before the filename, which tells the browser to look for the named file "one level before" the current level on the server:

```
<a href="../index.html"><img src="../images/arrow.gif">Home</a>
```

**Book III
Chapter 9**

**Making Websites
with Templates and
Server-Side Includes**

Site-root relative paths

Site-root relative paths require a little bit more code to tell the server to always look for the named file or object relative to the site's root. To do that, you add a slash before any link or sourced object. If you were to turn a site-root relative path into a sentence, you might read it as, "Starting always from the root level of the site, go to the contact folder and open the page called directions.html." Likewise, to display an arrow graphic, you might say that the path tells the browser to start at the root level, look for a folder called images, and display a graphic inside that folder called arrow.gif, as in the following:

```
<a href="/contact/directions.html"><img src="/images/arrow.gif">Directions</a>
```

Furthermore, when you open the Directions page, the path back to the home page from the directions.html page would look like this:

```
<a href="/index.html"><img src="/images/arrow.gif">Home</a>
```

The path to the image stays the same because in site-root relative lingo, it always tells the server to start at the root level, look for the images folder, and then find and display the named graphic.

In the case of the footer.html SSI example in the earlier section "Creating, Including, and Testing SSIs," all the links in the SSI file to the main navigation pages would need to use site-root relative paths for the server to parse the included data properly on all the pages of the site.

A good analogy to help you remember the difference between document relative and site-root relative paths is to think about giving directions. Document relative directions would tell you how to get to New York City from your current location, wherever in the world you might be. Site-root relative linking, by contrast, gives you directions to New York City, or any other destination for that matter, always starting from the same place in Los Angeles.

Adjusting paths in an SSI file from document relative to site-root relative

To adjust the paths in an external SSI file from document relative to site-root relative, follow these steps:

1. **Open the SSI file that you created in the earlier section "Creating, Including, and Testing SSIs" (ssi/footer.html) in your favorite HTML editor.**

   The footer file contains text and a handful of hyperlinks to other pages. As you can see in the code, each hyperlink lists just the filename and file extension, such as link1.html.

2. **In Code view, insert a slash before each linked filename in the document, as in `<a href="/link1.html">`. When you finish, save and close the file.**

Adding the slash makes the path to each of the hyperlinks site-root relative so that the server and browser can properly parse the SSI file data.

This file doesn't contain any graphics, and because you'd also need to modify the paths to graphics where they are part of the SSI code, in the next steps you add a graphic to the footer and then modify the path to be site-root relative.

3. **In the code of the `footer.html` file (directly before the word `Copyright`, for example), place your cursor where you want to insert a graphic. Then insert the graphic of your choice.**

For example, if you were to insert the graphic called `bluearrow.gif` located inside an `images` folder at the root level of your site, your code would look something like this:

```
<p><a href="/link1.html" title="Link 1" target="_self">Link 1</a> | <a
    href="/link2.html" title="Link 2" target="_self">Link 2</a> | <a
    href="/link3.html" title="Link 3" target="_self">Link 3</a> | <a
    href="/link4.html" title="Link 4" target="_self">Link 4</a> | <a
    href="/link5.html" title="Link 5" target="_self">Link 5</a><br />

<img src="../images/bluearrow.gif" width="20" height="20" alt=""
    />Copyright &copy; Sitename YEAR All Rights Reserved </p>
```

Normally, an image like this, which is located in an `images` folder, would use the default document relative path with the `../` before the folder name for the source of the image. However, because this image is now inside an external SSI file, the path must be converted to one that is site-root relative.

4. **Edit the path to the image from document to site-root relative by removing the `../` syntax and inserting a single slash before the `images` folder name instead:**

```
<img src="/images/bluearrow.gif" width="20" height="20" alt="" />
```

A lot of people forget about this step when creating SSI files; however, it is easy to remedy if you do happen to forget. In fact, as long as you're testing the page prior to publishing, you can catch any forgotten paths to graphics during your testing phase. The same goes for regular hyperlinks: Although the links themselves might look normal in the browser, when clicked, their paths won't bring a visitor to the correct page until you convert the paths into site-root relative paths.

To help you remember all the different things that must be done to ensure that your pages using SSI will parse correctly when displayed in a browser, here's a list of questions you can ask yourself when working with SSIs:

**Book III
Chapter 9**

Making Websites with Templates and Server-Side Includes

✔ Can the site's host server handle SSIs?

✔ Does the SSI link specify the proper type, *file* or *virtual,* for the host server?

✔ Are all the SSI include code links properly syntaxed?

✔ Do I need to change file extensions on pages containing SSI links from `.html` to `.shtml`?

✔ Are all the paths to documents and images in the external SSI file site-root relative?

As long as you can remember to check all these things, you should be able to use SSIs to construct your websites.

Book IV

Web Standards and Testing

The 5th Wave   By Rich Tennant

MIDTOWN

WHERE'S THE DANG DOOR?!

WebSite DESIGN Co.

C'mon in!

OUR AWARDS

*F*ollowing the World Wide Web Consortium (the W3C, www.w3.org) recommendations for writing standards-compliant, accessible code is a must for designers in today's Internet world. The more you can find out about this important topic, the more visitors will be able to access your sites.

Chapters in this minibook cover details about following web and accessibility standards and topics that relate to performing prelaunch testing, cleaning up and correcting common problems in your code, and validating your HTML and CSS markup.

Chapter 1: Following Web Standards

In This Chapter

✔ Following web standards

✔ Finding out about W3C standards online

✔ Using the right DOCTYPE

✔ Understanding the differences between HTML, XHTML, and HTML5

✔ Discovering why CSS is better than HTML for styling

✔ Writing Section 508–accessible code

*W*eb standards are an important part of the web design process that every designer, coder, and programmer needs to understand and use. The standards generally focus on how a web page works under the hood, but they can also have some significant implications for a site's design. Most importantly, these standards help ensure that anyone and any device (such as a screen reader or search engine robot) using the web — regardless of their browser, device, or operating system — can view the content on a web page.

In this chapter, you find out about the World Wide Web Consortium (W3C) and some of the goals it sets forth for web design. You also find an introduction to following some of these standards, including using DOCTYPEs, styling page content with CSS instead of HTML formatting tags, and writing valid semantic HTML, XHTML, and HTML5 code. In addition to the standards that keep pages accessible and running smoothly across the web, the federal government outlines another set of standards regarding making web pages *accessible* to people with disabilities. At the end of the chapter, you find a discussion about accessibility issues and how the federal government's Section 508 amendment to the Rehabilitation Act prescribes additional ways content should be coded for the web.

Frame A

Frame B | Frame C

Working with Web Standards

The early days of the web (which was developed in 1989) were a lot like the days of the Wild West. Anyone who was willing to take the time to explore its uncharted territories was welcome to do so, making up his or her own coding and presentation rules along the way to survive in the then largely unknown Internet world. Because these pioneers and designers had no rules to follow, website navigation took on any and every form, making many early Internet users feel frustrated and confused as to how they should go about finding the information they sought.

Yet as more and more artists and designers began to explore the depths of possibilities in the digital realm, while businesses started using the web space as a way to market and advertise their products and services, the urgent need for web standards became apparent. Thankfully, today, most of the big software companies are on board regarding standards compliance. This means that as you find out more about creating websites, your HTML and WYSIWYG code editors should be guiding you along the way by writing standards-compliant code that can easily adapt to a variety of devices and provide visitors with rich interactive experiences. Of course, you'll still likely encounter issues with incompatible scripts, IE-only features, and other browser- and device-specific coding concerns, but for the most part, standards have helped smooth a path to make your job a little easier. As with acquiring many new skills, if you follow the right way to do things from the start, you shouldn't have any bad habits to break later on as you keep improving your skills.

In the following sections, you find out more about the importance of designing sites that follow web standards, the W3C recommendations for web standards, and layering web content.

Understanding the importance of writing standards-compliant code

First and foremost, designing websites that follow web standards helps ensure that anyone using the web — regardless of their browser, device, or operating system — can view the content on a web page. Additionally, following web standards also makes sites easier to maintain and thus makes them an even more cost-effective method for communicating with site visitors than traditional methods of marketing and communication. The more all Internet software and hardware manufacturers comply with these World Wide Web Consortium (W3C) recommendations, which are described in the following section, the better all web visitors' experiences can be. That's where you come in.

As an added bonus, besides being accessible to the widest possible audience, standards-compliant websites are more likely to load faster in a browser and tend to have better search engine rankings than their non–standards-compliant counterparts. Ultimately, though, the number one reason to use web standards is that by following them, you can honestly and proudly present yourself as a professional web designer or developer. This not only makes you look good, but it also makes your clients look good too, and that's good for everybody's business.

To help be a part of this Internet utopia, you must do your part to follow the recommendations when writing the HTML, HTML5, XHTML, CSS, CSS3, JavaScript, jQuery, and other programming code for your websites. Most WYSIWYG code editors, such as Dreamweaver and Expression Web, do a respectable job of writing standards-compliant code — particularly when certain Accessibility preferences are set within the applications. However, it's ultimately up to the designer or developer how standards-compliant that code is. This is especially true for anyone who intends to hand-code, hand-edit, or use HTML code editors such as TextWrangler and BBEdit. Above all, you must do your part to ensure that the code is written in correct, valid, *semantic HTML* (code that uses tags to accurately define contents, such as <li> tags for list items) and that the code follows the recommendations of the *World Wide Web Consortium (W3C)*, the organization that helps develop these standards.

Taking a look at W3C recommendations

In 1994, Tim Berners-Lee founded the World Wide Web Consortium (W3C) as an international vendor-neutral group dedicated to bringing standards to the web with the ultimate goal of making all software and hardware web accessible. The W3C's mission is "to lead the World Wide Web to its full potential by developing protocols and guidelines that ensure long-term growth for the web." Since its founding, the W3C has published over 100 "W3C Recommendations" for web standards, including the following:

✓ **The conformity to uniform methods of coding HTML, XHTML, and HTML5:** HTML has new rules to follow that would improve the presentation of pages across a wider array of devices. *XHTML,* an enhanced version of HTML 4.01, follows stricter coding rules to improve the accessibility of pages across browsers, operating systems, and other devices that access the Internet. HTML5 is the latest version of HTML (and is the current standard, unless you have a good reason to write XHTML code instead) and further aims to improve how content gets delivered on the Internet. With it come many new features including new coding rules for improved parsing, new elements and input attributes, better support for audio and video, the addition of dynamic features like geolocation, and the deprecation of some less-effective tags and attributes.

✓ **The inclusion of DOCTYPEs in web code:** By adding a DOCTYPE tag to the code of all HTML, XHTML, and HTML5 pages, the browser can interpret a web page as an application in the XML programming language. As a standard, this is important because XML allows programmers to create proprietary markup languages through which even more information can be exchanged on the web. You find details about adding DOCTYPEs later in this chapter.

✓ **The use of Cascading Style Sheets to style web content:** Separating content (HTML) from presentation (CSS) and interaction (JavaScript, jQuery, and other programming languages) frees designers and programmers to streamline their code and centralize their presentation markup.

Figure 1-1 shows an example of an early, unorganized website from 1998, which was built with frames (which aren't used anymore) and offered three different navigation options for visitors, including a jump menu, graphic buttons, and hypertext links. Now that standards exist, the web is a much more organized, efficient place to shop, research, mingle, and interact.

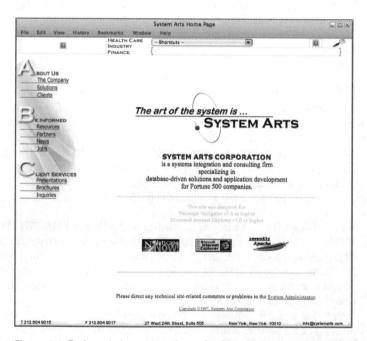

Figure 1-1: Early websites were often a jumble of links, graphics, and text.

Exploring the W3C website

Indisputably, the W3C website is the primary source for finding the latest information about anything web related, from CSS and document formats to browser compatibility and web graphic formats. You can even find documentation about more complex issues and initiatives that most designers have never even heard of.

If for some reason you haven't had the chance to visit the W3C website, shown in Figure 1-2, take a few moments now to explore some of the following areas of the site (www.w3.org):

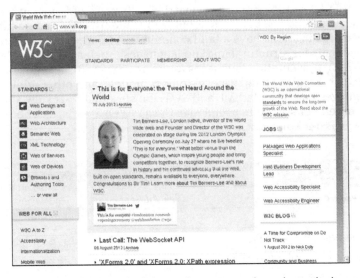

Figure 1-2: The w3.org site is your primary source for web standards.

- ✔ **Web Design and Application documentation:** On the left side of the screen, in the topmost section labeled Standards, click the link for Web Design and Applications. Here you can find summaries and links to all the areas related to building and displaying web pages such as HTML and CSS, Graphics, Accessibility, and Mobile Web.

- ✔ **Mobile Web:** To find out more about the Mobile Web Initiative, click the Mobile Web link located in the Web For All section of the left sidebar. This area of the site features all the latest developments and concerns related to designing for mobile web. You'll even find a section entitled "Check your site/your browser," where you can test whether a site is mobile ready.

✔ **Search feature:** To find information about a particular topic, return to the W3C home page and use the Google Search W3C feature in the upper-right corner of the page.

Spend some time understanding these standards. The more you can gain knowledge about them, the better you can build websites that are standards compliant and accessible to the widest possible audience.

In addition to the W3C, several other organizations exist to provide recommendations for following standards on the web, to fight for consistency and accessibility, and to offer suggestions and resources for compliance. As soon as you can, be sure to visit and bookmark the websites in Table 1-1 so that you can review their offerings and quickly return to them anytime you have a question about web standards and accessibility. All these organizations have a bold commitment to creating standards that set precedents for structural markup languages (such as HTML HTML5, and XHTML), presentation languages (such as CSS/CSS3), scripting languages (such as JavaScript and jQuery), object models, and other additional markup languages (such as MathML and SVG). Be sure to also review and bookmark the dated but still quite useful Max Design Web Standards Checklist at www.maxdesign.com.au/articles/checklist.

Table 1-1	Web Standards Resources
Resource	*Web Address*
W3C	www.w3.org
The Web Standards Project	www.webstandards.org
The Web Standards Group	www.webstandardsgroup.org
Section 508	www.section508.gov
Web Accessibility in Mind	www.webaim.org

Using DOCTYPEs (DTDs)

Though DOCTYPEs have been around since about 1999, only in the past few years have they started getting the kind of respect and attention they were intended to have. A *DOCTYPE* — also often referred to as a Document Type Definition, or DTD, or sometimes even a Document Type Declaration (again, DTD) — is a set of instructions in the top code of an HTML page that tells a browser how to identify the type of code that the page was written in as either HTML, XHTML, HTML5, or (for super old code) Frames. More importantly, the DOCTYPE informs the browser how the document should be interpreted as an application of the XML programming language. *XML,* which stands for eXtensible Markup Language, is an easily customizable programming language, like SGML (Standard Generalized Markup Language), for the communication of information and application services between people and computers using structured and meaningful semantic code.

By taking care to use the proper DTD on all your web pages, you can improve the accessibility of your website to both human and nonhuman visitors alike while also ensuring that your page code is valid.

Selecting a DOCTYPE

The DOCTYPE, as I mention briefly in Book III, Chapter 1, is a line of code that gets added to the top of each web page. The DOCTYPE must be placed at the top of the HTML code, before the opening <html> tag, as illustrated in Figure 1-3, which uses the old HTML 4.01 Transitional DTD. In addition to informing the browser which markup language the page uses, the DOCTYPE associates an XML or SGML file with a DTD. Before you learn about which DOCTYPE to use, take a look at the code.

```
1   <!DOCTYPE html PUBLIC "-//W3C//DTD HTML 4.01 Transitional//EN"
2       "http://www.w3.org/TR/html4/loose.dtd">
3   <html>
4   <head>
5   <title>My Page Title</title>
6   </head>
7   <body>
8   Page content goes here
9   </body>
10  </html>
11
```

Figure 1-3: Place the DTD above the opening HTML tag.

The DTD itself, whether it's for an HTML-, XHTML-, or HTML5-based page, is composed of two parts:

✔ **Definition:** The first half is the markup language identifier, which matches the DTD type to the type of code used in the web document. For example, the following DTD would be used when writing HTML 4.01 transitional code:

```
<!DOCTYPE html PUBLIC "-//W3C//DTD HTML 4.01 Transitional//EN"
```

✔ **Declaration:** The other half of the DTD specifies the URL of a web-accessible text file that contains more information about that DTD's usage, which for HTML 4.01 would look like this:

```
"http://www.w3.org/TR/html4/loose.dtd">
```

The W3C recommends that all HTML 4.01, XHTML, and HTML5 web pages include a DOCTYPE specifying a DTD. They used to require that Frameset pages use a DTD too, but those tags are now obsolete. The DTD identifies the type of code being used in the document so that a web browser knows how to interpret or process the information in the code and display the content on the page a little faster. The next three sections show you the differences between the DOCTYPEs for HTML, XHTML, and HTML5.

HTML 4.01 DOCTYPEs

You can use three types of DTDs with HTML 4.01 on your pages. The first can be used for most, if not all, of your pages because it tells browsers to use the strictest, most accurate, standards-compliant page rendering. Keep in mind, however, that it does require that the HTML contain no coding errors or deprecated tags:

```
<!DOCTYPE html PUBLIC "-//W3C//DTD HTML 4.01//EN"  "http://www.w3.org/TR/html4/
    strict.dtd">
```

The second HTML DTD should be used for pages that might contain legacy code, deprecated tags, and possibly some minor coding mistakes, such as improper tag nesting, all of which do not or cannot comply with strict DTD guidelines. The transitional and loose settings tell browsers to be a bit forgiving when interpreting any out-of-date tags and common code blunders:

```
<!DOCTYPE html PUBLIC "-//W3C//DTD HTML 4.01 Transitional//EN"  "http://www.
    w3.org/TR/html4/loose.dtd">
```

The third, now obsolete HTML DTD was for HTML documents that use frameset tags to display two or more pages within a single browser window:

```
<!DOCTYPE html PUBLIC "-//W3C//DTD HTML 4.01 Frameset//EN"  "http://www.w3.org/
    TR/html4/frameset.dtd">
```

XHTML DOCTYPEs

When working with XHTML code (which you may want to use exclusively instead of HTML 4.01 when working with programs that use XML), you must choose the correct XHTML DTD. You can choose from three kinds of DTDs when writing XHTML 1.0 code. The first can be used for most or all of your XHTML files that use CSS for page content presentation and adhere to the strictest possible interpretation of standards-compliant code. Note that with this DTD, the opening <html> tag is appended with the xmlns attribute:

```
<!DOCTYPE html PUBLIC "-//W3C//DTD XHTML 1.0 Strict//EN"  "http://www.w3.org/TR/
    xhtml1/DTD/xhtml1-strict.dtd">
<html xmlns="http://www.w3.org/1999/xhtml">
```

The second DTD is for XHTML files that might still contain styling and presentation code within the file as well as certain tags and attributes that the strict DTD disallows:

```
<!DOCTYPE html PUBLIC "-//W3C//DTD XHTML 1.0 Transitional//EN"  "http://www.
    w3.org/TR/xhtml1/DTD/xhtml1-transitional.dtd">
<html xmlns="http://www.w3.org/1999/xhtml">
```

Stepping outside the frame

By now you should already know what HTML is, and probably have a good idea that XHTML and HTML5 are more advanced forms of HTML 4.01. What you may not know, however, is what frames were. Frames refers to an old web page presentation technique that used `<frameset>` tags instead of `<body>` tags to make two or more pages display within a single browser window, as illustrated in the figure. The technology was an early attempt at a meta-organizational structure for a website, intended to speed the process of loading pages in a browser over slow modem connections. Frames have since been replaced first by using tables for layout and then eventually by CSS and `<div>` tags for layout. For anyone curious about how these primitive tags used to work, a free tutorial still exists at www. w3schools.com/tags/tag_frame. asp. In the rest of this chapter, you explore the DOCTYPE options for HTML, XHTML, and HTML5.

```
Edit and Click Me >>

<html>

<frameset rows="50%,50%">

<frame src="frame_a.htm">

<frameset cols="25%,75%">
<frame src="frame_b.htm">
<frame src="frame_c.htm">
</frameset>

</frameset>

</html>
```

Your Result:

Frame A

Frame B   Frame C

The third XHTML DTD was used for XHTML documents that included frameset pages with XHTML syntax rules:

```
<!DOCTYPE html PUBLIC "-//W3C//DTD XHTML 1.0 Frameset//EN"  "http://www.w3.org/
    TR/xhtml1/DTD/xhtml1-frameset.dtd">
```

In addition to these DTDs, you find two other XHTML DTDs. Strict XHTML 1.1 is a newer version of Strict XHTML 1.0 based upon the modularization of XHTML:

```
<!DOCTYPE html PUBLIC "-//W3C//DTD XHTML 1.1//EN"  "http://www.w3.org/TR/xhtml11/
    DTD/xhtml11.dtd">
<html xmlns="http://www.w3.org/1999/xhtml">
```

This DTD should be used only if you're certain that you can comply with the stricter coding requirements of this form of XHTML. In other words, if you think you may need to use some coding hacks to get your job done, don't use it.

Likewise, the Mobile 1.0 XHTML is a DTD used to describe XHTML code that's been developed for wireless display. Choose this form only if you're developing web page content with XHTML for wireless mobile devices:

```
<!DOCTYPE html PUBLIC "-//WAPFORUM//DTD XHTML Mobile 1.0//EN"  "http://www.
    wapforum.org/DTD/xhtml-mobile10.dtd">
<html xmlns="http://www.w3.org/1999/xhtml">
```

For a few years, there was a lot of debate about whether to switch from HTML to XHTML. Some designers firmly thought that no reasons existed to make the change, while others believed that following the recommendations of the W3C was the right thing to do, even if all the benefits of XHTML hadn't yet been fully realized. In fact, many designers made the switch to XHTML but then reverted back to HTML once they found out it was more trouble than it was worth. Today, that discussion is more often than not ignored as most designers and coders have moved on to working with HTML5. To find out more about the HTML/XHTML debate, check out `www.sitepoint.com/forums/showthread.php?t=393445#q7`.

HTML5 DOCTYPE

Surprisingly, the HTML5 DOCTYPE isn't much of a DOCTYPE at all! The main differences from HTML 4.01 and XHTML you'll notice are the use of all lowercase letters, the removal of a declaration of a URL for DTD usage, and the lack of an attribute appended to the opening `<html>` tag:

```
<!doctype html>
<html>
```

This simplification is mainly because, unlike HTML and XHTML, HTML5 isn't based on SGML (Standard Generalized Markup Language), an international standard for markup languages.

HTML5 is now the current standard used by web design and production professionals as browser and device support for it continues to grow. To see whether your browser or device supports HTML5, check out the test scores at `http://html5test.com`.

All in all, when a DOCTYPE is specified in the head of any HTML file, whether it uses HTML, XHTML, or HTML5 markup, a browser can recognize the code and parse it faster. Additionally, the DTD helps ensure that your web pages can be tested for accuracy by using an online markup validator like the one at `http://validator.w3.org`. (You find out more about testing, accessibility, compliance, and validation in Book IV, Chapter 2.)

Adding a DOCTYPE in Dreamweaver

If you're a Dreamweaver user, you almost don't have to think about the DTD because the program automatically inserts the selected DOCTYPE and DTD into the code each time you create a new document through the New Document dialog box. Of course, you have other ways to create a new file in Dreamweaver, and in those cases, the program's default DTD, as specified in the program's preferences, will be automatically inserted.

No matter which DTD you select, Dreamweaver automatically writes the appropriate DTD-specific code. For example, if you choose to build pages using the XHTML 1.0 transitional DTD, Dreamweaver's code editor automatically writes XHTML-compliant code. Likewise, when you choose HTML5, Dreamweaver writes HTML5-compliant code.

To select the appropriate DTD for your new documents in Dreamweaver, follow these steps:

1. **Launch Dreamweaver and choose File⇨New to open the New Document dialog box and select the Blank Page option from the top-left column, as shown in Figure 1-4.**

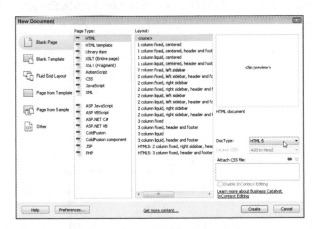

Figure 1-4: Use the New Document dialog box to select a DOCTYPE for your code.

2. **Select the HTML option from the Page Type Category, and choose <none> from the Layout column.**

   Dreamweaver opens a new blank HTML file.

3. **In the DocType area in the lower-right corner of the dialog box, use the menu to select the desired document type (DTD).**

Over the years, the default in the DocType area has changed from version to version in Dreamweaver. For a long time it was set to HTML 4.01 Transitional before Adobe switched it to XHTML 1.0 Transitional. At the time of this writing, the DocType area may be set to HTML5. The options in this list are None, HTML 4.01 Transitional, HTML 4.01 Strict, XHTML 1.0 Transitional, XHTML 1.0 Strict, HTML5, XHTML 1.1, and XHTML Mobile.

To modify the default DTD in your copy of Dreamweaver, open the Preferences dialog box by choosing Edit⇨Preferences (Windows) or Dreamweaver⇨Preferences (Mac), click the New Document category, and choose the desired Default Document Type from the DTD menu, as shown in Figure 1-5.

4. **Click the Create button to open the new, blank HTML or XHTML page in the Dreamweaver workspace.**

   If you check the code in Code view, you can see the selected DTD at the top of the page, above the opening HTML tag.

Older versions of Dreamweaver, including MX and earlier, either didn't provide an option to select the DTD or coded in only part of it automatically. If you're still using an old version of Dreamweaver or another code editor that doesn't include the DTD, be sure to hand-code the appropriate DTD into your pages or upgrade your software so that your program does it for you automatically.

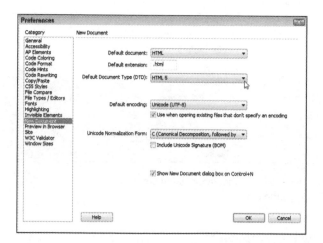

Figure 1-5: Set the default DTD in the Preferences dialog box.

Writing Semantic HTML Code

Most of the best code editors these days — whether you're using a code-only editor or one with a WYSIWYG view — automatically write code for you that conforms to HTML 4.01, XHTML 1.0, or HTML5 standards based on the DTD you select when creating your pages. That's a very good thing, especially for HTML newbies. Where your code can start to unravel, however, is when you "go rogue" by hand-coding, hand-editing, and using any free code and scripts that you find online. Another potentially complicating factor that may jeopardize the validity of your code can happen when you start working with legacy HTML pages (perhaps created by someone else a few years ago) that still use some of the older HTML tags that have been deprecated (phased out) over the past several years.

Whether or not you're hand-coding, either with or without the help of an editor, one of the best insurance measures you can take to avoid any potential browser rendering and code validation issues is to know the rules that govern HTML so that you can write valid, semantic markup.

If you aren't yet familiar with the rules of the HTML road, quite a few very good free online tutorials are available, such as those found at W3Schools. com and SitePoint. Getting yourself a good HTML handbook is another smart thing you can do so that you always have a guide at your fingertips when questions arise. You can find several wonderful titles at www.wiley.com.

Regarding the differences between HTML, XHTML, and HTML5, and deciding which markup language to use for your web pages, you might want to start coding your projects with HTML5 and use only XHTML or HTML 4.01 Transitional if you have a specific need to do so. Alternatively, you can start with HTML 4.01 and then easily transition to XHTML or HTML5 code, at which point the stricter and newer rules of XHTML and HTML5 might make more sense to you. Whichever version you decide to use, make sure to use it consistently throughout your site. One benefit of starting with HTML is that some tags and attributes are backward compatible with many older browsers, whereas XHTML and HTML5 are not supported in part or in full by many of the older browsers. In addition, programs such as Dreamweaver and Expression Web can code properly syntaxed semantic HTML, XHTML, and HTML5, but the programs aren't human, so you need to intervene occasionally to ensure that the code is properly formatted and remains that way anytime you make alterations to your code by hand.

Table 1-2 shows a side-by-side comparison of writing HTML, XHTML, and HTML5 code. Review the rules and use the markup that best meets your needs.

Table 1-2	HTML and XHTML Markup Comparison	
HTML	*XHTML*	*HTML5*

Code structure must be ordered correctly, but forgotten tags may be forgiven and cause a page to fail acceptably, such as forgetting to close the `<title>` or `<head>` tag.	All code elements must be closed and placed in the proper location hierarchically within the opening and closing `<html>` tags, as in
	
	`<html>`
	
	`<head>...</head>`
	
	`<body>...</body>`
	
	`</html>`
		Markup can be written in either HTML, XHTML, or a combo "polyglot markup" syntax that combines rules of HTML and XHTML.

HTML files should have, but aren't required to have, an HTML DOCTYPE declaration above the opening `<html>` tag.	All XHTML files must include an XHTML DOCTYPE declaration above the opening `<html>` tag, as in
	
	`<!DOCTYPE html`
	
	`PUBLIC "-//W3C//DTD XHTML 1.0`
	
	`Transitional//EN"`
	
	`"http://www.w3.org/TR/xhtml1/DTD/`
	
	`xhtml1-transitional.dtd">`
	
	`<head>`
	
	`<title>Add your title here</title>`
	
	`</head>`
	
	`<body>`
	
	`...`
	
	`</body>`
	
	`</html>`
		HTML5 files require the simple HTML5 `doctype` declaration above the opening `<html>` tag:
		
		`<!doctype html>`

HTML	XHTML	HTML5
Tags can be written in either uppercase or lowercase, but lowercase is preferred, such as `<title>` instead of `<TITLE>`.	Tags must always be written in all lowercase letters, as in `<head>`, `<body>`, and `<p>`.	Tags and tag attributes should be written in all lowercase letters, as in `<header>`, `<h2>`, and `<aside>`.
HTML cannot be an application of XML.	XHTML takes advantage of XML.	HTML5 is not an application of XML, but XHTML5 is the XML serialization of HTML5.
Tags and objects can be improperly nested with little consequence, so `<b><i>Citizen Kane</b></i>` would still be displayed in bold and italics.	Tags and objects must be properly nested to display accurately in a browser, so `<strong><em> Marshmallows </strong></em>` would be incorrect and `<strong><em> Marshmallows </em></b>` would be correct.	Like XHTML, tags and objects should be nested correctly to display accurately in a browser.
Tags needn't always have closing tag elements, as with the `<p>`, `<hr>`, and ` ` tags.	All tags and objects must be properly closed. Tags that didn't typically need to be closed in HTML should now be closed by placing a space and slash inside the tag, as in ` `, `<hr/>`, and `<img/>`. All other tags, such as `<p>`, `<td>`, and `<li>`, must also be properly closed.	In HTML5, the `/>` used in XHTML to close tags is unnecessary for void elements (elements that don't contain any content, such as ` `).

(continued)

Book IV
Chapter 1

Following Web
Standards

Table 1-2 *(continued)*

HTML	XHTML	HTML5
Values inside attributes of tags can be written either with or without quotation marks, as in `<img src="images/ dog.png "width=100 height=100>` or `<img src="images/dog. png "width="100" height="100">`.	Values inside attributes of tags must be written inside quotation marks, as in `<div id= "banner">` and `<span class= "special">`.	Values inside attributes of tags should be written inside quotation marks, as in `<img src="images/ logo.gif" width="100" height="25">`.
Attributes can use shorthand to minimize the code that needs to be written when the value matches the desired option, as with `<input disabled>`.	Attributes can no longer use shorthand and must always use the full syntax of the HTML code, as with `<input disabled= "disabled"/>`.	Attributes should always use the full syntax of the HTML code and attributes, as with `<input disabled= "disabled"/>`.
Objects use the name attribute, as in `<img src="max.jpg" name="max">`.	Objects use either the `id` attribute instead of name, as in `<img src="emily.jpg" id="emily">` or use both the `id` and the name attributes together, as in `<img src="emily. jpg" id="emily" name="emily">` Using both name and `id` attributes together helps older browsers interpret and display HTML data.	Objects should use both the `id` and name attributes together, as in `<img src="portugal. jpg" id="portugal" name="portugal">`

After reviewing Table 1-2, it might become apparent that XHTML and HTML5 follow a much stricter set of rules than HTML. This is true, but HTML5 is also the current recommended standard for the web, and both XHTML and HTML5 have many benefits that HTML lacks. For instance, because of all its standards, some say XHTML — and HTML5 by extension — is easier to learn than HTML. Not only that, but XHTML is both XML- and XSL-ready and HTML5 offers more control over content and new features. (XSL, which stands for eXtensible Stylesheet Language, is similar to CSS but is used exclusively to define the presentation of content in XML files in a browser.)

Whichever markup language you select, you can test the validity of the code for compliance to the W3C recommended standards using the techniques you find in Book IV, Chapter 2. Until then, as long as you tell your HTML/web editor to code in the desired markup language and pay attention to syntactical rules while making any code adjustments by hand, you should be able to code your pages properly.

Formatting with CSS Instead of HTML

Before CSS came along, all the presentation markup was added to the code using old HTML formatting tags. Today, although you can somewhat format your text in HTML, the standards-compliant way is to format your pages using CSS, and preferably with an external CSS file rather than internal or inline styles. When you use CSS, you can define sitewide styles for the tags used to mark up your content and create custom tags to selectively style page elements. This is in stark contrast to the old way, where formatting tags were applied to every single block of text, graphic, and other objects that required particular formatting.

Comparing CSS and HTML formatting

In the context of a chapter dedicated to following web standards, knowing the proper way to style your content is worthy of further explanation. To illustrate, I review the differences between old HTML formatting and formatting using CSS. This should give you a nice sense of appreciation for CSS.

First the old way. Using the old formatting and font styling tags, each line, paragraph, and block of text needed to be surrounded by its own set of `<font>` tags, which included styling attributes about the font's face, size, and color. Often, these tags and tag attributes (many of which have since been deprecated or completely omitted) were also used to handle formatting for things such as alignment, bold, and italics:

```
<p align="center"><font color="#FF3399" size="2" face="arial, "lucida console",
    sans-serif"><a href="meetourstaff.html"><i>Meet Our Staff</i></a></font></p>
```

Notice how much space the `font` tag with its attributes and the `center` alignment attribute in the `<p>` tag take up, relative to the amount of content. Now think about this: Each character and space in the formatting markup take up a fraction of a byte in file size, which means that when you add all the individual bits of code together, the styling markup can dramatically increase the size of an HTML file, thereby causing the page to load slower in a browser window.

Now take a look at the same content and code when styled using CSS instead, where the <p> tag style is redefined in the CSS:

```
<p><a href="meetourstaff.html">Meet Our Staff</a></p>
```

The styling and positioning for the <p> tag might look like this:

```
p {
    font-family: arial, "lucida console", sans-serif;
    font-size: 1em;
    font-style: italic;
    font-weight: bold;
    color: #ff3399;
    text-align: center;
}
```

Much simpler code! The alignment is now controlled by the text-align: center style for more consistent rendering in different browsers, the old <i> tag gets replaced by the font-style:italic attribute, and the rest of the font styling is handled by the remaining font rules within the style declaration.

Perhaps best of all, one of the greatest advantages of CSS is the reusability of the style; no matter where else on the page you have additional paragraphs, you automatically get this formatting rather than having to reapply all the font attributes to each <p> tag.

Taking a look at the benefits of CSS

The benefits of styling your HTML, XHTML, and HTML5 content with CSS are vast:

- ✓ **CSS is easy to learn and use.**

- ✓ **CSS makes HTML pages smaller** in file size, thereby speeding up page download times.

- ✓ **CSS is one of the W3C's core recommendations,** so your CSS-styled site complies with the current standards. Moreover, most HTML formatting tags are being deprecated by older browsers and may not even be supported in XHTML and HTML5 code, so you have no good reason not to use CSS for most, if not all, of your content styling and positioning needs.

- ✓ **CSS is infinitely editable,** giving you the flexibility of changing the look of your pages as often as you like without ever altering the content.

✏ **CSS helps separate *presentation* (how the page looks) from *content* (what's on the page)** by moving all the page-styling instructions into a centralized location. That location can either be in-line with the code (not recommended) or internal in the head area of the web page (better), or in an external CSS document (suggested) to which all the pages on a site are linked, the latter being the most useful and elegant method for working with CSS. The benefit of having an entire site's style information contained in a single external CSS file is that doing so allows for instant sitewide style updates.

✏ **CSS styles your content *semantically*,** which means that it requires fewer styles than the old HTML formatting tags. For example, CSS allows designers to redefine the presentation of content contained inside particular tags, such as automatically adding a particular color and font face to any content marked up with H3 tags or applying the same background color and border attributes to any sidebar layers on the site.

✏ **CSS can be used to style the look of text, images, layers, and objects as well as to position objects** on a web page. This feature alone drastically reduces the amount of code required to display objects on a page. For instance, `<div>` tags, and even objects contained within them, can be relatively or absolutely positioned on a page with CSS. Before, to place something in an exact spot on a page required code hacks involving the use of tables with empty table cells and spacer GIFs. All that extra code goes away with CSS. Other pre-CSS code hacks involved the unorthodox and creative use of HTML, CSS, JavaScript, and other code to manipulate objects on a web page and/or work around limitations of the web to achieve a desired visual effect.

✏ **CSS is an affordable solution for styling content** because it takes less time to implement and update than the older styling techniques did. With the old way, even simple changes might require the hand-editing of all the individual pages on a site. With CSS, one change to an external CSS file can update a style across an entire website.

After you begin styling your content with external CSS, you'll probably never want to go back to using internal or inline CSS, and certainly not ever use the old font tags for styling. In fact, if you inherit someone else's site and are hired to do a redesign, you can create new CSS styles for the content and strip the old formatting tags from all the existing pages on the site as part of the redesign project. You might even use this *font tags–to–CSS conversion* as a selling point of your services by explaining all the aforementioned benefits of CSS to your client. Not only should the client be impressed by the scope of your knowledge on the matter, but she might even feel somewhat inclined to hire you for her next redesign project sometime down the road if she ultimately likes your design and enjoys working with you this time.

Book IV Chapter 1

Following Web Standards

Exploring pages styled with CSS

To further illustrate how wonderful it is to use CSS for semantically styling content, these steps show you some really amazing examples of how the same content can look completely different when styled with different CSS.

1. **Point your browser to** www.csszengarden.com.

   What you see here is the site's home page developed by CSS mastermind, Dave Shea.

2. **On the right side of the page, under the red Japanese Torii gate where it says Select a Design, click any of the links.**

   Each link takes you to separate pages using the same content but styled with CSS created by different designers. This listing is updated occasionally, so the list you see the first time you browse the garden may be different from the list you find six months later. Regardless, each set of links shows how the same content can be styled with CSS to create a totally different look!

   Figure 1-6 shows a comparison of the CSS Zen Garden home page design (left) with one of the designs (right) available in the list at the time of publication. The HTML tags in the code are exactly the same on both pages. It's the CSS style definitions — which include fonts, colors, graphics, and positioning among other things — that have been changed to achieve the new layout and look.

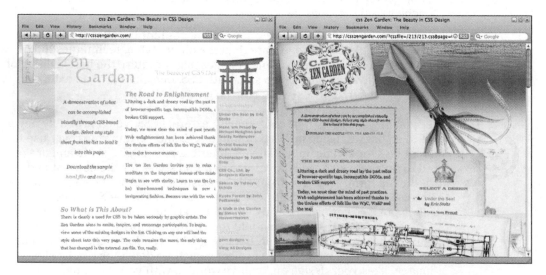

Figure 1-6: CSS magically transforms the appearance of the same content.

3. **Scroll down the page until you see the Select a Design section and click another link.**

   Same content, different design. At this point, you should be totally convinced of the amazing power of CSS!

4. **Click another link in the Select a Design column.**

   What makes this particular site extremely brilliant is that any designer who submits his or her design to the CSS Zen Garden agrees to make the CSS open source. This means anyone, including *you,* can go examine the CSS and find out how all the visual effects were created.

5. **To view the CSS for any particular design, look for a Resources section and click the View This Design's CSS link.**

   When you click this link, the CSS for that page automatically opens in your browser window. Figure 1-7 shows the CSS for the design on the right side of Figure 1-6. In the CSS, you can see how the General Properties styles format the appearance of the page background and text links, and the Text Properties styles define the look of paragraphs and headers. Likewise, in the DIV Properties section of the CSS, content contained in `<div>` tags with these named IDs (for example, `#preamble`) will be automatically styled by the style rules contained within them, such as the section on the page that contains preamble text, where it says "The Road to Enlightenment."

Book IV
Chapter 1

Following Web Standards

Figure 1-7: View the CSS code to find out how designers created different effects.

6. **Choose File⇨Save or File⇨Save Page As to save a copy of the CSS to your computer.**

   The filename you give the CSS is up to you, so feel free to change it to whatever you want. What matters is the extension; all CSS files must be saved with the `.css` file extension to work properly.

7. **To see even more designs using different CSS, return to the main CSS Zen Garden site and click the View All Designs link in the Archives section, which takes you to the CSS Zen Garden archive on Dave Shea's MezzoBlue site.**

   The CSS Zen Garden website is a truly inspired site with the ultimate goal of teaching you the benefits of styling with CSS. Spend a little time exploring as much CSS there as you can to find out about the various ways you can style your own pages.

Finding Out about Accessibility Standards

According to the W3C, people with disabilities who surf the web make up nearly 20 percent of the Internet's population. Believe it or not, that's a larger percentage than the roughly 8.2 percent of all Internet consumers using the OS X (as opposed to Windows or Linux). Without a doubt, then, people with disabilities make up a large enough group of potential website visitors that you should definitely pay considerable attention to them and their particular needs when designing websites.

To make your websites accessible, modify the code so that visitors with disabilities and search engine robots/spiders can access the information on the site's pages. Common coding enhancements include adding footer links, a site map page, alternative text attributes for images, page titles, meta tags, object labels, titles for links, link tags to the home and site map pages in the head, access and tab index keys, and form input labels.

One of the primary web standards organizations with an online presence devoted to the subject of web accessibility for people with disabilities is the Section 508 government site (`www.section508.gov`), shown in Figure 1-8. This organization is dedicated to compliance of Section 508 (29 U.S.C. 794d) of the Rehabilitation Act, especially with regard to the accessibility of websites to all people, whether employees of the federal government or not, including those with disabilities. Although their prescriptions for accessibility are technically legally applicable only to federal agencies using, developing, maintaining, and procuring information technology, many web designers and developers are now informally broadening the scope of Section 508 to include access to any and all information that is readily available on the web to anyone, with or without disabilities.

Figure 1-8: The Section 508 website recommends guidelines for making web pages accessible to visitors with disabilities.

The Section 508 amendment, which was passed in 1998, is often broken down into two parts: The first relates to HTML usage, and the second part deals specifically with JavaScript, jQuery, plug-ins, and other multimedia enhancements found on web pages. You can find a copy of the document in its entirety at www.section508.gov. When building pages for the web, each page must necessarily pass or fail each of the standards as set forth in Section 508. While only governmental agencies are currently bound to follow these guidelines, knowing about the various standards helps you become a more competent designer.

The benefits of designing for accessibility don't stop with making sites more accessible to those with disabilities. By following accessibility guidelines, the content on your pages can be more easily accessed using a larger group of lesser known or less popular (but no less wonderful) web browsers, such as Opera, Mozilla, Lynx, and Amaya. The more devices that can access a Section 508–compliant site, the greater the likelihood of increased visitor traffic and potentially increased sales of products and services.

**Book IV
Chapter 1**

**Following Web
Standards**

Chapter 2: Testing, Accessibility, Compliance, and Validation

In This Chapter

- ✔ Checking your code for errors
- ✔ Testing on different platforms and browsers
- ✔ Fixing common code errors
- ✔ Checking HTML syntax
- ✔ Making pages CSS, HTML, and 508 accessibility compliant
- ✔ Fixing noncompliant code issues

Congratulations on making it this far! You're almost to the finish line, and you have only a few more things to do before you can publish your site for all to see. At this stage, it's time to put all the pages on your site through a rigorous review to catch potential problems like spelling errors, code issues, broken links, and missing accessibility code attributes such as alt text attributes for images and title attributes for hyperlinks.

This chapter focuses on providing you with helpful tips and suggestions on validation, testing, standards compliancy, and more. Most HTML code editors have tools to assist you with testing your pages so that you can identify and fix any problems before visitors have a chance to see the site. For instance, in this chapter, you find out how to use several testing tools, including ones that clean up code and check spelling, and I discuss a tool to find and replace text and source code throughout a site. In addition, you discover how to clean up redundant and unnecessary code, apply uniform source formatting to pages, and fix some common coding problems such as identifying broken links and orphans.

> **Markup Validation**
> Check the markup (HTML, XHTML,
>
> **Jump To:** Con
>
> This document was successfully c
>
> **Result:** Passed
>
> **Source:**
> ```
> <!DOCTYPE html PUB
> Transitional//EN"
> "http://www.w3.org
> transitional.dtd">
> <html xmlns="http:
> <head>
> <meta http-equiv='
> charset=utf-8"
> <title>Web
> ```

A few examples in this chapter use Dreamweaver. However, if you're using another program, you should be able to find many similar tools. For details about any specific tools, be sure to consult your application's help resources.

While you're busy making all the corrections, remember that making your pages pass validation makes the site more accessible to more visitors, which can translate into more visitors overall and potentially more sales. Cleaner code also means faster page downloading times, improved search engine accessibility, and quicker page maintenance and site updates in the future.

Understanding the Process of Validating Your Code

When you take a patient and careful look at everything on your site, you can usually find and fix any display and functionality issues before your pages go online. That is not to say that the cleanup and validation process is a breeze. On the contrary, site testing can be a demanding task at times. In fact, it's quite common to find new coding issues at each phase of the validation and compliance testing process.

More than likely, however, what you'll find is that performing the validation testing is relatively easy, and though it may take you some time to research, retest, and fix any problems you find during the validation process, the whole experience will enrich you and refine your skills, ultimately making you a better designer for any future projects.

Validation offers many important benefits to both you and your site's visitors:

✔ Validation makes a site more accessible to the widest audience, which can translate into increased visitor traffic and potentially more sales of products and services.

✔ Validated web pages display faster in a browser window.

✔ Validated, clean code improves search engine accessibility and search engine results rankings.

✔ Validated pages are much easier to maintain and update.

✔ A well-validated site can be your calling card for obtaining future business.

To help you keep track of your progress, the validation process itself can be performed methodically over the course of several days. This chapter walks you through each of the steps. You begin by converting all the syntax on every page to match the specified DTD in the code. Then, you perform HTML, CSS, and accessibility testing on every page. If you find any errors, you spend time fixing them and then retest to ensure that you've either fixed everything or that problematic code fails acceptably. After that, you're done.

Performing Prelaunch Testing

Building a website is one of those activities that requires you to remember a lot of little details. Besides designing the mock-up, optimizing all the graphics, creating a template, building the individual pages, pasting in all the relevant content in every page, dropping in JavaScript, jQuery, and media files, and formatting everything with CSS, you have to remember to include meta tags in the code, add customized titles to every page, give all your images alternative text attributes, and add `target` and `title` attributes to your links, especially any that will open in separate browser windows. The list of tasks could go on and on. That's where good organization comes in handy.

In the following sections, you discover how to create your own web-testing checklist so that you can remember all the items on the site that you need to test. Additionally, you find out how to choose which platforms and browsers to test.

Creating a web-testing checklist

To help you remember all the tasks you need to do, consider creating your own web-testing checklist, like the starter list example shown here, and use it when reviewing every site you build prior to publishing:

- Have you performed a spelling and syntax check, included the correct DTD, applied source formatting, organized and commented your CSS, and cleaned up any HTML and Word HTML coding errors?

- Have you tested all the pages on your site in multiple browsers and browser versions on Mac, PC, and Linux platforms and found solutions for any glaring errors?

- Have you tested all the pages on your site on multiple handheld devices (such as smartphones and tablets) on Android and iOS platforms and found solutions for any glaring errors?

- Do all the pages on the site include appropriate meta tags?

- Does each page have a unique, descriptive title?

- Do all the images on the site include descriptive `alt` text attributes, including empty `alt` text attributes for decorative images that don't need `alt` text descriptions?

- Do all the hyperlinks include `title` and `target` attributes?

- Do all the instances of script on the page include `<noscript>` content so visitors without JavaScript enabled can access that content?

✔ Do links that open in a separate browser window or tab provide some kind of indicator to visitors that the link opens a new window or tab?

✔ Have you hand-checked all the internal and external hyperlinks for accuracy? Do the links go where you want them to go? Did you find any broken links that need fixing?

✔ Are the site's forms fully accessible and functional?

✔ Does the site have any unused "orphan" files, images, or folders that can be safely moved to another location or deleted?

For a comprehensive checklist that covers everything from code quality and accessibility to basic usability and site management, visit www.maxdesign. com.au/presentation/checklist.htm. Also, be sure to explore the fantastic list of tools at www.smashingmagazine.com/2009/06/29/45-incredibly-useful-web-design-checklists-and-questionnaires/.

Testing on multiple platforms, browsers, and devices

Possibly the most effective method for ensuring that your pages look and function the way you want them to is to test them in as many different scenarios as possible. Viewing pages in a browser is the best way to evaluate how your site's pages will look to visitors. Therefore, the wider the set of browsers, browser versions, and operating systems (Windows 8, Windows 7, Vista, OS X, and so on) you can test in, the greater the likelihood you will find any hidden mistakes in the code and fix them before you launch your site. The same goes for testing your site on multiple devices running Android and iOS operating systems, and all the new browser apps currently available for handheld devices.

Browser and device testing should be done regularly throughout the master page and site-building process and again at the end of the project prior to publication. Presuming that you've been previewing your pages in one or two browsers and devices (most new designers often mistakenly only test in just Internet Explorer or just Firefox on a PC) during the building phase of the site, you've probably already dealt with some of the more glaring display issues. However, at this stage, the focus is on how well the site displays in different browsers and operating systems. That means if you're a Mac person, you need to get your hands on a PC, and if you're a PC person, you need to do some testing on a Mac.

According to the statisticians at W3Schools.com (shown in Figure 2-1), as of July 2012, 84.5 percent of all Internet users use PCs running some version of Windows; 8.2 percent of all Internet traffic comes from OS X users; 4.9 percent comes directly from Linux OS users; and another 1.6 percent comes from mobile users. The remaining percentage of web users experience the

Internet with alternative tools, such as screen readers and text-only assistive devices. These statistics alone should tell you that to be fully thorough in your testing you must simulate how all visitors experience the site and correct any glaring mistakes prior to publishing.

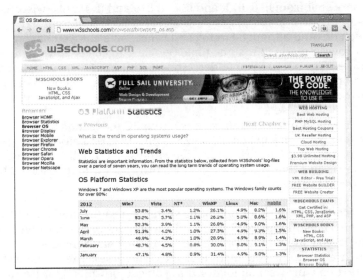

Figure 2-1: Most Internet users access the web on a PC running one of the Windows operating systems.

Deciding which platforms, browsers, and devices to test

Realistically, testing in every possible browser and device scenario isn't an affordable solution for the average web designer. At a minimum, try to test on both Mac and PC in the most popular browsers and browser versions, as well as on as many iOS and Android handheld devices as you can access, including smartphones and tablets. This means testing not only the most recent version of a browser but also the last few versions. For example, you may want to test IE 8, 9, and 10. Some designers even go back as far as IE 6 and 7! At the time of this writing, the most popular browsers and versions you may want to consider testing in are:

✔ **PC:** Firefox 13.0+, Chrome 20.0+, Safari 5.0, Internet Explorer 8+, and Opera 11.0+

✔ **Mac:** Safari 5.0+, Firefox 13.0+, and Opera 11.0+

Sure, this list still seems like a big one, but the time it takes for you to download, install, and test on these browsers will be well worth the effort. The main reason to do all this testing is that some versions of the same browser can display your pages drastically differently from other versions, depending on the platform. A case in point is the IE 6 browser. On a PC, IE 6 works pretty well, but no Mac equivalent exists because the IE developers chose to abandon the Mac platform altogether. IE 6 and IE 7 on a PC also present different display issues that must be dealt with until the majority of IE users shift from IE 6, IE 7, and IE 8 to IE 9 and IE 10. Likewise, Safari browsers often render pages — especially text — differently than IE and Firefox do. And although Firefox and Safari have enjoyed having a corner on the browser market for some time, Google Chrome is now the most popular browser. The sooner you understand the different display requirements of each browser, the sooner you can understand how to code your pages for nearly any browsing environment.

Because most Internet traffic comes from PC users, one useful strategy is to test your pages in a bunch of browsers on a PC first before testing everything again on several Mac browsers. Many times — though not always — any display issues that you fix for your PC browsers will be resolved by the time you begin testing on a Mac.

Don't forget about other operating systems besides the PC and Mac. Linux is the third most popular OS, and with 4.9 percent of the Internet population using it, you should test your pages in a Linux environment too. To do that, there are two tools you might look into. The first is the Lynx Viewer, which is a text-only browser simulator that you can download for free at Delorie. com. This browser simulator identifies how visitors using text-only browsers will see your site so that you can correct any issues that those visitors might experience. To use the free simulator, register on the Delorie site (`www.delorie.com/web/lynxview.html`) and install a test file on the hosting server before the simulator can function. The other is the free jsLinux simulator created by Fabrice Bellard at `http://bellard.org/jslinux/` which is a JavaScript emulator that runs Linux in a browser.

For the best, most thorough results of your testing, consider uploading your site to a test directory on the same server that will be hosting the site. Having the pages on the destination server can help you uncover unforeseen server issues before you publish the site.

Testing a page

For a testing strategy, try this: For each web page you review, ask yourself whether the page looks and functions the way you intended it to. If you need to resolve any display or functionality issues, go back into the code and make the appropriate changes:

  ✔ Review the home page first in every browser on a PC and a Mac, and again on as many smartphones, tablets, and other handheld devices as you can get your hands on.

✔ Review any pages on the site that include HTML forms and verify that the forms correctly process the data.

✔ Review any pages that contain dynamic data, such as a news item pulled from a database, and test the pages to ensure that the information is displaying correctly.

✔ Review the rest of the pages on the site and check the functionality of any interactive elements that use JavaScript, jQuery, or other scripts, programming languages, or applications, including any image viewers, galleries, sliders, accordions, widgets, links, and multimedia files.

Finding problems is one thing, but fixing those problems can be quite something else. When you identify problems with how the pages appear, exactly how to correct those issues might be a time-consuming matter of trial and error. In some instances, the problem will be easy to correct, as with a glaring coding mistake. However, in other instances, finding a way to make the page look right might involve several different solutions. Be patient and persistent, and remember that the more mistakes you make and correct, the better designer you'll become.

Using third-party testing tools

In addition to testing the pages yourself, other tools may be helpful. For instance, several third-party software tools can assist you with your cross-platform/cross-browser testing, regardless of whether you're testing pages on a Mac or a PC.

One of the most useful testing tools available today is Adobe BrowserLab, the free browser testing and previewing service offered by Adobe at `http://browserlab.adobe.com`. Although it isn't technically a browser simulator that can confirm whether your dynamic features work properly, the screenshots provided by this service can give you a good idea of page rendering in the different browsers and browser versions.

If you want an actual browser simulator, check out the desktop browser options in the Browser Sandbox at `https://spoon.net/browsers`. With this tool, you can run any browser in what's called an *isolated virtual environment*. In addition to Firefox, Chrome, Safari, Opera, and IE, you also find options for mobile browser testing in Firefox and Opera mobile.

Other third-party testing options you might want to try are BrowserShots.org, SuperPreview (PC only), Lunascape (PC only), and IETester (Windows only). You can find a comprehensive list of tools at `www.smashingmagazine.com/2011/08/07/a-dozen-cross-browser-testing-tools/`.

Cleaning Up Your Code

Whether you're hand-coding or working with a code/WYSIWYG editor, you must always make a practice of checking the hierarchical order, syntax, and spelling of your HTML, CSS, JavaScript, jQuery, and other programming code. Even when you use the best programs available, at some point your code could include errors because you are human. No matter how carefully you build a site, the HTML in your pages will probably inadvertently become cluttered with redundant tags, unnecessary markup, and outright detrimental code that can negatively impact the presentation and functionality of your web pages.

Many of these errors often happen when you paste content onto your pages from other sources such as a Word or an Excel file, a website, an e-mail, or another code editor or application. Other errors might happen from an honest typo or from coding mistakes that happened behind the scenes when moving elements around the page by clicking and dragging or cutting and pasting. One very common code problem is finding empty hyperlinks on your page, which some code editors occasionally leave in the code for no apparent reason when you move a link from one spot on the page to another. These empty links are essentially just bits of code that don't surround any content, such as `<a href="http://www.wiley.com"></a>`, which means they won't appear in the browser. As is often the case, such extra code might not be noticeable during the building phase of your site, but it will often rear its head during the testing phase prior to publishing.

To minimize coding errors on your web pages, be sure to perform code cleanup at least twice during the building phase:

1. **After building your master page(s) or template(s), clean up the code before building out any of the remaining pages for the site.**

2. **Do another round of cleanup on all the pages of the site at the end of the building phase, prior to site launch.**

To help with the cleanup process, take advantage of any special tools your coding application may recommend for this task. Dreamweaver, for example, offers several tools that can automate the cleanup process within any managed site, such as a Find and Replace tool, a Spell Checker, a Word Clean Up command, a Code Clean Up command, a Source Formatting tool, and a Convert Syntax tool. Although many of the examples you find here include step-by-step instructions specifically for Dreamweaver, most other coding applications may have similar tools you can use to perform these tasks.

In addition, you can find quite a few online tools to check your pages for certain errors and help you identify those problems in the code. The only drawback to online tools, however, is that many of them allow you to input only one URL at a time, which, though thorough, can make the cleanup process rather tedious.

Finding and replacing errors

By far, one of the most robust tools you'll find in most HTML coding editors is the Find and Replace tool. With this one tool, you can search for and optionally replace or delete any text, source code, or specific tag throughout an entire page, selected pages, a specified folder, or an entire managed site. Suppose, for example, you realize that the content provided by the client contains a certain word that's misspelled throughout the entire site. This tool can find that misspelling and replace all instances with the correct spelling on all the site pages. Pretty powerful stuff!

The only thing about this kind of tool that might be a deterrent to some designers is that often times these kinds of global operations typically cannot be undone, which can be especially critical when modifying pages sitewide. Therefore, to ensure that you can revert innocent mistakes should they happen, make a backup copy of your entire managed site *before* using this tool. That way, in the event that something does goes awry, you can always revert your site to the state it was in before you began making changes. After a few weeks, when you know you won't need to revert to that particular state of the site, you can safely delete the backup files.

To find a misspelled word or phrase and replace that text with new text throughout all the pages in a managed Dreamweaver site, open the document that contains the spelling error and select the misspelled word or phrase. Then choose Edit➪Find and Replace to open the Find and Replace dialog box, as shown in Figure 2-2.

Figure 2-2: The Find and Replace tool helps you fix coding errors.

Changing words and phrases is only one example of how to use a tool this powerful. You can also use the Find and Replace tool to edit whole chunks of code, replace filenames throughout the site, and remove tags and other unwanted coding like comments and other unnecessary markup.

Checking spelling

Notwithstanding you and your client's best efforts, spelling errors inevitably happen. Sometimes they take the form of regular typos and grammatical errors, like *htis* instead of *this* and *they're* instead of *their* or *there*. Other times, typos come in the form of commonly misused words, such as *accept* versus *except*. Occasionally your spelling errors might even occur as accurately spelled words that are contextually wrong, such as typing **moon** when you meant **noon**.

Possibly the best defense against most spelling errors is a two-pronged approach. First, check the spelling for errors using your own eyes and a spell checker. Second, enlist a group of volunteers, possibly even including the client, to read the site content in search of any spelling errors and grammatical mistakes prior to publishing. The more people who help with this task, the greater the likelihood that you'll find and fix all the errors. With luck, you may even discover some other site issues that need repair, such as broken links and missing images.

Checking the spelling of all the content on a site is quite a big task. If you'd rather not be responsible for the accuracy of the site's spelling — especially because clients often provide content that is rife with spelling errors! — you can include a stipulation in your design contract that states that the client is ultimately responsible for the accuracy and substance of the content. In any case, consider running a spell check to correct any obvious mistakes that you may have made while working on the pages, such as *the* misspelled as *teh*.

Be sure to take advantage of any automated spell checking commands that come as a standard feature of your HTML editor. Dreamweaver has a decent spell checker that works very similarly to the one found in Microsoft Word. To open the spell checker in Dreamweaver, choose Commands⇨Check Spelling, as shown in Figure 2-3.

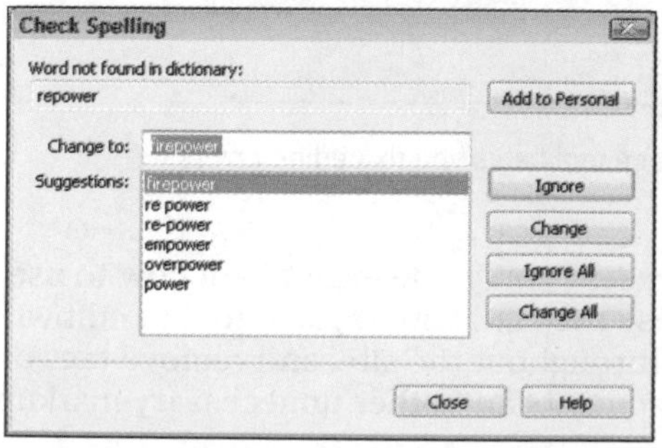

Figure 2-3: Dreamweaver's Check Spelling command is similar to the spell checker in Microsoft Word.

Removing unwanted formatting

Most code editors have a command that automatically cleans up the common errors in your code. For instance, the Clean Up Word HTML/XHTML command in Dreamweaver is a must for any web page that includes content that was copied from Word or any other Microsoft documents. The reason this is important is because Microsoft files often embed extra markup when pasted into a web page to make the file's content retain its formatting. Unfortunately, on the web, all this extra Microsoft HTML code is unnecessary. Therefore, you must use a tool like this to strip that extra markup out of your pages to ensure that your code — not Microsoft's — dictates the look of the site within the browser.

To access the Clean Up Word feature in any open document in Dreamweaver, follow these steps:

1. **Choose Commands⇨Clean Up Word HTML.**

   The Clean Up Word HTML dialog box opens, as shown in Figure 2-4.

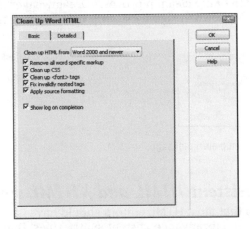

Figure 2-4: Clean up unnecessary markup in your code copied from Microsoft documents.

2. **Enable or disable the cleanup settings as desired on both the Basic and Detailed tabs of the dialog box.**

   By default, all the options on both tabs are automatically enabled to provide the most robust form of cleanup. Here's an overview of the options on the Basic tab:

   • *Remove All Word Specific Markup:* This setting deletes any special markup that is required to format the page in Word and Word HTML files but is unnecessary in a normal HTML file.

- *Clean Up CSS:* Enable this option to delete any Microsoft Word–specific CSS markup, such as `<p class="MSO Normal" style="Margin-TOP:3em">`. This type of markup can override your CSS, so be sure to leave this one turned on.

- *Clean Up <font> Tags:* This setting deletes any instances of old `<font>` tags for styling.

- *Fix Invalidly Nested Tags:* Word sometimes adds markup to a page outside normal heading and paragraph tags, which don't conform to valid tag-nesting standards. This option removes those tags.

- *Apply Source Formatting:* Source formatting is determined by the options specified in Dreamweaver's `SourceFormat.txt` file as well as the Code Format settings in the Preferences panel. Leave this one enabled.

- *Show Log on Completion:* Select this check box to see a summary of the cleanup results.

3. **Click OK to run the Clean Up operation.**

   Upon completion of the cleanup process, Dreamweaver displays an alert box, like the one shown in Figure 2-5, with details about the cleanup.

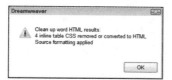

Figure 2-5: The cleanup alert message.

Applying consistent HTML and XHTML syntax

Another useful tool that most HTML editors should have is one that will clean up the HTML and fix any inconsistent syntax rules. Dreamweaver, for instance, has the Clean Up HTML/XHTML command. This tool looks for problematic code within an open document and automatically cleans up any errors that it finds. This tool is especially helpful in ensuring that your code uses consistent markup syntax to match your selected DTD. Inconsistent syntax can sometimes happen when Dreamweaver codes in one markup language (XHTML) and you code in another (HTML).

Most Clean Up HTML/XHTML commands take their cue from the stated Document Type Definition (DTD) in the open document and convert any tags and syntax that are inconsistent to the proper format.

To illustrate how this works, follow these steps to apply this command to an open document within the Dreamweaver workspace:

1. **Choose Commands⇨Clean Up HTML or Commands⇨Clean Up XHTML.**

   Dreamweaver automatically recognizes the DTD in the page code and displays the HTML Clean Up or XHTML Clean Up command in the Commands menu to match that DTD. The HTML option appears for both HTML and HTML5 DTDs.

   The Clean Up HTML/XHTML dialog box opens, as shown in Figure 2-6.

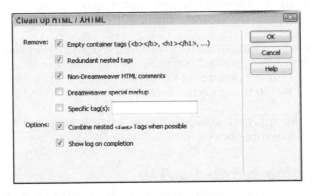

Figure 2-6: Clean your code of common syntax errors.

2. **In the Clean Up HTML/XHTML dialog box that opens, adjust the cleanup settings.**

   By default, a few of the options are automatically enabled, but you may disable them and configure the rest of the settings to suit particular cleanup needs. For instance, you can use the Specific Tag(s) field to clean up empty `<span>` tags.

   To view cleanup results after running the command, be sure to select the Show Log on Completion check box.

3. **Click OK.**

   If you enabled the Show Log on Completion check box, a small alert box appears, listing a helpful Clean Up summary.

Applying source formatting

In addition to allowing users to choose specific source formatting options for all newly created documents, another helpful tool that your code editor may have is one that will apply source formatting after the fact. This is a way of telling your code editor to automatically format pages in a particular way and to clean up any code that may not conform to the DTD you're using. For example, in Dreamweaver, you can adjust some of the settings in the program's Code Hints Preferences, which instructs the software to automatically create closing tags around selected content after typing `</` at the end.

Another fantastic Dreamweaver feature (which your code editor may also have) is the Apply Source Formatting option. This command applies the formatting options to the code of your page as specified in Dreamweaver's HTML format preferences and in the application's `SourceFormat.txt` file (itself an editable document that helps Dreamweaver determine how to code new files), thereby overwriting any coding inconsistencies that might have come about since the file was originally created.

To apply source formatting to any open document in Dreamweaver, choose Commands⇨Apply Source Formatting. Dreamweaver then applies the settings in the Code Format preferences to HTML, automatically updating any code that didn't match those preferences.

You can also apply the source formatting to a selection of contiguous code instead of an entire document.

Converting syntax by DTD

When most designers select a DTD for their web docs, they have all the intention in the world of writing code that's compliant with that DTD's syntactical rules. Sometimes, however, with all the cutting and pasting and inserting and hand-coding, the syntax gets out of whack here and there, and when the time comes to test and validate pages, you might find errors that cause the pages to not display exactly as you intended.

This is especially true when you make the shift to using an XHTML or HTML5 DTD but are still in the habit of hand-coding tags in HTML syntax. One of the easiest mistakes to make in this regard is forgetting to add the extra space and slash for certain tags in XHTML when their HTML counterparts don't require it, like forgetting to write `<br />` instead of `<br>`.

If you happen to be a Dreamweaver user, you're in luck because Dreamweaver has a sweet little Convert Syntax tool that automatically converts all the code in a single document to conform with the syntactical rules of any selected DTD. If you're using a different code editor, check that editor's help files to see whether you can find a similar command.

Using Dreamweaver's Convert Syntax command, you can change all the HTML syntax into XHTML or HTML5 and vice-versa. In other words, the code on any page — regardless of the original DTD and syntax used to code the page — can be automatically adjusted to match the syntax for any of the following DTDs:

- HTML 4.01 Transitional

- HTML 4.01 Strict

- HTML5

- XHTML 1.0 Transitional

- XHTML 1.0 Strict

- XHTML 1.1

- XHTML Mobile 1.0

- XSLT 1.0

To illustrate how this tool works, take a look at Listings 2-1, 2-2, and 2-3, which show an example of how the Convert Syntax tool converts a page using HTML 4.01 Transitional into the proper syntax for the XHTML 1.0 and HTML5 DTD.

Listing 2-1:   Before Syntax Conversion (HTML)

```
<!DOCTYPE HTML PUBLIC "-//W3C//DTD HTML 4.01 Transitional//EN" "http://www.
    w3.org/TR/html4/loose.dtd">
<html>
<head>
<meta http-equiv="Content-Type" content="text/html; charset=utf-8">
<title>Untitled Document</title>
</head>
<body><p>It's easy to change the syntax with<br>
 the Syntax Conversion Tool</p>
<hr>
</body>
</html>
```

Listing 2-2:   After Syntax Conversion (XHTML)

```
<!DOCTYPE html PUBLIC "-//W3C//DTD XHTML 1.0 Transitional//EN" "http://www.
    w3.org/TR/xhtml1/DTD/xhtml1-transitional.dtd">
<html xmlns="http://www.w3.org/1999/xhtml">
<head>
<meta http-equiv="Content-Type" content="text/html; charset=utf-8" />
<title>Untitled Document</title>
</head>
<body><p>It's easy to change the syntax with<br />
 the Syntax Conversion Tool</p>
<hr />
</body>
</html>
```

Listing 2-3: After Syntax Conversion (HTML5)

```
<!doctype html>
<html>
<head>
<meta charset="utf-8">
<title>Untitled Document</title>
</head>
<body><p>It's easy to change the syntax with<br>
 the Syntax Conversion Tool</p>
<hr>
</body>
</html>
```

To convert the syntax of any open document in Dreamweaver — which includes having Dreamweaver automatically insert the selected DTD when one isn't detected or overwrite any existing DTD — follow these simple steps:

1. **With your document open in the Dreamweaver workspace, choose File⇨Convert and select the desired DTD from the submenu, as shown in Figure 2-7.**

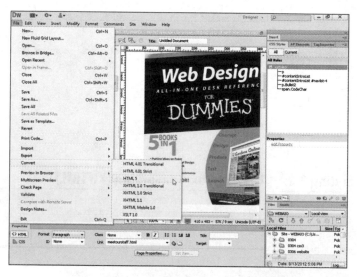

Figure 2-7: Use the Convert command to update a page's code syntax by DTD.

Dreamweaver immediately updates the DTD in the open file to match the one you just selected and converts any tags within the code of the page to match that DTD's syntax rules.

2. **Save the file and repeat this process on any additional open files to ensure that all the files within the same managed site use the same DTD and coding format.**

   Currently this tool doesn't perform any sitewide conversion; therefore, be sure to apply this Convert command to each document in your managed site.

If you happen to be working on a site that uses templates, feel free to apply this tool to normal documents, templates, and template-based files. Any changes made to the template should be automatically applied to any template-based pages upon save. However, be sure to also apply the Convert Syntax command individually to all the template-based files on the site after updating the template so that the content inside any editable regions of the template-based files will also be converted to match the selected DTD.

Fixing Common Code Errors

After you're done with the basic code cleanup, you can perform a handful of mini-tests to check your code's accuracy and functionality. Most of these tests help you check for things that need remembering but are easily forgotten, such as verifying that all the images include `alt` text attributes and all the links work properly, so checking for them at the end of the site-building phase makes good sense.

Although a lot of these tests can be automated for you when working in an HTML code editor, some must still be performed by hand. For those instances, using a methodical system of some kind can help you tackle the task in a more manageable way:

- ✔ **Checking page titles:** To check whether all the pages on a site include unique titles, open each page one at a time and verify that the title has been entered. Untitled pages display `Untitled Document` between the title tags in the code. Alternatively, you can run a Dreamweaver report instead to check specifically for untitled documents, but the hand-check is a more thorough method of verification because you might find typos that the report simply wouldn't identify.

- ✔ **Checking meta tags:** To verify that the desired meta-tag information has been added to the head area of each file's code, take a look at the template file(s). When you modify a template, all the template-based pages should be automatically updated with new information. For non-template–based pages, check each page one at a time. To streamline the process of adding or updating meta tag content, copy the updated content to the computer's Clipboard and paste the updated meta information into the `<head>` area of each file's code. When you're finished, save everything and close the files.

✔ **Using built-in testing tools and reports:** Check to see whether your code editor offers any kind of built-in testing tools and reports. Oftentimes these tools are grouped together in some kind of panel. For instance, you can open Dreamweaver's Results panel by choosing Window⇨ Results or by pressing F7. The Results panel contains eight different tabs, each of which provides access to special types of site information and testing tools. Four of them in particular are extremely useful for prelaunch testing: Validation, Browser Compatibility, Link Checker, and Site Reports.

In the case of Dreamweaver, each of the tools in the Results panel works in a similar way:

✔ To activate a tool, click the green Play button at the panel's upper-left edge.

✔ The selected task can be performed on the currently open file, all open files, a specified folder, selected files in the Files panel, or on all the files in the currently managed local site.

✔ Each tool can be customized to meet specific testing needs.

After running each tool's function, the tool's results display in the Results panel window. Results are often listed by filename first, then by the line of code containing the issue in question, followed by a description and any other pertinent details. Each issue identified also displays with one of three icons next to each line — Error, Warning, or Message — as shown in Figure 2-8. Errors should always be addressed and corrected, warnings need to be looked into but might not cause serious display problems, and messages (if you ever happen to encounter them) typically identify code issues that although incorrect, might not affect how the page displays.

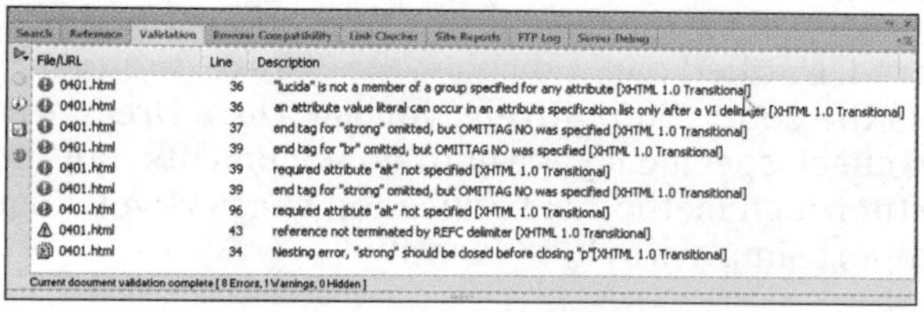

Figure 2-8: Validation results — errors, warnings, or messages.

For each problem identified in the code, you can right-click (Windows) or Control+click (Mac) the results line to access a contextual menu from which you can select further options, such as requesting more information about a particular issue. What's more, when you click any error in the Results panel, Dreamweaver takes you directly to the page that contains the error and highlights the exact line(s) of code that contains the error, making it easy for you to identify and correct.

Read on to find out more about the powerful Validator, Target Browser Check, Link Checker, and Site Reports features in Dreamweaver.

Validating your markup

No matter what code editor you happen to use, you absolutely must use a built-in or standalone validation tool to check the accuracy of your code. Most code editors have some kind of feature that allows you to validate code in the currently open file, a series of selected files, or the specified managed site, and you should be able to use this tool to validate a number of different markup languages, including HTML, XHTML, HTML5, JSP, CFML, XML, and WML. If your code editor does not include a code validator, use an online validator. You find out about online code validation in the later section, "Validating HTML and CSS Markup."

Over the past several years, Dreamweaver has included a built-in validation tool to help identify coding errors. The Validator tool, however, was deprecated in CS5 but then made a comeback in CS5.5 and CS6 by integrating Dreamweaver with the W3C's free validator tool. To illustrate how this built-in validator works, the following steps show you how to run Dreamweaver's Validator on a single open HTML file:

1. **From the Validation tab in the Results panel, click the green arrow button in the upper-left corner and select Validate Current Document.**

   Dreamweaver automatically runs the report and displays any problematic results in the bottom part of the Results panel.

2. **To view or correct any of the errors, warnings, or messages listed in the results area, double-click the filename of the error in question.**

   Dreamweaver automatically opens the selected document and highlights the line(s) of code that contains the error.

3. **Correct any errors within the HTML code as needed and rerun the report.**

   Occasionally, fixing one error can result in another, so it's always a good idea to rerun the report at least once to ensure that you've identified and corrected every error, warning, and message.

When no problems are found in the code, Dreamweaver displays the message `No warnings or errors found [DTD]`.

Checking browser compatibility

One of the biggest issues with building web pages is ensuring that those pages are cross-browser and device compatible. This means that they should look good and function properly in as many browsers and on as many devices as possible.

Many code editors include some kind of browser compatibility tool that takes a look at all the tags in your files and determines whether those tags and any attending attributes are compliant with the latest W3C recommendations for your selected DTD in the most popular current browsers. These tools should be able to quickly identify coding issues, such as whether the code contains any deprecated tags like <center> and <b>, which should be identified and changed or removed.

Though the browser compatibility test typically doesn't show you how any found errors will look in browsers that don't support a particular tag or attribute, the test results often list the browser type and version that may have difficulty displaying the identified content so that you can do your own testing to correct the error. For instance, using Dreamweaver's Browser Compatibility tool, you might see an error like the one shown in Figure 2-9. In the figure, the tool identifies and describes the Three Pixel Text Jog issue, which cannot be properly displayed in Internet Explorer 6.0.

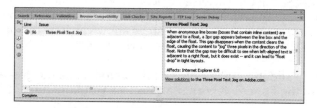

Figure 2-9: Identifying coding issues that can cause browser display problems.

To run the browser compatibility test in a single open HTML file in Dreamweaver, follow these steps:

1. **From the Browser Compatibility tab in the Results panel, click the green arrow button in the upper-left corner and choose Check Browser Compatibility from the drop-down menu.**

2. **Depending on the number of found issues, the report might take a few minutes to generate. Be patient.**

   Like the other tabs in the Results panel, the results for this tool display in a list at the bottom of the Results panel with an Error, Warning, or Message icon next to each issue found. In addition, this panel displays detailed results about each found issue along the right side of the panel.

3. **To correct any issues found, double-click the line in the Results panel that contains the issue, and Dreamweaver automatically opens the page that contains the error.**

The code in question is highlighted and/or displayed with a red or green wavy underline in Dreamweaver's Code view to assist in making a correction or adjustment. To reveal a pop-up tip window within the code that identifies the error and lists the browsers that don't support it, place your cursor on top of the wavy underline, as shown in Figure 2-10.

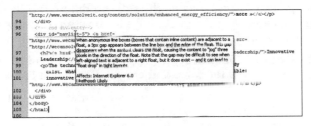

Figure 2-10: Displaying questionable code in Code view.

As great as the Browser Compatibility tool is, keep in mind that it checks only for the validity of code within a subset of browsers and browser versions. What it doesn't do is verify the accuracy of the code or of any functionality of any JavaScript, jQuery, or other code used in the file(s).

Verifying internal and external links

A link checking tool can help you to check your pages for broken internal links (for example, you misspelled `index.html` as `indez.html`). It can even display a list of all the page's external links and help you to identify any orphaned files (unused or unlinked-to files) that you can remove from the site to help save room on the server.

To illustrate how to use Dreamweaver's Link Checker tool on a single open HTML file, follow these steps:

1. **From the Link Checker tab in the Results panel, click the green arrow button in the upper-left corner and choose Check Links in Current Document from the drop-down menu.**

   To check links in an entire site or selected files in the Files panel, choose one of the other options from the drop-down menu.

2. **By default, broken internal links (if any exist) are displayed at the bottom of the Results panel. To correct a link, click the URL under the Broken Links column and edit the text to correct the link.**

   An internal link is any hyperlink that doesn't work because the link contains a typo, an incorrect path, or improper syntax, or the linked file is not on the server.

Corrected links automatically disappear from the listing.

If no broken links are identified, congratulations!

3. **Click the Broken Links drop-down menu at the top of the Link Checker area, just below the Results panel tabs, and choose External Links.**

   Any links going to pages outside the site to a different URL are listed here. Though you can't test these links from within Dreamweaver, the list can be a useful tool for identifying the links that need to be verified.

4. **Click the External Links drop-down menu at the top of the Link Checker area, below the tabs, and choose Orphaned Files.**

   An *orphan* is any file, image, or other asset in a website that isn't linked to any other files in the site and may therefore (in most cases) be deleted or otherwise relocated to a backup location.

   This report feature can be used only to check for orphans on an entire managed site, so when the alert box appears, click OK.

5. **Click the green arrow button in the panel again, but this time, choose Check Links for Entire Current Local Site from the drop-down menu. When the results appear, click the Broken Links drop-down menu and choose Orphaned Files.**

   Any file, image, or other asset saved to the local managed site that isn't being referenced by another file within the site (linked to) will be displayed in the Results panel.

6. **If you know that a particular file in this listing is unnecessary to the functionality of the site, either archive it in another location or delete it.**

7. **As a practice, rerun the report after making any changes to ensure that you've caught and corrected as many errors as possible.**

Generating site reports

Many code editors also include some kind of HTML reports feature you can run to help you find common code mistakes that can affect page download time and create performance and display issues. Run these reports for every site prior to site launch to make sure that you catch those little problems that might otherwise slip through the cracks.

Although each code editor may have slightly different reporting tools, most should have certain features in common. For example, Dreamweaver's reports can identify the following issues:

✔ Combinable nested font tags such as `<font face="verdana, arial"><font size="2">Hello</font></font>`, which could be either rewritten as `<font face="verdana, arial" size="2"> Hello</font>` or, better yet, stripped of font tags so that you can style the page with CSS.

✔ Accessibility issues, which identify ways the code can be improved.

✔ Missing `alt` text attributes for any `<img>` tags.

✔ Redundant nested tags that can be safely removed, such as deleting the extra `<strong>` tags around the words vernal equinox in the following sentence: `<strong>Spring begins on the <strong>vernal equinox</strong>, which is usually March 20 in the Northern Hemisphere</strong>`.

✔ Removable empty tags that are unnecessary and can be deleted from the code, such as a tag pair that surrounds no content (`<a href="monkey.html"></a>`) or an opening tag that's missing its closing tag, as in `<p>Hello world`.

✔ Untitled documents and files with empty `<title>` tags.

✔ Workflow reports for designers working within a group setting. These special reports help identify files that have been checked out by particular teammates, locate files with associated Design Notes, and display files that have been recently modified.

To run the HTML Site Reports feature on an entire managed site in Dreamweaver, follow these steps:

1. **From the Site Reports tab in the Results panel, click the green arrow button in the upper-left corner.**

   The Reports dialog box opens, as shown in Figure 2-11.

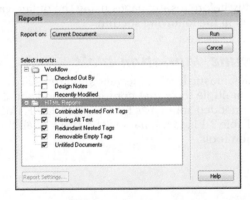

Figure 2-11: Run reports to find common coding mistakes.

2. **Select each of the options listed in the HTML Reports area of the dialog box.**

   Leave all the Workflow reports options deselected.

3. **Click the Run button to run the report.**

   Results are listed at the bottom of the Results panel and are each identified by filename, code line number, and a description.

4. **Make corrections directly inside the Results panel or double-click any of the entries to edit directly in the document in question.**

   For instance, one warning might be that a particular image is missing its `alt` attribute. To fix it, double-click the error and update the HTML code.

5. **When you're finished making corrections, save any changes in the file and then rerun the report with the same settings.**

   Rerunning the report can help you feel confident that all the errors have been addressed.

Validating HTML and CSS Markup

Validating your markup, both the HTML and the CSS, is the last step in the process of testing your pages before you publish your site. The validation process itself is automated, which means that you just run your pages through a system and then correct any coding errors that are found along the way.

Dreamweaver, as explained in the previous sections, has a good set of built-in code validation tools in the Results panel that help designers improve their code prior to publishing. Other code editors and online validators use similar tools to achieve the same goals. Although using these tools isn't mandatory, they can definitely help designers identify and fix problem code locally before testing pages using the online validation tools, which are described in the following section.

Using free online validation tools

Fortunately, several fantastic free online validation tools are at your disposal. The W3C provides multiple tools that conform to and validate against the W3C's latest recommended standards for CSS, HTML, XHTML, HTML5, and 508 accessibility. Table 2-1 lists the names and URLs of all the recommended free online validation tools.

Table 2-1	Online HTML, CSS, and Accessibility Validators
Validator Name	*URL*
W3C Markup Validator	`http://validator.w3.org`
W3C Link Checker	`http://validator.w3.org/checklink`
W3C CSS Validator	`http://jigsaw.w3.org/css-validator/`
W3C Log Validator	`www.w3.org/QA/Tools/LogValidator/`
W3C Unicorn Unified Validator	`http://validator.w3.org/unicorn/`
CSS Portal CSS Validator	`www.cssportal.com/css-validator/`
XHTML-CSS Validator	`http://xhtml-css.com`
Validator.nu Living Validator	`http://validator.nu`
WebAim WAVE Web Accessibility Evaluation Tool	`http://wave.webaim.org`
HiSoftware Cynthia Says Portal	`www.contentquality.com/Default.asp`
AChecker Accessibility Validator	`http://achecker.ca/checker/index.php`

Discovering what these tools test

Most of the free validators allow you to test in up to three different ways, depending on the location of the files being tested and the particular validator being used:

- ✔ **Validate by URL:** To test by URL, you must upload the page you're testing to a live, working server before you can use that URL in the validator. This means you could upload the files to a testing server or a hidden directory on the actual server that will be hosting the site, such as `http://www.`*mywebsite*`.com/test`, and validate by URL from there.

- ✔ **Validate by upload:** This method allows you to browse for (on a local computer or at some remote destination), select, and upload a single HTML file for validation. For more advanced options when using the W3C validator, go to `http://validator.w3.org/#validate-by-upload`.

✔ **Validate by direct input:** To test the code on a single web page before that file has been uploaded to a host server, copy the entire document — from DTD to closing `</html>` tag — and paste it into the Direct Input or other appropriate testing text area on the desired online validation page.

Although most of these tools are free, performing the validation on all the pages might take a while because you can validate only a single page at a time.

Using the W3C Markup validator

All the free online validators in Table 2-1 are quite easy to use. To illustrate, follow these steps to validate a web page using the W3C Markup validator:

1. **Point your browser to** `http://validator.w3.org`.

   This is the W3C's main Markup Validation page.

2. **In the Validate by URL Address field, shown in Figure 2-12, type the complete path of the following test page:**

   `http://www.luckychair.com/webaio/validation.html`

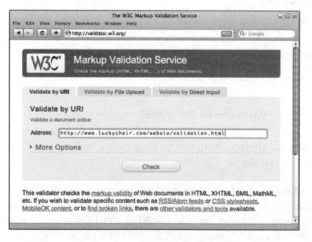

Figure 2-12: Enter your test URL and click the Check button to validate your code.

The remaining steps use this sample file to illustrate specific code validation issues. When you've completed this exercise, feel free to repeat the process using one of your own web pages.

3. **Click the Check button to validate the page.**

   The W3C server processes the validation and returns results in the same browser window.

The results display a big red bar across the top that reads `Errors found while checking this document as XHTML 1.0 Transitional!` Below the red bar, you see details of two found errors on lines 44 and 46 regarding the omission of `alt` text attributes on two of the page's graphics:

```
Line 44, Column 84: required attribute "alt" not specified.
... " width="100" height="30" id="dell" /></td>
Line 46, Column 84: required attribute "alt" not specified.
... " width="100" height="30" id="sony" /></td>
```

The W3C validator returns line numbers in the error descriptions. To see which actual line numbers the validator is testing against relative to your code, you need to resubmit the test page. At the top of the validation failed page, you should see an area labeled Options. Inside this area, enable the Show Source option and click the Revalidate button. When the results are returned, you see a new Source Listing area below the results that contains the line numbers in the code.

4. **In a new browser window, point your browser to** `www.luckychair.com/webaio/validation.html` **and save a copy of this page to your local computer by using the browser's File menu.**

   The Save option in your browser is typically something like File⇨Save Page As or File⇨Save Page.

   You're now going to correct the errors and retest the page.

5. **Open the downloaded** `validation.html` **page in your favorite HTML editor and add the** `alt` **text attribute to each of the images as indicated in the W3C failed validation results.**

   Insert descriptive `alt` text attributes to the code as follows:

```
<tr>
 <td><img src="images/b_dell.gif" name="dell" width="100" height="30"
    id="dell" alt="dell" /></td>
 <td><img src="images/b_mac.gif" alt="Mac" name="mac" width="100"
    height="30" id="mac" onclick="MM_goToURL('parent','http://www.
    apple.com');return document.MM_returnValue" onmouseover="MM_
    swapImage('superstore', '','images/new.gif','mac','','images/b_
    mac_over.gif','main','','images/mac.jpg',1)" onmouseout="MM_
    swapImgRestore()" /></td>
 <td><img src="images/b_sony.gif" name="sony" width="100" height="30"
    id="sony" alt="sony" /></td>
</tr>
```

6. **Return to the main Validator page at** `http://validator.w3.org` **and click the Validate by Direct Input tab at the top of the page.**

   In this area, you can validate the code by direct input without needing to upload a test file to a working host server.

7. **Save the changes to your updated** `validation.html` **file. Then select and copy all the code on the page (from DTD to closing** `<html>` **tag), paste it into the Validate by Direct Input field, and click the Check button.**

Pasting in the HTML code from a local copy of a file can sometimes be faster than the Validate by URL and Validate by File Upload methods.

When the results appear, you see a green bar across the top of the results page that reads `This document was successfully checked as XHTML 1.0 Transitional!` — like the one shown in Figure 2-13.

This tool, like most the others, can verify only one page at a time. Fortunately, single-page validators can often identify sitewide coding issues, which can be quickly fixed on all the pages of a site. For instance, if the validator finds a missing tag, you could use an automated process like Dreamweaver's Find and Replace tool to find the problematic code and replace it with the corrected code in all the pages of a managed sited.

What a validator won't catch are instances of code usage that, though valid, aren't standards compliant. Take the code in the preceding steps, for example, which has rollover graphics embedded inside table cells. In all likelihood, the table, graphics, and JavaScript rollovers could all be replaced with `<div>` tags and a few CSS styles.

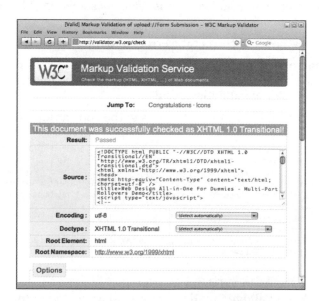

Figure 2-13: Pages that pass validation display a "passed validation" notice.

Fixing noncompliant code

For each coding issue identified by a validator, you need to determine what course of action to take. Although some culprits that repeatedly crop up are easy to fix, such as missing `alt` text and `<noscript>` tags, you're bound to find coding issues that completely baffle and stump you. For instance, if you get an error message that reads `XML Parsing Error: Opening and ending tag mismatch: br line 52 and body`, it might be difficult to figure out what that means, let alone why it was caused and how you should fix it. As a strategy then, try to fix the issues within the code from the top down, as they're listed in the validation results, because sometimes fixing one issue resolves another. With the XML parsing error, that issue might disappear when you correct for an omitted closing element on a `<br />` tag listed earlier in the error results.

The best way to find out how to code better and make fewer mistakes before validation testing is to make lots of honest mistakes and figure out how to correct them on your own. Most often, you can fix noncompliant code by hand or with the help of a good HTML editor. To help you identify some of the more common coding mistakes, Table 2-2 lists several code issues along with suggestions about how to fix them.

Table 2-2	Common Noncompliant Code Fixes
Problem	**Solution**
`alt` text attribute missing from `<img>` tag	Add the alternative text attribute, either with or without a description, as in `<img src="images/logo.gif" width="150" height="150" alt="Pete's Pizza"> <img src="images/flourish.gif" width="200" height="150" alt="">`.
`<noscript>` tags missing from code	Add `<noscript>` tags below each instance when JavaScript is present in in-line JavaScript or at the end of the content before the closing body tag. Between the `<noscript>` tags, insert HTML content (text, graphics, media files, and so on) that describes the function of the JavaScript and, when appropriate, how visitors can access the information revealed by it, as shown here:
	`<script language="JavaScript" src="bookmark.js" type="text/javascript"></script><noscript>The JavaScript used on this page provides a quick link that allows visitors to automatically bookmark this page. As an alternative, please use your browser's Bookmark This Page feature.</noscript>`

(continued)

Table 2-2 *(continued)*

Problem	Solution
Flashing or flickering element(s) detected, such as animated GIFs, Java applets, and other multimedia plug-ins	Adjust the speed of any animations to avoid causing the screen to flicker with a frequency between 2 Hz and 55 Hz. Animations that exceed these two measures may cause seizures in visitors with photosensitive epilepsy. For further details, see `www.access-board.gov/sec508/guide/1194.22.htm#(j)`.
No `DOCTYPE` specified	Add a valid `DOCTYPE` above the opening `<head>` tag.
No HTTP charset parameter specified	This special meta tag specifies the character set used in the HTML code. Some HTML editors include it automatically when generating new blank web pages. If validation finds that this tag is missing from your HTML or XHTML code, insert the following code by hand: `<meta http-equiv="Content-Type" content="text/html; charset=utf-8">`. For HTML5, insert `<meta charset="utf-8">`. For further information visit `www.w3.org/International/O-charset.en.php`.
No `<title>` tag specified	Add a unique title between `<title>` tags in the head area on each page.
No `<meta>` tags specified	Add meta keywords and meta description tags to the head of each page. These can be identical on every page on the site. If desired, you may also add additional meta tags as needed.
No Robots tags specified	Add the `Robots` `<meta>` tag in the head of the page to instruct web spiders and robots whether to index the page and follow any hyperlinks, such as `<meta name="Robots" content="All">`.
Deprecated `<font>` tags detected	Move all the presentation markup of the HTML (page, fonts, tables, links, and so on) to an external CSS file and remove all `<font>` tags and HTML and inline formatting attributes.
Deprecated table height attribute detected	Control table cell heights, when necessary, with CSS styles.
Style attributes detected in the opening `<body>` tag	Move `body` attributes, like margin attributes and background page color, to a BODY tag redefine style in an external CSS file.

Problem	Solution
`type` attribute not specified for JavaScript or CSS	Add the `type="text/css"` attribute for `<style>` tags and the `type="text/javascript"` attribute for `<script>` tags: `<style type="text/css"><script type="text/javascript">`.
Entity name used instead of entity number	Change the entity name to an entity number, such as using `$#169;` instead of `&copy;` to create the copyright symbol (c).
No background color attribute was specified for a CSS style that specifies text color	Provide each style that contains a text `color` attribute with an attending background `color` attribute. The background color should match, or closely match, the background color upon which the text will display on.

When you're finished identifying and adjusting all the noncompliant code identified by the validation tools, and have fixed everything that needed fixing, move on to the retesting and acceptable failure phase of the testing process.

Retesting and failing acceptably

Your ultimate goal when testing for code accuracy is to get a clean bill of health from the various HTML, CSS, and accessibility validators for each page on your site. To achieve that goal, you need to spend some of your time retesting each page after making adjustments to the code. Regrettably, you may run across some issues that are simply unfixable given your time frame and budget. These issues often crop up when you use special HTML and CSS hacks to make the page display a particular way in certain browsers.

For those times when a coding error causes a page to display an object not exactly as you intended, but the lack of styling doesn't alter the overall layout of the site, those pages are referred to as *failing acceptably*. Likewise, when an error in the code makes the page look completely jumbled in a browser, that page is referred to as having *failed*.

To illustrate how a page might fail or fail acceptably, think of a page that displays perfectly in nearly every browser on both a Mac and a PC but appears skewed when viewing it in Internet Explorer 6 and 7 on a PC and Safari 2.0 on a Mac. To resolve the display issue, you could create separate CSS files for each browser and use browser-detection JavaScript to automatically pair the right CSS with the viewer's browser. Alternatively, if the skewing is minor, say just a shift of about 10 pixels in one tiny area of the page, you could choose to live with the disparity.

When you can't find a solution to a particular coding error or display issue, you must determine whether you can live with the consequences of having a site that is either aesthetically inconsistent across multiple browsers and devices or not as accessible as it should be. Certainly if the page looks good in IE but looks funky in all the other browsers, your validation and testing work is far from finished. Yet if the page looks good in IE, Firefox, Opera, Safari, and Chrome but just doesn't seem to display exactly the same way in Safari on a Mac (as might be the case with the way text is rendered and how it wraps on the page, leaving orphans and widows within the text, as illustrated in Figure 2-14), perhaps you can live with that particular audience not being able to see your page in its ideal way. Ultimately, it's up to you. Before you give up, however, keep in mind that in most cases, you should be able to find a solution to your coding issue if you research the issue online.

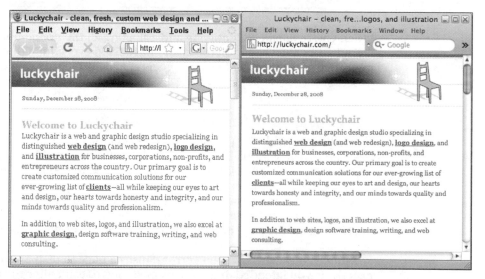

Figure 2-14: Text renders a little differently in Firefox (left) than it does in Safari (right).

Book V
Publishing and Site Maintenance

The 5th Wave — By Rich Tennant

"How long has he been programming our META tags?"

*G*etting your site online often starts with registering a domain, securing a hosting plan, and publishing your finished site on the web using File Transfer Protocol (FTP).

Publishing a site is often just the beginning of your website's existence. You also want to look for ways to improve your site's search-engine friendliness using search engine optimization (SEO) techniques as well as making sure that your site stays current with new information so that visitors will come back to your site regularly. This minibook covers domain registration, hosting, publishing, SEO, and site maintenance.

Local Files	Size	Type	Modified	Checked Out By
Site - Monkey Bars (C...		Folder	8/15/2012 1:31 PM	-
images		Folder	11/19/2009 3:24 PM	-
Templates		Folder	11/19/2009 3:24 PM	-
.htaccess	0KB	HTACCE...	10/21/2008 1:22 PM	
about.html	7KB	Firefox H...	10/21/2008 1:43 PM	
bookplates.html	6KB	Firefox H...	10/21/2008 1:43 PM	
contact.html	7KB	Firefox H...	10/21/2008 1:43 PM	
fundraiser.html	12KB	Firefox H...	11/13/2008 11:0...	
fundraiser.proce...	2KB	PHP Script	10/21/2008 1:22 PM	
getstarted.html	9KB	Firefox H...	10/24/2008 2:30 PM	
gifttags.html	6KB	Firefox H...	10/21/2008 1:43 PM	
i_bookplates.html	3KB	Firefox H...	10/10/2008 10:5...	
i_gifttags.html	3KB	Firefox H...	10/8/2008 10:30 ...	
i_journals.html	3KB	Firefox H...	10/10/2008 10:5...	
i_tshirts.html	3KB	Firefox H...	9/25/2008 2:55 PM	
index.html	5KB	Firefox H...	10/21/2008 1:43 PM	
journals.html	6KB	Firefox H...	10/21/2008 1:43 PM	

Chapter 1: Domain Registration and Hosting

In This Chapter

- ✓ Selecting a domain name for your site
- ✓ Getting help from domain name generators
- ✓ Registering a domain name
- ✓ Researching the best hosting plan
- ✓ Designing and uploading a placeholder page for the new domain

This chapter focuses on what you need to do to prepare your site for publishing on a host server. You find out about domain name selection, name generators, domain verification, and domain registration. You also discover how to find a good hosting plan, including what to look for in a plan, where to find a host, and general pricing structures. The last part of this chapter shows you how to create a customized placeholder page, which is a single, simple web page with company branding, an e-mail link, and a smattering of other contact information that can hold the place on a new domain until the new website is fully built and ready to publish.

Understanding How to Get Your Site Online

Before you can make a new website available on the Internet, it must first be assigned its own special web address, which is commonly referred to as the *domain name*. The process of acquiring a domain name can be a fun adventure and only requires a little bit of work. To start with, someone needs to think of a good name for the site and then check to see whether that name is available for use or has already been taken. If the desired name is available, the name needs to be registered, and that can be done either through a domain registrar or a host provider.

After the domain name is registered, the site needs a hosting plan so that it can reside on a server and thus become available to the public. All of this needs to be done before you can publish the site. Most people like to register the domain and get a hosting plan at the start of any new web project to ensure that the domain name is secure during the site-building process. And, because building a site takes a good bit of time, most folks also like to have a customized placeholder page designed and uploaded to the domain until the new website is ready for publishing.

If you are working as a freelance web designer, some of your clients will have already registered a domain and possibly even secured a hosting plan before contacting you about your design services. Other new clients, however, will not have done any of these things and will need a fair amount of hand-holding from you as you take them through each of the steps. Being able to provide information about these topics to your clients can both enrich your skills as a web professional and enhance their experience with you as a designer. This fact alone can be very good for business because happy clients are more likely to return to you for website maintenance services after their site gets published, as well as refer other friends and business acquaintances to you if they feel confident in all your web-related skills.

If this is your first time dealing with domain names and hosting plans, you may want to try setting up a domain name and hosting plan for your own website before handling these tasks for any clients.

Selecting a Domain Name

Choosing a domain name for a website is something that you, in your role as a designer, may or may not be involved in when working with clients, depending on their individual needs and how web-savvy they are. Some clients will have already selected a domain, registered it, and secured hosting, whereas others will say they don't really understand anything about all that stuff and are relying on your experience to help them figure it all out, or in some cases do it all for them because they don't care to know. Some clients, of course, will fall somewhere in between these extremes, needing a little help with some but not all of these domain-related responsibilities.

In the following sections, you find out more about domain names, how to help select a domain name for your client, and then how to check to make sure the name is available.

Understanding what a domain name is

Simply put, a *domain name* is a name that is used to identify an address on the Internet for a particular website and any e-mail addresses configured for that site. For instance, if your company is called Clean For Dreams, your domain name might be `http://www.cleanfordreams.com`, and your e-mail address could be `info@cleanfordreams.com`. The web address itself is composed of four distinct parts, as diagrammed in Figure 1-1:

- **Protocol:** The first part of a web address, `http://`, is the HyperText Transfer Protocol (HTTP), which identifies the protocol that allows a computer to browse the web by getting information from a remote server. Secure access to the Internet (that is, anytime a domain has an SSL [Secure Sockets Layer] certificate installed on the host server for encrypting private data) requires the use of the `https://` (note the *s* for secure) protocol.

- **www:** The second part refers to the World Wide Web and identifies the type of page that will be delivered in a browser window. Another type of web address includes domains where the `www.` is omitted, such as in `http://maps.google.com`. This type of address refers to a *subsite* or *subdomain* that resides on the main domain's servers but is separate from it.

- **Domain name:** The third part identifies the unique name of the website as registered by the owner of the site. Domain names may contain any combination of uppercase and lowercase letters and numbers. In addition, though less often used, domain names may also include hyphens but no other special characters, as in `www.jet-streamshowerhead.net`.

- **Extension:** The fourth part identifies the type of site visitors should expect to see at the address, such as `.com` for commercial business sites, `.org` for nonprofit organizations, and `.edu` for educational sites.

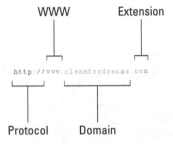

Figure 1-1: The four distinct elements in a web address.

Although several unrestricted top level domain (TDL) extensions are in use by all kinds of businesses around the world, the most familiar extensions should really be used as they were intended. For example, the `.org` extension should be used for nonprofit organizations, and the `.gov` extension should be used exclusively for government agencies. Table 1-1 lists the more common extensions from around the world.

Table 1-1	Common Web Domain Extensions
Extension	*Usage*
.com	Commercial, but is commonly used for just about any kind of business
.net	Internet administrative site, but is also commonly used for other types of sites
.org	Organization, most often used by nonprofit groups and trade associations
.info	Information, the fourth most popular extension
.biz	Business
.us	United States
.name	Personal websites
.at	Austria
.be	Belgium
.bz	Belize
.cc	Cocos (Keeling) Islands
.cn	China
.de	Germany
.eu	European Union
.gs	South Georgia and the South Sandwich Islands
.ms	Montserrat
.mx	Mexico
.nz	New Zealand
.tc	Turks and Caicos Islands
.tv	Tuvalu, but often used for television
.tw	Taiwan
.uk	United Kingdom
.vg	British Virgin Islands
.ws	Western Samoa, but is often used for websites

For a complete listing and description of all the domain name extensions available to you and your clients, visit the following website:

www.networksolutions.com/domain-name-registration/popup-
    extensions.jsp

In addition, ICANN (Internet Corporation for Assigned Names and Numbers at `www.icann.org`) is currently developing several new extensions slated for public use sometime in 2013. Many of the new extensions are industry related as well as geo/cultural, such as `.law`, `.futbol`, and `.solar`. You can view a complete listing at:

`www.newgtldsite.com/new-gtld-list/`

Finding a domain name for your client

The first thing to do when researching a domain name for a business is to see whether the name of the business is available. For example, if your client's company is Station Organization, the most fitting domain name for the company would be `www.stationorganization.com`. With an unusual or unique business name, selecting domains can be fairly quick and easy. When a client has a common business name, which is likely to have been already taken by someone else, things can become tricky.

If the desired domain name is already taken, you or your client needs to come up with a new name, and tinkering with the desired name is a good place to start. Easy solutions work best, such as adding a city name or state reference, inserting a hyphen between certain letters, or using common abbreviations within the name. For example, if the company name is Rochester Apartments and it's located in New York, the client could consider using `rochesterapartmentsny.com`, `rochester-apartments-ny.com`, `rochesteraptsny.com`, or `rochester-apts-ny.com`. Conversely, the client might also consider using a different domain extension, either with or without the other name adjustments, such as `rochesterapartments.net` or `rochester-apartments.info`. If your client gets really stumped trying to find the perfect domain name, you can help him find the right one using a domain name generator, as described in the next section.

Part of your job in helping a client choose a domain name also includes helping to select an appropriate domain extension. In some cases, the domain names with the chosen extension will already be taken by another company with the same name. In those instances, the client needs to use a different extension with the desired domain name, alter the spelling of the desired domain name, or come up with a similar but different domain name with the desired extension.

Using domain name generators

To get help finding a suitable domain name, whether the one you want is already taken or you're just interested in seeing what kinds of domains are available based on a few keywords, turn to one of the popular online domain name generators. In addition to helping you come up with new and unusual name ideas, these services can also suggest suitable alternatives based on real-time domain name availability. Most generators take whatever word or words you'd like to include in the domain name and then shake them out in a variety of combinations either with or without other words, and present a resulting list of potential names for you to choose from.

The most popular and useful domain name generators can be found at Network Solutions (`www.networksolutions.com`), DomainsBot (`www.domainsbot.com`), NameTumbler.com (`www.nametumbler.com`), Impossibility! (`www.impossibility.org`), Blungr (`http://blungr.com`), and Nameboy (`www.nameboy.com`). At Nameboy, shown in Figure 1-2, you can enter a primary and optional secondary word to begin the search and choose whether returned results include hyphens between characters and rhyming, which can sometimes make the domain name easier to remember. It also allows you to verify domains you're interested in with its handy WHOIS search form. You can even search for and register domains that have expired or are about to expire.

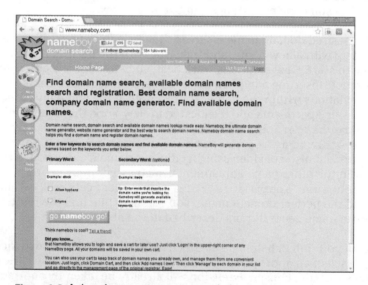

Figure 1-2: A domain name generator can help you find suitable alternatives for your ideal domain name.

No matter which service you use, be sure that you verify the domain name availability (as described in the next section) before plunking down any money to register the domain. You may also want to find out about registration services and hosting plans before you ultimately commit.

Checking domain name availability

Even if you don't require the services of an online domain name generator, you still need to verify that the domain name you have chosen for your website is truly available for registration. This means ensuring that no one else is currently using the domain you want or has already registered it but hasn't begun using it yet.

Thankfully, verification is free and quick to do on a number of websites, including many of the domain registrar and domain name generator sites. For example, Network Solutions (www.networksolutions.com) provides fast results along with providing automatic alternative name suggestions if the name you enter is already taken. With a good verification tool, finding the right name for your site should be only a matter of a having a bit of patience and open-mindedness while you perform the search and verification process.

To show how easy it is to use these domain name verification services, follow these steps to check for the same name on both Network Solutions and DomainsBot:

1. **Go to** www.networksolutions.com, **as shown in Figure 1-3.**

2. **In the Search for a Domain text box on the left side of the page, type the domain name you want to register (leaving the** .com **and** .net **options selected) and click the Search button.**

   For example, type **rochesterapartments**.

   In the search results that appear, you see that this domain is already taken for the .com, .net, .org, and .info extensions. Other extensions that are available include .co, .biz, .us, .us.com, .mobi, and .tv.

Figure 1-3: Network Solutions is a reputable place to register your domain name.

3. **Do another search. This time, enter a variation of the desired domain name in the Search for a Domain text box and click the Search button.**

For example, type **rochester-apts**.

Aha! This domain name is available with both the `.com` and `.net` extensions and could be registered today if you wanted it (presuming that no one has registered this domain since the time of this writing).

4. **Go to** www.domainsbot.com **and type the words your first choice of domain name into the search field.**

For example, enter **rochester apartments**.

Before you even click the Search button, notice how the page reconfigures itself, like the example in Figure 1-4, to reveal the availability of any domains that use the two words in the search field. The `rochester apartments.com` domain name is included in this list and is noted as Not Available.

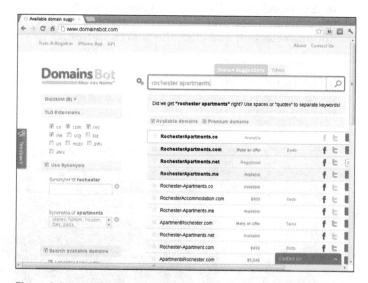

Figure 1-4: DomainsBot can help you find suitable alternatives for domain names that are already taken.

As you can see, these search results are more detailed than those from Network Solutions. In addition, the page includes extra tools to help you refine the search based on selected criteria.

5. **To modify the domain search results, adjust the settings in the various search fields located on the left side of the page.**

For example, adjust the following settings:

- Under TDL extensions, deselect all the extensions except .com.

- Under Synonyms of Apartments, delete all the keywords listed except *lofts* and *suites* and select the check box to save these edits.

- Deselect the Search Premium Domains option.

- Under General, select Exclude Offensive Keywords and Exclude Dash.

The list of domain options automatically updates the list of available domains as you make changes to the search criteria.

If the apartments are located in downtown Rochester and have an open floor plan, for example, RochesterLoftsDowntown.com and RochesterCityLofts.com might be good choices, for example. However, if the domain name really needs to exactly match the company name, the client may be out of luck and will need to come up with some other ideas to find a suitable domain name to register.

If you can't find exactly what you're looking for the first few times, be open to new ideas and try searching on other domain name generator websites. The more you search, the more likely you are to come upon a domain name that really works.

Registering a Domain Name

When you find the right domain name for your website, get it registered as quickly as you can. Think of registering a domain name like reserving a rental car: To reserve the car, you must provide the car agency with your name and contact info, credit card, car preference, and rental dates. To actually use the car, you must go to the rental car agency, sign a contract to rent the car for a predetermined period of time, and provide payment information before the agency gives you the car keys. Likewise, registering the domain is a means of paying for and placing the name on reserve for later use with a hosting plan for a specified period of time.

To register your domain name, you can go about it in one of two ways: Register your site with a domain registrar or sign up for a hosting plan and have the host provider register the domain for you as part of your hosting package. Both options have unique benefits and drawbacks.

Using a domain registrar

When registering a domain name through a domain registration service, you get the benefit of quick and affordable registration without having to worry about hosting until you're ready to publish your site. In most cases, you should be able to choose a time frame for the rights to use your chosen domain name. Typical terms for domain registration are for one, two, three, five, and ten years. Rates for the registration range from as low as $0.99 to over $35 per year. Many registrars include e-mail accounts and other services for this fee; however, some do not, so be careful to understand exactly what you're paying for. Most domain registration rates fall somewhere in the $10–20 per year range, and the rate often drops significantly when you increase the term of the registration to two years or more. The `.com` domains are usually the most sought-after domains and tend to cost more, whereas the less trendy `.info` and `.mobi` extension domain names can now be grabbed up for as little as $0.99 per year.

Choosing the right domain registrar — if you want to use one instead of registering your domain through your host provider — depends on your time frame, budget, and needs. The most popular domain registrars tend to be the ones that charge the least amount of money. Keep in mind, though, that while more affordable, the less expensive services may not necessarily provide the best customer care, which, depending on your level of knowledge, might be an important factor to you and your client. Therefore, shop wisely and do your research before you procure a domain for yourself or a client. Alternatively, you could pass on this part of the process and recommend that your client registers the domain on his own through a particular registrar or host provider.

In addition to domain registration, most registrars these days provide additional web-related services, including domain verification, domain name generators, domain transfers, hosting, and Internet access.

If you just need to register the domain name for a time before the site is ready to publish, but aren't interested in e-mail or hosting until right before the site gets launched, it would probably be fine for you to use one of the cheaper domain registrar services. However, if you know you need other services such as web hosting and e-mail, obtain an SSL certificate, and set up an e-commerce shopping cart, go with one of the companies that also provides those services, such as Network Solutions (`www.networksolutions.com`), eNom (`www.enom.com`), Tucows (`www.tucows.com`), HostGator.com (`www.host gator.com`), Lunarpages (`www.lpwebhosting.com`), directNIC (`www.directnic.com`), GoDaddy.com (`www.godaddy.com`), and Register.com (`www.register.com`), or any of the myriad hosting services that might have been personally recommended to you by friends and business associates.

Before you do that, however, consider your long-term needs:

✓ **Your site is ready, you want to post a placeholder page while you're building your site, or will have a short turnaround time (say, 30 days or less):** You may want to speed the domain registration process by registering the domain through the host provider that will be hosting the site.

✓ **Your site will not be ready for publishing for quite some time:** You can save some money by registering the domain and not worrying about hosting until you're ready to publish the site. If this is the route you decide to take, just make sure that you understand that if you register the domain with one company and use another company for hosting, you need to do a DNS transfer when the hosting plan has been secured. To avoid having to do a DNS transfer, simply register the domain name while you sign up for a hosting plan with your preferred host provider.

Using a host provider

When registering a domain name through a host provider, all you need to do is tell the provider your chosen URL when you sign up for your hosting account. The host then registers the domain for you as part of the hosting plan, often without any additional fees. To find out more about hosting, see the later section, "Finding the Best Hosting Plan."

Activating your domain

To use the registered domain name and allow visitors to access an actual website through that name, you must secure a hosting plan and activate the registered domain name. When you register a domain with one company and host with another (which a lot of people do to try to save a few bucks), the site can be activated for hosting only through a *DNS transfer*. By contrast, when you register your domain and host with the same company, the site becomes active almost immediately after payment.

The DNS (Domain Name Server or Domain Name System) helps create a permanent address for every domain name. Every computer and server that connects to the Internet has its own IP (Internet Protocol) address, typically written in four sets of numbers separated by dots, as in 123.45.67.890. By parking a domain name on a server and creating an alias for the IP to match the domain name, you let visitors begin to use the domain name to find a site.

To get the IP address of your computer, go to `http://whatismy ipaddress.com`.

A DNS transfer, therefore, means that the host provider's servers are pointing to the domain name as an alias for the server's IP address. For the host provider to create that alias, the domain must be transferred from the registrar to the host provider. This ensures that the domain name points to the server that hosts the site so that the site can be properly accessed by everyone on the web.

Finding the Best Hosting Plan

A hosting plan is like a parking space for a website that you rent out by the year on a host provider's server. While parked there, and as long as the domain name is pointing to the host's servers, the site is accessible to anyone surfing the Internet with knowledge of the web address or who happens to find the site listed in search engine results.

In the following sections, you find out how to find the right host provider and evaluate hosting plans.

Researching host providers

Like domain registrars, host providers are everywhere online, which means that finding the right one for your needs may require a little research. You could consult one of the hosting plan review sites, such as Hosting-Review. com (www.hosting-review.com), Top 10 Web Hosting (www.top10web hosting.com), or TheHostingChart.com (www-thehostingchart.com), to find the names of the most popular host providers. However, bear in mind that the host providers on those kinds of lists might be rated more for their pricing than for quality hosting and customer service.

Ideally, you'll want certain things from your host provider: a reasonable rate, great technical support and customer service, and enough web space on the server to host all your files. In addition, you should get the right number of e-mail accounts for your needs, have access to some good site-reporting tools, and be eligible for any special services and discounts that the host provider may have to offer, such as 1-click WordPress installation.

On a personal note, having worked with many different host providers over the years, and having experienced firsthand the difference between good and bad customer support, I can highly recommend Lunarpages (www. lpwebhosting.com) for both domain registration and hosting plans.

Lunarpages, shown in Figure 1-5, is a full-service web development and hosting company that offers competitively priced domain registration and hosting plans with top-rated 24-hour telephone and e-mail technical support. Lunarpages is offering two special discounts to readers of this book who sign up for new 12/24-month hosting plans.

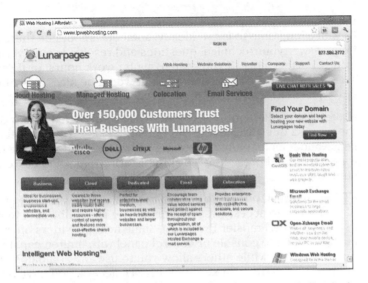

Figure 1-5: Lunarpages has fantastic customer support and offers both domain registration and hosting services.

Both discounts include unlimited storage, unlimited data transfer, and $700 worth of free bonus programs included with your hosting account:

- **Save $10:** Enter coupon code **WebDesign10** and save $10 when signing up for any 12- or 24-month Basic Hosting Plan.

- **Save $30:** Enter coupon code **WebDesign30** and save $30 when signing up for any 12- or 24-month Business, Windows, or LPQuicksite Plan, or any 3-, 6-, 12-, or 24-month VPS or Dedicated Account.

To find the right host provider for your (or your client's) project, keep the following tips in mind:

- **Referrals:** A friendly recommendation can often be the best method for finding a reputable hosting plan. Most people either love or hate their host providers. If you keep hearing praise for the same host provider from different people, that can be a good sign.

- **Customer service:** The most important feature of any hosting plan is customer service. Having 24-hour telephone and e-mail support is absolutely essential, so make sure that the host provider you are interested in offers this. If it doesn't, keep looking. Customer service is so important because you will, at some point, need help and shouldn't have to wait a long time to get it. Ideally, someone should be there 24/7 to help answer your technical questions and resolve any server-related issues. Furthermore, if you keep irregular work hours, or if your host is on one coast and you're on another, it would be nice to be able to have your questions answered anytime, day or night.

Make a list of all the host providers you're interested in and then call them to ask questions about their hosting plans. You can get a good sense about a company's customer service by talking to one of its customer service representatives about hosting plans and customer support.

✓ **FTP and control panel:** Be sure to inquire about ways that each hosting plan allows site access. At a minimum, you should be able to upload files using FTP (File Transfer Protocol). Some host providers offer only a custom-built site console or control panel with limited capabilities for uploading files, while others allow you to use any standalone FTP program to access the host server. With FTP access, you have better control over uploading files when it's time to publish the site.

✓ **Cancellation policy:** Be sure to also ask each company about its cancellation policy and whether that includes a refund. If for any reason you decide you want to switch plans to another host provider sometime in the future, it would be nice if you could get a refund for the unused balance of the plan. The host providers that do offer prorated or partial refunds are often the ones with the best customer service and hosting plans.

Evaluating hosting plan packages

While you're researching the different hosting plans from the various hosting companies, make sure to look for the type of hosting package that's appropriate to your needs. Shared hosting plans tend to come in four distinct flavors: the bare-bones starter plan, the small-business plan, the big-business or cloud hosting plan, and the e-commerce plan. Most plans have certain features in common, with tiered levels of benefits, as outlined in Table 1-2.

Table 1-2	Typical Web Hosting Plan Features			
Feature	*Starter*	*Small Biz*	*Big Biz*	*e-Commerce*
Monthly fee	$3.95–9.95	$19.95	$19.95–59.95+	$44.95+
Technical features	5GB hard drive storage space, 50GB data transfer, 20 million page views, dedicated IP address, 3 user accounts	400GB to unlimited hard storage drive space, 400GB to unlimited data transfer, 40 million page views, dedicated IP address, 6 user accounts	1000GB hard drive storage space, 400GB to unlimited data transfer, 60 million page views, dedicated IP address, 12 user accounts	1000GB hard drive storage space, 1000GB to unlimited data transfer, 100 million page views, dedicated IP address, 24 user accounts
E-mail	5 accounts and 1 GB hard drive space, spam guard, virus protection, online e-mail access, autoresponders, forwarders, and so on	500 accounts and 1.5 GB hard drive space, spam guard, virus protection, online e-mail access, autoresponders, forwarders, and so on	750+ accounts and 2GB hard drive space, spam guard, virus protection, online e-mail access, autoresponders, forwarders, and so on	1,000+ accounts and 3GB hard drive space, spam guard, virus protection, online e-mail access, autoresponders, forwarders, and so on
Database and indexing services	mySQL max, 25MB hard drive space	+ mySQL server, 2 ODBC data source names, Microsoft Access, unlimited hard drive space	+ mySQL server, 4 ODBC data source names, Microsoft Access, unlimited hard drive space	+ mySQL server, 6 ODBC data source names, Microsoft Access, unlimited hard drive space

In addition to the services listed in Table 1-1, most plans also provide or support the following:

- ✔ **Account:** 24-hour uptime, customer service, and technical support

- ✔ **Scripting:** MySQL, CGI-BIN, Perl, PHP, Ruby on Rails, Python, SSI support, and so on

- ✔ **Domains:** Dedicated domain name, domain transfers, registration of new domains, domain pointers, and so on

- ✔ **Site management:** Online control panel, website builder, FrontPage extensions (scripts that provide dynamic functions on sites built with Microsoft FrontPage or ExpressionWeb), 24-hour FTP access, free web-based statistics, access to raw log files, and so on

- ✔ **E-commerce services:** SSL secure servers, shared SSL certificates, merchant tools with and without credit card processing, Google Checkout, and so on

- ✔ **Data center:** Firewall and antivirus protection, daily backups, redundant servers with UPS features power backups, and so on

Although monthly rates can run as low as $1.50 and as high as $99, most plans range from about $4.95 to $39.95 per month and differ by the terms of service they provide:

- ✔ **Uptime:** The total time within any 24-hour period where the site is accessible to visitors on the Internet. Anytime a host provider's server goes down, for whatever reason, domains on that server go offline, which is commonly referred to as *downtime*. An uptime of 100 percent is the ultimate goal of all host providers, but most will only guarantee a 99 percent uptime rate.

- ✔ **Hard drive space:** This is the total number of megabytes (MB) or gigabytes (GB) of space allotted for the domain on the host provider's server. To determine your website's hard drive space needs, multiply the number of pages by 30K and then factor in enough space to account for all the additional files required for the site, including all the graphics, CSS, JavaScript, jQuery, PDFs, and multimedia files. You may also be able to estimate the total number of megabytes for your site through your HTML code editor. For example, in Dreamweaver, you can select all the files through the expanded Files panel and read the total byte count in the status bar. Typical small sites can make do with as little as 500MB–1GB of space, whereas e-commerce sites can require upward of 30GB, depending on the number of products being sold on the site.

- ✔ **User account:** Depending on the website's needs, the hosting plan can accommodate from one to several user accounts. Each account provides password-protected host server access to site management tools such as passwords, e-mail setup functionality, and billing information.

✔ **Data transfer and page views:** The data transfer and page view figures refer to the maximum allowable number of times that visitors can access the pages (that is, the text, graphics, and other content) on the hosted site within a given time frame, such as a 30-day period. If the site is very popular, there could easily be anywhere from several hundred to over 50,000 page views in a month!

✔ **Web-based statistics:** Web-based stats can help site owners track the number of visitors to their site, including such details as the entry and exit URLs, the number of hits and page views, keyword analysis, and the number of returning versus new visitors.

✔ **Dedicated IP address:** Domains with a dedicated IP address are hosted on their own servers as opposed to sharing a server with other domains. Dedicated IP plans are more expensive than websites that use a shared IP address, but they are also ultimately more reliable because a dedicated server can more accurately monitor its own web traffic and provide faster server response times. A dedicated IP address can also sometimes be a requirement if your site needs an SSL certificate, depending on the host provider's setup, so be sure to ask about this if you intend to get an SSL certificate.

✔ **Domain pointer:** This feature, which may cost a few extra bucks per month, allows one domain to automatically reroute visitors to another domain. Domain pointers can often be useful when a business wants to provide for misspellings of a domain name so that anytime visitors try to view the misspelled domain, they're automatically directed to the correctly named site, such as www.yahooo.com pointing to www.yahoo.com.

Shop around, do your research, speak to friends and business associates, and make your decision. After you choose a host provider, just sign up for the desired hosting plan. If you're also registering a domain for the first time when signing up for the plan, the site should be ready for use right away. If the domain was registered elsewhere, you can do the DNS transfer from the registrar to the host's servers as soon as you're ready to publish the site or a placeholder page. You (or your client) can also set up e-mail accounts and adjust them at any time after the plan is paid for. Later, if you (or your client) are not happy with a particular host provider, you can always switch to another provider.

Creating a Custom Placeholder Page

A *placeholder page* is exactly what it sounds like: It's the default home page that visitors see at a particular web address — your domain name — when you (or your client) have both registered the domain and set up a hosting plan, but have not yet published the new website or any of your own pages there.

The default placeholder page provided by the host provider can vary. Sometimes that page may identify the domain name and IP address of the domain, and sometimes it doesn't. More often than not, what you see are some instructions to the site owner on how to access the host's servers to manage the new hosting account. The rest of the page is usually filled with information and links to the services of the domain registrar or hosting company where the site is parked, as in the example from Lunarpages shown in Figure 1-6.

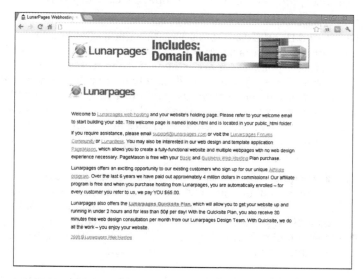

Figure 1-6: A host provider placeholder page often provides site setup tips to the site owner but no information to potential visitors about products or services.

Fortunately, the domain registrar or host provider placeholder page only stays online until it is removed or overwritten by either you or the site owner (or the webmaster or whomever else the client might hire to manage the site after you design it). The smartest thing to do, then, is to take advantage of this paid-for open advertising space and design a customized placeholder page for the domain that can sit there until the new site is ready to publish.

The best custom placeholders are simple HTML web pages that identify the site (logo, company/owner name, tag line, and other branding) and offer a means of contacting the site owner by both snail mail and e-mail. Anything else on the page, like a blurb about the company or some recent news items, is gravy. Figure 1-7 shows an example of a typical placeholder page that includes company name, an encrypted contact e-mail address, and general information.

In the following sections, you find out how to design your own placeholder and then publish it.

Figure 1-7: A customized placeholder page can include the company logo, an (encrypted) e-mail address, and a statement about the company's services.

Designing a placeholder page

To create your own custom placeholder page, you need access to the following things:

- ✔ A text, HTML, or WYSIWYG code editor to build the placeholder page such as Dreamweaver, CoffeeCup, Amaya, Kompozer, TextWrangler, or even TextEdit or Notepad

- ✔ The site owner's company name/logo in GIF, PNG, or JPG format

- ✔ The descriptive statement about the site that will be included on the placeholder page

- ✔ The site owner's e-mail address, which should use the new domain name such as info@*mysite*.com rather than a personal e-mail address from AOL, Gmail, AT&T, or Yahoo!

The following two sections show you how to create a simple customized placeholder page styled with internal CSS. By leaving the CSS inside the page, you only have to upload a single file rather than the HTML and the CSS.

Creating the page

Follow these steps to create the placeholder page:

1. **Create a new folder on your computer desktop called Placeholder, and inside that folder, create another folder called images.**

   The placeholder page and image you're about to create will be saved to this folder structure.

2. **Save the company logo with the `.jpg`, `.gif`, or `.png` file extension and place it into your new images folder inside the Placeholder folder on your desktop.**

   If you want to follow along with the example, download a copy of the logo graphic named Luau-a-go-go (`luauagogo.gif`) from this book's website.

   To save a copy of the graphic, as shown in Figure 1-8, right-click (Windows) or Control+click (Mac) the image and choose Save (This) Image As. Choose the images folder inside the Placeholder folder on your desktop as the save-to location.

3. **Using your preferred code editor, or your computer's text editing program, open a new blank document.**

   To use your computer's default text editing program, choose Start➪All Programs➪Accessories➪Notepad if you're using a PC, or on a Mac, launch your Applications folder and double-click the TextEdit icon.

Figure 1-8: Use this logo to create a sample placeholder page.

   A new untitled document should open automatically. If that doesn't happen, choose File➪New to open a new file.

4. **If you're using a text editor, type the following basic HTML5 page structure, including the HTML5 DTD and `charset` meta tag:**

```
<!doctype html>
<html>
  <head>
  <meta charset="utf-8">
  <title></title>
  </head>
  <body>
  </body>
</html>
```

Otherwise, if you're using an HTML code editor, which automatically drops in the structural code for you, skip ahead to Step 5.

5. **Between the opening and closing <title> tags, type a title for the page (for example,** Luau-a-go-go).

Your code should now look like this:

```
<!doctype html><html>
  <head>
  <meta charset="utf-8">
  <title>Luau a-go-go</title>
  </head>
  <body>
  </body>
</html>
```

This code sets the title for the page, which appears in the browser's title bar.

6. **Between the opening and closing <body> tags, type the company name, a descriptive statement or tag line, and an e-mail address (which you convert into an encrypted e-mail address in Step 10).**

For example, type the following bold text, making sure to add the paragraph <p> and break <br> tags where indicated:

```
<!doctype html><html>
  <head>
  <meta charset="utf-8">
  <title>Luau-a-go-go</title>
  </head>
  <body>
  <p>Luau-a-go-go</p>
  <br>
  <h1>Hawaiian Themed Catering</h1><br>
  <p>Luaus * Special Events * Birthdays * Anniversaries *Celebrations<br>
  Santa Monica, CA<br>
  For further information contact<br> info@luauagogo.com</p>
  </body>
</html>
```

The <body> tags hold the text and other content that appear in the browser window.

7. **Choose File⇨Save to open the Save As dialog box.**

You need to save the document to your new Placeholder folder.

8. **In the File Name field, type** index.html; **in the Save In field, select the Placeholder folder; and in the Save as Type field, select the All Files option. Then click the Save button.**

This document does not include any logo graphic yet, so you'll need to modify the code.

If you're using TextEdit, choose the Make Plain Text option from the Format menu. You also want to make sure that you include the .html file extension before saving so your document doesn't accidentally save as an .rtf or .txt file.

9. **Delete the line of code that says `<p>Luau-a-go-go</p>` and replace it with the following line of code, which inserts the logo graphic onto the page:**

   ```
   <img src="images/luauagogo.gif" alt="Luau-a-go-go" width="208"
       height="76">
   ```

   Replace the text in italics if you're using your client's logo.

10. **Convert the e-mail address into a working hyperlink using an e-mail encryption service (instead of the regular `mailto:` e-mail link, which is vulnerable to spambots), like the one found at** www.dynamic drive.com/emailriddler.

    Your page code should now look something like this:

    ```
    <!doctype html><html>
      <head>
      <meta charset="utf-8">
      <title>Luau-a-go-go</title>
      </head>
      <body>
      <img src="images/luauagogo.gif" alt="Luau-a-go-go" width="208"
        height="76">
      <br>
      <h1>Hawaiian Themed Catering</h1><br>
      <p>Luaus * Special Events * Birthdays * Anniversaries *Celebrations<br>
      Santa Monica, CA<br>
      For further information contact<br>
    <script type="text/javascript">
    /*<![CDATA[*/
    /***********************************************
    * Encrypt Email script- Please keep notice intact
    * Tool URL: http://www.dynamicdrive.com/emailriddler/
    * ***********************************************/
    <!-- Encrypted version of: info [at] ********.*** //-->
    var emailriddlerarray=[105,110,102,111,64,108,117,97,117,97,
        103,111,103,111,46,99,111,109]
    var encryptedemail_id62='' //variable to contain encrypted email
    for (var i=0; i<emailriddlerarray.length; i++)
    encryptedemail_id62+=String.fromCharCode(emailriddlerarray[i])
    document.write('<a href="mailto: '+encryptedemail_id62+'">'
        +encryptedemail_id62+'</a>')
    /*]]>*/
    </script></p>
      </body>
    </html>
    ```

For more on e-mail encryption, see the sidebar about protecting your e-mail addresses from spam in Book III, Chapter 1.

11. **Save the changes to your file and preview the page in a browser window.**

    To preview the page in a browser, drag and drop the icon of your new `index.html` page into any open browser window. No Internet connection is required to preview the page locally.

    The page looks okay, like the one shown in Figure 1-9, but it could definitely benefit from a little styling, as described in the next section.

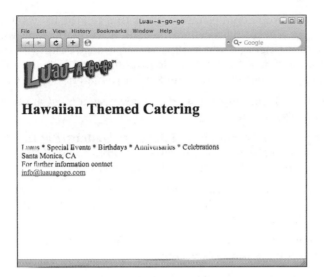

Figure 1-9: Before you add CSS styling, a placeholder page can often look bland with just graphics and text.

Styling the page

Follow these steps to add CSS styling to the placeholder page:

1. **Above the closing `</head>` tag in your code, type the internal CSS markup you want to use on your page.**

   See Book III, Chapter 3 for more on CSS.

   If you're following along with the example, type the following markup:

   ```
   <style type="text/css">
   <!--
   #luauagogo {
     height: 250px;
     width: 500px;
     margin-right: auto;
     margin-left: auto;
     margin-top: 15%;
     margin-bottom: auto;
     text-align: center;
     font-family: Georgia, "Times New Roman", Times, serif;
     font-size: 12px;
     color: #F60;
     padding-top: 20px;
     padding-right: 0px;
     padding-bottom: 0px;
     padding-left: 0px;
     background-color: #FFF;
     border: 1px dashed #0CC;
   }
   a:link {
     color: #0CC;
   }
   -->
   </style>
   ```

This CSS markup contains instructions that tell the browser how to style the content. These styles center the content in the browser window, style the text in the Georgia font in 12px and an orange color with the hexadecimal color of #ff6600 to match the logo, add a blue dashed border around everything, and use blue as the link color to match the border.

Before this CSS markup can work, however, you must apply this ID style to the page's content.

2. **Wrap a pair of DIV tags around the page content. Put the opening `<div>` tag directly after the opening `<body>` tag and the closing `</div>` tag directly above the closing `</body>` tag.**

DIV tags are container tags for layers that can be styled and positioned with CSS when you include the `id` or `class` attribute in the opening tag that matches the name of the style in the CSS markup.

3. **Add the attribute `id= " uniqueid "` (for example, `id= "luaua gogo"`) to the opening `<div>` tag.**

Replace `uniqueid` with the ID of your choice.

The `body` part of your code should now look like this:

```
<body>
<div id="luauagogo">
  <img src="images/luauagogo.gif" alt="Luau-a-go-go" width="208"
    height="76">
  <br>
  <h1>Hawaiian Themed Catering</h1><br>
  <p>Luaus * Special Events * Birthdays * Anniversaries *
    Celebrations<br>
  Santa Monica, CA<br>
  For further information contact<br>
  <!-- encrypted email address code here --></p>
</div>
</body>
```

4. **Save the file again to save the changes you just made and preview the page in a browser window.**

Figure 1-10 shows what the page example should look like after applying the CSS ID style.

When creating your own placeholder page, feel free to generate as many graphics and other CSS styles as needed to make the page look exactly as you'd like it to. If you've already created a mock-up for the website, you may even want to use some of the same design features within the placeholder page. When the page is finished, you need to upload the page and any graphics or other supporting files to the host server so that the placeholder page can brand and identify the domain until the new site is ready to publish.

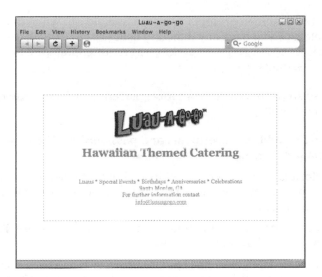

Figure 1-10: Use CSS to give your placeholder page more style and personality.

Uploading a placeholder page

When a custom placeholder page is created for a client, be sure you get your client's approval on the page before publishing it. This gives the client the opportunity to review your work and suggest any changes that may need to be made. After all, this page represents the client's company, and she will want to put her best face forward. If the client does recommend some changes, make any adjustments to the code as needed and then resubmit the page for approval. When the client grants approval, you can then upload the placeholder HTML file, the images folder that contains any graphics, and any other files needed to support the page to the host server.

To transfer the placeholder page and supporting files to the host server, you can use the host provider's control panel, a standalone File Transfer Protocol (FTP) program, an FTP program that is built into an HTML editor (Dreamweaver has one), or a browser that supports FTP. You discover more about FTP in Book V, Chapter 2, so for now, I discuss how to upload your files through a browser.

Before you begin, download and install the free cross-platform Firefox FireFTP add-on from `http://fireftp.mozdev.org`. If after clicking the Download button you see an alert that says "Firefox prevented the site from asking you to install the software on your computer," click the Allow button and follow the onscreen prompts to install the add-on. When finished, restart Firefox. (If you have any difficulty using FireFTP, view the Help files at `http://fireftp.mozdev.org/help.html` or contact the host provider for further assistance.)

Follow these steps to transfer your local placeholder files to the remote host server using Firefox:

1. **Get the FTP address, username, and password for the domain from the host provider or from your client.**

    This information is typically sent by e-mail to the person who signed up for the hosting account. The FTP address should be something like `ftp.domainname.com`.

2. **With a live Internet connection, open Firefox and choose Tools⇨Web Developer⇨FireFTP to launch FireFTP.**

    The FireFTP tool opens in a separate browser tab. Notice that the screen is split into two sides. Your local files are listed on the left and the remote files from the server will be listed on the right after a connection to the server is established.

3. **From the account menu at the top of the window, choose Create an Account to launch the Account Manager dialog box, shown in Figure 1-11.**

    This is where you enter the FTP access information to connect with the remote host server.

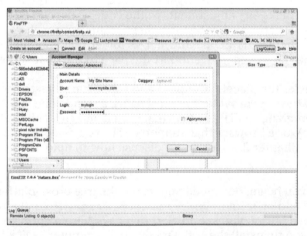

Figure 1-11: Enter the FTP username and password in the FireFTP Account Manager dialog box.

4. **In the Account Name and Host fields, enter a name for your site and the URL of the domain you want to access.**

   The name is for your eyes only so it can be anything you like. The URL should be the exact domain name as in www.*domainname*.com.

5. **Enter the FTP Login (username) and Password provided by your host provider.**

6. **Click OK to close the dialog box and click the Connect button at the top of the window to connect to your site.**

   After a connection is established, the browser window automatically refreshes and displays all the files on the host server for the domain. Those files will probably include a default placeholder home page named index.html, a CGI-BIN folder for processing scripts, and possibly a few other preinstalled files and folders that the host server requires to make the site accessible to visitors.

   Some host providers place your site's files inside of a folder named public-html or www. If you see one of those folders, double-click to open it. You should then see your host provider's default index.html file. If, for some reason, you'd like to save this file for archival purposes, select the file, right-click to open the context menu, and choose Rename file. You can rename it anything you like such as _hostindex.html or zhostindex.html so it will fall alphabetically at the top or bottom of the list of files.

7. **Drag and drop a copy of your Placeholder folder's index.html file along with a copy of the images folder from the Local files on the left of the screen into the Remote files listed on the right.**

   Your browser begins copying the files to the remote host.

8. **If prompted to overwrite the index.html page, click the Yes button so that your new custom placeholder page will appear as the new default home page.**

   When the files have fully been copied to the server, you are finished *ftp-ing* and can disconnect by clicking the Disconnect button.

9. **To test the success of the file transfer, type the URL of the domain into the browser's address bar, such as** http://www.*mydomainname*.com.

   Your new placeholder page should appear. If you don't see it, try refreshing the browser window (usually by pressing F5) and/or clearing your browser's cache.

For simple directions on how to clear your browser's cache, visit `www.bnl.gov/itd/webapps/browsercache.asp`. If you still don't see your placeholder page, your server might use the `default.html` homepage naming convention. To test that theory, rename `index.html` to `default.html` and upload the file to the server. The new placeholder page should appear if your theory is correct.

Chapter 2: Publishing Your Site

In This Chapter

✓ Finding out about FTP programs

✓ Establishing a remote connection

✓ Testing files in a test directory

✓ Transferring files with FTP

✓ Uploading your site

*t's finally time to publish your site! At this stage, you have done quite a bit of work. You've planned, organized, and gathered information for your site; designed a mock-up; optimized all the graphics; built all the pages; tested and validated an entire website; and registered a domain and secured a hosting plan. Now you are truly ready, at long last, to share your site with the world. To officially publish your site and get It online for all to see, you need to transfer all the files that make up the site — that is, all the HTML files, images, CSS, external JavaScript files, SSIs, media files, and any other site assets and documents for files that are accessible through the site — to the remote server that is hosting the site.

If you have registered a domain but have not secured a hosting plan, now is the time to do that and put in for the DNS transfer because you'll need the hosting plan to be up and running before you can transfer files to the server. Otherwise, if the hosting plan is ready, go dig up the information the host provider sent to you that shows the plan's username and password and includes any special instructions about FTP (File Transfer Protocol) and transferring files to the host's remote server. FTP is the most common way to transfer files to a remote server, so that's what I discuss in this chapter.

General	Advanced | Transfer Settings | Charset
Host:	Port:
Protocol:	FTP - File Transfer Protocol
Encryption:	Use plain FTP
Logon Type:	Normal
User:	anonymous
Password:	●●●●●●●●●●●●●
Account:	

In addition to finding out how to set up a remote connection to a host server with FTP, this chapter instructs you on how to transfer your local files both to and from the host server, create a test directory on the server, upload your site to the test directory for a final round of testing, and finally, upload the site to the root level of the host server to officially publish the site on the web.

Uploading Files with File Transfer Protocol

File Transfer Protocol (FTP) is the standard TCP/IP Internet protocol that allows the exchange of files between remote computers over the Internet. To initiate an FTP session, a client (you) must use special software or some kind of Internet interface to log on and gain access to the remote server. Logging on typically requires the input of a special username or ID and a password that the host provider furnished when you (or your client) purchased the hosting plan. For example, if your name is Mary Miller and your site is called `www.millercheesesticks.com`, your host provider might automatically generate a username/ID and password for you, such as mmillmiller and zc79ole7. Not all host providers generate the username and password combo for you. Some provide you with temporary account information and the opportunity of resetting your username/ID and password to something else after you log on to your site.

After access to the remote server has been established for the FTP session, you may begin *getting* (downloading) and *putting* (uploading) files between your local computer and the remote server. Remember, the remote server is the live host, which means that as soon as files are copied onto the remote server, they're live and publicly accessible on the Internet! When you finish transferring your files, to end the FTP session, log off or otherwise disconnect from the remote server. The whole process is surprisingly simple.

Choosing the right FTP program

You can use many different FTP applications to transfer your files. Although their interfaces may be somewhat different, most FTP applications allow you to do the same things with your files, such as viewing a listing of files by name, date, and size, creating directories, and allowing you to transfer, copy, rename, and delete files and directories on the remote server.

FTP programs come in four different flavors; a standalone application, an integrated feature of another software program, a tool on a host provider's website control panel, or a component of a browser interface:

- **Standalone programs:** Standalone programs, such as WS-FTP, FileZilla, Cyberduck, or Fetch, must be installed on your local computer and launched like any other program each time you need to access the remote server. You may use the same program to access as many sites as you like, as long as you have the correct URL, username, and password combination for each domain. Each site can have its own server profile. Saved profiles archive the FTP URL, username, and password information to make future logons faster.

  Though some FTP programs have a drag-and-drop interface where you can drag files from your local desktop into the remote view of the host server, most programs consist of a single window with two panes that represent views of the local site files and the remote site files, as shown in Figure 2-1. Data may then be transferred both to and from the remote server using common interface controls such as Get, Put, Change Directory, Make Directory, Rename, Delete, and Refresh.

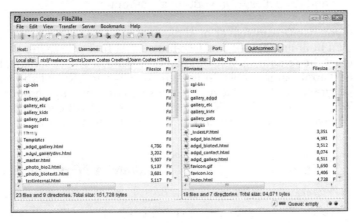

Figure 2-1: The standalone FileZilla program has a single, two-paned window for displaying local and remote files.

✓ **Integrated application:** Some FTP clients are built-in components within other programs that allow you to transfer files to and from a specified remote server through a special FTP panel. For example, Dreamweaver's Files panel can be used as an FTP tool. When you expand the Files panel, you can even see both the remote and local views of the files being transferred and can transfer files in either direction.

✓ **Internet control panel:** Your host provider may include some kind of special Internet control panel through which you can transfer files to and from the host server. These panels are often customized web interfaces developed by host providers and are composed of a handful of specialized web forms. These forms allow the host's customers (you or your client) to upload files to the remote server and occasionally to also select and download files from it. Most control panels restrict uploads to single files at a time, rather than enabling users to specify and upload several files or folders at once. Control panels also rarely let clients have full control over the files on the remote server and may even restrict access to certain tasks, such as renaming and deleting files.

✓ **Browser interface:** Many browsers include an FTP client interface that allows you to access the remote server with a simple Internet connection from your local computer. With some browser interfaces, you establish a connection to the remote host by entering an FTP address into the address bar, after which time the browser prompts you to enter a username/ID and password. Other browser interfaces employ the use of special browser plug-ins or add-ons, like the FireFTP add-on described in Book V, Chapter 1. After the FTP address, username, and password have been submitted, that information is then passed to the remote server and authenticated when the logon information is correct. After the connection is established, the same browser window is used to display the files and directories on the remote server, into which you may drag and drop files from your local computer.

If you use Dreamweaver or some other HTML coding application that has its own built-in FTP tool, feel free to use that tool to transfer your files to and from the remote server. On the other hand, if you're looking for a standalone FTP application, Table 2-1 lists the names and URLs of some of the better programs for both Mac and Windows platforms (my personal favorites are WS_FTP and FileZilla). Take a few minutes to visit each of these sites and download the application that appeals the most to you.

Table 2-1	Standalone FTP Programs		
Program	**URL**	**Price**	**OS**
FileZilla	`http://filezilla-project.org`	Free	Win/ Mac/ Linux
WS_FTP	`www.ipswitchft.com/products/ws_ftp_pro/`	$55	Win
CoffeeCup Free FTP	`www.coffeecup.com/free-ftp`	Free	Win
FlashFXP	`www.flashfxp.com`	Free/$29	Win
SmartFTP	`www.smartftp.com`	$36	Win
CuteFTP	`www.globalscape.com/products/ftp_clients.asp`	$59	Win/ Mac
Cyberduck	`http://cyberduck.ch`	Free	Mac
Fetch	`http://fetchsoftworks.com/fetch/`	$29	Mac
FTP Client	`www.ftpclient.com`	$35	Mac
Fugu SFTP	`http://rsug.itd.umich.edu/software/fugu`	Free	Mac
RBrowser	`www.rbrowser.com`	Free/$29	Mac
Yummy FTP	`www.yummysoftware.com`	$28	Mac

Setting up a remote connection

After you have chosen your method of FTP (which may include purchasing, downloading, and installing a standalone application), your next step is to set up the remote connection to the host server. This process involves configuring the FTP client with a session profile for the connection to your domain. Profiles normally include the following bits of information:

- The URL of the domain being accessed or a special FTP address provided by the host, as in www.*mywebsite*.com or ftp.*mywebsite*.com

- The host-provided username and password to access the site via FTP

- When applicable, additional host-related information that may be required by the FTP application or server to assist with making the connection to the remote server, such as the host type, account name, initial remote directory, and firewall information

To illustrate how this works, take a look at the interface for configuring a new session profile in FileZilla in Figure 2-2. Before a connection to the remote server can be established, each FTP session profile requires a profile name, host name/address, user ID, and password.

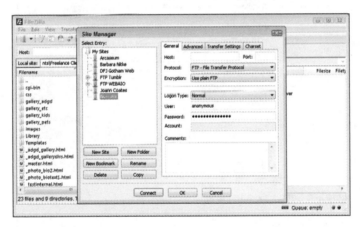

Figure 2-2: FTP sessions require a host address, user ID, and password before allowing access to a remote server.

By contrast, Dreamweaver users must manage a site and set up the remote access information before being able to use the program's built-in FTP tools. Follow these steps to set up a remote FTP connection in Dreamweaver. If you are using another coding editor for FTP, you should be able to easily adapt most of these steps.

1. **Launch Dreamweaver and choose Site⇨Manage Sites.**

   The Manage Sites dialog box opens. If you have already managed a site for the files you intend to transfer, that site's name should appear in the dialog box. However, if you haven't managed a site for this web project, you must manage a site before continuing.

2. **To create a managed site, click the New Site button in the Manage Sites dialog box.**

   The Site Setup dialog box opens with the Site category selected.

3. **Enter a name for the site in the Site Name text box and the location of the site on your local computer in the Local Site Folder text box, as shown in Figure 2-3.**

   The name you give your site is solely for your own use and does not appear anywhere on the published site, but it does help you identify the site by name within the Manage Sites dialog box. The local site folder tells Dreamweaver where to find the files for this site so that it can perform special functions like sitewide updates.

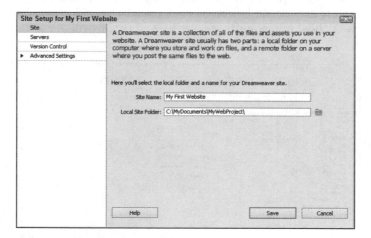

Figure 2-3: Set up a managed site.

4. **In the Category section on the left of the dialog box, select the Servers option. Then, on the right, click the Add New Server (plus sign) button.**

   The dialog box now displays FTP configuration fields, as shown in Figure 2-4. The Connect Using setting defines the protocol by which files will be transferred between your local computer and the remote server. In this case, it's preset to FTP.

5. **In the FTP Address field, enter the host address where the files will be uploaded to.**

   This can be either the domain name preceded by www or ftp, such as www.*mydomain*.com or ftp.*mydomain*.com, or the domain's IP address (which should have also been given to you by the host provider). If you're not sure which one to enter, try www.*mydomain*.com first, and if that doesn't work, refer to the information about FTP access furnished by the host provider or system administrator.

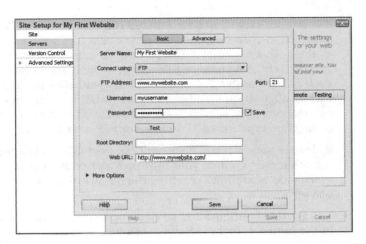

Figure 2-4: Set up your FTP connection by entering in your FTP profile information.

6. **(Optional) If your host provider requires the additional input of a host or root directory, enter that information in the Root Directory field.**

   A *host directory* or *root directory* is the location on the remote server where files for your domain will be kept. Typical host directories are often www, public_html, or some specialized name such as /b52/domainname.

   If this information is required for FTP access on your host server, your host provider would have furnished this information to you along with the user ID and password. Therefore, if you don't have (or think your site doesn't have) a host directory, leave this field blank.

7. **Enter the Username and Password information for the remote server.**

   Some host providers refer to this information as your Login ID, username, or user ID.

8. **Click the Test button to verify the connection to the remote server.**

   If the remote information you have entered is accurate and your computer can make an FTP connection to the remote server, Dreamweaver displays a Connection Established success message. Congratulations! You may proceed to Step 9.

   If, on the other hand, your computer fails to make a connection to the remote server, you see an error message. Go back and check the spelling of all the information you have entered in the dialog box to ensure that the information is accurate. Typos and incorrect letter case can prevent the connection from being established. Test again until a connection is established.

If you're sure that you have entered the Username and Password information correctly, click the arrow next to where it says More Options. This expands the More Options panel, where you can try successively using passive FTP and/or some of the other options available such as Use Passive FTP and Use Proxy, and click the Test button after each configuration modification to see whether you can establish a connection to the server. You may also want to try changing the connection type from FTP to SFTP or FTP over SSL/TLS.

If, despite your attempts, you still can't establish a connection to the remote server, contact your host provider or system administrator for assistance. Sometimes resetting the password allows you to establish a connection.

9. **To save this configuration so that you may use this remote connection in the future, select the Save check box next to the Password text box.**

   This is a very useful feature because it allows you to forget about the username and password and establish a connection to the remote server more quickly when transferring files in the future.

10. **Click the Save button to close the FTP settings pop-up window. Then click the Save button to close the Site Definition dialog box and return to the Manage Sites dialog box. Lastly, click the Done button to close the Manage Sites dialog box.**

If you've decided to use a different FTP client than Dreamweaver, take a moment to configure your chosen FTP client with the appropriate session profile details for your website. Most FTP tools allow you to either test the connection or make a live connection to verify that your session profile information is accurate. Should you need any help setting up or troubleshooting the connection, consult the FTP client help files and contact your host provider or system administrator.

After you have established a successful remote FTP connection with your domain's host computer, you're ready to transfer files between your local computer and the remote host. In the next section, you find instructions on setting up a test directory, transferring files, performing last-minute testing, and publishing your site.

Setting Up a Test Directory

Though you're undoubtedly very excited about publishing your website, you have one more task to perform beforehand: Set up a test directory where you can upload your site to the hosting server for one final round of quick testing.

A *test directory* is a folder you create that sits at the root level of the remote server, as shown in Figure 2-5. By uploading a copy of all the site files from your local computer to this remote test folder, you can review the remote files on the Internet, as though they are "live," for the final round of testing. This keeps the customized placeholder page (index.html) intact and visible to any potential visitors to the domain until you're ready to publish the site. (See Book V, Chapter 1 for the lowdown on creating a placeholder page.)

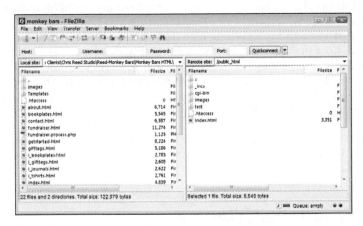

Figure 2-5: Test a site in a live environment by placing a copy of it in a test folder on the remote server.

To create a test directory on your remote server, follow these steps:

1. **Launch your FTP client and establish a connection with the remote server.**

   Though each FTP client is slightly different, they all should allow you to establish a connection by selecting the desired session profile and clicking an OK or Connect button.

2. **Create a new test directory with the name of your choice at the root level on the remote site.**

   You should see an option somewhere in the FTP interface to make a new directory (often called MkDir) or create a new folder using the File⇨New Folder command.

   Your test directory folder can be named anything you like, such as test, temp, dev (for development), secret, lab, check, wip (for work in progress), or trial. Alternatively, you could name the test directory after the abbreviation of the client's site, such as MBD for Monkey Bars Design.

When you create your test directory, you may notice that the host server already contains some files and folders. Most host providers display default home pages (usually called `index.html` or `default.htm`) that are used as placeholders for your domain until you're ready to publish your site. When those pages include graphics, you'll also likely see an images folder at the root level of the host server for your domain. If you have already designed and uploaded your own customized placeholder page to the server (as described in Book V, Chapter 1), you can see that file on the remote server too.

In addition to a default home page, many host accounts include a `cgi-bin` folder, inside which you can place script files to handle form processing and other programming. Anything else that you see there is probably required by the host provider for your site to be fully functional, so be sure to leave those files where they are. Creating a test directory should not affect those files, as long as you leave your customized placeholder page named `index.html` and the images folder in place at the root level until the fully tested site is ready for publishing.

Now that you have your test folder in position on the remote server, you are ready to discover the file transfer process, final-round testing, and publishing.

Getting and Putting Files

FTP file transfers are normally bidirectional, which means that you may send and receive files both to and from the remote server location. When you transmit your files to the remote server, you call that *uploading* or "putting" files, and when you receive files from the remote server, that is called *downloading* or "getting" files.

In most cases, the transfers put copies of your local files on the remote server for testing and publishing purposes. From time to time, however, you may want to get a copy of some of or all the files from the remote server for your local computer to, say, restore a broken version of a file or to get a copy of the site onto a new computer. In either case, file transfers via FTP are a useful way of making copies from one location to another. Like a document through a fax machine (if you even remember how those work!), the original files always stay in one location while the copies are transmitted to the remote location.

Putting files on the remote server

To put a copy of your local site files into the new testing folder on the remote server using FTP, follow these steps:

1. **Launch your FTP client and establish a connection with the remote server.**

   Ideally, your FTP interface should display and provide access to both your local files and your remote files, so you may need to configure your

FTP tool to display both locations. If your FTP client has a drag-and-drop-style interface, have the folder to your local site on your computer open in a window right next to it so that you can easily drag and drop files between the two locations.

2. **Open the test folder on the remote server by double-clicking the folder's icon.**

   This folder needs to be open so that the files can be transferred into it, rather than to the root level of your domain on the remote server.

3. **Put (transfer) all the local files that make up your site, including all HTML files, CSS, JavaScript, images, and other assets, into the test folder on the remote server.**

   Depending on your FTP client interface, this step can involve a drag and drop of all the selected files on your local computer into the remote test folder, or the selection of all the desired files and the clicking of a Copy, Put, or Transfer button.

While transferring files in some FTP clients, you may be prompted to choose whether to also transfer *dependent* files. Dependents are any additional files associated with the HTML document(s) being transferred, such as images, media files, PDFs, SSIs, CSS, jQuery, and JavaScript files. When the transfer involves sending information for the first time or uploading files that have been modified in some way, including dependents is a good idea.

Transferring files with Dreamweaver

In Dreamweaver, you have a number of ways to transfer files through the Files panel:

✔ Use the file transfer buttons that display along the top of the collapsed Files panel.

✔ Use the FTP commands in the Files panel's options menu.

✔ Expand the Files panel and use any of the FTP buttons that display across the top of the expanded Files panel window or any of the commands on the Files panel options menu, or drag and drop any selected files between the remote and local views of the managed site.

The smartest way to transfer files is to use the expanded Files panel so that you can view both the local and remote files at the same time, much like a standalone FTP client.

To transfer files to the remote server with Dreamweaver's expanded Files panel, follow these steps:

1. **Launch Dreamweaver and select the desired managed site from the drop-down list at the top of the Files panel.**

If you don't see your site listed here, you need to manage a site. Choose Site⇨New Site to open the Site Definition dialog box, inside which you can enter a name for the site in the Site Name text box and the location of the site on your local computer in the Local Site Folder text box. Then switch over to the Servers category and set up a new FTP profile for your site. When finished, click the Save button.

2. **Click the Expand/Collapse button in the upper-right corner of the Files panel to expand the panel, as shown in Figure 2-6.**

After the panel is expanded, the Files panel displays two separate panes, one for the local files and one to display remote files. By default, the local files display in the right pane and the remote files display on the left.

Most standalone FTP programs show the local files on the left and the remote files on the right. To swap the location of the local and remote files in Dreamweaver, collapse the Files panel by clicking the Expand/ Collapse button and open Dreamweaver's Preferences by choosing Edit⇨Preferences (Windows) or File⇨Preferences (Mac). In the Site category of the Preferences dialog box, modify the Always Show and On The drop-down lists to suit your particular needs, such as selecting Local Files from the Always Show drop-down list and selecting Left from the On The drop-down list. Click OK to close the dialog box with your new settings and expand the Files panel before proceeding to Step 3.

Figure 2-6: Expand the Files panel.

You won't see any files in the remote listing until you establish a connection via FTP.

3. **Click the Connect to Remote Server button on the toolbar at the top of the expanded Files panel to establish a connection.**

The button looks like a blue plug and socket. When clicked, the plug connects with the socket, and a green light appears next to it, indicating that the connection was a success. Upon connection, you also see all the files on the remote server appear in the Remote Site pane of the Files panel, as shown in Figure 2-7.

Connect to Remote Host   Put

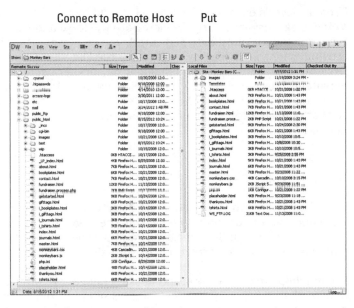

Figure 2-7: Create a connection to the remote server using the expanded Files panel.

4. **To transfer files from the local site to the remote site, select the file(s) that you'd like to transfer from the Local Files pane and click the blue up-arrow Put button on the panel's toolbar.**

To transfer your files to a specific folder on the remote server, you must open that folder (by double-clicking it) before transferring files from the local pane.

To select more than one file at a time for a multiple file transfer, press and hold the Ctrl (Windows) or ⌘ (Mac) key while selecting each additional file.

5. **Upon clicking the Put button, Dreamweaver displays a Dependent Files dialog box. Click the Yes button to upload dependent files or the No button to upload only the selected file(s).**

Depending on your Internet connection speed and the size of the files being transferred, the upload may take anywhere from one second to several minutes.

6. **To end the FTP session, click the Connect to Remote Server button to disconnect from the remote server, and then collapse the Files panel by clicking the Expand/Collapse button.**

   To reestablish a connection with the remote server for future transfer sessions, repeat Steps 2–6.

Dreamweaver's expanded Files panel can do more than just transfer files. You can also use it to sort and view both the local and remote files by size, type, and modification date. If desired, you can even set additional file attributes for the display by configuring the File View Columns category in Dreamweaver's Site Definition dialog box. Another useful feature of the expanded Files panel is the Synchronize command, which assesses both local and remote files and then transfers files to and from the remote site so that both locations contain the most recent version of each file in the managed local site.

Performing Final Site Testing

When you upload the site to the test directory on the remote server, you have one final opportunity to review all the pages before you make them accessible to the public. This gives you the time you need to do any testing and make last-minute corrections to your site.

Broken links, spelling errors, and missing images are often found during this final testing stage, so spend the few extra minutes, hours, or days, as the case may be, performing this most important second-to-last step before making your site live on the Internet. If you're working on a web project for a client, have the client get involved with this final review of the site before publishing. After testing and correcting any errors you may find, you can confidently publish the site, remove the test directory from the server, and start on another web project.

Although technically the pages are on the Internet as soon as they are uploaded to the test directory, no one else — including search engine spiders and robots — know about the presence of these live, published files in this test directory unless you give them the specific web address. Spiders and robots don't typically index sites unless you expressly request indexing or unless one or more of the pages is automatically indexed during a regularly scheduled crawl. For that reason, it is best to delete the test directory from the remote server as soon as possible after publishing the site.

To access the files on the Internet within the domain's test folder, enter the domain name and test directory in your browser's address bar. For example, if your domain name is `pumpkinsticks.com` and the test directory you created is called test, you'd enter **http://www.pumpkinsticks.com/test** in your browser's address bar. If your test folder is not set up properly within the host's server, you may see an error message that you cannot browse the directory.

After the directory is set up, be sure to enter the URL of your test directory correctly in the address bar, paying special attention to letter case, because on some host servers, entering an incorrect address can prevent you from accessing your files. For instance, if your host server only displays pages when the path uses the correct letter case, you might be able to access your files with http://www.pumpkinsticks.com/test but not with http://www.pumpkinsticks.com/TEST. If you don't automatically see the home page in your test directory (index.html), try entering the full path to that file, as in **http://www.pumpkinsticks.com/test/index.html**.

If you're designing a site for someone else, feel free to share the test URL with your client. This gives both you and the client one final opportunity to review the site prior to publishing. Though some issues may come up that require a pushback of the site publication by a few hours or days, it is far wiser to have more eyes previewing the site for errors before it goes live than to publish the site with even one missing image, glaring typo, or broken link.

If you do find a coding issue that needs correcting at this stage, update the file locally first and then send the updated file to the test folder by way of FTP. Then, after clearing your browser's cache, preview the updated page again in the test directory to ensure that the error was corrected to your satisfaction. If not, continue making adjustments and uploading the file again until the page looks and functions correctly.

For times when you provide a client with the URL to the test directory, be sure to have her review the entire site online and provide written approval of the site to you when she's satisfied with the work and agrees that the project is completed. Getting a signed Project Completion form officially marks the end of the web project so that you can submit any final invoices to the client and confidently publish the site.

With luck, this final testing phase shouldn't turn up too many issues related to accessibility or validation (though of course if you find any issues like that, you should certainly fix them). Instead, your focus should be on finding and fixing any interactive problems with links, graphics, and forms, creating any custom error pages as needed, and catching any last-minute typos that might have been inadvertently overlooked.

Unfortunately, there is one thing you can't test for within a test directory, and that's the functionality of any form processing that uses scripts copied into the remote cgi-bin folder, such as a Join Our Mailing List form on a Contact page with a forwarding Thank You page redirect. The reason that you cannot test pages with forms within a test directory is that those pages must reside at the root level of the site to process any scripts. To test form pages, then, put a copy of those pages with test filenames (such as testform.html and testthankyou.html) at the root level of the remote server and test them there. Even though these few files are at the root level and are technically publicly accessible to anyone with an Internet connection, no one knows about the presence of these files unless you give them the URL. When you are at the root level, you can safely test and verify the functionality of these files in a live site environment while testing the rest of the site in a virtually hidden test directory.

Keep in mind that testing your files in a test directory works well only when you have been creating your links to files and graphics using document relative links (such as images/logo.gif) instead of site-root relative links (like /images/logo.gif) or hard-coded links (such as http://www. mysite.com/images/logo.gif). For instance, if you happen to have used site-root relative links (which are most effective for sites built with SSIs), your graphics and links may not function properly in the test directory. In other words, your images will not appear and your hyperlinks will appear to be broken. To remedy this situation, you can go back into your files, modify the links in your code, and upload the files to the test server again for testing, or you can set up a special live testing environment where you can safely test your site before making it live on the Internet. For specific instructions for setting up a live testing environment for your domain, check with your host provider.

Creating Custom 401 and 404 Error Pages

When a web server receives a request from a browser that it doesn't know how to process, it typically returns one of several error messages to the visitor's browser window. Two of the most common errors are

- **401 Unauthorized Access:** This message gets displayed when people attempt without permission to access web pages that are password protected.

- **404 File Not Found:** This message appears when visitors click a broken hyperlink or type an incorrect web address in the browser's address bar.

You can customize these messages to match the design of your website, and with a little help from your host provider, you can have these custom error pages installed and in service on your domain within 24 hours or less after transferring the site files to the remote server.

Creating the error pages

The 401 Unauthorized Access page usually includes a short message to visitors along with the refresh meta tag that redirects visitors to the home page or some other location on the web after a specified number of seconds (see Figure 2-8).

Figure 2-8: The 401 Error page is used for pages that visitors are not authorized to access.

The meta tag goes in the head of the page and should be formatted like this:

```
<meta http-equiv="refresh" content="10;URL=http://www.yourdomainname.com">
```

The message can say anything you like, but typically, it says something like this:

```
You have attempted to access a page for which you are not authorized. This
page will automatically redirect to the [INSERT DOMAIN NAME] Home Page in
10 seconds or click the following link to manually redirect this page to
[INSERT DOMAIN NAME].
```

The 404 File Not Found message provides more space for a customized message and any additional information such as marketing and advertising, but generally should state something like this (see Figure 2-9):

```
The page you are seeking cannot be found:
The page you are looking for might have been removed, had its name
changed, or is temporarily unavailable.
Please try the following:
   * If you typed the page address in the Address bar, make sure that it is
     spelled correctly.
   * Open the www.DOMAINNAME.com home page, and then look for links to the
     information you want.
   * Click the Back button to try another link.
```

To customize your own 401 and 404 error pages, create two new web pages based on existing pages on the completed site. This ensures that the new pages use the same layout and graphics as the rest of the site. Save these files with the filenames error401.html and error404.html, and then edit the content areas for both pages by using the preceding examples. If desired, add more information to suit your site's particular needs. For example, rather than just displaying the URL of the home page on the 404 error page, why not also include links to all the pages on your site, similar to your site map page? The same technique would also work for the 404 error page. The customized content is entirely up to you, so be as creative and helpful as you can to the visitors (potential customers) that will be viewing these pages.

Figure 2-9: The 404 Error page is displayed when the URL cannot be found.

Editing the .htaccess file

Next, you need to edit the existing .htaccess file on your server (if one already exists) or create a new one. An .htaccess file is a hypertext file that provides directives to the server, such as password protection and serving error pages. This file needs to sit at the root level of your host directory to provide instructions to the server on how to serve up your new custom documents should either of these errors occur.

To see whether your server already has an .htaccess file, establish a remote connection to your server using your FTP client and take a look at the root level of your host server. If an .htaccess file already exists, download (get) a copy of it to your local computer so that you can make modifications to it. If you don't see an .htaccess file at the root level, create a new one.

In Dreamweaver, .htaccess files are often hidden or invisible in the Files panel. To reveal these hidden files, click the Options menu in the upper-right corner of the Files panel, choose View, then choose Show Hidden Files.

To create an .htaccess file, follow these steps:

1. **Open a text editor, such as Notepad or TextEdit, and type in the following two lines of code:**

    ```
    ErrorDocument 404 /error404.html
    ErrorDocument 401 /error401.html
    ```

2. **Save the file as htaccess.txt to the root level of your local site.**

3. **Establish a connection between your host server and your FTP client, and upload a copy of the htaccess.txt file to the root level of your host server.**

4. **While still connected to the remote server, change the name of the htaccess.txt file on the remote server to .htaccess by removing the .txt extension and placing a period *before* the filename.**

5. **Upload your customized error401.html and error404.html files to the root level of your host server.**

The final step, after creating your custom error pages and uploading them to the root level of your remote server, is to contact your host provider for further instructions on how to make these new files replace the server's default error message pages. The host provider typically needs to configure some software on the server end before the new pages will work. The provider might also request that you log on to your site's control panel or site utility and make some adjustments to your site's configuration.

Taking Your Site Live

To publish the site, establish an FTP client session and put a copy of the entire local site in the root level of the remote server, excluding any Template and Library folders that you may have generated to create the local version of the sites. These types of files are generated by your HTML code editor and are only necessary for site management within the editor; the files are therefore unnecessary for site functionality on the remote server. In addition to the main HTML files for your site, be sure to also upload any additional folders and files that support the functionality and presentation of the site, including images, media files, PDFs, downloadable files, SSIs, CSS, jQuery, and JavaScript.

Immediately after publishing the site, open a browser window with an Internet connection to access the site using the domain's URL. If you see the home page when you enter the URL (such as http://www.*mydomain*.com), your site is finally *live!* Take this moment, now that all the files are in their final destination, to test all the site's pages one more time. Check for any missing images, broken links, and anything else that might suddenly jump out at you as being not quite right. If you find any issues that need trouble-shooting or fixing, fix them right away on your local version of the site and upload the corrected files to the remote server as quickly as possible.

When you're absolutely, positively, 100 percent sure that the newly published site is fully functional, delete the test directory from the server. Deleting files can be as simple as selecting the directory (folder) within the FTP client session window and clicking a Delete button, or it can take a little more work. Some FTP clients require that you delete any contents inside a folder before the folder itself can be deleted. However you have to get it done with your FTP client, do it. The purpose of deleting the test directory after publishing the site is to prevent any visitors, human or computer, from accessing and indexing those test pages. Then, in the event that any of the test pages were indexed by search engines during your test period, should anyone attempt to access those URLs at a later date, your new customized 404 File Not Found error message page will display when those pages are not found by the server.

To maximize your efforts, turn to Book V, Chapter 3 to discover ways to improve search engine rankings with search engine optimization and to keep your customers happy with site maintenance services.

Chapter 3: Search Engine Optimization and Site Maintenance

In This Chapter

✔ Understanding search engine optimization (SEO)

✔ Seeing the benefits of ethical SEO

✔ Improving search engine rankings with HTML

✔ Submitting a URL to search engines

✔ Improving visibility and accessibility with a site map

✔ Performing site maintenance

✔ Keeping your site up to date

*Y*our site is up and running — give yourself a giant pat on the back, take a deep breath, and get ready to do a few more things to make the most out of all your hard work. Although additional work is not an absolute requirement, you can apply a handful of other useful techniques to your site to make it even more search engine and visitor friendly. As an added benefit, when you do the tasks outlined in this chapter, your design services will be more valuable to your clients and can help you stand out from the competition.

y Might Be
.ants

Typekit

Bobulate

Typedia

The Amanda Project

W.W. Norton

Theme Magazine

Objectifi

py Cog

Kongregate

AIGA

A List Ap

This chapter explains several search engine optimization (SEO) techniques that can help make your site more search engine friendly. In addition, you find out why every site should include an HTML Site Map page and how to create one. As a final note, this chapter shows you how to perform regular website maintenance and suggests ways to help you keep your site content fresh and up to date.

Dict

Understanding Search Engine Optimization

Search engine optimization (SEO) refers to any techniques applied to the code and/or content of a web page that assists with the indexing of a site by search engines and the improvement of the site's ranking order within them. Because search engines often rely on computerized bots to crawl the web and to develop and maintain their indexes, many of the SEO concepts can be easily implemented by thinking strategically about the site's content, `title` tags, meta tags, page structure, and accessibility coding. When the site has been optimized for search engines, the site's URL can be submitted to search engines, which itself can help visitors find the site and improve the site's ranking within the search engine results.

Attracting clicks with advertising

Depending on your (or your client's) budget, you can do a range of things to increase both web traffic and conversion rates. *Traffic* refers to the number of visitors to a site, while a *conversion rate* is the percentage of those web visitors who actually become customers by completing a valid sale or other online transaction.

If you have somewhat of a budget, spending money on pay-per-click advertising can be very useful and profitable. Pay-per-click Internet advertising, or paid placement, is a method of site promotion whereby the advertiser (you) bids on the keywords or key phrases you think will be used by potential site visitors and then pays a fee anytime a visitor clicks an advertising link that leads to your site. Google offers perhaps the most well known pay-per-click service, Google AdWords, which displays your advertised URLs along the top or right edge in the Sponsored Links areas of the Google Search Results pages, like the example shown in the following figure.

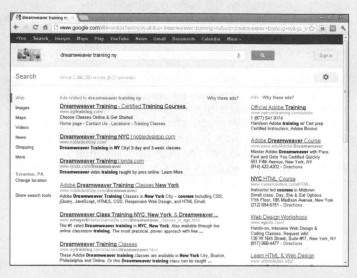

Additionally, if you sell any products or services, conversion rates have been known to increase when a site does everything it can to easily facilitate a sale. For instance, smart shopping sites are known for having clearly labeled Add to Cart buttons, making the checkout process easy to use, making clearly defined shipping and return policies available to visitors, and offering excellent customer service and sales support.

On the other hand, if you have no money set aside for marketing, it would be really smart for you to take a little time to make the site more search engine friendly.

The more you know about SEO, the more valuable your services can be to your clients, who often will want to rely on your knowledge and expertise to guide them through (or completely handle for them) the process of getting their site listed on search engines and attracting more visitors.

Practicing Ethical SEO Techniques

As with all things in life, there is a good way and a bad way to go about doing things, and when it comes to practicing search engine optimization on your site, the same holds true. There is a good way to go about improving your search engine rankings, and then there's a bad way.

Back when the Internet was new, when there weren't so many websites and blogs, and search engines were something new, you could add a few different meta tags to your code and then sit back and watch as your site hit the number one or number two spot in the search engine results rankings. Then, as more and more visitors began to rely on search engines that use web robots and spiders to build their databases, a new breed of Internet scam artists was born. These so-called SEO service providers had one aim: to make money by tweaking the HTML code on a site that would trick those search engine robots and spiders into showing certain websites at the top of the search engine rankings. The motivation to use this type of deception was that if your site was listed on the first or second page of search engine results, you'd get more site visitors, and therefore you'd sell more products and services. Of course, this hasn't proven to be true, but that hasn't stopped anyone from trying to cheat the system.

These sneaky tactics worked for a little while, until the search engines devised a way to improve the web robots and spiders to automatically detect and ignore sites that use common scams. As a matter of fact, some of these sneaky practices got so out of control that the search engines took even more drastic measures to ensure that their search results are as accurate and truthful as possible. As a consequence, it's no longer as simple as it once was to get good legitimate search engine rankings.

Because these questionable techniques fall into the realm of unethical practices, I don't discuss them in detail in this book. However, to educate you further about what kinds of things to avoid, the following list briefly outlines some of the more common unethical practices you should take extreme care to stay far, far away from:

- **Keyword padding:** Do not engage in padding keywords into the meta tags or body content of web pages that have nothing to do with the website's specific business.

- **Keyword listing:** Avoid listing keywords in the body of your site content when their purpose is not clear. The only legitimate place for a list of keywords is inside the keywords meta tag or when listing a site's products and services naturally within the content of a page. If you do list words in this capacity, do it carefully so that it doesn't appear to be a spam-like keyword listing. A safer method would be to write copy that logically includes all the products and services in paragraph form.

- **Tag padding:** Do not use multiple versions of the same tag within the HTML code, such as duplicate meta description or title tags, to try to get more information through to search engines than you can with one tag. This, too, is viewed as spam by search engines and puts the URL at risk.

- **Image padding:** Don't use words in your alternative (alt) text attribute for images that have nothing to do with the image being described.

- **Hidden text:** Don't add keyword-stuffed text to a page where the font color matches the background color of the page or other container tag that holds the text. Search engines can detect such slimy practices and treat those pages, and possibly all pages at the offending web address, as spam.

- **Oversubmitting:** Never, ever submit a URL to any search engine, index, directory, or listing more than once in any 24-hour period. Daily submissions are also too often. Be realistic and submit only when significant changes have been made to the layout or content of a site. Besides, resubmitting your site is often unnecessary because, after your site has been indexed, the search engine periodically checks on your site.

- **Duplicate page submissions:** Do not submit pages with identical content but with different filenames. This is viewed as spam and can put the web address at risk.

- **Cheating:** Don't trick people into visiting a site by using inaccurate keywords, meta tags, and content, or by false advertising or unethical page redirects. Do not try to outsmart the search engines. The people who create the search engine programs are always on the lookout for cheaters, and if they find unethical SEO techniques on a submitted URL, they have the power to blacklist a URL and prevent the entire site from being indexed.

Be forewarned that should you choose to attempt any of these practices on your own (or a client's) website, you may be putting all the pages on that domain at risk of being indefinitely blacklisted by search engines. Besides, trying to trick the system is counterintuitive because most of the traffic coming to any website is often generated through search engines.

Be smart and do the right thing. To be a good web designer today, you must educate yourself about the ethical ways to make a website visible to search engines and avoid unethical practices altogether.

Optimizing Your Site for Search Engines

The previous section shows you what not to do to improve search engine rankings; in this section, I'm happy to present some ethical and effective SEO techniques. To apply useful and ethical search engine optimization to your site, you can make several free and fee-based enhancements to your pages that can improve how the content inside them gets indexed by the web robots and spiders that crawl the web in search of new pages to add to their databases.

Robots and *spiders,* by the way, are the automated software programs that perform particular tasks, crawl the web on a mission to find new web pages, and then index the new pages in a large database. At minimum, when a new web address is found, that page (usually the home page called `index.html`) is automatically added to that robot or spider's indexing database. Furthermore, any hypertext links detected on that page may also be followed and indexed automatically as part of the process. Because you have very little control over whether this indexing actually happens, you can at least prepare for the possibility of it by paying special attention to all the textual content and hyperlinks on your site, especially the home page.

To get you on the right track, the following sections describe some simple ways to improve the ranking of your web pages in search results listings for search engines such as Google, Bing, Yahoo!, and others — all without spending any money.

Maximizing keywords

The first thing you can do to improve a website's search engine friendliness is to maximize your keywords. One of the things that search engine robots and spiders do is search for meaningful content within the text on pages that they crawl. This means that the sites you design need to help those bots find that content by including site-specific keywords that identify a company's products and services, especially on the home page.

Keywords can be any words or short phrases *(keyphrases)* that describe the product, service, or information on the site that needs to be advertised. If your site sells products, tell the world about them using clearly identifiable keywords that visitors might use. This can help visitors around the world using search engines to more readily find a particular website.

Keep in mind that the keywords within the text of the site's pages can be the same as any keywords listed in the `keywords` meta tag. However, because content keywords and key phrases can be integrated into the text in the body of the page, you have much more latitude for including the most popular keywords within the text that the site's target audiences are likely to use when doing a search engine search.

To evaluate your site's content and find ways to maximize keywords, look through each page on your site with the following key concepts in mind:

1. **Verify that the text on each page — especially the home page — includes descriptive keywords and key phrases.**

   For instance, if the website offers printing services and uses only chlorine-free 100 percent post-consumer recycled paper and vegetable-based inks, *Chlorine-Free 100% post-consumer recycled paper* and *vegetable-based inks* would be great key phrases to include in the page's text, as illustrated in Figure 3-1.

2. **Find ways on every page to hyperlink any keywords or key phrases to other relevant pages on the site. If you see keywords that aren't yet linked to somewhere else on the site when they should be, add them.**

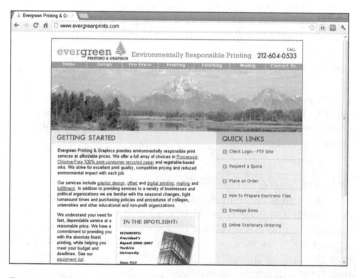

Figure 3-1: Maximize searchability by including keywords and key phrases in the text.

For instance, if the copy on a page includes the phrase, "Our services include graphic design, offset and digital printing, mailing and fulfillment," you can easily turn the words *graphic design, offset, digital printing, mailing,* and *fulfillment* into individual hyperlinks that link directly to those five pages on the site. (Refer to Figure 3-1.)

3. **To emphasize certain words or phrases within the page content, mark up headlines and bylines using headings tags such as <h1> and <h2> and mark up other important text with <strong> (bold) and <em> (italic) styles.**

   By using these heading and emphasis tags, you're alerting search engine robots that the content contained inside those tags is likely to be more relevant to search engine users than other content on the page.

If you're advising clients about improving the content on their pages, tell them not to worry about being too conservative with the amount of content placed on every page. Many site owners erroneously think that having too much copy will scare away readers. On the contrary, some SEO guidelines recommend having a minimum of 200 words of copy on every page so that the spiders and robots have something to read and index.

When you have finished reviewing and updating your site, the content should be well marked up with heading, italic, and strong tags for emphasis; the copy should include lots of descriptive keywords and key phrases; and when applicable, those keywords and key phrases should by linked to other relevant pages on the site.

Including descriptive text and hyperlinks

Take extra care to ensure that the copy reads legibly and doesn't have keywords haphazardly thrown into it. Avoid at all costs the appearance of *keyword spamming,* which is what happens when you list a bunch of keywords in a row with no context. All the keywords need to be logically embedded in the page copy. For example, instead of listing the words *shampoo, conditioner, deep conditioner, hair spray, hair products, hair treatments, hair accessories,* and so on, write something like "At X company, we sell only the best hair products and hair treatments on the market. We offer all the best high-quality shampoos, conditioners, and deep conditioners, along with hair spray and hair accessories."

Be sure to also include hyperlinks on the keywords to each of those product categories. If you feel stuck for different ways of presenting the content on the page, it's okay to reuse some of the content and wording found elsewhere on the site — just don't go overboard. You could, for instance, use "X Company — Your Online Shop for the Finest Hair Products, Treatments, and Accessories" in the title tag and then repeat "X Company is your online shop for the finest hair products, treatments, and accessories. We sell shampoo, conditioner, deep conditioner, hair spray, and more!" somewhere within the body of the page.

Embedding object and image descriptions

Another great SEO technique that attracts the attention of search engine robots and spiders involves using the HTML `title` and `alt` attributes to describe certain page elements and images.

You can add the HTML `title` attribute to several different tags, such as hyperlinks, tables, table cells, and table rows. This attribute also improves accessibility by describing the contents found within the structural element, as in the following two code examples:

```
<a href="shippingrates.html" title="View our UPS Shipping Rates">View our UPS
    Shipping Rates</a>
<table width="500" title="UPS Shipping Rates">
```

Similarly, the `alt` attribute describes in a few words or a short phrase what an image looks like or, when the image contains only copy, what that copy says:

```
<img src="images/p380logo.png" alt="Point 380 - Crucial Resource Strategy"
    width="341" height="112" border="0">
```

In addition to making your code more standards compliant, the inclusion of these tag attributes both helps to increase search engine relevance of targeted keywords and makes it easier for visitors using screen readers, text browsers, and other assistive technologies to experience visiting the site.

Adding keyword and description meta tags

Even though you may have had the best intentions of adding these valuable tags (which you read about in Book I, Chapter 3) when you were building the site, you may have forgotten to put them into the head of all your pages or to have updated them with accurate and relevant information.

You can add several meta tags to your code to assist with making the pages search engine friendly. However, two of them in particular can really help with site optimization:

✔ **Description:** The `description` meta tag provides a brief description of the website's products and/or services in 250 characters or less, including spaces and punctuation. This description is critically important because this text often gets displayed when the URL appears as part of a search engine's results listings. Therefore, whenever possible, try to include two to four keywords in the early part of the description statement. For example, the meta description for my photography website (`http://suejenkinsphotography.com`) is as follows

```
<meta name="Description" content="Fine art photography including
    abstracts, landscapes, holgas, and experimental low-res digital in
    black & white, color, and digital.">
```

and this same sentence appears as the site descriptor when listed in Google's search results, as shown in Figure 3-2.

✓ **Keywords:** The `keywords` meta tag provides a list of the seven most important keywords and key phrases (1,024 characters, including spaces and punctuation) that visitors to the site might type in a search engine to find the website's products and services. These keywords should be listed in order of importance and include any plural versions of keywords if visitors might search for both the singular and plural instances, such as *ipod* and *ipods*. The same goes for common misspellings of important keywords for any site, like *callender, callendar,* and *calander* for a site that sells calendars.

Figure 3-2: Your description meta tag appears in search engine results listings, so be sure to write a good one and include it in your code.

Keywords, unfortunately, are one of those tags that have been rendered almost completely useless by unethical SEO practitioners. Today, only one former search engine, Inktomi (which is now part of Yahoo!), still uses keywords in factoring search engine rankings. Whether you choose to include this meta tag in your code is up to you, but the prevailing thought is that as long as one search engine uses them, that's enough to warrant including the `keywords` meta tag in your pages.

Meta tags don't appear anywhere on the web page when viewed in the browser, and they are strictly used by search engine robots and spiders to index your site. The syntax for these two meta tags should be written as follows, where you fill in the specific content (shown in bold) for your particular website:

```
<head>
<title>Your Page Title</title>
<meta name="keywords" content="Your keywords">
<meta name="description" content="Your description">
</head>
```

One question a lot of new web designers want to know the answer to is whether they should use the same set of `keywords` and `description` meta tags on all the pages throughout a website. The answer is entirely up to you. Some SEO professionals suggest using customized descriptions and keyword lists for each page of the site to improve search engine rankings for individual pages. Although this is useful, keep in mind that this takes a bit more work to manage. For one, you need to come up with the customized meta tag content for each page. For another, if you are using a template system through your HTML code editor, you need to reposition one of the closing editable area template comment tags within the HTML code so that it includes the meta tags in question. Repositioning the closing tag would make that area of the code editable within any template-based files. For example, you'd need to change your code in your template from this:

```
<!-- TemplateBeginEditable name="doctitle" -->
<title>MindworkNY.com</title>
<!-- TemplateEndEditable -->
<meta name="Keywords" content="Psychologist,Therapist,Depression,Mood Swing
     s,Anxiety,Stress,Counseling,New York,Carolyn Ehrlich,Mindwork,New York
     City,Therapy" />
<meta name="Description" content="Mindwork was founded on the belief that those
     who seek therapy have the potential for psychological and emotional growth."
     />
```

to this:

```
<!-- TemplateBeginEditable name="doctitle" -->
<title>MindworkNY.com</title>
<meta name="Keywords" content="Psychologist,Therapist,Depression,Mood Swing
     s,Anxiety,Stress,Counseling,New York,Carolyn Ehrlich,Mindwork,New York
     City,Therapy" />
<meta name="Description" content="Mindwork was founded on the belief that those
     who seek therapy have the potential for psychological and emotional growth."
     />
<!-- TemplateEndEditable -->
```

For more on how to use these and other meta tags effectively, turn to Book III, Chapter 1.

Updating bland page titles

There is nothing more boring than a page title in the browser's title bar that simply repeats the name of the page, such as *Contact,* and doesn't identify the name of the site or provide any additional clues about what can be found on the page. `Title` tags are like free advertising spaces that allow you to highlight the page-specific content, which in turn can help visitors find that information more quickly when researching a topic of interest through a search engine. To take the fullest advantage of this free publicity space — yes, free publicity space! — be sure to add unique titles packed with keywords and key phrases to all the pages on your site.

Because your page titles do appear in the visitor's browser's title bar, as illustrated in Figure 3-3, you must pay special attention to the words you use there. Whenever possible, write complete sentences that accurately describe what can be found on each particular page.

Figure 3-3: Make the most of your page titles by writing complete, informative, keyword-rich sentences.

For example, instead of having a super-boring and unhelpful title, like this:

```
<title>Our Menu</title>
```

. . . you can use more site-specific keywords in the title to improve the chances of people finding particular pages on your site when searching for products, services, and information through a search engine, like this:

```
<title>Komi Organics :: Balanced homemade kid's meals, fresh to your doorstep! ::
       Our menu plan uses USDA Certified Organic ingredients!</title>
```

As with the other meta tags, try with your `title` tags to include a couple of keywords or key phrases near the front part while identifying the content on the page, but be careful not to simply list keywords. Keyword listing could be misinterpreted as spamming and could blacklist the domain from being indexed by search engines. Instead, each title needs to read like an enticing, informative sentence, not a laundry list.

Page titles can be any length up to about 70 characters. If your titles exceed this suggested length, any extra characters may be truncated in the title bar of some browsers, such as "Rockwood & Perry Fine Wine & Spirits offers fine wines, advice, accessories, direct imports . . ." instead of the full title as listed in the code. Still, for the extra bump that having well-written, keyword-rich, descriptive titles can do for your site rankings, seeing truncated titles in a browser's title bar may not be such a critical issue.

Submitting a Site to Search Engines

As soon as a new site is 100 percent complete and published on its domain, the URL can be submitted to search engines for indexing and listing. You do this by submitting the site's URL to the search tools that the target audience is likely to use. These tools include search engines, which use robots and spiders to crawl the web in search of new listings, and search directories, which are essentially categorized lists of sites that are sometimes compiled or edited by people instead of bots.

Hand-submitting the URL

Although it's a good idea to get the site listed on the most popular search tools that you think will assist the target in finding the site, it doesn't mean using some kind of submission tool or SEO service that will blast the URL, like spam, to any and all search engines around the world. Those kinds of submission techniques not only create tons of kickback spam e-mails to the submitting e-mail address, but they also rarely, if ever, increase site traffic.

What's more, some SEO submission tools and SEO services deliberately submit the URL directly to spam sites — web pages of site listings that clog up the Internet and have no purpose — which can jeopardize the integrity of the domain when it comes to listing the site legitimately on the major search engines. The best way to get a site listed, then, is to hand-submit the URL to the major search engines and directories yourself and, when additional exposure is desired, to pay a reputable listing service such as Google AdWords and Yahoo! Search Advertising Solutions (formerly Overture Keywords) for pay-per-click advertising. These services offer paid listing options for as little as $25 per month that can guarantee that your site is listed in the top search results or is listed in the sponsored advertising space directly above or to the right of the regular search listings.

Most search engines, search directories, and search listings (which use search engines and directories to compile their data) charge you a fee for submitting a URL with them; however, a few of them are still free. Table 3-1 lists the most popular tools for making search engine submissions.

Table 3-1	Search Engines, Directories, and Search Listings		
Service Name	*URL*	*Service Type*	*Free or Paid Service*
Google	`www.google.com/addurl`	Search engine	Free
Open Directory Project	`http://dmoz.org/add.html`	Search directory	Free
Yahoo!	`www.search.yahoo.com/info/submit.html`	Search directory	Free and paid service (requires registration with Yahoo!)
AOL Search	Submit URL to Google and your listing should appear in AOL's search listings	Search listing	Free
Bing	`www.bing.com/toolbox/submit-site-url`	Search listing	Free
Google AdWords	`http://adwords.google.com`	Search engine	Paid service
Yahoo! Advertising Solutions	`http://advertising.yahoo.com/contact-sales/` Yahoo! is now a hybrid of purchased indexes: Inktomi, AltaVista, and AlltheWeb	Search directory	Paid service

Submitting your site to a search tool usually only takes a minute or two, and although you have no guarantee of the submitted URL being indexed, a submitted page is better than no submission at all. As a value-added service, you may want to offer to submit your clients' sites to the free search engine submission tools as part of your web design package.

Most of the free submission tools request just the domain name and a valid e-mail address to complete the submission process. Google, for instance, only requests that you first create an account before you log into the URL submission page. Then simply provide the home page URL and complete the human submission validation field entry, as shown in Figure 3-4.

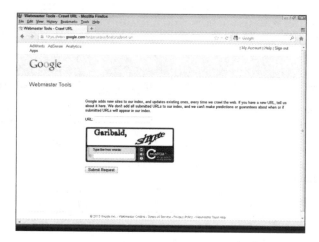

Figure 3-4: Enter the home page URL to submit a site address to Google.

Other tools require that you choose a submission category that matches the site's product or service offerings. For example, before submitting a URL to the Open Directory Project (www.dmoz.org), you must use that site's search feature to locate the most appropriate category for your site, and then submit the URL to the directory from within that specific section of the directory. To illustrate, suppose you've just designed, built, and published a new website for a children's mystery book writer who's just finished his second novel in a series about a fictional character. What would be the best category to list this site in? One for children's books, one for children's book authors, or one that promotes the sales of the children's books?

To find out, go to www.dmoz.org and, in the search bar, enter the keywords *children's books*. What are some of the subcategories that appear? Are some more appropriate than others? Type another search with the keywords *children series books*. Two suitable categories for this website might be "Arts: Literature: Children's: Children's Series Books" and "Business: Publishing and Printing: Publishing: Books: Children." Because you may submit the site to only one category, choose wisely because you have no second chances.

If you are submitting the site for a client, ask the client for her opinion about which category best matches her needs before submitting the site to the search tool. As soon as you have chosen the right category, select it and then click the Submit URL link at the top of the page. This brings you to a submission page where you can follow the online instructions for submitting the site.

Waiting for the site to be listed

After you make a submission, each search engine, search listing, search index, and search directory can take anywhere from one day to two months to get it listed. For instance, Google has claimed new listings occur within four weeks of submission, but listings can just as likely occur within a day or two. Tell your client to be patient while waiting for the listing to appear after the home page URL has been submitted. Just because a site gets published doesn't automatically mean it can be found instantly by any and every search engine. All that publishing a site means is that the content on the domain is publicly accessible to anyone with an Internet connection. It also doesn't mean the listing suddenly appears on the first page of search engine results after the URL is indexed. To be listed, a URL must be submitted to a search engine, search listing, search directory, or search index. Tell your client that as long as the URL submitted to the search engine directs visitors to her domain, the listing should happen within a reasonable time frame, typically between one and eight weeks.

With most search engine submissions, only the home page will be indexed, rather than all the pages on the entire site. If you are interested in finding out how many of the site's pages have been indexed, check with the search engine to see whether it has any method for verifying that information. Google, for instance, can show you how many of your site's pages have been indexed when you type **site:*mydomainname*.com** into Google's search field. The *For Dummies* website (site:dummies.com) alone boasts about 240,000 indexed pages on any given day!

Though some SEO professionals may encourage you to resubmit your URL to search engines, search listings, search directories, and search indexes daily, weekly, or any time you update even a single page on a site, understand that those search tools may treat multiple submissions like those as more of a form of computerized Internet harassment than a smart business practice. A more rational and courteous submission schedule to take for your site would be to make one initial submission shortly after the site gets published, and then make regular quarterly or slightly more frequent resubmissions when the content on the site is updated. In between those times, the search engines that already index the site should automatically take notice of any significant changes.

Giving Your Site an HTML Site Map

When you create a visual site map (as described in Book I, Chapter 3), you create a diagram of all the pages on a site, including the interconnectivity of the main pages through navigation and subnavigation. You then use that information to help gather and define site content, as well as serve as a useful guide when generating the mock-up of the site's design. After your site has been fully built, you can use this visual site map again to help you create an HTML Site Map page, which will be added to the site on the remote host server as a tool to help visitors navigate through the site using a list of hypertext links.

The following sections explain what an HTML Site Map is, how to create one, and how to make it easily accessible to all other pages on the site.

Deciding what to include on the HTML Site Map page

In its most basic form, the HTML Site Map page contains a list of standard hypertext links to all the pages on a website. This list should include links to the home page, to all the main pages and subpages on the site, and to any other pages on the site that might not be accessible through the main navigation, such as a Privacy Policy or Customer Service page.

For best results, save the page with the filename `sitemap.html` and present all the hyperlinks to the site's pages in a simple list format, like the one shown in Figure 3-5.

Figure 3-5: Keep your Site Map page links in a simple list format for easy navigation.

To make this finished page accessible, you should include a link to it in the footer as well as adding a link to it within the head of the page. These two actions will help make the site more accessible to

✓ Visitors with disabilities using screen-reading programs or other devices

✓ Visitors with other browsing preferences, such as text-only browsers and browsers with JavaScript disabled

✓ Visitors who want to be able to go directly to any page on the site with a single click, rather than using the site's main navigation system

✓ Visitors who want to see at a glance all the pages on a given site and know how they're virtually organized

In addition to helping human visitors navigate the site, a site map also helps search engines locate and (with luck) index all the pages of a site. Having hyperlinks to all the pages in one location does improve the chances of the entire site getting indexed, and when that happens, the contents of that site become more readily accessible to visitors, which can help increase web traffic. This is because some search engine robots and spiders ignore the images and other graphics on a page and instead only pay attention to the meta tags, marked-up text, and hyperlinks when indexing individual pages. Logically, then, because the Site Map page is really just a listing of hyperlinks to all the pages on a site, those pages have a higher likelihood of being indexed.

If you're still not convinced about the benefits of having an HTML Site Map page, think about how doing so might improve sales. Suppose your site has a page for products which links to several additional pages with further information about each of those specific products; you'd be wise to allow visitors to be able to find those specific pages from a search engine. For example, if your website sells custom hand-crafted silver jewelry that includes rings, necklaces, and earrings, you may be able to sell more necklaces by having a hyperlink on the Site Map page that takes visitors directly to your necklaces page. After a search engine indexes the pages listed on the Site Map page, a visitor searching for *hand-crafted silver necklaces* might more easily find your site in the search engine results listing and be able to go directly to your site's necklaces page.

Creating a Site Map page

Creating a Site Map page in HTML is fairly straightforward. It is just a matter of inserting a set of listed hyperlinks that lead to the rest of the pages on the site.

To illustrate how to convert your visual site map diagram (which you create for your site in Book I, Chapter 3) into an HTML Site Map web page, grab your site map. (See Figure 3-6 for an example site map.) Then follow these steps to create a Site Map page:

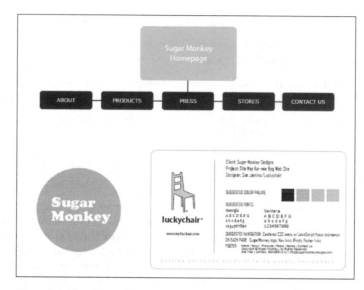

Figure 3-6: Use the architectural site map diagram to build the HTML Site Map page.

1. **Open the home page of your completed website in Dreamweaver or in your preferred HTML or WYSIWYG code editor.**

   If you use Dreamweaver, make sure that the Files panel lists your site as the managed site. If not, choose Site⇨Manage Sites to select your site from the listing.

2. **Choose File⇨Save As, and when the Save As dialog box opens, save a copy of the home page to the root level of your managed site with the filename `sitemap.html`.**

   The new page looks identical to the home page, including all the site's design elements, logo placement, and navigation.

3. **In the main editable area of the page, select and delete all the home page–specific content.**

   You now have room to insert a list of hyperlinks.

4. **Place your cursor at the top of the empty area and type the names of all the pages on the site, including the Site Map page, with one name per line, as they appear on the visual site map.**

   For example, use the page names Home, About, Products, Press, Stores, Contact Us, and Site Map.

5. **Select all the words and convert them into an unordered list, thereby converting each page name into a list item.**

   The HTML code for the Site Map page should use the unordered list tags, as shown in the following sample code:

   ```
   <ul>
      <li>Home</li>
      <li>About</li>
      <li>Products</li>
      <li>Press</li>
      <li>Stores</li>
      <li>Contact Us</li>
      <li>Site Map</li>
   </ul>
   ```

   When you create your own Site Map page in HTML, be sure to also include links in this list to any pages on your site that may not be linked through the main navigation. For instance, if your site includes Privacy Policy, Terms of Service, and Customer Support pages, add links to those pages to the bottom of the list, directly above the link to the Site Map page.

6. **If you have any subpages, add those pages to the list as a subset of the main page they should be listed under, as shown in this example:**

   ```
   <ul>
      <li>Home</li>
      <li>About</li>
      <li>Products</li>
        <ul>
        <li>Silver</li>
        <li>Gold</li>
        </ul>
      <li>Press</li>
      <li>Stores</li>
      <li>Contact Us</li>
      <li>Site Map</li>
   </ul>
   ```

   For example, the Sugar Monkey website has no subpages below any of the main navigation links, so you can skip this step.

7. **(Optional) If desired, type a descriptive sentence beneath each bullet item in the list to help visitors learn about what they can expect to find on each page.**

   A description like this can assist visitors viewing the pages as well as help search engines locate and index each of the pages on the site.

   For example, if you were to add descriptions to the Sugar Monkey Site Map HTML page, one of your list items might look like this:

   ```
   <li>About<br>
   Learn about the founders of Sugar Monkey and get the real story behind
      Sugar Monkey's success.</li>
   ```

8. **Convert each of the page names in the list into hyperlinks to their respective pages on the site, making sure that each link includes its own `title` attribute.**

   For instance, if the about list item became a link to the About page, your code might look like this:

   ```
   <li><a href="about.html" title="Learn About Sugar Monkey">About</a><br>
   Learn about the founders of Sugar Monkey and get the real story behind
        Sugar Monkey's success.</li>
   ```

9. **Save your changes, close the `sitemap.html` file, and upload a copy of this file to the site's remote host server.**

   Test the page as soon as possible and correct any typos or coding errors. If you make any changes, upload the corrected file to the remote host server.

   No one will know about this page until you add a few links to make the page accessible to site visitors.

Making the site map accessible

After you finish building your new HTML Site Map page and have uploaded it to the host server, you need to tweak your site a little bit to make that page easily accessible to all the other pages on the site. Specifically, the Site Map page should be linked in two key areas of a web page:

✔ **Footer:** The first place to add the Site Map link is in the footer of every page, next to the other footer links to all the main pages of the site, as shown in Figure 3-7.

✔ **Head of HTML code:** The second place to add a link to the Site Map page is within the head of your HTML code on every page of the site. If you use a template on your site, you should be able to add this link to the template, and your HTML editor should update all the template-based pages with this link when you save the changes to the template file.

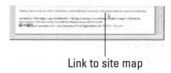

Link to site map

Figure 3-7: Include a site map link in the footer of every page.

The link itself includes both the `rel` tag attribute, which specifically defines the link as a site map link, and the `href` attribute, which allows you to specify the source (location) and filename of your Site Map page. Place the link code anywhere between the page's opening and closing <head> tags:

```
<head>
<link rel="Site Map" href="sitemap.html">
</head>
```

By adding this link to the head, you not only make the page friendlier to search engines, but you also make the page, and thus the entire site, more accessible to people using methods other than browsers to access the pages on your site.

Site Map pages are also especially useful for larger sites and sites that rely on graphics-heavy JavaScript, jQuery, or Flash navigation menus, all of which cannot be easily accessed by certain screen-reading programs, text-only browsers, other assistive technologies, or web robots or spiders. This isn't to say that you should never use JavaScript or other methods for your navigation. Rather, when you do use them, be sure you also include a link to the Site Map page in the footer of every page as an alternative method for site navigation. In addition, when the navigation uses JavaScript, be sure to also include <noscript> tags somewhere on your page (perhaps at the bottom of the body area) for visitors who have JavaScript disabled or use devices that can't read JavaScript. The following example shows how you might add a <noscript> tag to your code:

```
<noscript>
<p>This site uses JavaScript for the main navigation. To access the pages
without JavaScript, please use the links on our <a href="sitemap.html">
Site Map</a> page.</p>
</noscript>
```

To further enhance the usefulness of your Site Map web page, apply any of or all the following suggestions to your pages:

- On larger sites, in addition to including a descriptive sentence below each link in the list, consider adding a sentence below each main navigation area to describe the contents to be found within that section.

- Include the title attribute in every hypertext link on the site map, as in the following code example:

  ```
  <li><a href="freemp3s.html" title="Download Free MP3s">Download Free
      MP3s</a></li>
  ```

- Add the tabindex tag attribute (normally used for form fields, but they can also be used to add a tab index number to image maps and hyperlinks) inside each hypertext link to help visitors with disabilities access those links with a single keystroke, such as

  ```
  <li><a href="freemp3s.html" title="Download Free MP3s"
      tabindex="7">Download Free MP3s</a></li>
  ```

✔ Add a site search feature to your site to further assist visitors in finding exactly what they are looking for. Google has a nice free custom search engine tool you can use (www.google.com/cse), or you can find several other scripts online, for money and for free, that you can use to add the search functionality to your site.

✔ Consider adding context-specific navigational hypertext breadcrumb links, such as Home⇨Services⇨Search Marketing, to the tops of all the content areas on your site to show visitors where they are hierarchically within the site and to provide visitors with an alternative method of navigation, as shown in Figure 3-8.

Breadcrumb links

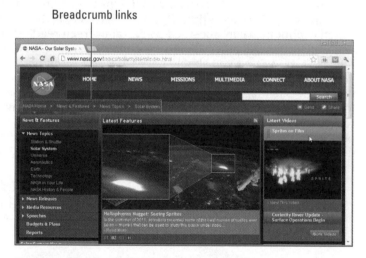

Figure 3-8: Breadcrumb links show visitors which page they are on relative to other pages on a site and provide an alternative method of navigation.

Keeping the Site Relevant

Finally, you've put your site online, SEO is taken care of, you're happy to be finished, and there appears to be nothing else to do with this particular project for the time being. Now is the time to celebrate, relax, and forget about the site for a little while . . . that is, until it is time to make some changes. Routine site maintenance is a must for any website, so before you get to that stage of running a website, take some time to plan out a method for performing your site updates. For instance, you may want to schedule updates at regular intervals rather than just haphazardly jumping in to make changes anytime they are needed. In addition to site maintenance, you need to think about how often to add new content to the site to keep it fresh and appealing to visitors.

Performing site maintenance

No matter how big or small your website happens to be, at some point, there comes a time when you need to perform some site maintenance. The changes may be as minor as updating the copyright year in the footer after January 1, as complex as adding a new page to the site and having to update all the site's navigation links to accommodate the new page, or as major as a full website redesign to give your site a fresh appearance.

Depending on the breadth of the site maintenance task before you, you can either leave the site online or take the site temporarily down while you upload the changed files to the remote host server:

✒ **Online site updates:** When your site changes are fairly minor, work on a local copy of the site and make your changes offline. Test your pages in a temporary directory on the host server to verify that the changes are accurate, and then upload all the updated files — including any images, media files, and external CSS, JavaScript, jQuery, and SSI files — to the remote host server. In most instances, uploads such as these will not significantly disrupt visitor traffic.

✒ **Offline site updates:** When your site changes are substantial, you can still work on a local copy of the site and make your changes offline. When you finish, test your updated pages in a temporary directory on the host server to verify that the changes are accurate. However, to avoid the possibility of negatively impacting your visitors' experience on the site during the transferring of all the updated files from your local computer to the root level of the remote host server, temporarily disable the site.

To temporarily take your site offline so that you can transfer updated files to the server without affecting visitors, do one of the following:

✒ Work with your host so that you can upload your updated site to an active server where you can do all your testing. Then change the DNS record so that instead of *mywebsite.com* pointing to the old server at 123.123.123.123, it now points to 123.123.123.124, where your new content is ready to rock.

✒ Create and upload a special Under Maintenance web page (such as the example shown in Figure 3-9) to the remote host server and then install a 301 Redirect script on your server so that access to any page on the site during the maintenance period automatically redirects visitors to the maintenance page. The 301 Redirect can be implemented in a variety of ways, depending on your skill level and coding preferences. For a tutorial on all the different ways you can create a 301 Redirect on your site, visit www.webconfs.com/how-to-redirect-a-webpage.php.

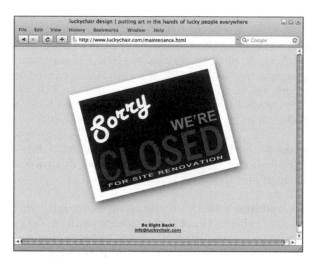

Figure 3-9: Let visitors know your site is offline to be updated.

Scheduling site updates

Some site updates may come with regular frequency, such as adding new files that can be downloaded by visitors each week or updating a monthly schedule of events. Other changes, by contrast, may come at less frequent intervals, which is often the case when you're maintaining a website for a client, family member, or friend.

To help you manage your time and make the most out of every updating session, you may want to limit site updates to a particular day of the week. For instance, by making Monday your site update day, you can combine multiple small tasks into one updating session. If you have multiple clients, this kind of system can also help you establish some ground rules with your client so that change requests aren't coming in all week long. Instead, your clients can take on the responsibility of compiling all their change requests into a single document that they can then send to you, say, each Friday afternoon. If your clients have less frequent site update needs, you can have them send in any change requests by a particular date each month, such as on the 1st or 15th.

Adding new content regularly

On the Internet, the well-ranked and popular sites are the ones that keep all their content fresh and up to date.

At a minimum, you should plan to make regular updates to the home page. If you have more time and are devoted to fine-tuning your site to attract your target audience and accommodate their specific needs, you may choose to make daily, weekly, biweekly, or monthly updates to both the home page and the other pages on the site.

In addition to updating content within your pages, you can do plenty more things to keep your content current, including the following:

- If you will be making regular updates, invite your site's visitors back at regular intervals and encourage them to participate in any special promotions, discounts, sweepstakes, and opinion polls.

- Regularly check your site statistics. Most host providers include some kind of site stat tool with your hosting plan that includes information like which URLs and IP addresses are visiting your site, their country of origin, and the entry and exit page URLs of your site.

- Anytime you make updates to your site, check all the internal and external links. Some of the links to external links may have changed or otherwise been removed from the Internet. When you find any broken or dead-end links, update them immediately or remove them.

- Periodically update your site's design. Change the color scheme or some of the photos, or put a new face on your site. Showcase your talents and keep visitors coming back for more.

- Revisit your page titles and meta tags and update any that no longer accurately describe the contents of the pages and your site.

- If your site lists a calendar or event schedule, make sure that it gets updated in a timely manner. People don't want to know about a class they can no longer sign up for or read about a product or service that isn't offered anymore.

- Got a new product or service? Shout about it on your website. Devote an area on the home page and either integrate the new item(s) into your site's other pages or create a new dedicated What's New page. This can help encourage visitors to return to the site more often.

- If your site sells products or services, ask yourself whether you can do anything to improve the ready-to-purchase and checkout cycles. If needed, add additional informational steps to help your visitors complete their purchases.

- Sites that get a lot of e-mails and phone calls that ask many of the same questions can often benefit from adding a FAQs page to the site. The FAQs page can list both the questions and the answers to these important customer inquiries.

- How about adding a blog to your site? Blogs can increase visitor traffic when you regularly post information that is of interest to the target audience. Blogs also provide a way for visitors to comment on your posts.

- If you have anything else on your site that is no longer relevant or is out of date, take it off the site. Taking care of your site includes making sure that your content is timely and relevant.

Each website warrants its own update schedule. Consider your own website's needs and create a custom calendar of things to remember to help you stay on top of site maintenance and content changes each month. Figure 3-10 shows an example of a yearly plan (from `http://lorelle.wordpress.com`) where you accomplish tasks each month.

Calendar for Website Maintenance and Submission			
January	**February**	**March**	**April**
• Site Submission • Check Site Statitics	• Check Link Popularity • Verify Links	• Check Site Statitics	• Site Submission • Add New Content
May	**June**	**July**	**August**
• Check Site Statitics • Update Headings and Tags	• Check Link Popularity • Check Tags	• Site Submission • Check Site Statitics	• Verify Links • Add New Content
September	**October**	**November**	**December**
• Check Site Statitics	• Site Submission • Check Link Popularity • Add New Content	• Check Site Statitics	• Review Web Standards and Update

Figure 3-10: Making a schedule for your website can help you stay on top of necessary site maintenance tasks.

Moving on

Congratulations! You've done it! You have published your first website. Although that feels fantastic in one sense, finishing a project can sometimes be a little anticlimactic too. You've put in so much work to design and build it and now, suddenly, you must let it go and move on. If you have done an admirable job, there is good chance that while you're working on your new web projects, the client will often come back to you to make minor (and sometimes major) adjustments to the site. Some clients need regular weekly or monthly site maintenance, whereas others might only contact you sporadically for small edits like a change of address or to modify the copyright year in the footer.

The more responsive and friendly you are in making site updates for your existing clients, the more likely those clients will continue working with you and be inclined to recommend your services to their friends, family, colleagues, and business associates. To help generate more business from your existing clients, consider sending your own periodic e-mail newsletters or making personal phone calls once a month or so to check in and say hello. Personal contact like this really means a lot in this fast-paced, impersonal, need-it-now society. To really stand out from the competition, send your client a handwritten congratulations card with a note saying how much you enjoyed working with him or her and how pleased you are with the launch of the new site.

Another thing you should do after finishing each new project is add information about the project to your own website. Some designers simply include a small screen shot graphic of the completed site's home page with a link to it and the name of the client's site or a detail page about the project, like Jason Santa Maria's site shown in Figure 3-11. Others combine a thumbnail listing with more in-depth case studies that detail the entire process from start to finish. (If you don't have your own website yet, you've just found your next project to work on.)

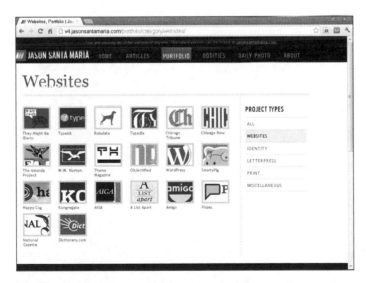

Figure 3-11: Showcase your talent with a portfolio page that contains a screen shot of all your completed web projects.

When word begins to spread about your services, hopefully you can spend less time and money on marketing. Until then, it's up to you to find new clients and build your portfolio. The more projects you have under your belt, the more you can feel confident about your skills and possibly charge more for your services. Best of luck!

Index

M

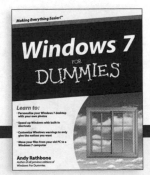

Math & Science

Algebra I For Dummies,
2nd Edition
978-0-470-55964-2

Biology For Dummies,
2nd Edition
978-0-470-59875-7

Chemistry For Dummies,
2nd Edition
978-1-1180-0730-3

Geometry For Dummies,
2nd Edition
978-0-470-08946-0

Pre-Algebra Essentials
For Dummies
978-0-470-61838-7

Microsoft Office

Excel 2010 For Dummies
978-0-470-48953-6

Office 2010 All-in-One
For Dummies
978-0-470-49748-7

Office 2011 for Mac
For Dummies
978-0-470-87869-9

Word 2010
For Dummies
978-0-470-48772-3

Music

Guitar For Dummies,
2nd Edition
978-0-7645-9904-0

Clarinet For Dummies
978-0-470-58477-4

iPod & iTunes
For Dummies,
9th Edition
978-1-118-13060-5

Pets

Cats For Dummies,
2nd Edition
978-0-7645-5275-5

Dogs All-in One
For Dummies
978-0470-52978-2

Saltwater Aquariums
For Dummies
978-0-470-06805-2

Religion & Inspiration

The Bible For Dummies
978-0-7645-5296-0

Catholicism For Dummies,
2nd Edition
978-1-118-07778-8

Spirituality For Dummies,
2nd Edition
978-0-470-19142-2

Self-Help & Relationships

Happiness For Dummies
978-0-470-28171-0

Overcoming Anxiety
For Dummies,
2nd Edition
978-0-470-57441-6

Seniors

Crosswords For Seniors
For Dummies
978-0-470-49157-7

iPad 2 For Seniors
For Dummies, 3rd Edition
978-1-118-17678-8

Laptops & Tablets
For Seniors For Dummies,
2nd Edition
978-1-118-09596-6

Smartphones & Tablets

BlackBerry For Dummies,
5th Edition
978-1-118-10035-6

Droid X2 For Dummies
978-1-118-14864-8

HTC ThunderBolt
For Dummies
978-1-118-07601-9

MOTOROLA XOOM
For Dummies
978-1-118-08835-7

Sports

Basketball For Dummies,
3rd Edition
978-1-118-07374-2

Football For Dummies,
2nd Edition
978-1-118-01261-1

Golf For Dummies,
4th Edition
978-0-470-88279-5

Test Prep

ACT For Dummies,
5th Edition
978-1-118-01259-8

ASVAB For Dummies,
3rd Edition
978-0-470-63760-9

The GRE Test For
Dummies, 7th Edition
978-0-470-00919-2

Police Officer Exam
For Dummies
978-0-470-88724-0

Series 7 Exam
For Dummies
978-0-470-09932-2

Web Development

HTML, CSS, & XHTML
For Dummies, 7th Edition
978-0-470-91659-9

Drupal For Dummies,
2nd Edition
978-1-118-08348-2

Windows 7

Windows 7
For Dummies
978-0-470-49743-2

Windows 7
For Dummies,
Book + DVD Bundle
978-0-470-52398-8

Windows 7 All-in-One
For Dummies
978-0-470-48763-1

Available wherever books are sold. For more information or to order direct: U.S. customers visit www.dummies.com or call 1-877-762-2974
U.K. customers visit www.wileyeurope.com or call (0) 1243 843291. Canadian customers visit www.wiley.ca or call 1-800-567-4797.

Connect with us online at www.facebook.com/fordummies or @fordummies

Dummies products make life easier

- DIY
- Consumer Electronics
- Crafts
- Software
- Cookware

- Hobbies
- Videos
- Music
- Games
- and More!

For more information, go to **Dummies.com**®
and search the store by category.

Connect with us online at
www.facebook.com/fordummies or @fordummie

FOR DUMMIES®
Making everything easier!™